## On Capitol Hill

### *The Struggle to Reform Congress and Its Consequences, 1948–2000*

Thirty years after the "Watergate Babies" promised to end corruption in Washington, Julian Zelizer offers the first major history of the demise of the committee-era Congress and the rise of the contemporary legislative branch. Based on research in more than a hundred archival collections, this book tackles one of the most enduring political challenges in America: barring a wholesale revolution, how can we improve our representative democracy so as best to fulfill the promises of the Constitution? Whereas popular accounts suggest that major scandals or legislation can transform government institutions, Zelizer shows that reform is messy, slow, and involves many institutions coming together at the right time. The short period of reform in the 1970s – one that rivaled the Progressive Era – revolved around a coalition that had worked for decades, a slow reconfiguration of the relationship among political institutions, shifts in the national culture, and the ability of reformers to take advantage of scandals and elections. Zelizer presents a new look at the origins of the partisanship and scandal warfare that characterize today's politics. The book also offers a warning to the next generation of reformers by showing how a new political environment can radically transform the political impact of government reforms, as occurred when the conservative movement – during its rise to power in recent decades – took advantage of reforms that had ended the committee era.

Julian E. Zelizer teaches twentieth-century political history at the State University of New York at Albany. His book *Taxing America* (Cambridge, 1998) was awarded the Organization of American Historian's 2000 Ellis Hawley Prize and the Lyndon Baines Johnson Foundation's 1998 D. B. Hardeman Prize. Zelizer is co-editor of *The Democratic Experiment* (Princeton, 2003) and editor of *The Reader's Companion to the American Congress* (Houghton Mifflin, forthcoming). His writing has appeared in the *New York Times*, the *Los Angeles Times*, and the *Albany Times Union*.

## Advance praise for *On Capitol Hill*

"*On Capitol Hill* deserves to become a landmark in the current revival of the study of American political history. It is a lucidly written, sensible, and wide-ranging survey of congressional reform in the post–World War II era and will provide nourishment for many a stimulating seminar, especially among readers who are eager to enlarge their perspectives beyond the presidential synthesis of American politics."

> – Nelson W. Polsby, University of California, Berkeley,
> author of *How Congress Evolves*

"*On Capitol Hill* asks a crucial question: Why does Congress appear less purposeful and effective than in the past? Julian Zelizer's persuasive answer should engage – and trouble – everyone concerned with the future of American democracy. With its massive research base and its fair-minded, cogent analysis, this book will remain a landmark in the history of American government."

> – Michael B. Katz, Walter H. Annenberg Professor
> of History, University of Pennsylvania

"A truly magisterial work, *On Capitol Hill* situates pivotal shifts in congressional procedures within the panorama of twentieth-century U.S. history. Analysts of Congress learn how broader social movements and political reorganizations contributed to congressional reforms of the 1970s and pushed their consequences in unintended directions. Students of social movements learn why they cannot afford to ignore governing elites and institutional rules of the game. This book deserves a wide and enduring readership within and beyond academia. Bravo, Julian Zelizer, on a landmark achievement!"

> – Theda Skocpol, Victor S. Thomas Professor
> of Government and Sociology and Director of the
> Center for American Political Studies,
> Harvard University

"With a sure touch, Julian Zelizer offers a comprehensive account of congressional reform during the last half century. It is all here: the Democratic Study Group, Common Cause, various outrages and scandals, the drive for civil rights, the packing of the House Rules Committee in 1961, the liberals' empowerment of the House Speakership, the structural moves by Speaker Newt Gingrich, campaign finance reform. The referencing is prodigious. Nothing like this impressive work has ever been done."

> – David Mayhew, Sterling Professor of Political Science,
> Yale University

"Steeped in detailed research and sensitive to the Big Picture, Zelizer tells a gripping story, full of large characters, innovative arguments, and savvy judgments. Zelizer not only analyzes the history of congressional reform and the political paradigm shifts in Congress, he also reinterprets the history of reform politics in twentieth-century America. Nobody has really explained what happened to the good-government, mugwump tradition in American politics after World War II. Zelizer changes all that."
– Bruce Schulman, Boston University

"Julian Zelizer's remarkable book offers us nothing less than a hidden history of our times, a parallel universe that explains why Congress was able to enact some of the most significant legislation of the twentieth century and why other equally popular bills were consigned to the dustbin. Zelizer demonstrates that the impact of procedural reform in the Congress has had enormous consequences all across the land. This book is essential reading, not just for policy historians but for all those concerned with American labor, race, media, and political culture during the last half of the twentieth century."
– Nelson Lichtenstein, Professor of History,
University of California, Santa Barbara

# On Capitol Hill

*The Struggle to Reform Congress
and Its Consequences, 1948–2000*

JULIAN E. ZELIZER

*State University of New York, Albany*

CAMBRIDGE
UNIVERSITY PRESS

PUBLISHED BY THE PRESS SYNDICATE OF THE UNIVERSITY OF CAMBRIDGE
The Pitt Building, Trumpington Street, Cambridge, United Kingdom

CAMBRIDGE UNIVERSITY PRESS
The Edinburgh Building, Cambridge CB2 2RU, UK
40 West 20th Street, New York, NY 10011-4211, USA
477 Williamstown Road, Port Melbourne, VIC 3207, Australia
Ruiz de Alarcón 13, 28014 Madrid, Spain
Dock House, The Waterfront, Cape Town 8001, South Africa

http://www.cambridge.org

First published 2004

Printed in the United States of America

*Typeface* Sabon 10/12 pt.    *System* AMS-T$_{\text{E}}$X    [FH]

*A catalog record for this book is available from the British Library.*

*Library of Congress Cataloging in Publication data*
Zelizer, Julian E.
On Capitol Hill : the struggle to reform Congress and its consequences, 1948–2000 /
Julian E. Zelizer.
p.   cm.
Includes bibliographical references (p. ) and index.
ISBN 0-521-80161-3
1. United States. Congress – Reform – History – 20th century.   2. United States – Politics
and government – 20th century.   I. Title.

JK1041.Z45   2004
328.73′076 – dc22                                        2003065614

ISBN 0 521 80161 3 hardback

*For Nora:*
*From sitting across the table at Levering*
  *to making our little darlings,*
*What a beautiful journey together,*
*I love you beyond words*

# Contents

# Acknowledgments

Writing this book has been a sheer delight. I am extremely grateful to the institutions that supported this research, including the Dirksen Congressional Center; Carl Albert Center; Gerald Ford Foundation; Gilder Lehrman Institute of American History; Hagley Museum and Library; Harvard University Shorenstein Center on the Press, Politics and Public Policy; National Endowment for the Humanities; and the State University of New York at Albany. Without their generous support, the research for this book would have been impossible to conduct. I likewise want to express my deep appreciation for the many archivists at the collections cited in this book. They helped me sort through the vast materials that were available and kindly tolerated my photocopying habits. Additionally, I would like to thank Walter Oleszek in the Congressional Research Service for sharing his personal collection on the Bolling Committee and Bill Cable for doing the same; Kristine Walseth of the House of Representatives for allowing me to see her Democratic Caucus hearing books; and Steven Frantzich for providing me the research materials he collected for his great work about C-SPAN. My thanks to Scott Alder, who put me in touch with Walseth and Oleszek and shared his oral history interviews. Nicole Mellow was very generous in helping me locate some archival data I was searching for. Ben Schwartz provided research assistance with some final improvements in the eleventh chapter of this book.

The Rockefeller College of Public Affairs and Policy at the State University of New York at Albany has offered me a wonderful intellectual home from which to complete this book. As the historian in a school of public policy and governance, I have benefitted from an exciting intellectual community and the warm reception from my colleagues. Working with sociologists, political scientists, economists, psychologists, and organizational analysts has pushed me to refine my arguments, strengthen my working assumptions, and clarify my analysis so that it could reach a broader audience. The Rockefeller College also provided me a special grant that helped obtain reproduction rights for some photographs in this book. A special thanks to Dean Frank Thompson, whose enthusiasm, optimism, and unwavering support have always made me feel welcome.

Furthermore, I am deeply grateful to the numerous colleagues who took the time to carefully read earlier drafts of this manuscript and provide me with penetrating (and sometimes painful) evaluations of the work. They include Scott Adler, Lew Bateman, Edward Berkowitz, Sarah Binder, Lizabeth Cohen, Jacob Hacker, Michael Katz, Ira Katznelson, David Mayhew, Bruce Miroff, Nelson Lichtenstein, Nelson Polsby, Eric Schickler, Michael Schudson, Bruce Schulman, and Don Wolfensberger. Hopefully, they will agree that the current version is vastly improved from those earlier drafts. They should know that all were instrumental in this creative process. Each person offered me distinct suggestions for moving this project forward and bringing out important aspects of the narrative. Another group of colleagues were kind enough to provide me with constructive comments about articles, proposals, and conference papers that grew out of this work, including Brian Balogh, Alan Brinkley, Marc Carnes, Joseph Cooper, David Farber, Daniel Fox, Gary Gerstle, Lani Guinier, J. Morgan Kousser, Scot Powe, and Brigitta Van Rheinberg. As always, Eric Patashnik kept me laughing throughout this process, and our many conversations pushed me to thinking more broadly about the implications of my particular historical story. His comments on the manuscript were very helpful.

In addition to reading this book, my close friend Meg Jacobs has constantly supported me and kept my spirits high. Meg is a wonderful friend. I have thoroughly enjoyed our time together at conferences. We have experienced the thrills of parenthood together while working through the challenges that face young historians. She also gave me terrific comments on this book, which made it a better product. Meg makes my world much brighter.

Pennsylvania State University Press gave me permission to reprint some material that appeared in an extended and different version of the story in Chapter 7, which appeared as "Seeds of Cynicism: The Struggle over Campaign Finance, 1956–1974" in the *Journal of Policy History,* vol. 14, no. 1 (Winter 2002), pp. 73–111. Duke University Press granted permission to reprint material that appeared previously as "Bridging State and Society: The Origins of 1970s Congressional Reform" in *Social Science History,* vol. 24, no. 2 (Summer 2000), pp. 379–93.

The people at Cambridge University Press have treated this manuscript with efficiency and class. Frank Smith has been excited about this project from the first time I mentioned it to him. Starting with our great lunch in St. Louis and continuing throughout the publication process, he has made sure that the completion of this book was an enjoyable process. Frank read each chapter with great care. I hope that he is pleased with the final product. Matt Darnell did a wonderful job of copyediting.

Most important, there is my family. My parents, Gerald and Viviana Zelizer, have remained big fans (as they say) of their son and have always pushed me to pursue my interests. Without a doubt, the best things ever to happen in my life occurred over the past few years: the birth of our delightful daughter Sophia Miriam and our adorable son Nathan Solomon. Sophia is an absolute joy and already a great person. She fills the room with her smiles and spirit. Every time that I hold her in my arms, she warms her daddy's heart. Pardon the cliché, but she will always be daddy's girl. Nathan arrived as this book went to press. I can already tell that he is wonderful and I can't wait to get to know him.

Finally, there is the person to whom this book is dedicated, the other love of my life, my beautiful wife Nora. I have always believed that the biggest challenge in human existence is to not be lonely. Once you have overcome that obstacle the rest is relatively smooth. Ever since our first date in 1991, when Nora and I sat together on the corner stools of Baltimore's Cat's Eye Pub and listened to a rocking version of "Me and Bobby McGee," I just knew that my own challenge was over. Nora is the most incredible person I have ever met. Brilliant, kind, fun, sexy, and loving, Nora is – to borrow a phrase from my favorite band – my Sunshine Daydream. Every moment we have shared has filled my heart with love. From taking the tape-recorded tours of the Louvre to tromping down Key West's Duval Street in the wee hours of the night, Nora always makes every experience festive beyond words. She has taught me to take a moment wherever we are to appreciate what is around us. Of course, on June 1, 2002, Nora offered me the greatest gift a person can give, our daughter Sophia, and for that I will always be indebted to her. And on December 26, 2003, she gave me that gift again with Nathan. As I said in my first book, Nora and I have many adventures left together and I hope this book is a small testament to my love for her. If this paragraph makes it sound as if I am ridiculously over the top about this woman, well, that's because I am. Thank you, my love.

# Key to Collections

*Boston College, Chesnut Hill, Massachusetts*
Thomas P. O'Neill Papers                                   (TOP)

*Boston University, Boston, Massachusetts*
John McCormack Papers                                      (JMP)

*Carl Albert Center, Norman, Oklahoma*
Carl Albert Papers                                         (CAP)
Page Belcher Papers                                        (PAB)
Andrew Biemiller Papers                                    (BP)
Happy Camp Papers                                          (HCP)
Fred Harris Papers                                         (FHP)
Mike Monroney Papers                                       (MMOP)
Tom Steed Papers                                           (TSP)

*Chicago Historical Society, Chicago, Illinois*
Paul Douglas Papers                                        (PDP)

*Columbia University, New York, New York*
Bella Abzug Papers                                         (BAP)
Herbert Lehman Papers                                      (HLP)

*Dirksen Congressional Center, Pekin, Illinois*
Robert Michel Papers                                       (RMP)

*Franklin Roosevelt Presidential Papers, Hyde Park, New York*
Harold Ickes Diaries                                       (HID)
Henry Morgenthau Diaries                                   (HMD)
President's Personal Files                                 (PPF)
President's Secretary's File                               (PSF)

*The Gallup Organization, Princeton, New Jersey*
Gallup Poll Archival Data                                  (GPA)

*George Meany Archives, Silver Spring, Maryland*
AFL-CIO Papers                                             (ACP)

*Gerald Ford Presidential Library, Ann Arbor, Michigan*
Philip Buchen Papers (PBP)
Arthur Burns Papers (ABP)
John T. Calkins Papers (JTCP)
James Cannon Papers (JCP)
Richard Cheney Files (RCF)
James Connor Files (JCF)
Gerald Ford Audio Collection (GFA)
Gerald Ford Congressional Papers (GFC)
Gerald Ford Vice Presidential Papers (GVP)
Gerald Ford Presidential Papers (GFP)
Gerald Ford Video Collection (GFVC)
Robert T. Hartmann Files (RTHF)
Robert T. Hartmann Papers (RTH)
Edward Hutchinson Papers (EHP)
Jerry Jones Files (JJF)
William Kendall Files (WKF)
Kenneth Lazarus Files (KLF)
Loen and Leppert Files (LLF)
Ron Nessen Papers (RNP)
William Timmons Papers (WTP)

*Hagley Archives, Wilmington, Delaware*
Chamber of Commerce Papers (COC)
National Association of Manufacturers Papers (NAM)
Sun Oil Company Papers (SOC)

*Harry Truman Presidential Library, Independence, Missouri*
Harry Truman Presidential Papers (HTP)
Harry Truman Oral History Collection (HTOHC)

*House of Representatives, Washington, D.C.*
House Rules Committee Hearings (HRC)

*Howard Baker Papers, Knoxville, Tennessee*
Howard Baker Senate Papers (SHBSP)

*John F. Kennedy Library, Boston, Massachusetts*
John Kennedy Presidential Papers (JKP)

*Library of Congress, Washington, D.C.*
Congressional Budget Office Papers (CBO)
Democratic Study Group Papers (DSG)
Earl Warren Papers (EWP)
Emanuel Celler Papers (ECP)
Joseph Rauh Papers (JRP)
League of Women Voters (LWV)
NAACP Papers (NAACP)
William Brennan Papers (WBP)

*Lyndon B. Johnson Presidential Library, Austin, Texas*
Drew Pearson Papers (DP)
Lyndon Johnson Collection (LJOH)
Lyndon Johnson Senate Papers (LJS)
Lyndon Johnson Presidential Records (LJP)

*Minnesota State Historical Society, Saint Paul, Minnesota*
John Blatnik Papers (JBP)
Donald Fraser Papers (DFP)
Hubert Humphrey Papers (HHP)
Max Kampelman Papers (MKP)
Eugene McCarthy Papers (EMP)
Walter Mondale Papers (WMP)

*National Archives, College Park, Maryland*
Federal Election Commission Papers (FEC)
Richard Nixon Administration Papers (RNA)

*National Archives, Washington, D.C.*
Democratic National Committee Papers (DNC)
House Administration Committee Papers (HAC)
House Judiciary Committee Papers (HJC)
Joint Committee on Legislative Reorganization Papers (JCLR)
Republican Policy Committee Papers (RPC)
Senate Rules and Administration Committee Papers (SRAC)
Sidney Waldman Oral History Interviews (SWOHI)
Supreme Court Records (SC)

*Princeton University, Princeton, New Jersey*
ACLU Papers (ACLU)
Adlai Stevenson Papers (ASP)
Arthur Krock Papers (AKP)
Common Cause Papers (CCP)
Frank Thompson Papers (FTP)
George McGovern Papers (GMP)
Justice Marshall Harlan Papers (JMHP)

*Senate Historical Office, Washington, D.C.*
Senate Oral History Project (SOHP)

*State University of New York at Albany, Albany, New York*
Gerald Solomon Papers (GSP)
New York State Conservative Party (NYSCP)
U.S. Government Publications (GP)

*Texas Christian University, Fort Worth, Texas*
James Wright Papers (JWP)

*University of Georgia, Athens, Georgia*
Richard Russell Oral History Project (RROHP)

*University of Michigan, Ann Arbor, Michigan*
James O'Hara Papers                              (JOP)
Phil Hart Papers                                 (PHP)
National Elections Study                         (NES)

*University of Minnesota, Minneapolis, Minnesota*
National News Council Records                    (NNCR)

*University of Missouri, Kansas City, Missouri*
Richard Bolling Papers                           (RBP)

*University of Montana, Missoula, Montana*
Mike Mansfield Papers                            (MMP)

*University of Virginia, Charlottesville, Virginia*
Harry Byrd Jr. Papers                            (HBP)
Harry Byrd Sr. Papers                            (HBSP)
Howard Smith Papers                              (HSP)
William Spong Jr. Papers                         (WSP)
Hugh Scott Papers                                (SHSP)

*University of Washington, Seattle*
Julia Butler Hansen Papers                       (JBHP)

*Unprocessed Materials*
Democratic Caucus Papers                         (DCP)
Steven Frantzich Research Materials              (SFR)
Walter Kravitz Papers (Legislative Research Service)   (WKP)
Walter Oleszek Papers (Legislative Research Service)   (WOP)
William Cable Papers (House Parliamentarian Office)    (WCP)

*Vanderbilt University, Nashville, Tennessee*
Television News Archives                         (TNA)

*Washington State University, Pullman, Washington*
Tom Foley Papers                                 (TFP)

*Wisconsin State Historical Society, Madison, Wisconsin*
Americans for Constitutional Action Papers       (ACA)
Americans for Democratic Action Papers           (ADA)
Congress of Racial Equality Papers               (CORE)
Leadership Conference on Civil Rights            (LCCR)
William Proxmire Papers                          (WP)

*Oral History Interviews*
Herbert Alexander
John Brademas
David Delquadro
Anita Perez Ferguson
Brian Lamb

# Transforming Congress

Senators John McCain (R-AZ) and Russell Feingold (D-WI) were an odd couple. McCain, an acerbic and explosive Vietnam veteran with a solid conservative voting record, and Feingold, a plainspoken midwestern progressive who was educated at Harvard, seemed to have little in common other than their willingness to act as mavericks. Yet they shared a passionate concern for government reform. The two men teamed up in 2001 and 2002 to push through Congress a widely celebrated reform that closed "soft money" loopholes in the campaign finance system and limited the amount that interest groups could spend on candidates. McCain, Feingold, and their supporters promised that the legislation would restore citizens' faith in the federal government and allow for fairer policy making. Although the spirit of reform that surrounded the bill dissipated amid intensification of "the war on terrorism," Senators McCain and Feingold joined a long list of elected officials who had wrestled with one of the most enduring challenges in American politics: Barring a wholesale revolution, how can we improve our representative democracy so as to best fulfill the promises of the Constitution? Given the tenacity of institutions, the answers to this question are far more complex than the rhetoric of politicians or reformers usually suggests.

The achievement of sweeping government reforms and the problems that emerge from such efforts are no artifacts of the distant past. To understand more about the history of government reforms we can look to the important period of the 1970s, a decade usually remembered for disco dancing, great movies, and swingers.[1] Government reforms were a central part of the 1970s as the federal government moved from the relatively insulated, hierarchical, and stable governing structures that had existed since the Progressive Era into a polity that was uncertain, fragmented, partisan, and highly conflictual. At the turn of the twentieth century, during what Richard Hofstadter called the "Age of Reform,"[2] politicians, business, good-government reformers, experts, and social movements introduced a period characterized by interest-group and congressional committee politics, a newspaper-based media committed to objectivity, and institutions and norms that nurtured bipartisan negotiation and constrained scandal.

A second wave of reform hit in the 1960s and 1970s when the institutional structures of the Progressive Era became the targets of change. In almost every political arena, a widespread consensus emerged that new leadership and policies required reconstructing the political process. Reformers changed the nomination procedures for presidential candidates to break the remaining hold of party elites. Access to information became easier to obtain in every arm of the government. Reformers also secured permanent rights for public interest groups in the administrative process, and the federal government embraced a proactive role in protecting the voting rights of citizens. At the same time, an Office of the Independent Counsel, grand juries, and the FBI institutionalized the investigation of political corruption. The result was a new era defined by strong partisanship without secure party leaders; a television-centered media with a 24-hour news cycle; scandal warfare and the criminalization of politics; a dependence on polling; and codified rules of ethics. By moving beyond the textbook depiction of 1970s institutional reforms and the current political atmosphere as a product of Watergate, this book demonstrates that reform has a much longer and more complex history. The reforms signaled a historic shift in eras.[3]

The government reforms of the 1970s helped create the Congress that we know today, one where political parties drive the institution with unprecedented force and vigor. In today's Congress, fierce partisanship erodes the kind of professional trust that is essential to bipartisan compromise. Party leaders find that they have a large number of institutional tools at their disposal. Yet these party leaders must remain highly responsive to their membership, contending with codified ethics rules, bold mavericks and junior members, committee and subcommittee chairs, and specialized caucuses. The external constraints on Congress that took hold after the 1960s have been equally severe. Legislators struggle under the 24-hour light of an adversarial media. They confront a fragmented universe of interest groups, think tanks, and activists that make it difficult to sustain coalitions. Notwithstanding promises of a resurgent Congress in the early 1970s, the executive and judicial branches have remained formidable adversaries on almost every issue.

The contemporary Congress looks very different than the institution that existed between the 1910s and 1960s. Most of those years were dominated by southern Democrats. Power rested on a larger infrastructure organized around autonomous, insular, seniority-based committees and congressional districts that privileged rural voters. The media usually refrained from aggressive investigative stories, technocratic expertise enjoyed unprecedented authority, and campaigns revolved around a secretive process that favored large contributors. Notwithstanding the differences between the House and Senate, there were vital consistencies that became the focus of attention for supporters of reform, including the fact that southern Democrats relied on the committee process in both chambers to achieve power.

So how did reformers bring to an end the committee era of Congress – and did the transformation satisfy their objectives? These are the questions that

frame my examination of how Americans have and have not been able to recon-
figure their democratic institutions in the second half of the twentieth century.
Besides the broader significance of institutional change to post–World War II
American history, the phenomenon is especially important to the trajectory of
congressional history.[4] The process in any given congressional era is more than
a technical backdrop to the *real* political action. Historical periods in Congress
revolve around sea changes in the legislative process. Congressional time does
not follow the conventional narratives about politics. After all, the elections of
legislators are staggered, the institution consists of two chambers, there is no
titular head or unified leadership in a split body with up to 535 members, and
Congress handles a massive number of policies that often have little to do with
one another. Therefore, each congressional era gains its character from the formal and informal rules of the game by which all participants operate.[5] In this
context it is helpful to think of Congress as an automobile. While drivers of
various skills can take the automobile in different directions and along various
types of roads, the internal machinery of the vehicle plays a crucial role in determining how smooth the drive will be as well as how far and fast the driver can
go. Each generation of legislators and their leadership becomes closely identified with the legislative process through which they worked. Struggles to reform
the process have thus involved battles over the power structure of the nation's
most vital representative institution.

## The Story of This Book

This book places the transformation of Congress at the center of postwar American history, building on the foundation of nineteenth-century and Progressive
Era historians who understood that institutional change has been as important
as presidents, policies, and movements in defining political eras.[6] In order to
understand the institutional changes that shaped Congress, it is essential to look
beyond the motivations of legislators – the subject that has dominated the attention of political scientists. In the most basic of terms this book posits that
reforming government is much harder work than most politicians or pundits
admit.

Reform is the work of the tortoise, not the hare. Whereas popular accounts
often suggest that one large scandal or piece of legislation is capable of fundamentally changing how government works, reform is a thoroughly *historical*
process that is messy, slow, and involves multiple institutions. Starting back in
the 1930s, the story about the end of the committee-era Congress revolves around
coalitions that worked for decades to obtain broad changes across the policy-
making process. Congressional change depended on a slow reconfiguration of
the relationship between different political institutions as well as on shifts in the
national culture. Just as important was the ability of reformers to take advantage
of windows of opportunity when those unexpected moments occurred. The narrative about congressional reform takes place in fits and starts. The changes were

not inevitable or automatic; they resulted from a fierce and protracted struggle. To recapture this history we must look outside the institution and then turn inward once again.

This history carries many warnings for those who today make bold promises about reforming government. The history of Congress shows how a new political environment can radically transform the impact of government reforms, as when the conservative movement took advantage of the postcommittee era in the 1980s and 1990s during its rise to power. It shows how sometimes the solutions obtained by reformers are little better than what was replaced or don't really get to the underlying forces behind public discontent with government.

### 1937–1946: The Conservative Committee Era

The first stage of this story took place between 1937 and 1946. During these tumultuous years, the committee process and southern Democrats came to be seen as one.[7] Amidst the New Deal and World War II, southern Democrats took advantage of the legislative process to defend their policies. Realizing their enormous strength in Congress, President Franklin Roosevelt's administration had crafted New Deal policies through an alliance with southern legislators. While southern Democrats supported most of the New Deal, a key condition of this alliance was to avoid southern unionization and civil rights for African-Americans. This was not problematic through most of the 1930s, since a majority of non-southern Democrats were not particularly concerned about racial inequality and focused on northern workers.

The alliance, however, started to strain toward the latter part of the 1930s as many southern Democrats found themselves in conflict with their northern colleagues. Roosevelt's court-packing plan was one of the first issues that angered southern legislators, who perceived the move as an unacceptable expansion of presidential authority and a flagrant attempt to undermine the traditional guarantor of states rights, the Supreme Court. Roosevelt's failed purge of key southern Democrats in the 1938 election locked the president into a confrontational relationship with the region. Thereafter, the decision by some northern liberals in WWII to fight for the rights of African-Americans and to encourage southern unionization exacerbated the feeling of isolation among those from Dixie.

Yet southerners were confident that they could not be pushed around. Although they lacked control of the executive branch, southerners claimed an overwhelming number of committee chairs. After 1938, they could count on an informal voting coalition with Republicans. Following the 1938 elections, southern legislators thus started to use the committee process to defend their agenda from the ambitions of pro–civil rights and pro-union Democrats. It is significant that the committee process was seen to involve a broader infrastructure than the mere power of committees (a flattened portrait that is often found in today's history books): it involved secrecy in deliberations, a particular type of campaign process, the structure of districts, seniority, norms and rules that guided behavior among legislators, and relationships with external institutions. By the start of the Cold War, most observers associated the committee process with southern Democrats. This identification imbued the legislative process with a distinct political character that made even the most technical procedures a subject of conflict throughout the next three decades.

### 1948–1970: *Building a Constituency for Congressional Reform*

Between 1948 and 1970, two pivotal developments propelled Congress into a new stage in its evolution: the formation of a liberal coalition that promoted congressional reform and a shift in the institutional environment surrounding Congress. These developments created an unfavorable political climate for the committee-era Congress.

Many historians have assumed that the reform tradition disappeared after the turn of the twentieth century or that the tradition survived only in rump form through groups such as Common Cause and the League of Women Voters. But the second half of the twentieth century revealed that the reform tradition was alive and well. Just as Progressive Era historians have shown that reform consisted of a far greater number of actors than the elite Yankee Protestants whom Hofstadter once described,[8] this book claims that the second wave of reform in the twentieth century was promoted by a diverse coalition that came from within the political arena, not from outside it. The coalition began with representatives from labor, the civil rights community, national elite organizations of New Deal liberals, academia, religious associations, philanthropic foundations, and the Democratic party. At first, the coalition was driven by a desire to obtain progressive legislation for African-Americans and blue-collar workers and not by moralistic concerns about the nature of democracy. This coalition believed that the deal their senior predecessors had made with southern Democrats over civil rights was untenable. They insisted on dismantling the process that empowered their opponents so that government could be moved into new areas of society.

In the 1950s and 1960s, this liberal coalition included legislators such as Hubert Humphrey (D-MN), Eugene McCarthy (D-MN), and Richard Bolling (D-MO), as well as interest groups such as the Americans for Democratic Action, the Leadership Conference on Civil Rights, and the National Committee for an Effective Congress. Notably, organized labor and their Democratic allies in Congress were key partners in the coalition. The partnership strengthened the cause of institutional reform by connecting it to a vibrant and well-established electoral constituency that was perceived to have political clout. Yet the primary concerns of unions were not those with the biggest impact on the coalition in these formative years. Civil rights brought the disparate elements of the coalition together in the postwar decades. The issue had more influence within the coalition than any other before the 1970s, since it offered a type of ideological clarity that did not exist with alternative policies and since it united northern Democrats.

The liberal coalition in the 1950s and 1960s drew on a shared understanding about the failures of the legislative process as they pressed for institutional reform, acting as (what political scientist Douglas Arnold called) *instigators* that helped "reveal citizens' stake in an outcome" on controversial issues.[9] Interacting as a network that worked across institutions, members of the coalition developed a sense of themselves as a permanent constituency collectively focused on congressional reform.[10] The coalition believed that institutions were propping up a small group of conservative politicians who did not reflect the wishes of a liberal nation. Regardless of whether their assertions were correct, this belief inspired most of them.

Unable to control the legislative process, this coalition relied on alternative tactics. At certain moments they made dramatic attention-getting gestures by ignoring political traditions or turning to sympathetic ears in the national media. Other times they tried to trigger congressional investigations and reached out to the membership bases of the affiliated organizations. Often, their goal was not so much specific legislation or procedures as it was to mobilize public opinion.[11] In order to obtain incremental measures, they formed voting coalitions in committee and on the House and Senate floors with other legislators and organizations who supported reform for different objectives, such as younger moderate Republicans who sought to improve the electoral fortunes of their party or civil liberties organizations who were horrified by Senator Joseph McCarthy's (R-WI) use of committees in Cold War investigations. Despite these alliances, the liberal coalition did more than any other faction to *politicize* congressional reform by linking procedure to the interests of burgeoning social movements and by placing the issue on the national agenda. Although the liberal coalition was influenced by political calculations, its members were also driven by a desire to promote ideological liberalism, to strengthen Congress as an institution and make it more efficient, and to make all legislators more accountable to their parties and more trusted by their constituents. Committee leaders who articulated their own ideas about Congress failed to sell their response as effectively.[12] For instance, senior members in the 1950s warned that opening the institution to the public and allowing the media to monitor legislative deliberations would result in a chaotic atmosphere where members played to reporters and the cameras instead of engaging in serious deliberation. In the end, however, these arguments failed to persuade in the face of overwhelming demands for democratic accountability and media access.

This coalition was not a tightly orchestrated network. Rather, at the same moment in history, this diverse group agreed that the committee process was at the root of their various dissatisfactions, and they drew from a common package of solutions. When the coalition broadened its membership in the 1960s, its character changed as it turned into a full-fledged "reform coalition" upon being joined by new Washington-based organizations and activists who believed that the process protected an entire class of elites – not just southern Democrats – whose power was untouchable barring a fundamental reconstruction of institutions. During these decades, the coalition absorbed more individuals and organizations who focused on what they saw as rampant corruption and the endemic weakness of Congress to shape policies that would benefit the suburban middle class. Common Cause, Ralph Nader, and younger suburban Democrats elected after 1968 embodied this newer faction.

Urban, labor, and civil rights forces were now sharing space in the coalition with those who were more concerned about protecting suburban consumers by wresting power away from all government officials. These latter groups, who displayed little interest in mass mobilization, wanted to reform the legislative and bureaucratic institutions of government in order to increase access for a larger number of Washington-based organizations. Although conservative southern Democrats were still a primary concern throughout the coalition, they were no longer the sole focus. Since these were organizations whose members generally exercised minimal influence and that received much of their funding from wealthy donors and foundations, they were willing to take controversial stands on reform that threatened major liberal interest groups, especially organized labor. The potential for internal conflict had increased as the unifying issue of civil rights diminished in intensity following the legislation of 1964 and 1965. The newer arrivals believed that *all* political power had to be reined in by using mechanisms beyond those specified in the Constitution. Although this fear of corruption stemmed from a tradition dating back to the Revolution, the sentiment intensified amidst Vietnam and Watergate.

Yet the newcomers were different from the mugwumps and good-government progressives in that this hardened generation of middle-class activists wanted to get its hands dirty through elected office, journalism, and interest groups. Entering into politics after federal institutions had become entrenched, these reformers did not share the idealistic visions of government that many of their predecessors once expressed before the federal government had ossified. Instead, the new generation believed that reformers needed to institutionalize themselves and their ideas because the flaws of government were systemic.

By 1970, the coalition had created a constituency for an issue that previously had none. The coalition made big promises about what reform could accomplish. Should they succeed, the reform coalition believed that they could create a Congress that made decisions with more efficiency and that would produce a greater number of progressive measures. According to the coalition, reform would create a Congress that the public trusted as well as a legislature that stood above the other branches of government. The challenges of containing multiple constituencies and objectives within a single coalition were usually overcome.[13] What was remarkable was that members of the coalition continued to agree on a similar target (committee chairs) and drew on the same package of solutions (empowering party caucuses, easing filibuster rules, strengthening subcommittees, codifying ethics, opening proceedings, creating fairer districts, etc.). Besides placing reform on the agenda, initial victories such as the expansion of the House Rules Committee in 1961 generated instability in an institution that was protective of its traditions and created the impression among politicians that the issue could matter electorally.

While the coalition mobilized and fought for incremental changes between 1948 and 1970, the institutional environment surrounding Congress turned hostile to the status quo. Although electoral competition would quickly diminish, the Supreme Court redistricting decisions between 1962 and 1964 had a powerful short-term effect. The Court openly attacked the legitimacy of the existing legislative process and placed conservative southern Democrats on the defensive. In 1969 the Supreme Court ruled that, under the Voting Rights Act, the Department of Justice was responsible for ending "vote dilution." In the long term, redistricting accelerated the liberalization of the Democratic Caucus and diminished the number of legislators who were wedded to the committee process. Moreover, the popularization of adversarial reporting that grew out of Vietnam and civil rights created a journalistic culture that was more willing to criticize legislators. This change was evident in press coverage of Senators Thomas Dodd (D-CT) and Adam Clayton Powell (D-NY). Opinion makers also devoted many scholarly pages to documenting how the committee system actually worked and prescribing ways to alter it. Finally, President Nixon's war with the Democratic Congress created an arms race of institutional attacks that focused national attention on the flaws of government.

### *1970–1979: The End of the Committee Era and the Start of the Contemporary Era*

The third stage of reform took place between 1970 and 1979, when political conditions were ripe for the coalition to attack directly the legislative process and the senior legislators who were in power. During these critical years, the committee process was gradually undermined by multiple forces, and the contemporary congressional era slowly took hold.

The construction of a new congressional process began while the remnants of its predecessor remained. Between 1970 and the election of 1974, the reform coalition laid the foundation for an alternative to the committee process. Although electoral self-interest was an obstacle to institutional reform, it was not insurmountable. Incumbents were susceptible to reforms that did not appear to have any immediate impact on them. When reformers were able to separate their proposals from the committee chairs who benefitted from the existing system, they often found enough support to enact a measure. The coalition obtained institutional reforms before November 1974, when congressional leaders believed that smaller changes would "buy off" those who were mounting pressure for reform and when they felt that – based on their short-term electoral calculations – the existing leadership would prevent the new procedures from being used against them. For instance, in 1971 the Democratic Caucus heeded the coalition's demand to do something about seniority by agreeing to select chairs on the basis of other criteria if a sufficient number of Democrats stood up publicly and demanded a vote on a chair. At the time, most senior members believed that junior legislators would be too intimidated to call publicly for such bold action. The coalition thus obtained reforms that did not appear threatening to those in power but that laid the foundation for long-term change.

Another critical factor to their success, which was most evident in campaign finance battles, was the coalition's ability to overcome growing internal divisions. The inclusion of organized labor in the reform coalition, a factor that had been so instrumental to its success at gaining attention and incremental reforms, became increasingly problematic over time. Some members of the expanded coalition wanted to tackle issues that threatened labor's needs. When the coalition found workable compromises, such as abandoning efforts to regulate political action committees, they moved forward with their proposals. When they failed to reach internal compromise, as with the battle over committee jurisdictions in the House, the coalition found that it did not have the strength to defeat opponents.

Reform was often a bipartisan affair. In many cases, reform-oriented Democrats entered into voting alliances with Republicans. Although the committee process granted certain benefits to the GOP in that they were junior partners in the coalition that dominated the process, many younger and moderate Republicans felt that their party would never reclaim majority status under the current leadership. Yet these bipartisan ties were frail, since Democrats frequently reneged on reforms that benefited the minority party or backed down from supporting such measures once GOP votes were no longer needed. Notwithstanding these tensions, bipartisan coalitions proved crucial to many reforms.

When election mandates and scandals created windows of opportunity between 1974 and 1976, the coalition was able to move even further by directly attacking committee chairs and the primary institutional mechanisms that they relied on. When these "focusing events" took place, the coalition was prepared to take advantage of them.[14] These were complex events. On the one hand, they revealed the impact of random and unpredictable events on the evolution of government. On the other hand, the existing reform coalition and favorable institutional environment had laid the groundwork for turning these events into something bigger than they might otherwise have been. These were just the kinds of conditions that distinguish eras such as the progressive period, when elections and scandals produce concrete institutional changes, from other decades in which they just fizzle. By the mid-1970s, a strong reform coalition was in place, the procedural world of the committee-era leaders had been significantly weakened, and external institutions no longer favored the status quo. Under these conditions, a scandal such as Wilbur Mills's escapades with a stripper or the 1974 electoral victories of the "Watergate Babies" opened windows to attack the leadership directly.

There were many dramatic moments in this climactic period for the committee era. Proponents of reform undermined many of the procedures and norms that had defined Congress for almost three decades. There were fierce battles during these years over weakening committee chairs, creating campaign finance regulations, codifying ethics, centralizing the budget process, reclaiming legislative war power, reforming filibuster rules, strengthening party caucuses, and authorizing a televised Congress. Even with the coalition in place, most victories were hard-earned given the remaining power of those who had thrived in the committee era. The most dramatic events were the downfall of four House committee chairs in 1974 and 1975 as well as the emasculation of the powerful Ways and Means Committee. Senate reformers were finally able to lower the number of colleagues required to stop a filibuster, and the entire budget process was centralized. Party leaders were empowered in both chambers. At the same time, new rules and norms ensured that individual legislators could pursue their interests and limit party barons who were seen as having gone too far.

The battles that rocked the committee-era Congress were the logical culmination of the Sixties. The domestic turmoil over civil rights and Vietnam – as well as Richard Nixon's presidency – had shifted attention away from long-standing problems (who had the right to vote, what kinds of policies did politicians pass) to alleged pathologies of the entire political process. This was one of those distinct moments in U.S. history when the mechanisms of our democracy came under heavy fire. It was this historical context that made the reforms in Congress so relevant beyond the institution, as they were linked to sweeping changes that reconfigured democratic government.

### The Contemporary Era

The final stage of our story took full shape by the late 1970s and continues today as the contemporary era congealed and the viability of watershed reforms diminished. The changes of the 1970s had created a Congress with new institutional supports that simultaneously fostered decentralized and centralized authority. Stronger parties were in place, but there were also many tools for keeping party leaders accountable and susceptible to pressure. The same process that granted party leaders procedures to pressure members into following their agenda offered new space for independent entrepreneurs and mavericks. The institutional changes had created a Congress that was more open to public and media scrutiny, where all legislators faced more rules and regulations, and where there were more entry points into the process for a greater number of interest groups and activists. The institutional changes had removed mechanisms of the committee era that had stifled partisanship and scandal warfare. As the reform coalition disintegrated and the institutional environment around Congress came to favor the postcommittee process, there was little momentum for moving beyond the existing procedural era. Although it is difficult to fully grasp the contours of the current era from a historical perspective (since we are still living in it), it is clear that Congress has not become the dominant, progressive, highly efficient, or trusted branch of government that reformers once hoped for.

The first factor behind this turn of events was that institutional changes in the 1970s did not replace autonomous committee chairs with any single source of authority that could drive the institution with greater efficiency, speed, or vigor. Whereas Congress had vacillated between centralized and decentralized eras throughout its history, the 1970s created a process that strongly buttressed both loci of decision making and so created competing centers of power: intense fragmentation and decentralization – through rules and norms benefitting subcommittees, caucuses, mavericks, and congressional minorities; and strong centralization – supported by components of the process that granted formidable tools to party caucuses. The hope of the reform coalition was to produce stronger congressional parties that were responsive to the rank and file. The institutional changes of the 1970s had ensured that those in power would have to contend with a variety of mechanisms that could be used against them if a sufficient number of colleagues were angered.

Neither source of legislative authority was conducive to bipartisan compromise. When Congress was operating under conditions of extreme fragmentation, as was the case in the late 1970s and early 1980s, it was extraordinarily difficult to bring different factions together around big legislative items other than the ever-popular tax cuts. Mavericks and congressional minorities were able to use the process to stifle legislative business in order to score political gains. When parties were strong, as has been the case since the mid-1990s, obtaining large legislative change under nonemergency conditions was equally daunting. Caucus leaders needed to obtain virtual unanimity among party members in both chambers, as well as a super-majority of senators, to overcome a filibuster. After that, they still faced the threat of a presidential veto in an era dominated by divided government.

Besides the hard-to-meet conditions that party governance required, trust among legislators diminished as a result of scandal politics. Scandal involved the revelation of corrupt (or allegedly corrupt) behavior by public officials. Of course, the relationship between politics and scandal has deep roots in American history because democracies always face the potential of being consumed by scandal – in contrast to state-centered nations, where a unified political elite controls politics, the media, and the legal system. What had changed in American politics by the 1970s was the erosion of countervailing forces – such as secrecy in government and autonomous committee chairs powerful enough to stifle unwanted investigations – that had held scandal in check during the committee era. Additionally, American culture had moved in a direction that was far more conducive to the investigation of corruption. Finally, many senior politicians had refrained from using scandal to their advantage during the 1960s and 1970s. During these two decades, the reform coalition had capitalized on scandals – and had helped produce revelations that became scandals – in order to broaden support for institutional reforms of the entire political process. Incumbents in the committee era thus had less reason to tolerate this form of warfare. Once scandal was decoupled from reform by the 1980s, however, there were fewer opponents to scandal politics. Since neither party maintained solid control of Congress in the current era, the incentives for conducting this form of bruising political battle were quite strong. When politicians felt the usual temptation to turn to scandal, the reconstructed legislative process placed few barriers in their way.

Furthermore, although the upheavals of the 1960s and 1970s had been expected to leave Congress as the dominant branch of government, most of the older external constraints that the committee-era Congress had encountered never disappeared while many new barriers to legislative hegemony emerged. For example, every legislator now faced an adversarial, 24-hour news media that showed little respect for Congress. Legislators had to scramble for alliances in a dispersed world of interest groups, think tanks, and activists, which necessitated a dependence on ad hoc coalitions. Divided government throughout most of this partisan period raised the barrier for enacting dramatic legislation. Additionally, diminishing federal revenue and increased precommitted spending made it difficult by the 1990s to create or retrench major programs, barring a national emergency. Meanwhile, Congress faced an executive branch that remained formidable as well as a proactive Supreme Court.

Ironically, many original members of the reform coalition would not enjoy the spoils of the procedural era they had helped to create. A majority of those in the reform coalition during the 1950s, 1960s, and 1970s failed to anticipate how the electoral landscape would be dramatically altered by the arrival in Washington of a generation of Republicans who quickly learned how to use the new political process to pursue an extremely conservative policy agenda. The Republican party reemerged as a force during the 1980s and 1990s. This new electoral context gave the contemporary process a political character that was at odds with what individuals such as Hubert Humphrey and Richard Bolling had hoped for when the battle over Congress began. The conservative movement around which the Republican party rebuilt itself succeeded not only because they were able to package a compelling set of ideas or tap into disaffected constituencies but also because they were successful at working in the new political institutions that had emerged in the aftermath of the 1960s.[15] Within Congress, as a minority and a majority, the GOP thrived at almost every aspect of the reconstructed legislative process – including cable television news, the campaign contribution system, codified and informal ethics rules, the redistricting process, and the procedural tools of party caucuses. In other words, the Republicans seized on the schizophrenic character of the new legislative process. During the 1970s and 1980s, they made use of the fragmenting and individualistic aspects of the process that were intended to constrain majoritarian power. Once they recaptured control of Congress, the GOP then reversed course by turning to those parts of the process that favored majorities.

To their frustration, conservative politicians in the Republican party had inherited a legislative process that did not offer much room for bold innovation and left politicians vulnerable to devastating attack. The 1970s reforms had created a system that featured many means of challenging the dominant source of power in Congress. This is an important part of the reason why the conservative movement did not realize many of its policy objectives besides tax cuts and emergency measures, despite controlling the institution between 1994 and 2000 and since 2002. Moreover, a significant number of GOP leaders were deposed.

Finally, the relationship between the internal democratization of Congress and the public's satisfaction with representation proved to be tenuous, belying the promise that institutional reform would improve public opinion about the institution. Because of reforms of the 1970s, Congress did become more democratic internally: more legislators participated in decision making, a greater range of interest groups and activists obtained access to deliberations, there was an increase in information available about Congress, and fewer legislators enjoyed unbound autonomy. However, public frustration increased. The reforms had failed to reverse broader political trends that were fueling this discontent, which included negativity in the media, the institutional separation of citizens from government, and the power of private money. Many citizens were turned off by the partisanship and the constant revelation of scandal that came out of the reform era. The messiness and volatility of the political process that the reforms had helped amplify – so that power would be made more accountable – exacerbated the perception of Washington as a town that seemed incapable of action.

2

# The Southern Gettysburg

Congress in the 1930s and 1940s seemed to be a relic from an earlier era: a de-centralized body where authority was scattered among committee chairs and policy making took an unusually long time. These characteristics were especially noticeable when contrasted against the aura of the modern presidency. Since Theodore Roosevelt, presidents have captivated public attention as citizens came to think of them as the embodiment of government. This was not the case with Congress, where elderly legislators representing sparsely populated rural areas held inordinate power in a century that many Americans felt was characterized by centralization, efficiency, youth, industry, and cities.

The committee era did not materialize out of thin air. The procedural pillars of the committee era started to emerge in the nineteenth century when parties were still the dominant congressional force, and the procedures had fully coalesced by the 1920s. Although southerners found themselves in command of many chairmanships after Democrats regained full control of Congress by 1933, for most of the Thirties southerners were relatively comfortable with the Roosevelt administration because they supported the New Deal.[1] The committee process obtained its infamous *political* reputation only toward the end of the Great Depression. It was after 1936 that southern Democrats began to stake their political fortunes on the committee process, when a coalition of urban and labor liberals attempted to move Democrats into new areas of labor policy and even civil rights (by WWII). When this happened, southerners turned to the committee process in order to defend their particular vision of the American state. Following the intraparty conflicts of these years, it would be difficult for most players in the national arena to separate southern Democratic legislators from the committee process. As a result, those who hoped to weaken the South politically saw it as essential to realign the structure of Congress.

## The Nineteenth-Century Partisan Era

During much of the nineteenth century, parties had been the dominant force in American politics.[2] Although the founding fathers had feared the factionalism of parties, partisan divisions took full shape by the 1830s. Mass parties became the primary institutions through which enfranchised Americans experienced politics.[3] Many participated in these activities only because of raw political intimidation or bribery, but mass political parties defined democracy. Congressional parties asserted themselves in several ways between the 1830s and 1890s, though the formal mechanisms of party leadership did not begin to evolve until the end of the century. Highly partisan electorates and state legislatures kept a close eye on the representatives and senators whom they sent to Washington. Since politicians were embedded in the party system, it was logical that their preferences would reflect partisan interests. Inside the House and Senate, informal norms discouraged maverick activity. Some formal procedural rules were important. For example, parties were willing to punish those who deviated from the party line. Because of rules enacted early in the century, the minority had difficulty obstructing the House's business.[4] In 1845, the Senate, where the tools of party leadership were never as strong as in the House, adopted new rules so that committee members were chosen by the party caucuses rather than by a secret ballot. There were many times when local and sectional interests prevailed, enabling congressional minorities to tie up the chamber. Yet, overall, the power of parties was impressive – as evidenced by the high rates of partisan voting.

Despite their success and power, the parties were unable to resolve the conflict over slavery. By the mid-1850s, sectional breakdown seemed inevitable, although partisan voting continued on many issues and legislators never fully abandoned their partisan identities. The situation reached a boiling point with the Kansas–Nebraska Act of 1854 as the Whigs and Democrats collapsed along sectional lines. The Civil War, which started in 1861, dissolved the union that had endured since 1789. Through this trauma, however, the war brought an end to slavery. Remarkably, the party system did not end with the Civil War. Republicans replaced Whigs and southerners seceded from the union, yet parties remained the primary vehicle of politics. During the Civil War, a GOP-controlled Congress and the president did not stop making domestic policy. During Reconstruction, the government experimented with unprecedented types of federal intervention to achieve social and economic justice. When President Andrew Johnson tried to capitalize on divisions between moderate and radical Republicans to block muscular Reconstruction, his strategy backfired. Resurgent partisanship among Republicans led to Johnson's impeachment in 1868.

During the decades that followed Reconstruction, the major parties were in better organizational shape than ever before.[5] Republicans and Democrats secured support among different social constituencies who believed that one or the other party represented their cultural outlook about the role of public institutions.[6] Each party also attracted a particular economic constituency.[7] Most important, both parties distributed patronage to their supporters. Neither party dominated: Republicans tended to control the Senate and Democrats the House between 1875 and 1895. Majorities were razor thin.

Party leaders had vastly strengthened their formal organizational capacity in order to keep their rank-and-file members as united as possible, given the slim majorities that existed. The Speaker of the House, for instance, had become extraordinarily powerful. Starting with Thomas Reed (R-ME) in 1890, the Speaker amassed enormous procedural authority through his chairmanship of the Rules Committee, control of the legislative agenda, and his power to appoint members to committees. After taking over the speakership in 1903, Joseph Cannon (R-IL) continued to expand its influence, which he used to stifle progressive legislation. Senators William Allison (R-IA), Nelson Aldrich (R-RI), Orville Platt (R-CT), and John Spooner (R-WI) had centralized decision making to improve the prospects for GOP legislation, limit growing internal party divisions, and strengthen the position of the Senate in relation to the House.[8] Formal Senate leadership positions would finally be put into place by 1915.[9]

Yet the partisan era was starting to wane by the 1890s. While mass parties would remain an important component of political life, their influence diminished. Strong presidents (such as Theodore Roosevelt) started to build commissions and bureaucracies as a way to free themselves from the stranglehold of parties. Electoral and civil-service reforms eroded the traditional tools that parties had used to influence voters and government officials. Moreover, parties were forced to compete with interest groups, which promised that they, too, could deliver solid voter support and ample campaign assistance.[10] The partisan press disintegrated as professional journalists maintained weaker allegiances to elected officials.

### The Rise of the Committee Era

The formation of the committee process started a new congressional era. Although there were multiple factors behind its emergence, the system's success ultimately hinged on the outcome of a political struggle against those who controlled the partisan process by the 1890s: northern Republicans representing the large business and financial interests of corporate capitalism. The Republican leadership in Congress and the party process upon which it depended came under attack from a coalition of progressive activists, politicians, journalists, and organizations who hoped to expand the federal government beyond what the existing Congress would tolerate. In 1909 and 1910, a coalition of insurgent Republicans and Democrats who were unhappy about repeated failures – and how they had been personally treated by Cannon – revolted against the Speaker. The coalition removed the Speaker from the Rules Committee and ended his control over committee assignments. They also passed reforms that allowed chairs to bring bills directly to the floor if they were bottled up in Rules. Parties, however, did not relinquish their power easily. President Woodrow Wilson enjoyed an unprecedented period of caucus government between 1913 and 1915. But this turned out to be a last hurrah for strong parties. By the 1920s, party caucuses waned. By ending party control over committees, seniority and committee autonomy were strengthened. This benefitted Republican and Democratic legislators in the South and in the Midwest, who were assured a degree of power regardless of who controlled the party caucuses.

Likewise, the enhanced partisanship that had existed under Senate Republicans during the 1890s ultimately foundered. Junior Republicans nudged the chamber back toward committees starting in 1899.[11] After 1913, the direct election of senators weakened the influence of state party machines, which no longer controlled their election. In 1920, the Senate strengthened its most powerful committees by eliminating forty extraneous panels. As party homogeneity broke down, conditions favored decentralized committees.[12]

Without strong party leaders, caucuses, or floor activism in either chamber, leadership rested in the hands of committee chairs after 1919. It is important to recognize that committees were not invincible. In the House, procedures such as the discharge petition enabled members to remove bills from recalcitrant committees under certain conditions. Senators could also talk a committee bill to death. While a filibuster could be stopped through cloture, this required the support of two thirds of the Senate "present and voting." Changing this procedure was extraordinarily difficult. Reform required a super-majority. Filibuster supporters successfully argued that, unlike the House, the Senate was a "continuing body" because its elections were staggered. According to this argument, the chamber was bound by the existing Senate rules. Thus, when proponents of reform tried to alter filibuster rules, opponents could filibuster their proposal.

Despite the influence that individuals and parties occasionally displayed, committees were at the heart of legislative politics by 1932. Committee chairs derived their power from controlling agendas, managing bills on the floor, distributing benefits to members, and using procedures to limit debate. Each committee developed a distinct style.[13] Party leaders deferred to committee chairs and caucuses were generally inactive. The Senate Democratic Conference met only seven times between 1917 and 1949.[14] Formal and informal rules favored autonomous committee chairs. If a committee refused to bring legislation to the floor, proponents needed 218 signatures to override them. Known as the "legislative gatekeeper," the Rules Committee possessed awesome authority by controlling the floor agenda, scheduling hearings on rules, establishing how much time legislation would be debated, and determining the rules for considering a bill. Furthermore, secrecy made it difficult for nonmembers to monitor the committee debates.

Norms of professional behavior also encouraged members to accept committee bills with the expectation that their committees would receive similar treatment. In both chambers, floor amendments were rare.[15] Respect for specialization encouraged members to defer to committee chairs who had mastered their areas of policy after years of experience. Younger legislators usually refrained from challenging senior members.[16] In most cases, individual senators did not filibuster or amend committee bills despite their procedural rights. With the exception of civil rights, filibusters declined after 1937.[17]

The committee process distributed decision-making responsibility: each committee took charge of a particular policy area, rather than relying on a handful of leaders or the entire membership to tackle every issue – whose numbers continued to increase with the expansion of government.[18] Standing committees also meshed with the needs of leaders who were trying to manage heterogenous party memberships.[19] Senate committees helped overcome the challenge of handling issues on the floor, where individuals and political minorities commanded enormous authority. As a result, the number of Senate committees proliferated from 23 in 1845 to over 55 in 1890.[20]

Similarly, the norm of seniority was seen to routinize decisions about committee assignments and individual promotion, creating harmony among legislators.[21] Congress had gradually adopted the norm after the Civil War, though it would not become a full-blown system until the early twentieth century.[22] Throughout the twentieth century, legislators rose through the committee ranks on the basis of length of service rather than skill or party loyalty. This situation differed from the early nineteenth century, when Henry Clay became Speaker of the House eight months after being elected.[23] Seniority meant that chairs tended to be older and held their position longer. After WWII, three fourths of committee chairs in the House would be over 60 years of age. Whereas the average tenure of chairmen was 1.4 years between 1911 and 1920, the average would reach 7.5 years by the 1960s.[24]

Seniority was based on similar values as professionalism. Experience and specialized expertise were seen as virtues. As members stayed in Congress for longer periods of time, it seemed desirable to reward those who possessed the greatest institutional knowledge. Moreover, everyone stood to gain: staying in office long enough would mean moving up the committee ladder. This was important because – as the rate of incumbency increased in the twentieth century – more members came to perceive Congress as a full-time career.[25] Seniority was a straightforward process. After Democrats took over the House in 1931, the Ways and Means Committee assigned members to committees in the House, whereas the southern-controlled Senate Democratic Steering Committee handled the same task. Members hoped to be placed on committees that dealt with policies relevant to their constituencies and policy interests. Freshmen received a committee assignment after their loyalty to certain policies was assured. Following the initial assignment, it was rare for parties to remove members from committees.

## The Institutional Environment

Although the committee process technically referred to the internal organization of the House and Senate, it really involved a broad institutional infrastructure that extended beyond Congress. This infrastructure ranged from the way in which candidates financed elections to the nature of the media. Reformers understood that they would have to tackle a much larger universe if they desired to truly end the committee era.

Throughout the twentieth century, campaign costs escalated with the advent of radio and television, so incumbents with access to private funds had a significant advantage. As the organizational strength of parties diminished, candidates were impelled to communicate to voters through the media and professional specialists. Campaign contributions to parties and candidates came from large individual and family contributions. The Progressive Era campaign finance laws that prohibited corporate contributions and required disclosure were rarely enforced.[26] Owing to a 1925 Supreme Court ruling, the federal government could not regulate state primaries – the main arena of electoral competition in the one-party South.

Given the electoral stability of incumbents from southern states, rural Democrats received substantial financial support from local business leaders and wealthy individuals known as "fat cats." Mississippi delta planters, for example, were a key source of money for the state's Democratic legislators. In Arkansas, liquor wholesalers and retailers were major party donors.[27] During the early 1940s, moreover, Lyndon Johnson (D-TX) revived the Democratic Congressional Campaign Committee by bringing in major contributions from Texas oil.[28] There were a host of techniques used to evade the laws: corporations often gave executives bonuses or inflated their salaries with the implicit agreement that the money would be used for campaign contributions; companies reimbursed individual expense accounts that were used for fund-raising events; and corporations paid public relations firms and lawyers that were used by candidates for campaigns.[29] Furthermore, the American Medical Association and American Petroleum Institute spent millions in the 1940s against hostile legislation. Unions had entered the campaign finance game when the Congress of Industrial Organizations (CIO) introduced the political action committee (PAC) in 1943. Finally, elite families such as the Vanderbilts, DuPonts, and Whitneys were major contributors.

Another procedure that protected rural southern Democrats was unfairly apportioned congressional districts. District lines favored sparsely populated rural communities over urban areas. State legislative bodies in the South, which were biased toward rural constituencies, apportioned and drew districts that benefitted Democrats who had little interest in urban constituencies.[30] Free from strong constraints, most states rarely altered federal or state districts in the twentieth century. Thus, over time, districts developed highly unequal populations. Nor did states reapportion districts when there were significant population shifts. Toward the middle of the century, constituents living in rural areas had proportionately more representation than city and suburban residents. Large cities fared worst in the South (although they did well in the northern states), while suburbs and smaller cities had the least representation nationally.[31] In the South this arrangement was born directly out of post-Reconstruction politics.[32] Georgia, for example, operated the notorious "county unit" system; this severely disadvantaged the urban areas, where most liberal voters were concentrated. Under Georgia's system, created in 1917, a majority of county unit votes (rather than popular elections) determined statewide government positions. The county units in Georgia were proportional to the seats in the state legislature, which privileged rural areas.[33] A similar system, unchanged since 1931, determined districts for seats in Congress. When new census figures resulted in a state gaining or losing representation, politicians in most states resorted to numerous tricks to reduce the impact of the change. The results of outdated districting in state government were most dramatic. More devastating to African-Americans were the voting laws that disenfranchised them. Committee chairs and senior GOP members, on the other hand, tended to benefit from these arrangements. In the mid-1950s, 39 percent of the 38 committee chairs and ranking minority members in the House hailed from districts that were overrepresented – in contrast to 25 percent for their other colleagues.[34]

The news media was hospitable or indifferent to the committee process between the 1930s and 1950s, as Congress received meager coverage outside of landmark investigations.[35] When writing about legislators, editors were respectful of the institution even when supporting the idea of making Congress more efficient and more active. As late as the 1950s, those reporters covering Congress still outnumbered those assigned to the White House. Congress had traditionally been more open as an institution than the executive branch, and the number of potential sources for the media were far greater. Since print reporters obtained so much of their exclusive information directly from congressmen and their staff, they had a strong interest in maintaining chummy relationships.[36] Most print correspondents perceived themselves as "pro-politician."[37] Speaker Sam Rayburn (D-TX) invited trusted reporters to attend his private afternoon meetings with select Democrats, but only on the strict condition that the conversations be off the record. Rayburn's daily news conference, attended primarily by the inner circle of reporters, relayed very little information and was conducted in technical jargon that intimidated writers who were not in his trusted circle. If a reporter dared to ask a question that he did not like, one of the Speaker's aides would say "Time, Mr. Speaker" and Rayburn would instantly depart.[38] If offended with reporters, legislators were known to break relations or make speeches condemning the journalist. In 1950, Senator Harry Cain (R-WA) was so furious about a negative statement about him in *Time* magazine that he attacked the reporter on the floor as a "smug, arrogant, self-centered, vain, and frustrated ... ulcer-burdened young American who could neither vote nor fight."[39]

There were examples of direct collaboration between politicians and reporters. In 1945, James "Scotty" Reston – who embodied the intimate relationship that existed between prominent elected officials and Washington reporters – and Walter Lippmann revised a floor speech for Arthur Vandenberg (R-MI) in which the Senator dramatically reversed his position on isolationism in foreign policy. The two reporters aimed to improve Vandenberg's chances for a presidential bid, and Reston subsequently published a column praising the speech. Three years later, Reston endorsed the senator as Republican candidate for president, citing that 1945 speech as evidence that Vandenberg would make a good president![40] On the other hand, many senior legislators avoided appearing in the press. Eugene Millikin (R-CO) was notorious for using profanity so that the press corps could not quote his statements.[41] Nor did legislators have to worry about regional and local media outlets, which tended to focus on the pork that legislators obtained. Politicians cultivated close relationships with the local media by providing them with a constant stream of press releases to enhance their image with constituents. At worst, for every reporter who championed reform, there was another who praised the institution. Local television would prove to be beneficial to incumbent legislators, at least through the 1960s.[42]

The professional norm of objectivity discouraged the press from taking an openly adversarial tone toward politicians, even though the reality of subjectivity had been long acknowledged.[43] This norm had arisen in direct response to the nineteenth-century partisan press that constantly covered sex scandals and to Progressive Era muckrakers who were unyielding in their exposure of corruption. The nation's first formal editorial ethics codes (1910), for example, stipulated that "offenses against private morality should never receive first page position, and their details should be eliminated as much as possible."[44] Nor was the private life of public officials considered to be legitimate material. Female correspondents kept to themselves the names of politicians who harassed them, while drunken legislators did not make the newspapers.[45] This rule was not ironclad. When Wisconsin's Republican Senator Joseph McCarthy and his allies attacked alleged homosexuals in prominent foreign policy positions during the 1940s and 1950s, the national press carried fairly specific reports from this campaign on its front pages.[46] Yet such cases were few and far between, and when they took place the issues were usually discussed in as muted and indirect language as possible – the result of reporters dutifully repeating the words uttered by politicians rather than uncovering the stories themselves.

There were exceptions in the press. Drew Pearson, whose syndicated column had appeared since 1932, was the most notorious. Born in 1897, Pearson was a Quaker pacifist. The son of a professor, Pearson received his education from such elite institutions as the Phillips Exeter Academy and Swarthmore College. After publishing two books with Robert Allen, Pearson launched a column entitled "Washington Merry-Go Round," a mix of Washingtonian gossip and hard news. Personally, he favored civil liberties and welfare. One of the nation's most widely distributed columns, it appeared in hundreds of newspapers with a total circulation of about 45 million readers. Pearson also hosted a weekly radio show. He made his name by attacking politicians. Steeped in the muckraking tradition, Pearson believed that his role was to expose corruption.

But Pearson was an exception. Few emulated his style before the 1960s. There were many mainstream reporters – such as William White, Arthur Krock, and Joseph Alsop – who openly praised Congress. *New York Times* columnist William White, for example, wrote a widely publicized book that complimented southerners for bringing stability to the legislative process and stifling partisanship.[47] Although the *New York Times* and *Washington Post* editorials frequently called for reform, their pieces were respectful of the institution, generally endorsing modernization so that the legislative branch could restore its place in relationship to the presidency. Modernization usually referred to a series of reforms that would speed up decision making in Congress by reducing the number of legislators involved with each issue while increasing the number of experts available to committees. Modernization thus entailed eliminating extraneous committees, centralizing decision making to some degree, and providing more staff and expertise. Conservative reporters and editors endorsed modernization as a means of retrenching the power that liberal presidents had amassed under Roosevelt, while liberal journalists saw modernization as a way to make Congress respond to presidential initiatives more quickly. Congress received strong support from smaller papers such as New York's *Daily News* and the *Chicago Tribune*.

Popular culture was ambivalent about Congress. There were numerous positive depictions. Even in movies about corrupt politicians, such as Frank Capra's *Mr. Smith Goes to Washington* (1939), virtuous figures were able to redeem the institution. Revealingly, in Capra's film the filibuster is an instrument used by the protagonist to fight corruption. On the other hand, the popular cartoon "Li'l Abner" featured a senator who slept through floor debates. Polls never showed very high support for Congress as an institution in the twentieth century, despite a few aberrational moments.[48]

The committee process was thus more than parliamentary rules and norms empowering committees and their chairs. All of the components examined in this section – campaign finance, apportionment and districting, the media, and popular culture – were part of the mix that defined Congress in this era.

### Southern Democrats and the Committee Process

The committee process obtained its political character during the late 1930s when it became identified with southern Democrats. When Democrats regained control of the House in 1931 and Congress in 1933, rural southerners were in an excellent position to obtain valuable chairmanships. A large number of them had remained in office for sufficient periods of time, since they represented noncompetitive one-party districts and states. As a result, seniority propelled southerners into top committee chairmanships. For example: Robert Doughton (D-NC), elected to the House in 1910, and Mississippi's Pat Harrison, who entered the Senate in 1919, were automatically named as chairs of the House Ways and Means and the Senate Finance Committees (respectively) in 1933. Southerners also chaired almost 50 percent of the House and Senate committees, since they constituted almost 50 percent of the Democratic party throughout this era.[49] Southern Democrats claimed 48 percent of Senate chairs and ranking minority posts from 1933 to 1952, and 51 percent in the House.[50] As added insurance for their power, southern senators had the filibuster.

Another reason that southern Democrats thrived in the committee process was that they were skilled at legislative politics. Although the reason for their skill is difficult to determine, it was important that they learned about governing through the intra-party factional Democratic politics of the South. Most southern legislators were also comfortable with the secretive nature of the committee process. Few felt any urgency to steal the spotlight. Richard Russell (D-GA), who tenaciously avoided the media, hung a sign in his office that read "You ain't learning nothing when you are talking."[51] Finally, younger southerners received preferential treatment. Martin Dies (D-TX) was placed on the House Rules Committee only four years after taking office in 1931.

Almost every southern Democrat opposed civil rights for African-Americans and unionization in their region. These legislators were convinced that voters would punish any official who tampered with racial laws. A large number of them were raised in segregated communities and personally opposed African-American equality. Furthermore, southerners believed that unionization would increase labor costs in their impoverished states and eliminate any competitive advantage with the North. The CIO, which formed in 1937, caused southerners to fear that unions would try to organize along interracial lines. Because efforts to organize the South had continually failed, unions were never able to create countervailing electoral pressure.

Outside of civil rights and unions, however, the diversity of southern Democrats during the Great Depression enabled them to agree with northern colleagues on many initiatives. This diminished conflict over the legislative process for most of the 1930s.[52] To be sure, there were some southerners – such as Carter Glass (D-VA) and Harry Byrd (D-VA) – who vehemently opposed almost every part of the New Deal. Yet they constituted a minority before 1937.[53] There was nothing inherently "conservative" about the southerners who worked within the committee process if conservatism is defined as opposition to the modern state. More common were individuals such as Martin Dies and Graham Barden (D-NC), who tentatively supported New Deal policies despite their reservations. Southerners were simply hard to categorize. Mississippi's John Rankin was a leader of the "public power bloc" in the House; he co-sponsored the bill creating the Tennessee Valley Authority and was initially a strong advocate of World War I veterans in their fight for higher benefits. Mississippi's Theodore Bilbo, who became a leading voice of southern racism, was seen by his white constituents as a defender of the New Deal social welfare agenda. His colleague Pat Harrison, who opposed civil rights for African-Americans, backed federal education assistance for African-American students and spoke highly of the Federal Emergency Relief Administration.[54] Harrison was crucial to such keystone New Deal measures as the National Recovery Act (1933) and the Social Security Act (1935). Senate Majority Leader Joseph Robinson (D-AR) was instrumental to the success of New Deal agricultural programs and greatly assisted in brokering support for other presidential proposals. Then there were several prominent congressmen, such as

Sam Rayburn, who were among Roosevelt's strongest allies in Congress. Prominent southern New Dealers included Hugo Black (D-AL), Lister Hill (D-AL), Claude Pepper (D-FL), Maury Maverick (D-TX), and Lyndon Johnson. As a whole, southern legislators were more liberal than northerners between 1933 and 1937.[55] The one additional issue that tended to unite southern Democrats was the strong concern that federal funding should not be biased against their region. From a practical perspective, seniority and large Democratic majorities ensured that the most conservative chairs would continue to control committees.[56] There were also many southerners, such as North Carolina Senator Josiah Bailey, who were known for taking contradictory positions on issues depending on which way the wind was blowing.[57]

As a result, the New Deal coalition had little trouble coexisting with the committee process before 1937. Roosevelt nurtured this alliance with southern legislators by proposing bills that respected their local racial and economic institutions while pouring funds into rural development.[58] Even the most progressive liberals avoided direct attacks on racism until WWII.[59] Nor was there any electoral reason for southern legislators to defy Roosevelt, since the region's voters did not signal disaffection from the administration.[60] Between 1932 and 1935, southerners helped to pass federal means-tested social welfare programs for the elderly and widows as well as work-related social insurance for retired males and the unemployed. Congress distributed money to farmers and underdeveloped rural populations. Southerners accepted hesitantly the new regulatory protections for labor on the assumption that unions would remain outside the South. Finally, Congress created emergency public works programs that were generous by international standards.[61] With WWII, Congress expanded America's role overseas with the support of most southerners, many of whom fell in line with national sentiment or whose constituents profited disproportionately from military spending.

The committee process thus facilitated a significant expansion of the state, with southern Democrats at the helm. State-building success depended on the construction of national programs that respected local southern institutions and did not require exorbitant income-tax increases.[62] Just as the diversity of southern Democrats enabled them to accept programs that adhered to particular structural constraints, the persistence of antistatism throughout the political spectrum meant there were many other forces who were willing to agree to restrictions on state expansion – albeit for different reasons.[63]

Furthermore, the committee process did not benefit only southerners and so there were many northern and western legislators who had a big investment in the system. For example, Emanuel Celler (D-NY) served on the House Judiciary Committee, where he used his position to promote liberalized immigration and civil rights. Another powerful legislator was New York's John J. O'Connor, a product of the notorious Tammany machine who became chairman of the House Rules Committee in 1935. Elected to the House in 1928, John McCormack – a self-taught lawyer and veteran of the Massachusetts legislature – was placed on

President Roosevelt signing the Social Security Act on August 14, 1935. The President is flanked by the chairmen of the tax-writing committees: North Carolina's Representative Robert Doughton (standing on the far left of the photograph) and Mississippi's Senator Pat Harrison (the second from the right in the photo, in the white jacket). This New Deal alliance between northern liberals and the southern committee chairs would become the focus of conflict after WWII (Library of Congress).

Ways and Means just three years after taking office. As chair of the Commerce Committee, Montana's Senator Burton Wheeler fought for most of Roosevelt's programs until 1937.

## The Committee Process under Strain

The problems with the committee process began around 1937, when some proponents of the New Deal concluded that it was politically "conservative" because of southern opposition to recent proposals. This shift started after 1937 as southern legislators began using the committee process to stifle bills and voting with Republicans on the floor. Thus, although the committee system had taken form as a result of multiple interests and forces earlier in the century (including, ironically, progressive legislators), southern conservatives had captured the process by the end of the Depression.

Several incidents pushed many southern legislators to oppose FDR's administration. First, events in the 1936 election frightened them. At the Democratic convention, Roosevelt supporters persuaded the party to abandon the rule requiring presidential and vice-presidential nominees to obtain two thirds of the delegate vote. That rule had protected the South. Moreover, southerners constituted less of the overall Democratic vote in 1936 than in previous elections. Combined with the landslide victories by urban liberals and with high rates of African-American voting, conservative and moderate southerners were concerned that the president might start courting African-Americans.[64] Second, Roosevelt's controversial proposal to expand the Supreme Court infuriated southerners, who believed that such action threatened the branch of government that traditionally protected states' rights. Third, the CIO, which coupled its militant sit-down strikes with a campaign to unionize Dixie, caused southern legislators to fear that labor organizing might succeed in their territory. Roosevelt had started to reach out and meet regularly with young southern liberals in order to push forward a bigger presence for the federal government in the southern economy by fostering unions and imposing national labor standards and a minimum wage.[65] Fourth, the recession of 1937 undermined claims that Roosevelt's programs could sustain economic recovery.[66] Finally, controversy surrounded the selection of a new Majority Leader in 1937. Although party loyalist Alben Barkley (D-KY) had temporarily replaced the deceased Joseph Robinson, most legislators expected that the senior Pat Harrison would succeed him. Harrison was the preferred candidate of most southerners, since they believed he would be faithful to the policy positions that concerned them in the mid-1930s. When Barkley won the election by one vote – after one senator switched his vote under White House pressure – southerners were livid.[67] During his first few months as Majority Leader, Barkley confirmed their worst fears by supporting Roosevelt's proposed reorganization of the judiciary as well as several other controversial policies. Some legislators who had generally backed Roosevelt before, such as Senator Josiah Bailey, came out strongly against the president with such statements as "We are engaged in a great battle in America. The lines are drawn. The socialistic forces of America are not confined to the Socialistic Party."[68] The shift of standpat liberals away from the president was a source of great distress for Roosevelt's advisors.[69]

Southerners (along with some conservative northerners) responded by flexing their procedural muscle. In May 1937, Roosevelt warned Secretary of Treasury Henry Morgenthau that conservative legislators were slowly trying to form a "Conservative Democratic Party."[70] By December, Roosevelt was so concerned that he had a private meeting with eight top Senate liberals to plan a strategy in response to the "conservative coalition" that had been formally proposed by Senators Bailey, Vandenberg, and others.[71] During 1937 and 1938, the House Rules Committee adopted an adversarial stance toward the administration. Allying with four Republicans, a block of five southern Democrats who had taken control of the committee turned the panel into an institutional base for conservatives. Southerners caused enormous difficulties when they bottled up a bill to provide minimum wages and maximum hours in the Rules Committee (there were other opponents, including the AFL) and prevented coverage of agricultural, domestic, and service workers. The leading figures in these and other incidents were southerners from uncompetitive seats who represented conservative rural populations and held high-ranking committee positions.[72] Yet there were northerners involved as well. House Rules Committee Chair John O'Connor wrote the president in April 1938 to say that he was at odds with most of the programs that Roosevelt was proposing to revive the economy. O'Connor ended by saying: "Please pardon the presumption of mere me entertaining these views and daring to frankly express them to you. But that is just the way I feel."[73] Many liberal Democrats in Washington were deeply despondent. In his diaries, Harold Ickes noted that "The President appears to have lost all his fight since he was beaten on his court bill ... liberals are becoming rapidly more and more dispirited."[74]

Matters came to a head when Roosevelt campaigned against five prominent conservative Democrats in the 1938 primaries. The primaries were perceived by several members of the administration as an attempt to rescue liberalism from "reactionaries" in Congress. "The Democratic Party is ... engaged in a great struggle against reaction within the party as well as without the party. Reactionaries within the party," Harold Ickes wrote Maury Maverick, "are attempting to gain control of the party in order to destroy the party's devotion to the great liberal principles."[75] Liberal Democrats believed the "old guard" that was causing so much trouble for the administration was a minority that was simply out of touch with the pulse of the nation.[76] In an unprecedented campaign, Roosevelt attempted to purge unsympathetic elements from his own party.[77] His efforts to unseat Walter George (D-GA), Ellison Smith (D-SC), Millard Tydings (D-MD), and John O'Connor elicited the most widespread attention. In some respects the campaign was as important as the outcome since, as Ickes noted, "we do not want to go into 1940 without the issue having been drawn between the New Deal and the Old Deal in the Democratic party."[78] The President went so far as to confront Walter George directly while appearing with him at a public event in his district. Urging the audience to vote for George's opponent, Roosevelt said that "the senior Senator from this State, cannot possibly, in my judgement, be classified as belonging to the liberal school of thought" and that he was one of the senators listening to a small "dictatorship" that had recently emerged in Congress.[79] Roosevelt boasted that he had "stepped on the gas in Georgia and South Carolina."[80] Senator Vandenberg warned that "the 'purge' that has come to America has utterly sinister implications.... It is one thing for a political leader to seek sympathetic political supporters, but it is a totally different thing for a President of this still free Republic to seek control of the legislative and judicial branches of a constitutional government."[81]

There were troubling signs for Roosevelt early on. In the Virginia primaries, the conservative anti–New Deal Democrat from Virginia, Howard Smith, defeated Roosevelt supporter William Dodd, Jr.[82] Despite Roosevelt's dramatic campaign, four of the five men were reelected. Roosevelt helped defeat John O'Connor, which was not insignificant since he chaired the Rules Committee and had been the prime target. But the overall failures of Roosevelt were still perceived in the media as a blow to his administration.[83] Making matters worse for the president, Republicans in the 1938 general elections achieved sizable gains in both chambers. In several southern states, conservative Democrats replaced New Deal liberals. While more than 20 percent of the Democratic incumbents lost – most facing experienced and qualified challengers – not one Republican incumbent suffered the same fate.[84] The mood on Capitol Hill changed. Senator James Murray (D-MT) lamented: "There was a time when I would have bled and died for him [FDR], but in view of the way he has been acting I don't want to have any more dealings with him and I just intend to stay away from him and he can do as he pleases."[85]

The conservative coalition was born in 1938. Besides controlling most prestigious committees, southerners entered into a voting alliance with Republicans who were opposed to many parts of the New Deal. Although these dyed-in-the-wool Democrats refused to enter into a formal coalition,[86] they cooperated in a marriage of convenience since the GOP was nonexistent in their region. The GOP needed southern Democrats on labor and tax policies. "The Republican–Southern Democratic coalition was an unnatural alliance that existed only because the Southerners were prisoners of the race issue," Lyndon Johnson's advisor recalled.[87] The coalition operated through private meetings, yet they publicly made their presence known.[88] Tensions became worse during WWII as Roosevelt's personal relationship with Congress deteriorated. One Senate reporter explained that "there was an ugly hostility, a bitter jockeying for political advantage and power, a mutual distrust and dislike that constantly clouded his relations with Congress."[89] The war had also stimulated proposals to deal with racial inequality.[90] In April 1944, one southerner explained that when colleagues from his region warned that they would soon ignore Congress and the Supreme Court, "the South isn't joking anymore.... Back them into the corner a little further and see what they do."[91]

The struggle that emerged between southern legislators who controlled the committee process and New Deal liberals between 1937 and 1945 centered on what type of state should exist. Most southern Democrats did not seek to dismantle the government because they continued to support most of its programs that did not affect race relations or unionization.[92] What southern chairs defended was a particular type of state that respected regional institutions, limited taxes and deficits, funded rural development, and ensured a strong oversight role for Congress.[93]

Southern Democrats were not seeking much that was new after 1937. Rather, the left wing of the Democratic party was insisting that their colleagues act more boldly on civil rights and on behalf of industrial workers. Roosevelt himself was sometimes more willing to take an adversarial stand against southern Democrats, telling Sam Rayburn that "good fellowship for the sake of good fellowship alone, an easy life to avoid criticism, an acceptance of defeat before an issue has been joined, make, all of them, less for Party success and for national safety than a few drag-down and knock-out fights."[94] The fight against fascism had stimulated many U.S. activists to call on the federal government to fulfill its democratic rhetoric on the home front by protecting the civil rights of African-Americans. Labor liberals, moreover, believed that the wartime mobilization programs offered an unprecedented opportunity for the government to

Elected to Congress in 1930, Virginia's Howard Worth Smith became one of the most infamous members of the conservative coalition (Library of Congress).

vastly expand its planning apparatus on behalf of industrial workers and consumers, including those located in the South.[95] The accord reached during the New Deal was thus being tested – not so much by southerners seeking a new conservative agenda as by left-wing Democrats hoping to move beyond the New Deal accord.

Although there were many explanations (including tepid electoral support) for why liberals did not succeed in obtaining many of their proposals after 1937, they blamed their failures on a legislative process that protected southern Democrats. In their minds, Congress was lagging far behind ideological trends and social movements and had produced an undemocratic situation in which the most powerful members of the legislative branch did not reflect the national will. This equation triggered a heated battle over the structure of Congress.

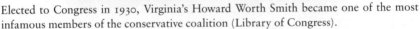

### The Legislative Reorganization Act of 1946

The first major postwar reform effort in 1945 and 1946 strengthened the committee system. The move toward reform started with an outpouring of scholarly research outlining proposals for improving Congress. Many political scientists viewed congressional decentralization as an anachronism in the age of large-scale organizations and scientific management.[96] Scholars sought partisanship, looking to Britain's parliamentary system as an ideal. One popular proposal was to create party committees that would craft coherent agendas. A report by the American Political Science Association (APSA), authored by George Galloway, targeted the excessive time legislators devoted to constituent issues; meager staff; decentralized responsibility; inadequate communication with the executive branch; interest-group influence; a maldistribution of decision-making power; and meager compensation for personnel. Appealing to conservatives and liberals, APSA claimed that a stronger legislative branch would be a more democratic alternative to bigger bureaucracy.[97] The report received an unusual amount of attention for an academic analysis. Galloway equated Congress to a "body without a head," warning that reform would have to come from "within" because of "vested interests, political inertia, and public apathy."[98] Galloway pondered: "Even before the Atom Bomb was invented, critics were saying that Congress was an anachronism – the political instrument of an individualistic era in an age of collectivism … now they are characterizing Congress as an 'oxcart in the age of the atom'."[99] The legislative process would receive more attention in 1946 when southerners used it to stifle a proposal by President Truman that would have made the wartime Fair Labor Employment Commission permanent.

A bipartisan coalition – including Mike Monroney (D-OK), Everett Dirksen (R-IL), Jerry Voorhis (D-CA), and Estes Kefauver (D-TN) – spearheaded the reform. Monroney and Senator Robert La Follette, Jr. (I-WI) co-chaired the Joint Committee on the Organization of Congress (JCOC). Monroney was a moderate Democrat who had spent much of his career since 1938 focusing on the reorganization of government; La Follette was a staunch liberal who had openly supported Roosevelt's court-packing proposal. The hearings in 1945 featured politicians and experts suggesting how Congress might become more efficient and publicly appealing. *Life* magazine devoted twelve pages of pictures to the JCOC, and the League of Women Voters placed the issue at the top of their agenda.[100] To build support for the elimination of certain committees, proponents of reform assured the chairs of the soon-to-be-inactive committees that they would benefit from increased staff and also promised some current chairs that they would obtain better positions.[101]

Democratic leaders did not authorize the JCOC to tackle issues relating to the internal power structure of Congress, and proponents of reform were not yet strong enough to force them to do so. Seniority, filibusters, and committee power were not considered to be fair game.[102] When the bill came to the House from the Senate, Rayburn buried it on his desk for six weeks until proponents dropped the party-strengthening provisions.[103] The long delay in the House that occurred as opponents whittled down the bill left Senate proponents with no choice but to pass the measure as they received it before Congress adjourned.[104] Moreover, internal divisions on marquee issues such as seniority and the Rules Committee caused reformers to voluntarily leave them off the table. The reformers were also ambivalent about parties, since they feared a return to Speaker Cannon.[105] The final reforms were so innocuous that southern conservatives supported them on the grounds that Congress had abdicated too much power to the executive branch.

The reorganization streamlined the committee process rather than dismantling it. Southern chairs retained control of the most important committee chairs and an increasing number of subcommittees (temporary GOP control did not diminish their position). The Legislative Reorganization Act of 1946 reduced the number of standing committees, increased committee staff, and limited committee assignments. The bill slightly improved congressional oversight and created joint committees to advise on economic and budget policy. In the Senate, the number of standing committees declined to 15 from 33, and the reorganization reduced the number of seats on each committee. The Act codified specific jurisdictions for House and Senate committees, aiming to rationalize the ad hoc process that had been used to determine jurisdictions until that time. Although media coverage was limited, the press praised Congress for addressing its problems without external pressure but continued to criticize its failure to tackle seniority.[106]

In the long run, the reorganization became a negative symbol to future reformers. Besides the reform proposals that were excluded, some of the biggest anticipated changes fell flat. The House Appropriations Committee teamed up with Ways and Means, for instance, to make certain that the legislative budget and the Joint Committee on the Budget were never operational.[107] Hence, discussions about reform began to feature the notion that reform would have to undermine the foundations of the committee process and directly attack the southern legislators who controlled it, rather than tinkering around the edges. Over the next decade, modernization faded as the focus of reform shifted to civil rights.

### The Committee Era

Southern Democrats had forged a close connection to the committee process by the end of WWII. William White wrote that "the Senate might be described without too much violence to fact as the South's unending revenge upon the North for Gettysburg."[108] Filibusters, procedural rules, apportionment, campaign finance, secrecy, committees, and norms strengthened the southern hand. Although southerners did not create the committee process, they did take over the top positions in this era. Following the Great Depression, it would be hard for most observers to separate the committee process from southern Democratic power. Conservative gains in the elections of 1942 and 1946 strengthened their standing.

The marriage of southern Democrats to the committee process planted the seeds for a fierce struggle. When some younger Democrats and Republicans attempted to introduce domestic policies that had been excluded from the New Deal accord in the 1940s, southerners instinctively turned to their institutional advantages as a defensive tactic and – suddenly – the legislative process became the focus of bitter conflict. When a liberal coalition forced Democrats to squarely confront the race issue in the 1948 election, all of the latent tensions over process were brought out of the smoke-filled back rooms of Capitol Hill and dropped onto the front lines of national debate.

# 3

## Bomb-Throwing Liberals

At the 1948 Democratic convention, delegates witnessed an explosive confrontation. With President Truman ambivalent about placing a strong civil rights plank on the platform, the young Senate candidate Hubert Humphrey delivered a thunderous speech demanding that the party embrace a forceful position on civil rights. Humphrey ignited the crowd when he declared: "to those who say that this bill of rights program is an infringement of states rights, I say this: the time has arrived for the Democratic party to get out of the shadow of states' rights and walk forthrightly into the bright sunshine of human rights."[1] Humphrey was one among a group of liberals – which included former Wisconsin Representative and future AFL-CIO lobbyist Andrew Biemiller as well as Joseph Rauh of the Americans for Democratic Action (ADA) – who had been fighting to extend civil rights protections at the federal, state, and local level throughout the 1940s. Humphrey's passionate and succinct ten-minute oratory played perfectly to the television cameras, which were covering the party conventions for the first time. After Truman announced his support for this plank, the Mississippi and Alabama delegations stormed out of the convention to form the States' Rights Democratic Party. Their candidate for president would be the person who directed the revolt, South Carolina Governor Strom Thurmond. Under Henry Wallace, the Progressive Party challenged Democrats from the left. Although the Dixiecrat candidate won only Alabama, Louisiana, Mississippi, and South Carolina in the general election, the conflict accelerated the internal war that was brewing among Democrats, shattering the tenuous truce that southerners had maintained with their northern colleagues and causing more Democrats to embrace "left-wing" issues that once were off the agenda.

A liberal coalition of legislators and organizations that formed after 1948 attacked the committee process. This coalition included the American Federation for Labor and Congress of Industrial Organizations (AFL-CIO), National Association for the Advancement of Colored People (NAACP), American Jewish Congress (AJC), American Civil Liberties Union (ACLU), Leadership Conference on Civil Rights (LCCR), and ADA. It began as a "liberal" coalition as they directed the drive for civil rights from inside the nation's capital before there was strong presidential support.[2] These organizations were the legislative team in a broader northern front of activists in the 1950s who were trying to change the hearts and minds of Americans on the question of race.[3] While civil rights was a principal concern, this generation of liberals championed a whole host of policies that angered many southern committee chairs: liberalized unemployment compensation benefits, federal health care for the elderly, urban renewal, macroeconomic intervention, and liberalized immigration.[4]

Yet the civil rights issue elicited the most consistent support from the coalition, papering over internal differences and bringing the greatest coherence to this alliance for reform. Since civil rights was also the one issue that could really unite southern Democrats, it brought out the ways in which the region depended on the committee process to protect their agenda. Most members of the reform coalition were genuinely committed to ending segregation on the grounds that institutionally sanctioned racism violated the principles of the nation. At the same time, the coalition warned on partisan grounds that if Democrats ignored civil rights much longer, core northern voters would become disenchanted and might find the GOP more appealing.

Pundits called these postwar liberals "bomb-throwers" because of their strong-armed tactics. Based on a keen awareness of the inner workings of legislative institutions, they targeted the procedural weapons of congressional conservatives, defined as Republicans and Democrats who opposed civil rights. Members of the liberal coalition wanted to create a legislative process that southern conservatives could not use to block their policy agenda and also to foster a style of politics that was more partisan and majoritarian. The liberal coalition equated the internal reform of Congress with a more democratic government. As a minority within their own party, Democrats such as Hubert Humphrey, Eugene McCarthy (MN), Paul Douglas (IL), and Richard Bolling (MO) worked with liberal interest groups to exert pressure on the leadership. Born out of internal party warfare, the legislative process was at the center of their struggle. According to the liberal coalition's discourse, conservative power rested on unfair institutional protections rather than strong electoral support. Members of the coalition underestimated the deep strands of conservatism – such as racism – that existed among many classes of citizens, including ethnic blue-collar workers in the North.[5]

These were not starry-eyed elite intellectuals pursuing clean government. Rather, they were thick-skinned players who were comfortable in the trenches of politics and who believed that they could be victorious only by undermining the main tool of their opponents: institutional structures. These liberals were committed to taking control of the legislative process, just as southerners had done since the 1930s. As Richard Bolling said: "one of the greatest weaknesses of the North, East and West group in the Democratic Party is the great lack of legislative technicians. The obscure Congressman from the South knows the tools of the trade pretty well.... Ideals are like the stars – you use them to guide you, but you never reach them. Learn the methods that get you there."[6] Most of these liberals believed in strong centralized parties as offering the best hope for a strong federal government and a political system that did not alienate citizens or privilege interest groups.[7]

What's more, most of these individuals and organizations could exert influence among elites: they had secured the necessary credentials to participate in the mainstream political culture by helping purge the most left-wing colleagues from their networks, all as part of the anticommunist effort. They sought to balance a rigorous attack on American communism and support for a strong anti-Soviet foreign policy with a cautious avoidance of what Richard Bolling called "the McCarthy technique [Senator Joseph McCarthy (R-WI)] of big lies, little lies, half truths."[8] From within the mainstream Cold War framework, however, the coalition pushed for controversial changes that aimed to do more than show that liberalism was not communism. As Humphrey's close ally (from the ADA) Joseph Rauh explained: "if the essentially negative task of establishing American liberalism as permanently opposed to Communism has been accomplished, the equally compelling task of building liberal forces within both major political parties is only just beginning."[9] Civil rights was an issue through which they could accomplish this. They saw antiracism as the issue that could unify the nonsouthern elements of the party, define Democrats around a moral issue rather than patronage and machines, and allow for the emergence of a strong centralized Democratic party by siphoning off significant support from the left – both locally and nationally.[10]

Situated on the perimeter of power, the liberal coalition relied on two tactics. The first was to mount a public relations campaign for congressional reform. They interacted with reporters, legislators, staffers, interest groups, experts, think tanks, and other key actors who tended to shape the political agenda. From providing the media with data for editorials, to producing radio and television shows for local stations, to taking bold action and making controversial statements that caught the attention of reporters, the liberal coalition turned congressional reform into a viable political issue. The second tactic was for members of the liberal coalition to serve as de facto lobbyists. In the same fashion that business and labor maneuvered to obtain legislation, the liberal coalition spent much of its time mobilizing support for reform measures in the halls of Capitol Hill. Whenever congressional reform was being considered, the liberal coalition lobbied legislators – and legislators in the liberal coalition lobbied their own colleagues – while keeping allies aware of any vital developments.

The liberal coalition argued that institutional change, racial equality, and the future of the Democratic party were intertwined. From 1948 to 1965, they slowly laid the foundation for an alternative to the committee process. Although this period did not witness the sorts of dramatic institutional changes that would take place in the mid-1970s, the liberal coalition's success at defining the problem of congressional reform and building a network that fought for these issues launched the critical agenda-setting stage of policy making. By the time that

John Kennedy began his presidency, the liberal coalition had placed reform on the national agenda – a difficult task, given public apathy toward these issues.


## The Liberal Coalition

The 1948 campaign was a raucous affair that revealed deep divisions in America. The Democratic party split apart as some southern conservatives and progressives formed their own respective parties for the presidential contest. In the congressional elections, northern voters elected a group of fervent Democrats who were determined to pass civil rights and other progressive measures. Democrats gained nine seats in the Senate, raising their total to 54, and enjoyed a net gain of 75 House seats, leaving their total at 263. Together with the interest groups that supported them, they were convinced that institutional reforms were essential to achieving their policy objectives. Since they entered politics in a period where majorities that supported New Deal programs were perceived as normative, they believed that a majority-based legislative system would be in their favor.

In contrast to southern conservatives, the postwar liberals elected in 1948 came from districts and states with large urban and industrial constituencies.[11] Most of them won electorally competitive seats with the strongest support from small urban and suburban areas. Their competitive seats and bold campaign promises combined with an unusual level of media attention to give them a strong incentive to make a name for themselves quickly rather than waiting through the lengthy process of seniority.[12] Reared in an eclectic tradition that fused independent politics with labor-based liberalism, a large number of them held graduate degrees in political science or economics. Many were elected over the opposition of local Democratic machines. The 1948 class was joined in 1952 and 1954 by other politicians who shared their concerns, such as Frank Thompson (D-NJ) and Lee Metcalf (D-MT).

One leading liberal was Eugene Joseph McCarthy, who was born in central Minnesota in 1916. McCarthy's mother raised him within the Catholic tradition. After college, McCarthy obtained a master's degree in sociology and economics. While teaching at a Catholic liberal arts college in St. Paul, his friends encouraged him to run for office. Running against the Democratic machine in 1948, the charismatic McCarthy won election in the Fourth District by uniting a coalition of academics, left-wing activists, and progressive unionists. McCarthy warned that institutional change could produce only limited results and that "a committed majority can circumvent or override procedural and personal obstacles."[13] McCarthy emerged as a leader among younger liberals.

Another leader of the liberal coalition was Richard Bolling. Like McCarthy, younger liberals saw him as a mentor. Bolling was born in Manhattan in 1916. His father was a conservative southern Democrat and his mother a LaFollette Progressive. When his father died at an early age, the family moved back to their hometown of Huntsville, Alabama. He studied at the University of the South at Tennessee and earned his master's degree at Vanderbilt. He served in various military posts during WWII before settling in Kansas City. Bolling was the midwestern director of the Americans for Democratic Action and the national chairman of the American Veterans Committee.

When Bolling decided in 1948 to run for Congress, he found little support from James Pendergast's powerful Democratic machine. However, the machine accepted Bolling in 1948 as a "face saving" candidate after the party had been shaken by scandal. Speaker Rayburn took a personal interest in Bolling by schooling him in his "Board of Education," where Democrats met over bourbon and water. Colleagues perceived Bolling as arrogant, aloof, and brilliant. A firm advocate for labor and civil rights as well as a Cold Warrior, Bolling's passion was institutional change.

These new liberals were not limited to the House. The Senate had its own renegades. After his splash in Philadelphia, Humphrey began his career as an opponent of Senate procedure. Growing up in South Dakota, Humphrey idolized William Jennings Bryan and Franklin Roosevelt.[14] Humphrey graduated magna cum laude from the University of Minnesota in 1939 and obtained his master's degree at Louisiana State University; his thesis was on the philosophy of the New Deal. His encounter with the South shaped his concern with racism, and his training as a doctoral student in political science at the University of Minnesota stimulated his interest in parliamentary procedure. At 30 years of age, while a professor in political science at Macalester College, Humphrey ran for mayor of Minneapolis. Although he lost, incumbents saw him as a threat since he had targeted illicit union contributions to the city council. Humphrey worked on the merger of the Democratic and Farmer-Labor parties, where he was criticized for purging the left wing from the party. Like others in this network, Humphrey shared the anticommunist sentiment of the 1950s. He perceived communism to be a dangerous threat to civil liberties, individual freedom, and democratic politics. While opposed to the bullying tactics of Senator Joe McCarthy, Humphrey's generation was willing to purge individuals associated with communism from their own ranks. They did so because of an ideological belief that communism was dangerous and as a practical strategy to ensure their own mainstream legitimacy.

Undeterred by his initial electoral loss, Humphrey ran again for mayor of Minneapolis in 1945. With strong labor support, he won election by campaigning against municipal corruption. His administration created the first Fair Employment Practices Commission in municipal government. Following his reelection as mayor, Humphrey decided to run for the Senate in 1948 and earned national attention at the Democratic convention. The Americans for Democratic Action worked closely with Humphrey while he promoted civil rights.[15] Based on his dramatic convention appearance in Philadelphia, *Time* featured Humphrey on its cover in January 1949, and he was named chairman of the ADA. Senior southerners treated Humphrey disrespectfully. In his first year as senator, Humphrey enraged southern conservatives by championing civil rights and legislative reform. In the *American Political Science Review*, Humphrey went so far as to call the "undemocratic" filibuster "evil."[16]

The Minnesotan brazenly defied congressional norms and procedure. Days after starting in office, Humphrey went to the Senate dining room with an African-American aide. When an African-American waiter informed Humphrey that there was only service for whites, the senator protested in front of his colleagues and insisted on eating with his aide.[17] Humphrey attacked senior legislators on television, on radio, and in print.[18] The most famous incident took place when Humphrey delivered a speech on the floor that called for the elimination of Harry Byrd's Joint Committee on Reduction of Nonessential Federal Expenditures.[19] Byrd was one of the most respected senior senators. Since entering the Senate in 1933, this fiscal conservative had spent his career fighting for tax reduction and downsizing government, except for Virginia.[20] Humphrey went so far as to criticize Byrd for not attending session on the day of a key spending vote. The speech outraged senior members of the institution. It turned out that Byrd was visiting his sick mother in Virginia. One senator after another stood up to denounce Humphrey. When Humphrey attempted to respond and was prevented from doing so by the leadership, senators stormed out of the chamber. For years, Byrd's allies refused to speak to him. Senior senators whispered nasty comments about Humphrey as he passed them in the hall to make certain that he could hear their thoughts. Humphrey moderated his position toward the leadership since he believed that Lyndon Johnson (who became Majority Leader in 1955) was more cooperative with liberals than any previous Majority Leader.[21] Johnson warned Humphrey that if he was not more pragmatic, "you'll suffer the fate of those crazies, those bomb-thrower types like Paul Douglas, Wayne Morse, Herbert Lehman. You'll be ignored, and get nothing accomplished you want."[22] Johnson believed that Humphrey could help him obtain the support of liberals and shed his sectional label,[23] while Humphrey felt that Johnson would endear him to southerners. The Minnesotan remained the principal bridge between the liberal coalition and the Senate leadership.

Humphrey's ally Paul Douglas was born in Salem, Massachusetts, and raised in a Quaker family. Douglas grew up in difficult personal and economic circumstances. His mother died of tuberculosis in 1896 when he was only 4. His alcoholic father abandoned his family and passed away in 1912. But Douglas persevered by working his way through college to obtain an undergraduate degree at Bowdoin College and a Ph.D. in economics from Columbia University. As a scholar, Douglas's publications called for the creation of a progressive party. While teaching at the University of Chicago between 1920 and 1948, he researched old-age policy and unemployment compensation. He also took time off from his teaching and research to serve in government positions during the New Deal. By the 1930s, his earlier romance with communism had ended. Following a trip to the Soviet Union, he was disheartened by the conditions there. A pacifist in WWI, Douglas enlisted in the Marines during WWII and was awarded

Strategy session for rules-change fight on January 2, 1953. From left to right: Senators Herbert Lehman, Hubert Humphrey, Irving Ives, and James Duff (Library of Congress).

the Purple Heart. He emerged as an avid supporter of America's military outlook in the Cold War. After time in Chicago and Illinois politics – where he fought for reform against the party machines that dominated government – he won election to the Senate in 1948 and thereupon devoted inordinate energy to filibuster reform.[24] Like Humphrey, Douglas praised England's Parliament, where cohesive parties pushed coherent agendas.[25]

Despite being a minority within their own party, this network of young liberal Democrats enhanced their political muscle through an alliance with Washington- and New York–based interest groups that had formed or expanded in the 1940s and 1950s. These organizations included the NAACP, ADA, AJC, ACLU, United Auto Workers (UAW), National Committee for an Effective Congress (NCEC), LCCR, and the AFL-CIO (produced by the merger of two unions in 1955). The groups in what was called the "liberal lobby" all supported reform on filibuster, committee, and seniority issues.[26] The lobby was composed of an amalgam of traditional interest groups with relatively strong grassroots networks (AFL-CIO and UAW); political action committee–type operations that provided financial assistance to politicians and mounted public relations campaigns (NCEC); and Washington- or New York–based organizations that focused on lobbying, media relations, and mobilizing a cadre of highly active local chapters – but that maintained minimal grassroots participation outside of financial contributions (ADA and LCCR). The liberal lobby offered allied legislators full-time lobbyists, public relations departments, researchers, campaign operations, and a national membership base. They distributed ratings of legislators that were based on roll-call tabulation and file-card records. There were interlocking relations between the groups, as individuals often served in multiple organizations and the organizations themselves were often jointly part of broader associations. When the Americans for Democratic Action formed, for instance, labor unions constituted one of their three major funding sources.[27] The AFL-CIO created the Committee on Political Education (COPE). Using voluntary member contributions for political education – indirect spending that was allowed by the campaign finance laws – COPE distributed publications about candidates and provided campaign volunteers. The organizations employed respected lobbyists such as the ADA's Violet Gunther and Joseph Rauh. AFL-CIO lobbyist Andrew Biemiller was known as a tough voice for labor and liberalism; so was Clarence Mitchell, the NAACP lobbyist from 1950 to 1978 and legislative chair of the Leadership Conference on Civil Rights. Most of these groups were in the mainstream Democratic camp and were firm anticommunists. But they were willing to criticize party leaders and to interact with left-wing activists.[28]

To some extent, the media offered younger liberal Democrats support. Television enabled younger politicians to gain public attention without the support of their senior colleagues. During the 1950s, maverick legislators in the Senate received ample press coverage.[29] Ironically, even though he was one of the legislators they despised and attacked, Senator Joseph McCarthy demonstrated to many liberals how a legislator could manipulate the press in order to gain instant attention.[30] Another example of television's ability to promote unestablished legislators was the congressional investigations into organized crime in 1950 and 1951, chaired by Senator Estes Kefauver, a member of the 1948 freshman class. Kefauver gained more exposure after two years in office than legislators who had been in office since the 1920s. Nearly 30 million viewers watched the proceedings. The senator earned $20,000 through lectures and lent his name to a book that landed on the *New York Times* best-seller list.[31]

Although most reporters did not take an adversarial stand toward Congress, there were notable exceptions. Drew Pearson continued to publish his columns. He remained in close contact with legislators (such as Paul Douglas) who sent him information they hoped to get into the press, and he kept in close contact about the issues that they believed were troubling the Senate. Hearst newspaper reporters Jack Lait and Lee Mortimer published the best-selling *Washington Confidential*, which exposed a scandalous Washington filled with prostitution, homosexuality, alcohol, and corruption.[32] CBS's Edward Murrow pioneered an investigative television show, "See It Now," which he used to attack Joe McCarthy in 1954 by juxtaposing pictures and audio to present a devastating portrait.

Yet there were limits to how much legislative liberals could rely on the media. Besides customary norms that discouraged younger members from appearing on TV, the leadership clamped down on television. Rayburn detested how television had turned Estes Kefauver into a celebrity and feared that the medium would allow younger members to short-circuit seniority.[33] When "Meet the Press" invited Rayburn to appear in 1957, the Speaker replied: "The trouble about my going on one program is then I would have no excuse to say to others that I could not go on their program. It is a chore that I have never relished and one that I doubt if I would be very good [at]."[34] Legislators of all political persuasions tended to dismiss the medium, along with radio, as merely distracting entertainment. Emanuel Celler warned that "the crowd-pleasing artists, the pie-in-the-sky promisers, the demagogues, and the gagsters would do everything in their power to get the cameras focused their way. But the responsible, shy, the patient, the modest and the self-effacing legislator would get the dirty end of the stick."[35] In 1952, Rayburn banned television in the House. The Senate did allow for some televised hearings but it, too, protected the floor and committees. As Minority and Majority Leader, Lyndon Johnson usually turned down invitations from Sunday-morning talk shows. The first time that Johnson agreed to appear on the CBS Sunday-morning roundtable, he entered the studio fifteen minutes before the show went on the air, handing the reporters some papers and explaining, "Boys, here are the questions you'll ask me." When the moderator Walter Cronkite replied that this was against their ethics, Johnson walked out. Cronkite chased him and promised that they would focus on the issues he suggested although not the exact questions. When Cronkite's fellow reporters refused to abide by the agreement, Johnson gave curt answers and didn't reply to most questions.[36]

Equally important, investigative reporters such as Pearson were professionally marginalized. The *Washington Post* published his work in the comic section; contemporaries compared him to a gossip columnist. There were not many others like him. While Pearson threatened Congress, leaders could rely on mainstream journalists. Freshman senators, for example, were given autographed editions of William White's classic book *Citadel,* which praised the Senate. Many television executives during the Cold War maintained working ties to government and were not interested in humiliating leaders.[37]

Reformers in Congress found some of their strongest support in the academic community. Political scientists and historians, enamored with European parliamentary systems and the New Deal presidency, tended to oppose the committee process. The landmark work of E. E. Schattschneider had offered a rallying cry for those who believed America needed to create strong centralized parties that would connect citizens to government and limit the power of interest groups.[38] Third parties were dismissed in this literature as largely ineffective.[39] The American Political Science Association published a report in 1950 that lamented the lack of congressional partisanship. Many senior academics communicated with northern legislators and were prominent members

of liberal interest groups. James MacGregor Burns wrote that Congress was a
"target of the nation's lampoonery."[40]

Ironically, the liberal coalition obtained some victories when Lyndon Johnson accepted processes that circumvented committee chairs. Johnson did this because strengthening the hand of the party leader was a mechanism to enhance his own power.[41] Since southerners trusted Johnson they gave him leeway, revealing how short-term calculations often cause legislators to act against their long-term interest. Johnson adopted other party-building measures that accelerated practices begun in the 1930s under Joseph Robinson and Charles McNary (R-OR), such as having the Majority Leader play a bigger role in scheduling committee legislation, occasionally ignoring seniority, and crafting Unanimous Consent Agreements that limited extended floor debate and nongermane amendments.[42] Seeking to gain the support of more young members even while weakening the hand of senior chairs, Johnson guaranteed that freshmen would be placed on one major committee before anyone else received two assignments.

The generation of liberal legislators elected after 1948 placed congressional reform at the top of their agenda. Sensing that procedure was integral to policy success, they were determined throughout the 1950s not to repeat the watered-down reforms of 1946. Working with interest groups and receiving some support from academia and the media, the liberal coalition launched a frontal assault against the committee process.

### The Liberal Discourse about Congress

The liberal coalition developed a discourse that made institutional structure a central political problem. Their rhetoric depicted a world where noncommittee members were prevented from influencing decisions and where southerners were privileged because of how institutions were structured. Although genuine in their convictions, members of the coalition tended to downplay (or ignore) most of the other obstacles they faced and to exaggerate the impact of the committee process – to the point that it became the sole explanation for virtually all their discontent and failures.

In the discourse of the liberal coalition, almost every political problem centered on the committee process. One of the most frequent and potent complaints was that southern control of Congress through the legislative process was preventing Democrats from making necessary gains in liberal areas at a time that Republicans were succeeding among conservatives as well as moderate regions. For instance, liberal Democrats warned that a conservative Congress harmed Democratic chances in presidential elections, since the northern and western industrial states constituted two fifths of the electoral college. Southern Democrats, they said, were threatening the party's appeal to African-Americans, who were considered the crucial voters in the six major swing states of New York, Michigan, California, Pennsylvania, Ohio, and Illinois. The electoral problem had been evident in 1952, when Democrats lost control of the White House and

Congress with unexpected losses in urban constituencies and with Republican gains among African-American voters[43] – and this in an election where Eisenhower had won four southern states (Florida, Tennessee, Texas, and Virginia) to become the first Republican since Hoover to break through the solid Democratic South. Republicans took over Congress for the second time since WWII. Although Democrats regained control of Congress in 1954, their majority was thin (48-47-1 in the Senate and 232-203 in the House).

While the Democratic leadership defended intraparty cooperation as the best electoral strategy, the liberal discourse stressed the need for a new progressive agenda. Humphrey expressed the mixture of practical and ideological concerns that motivated his generation when he explained: "the Republicans are going to proceed on the civil rights front ... I don't intend to let them walk off with those honors.... Either we are going to act in this area of civil rights as Democrats, or we are going to suffer the consequences on the political front for years to come. More important, it is morally right that we take action."[44] Without Franklin Roosevelt, Democrats could no longer rely on a powerful president to push a programmatic vision through Congress. After Democrat Adlai Stevenson lost the 1956 presidential election, the liberal coalition publicly blamed Democratic congressional leaders. The ADA charged on television that Lyndon Johnson was "running the Democratic Party for the benefit of the Southern conservative viewpoint. It is the Northern liberal viewpoint that has won the elections when the Democrats have won."[45] Rauh told an audience that Democrats had sunk to their "lowest point in 25 years."[46] Despite warnings that the attacks benefitted Republicans, the ADA determined they were necessary.[47]

Process and policy were intimately connected, according to the liberal discourse, because an elaborate chain of procedures kept southerners in power. The procedures ranged from districts that favored conservative rural voters to seniority rules. The filibuster was the ultimate symbol of how procedure blocked civil rights, since legislation could not even move through the chamber unless its proponents employed parliamentary tricks and accepted compromise. Procedures in some cases seemed to become more problematic over time. In 1949, Republicans and southern Democrats had teamed up to make it more difficult to end a filibuster. They obtained a rule that required two thirds of the *entire* Senate to invoke cloture, rather than the existing requirement of two thirds of those present and voting.

Senate liberals discussed the filibuster in the same breath as civil rights[48] even though they, too, sometimes relied on the technique to block bills that were being pushed by more conservative legislators. Writing for the *New Republic,* Paul Douglas explained that filibuster reform "may seem to be a barren and arid matter of parliamentary procedure. It involves, however, the whole question as to whether Congress will ever be able to pass civil-rights legislation."[49] The American Jewish Congress warned that civil rights was "impossible" to obtain under existing procedures.[50] Even when procedures did not stop a bill, the liberal coalition argued, the conservative coalition did the job on the floor.

The liberal coalition was frustrated that Rayburn and Johnson deferred to committee chairs. House members did not use the Democratic Caucus except for ceremonial purposes.[51] Rejecting the suggestion of former Speaker John Nance Garner (D-TX) to bind members to the party agenda, Rayburn said: "John, you haven't been around the House in twenty years ... a wild man from the North will get up and make a wild speech. Then someone from another section will answer him with a wilder speech. First thing you know you've got the Democratic party so divided that you can't pass anything."[52] Rayburn preferred to leverage informal relationships rather than the prerogatives of the speakership.[53] Under Johnson, the Senate Democratic Party Conference was dominated by southerners such as Russell. Johnson was determined to avoid the fate of the previous Majority Leaders, Scott Lucas (IL) and Ernest McFarland (AZ), neither of whom survived very long in the position.[54] Russell was so powerful that Jacob Javits (R-NY) claimed he was able to block liberal Republicans from obtaining committee assignments.[55] This situation contrasted to the Senate GOP, which – starting with the leadership of Robert Taft (R-OH) – vastly strengthened their party apparatus.[56]

Procedural issues became so important that civil rights organizations in the 1950s placed committee and filibuster reform at the top of their political agenda. Since civil rights was at the core of the liberal agenda in these years, procedural issues took on significant importance. As civil rights activists explained to Vice-President Nixon when he was trying to decide how to rule on the Senate's ongoing "continuing body" debate, to support civil rights without reform was "meaningless and misleading."[57] Memories of southerners having defeated the Fair Employment Practices Commission through these tactics since 1946 were very much on their minds. Although President Truman had told Congress that he favored a permanent FEPC in February 1948, he did not move forward with legislation because he feared a filibuster. A few years later, a filibuster did kill a watered-down version of the proposal after it had passed the House. In 1951, the NAACP listed filibuster reform as equally important as fighting employment discrimination. The Leadership Conference on Civil Rights, an umbrella organization that included approximately sixteen major civil rights, religious, and liberal organizations, ranked filibuster reform with criminalizing lynching and ending segregation.[58] "Until this obstacle is removed," the Conference said, "there can be no hope for congressional action against the forces of bigotry."[59] The groups organized a rally in Washington and launched a public relations campaign to stimulate grassroots interest.[60] They were frustrated at the start of every session when a bipartisan coalition of liberals and moderates (that included New Mexico Democrat Clinton Anderson and Vermont Republican George Aiken) ritualistically suffered defeat of their proposal that a simple majority be able to vote for cloture. The northern liberals had worked with (and through) Anderson and Aiken to get this item on the agenda.

Although the House passed civil rights legislation several times between 1949 and 1956, the liberal coalition claimed that each instance had required extraordinary parliamentary efforts.[61] They accused the Rules Committee of delaying

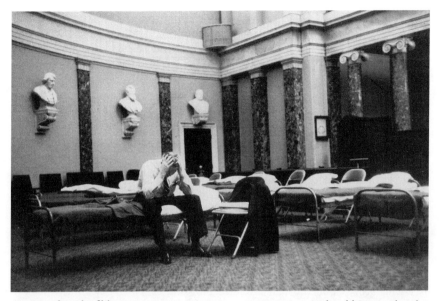

During a lengthy filibuster, a weary senator rests on a cot set up in the old Senate chamber (U.S. Senate Historical Office).

each civil rights bill so that it could not be considered until late in the second session, thereby severely limiting time for Senate debate.[62] In the end, the most they would obtain was a civil rights bill in 1957 that had been severely watered down. This was but one bill in an unfulfilled agenda. Furthermore, the liberal coalition realized that their limited success in the House depended on the supportive chairmanship of Emanuel Celler in the Judiciary Committee and on the desire of Republicans to take credit for civil rights. Without these exceptional circumstances, they would have no chance. The purpose of the reform campaign was to create a legislative environment where, under normal conditions, southern conservatives would not be dominant.

The anticommunist crusade became another example to the liberal coalition of how committee chairs could abuse their power. Many core southern conservatives had been major players on the relevant investigations at one time or another. On the notorious House Un-American Activities Committee, Martin Dies and John Rankin used the panel to hammer away at liberal institutions and political leaders. Joe McCarthy was perceived to share much of the same ideological outlook and agenda of the conservative coalition. In response to the congressional anticommunist brigade, the AJC and ACLU developed procedural codes to curb committee investigations. The codes were unsuccessfully proposed by House and Senate liberals.[63]

Through these and other arguments, however, the coalition revealed their limits. These were not unrealistic radicals. For instance, their discussions acknowledged that filibuster reform would have a limited impact because the constitutional design of the Senate itself favored small states. But members of this coalition were determined to obtain changes that were feasible within the near future. They downplayed more dramatic reforms that seemed unrealistic.

While southern conservatives were the most obvious opponents of liberals, moderates in the leadership were just as hostile to congressional reform. Because of their success, Democratic leaders by the 1940s were fighting to preserve the status quo, stifling the kinds of issues that would bring out the internal tensions in their party. As Samuel Lubell wrote in 1951, "the inner dynamics of the Roosevelt coalition have shifted from those of *getting* to those of *keeping*."[64] For Johnson and Rayburn, the legislative process served as an institutional check that fostered compromise and stability. The committee process had offered insulated forums to resolve intraparty regional conflicts by stopping controversial measures from reaching the floor.[65] At a time when the leadership was trying to build bridges within the party and survive narrow margins, removing these institutional mechanisms threatened to exacerbate internal tensions. Rayburn and Johnson also felt that most committee chairs were not that far away from the preferences of the median voter in each chamber. Democratic leaders feared that reform would create a style of politics that favored unproductive extremists, which they claimed voters had rejected through divided government.[66] Both Rayburn and Johnson strongly believed, as Johnson's advisor George Reedy once explained, that liberal and conservative mavericks threatened to "split the Democratic Party irretrievably and doom it to a long-term status as a minority."[67] Johnson and Rayburn had undertaken a conscious effort to design legislation that Eisenhower would support, since they believed that legislative productivity (in contrast to obstructionism) would improve the image of the Democrats.[68] The goal was to make old-guard congressional Republicans such as Robert Taft appear as obstructionists, with Democrats claiming joint credit with Eisenhower for popular positions.[69] The strategy had worked in 1953 when senators defeated an amendment by Ohio Republican John Bricker to curtail the treaty-making power of the president.

A crucial factor in the desire of legislators such as Rayburn and Johnson to maintain a centrist policy course was the serious political threat that existed from the right wing of the Republican party. Most Democrats during this period were concerned about avoiding actions that the right wing could capitalize on. This right wing had caused considerable damage during the congressional anticommunist campaigns of the early 1950s.[70] While younger northern liberals argued that Democrats needed to move to the left, a large number of prominent moderates believed that their party had to avoid veering too far to the left on foreign and domestic policy lest they become susceptible to the conservative mobilization being mounted at the local and national levels.

The discourse that members of the liberal coalition used when speaking about issues such as anticommunism and civil rights linked policy to process. Moreover, the liberal coalition added that a passive Congress would never reclaim its power in relation to the president unless the institution's leaders became assertive. Whereas congressional leaders warned of the dangers of extremism, the liberal coalition argued that moderation meant preserving the failed status quo.

## Politicizing Procedure

Between 1956 and 1958, battles over civil rights and campaign finance demonstrated that the liberal coalition could be an effective force even when the conservative coalition displayed its muscle. During these battles, the liberal coalition made critical choices that influenced how the reform agenda unfolded. The battle culminating in a civil rights bill in 1957 indicated to liberals how important it was to change the legislative process and how this issue gave them their greatest unity as a coalition in the pursuit of reform. Campaign finance dropped off their agenda because it divided the coalition.

The first struggle took place over civil rights. While there were many policies that animated the liberal coalition in the 1950s, there was none other as capable of uniting the ranks of liberal Democrats and which so isolated the southern Democrats whom they were targeting. The civil rights issue evoked strong reactions since it was gaining ground from multiple sources, including Supreme Court decisions, newspaper editorials, and local citizen conflicts. Southern Democrats were irate with the Supreme Court's 1954 *Brown v. Board of Education* decision, which outlawed segregation in southern schools.

Born in 1887 into a prominent Atlanta family that held great respect for the Confederacy, Richard Russell headed the Southern Caucus, which directed the attack on his party's civil rights agenda. The Southern Caucus was composed of 22 conservatives who had been elected by citizens in former Confederate states. Although opposing unlawful acts of resistance, Russell said of liberal opponents: "Any white man who wants to take the position that he is no better than the Negro is entitled to his own opinion of himself. I do not think much of him, but he can think it."[71] Russell proved to be a shrewd tactician who convinced his colleagues to package their arguments in the language of states' rights and individual liberties rather than blatant discussions about race.

Southern congressmen released the Southern Manifesto on March 12, 1956, denouncing the court's *Brown* decision as an unconstitutional "abuse of judicial power." The widely publicized document, written by Strom Thurmond with the assistance of Russell, John Stennis (D-MS), and Harry Byrd, was signed by 19 senators and 77 House members. The only southern senators who refused were Albert Gore (D-TN), Estes Kefauver, and Lyndon Johnson. Although southerners excused Johnson since he was Majority Leader and because of his presidential aspirations, they harassed Gore and Kefauver. Thurmond approached an unsuspecting Gore on the Senate floor and proceeded to jab him in the chest with the manifesto. When Thurmond asked him to sign it, Gore replied "Hell, no." Gore looked up at the press gallery only to realize that Thurmond had alerted southern reporters who were there to cover the story.[72]

Democrats proposed a voting-rights bill in 1956. Following *Brown*, the NAACP orchestrated a public relations drive with the ADA, the Leadership Conference on Civil Rights, and the United Auto Workers to build support for this legislation. National events were forcing the issue onto the congressional agenda. The bus boycott in Alabama and the lynching of a 14-year-old named Emmett

Till in Mississippi had stimulated demands in some northern states for legislation. But those events alone were not sufficient to turn the issue into a full-blown
national problem. The flow of information, draft editorials, and lobbyists that
the liberal coalition produced about these events and other issues was essential.
This network linked these tragedies to congressional reform, a connection that
was not evident to most citizens and many reporters. From the start of their
campaign, the Leadership Conference on Civil Rights warned that "procedural
roadblocks" would be the key to the civil rights battle.[73]

The year began ominously for liberals. Johnson adhered to seniority in replacing the recently deceased chair of the Senate Judiciary Committee with James
Eastland (D-MS), who was an ardent segregationist and racist. Eastland once
bragged that, as chair of the Subcommittee on Civil Rights, he used his power
to prevent legislation from passing: "You know the law says the committee has
got to meet once a week. Why, for three years I was chairman, that committee
didn't hold a meeting. I had special pockets in my pants, and for years I carried those bills around in my pockets everywhere I went and every one of them
was defeated."[74] In the House, Bolling, James Roosevelt (D-CA), Adam Clayton
Powell (D-NY), and Hugh Scott (R-PA) proposed voting-rights legislation on
April 9. The liberal coalition scored a victory when opponents failed to prevent
the bill from coming out of committee. Mitchell, as well as ADA and the AFL-
CIO, monitored deliberations and disseminated information about vote counts.
When Rules Committee Chairman Howard Smith (D-VA) turned to familiar procedural tricks, Rayburn intervened at Bolling's urging. On June 18, the House
passed the legislation by 286-126. Knowing that Johnson planned to send the bill
to Senator Eastland's committee, Douglas and Lehman monitored the bill so that
one of them would be present when it was delivered to the Senate. They planned
on using an obscure procedure for objecting to the committee referral to avoid
Eastland and have the bill placed directly on the legislative calendar. But Johnson outsmarted them by manipulating the printing and delivery of the House bill
so that neither was present when it reached the Senate.[75] Eastland buried the bill.

The initial loss was frustrating to many Democrats who sensed that Republicans were seeking to take over the civil rights issue.[76] With Republican Dwight
Eisenhower firmly in the White House, congressional Republicans were less dependent on southern Democrats to block economic legislation and so could
afford to be more supportive of civil rights.[77] Although still a minority of their
party, liberal Republicans from the West and Northeast – including Thomas
Kuchel (R-CA), Jacob Javits, Clifford Case (R-NJ), and George Aiken – were
outspoken civil rights advocates. They and other Republicans, Humphrey told
one Democrat, were "taking full credit" for the *Brown* decision and said that
African-Americans were "sick and tired" of broken promises from Democrats.[78]
The NAACP's Clarence Mitchell was making overtures to Republicans if they
would support civil rights. Mitchell said that Eastland was the best GOP "vote-
getter."[79] African-American Democrat Adam Clayton Powell had supported
Eisenhower in the 1956 presidential campaign because of Democratic failures

with civil rights and personal snubs by Adlai Stevenson. At a minimum, according to Paul Douglas, Republicans were going to favor civil rights while allowing southern Democrats to protect existing congressional rules in order to ensure that a bill would never actually pass, allowing the GOP to blame the "Naughty Democrats."[80] At the exact same time these Republicans gained prominence, Americans were hearing about Democrats blocking school integration in Arkansas. Johnson's failure to gain the 1956 nomination – after being tagged as a southern candidate – convinced him that he needed to pass civil rights legislation.[81]

Democratic fears were confirmed in the 1956 elections when Eisenhower won a significant number of African-American votes. When Congress reconvened in 1957, Eisenhower renewed his appeal to African-Americans by endorsing voting rights. The strongest component of the administration proposal empowered the Attorney General to seek injunctions against those who violated individual civil rights.

Democrats were now under great pressure to pass a bill or their party would be to blame. Senate reformers once again proposed that a majority be able to vote for cloture. When Vice-President Nixon issued an advisory ruling that the Senate was *not* a continuing body, Johnson and Russell responded with hardball tactics (such as delaying committee assignments) until the issue was resolved.[82] Although the liberal coalition failed to reform the rules governing filibusters, their attempt to do so influenced the legislative debate. The proposal for allowing a majority to end filibusters was only defeated by a vote of 55 to 38, with five Democrats and twelve Republicans having joined the liberal coalition since 1953. The vote signaled that opposition to southern filibusters was increasing and that proponents of reform were on the verge of having enough votes to impose majority rule. Southern opponents of civil rights thus had to tread very carefully. A refusal to compromise could result in an institutional environment that would be devastating to them.

The liberal coalition also continued its work in the House. On January 8, 1957, Eugene McCarthy and Frank Thompson, a labor-backed liberal Democrat from New Jersey, produced a Democratic Manifesto that endorsed a strong civil rights agenda and condemned the procedural tactics of southerners. While Rayburn refused to publicly support the document for fear that it would cause irreparable divisions, he privately admitted that the group's concerns were legitimate. Rayburn was being more supportive of younger members to maintain peace within the party.[83]

Calling themselves McCarthy's Mavericks, over 80 members from 21 states joined this effort, including John Blatnik (D-MN), Stewart Udall (D-AZ), Lee Metcalf, and Chet Holifield (D-CA). Meanwhile, Humphrey, Douglas, and five other senators released a similar document. McCarthy's Mavericks, working with Bolling, moved the bill out of Rules. Liberal interest groups publicized the legislation and the tactics being used against it. McCarthy's Mavericks functioned as an informal whip system by gathering votes and counteracting procedural tricks. Convinced that the legislation was popular in the House, Rayburn lobbied undecided southerners behind the scenes to take a position that would anger many constituents. Besides political calculations, Rayburn – who had helped block most civil rights legislation and favored segregation – had been slowly reassessing his beliefs since the *Brown* decision.[84] Although tepid, his support was nonetheless essential to the bill. The House passed the legislation 286-126.

Senator Douglas and his allies applied pressure to bypass Judiciary through special rules that placed the bill directly on the Senate calendar. They were assisted by Republican leader William Knowland (CA), who initially opposed such legislation but changed sides once Eisenhower had backed it. Even though Knowland was in the right wing of his party, he had come to believe that the GOP could make major electoral gains by courting African-Americans. Knowland was also planning to run for governor of California in 1958 and would need African-American votes.[85] The biggest threat to civil rights was a handful of western legislators who had traded their vote on civil rights to southerners in exchange for support on a dam construction bill.

Most southern Democrats relied on the threat of a filibuster to gain concessions. But they decided there was not enough support to sustain a filibuster and feared that a filibuster might trigger support for dramatic rules changes.[86] Russell also wanted Johnson to become president. To do so he realized that Johnson's ability to pass civil rights was integral. Seeking to pass legislation without losing the South, Johnson pushed through several crucial changes. He watered down the bill so that it focused only on voting rights, had a provision deleted that would have strengthened the Attorney General's ability to prosecute violations, and was able to remove another provision that required the use of judge trials (rather than juries, which in the South were biased against African-Americans). As Robert Caro has recounted in vivid detail, Johnson devoted all of his energy to brokering deals and forming voting coalitions to pass the first civil rights bill since Reconstruction.[87] Johnson's work proved crucial to the success of the legislation. Although at many points it seemed that he would be defeated, in the end he was able to find a bill that could pass. The bill's proponents were infuriated, but most decided to accept this version. The Senate passed the modified legislation 60-15 after one of the southern holdouts (who defied Johnson's negotiated agreement with southerners that they would not filibuster), Strom Thurmond, unsuccessfully mounted the longest filibuster (24 hours and 18 minutes) in American history. He did this on his own accord after failing to obtain support form the Southern Caucus. Mimicking southern filibuster tactics, Douglas organized four close-knit teams that monitored the floor at different times and who were responsible for bringing people back for a quorum quickly, thereby limiting how much rest southerners could enjoy.[88] Douglas also tried old-fashioned trickery. When Thurmond's voice became parched Douglas brought the southerner a pitcher of orange juice. Thurmond started to guzzle. Realizing that Douglas was trying to force the senator to go to the bathroom (the filibuster would end if his feet left the chamber), Thurmond's aide seized the pitcher from his boss.[89]

The Civil Rights Act of 1957 sent a mixed message to the liberal coalition. On the positive side, it was the first major civil rights measure since Reconstruction. The victory showed that conservatives could be defeated through procedural warfare and that the liberal coalition could get issues onto the agenda. Civil rights also united the factions in the coalition like no other issue. The leading newspapers praised Johnson and Congress for reaching this compromise.[90] Through this protracted struggle, congressional Democrats were able to reclaim civil rights: the GOP could no longer tell urban liberals and African-Americans that a Democratic Congress would never obtain this kind of legislation. At the same time, the watered-down bill served as a powerful reminder that procedural reform was a precondition for bold legislation. The final bill contained numerous loopholes and lacked enforcement mechanisms; the bill's impact on black voting would be negligible.[91] Committees and filibusters had been overcome at the cost of weak legislation. Senator Wayne Morse (D-OR) confided to Senator Lehman that "I am fed up with the argument that the civil rights bill the Congress passed is better than no bill at all. I deny that premise."[92]

While the struggle against committees and filibusters received strong support from the liberal coalition, the issue of campaign finance revealed how internal divisions would determine the boundaries of the reform agenda. Unlike the committee system and filibusters, which were clearly linked with the conservative coalition, campaign finance touched on the power of key members in the liberal coalition. The issue also touched on the political rights of unions at a time when organized labor's moral standing was being battered by congressional investigations into union corruption.[93] Campaign finance reform became tied up with legislation to deregulate the gas industry in the mid-1950s. In 1955, the liberal coalition attacked the political power of southern and southwestern gas companies when Eisenhower and Congress attempted to revoke the regulatory authority of the Federal Power Commission.[94] For representatives and senators of northeastern states, deregulating this industry would mean higher consumer prices. In 1950, Paul Douglas and other liberals had convinced Truman to veto a similar proposal.[95]

The battle over deregulation intensified in 1956 when Senator Francis Case (R-SD) admitted that he had been offered a $2,500 campaign contribution from Superior Oil to support the gas legislation. Although Case rejected the payment, the press jumped on the natural gas industry and its ties to Congress.[96] This caused Eisenhower to veto the bill. Johnson warned that the Senate had to be cautious since reporters like Drew Pearson would capitalize on leaks. Reminding colleagues that every senator had something "embarrassing if used by a sensational committee," he advised against hearings.[97] Johnson blocked an investigation into oil-industry lobbying, but Senators Douglas, Thomas Hennings (D-MO), and Albert Gore kept the issue alive. Hennings and Gore had regularly conducted hearings on campaign finance and sponsored "Clean Elections" bills that aimed to foster small contributions and eliminate secrecy in campaigns. Although Johnson prevented hearings into the oil industry, Gore headed a 1957 investigation into campaign finance through the Privileges and Election Subcommittee of the Senate Rules Committee. The senator hired Professor Alexander Heard as a consultant. Gore's subcommittee conducted a study by sending out questionnaires to political committees, 500 television and radio stations, and 275 individual contributors. The committee produced an extensive analysis of campaign contributions that provided stunning data on the major contributors to elections. At this time, the only other source of information was *Congressional Quarterly*. Yet Congress still did not pass legislation.

The biggest problem that Gore and Hennings faced was that many in the liberal coalition were ambivalent about campaign finance reform. Most Democratic legislators had learned from experience that campaign money was necessary. Paul Douglas believed that "we must reform our election procedures by providing new sources of revenue, rather than by increasing penalties."[98] Morse felt that "liberals have to constantly be on guard in respect to the raising of their campaign funds with respect to attempts to embarrass them financially."[99] But the strongest hesitancy in the liberal coalition emanated from labor, which felt that its political standing was under attack from business and congressional conservatives. The National Association of Manufacturers (NAM) had embarked on an intense public relations campaign attacking labor's political power.[100] "The labor unions themselves have blazed the trail for the rest of us," said Charles Sligh, Jr., the executive vice-president of NAM, "We must do as they have done."[101] Conservative organizations were forming their own political groups, such as the Americans for Constitutional Action (1958).

In this context, union leaders saw proposed reforms on PACs as a tool for conservatives to emasculate labor's political power. There was historical precedent for union concern. Congressional investigations into CIO contributions during the 1940s had resulted in permanent wartime prohibitions on union usage of general funds for campaigns. While unions supported publicly financed elections in the 1950s, they were against restrictions on PACs. By pooling contributions, unions created a lobbying presence in a way that workers could never achieve individually. Unions argued that conservative legislators were using reform to combat labor's political power without doing anything about their own contributions.[102] The steelworkers wrote Senator Lehman about a bill that would prohibit union members from contributing voluntarily to campaign funds: "In view of the recent natural gas scandal ... I cannot see why a penalty should be placed on the working people ... big business can knowingly and outwardly place large sums of money in political hands for purposes of individual gain."[103]

The debates between 1956 and 1958 demonstrated how the liberal coalition was framing the issue of institutional reform, in terms both of tying it to particular policies (such as civil rights) and of making other issues (such as campaign finance) more marginal to their agenda. The legislation also established the liberal coalition as a serious force in light of their success on civil rights. The ferocity of the congressional leadership in defending itself, however, indicated to them that stronger reforms were still needed.

## Organizing Congressional Liberalism

As the 1958 election approached, the liberal coalition worked with candidates in northeastern and midwestern states. Just as southerners had traditionally formed personal connections with incoming Democrats, younger liberals wanted to forge durable bonds with potential freshmen. McCarthy's Mavericks provided campaigns with money, polling, and research, as did organizations such as ADA. The 1958 election was a landslide for Democrats, whose advantage in the Senate climbed to 64-34 and in the House to 282-153: Democrats gained 39 House seats and 12 in the Senate. Most of the freshman Senate Democrats in 1958 were elected from states outside the South, and the number of junior senators was higher than at any time in the 1950s.[104] The discrepancy between Senate committees and the ideological center of the chamber increased.[105] Younger candidates from competitive urban districts did exceptionally well in the House.[106]

The 1958 election drew unprecedented attention to procedural issues and to the liberal coalition that was promoting them. The returns renewed hope for the liberal coalition, which had been reeling from conservative John McClellan's (D-AR) televised hearings into union corruption in 1957 and 1958. Liberals believed that because of the election they now had sufficient numbers to pass legislation if procedural roadblocks were overturned.[107] McCarthy's Mavericks sent a letter to liberal Democrats hailing the election as an opportunity to pass a bold agenda.[108] The Democratic National Committee's liberal advisory council called the election an "unmistakable" mandate for progressivism.[109]

In the postelection environment the Democratic leadership found itself under attack from the left and the right. Paul Butler, who headed the DNC's advisory council, joined with ADA to criticize Johnson's moderation. Butler was a brash and idealistic liberal. He went on a television show with Indiana congressman John Brademas to castigate Democratic congressional leaders for being so timid on civil rights.[110] Following the appearance, a well-publicized internal poll of the House revealed weakened support among young northern liberals for Rayburn.[111] Many younger senators were unwilling to abide by behavioral norms that had constrained rank-and-file activity.[112] At the same time, conservatives mobilized within the GOP and Eisenhower shifted to the right by intensifying his attacks on congressional spending. Republicans unexpectedly replaced the moderate Joseph Martin (R-MA) with conservative Charles Halleck (R-IN) as their leader. High expectations among liberals would make it devastating when Congress passed restrictive labor legislation in 1959 that the liberal coalition had blocked one year earlier.

The Democratic leadership derided liberal claims of an electoral mandate as sheer exaggeration. They noted that, since Eisenhower had been reelected only two years earlier, it was dangerous to read anything into the mood of the public.[113] In their minds, mistaking the election for a genuine demand for extreme legislation could undermine the Democrats' electoral standing. Rayburn and Johnson nonetheless placed several younger members on good committees and scheduled a few of their bills onto the calendar. Johnson and Rayburn simultaneously threatened opponents with unfavorable treatment on pork and worked through allies in the press – such as Joseph Alsop, Arthur Krock, Roscoe Drummond, and Marquis Childs – to attack Butler and his allies.[114]

McCarthy's Mavericks took on a formal structure in 1959 when they organized into the Democratic Study Group. The DSG perceived themselves as representing the "voiceless" younger northern and western Democrats who had been elected in districts that were Republican before the New Deal. Members of DSG felt that these Democrats were not represented by either of the two major factions in the Democratic party: southern Democrats such as Howard Smith or northern machine congressmen such as John McCormack. Neither of the two dominant factions, DSG said, had much interest in addressing new issues but rather sought to maintain their power.[115] Operating as a guerilla operation, DSG focused on three functions: lobbying the Democratic leadership to place liberals on committees, mobilizing votes for legislation, and disseminating research to members. Wendell Phillips, an administrative assistant to Representative George Rhodes (D-PA), served as the first staff director and organized the research efforts. One of the first studies they released provided a statistical analysis of the conservative coalition in the first session of the 86th Congress (1959–1960). According to the study, the 86th Congress appeared to have a massive Democratic majority with 281 Democrats, 154 Republicans, and two vacancies. But these numbers did not tell the real story. Despite the 1958 election, the study indicated that the conservative coalition claimed 225 votes compared to 196 for liberals. The conservative Democrats had voted 82 percent of the time with Republicans against their own party. On 86 percent of their votes, the twelve southern Democratic chairs voted with Republicans. The study emphasized that "procedural road-blocks" were crucial to conservative strength.[116] Functioning as a whip system, DSG used aggressive tactics. For instance, while trying to obtain enough signatures for a discharge petition in 1960 to allow liberals to force a civil rights bill out of Rules, DSG leaked the names of those Democrats who had signed the document to the *New York Times* and civil rights organizations. Knowing who their opponents were, civil rights advocates were able to campaign against them. Communicating through Bolling, DSG even persuaded Rayburn and Wilbur Mills (D-AR) – chair of Ways and Means, which made committee assignments – to weaken the conservative Education and Labor Chairman Graham Barden by packing his committee with liberals.[117]

Although Senate liberals did not formally organize after the 1958 election, they intensified their attacks. The election, combined with momentum building for stronger civil rights legislation, made filibuster reform seem more critical than ever. Between 1959 and 1961, Douglas and Humphrey were joined by ten Republicans in the fight to liberalize filibuster rules. Senator Joseph Clark (D-PA) wrote Harry Byrd: "Can there be any justification for continuing the dictatorial power now given to a single Senator ... ?"[118] While liberals mobilized in the

Senate, allied interest groups intensified their efforts. Civil rights activist Roy Wilkins noted that filibuster reform was an "enormously complex and technical matter little understood by the general public and, as the recent debate proved, by many newspaper men and some senators. But the question of human rights in our country is one demanding attention despite technicalities and parliamentary skirmishes."[119] But Johnson told each northerner that he would never support majoritarian filibuster reform because it would destroy the party's southern base and benefit Republicans.[120]

While pointing to the 1957 civil rights bill as proof that reform was not needed, the leadership sensed that the filibuster was losing support and that southern conservatives were isolating themselves.[121] Under pressure for some type of change, Johnson offered a reform in 1959 that changed cloture rules from two thirds (66 senators) of the Senate membership to two thirds of those present and voting. This was a return to the rules that had existed before 1949. Most liberals agreed that the reform was negligible.[122]

Senate liberals were once again frustrated by the filibuster during a debate over civil rights in 1960. When new civil rights legislation reached the Senate in 1960, Johnson decided to conduct 24-hour sessions in order to wear down the southern opposition. In response, Senator Russell organized four teams under the supervision of captains. Each team was ordered to retain the floor during 24-hour periods. During that time, the other teams left the chamber to rest. The team on the floor subdivided. One group filibustered while the other prepared to relieve them. The filibustering southerners would demand that members be counted to see if a quorum was present. Southerners asked for quorum calls at the most inopportune moments, such as the very early morning hours. Except for the person speaking, the rest of the team left the chamber. It took up to three hours for a sufficient number of senators to return to obtain a quorum.[123] The tactic wore down northerners who were forced at all hours to keep returning.[124] In the end, northerners were forced to accept watered-down legislation.

Often called "Douglas's group," Senate liberals also attacked Johnson for making committee assignments that favored southerners and for muting the party's caucus. In 1959, Johnson had refused to place two liberals, William Proxmire (D-WI) and Joseph Clark, on the Democratic Policy Committee or the Finance Committee. Outraged, Proxmire and Clark claimed that committee assignments did not reflect the industrial base of the party.[125] Clark wrote Johnson: "I don't believe you can indefinitely 'sit on the lid,' supporting the chairmen of standing Committees selected by seniority, many of whom are not in sympathy with the principles and platform of the modern Democratic party."[126] Proxmire's mail ran 30 to 1 in support of his attacks.[127] These senators also tried unsuccessfully to make the Democratic Conference meet more often and for the Democratic Policy Committee to propose bolder agendas.[128] Rejecting Gore's proposal to strengthen the committee, Johnson did agree to place three freshman senators onto the Legislative Review Committee, and all were made *ex officio* members of the policy committee.[129]

Although substantive reform did not pass during these years, the liberal coalition had expanded in size, its organizational structure had thickened, and they had defined the problem of congressional reform within the politicized context of progressive policy. In particular, the civil rights issue enabled the coalition to make explicit in its public appeals the link between the most arcane procedures (such as the filibuster) and the dramatic struggles that were shaking the nation. That context was becoming all the more potent in these years as numerous forces in the polity pushed controversial issues to the forefront of national discussion.

### Taming the House Rules Committee

The liberal coalition obtained its first significant institutional change in 1961 when the House temporarily expanded the Rules Committee, which had been a bastion for the conservative coalition. Although the final reform was the mildest option, the liberal coalition thus struck one of the first blows to the authority of committees. Known as the "legislative gatekeeper," the House Rules Committee controlled the floor agenda, scheduled hearings on rules, established how much time legislation would be debated, and determined what rules would be used when considering a bill. The Rules Committee had become more obstructionist after 1955 when Howard Smith took over the chairmanship. Smith fit the bill of the classic southern conservative, still living in a home where his mother had resided during the Civil War.[130] Adding to the committee's conservative bent, Republican leader Charles Halleck encouraged committee Republicans to vote with the conservative coalition.[131] Republicans named two conservatives, Hamer Budge (R-ID) and B. Carroll Reece (R-TN), to fill the vacancies created by departing moderates.

Republicans and southern Democrats insisted that the Rules Committee provided a shield against reckless legislation. Downplaying procedure, they contended that a majority could assert its will through mechanisms such as Calendar Wednesday, which enabled committees to circumvent Rules.[132] When Chet Holifield took over DSG in 1959, he targeted the Rules Committee. The DSG proposed to Rayburn that the House reinstate the 21-day rule and expand the committee so as to include more liberals. The decision to focus on Rules reflected how the agenda had changed since 1945, when reorganization proponents consciously avoided discussing the issue.[133] Rayburn promised DSG that Smith would be more flexible; Rayburn and Smith had maintained a gentleman's agreement whereby the chair released bills that were of special interest to the Speaker.

Rayburn's promise did not come to fruition. After 1959, Rules became even more obstructionist. For example, the committee prevented a federal education bill from going to conference committee. DSG brought small provisions before Rules (which they knew would not be brought to the House floor for a vote) just so Smith would antagonize key interest groups. *U.S. News & World Report* published a survey of 28 senators and 90 representatives on "What's Wrong with

Congress." There were many disagreements, but almost everyone agreed that Rules needed to be tamed.[134]

The election of John Kennedy as president in 1960 heightened interest in congressional reform. As a result of the 1960 election, the new House had 261 Democrats and 174 Republicans. Liberals insisted that there were enough Democrats and liberal Republicans to pass legislation if institutional rules did not prevent them from doing so.[135] "Stripped of the Senate filibuster and the House Rules Committee veto," the New York ADA promised, "the conservative coalition will no longer stand as a roadblock to the New Frontier."[136] Legislators and interest groups in the liberal coalition, who had promoted reforming the Rules Committee as a major issue for several years, now moved into high gear. Forty liberal interest groups met in Washington, for example, to map out a strategy for promoting majority rule.[137]

Tensions became more severe when Smith bragged to reporters that he would "exercise whatever weapon that I can lay my hands on" to stifle Kennedy. He refused to tolerate "radical, wild-eyed spendthrift proposals that will do the country severe damage."[138] Rayburn became openly frustrated with Smith. Following the election, Kennedy met with the Speaker in Florida. While refusing to take a public position on legislative procedure, Kennedy implied to Rayburn that he endorsed weakening the Rules Committee. Kennedy told his closest aide Lawrence O'Brien that "we can't lose this one Larry.... The ball game is over if we do."[139] When Rayburn returned to Washington, he suggested to Bolling that he would support reform.

The Democratic Study Group made four primary proposals. One reform would alter the party ratios in all committees by adding more Democrats and reducing the number of Republicans. The number of Democrats on the Rules Committee would thus increase. However, this option conflicted with a deal that Rayburn had made with Republican leaders to maintain committee ratios. The second proposal was to expand the committee so that Democrats could place more liberals on Rules without reducing the number of Republicans. This was the least controversial. The third option was to purge Smith's leading ally from the committee, William Colmer (D-MS), since he had not supported Kennedy in the election. This was a dramatic proposal insofar as party purges had been rare since 1925.[140] While this was the measure DSG preferred, its leaders understood that the purge of a southern conservative would provoke a fierce response and endanger Adam Clayton Powell for having supported Eisenhower in 1956. Two staunch Mississippi conservatives warned of retaliation.[141] The most institutionally radical proposal was to move the committee's rule-making authority to a party policy committee.[142]

The battle over the Rules Committee brought the problem of institutional procedures and their relation to southern Democrats to the forefront of media attention. The leadership had always found comfort in the fact that procedural reform had "very little sex appeal to the average Washington correspondent."[143] But after 1960, the press regularly published editorials and stories about how conservatives used procedure for power.[144] The liberal coalition provided reporters with all the material they needed to document the committee's power. Smith became a tangible villain in a battle that revolved around complex and abstract rules. Whereas procedures were often too complicated for reporting, the threat of Smith to Kennedy was simple to explain. It offered a foe and a hero. Tom Wicker wrote a feature story for the *New York Times Magazine* that focused on Smith; it was entitled "Again That Roadblock in Congress."[145] A CBS show on Smith triggered a massive inflow of mail from around the country – ranging from conservatives who praised him as a patriot fighting against dangerous legislation to opponents who called him a tyrant working against the national interest.[146] A Herblock cartoon entitled "Gateway to the New Frontier" depicted Kennedy standing before a gate being blocked by an angry bull. One of the bull's horns said "House Rules Committee" and the other "Senate Rules."[147]

There were troubling signals for Smith. Wilbur Mills called Smith to tell him that he opposed removing Colmer. After a private meeting with the Speaker five days later, Mills called Smith back to let him know that Rayburn was so "irritated" with Colmer that he was considering the purge.[148] Majority Leader John McCormack, Majority Whip Carl Albert (D-OK), and Bolling all endorsed this action. Rayburn searched for a viable compromise. Rayburn met privately with Smith to urge him to accept committee expansion in order to avoid a protracted conflict. Smith refused. Strategically, Rayburn was pleased since he wanted to be able to tell the House that Smith had been given the option to avoid an open fight but had decided against this path.[149] After his meeting, Rayburn informed DSG that, since Smith would not accept enlargement of the committee, Colmer should be purged. He asked DSG to remain silent before the press.[150] Smith received strong assurances that most southerners would not endorse a purge, especially since they were facing district pressure. Hale Boggs (D-LA), one of the stronger southern supporters of civil rights, received more mail on this issue than any other. Most of the letters opposed the expansion.[151] Yet Smith also realized – based on conversations with Carl Vinson (D-GA) and Clarence Cannon (D-MO) – that there was little chance of blocking committee expansion.[152]

Over the next two crucial weeks, high uncertainty reigned over the outcome of the vote. Vinson worked with Francis Walter (D-PA) to find a compromise that would avoid an open confrontation.[153] Liberals bombarded undecided members by sending out allied interest groups and representatives. Behind the scenes, Smith said he would accept limits on committee power as long as the conservative coalition retained control.[154]

Ten days after the session started, Rayburn revealed to the media that he was going to push for a *temporary* expansion of the Rules Committee. Reversing his position, he had decided not to purge Colmer. Rayburn said this was the easiest way to resolve the controversy without embarrassing anybody. Rayburn also sensed this was the most politically viable reform, since his vote counts indicated that none of the reforms was secure. Furthermore, the expansion would only be temporary. Future congresses would have to decide whether to adhere to the change. The Democratic Caucus ordered the Rules Committee to report a resolution to the House that enlarged their committee to fifteen members. Rayburn obtained the last-minute support of key southern conservatives by promising money for their districts and warning of worse alternatives.[155] Together with the assistance of Vinson, North Carolina Governor Terry Sanford, and the president, Rayburn persuaded one third of the southern Democrats in the House to support the committee expansion.[156] Deciding to push for what was possible rather than perfect, DSG kept quiet about Rayburn's private promise to purge Colmer, and they persuaded the White House to apply pressure in support of Rayburn's plan. Before the vote, Kennedy advisers leaked to the media that the president feared he would be unable to deal with Soviet Premier Nikita Khrushchev should the committee reform fail. This was a common argument at the time among civil rights supporters, who argued that racism severely undermined the nation's international standing in the Cold War.[157] On January 28, days before the House vote, Smith desperately tried to obtain Vinson's support by promising him that he would not "interpose" any obstacles to the five major bills that Kennedy had announced for the first session.[158] Going into the floor debate, Rayburn was still not fully certain he had all the needed votes.[159]

The final debate was intense. Opponents attacked the reform as an attempt to force unpopular legislation through Congress. They warned that the reform would weaken representative democracy by making legislators more susceptible to political pressure and less capable of reaching deliberative judgments. Denying the existence of a conservative coalition, opponents warned that the reform would take the House back to the days of "tyrannical" Speaker Joe Cannon. Smith blamed the reform on liberals who wanted to force representatives to vote for their bills rather than to vote on the basis of conscience or constituency. Waving a copy of the monthly ADA newsletter, Smith said cynically: "Now I have in my hand the monthly issue of Americans for Democratic Action. Have any of you ever heard of that? They claim credit for all this ruckus that is going on here now."[160] In a dramatic moment, Rayburn made a rare floor speech. He argued that every president should have an opportunity to have his proposals voted on and that a majority should be able to work its "will" by voting on legislation. Personalizing the conflict, Rayburn criticized Smith for writing a letter that accused the Speaker of wanting to "stack" the committee for partisan purposes.[161]

The House passed the resolution 217-212. The liberal coalition was successful because of 22 northern Republicans who supported the reform. Eighteen of these Republicans represented northeastern urban and industrial districts. They ignored Minority Leader Charles Halleck and the unanimous position of the party's policy committee. These Republicans were no longer comfortable with the conservative coalition. As they explained in a formal statement: "We repudiate any suggestion of a coalition with Southern Democrats.... To attempt to narrow the base of our party, to dull its conscience, to transform it into a negative weapon of obstruction can only succeed in projecting an image which has consistently been rejected by the Republican party and by the American people."[162] The reform drew unanimous nonsouthern Democratic support as well.[163] Thirty-six southern Democrats – most from Alabama, Arkansas, Louisiana, Tennessee, and Texas – voted in favor of the expansion. Two thirds of this southern Democratic contingent came from rural districts with small African-American populations, where race relations was not as prevalent an issue. Most important, Rayburn obtained the support of most southern committee chairs, including the powerhouses Vinson, Mills, and Oren Harris (D-AR). There were only two important chairs that did not support Rayburn, and one was Howard Smith.

Although the final reform was the least controversial alternative and though the final vote was narrow enough to indicate that southern strength remained formidable, the victory was significant to the liberal coalition. Democrats gained two additional members on the Rules Committee while the Republicans gained one seat. Two Democratic liberals, Carl Elliott (AL) and B. F. Sisk (CA), as well as moderate William Avery (R-KS), were placed on the committee, and the reformers showed that the legislative process was malleable. The expansion of Rules offered liberals evidence that the conservative coalition could be defeated. In 1963, the House would vote to extend the expansion by a larger margin of 235 to 196. During the battle over civil rights, Rules would not be a major obstacle, and the panel dropped off the liberal coalition's agenda. After the House weakened Smith, party leadership changed. Rayburn died in 1961 and Johnson became vice-president. John McCormack was elected Speaker, while Mike Mansfield (D-MT) took over as Senate Majority Leader.

## The Civil Rights Act and the Election of 1964

Like Howard Smith, southern senators were reminded that their power was fragile when – in the summer of 1964 – northern Democrats overcame a Senate filibuster to pass the Civil Rights Act of 1964. During this year the nation witnessed the powerful convergence of a vibrant grassroots civil rights movement, charismatic leaders such as Martin Luther King, and the liberal coalition that had been fighting to weaken institutional roadblocks from within Washington.

While the civil rights movement created national electoral and media support for federal intervention into the issue of southern race relations, the liberal coalition (which included several Washington-based civil rights organizations) was a key factor in the success of the bill once it was in Congress. The liberal coalition had already been instrumental in making sure the bill had not been bottled up in the House. Once it was in the Senate, members of the liberal coalition joined their resources to fight the southern response. The Leadership Conference on Civil Rights, for instance, served as an informal whip and gathered data that could be used in campaigns. Clarence Mitchell and Joseph Rauh met every night with Humphrey's staff to keep strategic communications open between the organizations in the liberal coalition.[164] Humphrey mounted a response to the filibuster by dividing allies into rotating troops to counteract the southerners with procedural warfare. The Senator had a baseball stadium manager inform a group of attending pro–civil rights legislators on the public address system that southerners were calling for a quorum call and they needed to return to work immediately. The LCCR arranged for a police escort to drive the senators back.[165] When President Johnson and Humphrey persuaded Minority Leader Everett Dirksen to accept cloture, enough Republicans lined up to end the filibuster. LCCR wrote its members, "Cloture At Last!"[166] The Civil Rights Act of 1964 ended segregation in public accommodations, improved the federal government's capacity to fight employment discrimination in government projects and education, and banned gender discrimination in employment.

The landslide election of 1964 increased the Democratic majority in the House to 295 and in the Senate to 68. Democrats used the opportunity to push for further institutional reforms. Northern legislators pointed to the fact that the greatest net losses for Democrats came in Alabama, Georgia, Idaho, and Mississippi, while the largest net gains came in northern and western states.[167] The postelection changes centered in the House. In January 1965, the Democratic Caucus recommended – and the House adopted – rules changes to reinstate the 21-day rule and a rule permitting bills to be sent directly to House–Senate conference without Rules Committee clearance. The caucus also recommended the creation of a joint committee to study congressional reform and propose recommendations, and it altered committee party ratios to reflect increased Democratic strength. The caucus stripped John Bell Williams (MS) and Albert Watson (SC) of their seniority for having supported Republican Barry Goldwater. Senate Democrats expanded the Steering Committee to seventeen members and included liberals Eugene McCarthy and Pat McNamara (D-MI). Republicans abandoned their strict adherence to seniority in making committee assignments.

## The Redefinition of Congressional Reform

During the 1950s and early 1960s, congressional reform was connected to a heated struggle over civil rights. Targeting southern chairs and the conservative coalition, the liberal coalition insisted that a new legislative process was integral to the success of postwar liberalism and to strengthening Congress. The reforms aimed to create institutional incentives that forced legislators to be accountable to their party and constituents. The major operating assumption of the liberal coalition was that the failure of their legislative proposals did not reflect weak electoral support so much as the influence of a small group of conservative legislators whose power rested entirely on unfair institutional protections. If those institutions were dismantled, the coalition insisted, progressive legislation would inevitably flow smoothly out of Congress since (the coalition believed) most Americans supported their positions. The evidence for this proposition remains dubious, particularly after years of historical research have recently started to reveal the broad-based support of conservatism at the height of the "New Deal Order." At the time, however, this assumption shaped the ideas of the coalition.

The liberal coalition helped place congressional reform on the agenda, linking technical procedures to the national social struggle taking place over civil rights, and they acted as hard-nosed lobbyists in the halls of Congress. Liberals envisioned an assertive Congress capable of responding to majority interests and the executive branch. They warned that Democrats would suffer politically should they remain under the grip of conservatives. To reform the House Rules Committee, they formed an alliance with moderate Republicans. The liberal coalition itself had altered the interest-group environment that legislators faced by creating more organizations focused on changing the actual political process and not just the policies Congress enacted. While there were unaffiliated moderates who pressed for reform, the liberal coalition politicized procedure by framing this issue within the context of progressive policy.

Yet the liberal coalition was not satisfied. The expansion of the House Rules Committee had failed to prevent the legislative logjam that frustrated President Kennedy until his death. Howard Smith continued to pose problems by bottling up legislation for as long as he could. Most of the Great Society victories in 1964 and 1965 were perceived as having been dependent on the highly exceptional circumstances surrounding those years (such as Kennedy's assassination and the existence of a mass civil rights movement). Liberal Democrats had relied on support from Republicans, a party with a decidedly mixed record on civil rights since the Civil War. Further, the sizable conservative gains in the 1966 congressional elections made the huge liberal Democratic majorities of 1964 seem aberrational rather than normative. The liberal coalition thus believed that more congressional reforms were needed to ensure passage of their legislation under normal working conditions, which was their ultimate goal. The chances of the coalition to obtain further reforms increased exponentially as the institutions surrounding Congress, including the Supreme Court and the news media, changed dramatically throughout the 1960s and created an unsympathetic environment for the committee system.

# 4

## Into the Political Thicket

In his memoirs, Supreme Court Chief Justice Earl Warren hailed *Baker v. Carr* as his greatest accomplishment.[1] Starting with the *Baker* decision in 1962, the Supreme Court issued a series of rulings that altered the electoral system which had protected senior southern Democrats. The Court decisions centered on the idea that Congress could be more representative if districts were equitable to urban and suburban voters. Improved voting rights, in the minds of proponents, would produce a Congress that was responsive to what they believed was the nation's majority wishes. The decision extended the concept of voting rights beyond the concern with the right to cast a ballot and toward every individual's vote counting equally.[2] When combined with the Voting Rights Act of 1965, the decisions shook the electoral base of southern Democrats and injected the judicial branch into legislative politics.[3] While the liberal coalition continued its efforts to mount pressure on legislators to enact further reform, the Supreme Court redistricting decisions constituted the first major alteration to the institutional environment surrounding Congress that favored a new era.

Between 1962 and 1964, the Supreme Court required state and federal legislatures to create voting districts with equal populations. In the short term, the decisions put conservative southern Democrats on notice. Until the 1960s, congressional reform had been championed by a coalition of legislators, interest groups, and academics. With the exception of President Kennedy's backroom support for the House Rules Committee expansion, the executive and judicial branches had avoided these matters. Now the highest court in the land challenged the legitimacy of sitting legislators by articulating the idea of "vote dilution," which meant the practice of using apportionment and districting to diminish the value of one vote in relation to another. Without the advantage of a crystal ball, there were fears in the 1960s among southerners that redistricting would have a profound effect on them. The primary defeat of Howard Smith in 1966 had resulted directly from the liberalization of his constituency through redistricting. Smith's downfall sent out shock waves because of his preeminent role in the committee era. In the battle for institutional reform, this kind of dramatic attack by one institution on another – even when the long-term impact on the system's leaders turned out to be far less or quite different than initially anticipated – was integral to reform politics. They provided reformers momentum and placed incumbents on the defensive.

The long-term impact of the Court decisions was equally significant, although it would not always serve the initial objectives of the liberal coalition. Redistricting helped create a Democratic Caucus that was more unified ideologically. As a result, there were fewer incentives and opportunities for legislators to rely on the committee process. Although most senior conservative southern chairmen from the 1960s retained their seats until retirement or death, many were replaced by liberal and moderate Democrats in the late 1970s and 1980s as well as by conservative Republicans in the 1990s.[4] Many younger Democrats were more conservative than their colleagues on fiscal and military issues, but they tended to vote the party line; there was no longer an issue as polarizing as civil rights to divide them from the caucus. Furthermore, Republicans were capturing the vote of conservative suburban and rural citizens. Almost nobody in the new generation of Republicans and Democrats had much interest in the committee process, since they were more committed to the emerging partisan style. The main impetus behind the unification of Democrats was the surge after 1965 of African-American voters, who tended to elect moderates and liberals instead of conservatives.

This development was not inevitable. A large body of political science scholarship has recently focused on the ideological unification of Democrats in the 1980s to show how electoral changes rather than procedural reforms naturally transform Congress.[5] But a comprehensive history reveals that the relevant electoral changes in the South were rooted in concrete reforms that removed institutional barriers and allowed natural electoral forces, such as African-American and suburban voters, to have an impact. The rise of liberal and moderate southern Democrats who voted the party line depended on the Voting Rights Act and the elimination of vote dilution through court orders, litigation, and Department of Justice actions. In Alabama, Georgia, Louisiana, Mississippi, North Carolina, South Carolina, Texas, and Virginia, the demise of legislative systems that were dominated by rural legislators depended on the enforcement of the Voting Rights Act – as modified by the Supreme Court in 1969 to include the problem of racial vote dilution, which the Court had defined in the early 1960s.[6]

### "The Biggest Thing to Hit Georgia Since Sherman"

The liberal coalition had always claimed that districting was an integral component of congressional reform. The ADA warned in 1959 that "the character of the legislature – its composition, its social outlook, its economic philosophy – is directly determined by the system of legislative representation."[7] This was not just a southern issue. In states such as Minnesota and New York, rural-based legislators enjoyed equal if not greater standing than those who represented urban areas.

Fulfilling their public relations function, the liberal coalition tried to generate political concern by framing this procedural issue in a way that would resonate with broad audiences. They depicted districts as a tool used by conservative legislators to stifle majoritarian policy desires: "The popular character of the House has been destroyed," complained Eugene McCarthy in 1952, "by the failure of the state legislatures to provide for Congressional districts of approximately the same population and by the practice of electing Congressmen at large."[8] The AFL-CIO's Gus Tyler said that "unfair representation is a vast and well fortified political roadblock to the legislative progress of twentieth century America."[9] Andrew Biemiller told the House Judiciary Committee that America had "taxation without *fair* representation – an evil only one step removed from the one which caused Colonial America to rise in righteous revolt."[10] The coalition rejected claims of the system's defenders that the current process protected rural minorities against urban power. The National Municipal League, whose committee on districting included Biemiller and the ADA's Edward Hollander, worked with the League of Women Voters, AJC, ACLU, and ADA to raise awareness about the problem.[11] The American Political Science Association called for districts to "contain as nearly as practicable the same number of individuals."[12]

Failing to obtain legislation in the 1950s, the coalition turned to the courts. In a series of historic cases between 1962 and 1964, the Supreme Court ruled that it had a right to intervene in apportionment and districting to ensure fair representation. The justices were aware of the connection between race, congressional power, and legislative districts. Earl Warren said that equitable reapportionment "would have saved ourselves acute racial troubles. Many of our problems would have been solved a long time ago if everyone had the right to vote and his vote counted the same as everybody else's. Most of these problems could have been solved through the political process rather than through the courts."[13] The ties between civil rights and the reapportionment issue were widely discussed in these decades. Speaking of his state's notorious county unit system, the avidly racist Georgia Governor Herman Talmadge warned in 1950 that "the very future of our entire pattern of segregation in Georgia is tied closely and inseparably to our County Unit System."[14]

Before 1962, the Supreme Court had refused to intervene because several justices did not believe that the Court had authority over what they saw as a state decision. Since the problem involved vote dilution rather than the outright denial of voting rights, justices were skeptical that the Court could offer a clear and manageable standard regarding how much a vote was worth. Justice Felix Frankfurter directed the opposition to court-ordered reapportionment and redistricting. As a strong advocate of judicial restraint, Frankfurter did not believe that the courts should interfere in what he called the "political thicket." If the Court intervened, he said, justices would have to confront endless cases to decide whether districts were equitable.[15] Frankfurter appeared to shift his position in the 1960 case of *Gomillion v. Lightfoot*, which involved Alabama legislators who had created a district in Tuskegee with the explicit intention of denying the vote to African-American residents.[16] But Frankfurter agreed on court intervention in that case because it involved outright denial of the right to vote.[17]

Although civil rights activists claimed the case was a precedent for court action against vote dilution, most were pessimistic that the Court would deal with the issue.[18] In 1961, Justice Harlan warned that intervention would undermine the integrity of the Court since its "aloofness from political vicissitudes" had been integral to the stability of the nation. "Those attributes," he insisted, "have been assured not alone by the constitutional and statutory safeguards which surround the Court, but also to a large extent, I believe, by the wise restraint which, by and large, has characterized the Court's handling of emotionally-charged popular causes." But were the Court to endorse a proposal driven by Democrats, Harlan predicted, cynics would start considering the "political backgrounds or ideologies" of the justices:

were we now to enter this "political thicket," would we not inevitably be courting such appearances, however unfounded, as all manner and gradations of apportionment cases come to our door? The only sure way of avoiding this is to keep the gate to the thicket tightly closed. Politics being what they are it seems to me that it would be almost naive to blink at the dangers of this situation.[19]

The Court began to take action with the state government of Tennessee, where rural counties dominated state politics. Despite demographic changes, Tennessee had not reapportioned the seats for its general assembly since 1901 – even though the state constitution mandated that it do so every ten years.[20] Plaintiffs from urban Tennessee argued that, because of this situation, rural areas received a disproportionate share of federal tax dollars. The issue gained a sympathetic ear from President Kennedy, who had highlighted the problem in 1958 with an article entitled "The Shame of the States."[21] Solicitor General Archibald Cox argued that urban citizens did not have equal access to the laws since they did not play an equal role when selecting their legislators. Some members of the Court urged caution. On April 20, 1961, Justice Frankfurter warned that "the solicitor general was irresponsible in stating there was a permissible remedy ... how can courts determine what is fair in this area?"[22] Justice Clark added: "Equality is not a basic principle in American political voting."[23]

Ultimately the Court could not reach an agreement and set *Baker* aside to be reargued the following term. In 1962, the Court ruled that Tennessee apportionment violated the Fourteenth Amendment by "debasing" the value of the plaintiffs' votes. Written by Brennan, the opinion concluded that certain Tennessee citizens were denied equal protection since they had less influence over their elected legislators. The majority left it to the lower courts to decide what would constitute an equitable district. Dissenting with Harlan, Frankfurter warned that "there is not under our Constitution a judicial remedy for every political mischief ... there is nothing judicially more unseemly nor more self-defeating than for this Court to make *in terrorem* pronouncements, to indulge in merely empty rhetoric, sounding a word of promise to the ear, sure to be disappointing to the hope."[24] Despite Frankfurter's objections, *Baker* determined that the federal courts would take on cases where citizens claimed that existing apportionment had denied them equal protection under the Fourteenth Amendment. It was a major blow to American federalism.

Days after *Baker*, Frankfurter suffered a stroke and retired. Kennedy replaced him with Secretary of Labor Arthur Goldberg, who was sympathetic to Warren's position on *Baker*. To replace Justice Whittaker, who had resigned right before *Baker*, Kennedy appointed his deputy attorney general Byron White, a supporter of the Court's redistricting decisions.

"It's the biggest thing to hit Georgia since Sherman," proclaimed the former Mayor of Atlanta William Hartsfield.[25] Reapportionment took place in 34 states while 11 others were working on plans by the summer of 1965.[26] Hours after the Supreme Court had filed its *Baker* decision in 1962, James O'Rear Sanders, a local businessman in Georgia, sued to overturn Georgia's notorious county unit system. John Sheffield, who represented a county where the number of African-Americans registered to vote remained at only 12 percent, warned that "changes in the county unit system will lead to other compromises with the NAACP on the integration question and to consolidation of counties."[27] A three-judge federal court declared the entire county unit system invalid. The Supreme Court concurred in 1963.[28]

For many southerners, the decisions appeared to be a revolution in southern politics. Future President Jimmy Carter recalled that his family followed these events with great attention: "This was the major news item to be read and discussed at our peanut warehouse, at church, at Lions Club meetings, and in the small county newspapers. The system was so firmly entrenched that we had never really considered the possibility or advisability of its being changed."[29] Most leading newspapers praised the decisions.[30]

The next targets of the Supreme Court were districts for the U.S. House of Representatives. Justice Stewart realized that "we are hitting Congress where it lives. Their jobs are involved."[31] Georgia's federal districting system was shattered by *Wesberry v. Sanders* (1964). This case was easier to justify because the Constitution stated that population was to be the basis of representation in the House. Plaintiffs from the Fifth District alleged that they were unjustly treated, since their population was three times as large as the population of the Ninth, the smallest district in Georgia. The Fifth District was the second most underrepresented in the nation. Residents of Atlanta had challenged districting on four occasions, yet each time their case had been rejected. But the *Baker* precedent and Frankfurter's retirement transformed the legal landscape.

The Court ruled 6-3 that populations in each congressional district must be roughly equal so that the vote of each citizen carried the same weight. Justice Black's majority, which included Chief Justice Warren and Goldberg, Black, Brennan, Douglas, and White, proclaimed that "It would defeat the principle solemnly embodied in the Great Compromise – equal representation in the House for equal numbers of people – for us to hold that, within the States, legislatures may draw the lines of congressional districts in such a way as to give some voters a greater voice in choosing a Congressman than others. The House of Representatives, the Constitutional Convention agreed, was to represent the people as individuals, and on a basis of complete equality for each voter." Harlan warned that the decision "casts grave doubt on the constitutionality of the composition of the House of Representatives."[32] According to opponents, "the abstract claim to equality cannot be brought down to earth except in the context of the struggle for power between the two political parties on the *national* level. And, a requirement of equal size is meaningless without a concomitant requirement of shape, which would bring the Court into the thickest part of the political thicket."[33]

The decisions attracted the attention of the media, playing a role similar to the battle over the House Rules Committee in 1961. Editorials were generally supportive except in a few hostile southern papers.[34] Based on thin evidence, the Democratic National Committee credited redistricting for contributing to the liberal landslide in 1964.[35] There was never as much opposition as to *Baker,* since it was clearer why districts for the House were of national concern. *Baker* also had altered perceptions about what types of judicial intervention were legitimate. By 1965, eighteen states had re-created districts as a result of the courts.[36] The liberal coalition played an integral role as part of the legal team behind this fight, as the ACLU, AJC, and NAACP brought suits against unfair districts.[37]

The final stage in this constitutional revolution extended the "one person, one vote" principle to both chambers of state government in *Reynolds v. Sims* (1964). *Reynolds* stated that both houses of state government had to be determined by population, not geography.[38] By empowering urban and suburban voters in the election of both chambers, the court could prevent one body from acting as a veto on behalf of rural interests.[39] The case created a new constitutional right by mandating "one person, one vote" as the basis for legislative apportionment.[40] The decision was a dramatic extension of federal power into the states by forcing particular district arrangements in both chambers. Most significantly, the Court equated vote dilution with the outright denial of the vote. In a companion case, the Court overturned a popular Colorado referendum in which citizens voted to allow one chamber to be based on factors other than population.[41] Through subsequent decisions, the Court applied the one person–one vote criterion to virtually all bodies of local government.

Just as the courts were defining and attacking the problem of vote dilution, Congress passed the Voting Rights Act (VRA) of 1965. Unlike redistricting, this was an issue driven by grassroots activism. Johnson and Congress moved on the legislation only after the nation watched a brutal attack on March 7, 1965, against civil rights marchers in Alabama. The legislation committed the federal government to appointing voting registrars to monitor areas with a large percentage of disenfranchised voters and suspended the literacy test that had been used to prevent African-Americans from exercising their right to vote. The boldest component of the legislation was Section 5, which stipulated that voting practices in areas with a history of past discrimination had to be preapproved by the

U.S. Attorney General or the Federal District Court for the District of Columbia. By 1966, voting-rights legislation and registration drives by civil rights organizations gave muscle to the new system by dramatically increasing the number of southern African-Americans who were registered and who voted.[42] In Mississippi, for example, black registration jumped from 6.7 percent before 1965 to 59.8 percent in 1967.[43] Whereas black registration had hovered at an average of 29 percent for each election in the seven states covered by VRA, none of the covered states had less than 50-percent black registration two years after Congress passed the bill.[44] At first, the redistricting decisions and the voting-rights legislation were not clearly related. But this changed at the end of the decade.

## Aftermath

The short-term effects of the decisions were primarily symbolic. The Supreme Court had attacked the legitimacy of another pillar in the existing legislative system just when southern Democrats were under fire from the liberal coalition and a national, grassroots civil rights movement. Whatever the long-term impact would be, in the mid-1960s the future was uncertain. There were many predictions by conservatives and liberals that court-ordered redistricting, when combined with the voting-rights legislation, would end the dominance of southern conservative rural Democrats. As a result, the liberal coalition was emboldened while their opponents were apprehensive.

By 1964, several politicians and organizations were openly attacking the justices. Many southern conservatives saw the decisions as the continuation of expanding judicial authority that had started with *Brown*. Richard Russell called *Reynolds* "another major assault on our constitutional system."[45] Representative Joseph Waggonner (D-LA) warned that redistricting would cause rural voters to lose power to urban residents "with their special problems of mass transportation, urban renewal, illiteracy, lawlessness, staggering welfare projects and industrial expansion."[46] Criticism was not reserved to southern conservatives. Majority Leader Carl Albert, who represented one of the smallest districts in the country, warned that population equality ignored the social, economic, and political factors that politicians considered when creating districts. Albert asked if the Court could also abolish seniority.[47]

There were two lines of attack by defenders of the status quo. Representative William Tuck (D-VA) proposed the most radical legislation in 1964, which would have stripped from the federal judiciary the right to interfere in any districting matters. Southerners had attempted to pass similar legislation in response to *Brown*. The bill encountered resistance from the House Judiciary Committee, chaired by Emanuel Celler. Howard Smith took the bill out of committee and brought it directly to the floor. Emotions were high. Celler called the Rules Committee a bunch of "angry men" who were frustrated with the "judicious decisions" of Judiciary and the Court.[48] The House passed the measure on August 19, 1964 by a vote of 218 to 175. However, when Strom Thurmond offered

Tuck's bill as an amendment, the Senate defeated it 56-21. Even many southern senators were willing to accept the Court decisions. Nor were they as directly threatened as representatives.

Most of the active opposition from Congress centered on the court-ordered redistricting of both chambers in state government. The *Reynolds* decision, in their minds, had gone too far and implicitly threatened the U.S. Senate. Minority Leader Everett Dirksen proposed postponing redistricting for two years to grant Congress time to consider the issue more fully. Dirksen's strongest supporters were conservative Senators James Eastland, John McClellan, Sam Ervin, and Roman Hruska (R-NE). Yet concern within the Senate extended beyond partisan or ideological lines. Liberal Republican Jacob Javits and Frank Church (D-ID) also backed Dirksen. The attack received support from numerous conservative interest groups, including the National Association of Manufacturers, which argued that "the delicate balance of power in federal–state relations was seriously upset when, for the first time in the history of our nation, as a result of the Supreme Court decision, states are no longer permitted to constitute their state legislatures on a basis other than population."[49] After the Senate Judiciary Committee approved the legislation by 10-2, Dirksen offered the bill as an amendment to a foreign-aid authorization bill. Celler denounced the tactic, warning that "an attempt to rob the Federal courts of their jurisdiction, as this rider would, of apportionment cases, conceivably could open the door to depriving the Federal courts of jurisdiction over any classification of cases, over labor cases, anti-trust cases, and we could wind up, if Congress saw fit, to render the Supreme Court a complete cipher and thereby destroy our republican system of government."[50] The DSG found sixty House Democrats who promised to oppose the bill. Liberals – including Douglas and Clark – conducted a six-week filibuster, an irony that conservatives enjoyed noting.

After the Senate rejected the measure, Dirksen proposed a constitutional amendment that would allow states to retain one chamber that did not reflect population size as long as citizens voted for such a compromise through a referendum or initiative. Mansfield co-sponsored the proposal. According to Dirksen, the states should be allowed to replicate Congress in that the Senate was not elected on the basis of population. Redistricting proponents feared that the amendment would place "any reapportionment plan beyond the reach of court review and saddle a state with it in perpetuity." The threat to overturn some redistricting decisions was real. In June 1965, the amendment had 37 co-sponsors from both parties, and polls showed that there were 60 senators (and 250 House members) prepared to support the measure or something resembling it.[51] Union activist Gus Tyler warned that, with the Dirksen proposal, "the 'one man: one vote' principle would be denied totally."[52] When Dirksen offered his proposal as an amendment to unrelated Senate legislation, Douglas spearheaded an attack that left it short of the needed votes. Once Dirksen's bill failed, he focused on backing a campaign in the states to call for a constitutional convention. Supporters hired the conservative public relations firm Whitaker and Baxter.[53] Although

Senator Everett Dirksen (second on right) stands with a group of colleagues on May 25, 1965. Besides Senate Majority Leader Mike Mansfield (who is in the center of the photograph), Dirksen is joined by Jacob Javits (far right), a liberal Republican who supported Dirksen's attacks on *Reynolds,* and liberal Democrat Edward Kennedy (third from the left), who backed the Supreme Court (Dirksen Congressional Center).

32 state legislatures had called for a constitutional convention by 1967, this was short of the needed 34, and opponents prevented any other states from joining.

Just as the liberal coalition had helped bring attention to districting, its members responded to the attacks against the Court. President Johnson refused to interfere on this issue because rural and conservative Democrats, whose support he needed on domestic legislation, adamantly opposed the Court. So did Dirksen, whose support the president felt was essential on foreign and domestic policy, as had been evident with civil rights in 1964.[54] Liberal legislators fought against the proposed legislation in Washington. Allied interest groups pressured state government officials against supporting an amendment. Proponents of redistricting formed the National Committee for Fair Representation (NCFR) to lobby their cause. Headed by the ACLU's Lawrence Speiser, NCFR included the AFL-CIO, AJC, ADA, CORE (Congress of Racial Equality), and the ACLU.

The public relations campaign of the liberal coalition highlighted the link between the conservative coalition and the attempt to nullify the one person–one vote principle. The AFL-CIO warned that conservatives were using "distorted history to camouflage their basic goal of denying to urban residents equal representation in state legislative halls."[55] The American Jewish Congress called this a conflict over "democratic principle."[56] While some critics considered warnings about Dirksen to be exaggerated, the coalition's dramatic rhetoric was logical in the context of their larger struggle against the procedural power of southern Democrats and compromises that had subverted previous reforms.

To build support for the Court decisions, the liberal coalition continued to emphasize the relationship between redistricting and race. As with filibusters, civil rights offered compelling rhetoric through which to discuss procedural controversies. This was not just political strategy. Civil rights was *the* central issue that motivated the coalition, and they truly believed the two causes to be inseparable. The coalition claimed that vote dilution was as noxious as denying citizens the vote.[57] The National Committee for Fair Representation added that, "Given control of one house of their state legislature, die-hard segregationists could easily veto attempts to win a full voice in state affairs for Negroes and other minority groups."[58]

There was a high-profile primary in 1966 that sent chills through the spines of senior southern Democrats concerned about what the decisions might mean to them. Virginia's 1966 Democratic primary was characterized in the media as a struggle between old-line conservatives – Howard Smith and Senator Willis Robertson – and their maverick opponents. Robertson was the conservative chair of the Senate Banking Committee. The *Richmond Times-Dispatch* warned that the challengers were "supported by the AFL-CIO, and by those who undertake to control and direct the Negro vote."[59] Smith claimed that a "vicious and unscrupulous" as well as "well-organized assault on the State organization" was underway with the "concerted support of the labor organizations, the Negroes, and many of the young liberals who have been educated in our state institutions to more liberal ideas."[60] As a result of court-ordered redistricting, Smith's Eighth District came to include suburban Fairfax county near Washington and four areas near Richmond. These new areas had a sizable African-American population relative to his old constituency. Elimination of the poll tax facilitated a large increase in the number of African-American voters. Smith was defeated by the liberal Democrat George Rawlings, Jr., a 44-year-old Fredericksburg lawyer. Because of the surging African-American vote, the 79-year-old Willis Robertson, whose campaign had boasted of his conservatism,[61] lost to Democratic state senator William Spong, a 45-year-old moderate liberal who was endorsed by the AFL-CIO. Spong had appealed to urban areas and African-Americans.[62]

Since Smith had been the target of reformers and had just been redistricted, his loss had tremendous symbolic impact. His campaign had received national press coverage. If he and the Virginia machine could fall, it seemed that nobody was safe. One of the foremost conservative southern journalists, a mentor of future North Carolina Senator Jesse Helms, reacted to the changes as follows:

political revolution in a state where revolutions or even raised voices, are regarded as downright uncouth.... Tuesday's earthquake in Virginia is part of a fault-line that runs down the east coast to Florida, and over to Louisiana and Arkansas.... What has become of stability in the South? It is gone with the wind, to borrow a famous line – the winds of urbanization, Negro voting, reapportionment.... Nothing is sacred in Dixie anymore.

The success of Spong and Rawlings in Virginia, piled on top of other alarms and excursions, is bound to stimulate young woodsmen to sharpen their axes elsewhere. If Willis Robertson and Howard Smith could be felled, why not Russell, Ellender, Hill, Eastland, McClellan, Stennis, and Long of Louisiana. And in the House, why not tackle Colmer, Gathings, McMillan, Mills, Hebert, and Rivers.[63]

The *Richmond Times-Dispatch* called the primary a "political earthquake."[64] The *Washington Post* concluded that "the most powerful force for congressional reform in this generation is the Supreme Court and its representation decisions. The old rural enclaves of seniority are no longer safe."[65] Revealingly, Rawlings lost in the general election to a Republican, William Scott, who built a coalition of Republicans, conservative Democrats, and suburban voters. The state's famous rural-based Democratic machine collapsed in these years as a result of reapportionment, the end of the poll tax in 1964, and voting rights.[66]

During the 1966 elections, Republicans scored big victories with a net gain of 47 seats in the House, three in the Senate, and a few important wins in the South as well. Knoxville attorney Howard Baker won an upset against the incumbent Democrat. Baker was the first Tennessee Republican popularly elected to the Senate. Although he was fairly conservative on economic issues, Baker had made an explicit appeal in his campaign to African-Americans. The GOP secured their strongest grip yet on Kentucky when Republicans William Cowger and Marion Gene Snyder won two seats from Democrats (Snyder won in the Fourth District, which had been reapportioned) and the incumbent Republican Tim Lee Carter was reelected. Another outcome that was highly symbolic, given his role in the civil rights struggle, was Dixiecrat Strom Thurmond's reelection victory in South Carolina, this time as a Republican (he switched parties in 1964). By the 1970s, about 25 Republicans had replaced southern conservative Democrats.[67]

Before the 1980s, the impact of the decisions was primarily ideological and symbolic. Smith's loss was exceptional. Only 31 representatives lost their seats because of redistricting in the 1960s, and there were no other cases as dramatic as Smith's.[68] Moreover, opponents of redistricting found more subtle ways to limit the impact of the Court decisions through methods such as political gerrymandering (which Warren thought would be prevented by population equality) and at-large elections.[69] What the Court had accomplished right away was to define a new problem in voting rights – vote dilution – that targeted the electoral foundation of Congress and created hope within the liberal coalition (as well as fear among committee chairs) about the future of the legislative process.

## Creating a Bipartisan South

The long-term effect of the Court decisions was equally significant: they were part of a process that removed southern conservatives from the Democratic Caucus and diminished the incentives for legislators to rely on the bipartisan committee process. There was already a decline in the number of rural-based representatives at the federal, state, and local level by 1969. In 1964, there were

214 congressional districts with a rural majority. That figure had dropped to 155 by 1968 and, only four years later, to 130.[70] Every state reapportioned its legislature at least once in the era that followed *Baker.* In Alabama, the industrial and urbanized portion of the state took control of the legislature from rural areas. In Maryland, the Eastern Shore as well as western and southern regions saw power shift decisively to Baltimore County and surrounding suburbs of Washington.

The real change started in 1969. This was when the Supreme Court decisions converged with the Voting Rights Act. In *Allen v. State Board of Elections* (1969), the Court proclaimed that the problem of vote dilution was covered under the Voting Rights Act. The justices concluded that the intention of Congress in the Voting Rights Act had been to require covered states to receive preclearance for changes to *any* of their voting practices. As a result, the Department of Justice – which was using its authority to end direct voting discrimination – was able to employ its resources against inequitable redistricting.[71] Although the executive branch was the "primary arbiter" of southern redistricting plans as a result of the preclearance rules imposed on seven southern states through the Voting Rights Act,[72] the problem of vote dilution had been given constitutional legitimacy by the Court through its interpretation of legislative intent. Moreover, the Department of Justice did not tackle the issue until *after* the Court instructed them to do so.

Over the next three decades, state legislatures and the courts dismantled the white and rural electoral base of southern conservative Democrats. African-American voting increased throughout the region, while population equality among congressional districts became the norm. At the federal level, redistricting increased the number of metropolitan and suburban House Democrats.[73] With the postwar influx of African-Americans to cities and with courts that tended to be Democratic, northern urban Democrats found themselves with the type of safe seats that southerners had once enjoyed. But the most dramatic story was in Dixie. When conservative southern chairs retired, died, or were defeated in the 1970s and 1980s, they were replaced by moderate and liberal southern Democrats who nurtured biracial coalitions. Black voters were their pivotal constituency. The number of conservative safe-seat Democrats in the South would fall to about 15 percent of the elections between 1982 and 1991. In contrast, moderate safe-seat Democratic incumbents in the South doubled their victories in the 1960s and 1970s.[74] Concurrently, the redistricting process would help gradually breathe life into a two-party system in the South. Redistricting eventually benefitted southern Republicans by moving African-Americans into concentrated areas and empowering suburban middle-class voters elsewhere, who were many times solidly Republican. In a few cases during the 1970s and 1980s, and usually during the 1990s, conservative southern voters elected Republicans.

The result was that the South became an arena of partisan competition as southern Democratic conservatives practically vanished. The changes in southern politics could be seen with Georgia's Democratic Representative John Flynt, chairman of the House Ethics Committee. Elected to the House in 1954 after serving in the state government and court system, Flynt was a quintessential southern conservative who had signed the Southern Manifesto. Flynt represented a thoroughly rural district, but court-ordered redistricting in 1964 forced him to deal with his first urban constituents and the growing suburban populations that surrounded Atlanta. Flynt, who knew the history and population of each rural county in his district, didn't understand even how to socially interact with new suburban constituents. After surviving one reelection by slim margins, Flynt retired before 1978. Confronting constant Republican opposition and uncomfortable with media and poll-driven politics, Flynt decided to leave.[75] In 1978, Republican Newt Gingrich won election to represent Flynt's district.

## Southern Impact

The Supreme Court redistricting decisions challenged the electoral legitimacy of committee-era leaders. During the 1960s, shortly after the decisions were made, senior chairs who had been under attack from the liberal coalition feared the potential – or, in a few cases, the reality – of reconfigured districts that threatened their careers. There were many debates over the impact of redistricting, and most observers in the 1960s agreed that the future was uncertain.[76] This was sufficient to cause concern among legislators accustomed to easy reelection. There were also tangible threats: the collapse of state political machines, a decreasing number of rural legislators, the defeat of Howard Smith, and few GOP gains in the South. Redistricting energized the coalition that was fighting against the committee process and appeared to strike another blow to southern conservative Democrats.

Over time, redistricting and the Voting Rights Act (which were combined by a 1969 Supreme Court ruling) allowed broader social changes – such as suburbanization, urbanization, and industrialization – to find expression in the composition of Congress. The decisions helped produce a new generation of southern Democrats and Republicans who were loyal to their respective parties. By the 1990s, in large part because of redistricting and voting rights, Democrats and Republicans would be relatively homogenous when voting. The old southern conservative Democrat would become a relic from an earlier era, and there would be fewer legislators who retained an interest in a strong committee process that could be used against party leaders. The Supreme Court attack on vote dilution was an integral trigger in the chain of events that ultimately made this happen.

# 5

## Exposing Congress

During the 1960s, academics, journalists, and scholarly politicians produced a voluminous literature about the committee process. These opinion makers partook in another important change in the institutional environment surrounding Congress. Their writings helped define the reform agenda by providing a comprehensive portrait of the committee process and popularizing the discourse that had been introduced by the liberal coalition.

Opinion makers argued that reconstructing the internal power structure of the House and Senate was essential to a series of interconnected goals. Reform would restore the role of the Congress relative to the president and make legislators more accountable; it would also facilitate progressive legislation. These opinion makers broadened the reform discourse by making congressional reform an end in itself and not just an avenue toward a set of policies. In doing so, they loosened the connection between congressional reform and postwar liberalism. Their broad attacks on institutional corruption were capable of ensnaring politicians of all ideological stripes, not just southern Democrats.

Their publications resonated in the 1960s popular culture. Although the New Left is often credited with giving rise to attacks on national institutions and leaders, the rebellion against institutions in the 1960s was more widespread than such accounts suggest. The political and economic institutions that been revered for much of the twentieth century came under severe attack from numerous quarters: leftist students protesting the military–industrial complex; conservatives who condemned the role of the federal government and the liberalization of social values; Hollywood movie producers and directors who used films such as *Dr. Strangelove or: How I Learned to Stop Worrying and Love the Bomb* to mock Washington policy makers.

Each voice of protest had a different angle, but all of them converged in this decade on a full-scale attack against the nation's institutions. A major tension among liberals who participated in this debate revolved around whether the best course was to construct a new system of direct democracy or to repair the existing tools of representative democracy.[1] Most opinion makers, like members of the reform coalition, came down in the latter camp. They were thus as much defensive as critical in that they perceived themselves as offering a way to protect the nation's representative institutions from being dismantled.[2]

The opinion makers who included sitting members of Congress synthesized arguments that had been floating around for two decades. In an age when congressional reform still generated lukewarm public interest, these experts maintained external pressure and monitored politics in lieu of government enforcement. Opinion makers helped create a perception among politicians that there was a burgeoning interest in reform. This was important since legislators were concerned with determining the *potential* preferences of voters.[3] They monitored the press carefully.[4] Savvy politicians realized that there was always the possibility that opinion makers would themselves stimulate interest in reform.

### Scandal and the Media

In the 1960s, the mainstream news media became more aggressive in its coverage of Congress than at any time since the Progressive Era. The media examined a series of major scandals that rocked Congress. Scandal offered a more accessible method for writing about the procedural problems of Congress, problems that the media believed were making it difficult to pass needed legislation while enabling legislators to remain unaccountable to constituents. Using individuals who were implicated in scandal, editors and reporters discussed legislators who seemed incompetent, corrupt, and powerful as a result of their years in office and ability to please powerful interests. The nightly television news shows, which expanded from 15 to 30 minutes in 1963, were interested in scandal since the stories fit into the narrative structure preferred by the networks.[5] There were a series of scandals that occurred in rapid succession that involved Robert "Bobby" Baker, Representative Adam Clayton Powell, and Senator Thomas Dodd. Although they did not focus on southerners, the scandals fostered an ongoing discussion about how institutions like Congress encouraged abusive behavior.

These scandals occurred at a specific moment in the evolution of the media. A younger generation of journalists and editors (as well as sympathetic middle-aged reporters) were adopting a critical outlook toward politicians. Driven by similar concerns as university students, they hoped to use the press as a means for uncovering the misdeeds of politicians and to disseminate this information for public knowledge. Between 1966 and 1974, according to one study, reporters shifted from a "lapdog" mentality grounded in norms of objectivity to an investigative "watchdog" mentality.[6] Although the impact of this transformation did not become fully apparent until Watergate, it could be discerned in how the media treated Congress in the 1960s.

There were many occasions when this journalistic generation wrote about congressional reform outside the context of scandal. The battle over Howard Smith had directed attention toward the power of the House Rules Committee. *Congressional Quarterly* released a lengthy special report in 1964 about congressional reform.[7] Shortly after Kennedy's assassination, there were many articles about why Congress had failed to pass most of his proposals, with editorials endorsing reform to prevent more logjams.[8] The civil rights filibuster in 1964 provided the most vivid example. CBS television assigned Roger Mudd to cover the Senate live every few hours of the filibuster. One reporter believed that senators were scared by Mudd since "his continued presence at the scene of Washington inaction has personalized and dramatized the halting processes of our government to the average viewer in a way no amount of words or secondary reports could have." Through their coverage of Vietnam, reporters would also adopt a more skeptical outlook about government.[9]

Yet it was through scandal that the legislative process regularly commanded the most attention. While discussing the incidents, the media frequently employed the term "establishment" to describe senior legislators who had obtained their power through procedure. In a decentralized institution, stories about a congressional establishment provided readers with a vivid picture of a unified leadership comparable to the image of the president. As opposed to technical changes or even policy-based stories, scandal enabled reporters to present congressional reform as an attempt to restrain a cabal. Through riveting tales of corruption, the media provided unprecedented coverage of how legislators operated behind the scenes. Scandal offered stories that were full of intrigue. The print media needed stories that would sell in an age when competition from television was more pronounced.[10] Unlike hearings or floor debates, editors placed these stories on front pages with photographs and large headlines.

One of the first scandals that broke in this decade involved Robert "Bobby" Baker, who had served as secretary of the Senate under Majority Leader Lyndon Johnson. Following a lawsuit in 1963, it became clear through court investigations and congressional hearings that Baker had engaged in highly suspect economic transactions. As secretary of the Senate Majority Leader, he accepted favors from interests in exchange for providing access to powerful congressmen. The Baker stories revealed the connections between powerful interests, staff, and legislators. Editorials criticized senators for conducting a limited investigation of Baker that ignored the senators for whom he worked.[11] The atmosphere in the Senate had become quite tense. Mansfield told Democrats: "I can understand it when the press and others seek to inflate the wickedness of the Senate to make its name synonymous with evil but I am appalled by the tendencies to do that ourselves by thoughtless words and panic responses."[12] As a result of the scandal, the Senate created a Select Committee on Standards and Conduct to investigate future wrongdoing. In 1967, Baker was found guilty. The judge sentenced him to eighteen months in prison for stealing $100,000 in campaign contributions. The Senate did not take action against the senators implicated in the incident.

Another politician who received media scrutiny in the 1960s was Adam Clayton Powell. Born in 1908, Powell was the first African-American representative from New York City. He took over the chair of the House Education and Labor Committee in 1961. Controversy followed Powell, who also served as a minister in Harlem's Abyssinian Baptist Church, from the moment he entered office.

Upon being elected, he angered colleagues by sitting in the "wrong" section of the segregated House dining room and barber shop. He antagonized southerners by offering amendments to spending legislation that would ban federal funds from supporting racially segregated institutions; the amendments eventually became Title VI of the Civil Rights Act of 1964. He angered Democrats in 1956 by endorsing Eisenhower's reelection campaign; Emanuel Celler called him a "turncoat."[13]

However, Powell's flamboyant personality and questionable ethics attracted the greatest attention. Powell's saga began in 1960 when he found himself on trial for income-tax fraud. Evidence emerged about how Powell, who was in his third marriage, deducted expenditures at lavish New York nightclubs that he frequented with beautiful women. While the trial was in progress, Powell publicly attacked police corruption. Critics called this an attempt to distract. On the House floor, he charged that high-level criminal operators were never arrested because of their connection to the police even as low-level runners were being imprisoned. On February 25, 1960, Powell publicly branded Harlem widow Esther James a "bag woman" who extorted money from gamblers that she distributed to the police. Outraged, James sued Powell for defamation of character. The tax trial ended in a hung jury, but the jury in the James case ordered Powell to pay her more than $200,000. Over the next three years, however, Powell refused to comply with court orders or civil citations. Powell was not even allowed to set foot in New York since he would face arrest – except on Sundays, when he was able to return to preach because state laws were not enforced on that day.

The controversy escalated to include Powell's activities as a politician. Colleagues accused him of using House funds to finance extravagant trips for himself and his female companions, placing family members on the government payroll, and missing crucial votes. Southern conservatives who despised Powell because of his civil rights advocacy jumped into the attack. Yet liberals were likewise frustrated with Powell for his chronic absenteeism and inability to manage Education and Labor. Sam Gibbons (D-FL), a southern liberal and civil rights proponent, proposed an investigation into Powell. A subcommittee formed in September 1966 under Wayne Hays (D-OH). On January 3, 1967, the subcommittee issued a stinging report that included the allegation that Powell's wife (with whom he no longer lived) received House paychecks that the chairman signed and cashed.

Powell's flamboyance and wild escapades offered the media a perfect foil to discuss corruption. In January 1967, *Newsweek* ran a cover story showing Powell standing next to his boat, *Adam's Fancy,* wearing leisure clothes and holding his pipe. The story noted that the "end of Adam's Eden" was near since "it seemed too late for Powell to overcome the tide that has built up against him."[14] *Life* published pictures of their photographers chasing Powell in a boat off his residence on a Bimini island and of Powell threatening the photographers with a shotgun. "The ingredients," wrote the reporter alongside the pictures, "were like a parody of an Ian Fleming adventure: burning Caribbean sun; a beachfront hideaway; a congressman in knee socks, gun in hand; an island of supporting

President Lyndon Johnson meets with Adam Clayton Powell in the Oval Office on June 18, 1965 (LBJ Library).

natives; a reckless boat duel in sparkling waters."[15] Donald Rumsfeld (R-IL), one of the younger Republicans who was fighting for congressional reform as a way to strengthen his party's standing, pulled reporter David Broder into his office and showed him two piles of clippings. The deep pile was composed of articles about Powell while the small pile included three stories about Republicans fighting for reform. Rumsfeld, Broder recalled, asked "why Powell is worth this much attention and our effort is worth this ... our effort to change the system that allows Adam Powell and a lot of others you don't write about to abuse power in ways that are just as bad, why that effort doesn't get any coverage?" Broder, who agreed, responded: "You're not as sexy as he is."[16]

Yet discussion in the media of the Powell scandal was coupled with calls for institutional reform. The media constantly pointed to Powell as an example of how seniority elevated incompetent leaders. The *New York Times* insisted that eliminating future abuses required taming the committee system, imposing ethics rules, and monitoring seniority: "Powell is not alone in stalling bills that the committee majority favors, packing the staff with his own retainers and spending committee funds in a high-handed manner."[17] The *Times* argued that Powell had called attention to a

fundamental source of mischief and irresponsibility on Capitol Hill. That is the automatic working of the seniority system. A member of the House or Senate may be a cynical playboy or a hopeless crank, an acknowledged dimwit or a totterer on the edge of senility, but – whatever his defects of mind, character or capacity – he will become chairman of some committee if he stays in Congress long enough.[18]

One of Powell's chief defenders in the House, Celler, warned his colleagues that they should be wary of casting the first stone because so many of them had "dear ones" on the payroll.[19]

Numerous critics charged that racial bias motivated legislators to focus on Powell. They correctly postulated that many southern Democrats were simply using these charges to punish Powell. Joseph Rauh of ADA said that his organization opposed a "one-shot reform aimed at one Negro Congressman" while nonetheless deploring his actions. He pointed out that the new chair of the Rules Committee, William Colmer, would be "far more dangerous to the national interest than Mr. Powell" and that the chair of the Armed Services Committee's "habitual drunkenness threatens the national security."[20] But this criticism furthered the discussion on the relationship between individual wrongdoing and procedure. Journalists claimed that the charges against Powell were unfair by revealing how other legislators committed worse abuses.

Democrats were divided about how to punish Powell. The Constitution offered three options. The House or Senate could *expel* a seated member for improper behavior with the consent of two thirds of the membership. *Exclusion,* which prevented an elected member from taking their seat because they lacked technical credentials, required only a majority vote. Finally, either chamber could *censure* a member by majority vote. This constituted a formal condemnation that still allowed the person to remain in office. On January 9, 1967, the House stripped Powell of his chairmanship and established a committee to investigate further punishment. The committee recommended that Powell should be censured, made to pay $40,000, and lose seniority. But on March 1, the House went further by excluding him through an overwhelming majority of 307 to 116. There was immediate opposition to this vote. Despite agreeing that Powell should be punished, many liberals and moderates complained that the House could not "second-guess an electorate which was fully aware of the charges" because Powell actually had fulfilled the technical requirements needed to be seated.[21]

Editorials concurred that the House had gone too far.[22] The NAACP warned Speaker McCormack that a punishment that "can be interpreted as tailor made to apply to him and to no other member of Congress will be fuel for appeals based on prejudice rather than reason."[23] During a series of acrimonious public demonstrations, Harlem residents complained that the House had disenfranchised them while allowing southerners to be represented by worse politicians. Powell sued the House to regain his seat and salary. After a court of appeals dismissed the case as not justiciable and as the case was pending before the Supreme Court, Harlem constituents reelected Powell in a special election held to fill his seat. The election would be one among many to highlight the complications of making Congress more "responsive" through reform, since voters often did not agree with the conclusions of reformers. Powell also paid Esther James so that he was no longer under threat of arrest. Rather than returning to Washington, however, Powell went to the Bahamas.

In January 1969, after he was reelected in the November elections, the House voted to seat Powell, fine him, and strip him of his seniority. In June, the Supreme

Court ruled that – since Powell fulfilled the legal requirements regarding age, citizenship, and residence – the House had misused its power of exclusion.[24] The decision angered many legislators, who believed the Court was interfering in their internal business as it had done with redistricting.[25] The decision did not do much for Powell, who no longer had any power and was ill with cancer. The following year, Powell lost the primary to Charles Rangel.

Whereas in the Powell case the media fueled a scandal driven from within the House, in the case of Connecticut Senator Thomas Dodd it was the reporters who were principals in the event. Elected to the Senate in 1958, Dodd had obtained a valuable seat on the Senate Foreign Relations Committee and had attracted attention through his hard-line anticommunism and support for U.S. military operations in Vietnam. The senator's problems began in 1966 with Drew Pearson and Jack Anderson's syndicated column, the "Washington Merry-Go Round." As the nation's most widely distributed column, it appeared in 625 newspapers with a total circulation of about 45 million readers. Over thirty installments, Pearson and Anderson exposed the content of more than a thousand documents from the senator's files that Dodd's top staff had secretly photocopied.[26] They were stolen from his office and distributed to the reporters by two former employees, James Boyd and Marjorie Carpenter. The stolen documents showed compelling evidence of corruption.

*Newsweek* and *Time* were initially critical of Anderson and Pearson. The *Washington Post* declined to publish editorials on this issue.[27] Pearson and Anderson wrote to the *Post*'s Katherine Graham, whose paper had not offered an editorial opinion on Dodd even while being critical of the journalists. The muckrakers wrote Graham that the public was "disillusioned by the Bobby Baker affair and felt that the senators themselves were exempt from investigation, while a functionary of the Senate was made the scapegoat. Should the final action in the Dodd affair turn out similarly, there would be much greater cynicism on the part of the public."[28] On his radio show, Pearson charged that *Time* did not want to expose Dodd because the publisher's wife was a friend of the senator.[29]

Despite this initial hesitance, most editors could not resist the lure of the scandal. The fact that the Powell and Dodd stories occurred at the same time played a role in the increasing media coverage of both scandals. Since the stories culminated with congressional action in the same months, the media reported on them side by side.[30] William Buckley, Jr., noted that "The clamor was incessant: Powell and Dodd, Powell and Dodd, Powell and Dodd – they became as inseparably linked in the public mind as Abbot and Costello."[31] Nor was coverage limited to national publications.[32] Sounding like a Hollywood movie, the documents stolen by Boyd and Carpenter contained shocking information. The memoranda detailed numerous favors Dodd had performed for the wealthy lobbyist Julius Klein, a registered agent for the West German government. These favors included trips to West Germany, where Dodd lobbied as a U.S. Senator on behalf of Klein. The documents also revealed that Dodd had frequently misused campaign funds. The senator made personal use of money that had been

raised on a tax-free basis in campaign events that were called "testimonial dinners," including one where President Johnson had appeared. The revelations
were particularly damaging in the context of news scandals about campaign finance published in 1965 and 1966.[33]

The Senate Ethics Committee opened its first investigation by taking up the
Dodd case. Committee chairman John Stennis limited the inquiry to Dodd rather
than larger institutional problems. Following closed-door hearings, the committee issued a report on April 27, 1967, recommending censure on the basis that
Dodd had misused campaign funds. The *New York Times* speculated that "were
there a clear code of ethics and a full financial disclosure law, along with an independent tribunal to enforce them, scandals such as the Dodd, Powell and Baker
cases would occur far less often and would be investigated more swiftly and
thoroughly."[34]

As with Powell, Dodd's case stimulated demands in the press for stronger disclosure, ethics codes, and campaign finance reform. Scandal and congressional
reform were closely connected. One story warned that senators were as "unen-
thusiastic" as Dodd "about keeping the issue on the front pages. They find few
things more unpleasant than questioning the integrity or good judgment of club
members."[35] When the Senate passed an ethics code in 1968, *Life* dismissed it as
"toothless."[36]

On "Firing Line," Dodd accused Boyd and Carpenter of stealing documents in
retaliation because he had fired the two staffers.[37] He said that he was being punished for legal activities that most senators engaged in.[38] He told his constituents
that the campaign against him was being driven by "hateful and vengeful" interests that included four "dishonorable and vindictive ex-employees" and a "minor
press wolf pack" angered by his strong stand against communism. He labeled the
technique being used against him as "multiple untruth," which forced the person
being challenged to prove that they were innocent.[39] Dodd did have supporters.
William White warned that Boyd and Carpenter had "poisoned the air of the
United States Senate and have caused every man sitting there to wonder whether
in his own office and in his own house there may be traitors to his person."[40]
A group of prominent citizens formed the National Committee for Justice for
Dodd. Russell Long (D-LA) was Dodd's strongest defender in the chamber.[41]

In response to the articles about his actions, Dodd unsuccessfully sued the
columnists for $5 million in libel. Accusing them of trying this case in the media
rather than the courts, Dodd said that Pearson and Anderson were the most "unscrupulous character assassins ever spawned by the American press."[42] Dodd allegedly hired a private detective to dig up dirt on the reporters.[43] Lobbyist Julius
Klein wrote Pearson to deny each specific charge. Klein said that "you only
picked points that suited you, as usual, out of context trying to make a case for
yourself but this time you won't get away with it."[44] He refuted each charge.[45]
Dodd's counterattack revealed the important role of the media in this scandal.
Pearson and Anderson were furious, since they felt they were fulfilling the responsibility of journalists to uncover corruption.[46] The columnists dismissed Dodd's

lawsuit against them as nothing more than a "Madison Avenue–minded public-ity stunt" calculated to "confuse and sidetrack" and "intimidate libel-conscious newspapers."[47] In the end, the libel charge fizzled.

Pearson and Anderson's role became part of the national press coverage.[48] Many colleagues praised them as models for investigative journalism. The *Nation* noted that Pearson practiced "a difficult but necessary kind of journalism.... Sometimes he misses, but there is no denying the unique service he has performed in an age in which newsmen play it safe more often than not."[49]

The scandal ended when the Senate censured Dodd on June 23, 1967, by a decisive vote of 92 to 5. Dodd became the sixth senator to be censured or con-demned. Within the Senate, the opposition to Dodd was not as deep as that to Powell had been. Unlike Powell's exclusion, the Senate did not impose any penal-ties and allowed Dodd to retain his seniority.

Toward the end of the 1960s, reporters started to focus their investigative lenses on the private lives of politicians. Ten years of covering scandals such as Powell and Dodd had motivated the media to dig deeper into the conduct of politicians. Whereas reporters had refused to write about the sexual escapades of John Kennedy in 1961, his brother Senator Edward Kennedy (D-MA) faced a new breed of reporters. Kennedy had been elected to the Senate in 1962. His career took a bad turn in the early morning of July 18, 1969, when Kennedy drove his car off a bridge and companion Mary J. Kopechne drowned. Kennedy escaped but did not tell police about the incident until the next morning. Al-though Kennedy claimed that he immediately went to seek assistance, the media discovered this to be false. Kennedy's travails received massive coverage. Re-porters openly speculated that Kennedy was afraid the scandal would destroy his career. The married Kennedy insisted that he was not sexually involved with Kopechne. Nixon had his staff spread information about the unfolding scan-dal. Pulling a page from Nixon's famous "Checkers" speech, Kennedy went on television to defend himself. He blamed his failure to report the accident on his disorientation after the crash. Voters returned Kennedy to the Senate. For the media, Chappaquiddick helped legitimate the notion that the private behavior of officials could be reported.

There were also a few journalists who published books on Congress. Some were moderates like Neil MacNeil, who argued that the House embodied repre-sentative democracy.[50] Pearson and Anderson's best-selling *Case Against Con-gress* presented legislators as criminals.[51] Robert Bendiner, whose articles had appeared in *Harper's*, the *Saturday Evening Post*, the *New York Times*, and *Life*, described Congress as dysfunctional.[52]

By the time the turbulent 1960s ended, the media was devoting extensive cov-erage to Congress. Scandals offered readers an unprecedented glimpse into how senior legislators wielded power. The Dodd story was so intriguing that in 1968 a play ran on television based on the case. James Boyd, the staffer who stole the documents, published a lurid account detailing Dodd's fall from grace.[53] In most of these cases, the media was not simply a passive observer; reporters were playing a central role in exposing corruption, and investigative journalism was establishing a sound footing in journalism.[54] Before the nation had ever heard of Woodward and Bernstein, reporters were investigating scandal on a regular basis and were prepared to take on powerful politicians.

### The "Boys of Congress"

Academics and scholarly politicians were also important opinion makers. The 1960s witnessed an "extraordinary reawakening of scholarly interest" in Congress.[55] There were numerous arenas where scholars and politicians mingled. For example, the famous Brookings Institution think tank organized and published proceedings of a roundtable where congressmen and scholars discussed the ins and outs of the legislative process.[56] The publications by political scientists and scholarly politicians provided a comprehensive picture of the committee process and offered a range of proposals for improvement.

Since the 1885 publication of Woodrow Wilson's *Congressional Government*, political scientists had always tended to favor congressional reform.[57] During the post-WWII period, there were different objectives in reform-oriented scholarship. One group endorsed strengthening the committee process so that Congress could move out of the presidential shadows.[58] A presidential-centered theory, on the other hand, contended that institutional reform should aim to make Congress more responsive to the liberal executive branch. Finally, the "party government" theory proposed to make Congress more responsive and more equal to the president by granting parties greater control, as was the case in England.[59]

There were several persistent themes running through the writing that endorsed institutional reform. One was that a conservative "establishment" dominated the House and Senate. Senator Joseph Clark published a series of books that depicted a conservative establishment of southern Democrats and Republicans who manipulated rules to block legislation. Clark lambasted them as the "antithesis of democracy ... a self-perpetuating oligarchy with mild, but only mild, overtones of plutocracy."[60] His writing contended that the establishment believed in an ethos of "white supremacy; a stronger devotion to property than to human rights; support of the military establishment; belligerence in foreign affairs; and a determination to prevent Congressional reform."[61] To prove this same point, Richard Bolling wrote historical case studies on the conservative coalition and their battles with liberals.[62] While explaining the differences between the two chambers, these publications focused on the similarities that defined Congress.

Williams College professor James MacGregor Burns remained one of the most articulate spokesmen for congressional reform. Burns explained that the nation was hampered by a fragmented government in a century when most institutions were centralized. Through widely publicized books and articles published in the 1960s, Burns contended that the nation was governed by a four-party system: the Democratic-Congressional party, the Democratic-Presidential party, the Republican-Congressional party, and the Republican-Presidential party. The Democratic-Congressional party had a distinct ideology of states' rights, white supremacy, and antigovernment conservatism. Its members responded to local rather than national interests. Whereas the Democratic-Presidential party championed centralized power, he explained that the Democratic-Congressional party valued countervailing forces and nonmajoritarian compromise. Headed by individuals such as Byrd and Smith, the power of this congressional party rested on a "whole system of local power patterns, electoral arrangements, voting behavior, career lines, and institutional arrangements and norms in Congress that together form an operating political system."[63] Although the presidential party had some sympathetic legislators, the structure of Congress rendered them impotent. Burns stated that reform was essential to ending the "deadlock" of democracy.

To bring the power of the congressional establishment alive to readers, political scientists in the 1960s were determined to provide data about how conservatives exercised power. For example, James Robinson catalogued the specific mechanisms through which the House Rules Committee blocked legislation. George Goodwin confirmed statistically that seniority produced older chairmen and that southerners were overrepresented in those positions. James Sundquist explored how the conservative coalition had blocked a progressive party agenda until 1964 and why the Democratic party was becoming more liberal. Historian James Patterson published the first comprehensive history of the conservative coalition.[64]

The research that was published after the 1964 election claimed that liberals were finally gaining strength, as evidenced by the enlargement of the Rules committee, the Democratic landslide, the procedural reforms of 1965, and the passage of Great Society programs. Stephen Bailey believed that, as a result of a "revolution," seniority and committee autonomy – along with the rural southern Democrats and midwestern Republicans who benefited from those procedures – were quickly giving way to strong parties in the House and Senate that were controlled by a coalition of "benign" northern Democrats and metropolitan Republicans.[65] Comparing the revolt against Joseph Cannon in 1910 and Howard Smith in 1961, Charles Jones said that leaders who thwarted procedural majorities faced the risk of being overthrown.[66] Expectations kept rising. Robert Dixon, Jr., lamented that the Warren Court had not gone far enough in *Wesberry v. Sanders* because the decision tolerated partisan gerrymandering.[67]

The literature appeared in all sorts of venues. Bolling published an article in *Playboy*, which in those years was known for controversial articles about national politics in addition to its more famous visual items. Amidst pictures of nude women stood Bolling's trenchant attack on "Republicans with Southern accents" who thrived because of the process. Linking policy to process, he said that the House had to assume its part "of the blame for ghetto fires and riot-ing, Birmingham bombings and the Little Rock school confrontation." Bolling cynically explained that,

for a Democrat to become a chairman, he need only live long enough and get re-elected often enough to outdistance his colleagues. Eventually, he'll make it, although he may have the morals of a Mafia *capo* or the mind of a moron – or both. And who among Democrats is most likely to achieve the cherished goal of chairman? The answer is easy: He is a member from a one-party Congressional district, usually in the rural South – in-sular, suspicious and racist.

The article pulled no punches, attacking John McMillan (D-SC), chair of the District of Columbia Committee, for making Washington "a national disgrace."[68]

In discussing this congressional era, these publications stressed the link be-tween the legislative process and political power. Institutions were at the heart of every problem. The assumption was that if institutions were fixed, liberalism would flourish and Congress would be revitalized: current institutional design discouraged policy innovation, shielded leadership, and weakened Congress. The writers were convinced that congressional conservatism did not reflect na-tional opinion. "The conservative bias of Congress can be attributed primarily to the operation of the seniority system, the senatorial filibuster, and the power of the House Rules Committee," explained one book.[69] Another text stated: "the major shortcomings of the legislatures seem to be due more to fundamental weaknesses in institutional design and to traditional practices than to the qual-ity of legislators or to the absence of legislative vision."[70]

Writers acknowledged that the public rarely placed pressure on politicians to change the institutional structure of Congress. The authors aimed to reverse this situation through their publications. If boredom was not the cause of public inaction, the other common explanation was lack of knowledge about proce-dure. Congressional reform, Bolling said, required "prodding from representa-tives of powerful interest groups, the liberal press, and political scientists who can inform the American people about the wretched condition of their national legislature."[71] Equally important, authors noted that members avoided reform because they perceived procedures as convenient or because they feared attack-ing those in power. The one explanation of inaction that few writers assumed was public acceptance of the process.

Almost every publication shared the belief that Congress had become a weaker branch of government in the twentieth century. The perception of an "Imperial Presidency" was integral to American political culture in the 1960s. The decen-tralized structure of representative government, most authors concluded, could not keep up with modern policy demands. The discourse of 1960s opinion makers moved beyond the liberal coalition by restoring modernization as a cen-tral objective. Observers pointed to polls that revealed sharp declines in con-gressional approval ratings. The common argument was that the problems of industrialization, urbanization, and the Cold War had created a major dilemma since Congress retained its nineteenth-century structure.[72] In this interpretation, Congress was capable of wielding only *negative* power, defined as the power to block legislation, rather than *positive* power, meaning the ability to initiate proposals. Political scientist David Truman wrote that the twentieth century

> has been hard on legislatures. Compelled in some fashion to deal with the complexities of increasingly urbanized, rapidly industrialized, and irrevocably interdependent societies, they have found themselves alternating in varying degrees between two equally dangerous and distasteful situations: yielding the initiative as well as implementing responsibilities to bureaucrats whose actions might be imperfectly mediated by political officials, or attempting to retain one or both of these functions at the expense of delay, indecision, and instability.[73]

The authors were determined to show the connection between changing the internal power structure and restoring the strength of Congress relative to the presidency. The failure of the 1946 reforms, they said, had been to leave intact the internal composition of Congress while focusing on promoting efficiency. These authors argued that, in order to regain power from the executive branch, the power structure needed to change. As long as conservatives maintained control, the institution would pale next to the president. This antipresidential argument became increasingly popular among liberal opinion makers in the late 1960s, as Vietnam made many of them disillusioned with Lyndon Johnson; they became all the more fearful after Republican Richard Nixon won election as president in 1968.

To strengthen Congress, the literature proposed weakening individual legislators by enhancing party discipline, centralizing legislative power, and codifying ethics. Party majorities acting through the leadership, according to this literature, would gain the ability to bind members on certain issues. The books were concerned that the existing procedural power of the Speaker was insufficient. Conditions were even worse in the Senate, the literature explained, where southerners relied on the filibuster as well. In this analysis, strong congressional parties would allow Congress to become more proactive and to coordinate action with the president. Seeking a balance between centralization and individual rights, most proposals sought to make the Speaker and Senate Majority Leader instruments of the rank-and-file party members.

Information was itself a central objective. Proponents of reform assumed that voters, armed with adequate information, would punish those who abused the laws.[74] The producers of knowledge hoped to fulfill the Progressive Era vision of an "informed citizen" who would make educated choices about politics without having to depend on parties or experts.[75]

There was another body of research about Congress that was rooted in the pluralistic outlook on American politics. This research consisted of up-and-coming political scientists in the subfield of congressional studies. The American Political Science Association (APSA) organized a project between 1964 and

1969 that was called "The Study of Congress." The project took form in informal meetings with political scientists that were conducted by Chet Holifield and Thomas Curtis (R-MO). APSA Executive Director Evron Kirkpatrick, an intellectual mentor of Hubert Humphrey, managed a $230,000 grant from the Carnegie Foundation.[76] Director of the study Ralph Huitt embodied the ethos of his political science colleagues, as he was a respected scholar who also served in government positions. Political scientists in the 1940s and 1950s had used Congress to understand other issues, such as the presidency, interest groups, parties, or democratic theory.[77] But in the 1960s, they focused on Congress itself. Richard Fenno recalled that "We met in the early 1960s, as members of a small group of young political scientists who came together to share the excitement of our budding research on Congress. We got a grant to get together periodically in Washington to take members of Congress to dinner and talk about how to study Congress ... the 'Boys of Congress'."[78]

Methodologically, their research was grounded in the behavioral approach popularized after WWII that stimulated scholars to develop empirical studies – rather than just theoretical arguments – about how institutions worked. This approach called for scholars to put forth in more systematic fashion the theories that they would be testing and to draw on scientific techniques of quantitative data collection to prove their hypotheses.[79] They believed that theories of human behavior could be identified that worked across time and space. Many scholars in 1960s embraced sociological concepts as a means of understanding political systems and norms.[80] They used the equilibrium model, which aimed to explain why social systems did not collapse and how different parts of a social system functioned to maintain stability among its members and with its external environment.[81]

Applying this theory to Congress, scholars studied the roles that guided individual behavior within committees and on the floor. Normative expectations of behavior were said to foster committee integration and bargaining. Students of political systems were also interested in how committees adapted to external demands on the floor. Instead of presenting committees as autonomous bodies dominated by tyrannical chairmen, this scholarship tended to depict committees as "subsystems" that responded to members inside and outside the panel.[82]

Scholars contended that procedures and norms created an internal system of authority that could not be "overturned by every gust of wind from the outside." The system, they said, was essential so that legislators "can act in an authoritative capacity, adjusting conflict between groups and developing an ordered pattern of action under which various parts of society can interact productively and harmoniously ... in which contentious types of conflict can be discussed calmly and determined rationally."[83] Donald Matthews postulated that Senate norms "provide motivation for the performance of legislative duties that, perhaps, would not otherwise be performed.... They encourage senators to become 'compromisers' and 'bargainers' and to use their substantial powers with caution and restraint."[84]

Although their research tended to refrain from explicit recommendations, their findings supported incremental (as opposed to dramatic) change. As Dale Vinyard noted, "Critics, in their zeal for reform, may sometimes overlook the values of existing practices ... a certain amount of inefficient behavior may be necessary as part of the process of building a consensus out of a diversity of philosophical, practical, and personal conflicts."[85] The directors of "The Study of Congress" believed that Congress changed slowly, "adaptively in things that matter, and seldom according to blueprint."[86]

Ideologically these scholars emerged out of the pluralist arguments of the 1950s. Although this bias was usually implicit, their research shared a common concern for how political stability was ultimately achieved in America. Pluralists had claimed that American politics revolved around an ongoing struggle between interest groups. Over time, they said, the competition between these groups – refereed by the federal government – achieved an equilibrium by distributing benefits to different sectors of society. The struggle in American history centered around marginal groups fighting for and eventually obtaining organized representation. Historians and political scientists who wrote about pluralism praised it for creating the type of long-term stability that seemed absent in other parts of the world. In their minds, competing interests eventually balanced each other out even if they created short-term conflict. The balance prevented the type of radicalism that had destroyed Germany and Russia. According to pluralists, the New Deal was the ultimate example because it empowered workers and farmers by supporting their organization into interest groups, creating a countervailing power to business that was not socialism. Pluralists tended to agree that there was a consensus in America that centered on the liberal values of private property, individualism, and localism. For a generation of scholars who had come of age learning about pluralism in their studies and hearing these arguments as they were refracted through the popular culture, the social conflict of the 1960s was unsettling. Their search for stability thus took on new meaning in this context. Hinting at the link between pluralism and congressional studies, Richard Fenno wrote that "concern for the internal workings of Congress leads to a preoccupation with the degree to which internal elements harmonize, with the ways in which the Congress holds itself together as an institution, and with its capacity as an institution to minimize conflict."[87]

The scholars associated with congressional studies complicated stereotypes that had been put forth by many in the liberal coalition. These authors stressed the unintended consequences of reform, differences between the House and Senate, the functional purpose of the committee system, differing types of committee leadership, and the ability of Congress to naturally change itself in response to electoral pressure without procedural reform.[88] Nelson Polsby, for example, presented another side of the House. He showed how seniority was part of the institutionalization of the House as the chamber adopted automatic and standard methods to conduct business similar to professionalization in the world of business. Seniority was part of this maturation process.[89] Polsby also challenged the argument that a southern cabal ran the Senate by pointing out that maverick northerners such as Hubert Humphrey had become leaders and that individual senators retained significant leverage.[90]

While accepting that moderate change was important, these scholars highlighted what they saw as the ability of the legislative process to mute fractionalizing and partisan tendencies. Although their conclusions often differed from the opinion makers calling for dramatic changes, their work was nonetheless integral to the evolution of congressional reform. Their publications provided the most thorough existing body of knowledge – and one that entered into committee hearings and congressional studies – about how the committee system worked and how it might be changed.

## Toward a Common Cause

The work of these journalists, legislators, and political scientists in the 1960s came at a crucial historical moment: after a liberal coalition had formed and was applying political pressure for change and before the broader political conditions had shifted to favor dramatic institutional reform. Like the court redistricting decisions, their writing constituted another important realignment of the institutional environment surrounding Congress (in this case, the news media and academia were the external institutions) that favored institutional change. There was also direct interaction between opinion makers and the liberal coalition through individuals such as Richard Bolling.

Opinion makers synthesized multiple arguments into a powerful discourse that filtered into newspapers, television, books, and university classrooms. The discourse brought together the various arguments for reform that had been articulated since WWII, including the ways that reform could modernize and revitalize Congress, reduce corruption, and facilitate the passage of progressive domestic and international policies. Younger congressional studies scholars offered the meat and potatoes of this literature by revealing in vivid detail the connections between policy, process, and leadership that made up Congress. Although more sympathetic to the virtues of the committee era, they complemented the rhetorical strengths of other opinion makers with their unprecedented data about how the committee process actually functioned. Popularizing the discourse about reform that had been brewing for over a decade, opinion makers helped generate the perception of expanded support for an issue that still did not elicit strong public activism.

# 6

# A Window of Opportunity

After suffering a narrow defeat to John Kennedy in 1960 and failing to become governor of California in 1962, Richard Nixon was psychologically elated when he took the oath of office in 1969 to become the 37th president of the United States. Amidst the celebrations, however, it was difficult for Nixon to fully grasp the explosive atmosphere into which he was entering. The domestic turmoil rattling the nation began its most intense period. Nixon started his presidency at the moment that America's governing institutions were under a glaring spotlight and when demands for government reform had reached their most intense pitch. This was certainly a bad time to be president for an individual who had difficulty controlling himself from using every ounce of power formally available to him – in addition to those that were not.[1]

Although all institutions were vulnerable by the time Nixon became president, congressional reform in particular had gained tremendous steam. This was due to the emergence of the liberal coalition and to a profound shift in the external environment surrounding the legislative branch, a result of the redistricting decisions of the Supreme Court and the intense focus on the operations of Congress by opinion makers. Between 1968 and 1970, all these forces accelerated to create a favorable political situation for the expanding number of legislators who sought to move beyond the committee era.

The confluence of three trends in this period created a window of opportunity for constructing a new procedural era in Congress. These developments were not random happenings. Rather, they were rooted in deeper struggles and developments that had been taking place since the late 1950s as the institutions, policies, and leaders who had governed since the New Deal came under challenge. The first was the crisis facing Democrats, as events in the 1960s had created a bitter internal battle over their party identity and had also brought financial instability. The second was the strengthening of the liberal coalition when it mutated into a reform coalition. It became a "reform coalition" owing to the entrance of individuals and organizations who believed that institutional reform was a primary goal and not simply a path to achieving a certain policy agenda (although they were certainly concerned about the interests of the suburban middle class). Significant components of the coalition were now willing to tackle a broader set of procedures – even when they tampered with liberal interests. The rhetoric of the coalition, moreover, focused as much on corruption as on how institutions favored specific policies or caused ineffective decision making. Finally, the institutional environment surrounding Congress continued to strain the committee process. President Nixon's war on the Democratic Congress turned the perceived weakness of the legislative branch into a political and constitutional crisis.

### Democratic Mavericks: The Second Generation

Liberal Democrats had been promoting institutional reform since the 1950s, but they always ran up against the prevalence of senior Democrats who had no interest in threatening the stability of the committee process. After 1968, however, the Democratic party entered a period of internal and financial instability that shook political support for the status quo across institutions. The liberal grassroots activism of the 1960s had been directed toward established Democrats. In the minds of the New Left, the liberalism of mainstream Democrats was duplicitous and unrealistic. University students charged that Democrats only pretended to be progressive: their true interests were protecting corporations and promoting imperialist foreign policies.[2] Despite the legislative accomplishments of 1964 and 1965, the sizable election victories of congressional conservatives in the 1966 elections shrunk the unusually large majorities that liberal Democrats had enjoyed and thus reinvigorated the interest of liberals in procedural reforms. Democrats were simultaneously under attack from a growing grassroots conservative movement that offered an equally harsh critique of the political center. The civil war brewing among Democrats reached a climax in the summer of 1968. Outside the Democratic convention, protestors demanded the inclusion of an anti-Vietnam plank and opposed Hubert Humphrey's nomination. When television networks broadcast dramatic footage of chaos around the convention, the party's problems became visible to the nation.

After Nixon won the election, Democrats feared for their electoral future. Not only were there deep divisions within the party, but now a Republican inhabited the White House. Independent candidate George Wallace, moreover, had made deep inroads into traditionally Democratic southern and northern constituencies. "By the end of the decade," according to one analysis, "liberalism was in full rout."[3]

The fact that the 1960s ended with a Republican triumph greatly frustrated many Democrats. Some officials, including Robert Strauss, wanted to push the party further toward the ideological center. For Strauss, the success of Nixon and Wallace signaled that Democrats had to moderate their agenda or risk losing more core support among southerners, northern blue-collar workers, and corporate America. Yet other liberals perceived the message of 1968 as being that Democrats needed to move to the left. The ADA, for example, warned that "the

liberal forces inside the Democratic Party are not going to accept a party leadership that veers right."[4] Both sides scored victories. Centrists such as Senator
Lloyd Bentsen (D-TX) and Robert Strauss retained control of the party's fund-
raising organs. Yet the party's left obtained rules for the Democratic nomination
process that weakened traditional urban machines and empowered a more socially diverse constituency in the presidential nominating process.[5] In 1972, the
Democrats nominated McGovern for president, one of the most liberal candidates in the party's history, who made government reform a centerpiece of his
campaign.[6]

Although neither side seized total control of the party, the contest over Democratic identity provided an unexpected opportunity for reform-oriented liberals
to gain influence. These liberals now constituted a sizable voting block among
congressional Democrats. A succession of elections since 1958 had brought
large numbers of Democrats into Congress who did not feel loyal to the committee process. Even the conservative resurgence of 1966 did not overturn the
gains that had been made. The new Democrats saw Eugene McCarthy, Hubert
Humphrey, Paul Douglas, and Richard Bolling as their mentors rather than Sam
Rayburn or Richard Russell. The existence of organizations in the House such
as the Democratic Study Group (DSG) – together with the influence of established senior liberal senators such as Eugene McCarthy – helped them to obtain
a stronger foothold within the congressional process than their predecessors.
Battles over civil rights and Vietnam, rather than the New Deal, were the formative events in their careers. "The new members are not exactly exponents of
Theodore Roszak's 'counter-culture'," noted one journalist, "but they do represent a marked generational break with the waxwork political traditions that
hold the House in bondage to the plunderers."[7]

Elected between 1958 and 1970, the second generation of reform-oriented legislators quickly made their presence known in the House and Senate by fighting
for congressional reform, progressive domestic policies, and an end to the Vietnam war. One member of this generation was Phillip Burton. Born in Ohio in
1926, Burton attended the University of Southern California and earned a law
degree at the Golden Gate Law School. Burton learned a tough lesson when the
San Francisco boss William Malone blocked his first election bid to the California State Assembly by supporting a deceased candidate in the primary. Yet
within two years Burton defeated an incumbent assemblyman by tapping into
the African-American and Chinese electorate. Burton forged strong ties to the
labor and student movements, defended Mexican-American farm workers, and
opposed anticommunist campaigns against American citizens. After helping
to create a politically favorable district in San Francisco, Burton won election
to Congress in 1964. He became a leading voice in DSG and the Democratic
Caucus. An arrogant, hard-drinking, chain-smoking politician, Burton always
understood the intimate relationship between process and policy success.[8]

John Brademas was the first Greek-American elected to the House. Born
in 1927 and raised in Indiana, Brademas was the son of a school teacher and

restaurant owner. Brademas obtained a strong belief in social justice through the Methodist Church. One of his lasting memories was hearing as a youth that his father's business was being boycotted by the Ku Klux Klan. He attended Harvard University. When working back in Indiana during the summer breaks, he was a member of the local UAW. He later received a doctoral degree at Oxford University. Balancing the life of politics and academics, he worked as an assistant to Adlai Stevenson in 1955 and 1956 and as a political science professor at Saint Mary's College. Paul Butler helped Brademas win election in Indiana in 1958. Entering with that historic freshman class, Brademas was one of the first members of DSG.

One prominent House liberal who displayed no loyalty to the committee process was Shirley Chisholm. Elected in 1968 from a newly drawn district that included Bedford-Stuyvesant in New York City, Chisholm was the first African-American woman to win a seat in the House. Her path to power had not been easy. Chisholm was born in 1924 in Brooklyn to immigrant workers from the West Indies. She spent part of her youth with her sister in Barbados living with her maternal grandmother while her parents saved money for their daughter's education. Returning to Brooklyn, she excelled in public school. Chisholm went on to earn a B.A. from Brooklyn College and a master's degree from Columbia University. Before entering politics, she worked as a school teacher, educational consultant, and administrator. Her twelfth district, with a large African-American and Puerto Rican population, was a direct result of the "one person, one vote" Supreme Court rulings. The House Ways and Means Committee assigned her to serve on the Agriculture Committee. She brazenly protested this decision because she did not feel that it would help her constituents. Because of her protests, Chisholm was reassigned to another committee. Chisholm emerged as a defiant voice in the Democratic Caucus by lambasting committee chairs and their power. She broke many institutional traditions – for example, by hiring a staff composed of many women and African-Americans.[9]

The Senate had its share of young and assertive liberals. Walter Mondale was one of this group's shining examples. Born in 1928, Mondale was raised by a Minnesotan family that was socially active and religious. During his college years, Mondale was a student activist in Minneapolis and became an avid follower of Hubert Humphrey. Working as an attorney in the 1950s, he helped to build the Democratic Farmer-Labor party, which remained the state's leading voice of mainstream liberalism. After serving as the Minnesota attorney general, in 1964 Mondale was placed in Hubert Humphrey's vacant senatorial seat. Mondale embodied the liberalism of this generation as an active participant in the struggle for civil rights, housing, child welfare, and limits on Cold War military operations.[10]

Another like-minded senator was Ted Kennedy. The brother of John was elected to the Senate in 1962. Although Kennedy spent his early days in office ingratiating himself to senior southerners, he devoted the next few years in the Senate to supporting several controversial issues. In 1965, he led the charge against the southern poll tax and helped craft a bill that liberalized immigration. Moreover, Kennedy headed the counterattack against Everett Dirksen's effort to postpone court-ordered redistricting. Though Kennedy's legislative record was modest, in the 1960s he captured the attention of reporters as an up-and-coming star of the institution. Before Chappaquiddick forever tarnished his reputation, Kennedy was emblematic of the emerging activist legislators who were committed to building a unified and progressive party.

Some of these legislators were even able to gain leadership positions. An important change in the Senate occurred in January 1969 when the 36-year-old Kennedy unexpectedly deposed the veteran Russell Long as Democratic Whip. Long had been vulnerable because he had not devoted much time to the position, focusing instead on his chairmanship of the Senate Finance Committee and suffering from alcoholism. When Maine's Edmund Muskie decided that he would not challenge Long, Kennedy accepted an offer from Majority Leader Mike Mansfield's top aide Charles Ferris to run for the position. Given his family and speculation about his future presidential ambitions, Kennedy's entrance into what was a normally unexciting race turned this competition into a matter of intense media interest. The contest came at the same time Morris Udall of Arizona was challenging John McCormack for the House speakership, so the two contests were coupled together in the news as a broader challenge to the senior southern establishment. The younger moderate senator Hugh Scott was also challenging the conservative Roman Hruska to be the Whip of the Senate Republicans.

Kennedy was excited about the possibility of reshaping the party caucus into a weapon that could be used against Nixon.[11] When the news circulated about this challenge, however, it was not clear that Kennedy could defeat the senior southern leader. But Kennedy defeated Long by a solid vote of 31 to 26. Additionally, Scott was elected Whip of the Senate Republicans (Udall's challenge was unsuccessful). "Yesterday was a rough day for the Old Guard in the Senate," remarked the *Washington Post* editors.[12] A *New York Times* reporter added that "a declining but still powerful Old Guard is losing its grip on the Senate it has so long dominated."[13]

Of course, legislative mavericks had been entering Congress since 1948. But never had they amassed such a sizable block of votes in both chambers, nor had they ever achieved such proximity to or participation in the leadership. Mike Mansfield had succeeded Johnson as Majority Leader in 1961 and now took an accommodating stance toward younger liberals following Nixon's election. Besides becoming more sympathetic ideologically, Mansfield feared that if he did not compromise with reform-oriented colleagues then more radical proposals would be put forth in the coming years. His leadership style, moreover, was more laid-back than Johnson's since he believed in responding to as many voices as possible. Mansfield made greater use of the Democratic Policy Committee and the Democratic Conference rather than relying on committee chairs to formulate the party agenda. Equally important, he broadened the regional representation

Senate Majority Leader Mike Mansfield in a group photo with Senate committee chairmen in September 1967. The senior age of most committee chairs became a symbol for many reformers of the problems facing Congress (University of Montana at Missoula Library, Special Collections Department).

on these bodies to reflect nonsouthern interests. The Democratic Policy Committee staff cooperated with younger liberals. On foreign and domestic policy, the committee's proclamations shifted to the left after Nixon's election; the feeling was that Democrats needed to be more forceful in order to retain their core constituents and attract newer suburban groups who were not yet committed to either party.

There was even a slight (albeit noticeable) change in the social composition of Congress. The elections between 1968 and 1972 brought African-American and female representatives into the House. Even though it was an extremely small percentage of the chamber, in 1972 fourteen women were elected to the House. Unlike most women who had previously held office, these individuals did not gain their power through the authority of their deceased husbands.[14] By 1973, moreover, there were thirteen African-Americans in the House and one, Edward Brooke (R-MA), in the Senate. One of the major immediate effects of the Supreme Court redistricting decisions was the creation of more inner-city House districts composed of black voting majorities. Redistricting resulted in the victory of seven African-Americans between 1963 and 1970.[15] As their numbers increased, African-American and female legislators formed the Congressional Black Caucus (1970) and National Women's Political Caucus (1971). The growth of caucuses during the 1970s (from three before 1969 to over thirteen by 1974) weakened the committee system by enabling junior members from nonsouthern states to establish themselves outside of committees while also help-ing them get on those panels.[16]

### Democratic Party Finances

In addition to the struggle over their identity, the Democratic party faced a major financial crisis. The Democratic fund-raising apparatus had been noto-riously sloppy. The party depended on informal contacts and ad hoc solicita-tions. Other than organized labor and agriculture, nonsouthern Democrats had depended on unorthodox businessmen, liberal wealthy families, and generous entertainers to fund them.[17] For several decades, however, Democrats had en-joyed contributions by virtue of their incumbency. Then, as the party's political fate changed during the late 1960s, Democrats faced dwindling funds.

Campaign costs skyrocketed in the 1960s, and television was the culprit.[18] The networks provided only limited amounts of free airtime to candidates. As a result of the Federal Communications Act, stations were required to provide equal time to opponents of those politicians who received free airtime. Only when those provisions were temporarily suspended, such as in 1960, were sta-tions willing to broadcast debates that included just some of the candidates in an election. These provisions, according to broadcasters, created an economic disincentive for stations to provide free airtime beyond a bare minimum.

The parties responded to rising campaign costs in the 1960s with different fi-nancial strategies. Republicans supplemented their traditional large donors by broadening their contributor base to conservative groups and individual citizens. Conservative campaign specialist Richard Viguerie used computer technology to send out personalized mail (or "direct mail") to Republican voters, requesting small donations for candidates. In 1964, individuals and single-issue groups funded much of Barry Goldwater's presidential campaign.

Because they controlled the presidency and Congress, Democrats felt less pres-sure to innovate in the 1960s even though the party had accumulated significant debt. Democrats stuck with their old tactics by leaning harder on large contrib-utors. Nonsouthern congressional incumbents continued their reliance on labor and liberal interest groups. In 1961, Democrats launched the President's Club; over 4,000 members made donations in exchange for invitations to monthly events with prominent officials, including the president.[19] The Democrats also raised money through corporate advertising books for conventions. Without supporting candidates outright, corporations purchased tax-deductible ads. Re-publicans copied this method although not as effectively. To a limited extent, Democrats expanded their small contributor drive in 1966.[20] Their efforts paled, however, in comparison to the Republicans. Their plan worked so long as Democrats controlled the White House and labor controlled political action committees. There was little pressure to innovate. But after Nixon's victory in 1968, large contributors quickly turned away from the party, leaving Democrats without a solid contributor base. Meanwhile, congressional Republicans were benefitting from the PACs formed by the American Medical Association in 1961 and the National Association of Manufacturers in 1963.

In 1970, Mansfield lamented that "the Republican coffers were filled and the Democratic cupboard was bare."[21] Warning members that they were facing a serious "campaign fund crisis," the Democratic National Congressional Committee asked incumbents from safe districts to donate part of their funds to those in marginal districts.[22] Democrats scrambled to build a computerized database of voting statistics and social demographics.[23] Under the leadership of Robert Strauss, the party increased its small contributor base from 16,000 to 45,000 and the Democratic National Committee developed new fund-raising methods such as a national telethon. Democrats nonetheless found themselves both in desperate need of campaign funds and also much more sympathetic to proposals for campaign finance reform.

### The Reform Coalition Broadens

During the late 1960s, the liberal coalition transformed into a reform coalition. Like opinion makers in the 1960s, associated organizations and individuals broadened the outlook of the coalition to focus on the need for government reform in itself, rather than as just a means to obtain legislation. They placed a greater rhetorical emphasis on the problem of corruption than had the coalition in the 1950s and 1960s. Whereas the liberal coalition in the 1950s was willing to live with more aspects of the existing process, since their primary target was the southern Democrats and their policy preferences, the coalition by the 1970s was equally concerned with wholesale institutional changes regardless of who was brought down in the process. The newcomers came out of an anticorruption tradition that had flared in various eras. They also saw themselves as champions of suburban middle-class citizens, who were considered to have been disempowered by the senior Democrats and Republicans who were allied with unions, business, or conservative elements of the South and West. Since the suburban middle class was an amorphous body and since most public interest groups were neither dependent on nor connected to a grassroots membership base, their proposals for institutional reform were not closely tied to the direct needs of an identifiable constituency (as was the case with unions and blue-collar workers, for example). The result was that they were more comfortable calling for broad reforms that might conceivably be against the interests of those they claimed to represent.

The national culture in the 1960s favored institutional reform. Even before Watergate, citizens were becoming distrustful of political institutions as a result of Vietnam.[24] Trust in Congress fell from 42 percent of those polled by Louis Harris in 1966 to 19 percent in 1971.[25] The New Left's reaction against the Democratic party – as well as their decision to concentrate on more vibrant political participation by citizens as a primary objective – had generated more intense concerns with how the democratic process actually functioned. The revolt against corruption extended beyond the New Left, as it was a response by many Americans to revelations of secretive foreign policy making and abusive presidential power. The burgeoning conservative movement was equally troubled by national institutions, although they argued that these "corrupt" institutions protected left-wing political and cultural causes. In this tense atmosphere, many established political players turned to government institutions as the answer. If institutions changed, they argued, a more satisfying style of politics would follow. Although active electoral pressure for reform remained tepid, indications from polls and other cultural markers consistently provided tangible evidence that institutional reform was politically appealing.

In this context, new public interest groups began to apply pressure for institutional reform. Though groups such as ADA, the League of Women Voters, and the National Committee for an Effective Congress (NCEC) had championed similar proposals since the 1950s, the size and organizational strength of the reform coalition now grew dramatically, as did their ambitions. The prototype for the new activism was Common Cause. Lyndon Johnson's former secretary of HEW, John Gardner, founded the group in 1970. Gardner was no political outsider. A liberal Republican, Gardner had spent many years in academia. In 1955, he was named president of the Carnegie Corporation. An early supporter of federal civil rights legislation, Gardner joined Lyndon Johnson's administration but resigned on March 1, 1968, because of his opposition to Vietnam and personal tensions with the president. He then founded the Urban Coalition Action Council, a group of civic, religious, labor, and business leaders who sought a solution to the urban crisis. When the Urban Coalition's funding dwindled, Gardner launched Common Cause.[26] During his time in Washington, Gardner had become frustrated with the political process. Right away some charged that Common Cause was a promotional vehicle for Gardner's presidential aspirations. Other critics found these activists to be arrogant. William Frenzel (R-MN) quipped that their newsletters sounded "like a congressman seeking re-election."[27] Although Gardner's elite background caused some to scoff at his activism, he followed a long tradition of dissatisfied insiders who turned their attention toward institutional reform. His experience and connections to national politicians enabled Common Cause to gain attention quickly.

The organization was part of a boom in nonprofit advocacy organizations after 1968.[28] While Common Cause relied on individual contributions, foundations (especially the Ford Foundation) provided sizable contributors that allowed them to exist. The leadership of Common Cause tended to be Democratic or independent, financially well-off, and in possession of undergraduate and graduate degrees. Most of the leadership was politically well connected and able to reach powerful politicians with relative ease. Members tended to be middle-class professionals. Ninety-four percent of them did little more than contribute money and receive mailings, as was common with many civic organizations in this part of the century.[29] By 1974, Common Cause claimed to have more members than the League of Women Voters or ADA. These organizations resembled the Washington-based elite groups that had been part of the liberal coalition in the 1950s and early 1960s, although those older organizations (such as ADA) had been more closely connected to interest groups with strong local ties, such as the AFL-CIO and UAW; mass political movements, such as civil rights; and the Democratic party (even if some of those groups were often at odds with the party leadership). Not only did the newer public interest groups develop little organizational infrastructure for democratic participation, they were rather isolated from broad-based groups other than those seeking institutional reform.

Their focus was on opening up the national political process through institutional reform (rather than mass mobilization) to a greater range of Washington-based organizations who claimed to represent various constituencies. The one political movement many of the public interest groups were involved with was environmentalism, yet this too was dominated by organizations that shared a similar top-down model. In addition, the newer arrivals maintained a strained relationship with unions, who were often at odds with their agenda. Since the majority of the public interest groups of the late 1960s and early 1970s were driven by their national leaders, they enjoyed flexibility in defining what issues and positions they would take. While tending to be on the "liberal" side of the political spectrum, John Gardner, Ralph Nader, and others were willing and able to depart from standpat New Deal positions.

Despite lacking a strong grassroots base, public interest organizations succeeded in attracting media attention. Legislators were aware that the groups could cause serious problems if they decided to target them. Common Cause established reputational strength within the network of people who were fighting for institutional reform. In terms of their policy objectives, the organization's leadership tended to align rather closely with younger Democrats and liberal Republicans, who were more likely to support programs of concern to suburban middle-class voters – particularly environmentalism and consumer protection. Less committed to union-based policies or the embrace of public authority that had been so important since the New Deal, these activists stemmed from an ideological tradition that was uneasy about any form of centralized power. In Common Cause's first decade, its overwhelming interest centered on the political process. Many of its leaders were Democrats and Republicans who were tired of the failure to craft programs that satisfied broad constituencies in their divided parties. They responded to critiques that had arisen in the 1960s, on the right and left, with a solution that avoided radical economic or political cures – one that repaired, rather than eliminated, existing political institutions.

In doing so, Common Cause articulated a critique of pluralism. Gardner's colleagues claimed that interest groups had disempowered a majority of individuals, including those they claimed to serve. From the start, the executive committee of Common Cause targeted campaign finance and congressional reform.[30] Common Cause warned that Congress would be unable to handle the nation's most pressing policy concerns unless the political process changed. It would be impossible to tackle issues (e.g., the environment) that were of importance to the suburban middle class under the existing system. They called themselves a "citizen's lobby – concerned *not* with the advancement of special interests but with the well-being of the nation," a lobby that aimed to "revitalize politics and government."[31] Gardner contended that an "institution's resistance to change is anything but capricious" since insiders protected themselves by "weaving a tough web of custom, rules, institutional structure and process. To cut through that web is to breach the castle walls and leave privilege unguarded." Contrary to conventional wisdom, Gardner firmly believed that institutions could change and had done so before.[32] Gardner insisted that a "renewal of institutions and processes" was needed to regain citizen confidence.[33] Leaders of Common Cause constantly cited polls as evidence that citizens supported them even if there was no groundswell of activism.

Common Cause shared the Progressive Era fear that corruption was undermining democracy. The organization was deeply suspicious of parties and attacked the organizational mechanisms that had traditionally served as intermediaries between voters and elected officials. Gardner said the major parties were no longer instruments of the popular will. But he distinguished his group from Progressive Era good-government predecessors and Gilded Age mugwumps. Foremost, he said that the Progressive Era reformers believed it was possible to fix politics permanently so that government could be pure. In contrast, Common Cause assumed that politicians would always be tempted by corruption. "They didn't understand that somebody always has too much power and somebody always has too little," Gardner explained of his predecessors, "and that if you drive the bad guys out of power the good guys who replace them will soon get accustomed to power and grow to love it and may eventually abuse it. So the struggle never ends." Therefore, he felt that reformers needed to establish a permanent base from which to monitor politics.[34]

Legislators paid attention to Common Cause not only because it represented politically active citizens but also because the group was quite skilled at Washington politics and media relations.[35] The new public interest groups had emerged in a period when there were thickened government institutions at the federal level. Since their leadership felt there were significant limits to how much they could transform institutions, they needed to institutionalize themselves and their ideas into the political process: the fight against corruption would be ongoing and unending. Common Cause secured a talented group of Washington lobbyists and public relations experts and also attracted prominent philanthropic benefactors. They adopted the techniques of interest groups to fight against interest-group politics. Like their Progressive Era predecessors, they relied heavily on the media.[36]

Building on the precedents of the liberal coalition, who had seen the media as an avenue around congressional leaders, Common Cause was much more aggressive in terms of the amount of time, money, and manpower invested into these efforts. Their strategy was even more powerful because they were taking their campaigns to the media after reporters had already embraced a more adversarial outlook toward politicians and were thus far more sympathetic than a decade earlier to demands for reform. The organization placed advertisements and op-eds in newspapers, bombarded legislators with position papers, and orchestrated "mass" letter-writing campaigns. Common Cause used almost all the weapons of a traditional interest group in the name of reforming government. "In a power arena like the Congress or national politics, either huge contributions, very widespread grass roots pressure, or media clout have to be brought to bear," explained a prominent Washington attorney;

Common Cause is seeking to rely primarily on the lobbying techniques of "special interest politics" but in truth belongs to the developing body of "opinion or value-judgement politics." It can never generate the close-in pressure or persuasion that special interest groups can with politicians. But it can top that approach by going to the public and having that apparent pressure feed back, with your Hill lobbying then a secondary but still essential follow up.[37]

Common Cause devoted resources to influencing public opinion by hiring public relations assistants and media specialists. During elections, leaders worked with local activists to pressure candidates into taking public stands on reform and stimulating local media coverage. They sent information packets to familiarize editors and reporters with the issues. By 1971, Common Cause commanded significant institutional and financial resources, claiming over 100,000 members and $1.75 million.

There were many similar organizations and individuals who were applying pressure to changing institutions. Philip Stern, heir to the Sears Roebuck fortune, founded the Center for the Public Financing of Elections. Stern hired Susan King, who had been the Washington spokeswoman for the National Committee for an Effective Congress, to lobby Congress and work with other reform groups.

The most well-known activist was Ralph Nader. Born in 1934 to Lebanese immigrants, Nader had been an avid reader of Progressive Era muckrakers while growing up in Connecticut. He graduated from Princeton in 1951 and from Harvard Law four years later. Dissatisfied with the professional life of a lawyer, Nader decided to become a political activist. His new career began in 1965 when he published a book about how the automobile industry designed unsafe cars.[38] Together with a group of idealistic college students who worked for him, called "Nader's Raiders," Nader broadened his activities to include institutional reform. He founded the Center for the Study of Responsive Law in 1969 while raising money through the nonprofit foundation Public Citizen. Nader's Congress Watch dedicated itself to providing voters with detailed information on each member. Reporters enjoyed covering his activities. He applied the New Left ideals to the world of legislative politics.

Existing reform-oriented groups such as ADA, DSG, and the League of Women Voters reenergized their efforts as well. ADA regrouped after the bitter fight over whether to endorse Eugene McCarthy or Hubert Humphrey. The more conservative leaders abandoned the organization after the decision to endorse

McCarthy. Under the control of reformers after 1968, the ADA agenda moved sharply to the left and became more confrontational toward the Democratic party.[39] In September 1970, the national board decided to make congressional reform its top priority.[40] The ADA closely monitored the press and exchanged information with editors. The League of Women Voters conducted an ongoing study into the committee process and distributed this information to its members.[41] With an estimated 140 members in the House, DSG distributed more than $150,000 in 1968 (up from $63,000 in 1964) to candidates.[42] Using direct mail, DSG was able to raise more funds than ever before. They provided resources other than money, including issue brochures used by candidates and a campaign photo service whereby all members were given the chance to have useful pictures taken, such as next to Vice-President Humphrey. Richard Conlon, the new staff director in 1968, had experience as a reporter and staffer on Capitol Hill. Conlon promoted his studies to the press. DSG also started a project with Hollywood notables (Henry Fonda, Robert Ryan, and Rod Serling) who cut radio ads for campaigns.[43]

The new and old organizations in the reform coalition enjoyed favorable media coverage. If legislators hoped that the media might become more timid after the 1960s, they were wrong. Nixon's attacks on the media fueled this adversarial relationship. When the Supreme Court defended the right of the *New York Times* to publish the top-secret "Pentagon Papers" on June 30, 1971, the decision encouraged reporters to continue on their investigative path. It was not just that journalists were taking a more adversarial stance toward politicians; they were also adopting an interpretative style of journalism. Reporters were less comfortable describing stories and letting the facts speak for themselves. They frequently injected their own analysis into the writing. During the late 1960s, for example, network news introduced commentary segments where former policy makers, journalists, and reporters presented opinionated comments on pertinent issues.[44] One of the fads of this period was called "instant analysis," where commentators criticized speeches immediately after they were finished. Feeling competition from the networks, print reporters mimicked the style.[45]

One final source of support for the coalition's critique of Congress emanated from the antiwar movement. Whereas committee chairs and party leaders in the 1950s had attacked legislation sought by the liberal coalition, with Vietnam they were seen as facilitating the continuation of controversial military operations even as there were mounting protests on the streets. Of course, there were many reasons why Congress did not try to slow the war in the 1960s, including the fact that the legislative branch had delegated considerable authority to the president in foreign policy. But it was clear that legislators had ignored many vocal critics of the buildup in the crucial years between 1963 and 1965. Most Americans were not aware (or forgot) that some of the most powerful committee-era legislators, including Senators Richard Russell and Mike Mansfield, had expressed strong warnings before 1965 against a military escalation in Vietnam (most of those warnings were made only in private).[46] Most of those top legislators had become quiet, moreover, once the ground war began.

Proponents of reform were also aware that senior southern chairs had long supported Cold War military operations. Southerners controlled the military committees and came from a region whose constituents were generally hawkish on foreign affairs. Their states and districts were deeply dependent on the military establishment, given the inordinate level of federal funding that flowed into their region. Referring to the vast number of military contracts located in his district, Georgia's Carl Vinson once joked to South Carolina's L. Mendel Rivers, chair of the House Armed Services Committee, that "you put anything else down there in your district, Mendel, it's going to sink."[47] An attack on American foreign policy was thus inevitably connected to the legislative process and the legislators who controlled the major committees. By the early 1970s, more legislators were openly critical of the war, but in the minds of the war's opponents there remained too many who were not. Even the legislator who took the most prominent antiwar stand, Senator J. William Fulbright (D-AR), was seen by many young liberals as a southern anti–civil rights conservative who thrived on the committee system.[48]

## Nixon's Attack

Divided government aggravated the internal tensions confronting Democrats. During Nixon's first term, the president decided to unleash an assault against Congress. His harsh criticism of the legislative process and brazen attempts to expand executive power turned the weakened status of Congress into a full-blown political crisis.

The president believed that he faced a more difficult political atmosphere than the last Republican president, Eisenhower. Despite Nixon's victory in 1968, Democrats had retained control of the House (245-187) and Senate (57-43). Nixon and his advisors believed that congressional Democrats were being driven by the party's most partisan figures and that the administration should use this in its public relations campaigns.[49] Nixon was infuriated when Senate liberals blocked two nominations for the Supreme Court in 1969. Top advisors lamented that "not since Zachary Taylor has a new President had to try to form a new Administration with a hostile Congress second-guessing every move."[50] In October 1969, Nixon told congressional Republicans that he wanted a "systematic program of putting the blame on Congress for frustrating the legislative program."[51] Nixon targeted the "super-partisans" and presented Congress as inefficient and incapable of governing.

Tension between the branches flared over access to television, which since the early 1960s had become the central medium of political communication and news. The president made unprecedented use of prime-time network appearances even as he cut down his televised press conferences. In the first eighteen months of his administration, Nixon appeared on prime-time television as much as Eisenhower, Kennedy, and Johnson combined.[52] From 1969 through 1970, Nixon preempted scheduled programs seven times to promote his Vietnam policies. Frustrated Democrats did not have an equal opportunity to respond; this was a problem that the opposition party in Congress had encountered with television ever since the industry's advent.[53] A big Democratic contributor wrote that "the Democrats find themselves like Spanish Loyalists huddling in trenches while the enemy bombers fly overhead at will."[54] Legal challenges by the DNC to obtain equal time failed even though the networks occasionally carried DNC Chairman Lawrence O'Brien's comments on a voluntary basis.[55]

Legislators also fought for equal airtime. Although Senate Democrats purchased airtime on one network in 1970 to protest the administration's policy in Cambodia, the networks refused to sell airtime to legislators after Nixon's next appearance. Some networks offered Senator Mansfield response time to Nixon's speeches, but these were not guaranteed. Liberals filed a complaint with the FCC that they deserved equal time. However, the FCC ruled on August 14, 1970, that the networks did not have to grant equal time to Congress. Fulbright attempted to use the "public service" provision of the 1934 Communications Act to force the networks to carry legislators. His resolution came under fire from network executives, who felt they were being coerced by politicians to play certain programs. Other broadcasting officials raised questions about who could be selected as spokesperson for Congress, given its decentralization.[56] Lack of bipartisan support, fears about tampering with media freedom, and the hesitance of legislators to anger the media during an election all contributed to the proposal's failure.[57] In the end, Congress did not obtain any legislative right to respond to the president.

The debates over television in Nixon's first year as president highlighted how he seemed to be expanding executive power. This was just a hint of things to come. Over the next four years, Nixon would continue to put Congress on the defensive as he usurped authority over budgeting and war-making.

Just as Nixon assailed the weakness of Congress, liberals attacked the president by focusing on the corruption of the executive branch.[58] Liberal Democrats who had defended presidential power in the twentieth century as an instrument of progressivism now started to warn of an "Imperial Presidency."[59] Democrats had already critiqued presidential power during the 1960s in response to the congressional abdication of war-making authority with Vietnam. But Democrats were unrestrained with Nixon. Together with Vietnam, Nixon thus undermined support for a strong presidency among the institution's greatest supporters. The flawed legislative process, argued John Conyers (D-MI), was more debilitating than ever since Democrats could no longer "rely on a progressive President or a liberal Supreme Court to assume the obligations of leadership which the Congress has been unwilling or unable to meet."[60]

The volatile atmosphere resulted in an arms war of institutional criticism. Each side escalated its attack on the other by making a public issue of procedural problems. The battle turned relations between the executive and legislative branches into a political and constitutional crisis. This placed the political process at the center of the national agenda. At the same time, Nixon's confrontational stance convinced liberal Democrats that it was essential for Congress to become more assertive. This required bringing down committee chairs and the process they relied on. Otherwise, they feared that Nixon would render their institution irrelevant. The "Imperial Presidency" was no longer just a theoretical argument. Under Nixon, it had become a constitutional crisis.

## The Advantages of Instability

The disintegration of the "New Deal Order" as it came under attack from the left and the right created a moment in history when substantive institutional reform was possible though not inevitable.[61] This moment marked the beginning of the decline of the political policies, ideologies, movements, and institutions that had been put into place during the Progressive Era. Within Congress, the committee era lurched toward its demise. The crisis of the Democratic party, an emboldened reform coalition, and an external institutional environment unfavorable to the legislative process all combined to provide a window of opportunity for proponents of congressional reform.

The legislators who opposed the committee process now had more room to maneuver. Suddenly it seemed politically feasible to move forward with reforms that were far more ambitious than efforts between 1961 and 1965. By this time, the reform coalition was promising that changing the way Congress worked would create a more efficient, progressive, trusted, and stronger legislative branch. The coalition seized this opportunity to tackle two explosive issues: the role of private money in elections and the autonomous power of committee chairs.

# 7

# Money in Politics

The beginning of the 1970s launched the third stage in the disintegration of the committee-era Congress. The political battle over Congress had started back in the late 1930s when the committee process of the House and Senate became inextricably identified with conservative southern Democrats. The second stage took place from 1948 through the 1960s with the formation and expansion of a coalition that perceived congressional reform as essential to achieving multiple objectives. The coalition included several constituencies (that were sometimes in conflict) and entered into voting alliances of convenience with such groups as moderate congressional Republicans. The coalition was able to overcome most internal conflicts before the mid-1970s because of a consensus on their targets and an agreement to draw on a common package of solutions. The members of the coalition had also made calculated compromises on certain issues, such as tempering their ambitions for changing campaign finance rules, that helped preserve the coalition. Furthermore, throughout the 1960s, the major institutions surrounding Congress changed in a manner that did not favor the committee process. The momentum for reform reached a new level of intensity in the late 1960s as political conditions for reform improved dramatically.

Between 1970 and 1974, the reform coalition took advantage of these conditions to accelerate its fight for a new legislative process even before a momentous scandal or election allowed them to directly take on the leadership.[1] During these years, Congress enacted the most expansive campaign reforms in American history, including stronger disclosure laws, public financing for presidential elections, contribution and spending limits, and an independent commission. The regulatory system revolutionized the disclosure of information, ended the dominance of large individual contributors, and injected public funds into campaigns.

In the process of fighting against opponents and trying to overcome the deep internal tensions that existed within their coalition, reformers continued to make important compromises during these battles that left considerable room for private money to influence congressional campaigns – although in a more fragmented, transparent, and decentralized manner. Foremost, many members of the reform coalition were still hesitant to tackle PACs, given the tensions between unions and the rest of the coalition. Most of organized labor was unwilling to compromise on the PAC issue, especially since the business and conservative communities were conducting a second wave of intense mobilization and organization (similar to the one that occurred in the late 1950s) by forming political action committees and similar organizations to funnel funds and resources toward sympathetic candidates. Since institutional reform was no longer as closely linked to revitalizing liberal policies, internal tensions flared during the battle over campaign finance, as they would with the struggle over committee power. The resulting compromise, which left PACs intact, was legitimated by the Supreme Court in June 1972.

The reform coalition was also crucial to enforcing the laws. Since the first round of campaign finance legislation did not include any independent commission, the coalition was forced to take responsibility for making certain that the laws were followed and that the public learned through disclosure about how campaigns were financed. Third, the coalition helped pass a second round of legislation by mobilizing when Watergate erupted. The Federal Election Campaign Act Amendments of 1974 created the modern campaign regulatory structure. But in the process of obtaining legislation, reformers made another big compromise by temporarily abandoning publicly financed congressional elections. This chapter also explores how the Watergate scandal impeded efforts to change Congress, since it directed energy toward the executive branch at the exact moment when the coalition was struggling to reconstruct the legislative process.

### The First Victory: Cost Control and Disclosure Legislation (1972)

The initial debate over campaign finance reform centered around the issues of cost and disclosure. The cost of campaigns in the television era had placed enormous pressure on candidates to rely on wealthy contributors.[2] The Citizens' Research Foundation reported that election spending in 1968 was 25 percent higher than 1964.[3] The National Committee for an Effective Congress (NCEC) proposed legislation that would enable congressional candidates to purchase airtime at a reduced rate. They wanted to eliminate the equal-time provision of the Communication Act of 1934; network executives said this would give them more flexibility in allocating time for select candidates who were seen as the frontrunners.

Until the 1970s, comprehensive information was almost impossible to obtain. Most reformers in 1970 favored stronger disclosure laws combined with selective cost controls. Existing spending and contribution limits were widely perceived as unenforceable and unconstitutional.[4] Democrats also feared that contribution limits would harm their party, given its need for funds. Advocates of reform doubted that campaign spending limits would survive constitutional challenge. Although the Supreme Court did not review any cases directly and sent mixed messages, several rulings in the 1950s and 1960s indicated a bias toward protecting speech in elections.[5]

In an era when citizen access to information was a primary goal of reformers, disclosure of campaign contributions offered a viable solution that avoided most constitutional and implementation problems. As a staff member for Senator Hugh Scott explained:

> Once a potential donor realizes that his name (as a donor) will become public property, he will think twice about making that contribution. "Dirty money" will stay away from campaigns and so will "dirty donors." Generally speaking, a rather large hunk of campaign income will never surface simply for fear of disclosure. Such a *self-imposed ceiling* is a much sounder approach than an arbitrary ceiling, of any kind, be it selective or general.[6]

Disclosure was one of the few issues that received nearly unanimous support within the reform coalition.

In 1970, Congress considered legislation that included free ads for candidates and additional airtime at reduced rates. Senators Philip Hart (D-MI) and James Pearson (R-KS) and Representative Torbert MacDonald (D-MA) introduced a bill based on the recommendations of the National Committee for an Effective Congress.[7] In response, network executives promised to discount rates voluntarily while adamantly opposing free airtime. The Commerce Committee reported a bill that suspended the equal-time provision and limited the rates broadcasters could charge candidates. On April 14, the Senate passed the legislation 58-27 with eight Republicans in favor. Democrats were aware that the bill could change their fortunes, especially in marginal districts.[8] The House passed a measure that also guaranteed reduced advertising rates for all candidates and mandated stronger disclosure regulations for campaign committees.

The conference committee eliminated the independent commission, which had been the most controversial provision. Most Democrats opposed a commission because it would increase enforcement of the laws. Republicans feared that, without a commission, Democrats would use disclosed information for partisan purposes. The committee also settled on watered-down cost control through reduced rates for candidates and repealed the equal-time provision for presidential and vice-presidential campaigns. Divided government once again fueled the debate over institutional reform, as it had in the 1950s. Nixon used the limitations as an excuse to veto the legislation on October 12, 1970. He said that the bill opened more loopholes than it closed, discriminated unfairly against the broadcast media, and benefitted incumbents.[9] Democrats charged Nixon with sacrificing campaign finance reform for partisan interests, and Common Cause equated him with "a man who decided not to undergo a much needed appendectomy because the doctor was not prepared to deal with his liver and back problems at the same time."[10]

The reform coalition continued to experiment with different tactics. They sometimes tried to make an end run around an intransigent Congress through the courts. Class action lawsuits served the dual purpose of enforcing laws and generating media publicity. On January 11, 1971, Common Cause filed a lawsuit in U.S. District Court against the Democratic and Republican National Committees and the Conservative Party of New York to enjoin them from violating the federal campaign laws. Common Cause claimed that the parties regularly flouted the 1925 laws that limited contributions and spending and that the public was angry.[11] Common Cause was joined by the ADA, the Twentieth Century Fund, and the NCEC. The Court ruled that since the government was failing to enforce the campaign finance laws, these public interest groups had the "right of private enforcement" and could bring class action suits against the parties as representatives of the voters.[12]

As reformers turned to the courts, the media continued to report on campaign finance abuses. Reporters in television and print media could now draw on a wealth of data from the reform coalition and the campaign finance experts who had come into existence one decade earlier. The media produced a number of articles and editorials endorsing reform.[13] The NCEC warned that each story "stokes the fires of public cynicism and the common suspicion of widespread wrong-doing."[14]

In addition to reformers and an aggressive media, partisan interests energized the drive for campaign finance reform.[15] By 1971, the Democratic party generally supported most campaign finance reforms.[16] They did so in large part because they needed campaign funds. AFL-CIO lobbyist Andrew Biemiller believed that, without publicly financed elections, "the Democratic Party will be in desperate shape." Biemiller captured the mix of motives in play at this time when he added that "both parties have looked primarily to large contributors, the Democrats even more than the Republicans. It is generally believed that this is not in the best interests of good government. Moreover, it gives the Republicans a substantial edge, which is currently accentuated by the advantages that accrue to an incumbent President."[17] Just as partisan interests stimulated Democrats to support public finance, Republicans sensed by late 1971 that it was against their electoral interest to appear as the party of obstruction in light of increased media attention on campaign corruption. Working with Democrats, moderate Republican Senators Scott and Charles Mathias (R-MD) proposed overall cost limits, media spending ceilings, and improved disclosure.

One recurring debate during this period concerned the impact of campaign finance reform on incumbents. There was a strong sentiment that congressional reform should make elections more competitive, thereby reversing the trend of incumbency that had been evident since the early 1950s. But it was unclear how changes to the campaign finance system would affect this trend. Public interest groups argued that the existing process favored incumbents, who had free exposure to the public and an easier time raising funds. In their minds, any effort to limit the cost of campaigns and provide free television exposure to all candidates would help competitors match those in office. But Republicans feared that reform would solidify Democratic majorities by establishing low spending ceilings, since incumbents had more free public exposure. There was no decisive resolution to this issue, but the debate was politically useful to opponents of reform who did not want to appear as protectors of vested interests. The argument strategically pitted campaign reform against the other institutional problem of noncompetitive elections.

In January 1971, the administration sent Senator Scott signals that they were willing to accept a revised bill. Scott's staff met with presidential counsel John Dean, who said the administration supported a tax credit for small contributors, a reduction in airtime costs, and a commission.[18] In March, Republican National Committee chairman Robert Dole (R-KS) told reporters that the president would not repeat his veto.

The television networks recognized the desire to impose ceilings on campaign costs. However, they insisted that the limits cover all types of media ads, not just television. At the same time, the networks did not want the government to impose specific costs. Instead, officials said that they would voluntarily provide candidates with the lowest possible commercial cost in the final weeks of campaigns.[19]

The Senate passed the regulations by a vote of 88-2 on August 5. Since senators faced more competitive elections than representatives and also needed to finance statewide media, they tended to be more concerned about campaign costs than representatives. The bill removed limitations on private contributions, created a commission, required television and radio stations to charge the lowest price possible to candidates, and strengthened disclosure laws. The Senate bill repealed the equal-time provision for all federal candidates, including those running for Congress. Common Cause had worked behind the scenes to obtain Senator Pearson's amendment for a commission (a measure based on language it had drafted).[20] Common Cause warned that eliminating the commission would create the "appearance of reform without the reality."[21] To obtain Democratic support, they had accepted expanding the commission from five to six members, with three from each party, to achieve a balance. However, reformers realized that many key measures were in trouble. Most important, the commission had weak support despite its passage in the Senate. Campaign spending limits, besides being constitutionally suspect, had also become highly partisan since Republicans argued that the regulations were pro-incumbent. Nor were individual contribution limits or public campaign subsidies very popular in either the House or Senate, as proponents came to realize by late July.[22]

When the Senate legislation reached the House, two committees had jurisdiction over the measure: the Interstate and Foreign Commerce Committee and the Administration Committee. Whereas the former committee was sympathetic to reform, the latter was chaired by Wayne Hays – an avid opponent. Since becoming chairman of the House Administration Committee in 1970, Hays had turned the position from one of administrative supervision into a center of power by expanding committee jurisdiction to include federal elections, allowances for the office expenses of members, and parking. Starting in 1973, he had taken over the Democratic Congressional Campaign Committee, which distributed campaign funds to House members. The acerbic Hays displayed little respect for what he called "Common Curse." He castigated and threatened colleagues, while bullying subordinates. But Hays was not alone in opposing the bill. Republicans on the Administration Committee were concerned that spending limits would protect incumbents.

The broadcast industry lobbied against the requirement that television stations had to sell airtime to federal candidates at the lowest unit rate.[23] But the pressure to impose selected cost controls was even greater than their lobbying efforts. The networks were also unable to prevent the House from knocking out the repeal of the equal-time provision, which in the minds of incumbents would have helped only challengers.

At the same time, the AFL-CIO was pressuring Democrats to oppose any amendments to regulate PACs. Unions still feared for the future of their PACs. The Supreme Court was considering a case of union leaders convicted of violating the prohibition of using general fund money for contributions to federal elections. Evidence revealed that the St. Louis Pipefitters Local Union No. 562 maintained a fund between 1949 and 1962, to which union members were required to contribute. The jury found the union guilty, since union officers who were paid by general funds administered the organizational money. When the case reached the Court, the Justice Department claimed it was not legal for unions to engage in any political activities even with voluntary funds. Unions were convinced that the Court would rule against them and saw "ominous" signs of growing congressional support to "hamstring" labor. Al Barkan, the head of the AFL-CIO's Committee on Political Education (COPE), outlined the situation when he told George Meany that "between the Supreme Court, the Mitchell Justice Department and the congressional snipers, the possibility that we will have to rely wholly on voluntary funds cannot be lightly treated."[24]

House and Senate liberals were also facing pressure against PAC reform in 1971, since conservative and business associations had greatly expanded their organizational political power in the 1960s. By the time that reform was being considered by Congress in 1971, there was an all-out war over financing elections.[25] Hundreds of major corporations had hired public affairs officers. The American Medical Association established a PAC in 1961, and the Business-Industry Political Action Committee was instrumental to conservative election victories in 1966. "The U.S. corporation's flirtation with politics that began shyly enough in the late 1950s," reported the *Wall Street Journal,* "has blossomed into a warm romance."[26] The rise of these PACs, combined with the pending Supreme Court case, made labor defensive. Nor did cash-starved Democrats want to lose union contributions. The result was that a majority of Democrats rejected strict limitations on PACs.

In January 1972, Congress passed the Federal Election Campaign Act Amendments, which strengthened cost control and disclosure. The amendments limited media spending, forced broadcasters to sell reduced-cost advertising, reasserted the right of Congress to regulate primaries, strengthened reporting requirements for all campaign committees, and deemed contribution limits to be illegitimate.

The legislation authorized labor to seek contributions for campaigns as long as they were voluntarily donated without intimidation. To gain administration support, Democrats inserted a 60-day delay to the law, which would take effect after the New Hampshire, Florida, Illinois, and Wisconsin primaries. Nixon signed the legislation on February 7 after realizing that he no longer had support for a veto.

Public financing proposals suffered a mixed fate. Senate Democrats unexpectedly attached language to tax legislation that authorized public financing of presidential elections. House Ways and Means Committee Chairman Wilbur Mills said he would support the amendment, but Republicans were fighting it "tooth and nail" because it would be a financial boon to Democrats. Nixon threatened a veto, saying it would be too costly. Mills felt that the tax legislation – which included accelerated depreciation for businesses – was too important to risk, so he engineered a compromise.[27] Taxpayers could allocate money in 1972 but Congress could not distribute funds until 1976. For reformers, Mills's compromise effectively killed public financing through postponement, just as in 1966.

### The Reform Coalition Finds Itself Divided: 1972

Following the passage of disclosure and cost-control legislation, the reform coalition could not let down its guard. Since the legislation failed to create adequate enforcement mechanisms, the coalition had to fulfill this duty. Coalition members spent 1972 making sure that the laws were followed in the November election. At the same time, continued conflicts within the reform coalition revealed that campaign finance had not obtained unanimous support. The conflict stemmed from the fact that labor wanted to defend its hard-earned political capital from reformers. This split helped produce significant compromises in any effort to reform the ties between money and politics. Most important, public interest groups postponed their quest for PAC limitations and instead decided to focus on public financing.[28] Though united on most issues, the reform coalition remained divided on campaign finance.

One immediate effect of the new campaign finance law was to stimulate intense fund-raising before the laws were activated. Nixon's team led the way, as Maurice Stans went on a whirlwind tour to solicit contributors. The press intercepted administration letters urging donors to make anonymous donations before the disclosure laws went into effect. Responding to a challenge from Common Cause, a few Democrats voluntarily disclosed campaign finance information before April 7. Candidates Wilbur Mills, Henry Jackson, and Richard Nixon refused.

Since the new law did not create an enforcement commission, the reform coalition took this responsibility upon themselves. While an investigation by the House Banking and Currency Committee revealed some of the illicit activities of Nixon's fund-raising, the reform coalition garnered the most publicity for these issues. The courts were a key avenue for enforcement. As soon as Nixon signed the legislation in 1972, Ralph Nader's Public Citizen, the Federation of Homemakers, and the D.C. Consumer's Association filed a lawsuit claiming that the president accepted money from the milk co-ops in exchange for reversing a decision by the Department of Agriculture that had lowered milk prices. In a separate action, Public Citizen filed a suit claiming that the Department of Justice had not enforced campaign finance legislation. Public Citizen and the NCEC filed a petition in March 1972 requesting that the Securities and Exchange Commission force corporations with "voluntary" committees to disclose their transactions fully. The petition resulted in an investigation by the SEC into campaign contributions from corporations. Finally, Common Cause filed a lawsuit on September 6 charging that the Committee to Re-Elect the President had violated the 1925 election disclosure laws. The suit was partially settled on November 1, 1972, with Nixon revealing the sources of $5 million in donations. On July 24, 1973, the court ruled that Nixon had to disclose the remaining donations. The information that emerged from these suits was soon on the front pages of newspapers. Under the new law, Common Cause filed complaints against 120 Democrats and 98 Republicans and called on presidential candidates to disclose pre–April 7 contributions.[29]

Besides the courts, the reform coalition called on its members to enforce the laws. Common Cause launched a national monitoring project of the 1972 election. The project aimed to determine how much was being spent and who was contributing. Common Cause trained more than a thousand volunteers throughout the states to analyze election reports. The volunteers established networks in state capitals and near offices of the major congressmen who would be the focus of the study. The group released its initial findings through carefully planned encounters with reporters.[30]

Common Cause also warded off attempts to undermine the regulations. When Wayne Hays attempted to subvert the regulations, Common Cause responded. Without public hearings, Hays's Administration Committee voted to exempt union and corporate contractors from the provision that had barred them from making voluntary campaign gifts. A few senators – under intense pressure from the reform coalition – killed the exemption.[31] Common Cause also reported that TRW, a large company with major government contracts, maintained an illegal campaign fund composed of money from employees. Common Cause filed a suit against TRW, which led the company to end the practice. According to John Gardner, scandalous revelations were essential to building public support for further reform.[32] Before the 1972 election, almost every reform organization pressured candidates to take positions publicly on campaign finance reform. The elections, which brought in a number of liberals to the House and Senate, left reform organizations with more votes.

Despite the public support of unions for campaign finance reform, labor was wary of additional legislation. The unions complained that "there has been planted in the public mind the vision of 'labor bosses' directing a vast paid army into political battle. Nothing could be further off the mark."[33] Although the

AFL-CIO supported subsidies for presidential elections and felt that "Watergate provides a rational basis for believing that legislative progress can be made on this subject at this time," they wanted a system that included some private contributions. One senior counsel for the AFL-CIO candidly wrote, "even though we are normally outspent, the opportunity to make contributions to our friends is one which repays us during the course of the legislative and executive processes."[34] Nor did the unions lend private support to subsidies for congressional elections, where labor actually spent most of its campaign funds.[35] COPE had provided more assistance in the 1972 congressional elections than in any other year.[36] Like most campaign finance experts at the time, the AFL-CIO believed that contribution limit laws would not be enforced. But if they were, AFL-CIO leaders feared that union campaign donations, which aggregated small contributions from individuals with modest incomes, might be treated in the same fashion as a large contribution from a single wealthy citizen.

There were other conflicts taking place in 1972 between labor and public interest groups. Many Common Cause proposals, unions feared, would result in a "crippling blow to the labor movement."[37] Like Wayne Hays, unions opposed banning corporate and union contractors from making voluntary campaign gifts. Moreover, labor was angry with state-based Common Cause efforts, such as California's Proposition 9, that enacted stringent disclosure and lobbying measures.[38]

These fights were not isolated to campaign finance; unions were often finding themselves in conflict with former allies. The diversification of the Democratic party to include more representatives of the suburban middle class was causing many rifts. Under president George Meany, for example, the AFL-CIO had angered many liberal and moderate Democrats by supporting Nixon's 1972 campaign and the continuation of Indochina military operations – all the while opposing many popular domestic initiatives in areas such as environmentalism. There were also an increasing number of blue-collar workers who had lost any sense of connection between their own shop-floor interests and the organizations that represented them in Washington.[39] Furthermore, under pressure from reform-oriented members of the party, the Democratic party had changed the rules for selecting delegates to the party convention despite AFL-CIO opposition.[40] The struggle exacerbated splits within the labor movement, as some unions (such as the United Auto Workers) endorsed the plan.[41] The new rules improved the representation of women, minorities, and youth at the expense of traditional power brokers such as unions and urban machines. The first Democratic candidate to benefit from the rules, George McGovern, did poorly with most unions while thriving with the newly empowered constituencies.

Notwithstanding tensions between labor and the reform coalition, one development calmed the situation. The Supreme Court decision in June 1972, *Pipefitters v. United States,* protected the right of unions to establish PACs as long as donations were voluntary and maintained in a separate account. The basis of the prohibition against unions and corporations, the Court explained, was that large

organizational money corrupted politics. But if the money was voluntarily contributed by individuals, the rationale did not apply. Based on the 1971 legislation
and precedents since the 1940s, the Court did not deny unions this right. Union
officers, moreover, could administer the funds as long as they were maintained
in a separate account. In effect, the Court had legitimated PACs. Dissenting,
Justice Powell warned that this opinion provided a "blueprint" for corporations
and unions to make contributions without regulation.[42] The AFL-CIO happily
reported that "the Pipefitters decision has been most helpful in finally disposing
of any question about a union's legal right to expend political funds collected
from its members."[43]

## Watergate: 1973

A significant part of Watergate, the scandal commanding national attention
by 1973, involved campaign corruption. The story started with the break-in
of Democratic National Committee headquarters in June 1972. Five men were
arrested and charged. *Washington Post* reporters Bob Woodward and Carl Bernstein reported within a few days of the break-in that the burglars might have
links to President Nixon's Committee to Re-Elect the President (CREEP). Federal District Judge Sirica, who handled the trial of the burglars, concluded that
the crime was somehow related to the presidential campaign. The courts and
press revealed throughout 1972 and 1973 that high-level officials in the Nixon
White House had orchestrated the break-in. The first congressional investigation
into the matter focused on Nixon's campaign finances. Gradually, the story expanded to include other campaign abuses including illicit contributions. Nixon's
scandal reverberated in the context of a preexisting coalition that was seeking to
enforce new laws. The revelations also occurred in an explosive partisan environment that pitted the Democratic Congress against a Republican president –
and with the media looking to flex its muscle.

Congress, the courts, and the media furthered the effort to make existing
campaign laws effective through the Watergate investigations. Mike Mansfield
formed the Select Committee on Presidential Campaign Activities to investigate
these allegations. He chose Sam Ervin (D-NC) to be chairman because of his
strict constitutionalism and reputation for legal knowledge. The Democratic
Caucus granted the committee the power to subpoena witnesses and records. In
addition, the committee included such respected Republicans as Howard Baker
(TN) and Lowell Weicker (CT), as well as a skilled chief counsel, Samuel Dash.
Ervin's committee conducted the much-discussed televised hearings that started
in May 1973 on the 1972 presidential campaign. When the Senate conducted
these televised hearings, high numbers of viewers tuned in to watch Congress investigate the scandal; the hearings led still more Americans to believe that Nixon
had known about the coverup while it was taking place.[44] Polls demonstrated
public approval of the hearings. Ervin became an overnight celebrity. Once John
Dean reached an immunity deal with the committee in exchange for his testimony

Watergate hearings: Senator Howard Baker (left) and Senator Sam Ervin (middle); staff member on right (U.S. Senate Historical Office).

about the president, the networks decided to undertake full-time coverage and forgo their soap-opera revenues. Although most of those polled continued to express opinions they had formed prior to the hearings, the televised event altered their understanding of what Watergate was about – namely, that Nixon's wrongdoing was potentially far more serious than they had thought. Like Senate hearings that preceded them, these gave Americans unprecedented insight into how the institution operated. The same would be true in the summer of 1974 when Americans tuned in to watch the House Judiciary impeachment proceedings. Chairman Peter Rodino (D-NJ) became a household name and, to some, a modern political hero.[45]

Watergate was a turning point in the politics of institutional reform. Nixon embodied the corruption that reformers had attacked since the 1960s. The media could not get enough of Watergate. After a respite around the 1972 elections, by 1973 the networks covered the events daily. Shortly before the Senate began its investigation into Watergate, CBS played a one-hour special that presented the events leading up to the hearings in the same fashion as a detective story.[46] The story was frequently presented in conjunction with discussions about the campaign finance system, just as reporters had covered Adam Clayton Powell and Thomas Dodd in the context of seniority.[47] In October 1973 Nixon fired the special prosecutor, Archibald Cox, which seemed to confirm that politicians would never police themselves. Nixon's activities also served as an argument for stronger laws to enforce ethical behavior among public officials. There was a sense, as NBC's David Brinkley said, that Congress could take this opportunity to do something about campaign corruption "while the heat is on, or it can let it slide, as it so often does, until the public attention turns to something else."[48]

Many of the reporters who handled Watergate were the same individuals who had been physically and legally threatened by southern politicians for covering civil rights in the early 1960s; they had been lied to by military officials about the Vietnam conflict, and they had lived through landmark Supreme Court cases where the justices protected journalist rights. Watergate culminated a gradual progression within the journalistic profession, from which reporters emerged more determined than ever to investigate and expose political corruption.

Watergate also turned campaign finance into a political grenade for Republicans, as many Democrats were preparing to make it a campaign issue in 1974. As Senator James Abourezk (D-SD) told colleagues: "it is very possible you will find that if you are against public financing you might be accused of being in favor of what has just happened in Watergate; in other words, it may be the most popular thing right now for everybody to be in favor of public financing rather than to think that you are being accused of wanting a slush fund. I think attitudes have changed that much."[49] To separate themselves from the scandal, Republicans stressed that Watergate was the product of a corrupt system and not of a corrupt individual or party. More congressional Republicans called for reform. William Brock, chair of the Republican Senate Campaign Committee, proposed stronger disclosure laws, restraints on campaign costs, and a single financial institution to handle campaign contributions.[50] Nixon even called for a nonpartisan commission (the day before Senator Ervin opened his hearings). In May 1973, William Frenzel (chair of the Republican Task Force on Election Reform) concluded that "Congress has a real incentive and a real mandate to act."[51] Most Republicans still opposed publicly financed campaigns as unconstitutional, costly, and protective of incumbents. They had less need for funds and did not want Democrats to benefit.

By 1973, most congressional Democrats agreed on the need for public subsidies, contribution and spending limits, and an independent commission. Watergate had placed contribution and spending limits back on the agenda after they were abandoned in 1971. Yet there were still serious divisions within the Democratic party. One disagreement revolved around the relationship between Watergate and institutional reform. Some Democrats, such as freshman Senator Joseph Biden (DE), wanted to target Nixon; others, such as John Pastore (RI), stressed the need to keep the issue bipartisan. A second division was over whether to call for public financing in congressional or just presidential elections. Pastore warned of the need to limit the reforms in terms of cost and coverage, or risk losing support. Likewise, Long believed that public financing for congressional elections, based on his past experience with this issue, would be seen by legislators as guaranteeing "them a well financed opponent." Public finance for presidential elections, though, could pass: "you ought to start right out with the Presidency where the people can understand it. That is where we have already acted and where we have already managed to put something on the statute books and the public has come to accept it."[52] James O'Hara (D-MI) argued that campaign finance had to be completely subsidized by the government.[53] Support for an independent commission had also become much stronger, since Watergate made it difficult to contend that the Justice Department could uphold the laws.[54]

In July 1973, the Senate Rules and Administration Committee reported legislation limiting campaign spending, restricting contributions, and creating an independent commission to regulate elections. Though the Senate rejected public subsidies for presidential elections, they did so by a narrow vote. In the House, John Anderson and Morris Udall received more support for public finance than ever before but were unable to get it through committee. A bipartisan coalition of senators did attach a rider for publicly financed elections to legislation that had obtained the support of the Democratic leadership (including Hays), but they were forced to drop the measure as a result of Senator James Allen's (D-AL) filibuster.

Although Allen blocked the campaign finance bill, the rising tide of support for publicly financed elections surprised reformers.[55] Common Cause established a "Watergate countdown" program. Volunteers met with the editors of local papers and trade associations in order to provide them with background memoranda and press conference packets.[56] Common Cause held press conferences releasing the findings from its campaign monitoring activities.[57] The Center for Public Financing published studies stressing that publicly financed campaigns, which would cost 69 cents for every adult of voting age, were essential.[58]

Watergate scared Democrats, who sensed the scandal was having a detrimental impact on how the public viewed all political leaders – not just Republicans. "It is a cesspool, it is a source of infection for the body politic," Hubert Humphrey warned his fellow senators in 1973 about the private financing of elections, "if it doesn't stop, there are going to be good men in this hall right here today who are going down the drain, not that you are guilty, not that you have done anything wrong, but that the public is disenchanted with all of us, and they are going to want somebody new and say I want a fresh one here."[59]

Polls confirmed that Watergate had heightened public anger with political corruption. But they also dated the trend back to the escalation of Vietnam. The problem with government was thus bigger than Nixon. According to Gallup polls, Americans now ranked government corruption as one of the most important problems facing the nation. Sixty-five percent of those polled said that they favored the use of public funding in presidential and congressional elections. Support for public financing had risen from 11 percent in 1964 to 67 percent in 1974.[60] When Gallup asked 1,560 Americans whether they believed there were sitting legislators who won election by using unethical and illegal means, 65 percent responded Yes.[61] Mansfield warned the Democratic Caucus in May 1973 that "A cloud hangs over the nation. It is Watergate and larger than Watergate.... The political disaster of Watergate has coupled with a shaken economy to create a dual crisis – a crisis of conscience and a crisis of confidence."[62]

Watergate offered a focusing event for the coalition to push their proposals that had incubated over many years. When the press publicized Nixon's misdeeds, there was a strong coalition prepared to move forward with legislation. As Senator Biden explained: "Watergate isn't the question. Watergate is merely a vehicle through which we can get through what we originally could not get through because the fellows on the other team are in a very compromising position as a consequence of it."[63]

Without the coalition, Watergate might have produced less legislation and the scandal itself might not have been as dramatic. But without a scandal as shocking as Watergate, the reform coalition might not have been able to secure legislative support for extensive reform. There was a perception that reform could finally pass, which was given support by a burst of regulations in the states. Forty states enacted measures to limit secrecy in politics and reduce the influence of private money in the eighteen months leading up to the climactic summer of Richard Nixon's resignation.[64] The impact of the disclosure laws that Nixon signed in 1972 encouraged politicians that reform worked. To illustrate this, Senator Claiborne Pell (D-RI) pointed out that the disclosure bill was "a pretty darn good law, because a lot of things exposed in the Watergate would not have come up if it hadn't been for the present law."[65] Indeed, the disclosure law was instrumental in forcing the revelation of controversial campaign contributions that demonstrated a pattern where Nixon took specific policy positions in response to campaign assistance from interest groups and where he used his power to coerce people into backing him.

### The Second Victory: Bifurcated Reform (1974)

Most Democratic leaders saw campaign finance as a defining issue of 1974. Mansfield said on television that, "If it was in 1972 that Watergate arose, and in 1973 that it was investigated, may it be said that it was in 1974 that the matter was finally ended in a new system of open elections openly paid for."[66] Watergate was seen not just as a presidential crisis, as confirmed by most polls. Mansfield explained: "Not only the Presidency, but all politics, politicians and political institutions – the entire government – have suffered a devastating blow."[67]

The drive for legislation gained momentum in April 1974 when the Senate passed a bill mandating public funds for all federal elections and creating a commission. Nixon could no longer afford to oppose these legislators as Congress deliberated his impeachment. Several weeks after Nixon's key fund-raiser, Maurice Stans, pleaded guilty to managing illegal contributions, the president called for an independent commission, stronger disclosure laws, rules against "dirty tricks," and strict reporting requirements for PACs.[68] By this time, however, Watergate had led Senate Minority Leader Hugh Scott to reverse his position on publicly financed presidential elections.[69] When Allen mounted another filibuster to water down the bill, Senators Kennedy, Scott, Walter Mondale (D-MN), and Alan Cranston (D-CA) – with the assistance of Common Cause, the Center for Public Financing of Elections, the AFL-CIO, and Congress Watch – rounded up votes for cloture.[70] The Senate passed a bill on April 11 by 53-32 that included public financing for congressional and presidential elections, an independent commission, contribution and spending limits, and repeal of the equal-time provision.

But there was trouble ahead in the House, where campaign finance proponents had to square off once again with the cagey Wayne Hays. Furious with the House Democratic leadership for allowing Hays to bottle up the bills in committee in previous years, Common Cause placed ads in the *Washington Post* and threatened to go on the campaign trail to link campaign corruption with congressional decisions.[71] Sensing that federal subsidies for presidential elections were inevitable, Hays persuaded his committee to report legislation that included public financing for presidential (but not congressional) elections. It was a dramatic step for Hays to support any type of public finance. Committee members John Brademas and Frank Thompson, who supported the congressional provision, brokered the compromise. Anderson and Udall vowed to fight for an amendment to extend public finance to congressional campaigns. Frenzel, along with other Republicans, attacked public financing and the absence of an independent commission. While the committee deliberated, the Watergate committee released its stunning 2,217-page report in June. Although Ervin's committee opposed public financing, the publicity surrounding this report centered on evidence of campaign corruption.

During the final stages of this battle, DSG's Phil Burton attempted one last time to obtain public funding for congressional campaigns. He negotiated a deal whereby Common Cause would not oppose Wayne Hays's final measure. In exchange, Frank Annunzio (D-IL) from Chicago's Democratic machine would introduce an amendment by Udall and Anderson for publicly financed congressional elections. Based on the amendment, the Democratic Congressional Campaign Committee (Hays's panel) and its Republican counterpart would be responsible for distributing the funds. This compromise would strengthen Hays's position while providing reformers something they wanted. Burton, Hays, Common Cause's Fred Wertheimer, and a staffer of Tip O'Neill agreed to the package. Burton posted Annunzio's amendment in the *Congressional Record*, as required by recently imposed caucus rules. But since Annunzio had sponsored the amendment, colleagues immediately became suspicious. Once they saw that Hays would control the funds, O'Neill, Richard Bolling, and other Democrats killed the amendment.[72]

The House passed the legislation on August 8 with 355 votes, only a few hours before Nixon resigned. It included contribution and spending limits, publicly financed presidential elections, and a part-time independent commission. The House legislation created two regulatory systems: public financing would attempt to constrain private contributions in presidential elections, while strict contribution limitations would theoretically achieve the same goal in Congress.

After rejecting an amendment for publicly financed congressional elections, the House had accepted an amendment to create a commission.

As late as August 21, key advisors to President Ford believed that Hays might block the legislation in conference committee.[73] The Republican National Committee warned that the House bill "virtually guarantees the end of the Republican Party" because of its limits on party activity.[74] Hays still wanted to stop the bill but believed that he could no longer afford to take the blame.[75]

The bills went to conference with two unresolved issues: public finance for congressional elections (in the Senate version but not in the House bill) and the strength of the independent commission (stronger in the Senate version). Enough Democrats were willing to abandon public financing for congressional elections in order to obtain other reforms – or because they were not interested in reforming themselves. In conference committee the House accepted a stronger enforcement commission in exchange for dropping publicly financed congressional elections. Spending limits were set low so that incumbents would remain confident that they could defeat unknown challengers.[76] The Senate passed the bill 60-16 and the House by 365-24.

The final legislation established contribution and spending limits, public financing for *presidential* elections, and an independent commission. The equal-time provision remained intact. Public funds were not to be distributed to congressional candidates. The legislation did not impose restrictions on PACs, and it permitted corporations with government contracts to establish them. This was the result of an intense lobby by labor groups – assisted by business lobbyists who saw this as an opening for them to flood the system with money.[77] Candidates could not spend more than $50,000 from personal funds. Independent expenditures (i.e., those made on behalf of a candidate but not in any way solicited or connected to his or her campaign committee) were limited to $1,000 a year. The Federal Election Commission was given the power to conduct investigations, initiate civil actions, and refer criminal violations to the Attorney General. The House, Senate, and president would each nominate commissioners. Congress retained the power to veto regulations. Ford opposed public finance but realized that he had little choice. A veto, said one top presidential advisor, was now politically dangerous and Congress would override it.[78] Democrats warned that a veto would "misread the lessons of Watergate."[79] On October 15, 1974, Ford hesitantly signed the legislation.

Although the legislation of 1974 did not provide public financing for congressional elections, reformers claimed victory. John Gardner told reporters that, while this was only a "half loaf," it was a "great half loaf." He explained that Congress would soon be forced to reform themselves because of the inconsistency in the two election systems.[80] However, he acknowledged that reform would fail unless it eventually covered congressional elections.[81] Others were not happy with the bill. Frenzel called the bill a "hoax" that would be a boon for incumbents.[82] The final compromises had raised questions about legislators who were balancing the various interests within the reform coalition and so settled for legislation that could pass. Common Cause, for instance, attacked DSG founder Frank Thompson for having compromised on publicly financed congressional campaigns, saying that he was a reformer only "up to the point that his positions do not alienate his patrons in the labor movement or interfere with his own prerogatives as a senior incumbent Congressman."[83]

## Transformed Campaigns

The reform coalition had undermined several important components of the committee era. They had worked to push through reforms that the leadership did not consider threatening but that nonetheless reconfigured the operations of the legislative branch. Taking advantage of instability in the Democratic party and a volatile political environment, reformers revolutionized the disclosure of political information. Until the 1960s, there was little public knowledge about contributions. After 1972, the United States imposed some of the most stringent disclosure regulations in the world.[84] Aided by public interest organizations who analyzed the data, it became much easier for interested citizens to learn of the contributors behind campaigns. The coalition had also obtained stringent contribution and spending limits as well as a public financing system for presidential elections. At the end of this period, the campaign reforms created a more transparent and porous process wherein single contributions could no longer dominate the system without public knowledge. There was now a precedent for using public funds in federal campaigns. After 1974, politicians were forced to seek smaller contributions from a broader base of donors. No single entity now wielded the amount of influence once held by the Rockefeller or DuPont families.

Yet the coalition also wrestled with their limitations, as they were unable to unite on campaign finance. The broadening of the coalition's agenda and membership – a key to its success – also brought more internal tensions. Confronting the same debates that emerged in every struggle since the 1950s, labor insisted on a more limited agenda than that pursued by public interest reformers. Since so many other interests and incumbent politicians were opposed to campaign finance reform, this split was costly. The acceptance of PACs was a deliberate compromise made among reformers, not an unanticipated consequence. Furthermore, Watergate temporarily deflected negative attention away from Congress. Sensing that public concern was centered on the president, reformers concentrated their firepower on that office. The result was a two-tiered regulatory structure that created strong incentives for donors to concentrate on Congress.

Nor had the final regulatory structure managed to curb the costs of congressional campaigns. Financial pressures continued to intensify for incumbents and challengers, and they now had to seek smaller contributions from a much broader base of donors. Spending caps were in place, but few considered them effective and there were serious constitutional concerns. Although there was still an opportunity to obtain publicly financed congressional campaigns, reformers understood they had only limited time before that window closed.

# 8

## Reforming the Future

Tackling the role of money in elections was not sufficient. To truly move into a new congressional era, the reform coalition needed to rein in the procedural power and autonomy of committee chairs. But committee chairs were still the dominant force on Capitol Hill, posing quite a challenge to those seeking substantive change. Reformers had to take big risks in this fight, and it was by no means clear that a sufficient number of legislators would join them when the time came for action.

Nonetheless, between 1970 and 1974, Congress adopted procedural alternatives to the committee process. Although not a single committee chair was removed from office before December 1974, the coalition obtained many procedures that could be used to overcome committee chairs in the future. Though changes were most dramatic in the House, both chambers implemented a host of new procedures: party caucuses gained a stronger role over committee chairs, secrecy was curtailed, televised hearings were authorized, and the budget process was centralized.

The blend of reforms started to create a process aiming to favor *responsive parties.* This meant congressional parties with the tools needed to serve as centralizing forces and yet required to remain responsive to formal rules, mavericks, caucuses, the rank and file, and (to a limited extent) congressional minorities. Toward these ends, the coalition simultaneously obtained mechanisms of centralization and decentralization. Whenever an issue came before Congress, the reform coalition formed alliances with moderate Democrats, Republicans, and fiscal conservatives whose objectives ranged from strengthening parties to expanding the rights of the minority party to enhancing the status of Congress.[1]

The slow transformation of the legislative process began with the Legislative Reorganization Act of 1970 and accelerated a year later when both parties decided to consider factors other than seniority when determining a member's standing on committees. During the congressional and presidential campaigns of 1972, the coalition applied pressure on all legislators by injecting congressional reform into electoral politics. As in every election since 1968, voters increased the number of legislators who were uneasy with the committee process. The next two years were turbulent, as Democrats empowered parties while Congress reconstructed budgeting.

The key to the reform coalition's success was a strategy that combined publicity campaigns, forcing legislators into taking public stands on specific reforms, avoiding proposals that aggravated growing internal divisions within the coalition, finding ways to attract bipartisan support, and separating procedural changes from direct attacks on committee chairs and senior legislators. When the coalition did not follow this strategy – as with the attempt to realign House committee jurisdictions – the combination of internal divisions and fierce opposition resulted in disaster.[2]

## The Legislative Reorganization Act of 1970

The drive to reform the procedural power of committees started with a whimper, not a bang. Most of the items contained in the Legislative Reorganization Act of 1970 were not priorities of the reform coalition. Instead, they were similar to the types of measures passed in 1946 that did little to alter the institution's internal power structure. Emerging from the hearings conducted by the Joint Committee on the Organization of Congress in 1965, the proposal was managed in the Senate by Mike Monroney. Monroney was a moderate liberal from Oklahoma who had been a key player in the 1946 legislative reorganization, someone who believed that improving the efficiency of Congress was essential to strengthening the institution in relation to the president and to increasing the chances of passing progressive legislation (he departed from many liberal Democrats, though, with his tepid support for labor). Monroney had made a name for himself in Washington since the 1940s by specializing on this issue. The reorganization also received active support from liberal Democrats such as Lee Metcalf, who perceived this as an opportunity to rein in committee power. In 1967, to ensure that the proposal did not suffer defeat, Monroney blocked many controversial proposals such as Joseph Clark's amendment to set an age limit of 70 on committee chairs. Although the Senate passed the bill by 75-9 on March 8, 1967, the reorganization stalled in the House Rules Committee because of several provisions. The "committee bill of rights" angered many senior southerners since it would enact procedures that freed a committee to overcome its own chair.

But the reorganization bill gained momentum in the House in 1969 as a result of the reform coalition and another scandal. Speaker John McCormack found himself in a precarious position to oppose reform after 1969 when the media uncovered a scandal involving his top assistant, Martin Sweig. Reporters charged that Sweig had distributed favors for lobbyist Nathan Voloshen from the Speaker's district office on Capitol Hill. Voloshen and Sweig were indicted by a U.S. District Court for fraud. Sweig was sentenced to thirty months in jail for perjury. Although McCormack was not directly implicated in any wrongdoing, the media used its coverage of the scandal to talk about the problems with the Speaker and the legislative process.[3]

Younger liberal Democrats from the reform coalition renewed their drive for internal change. In 1968, Morris Udall urged McCormack to retire before mounting an unprecedented challenge to the incumbent Speaker.[4] One year later, Jerome Waldie (D-CA) offered a "no-confidence" resolution for McCormack. Although the Democratic Caucus put aside the resolution by a vote of 192 to 23, DSG perceived the incident as a victory because their issues were forced into media discussions. The DSG also called for a special committee to study seniority and to recommend ways for making committee chairs more responsive to the caucus. One-term congressman Allard Lowenstein (D-NY) went so far as to threaten that liberals would withhold their votes during the organization of the House if his party did not embrace reform, thereby allowing Republicans to help determine the leadership.[5] Meanwhile, Republicans such as Barber Conable (R-NY) and Don Rumsfeld were urging colleagues to claim reform for themselves.[6] Confronted with an internal revolt, scandal, and Republican machinations to take credit for this issue, in March 1970 the Democrats finally voted to set up a special committee to study seniority. Two months later, McCormack announced his retirement.

This was the political context within which the House finally started to reexamine the reorganization proposal that had been stalled in Rules since 1967. The measure did not include many items that were central to the reform coalition, but their campaign against the House leadership, as well as the Speaker's scandal, allowed the issue to regain political footing. The Rules Committee approved a legislative reorganization bill in May 1970 that included an end to the House ban on television and radio coverage, a provision opening most committee hearings to the public, and improved computer facilities and professional staff. Rules avoided the changes to seniority that were being pushed by DSG, and they removed the controversial provisions that had previously held up the bill.

Besides generating pressure for the House to pass some type of reform, the coalition obtained a few provisions of its own. The most important centered on secrecy, an issue that groups such as DSG and the National Committee for an Effective Congress had been attacking for years.[7] The media was usually sympathetic to reforms that curbed secrecy since, as one Senate staffer understood, "the ability of reporters to do their jobs depends always on accessibility."[8] The most concrete manifestation of their antisecrecy campaign came when the House changed the process through which members took unrecorded votes on amendments. Conservatives had used the tactic to obtain votes from liberals who would not publicly take the same position that they might in secret. Reformers convinced Tip O'Neill and Charles Gubser (R-CA) to co-sponsor the amendment since neither was identified as a "reformer." Yet both supported the change on the grounds that unrecorded votes were egregious and generated public concern. The practice had gained notoriety when 1960s peace activists sat in the galleries to try and determine (usually unsuccessfully) how representatives were voting on legislation related to the military operations in Vietnam. Privately, DSG staffer Richard Conlon lobbied in the House and conducted a media blitz. The House added an amendment instituting a recorded teller vote to the reorganization bill by a nearly unanimous voice vote in July.

The passage of the recorded teller vote strengthened the ties between the reform coalition and the gregarious O'Neill, who began his House career in 1952 under Speaker Rayburn. From the start, O'Neill served as a broker between young Democrats and the leadership. This was a role he tested since his days in Massachusetts politics, where he balanced the demands of his ethnic working-class constituency and independent-minded residents of Cambridge. O'Neill shocked Democrats in 1967 by opposing the Vietnam war. His work for the recorded teller vote earned him the respect of the reform coalition. According to David Cohen of Common Cause, "the younger guys just loved him, yet the older guys still trusted him." O'Neill "believed that good government was good politics."[9]

Despite what some saw as its shortcomings, the legislative reorganization passed by wide margins. The House passed the bill by a resounding vote of 326-19 on September 17, 1970. Within a few weeks, the Senate passed the bill by 59-5. In October, Congress adopted the Legislative Reorganization of 1970, which increased the opportunity for noncommittee members to challenge committee bills, implemented electronic voting on the floor, forced committees to make recorded votes public, authorized recorded teller votes, limited proxy voting, permitted television and radio coverage of House hearings (based on the approval of a committee majority), encouraged committees to hold open hearings, required better committee assignments for junior senators, spread staff among more committees, and stipulated that one third of committee funds would be used for minority staff – a compromise that DSG member Frank Thompson had engineered to expand bipartisan support. Many of these changes empowered committees to function in the face of unresponsive chairmen. Clearly the reorganization did not overturn the committee system. Nonetheless, as one study noted, the legislation marked "the end of an era when powerful committee chairs and other senior members could forestall structural and procedural changes that appeared to undermine their authority."[10]

Because this legislation passed, the reform coalition saw a window of opportunity to obtain more of their agenda.[11] Although the managers of reorganization had avoided most of the key items that the top reformers sought, the coalition had been instrumental to building political pressure in the House for some type of bill to pass in 1970. The coalition had also generated media discussions about the failed reforms and had triggered congressional studies about the committee process. By opening committee hearings and obtaining the recorded teller vote, moreover, the coalition obtained a few of its key items. Nonrecorded teller votes would decline from 51 in 1970 to 2 in 1971.[12]

## Party Reform (1971–1972)

The next major modifications took place in the party caucuses. In the reform discourse, strengthening parties was crucial to institutional reform.[13] According to DSG's John Culver (D-IA), Congress needed institutional incentives to "force" party leaders to be responsive to a party's majority rather than to committee chairs.[14] The chances for obtaining such reforms had improved as a result of the 1970 election and alterations in the leadership. Within the House, the election expanded the Democratic majority to 255, with 56 freshman Democrats and Republicans. The new generation of leaders was more attuned to the recently elected legislators. Democrats selected the moderate Carl Albert to replace McCormack in 1971. Born in 1908, Albert was younger than most of the committee chairs. Rayburn appointed Albert as Majority Whip in 1955. Ever since he had defeated Bolling in 1962 to become Majority Leader, liberals suspected that Albert was sympathetic to senior southern chairs and the maintenance of the existing committee process, even though he supported the Great Society. Although the "little giant" believed that the committee process served a valuable function, he also understood that he could not afford to alienate younger members. Albert thus found himself straddling two legislative worlds in transition.[15]

Democrats elected the conservative Hale Boggs as Majority Leader, but liberals anticipated that, as Speaker, Albert would be more accommodating than McCormack had been. Albert's whip was Tip O'Neill, who energized the office by publishing weekly "whip packets" that contained information about bills that were scheduled for floor debate and by providing analyses of legislation. O'Neill had also earned the gratitude of young and senior Democrats by improving the fund-raising tactics of the Democratic Congressional Campaign Committee (DCCC) – which distributed campaign funds – after he took over in 1970.[16] O'Neill became Majority Leader after Boggs disappeared in an airplane crash in October 1972.

The Democratic Study Group was also under new leadership. In 1971, Phillip Burton took over as chair. Burton had earned his liberal credentials in the 1960s by fighting for progressive legislation. Known for his hardball tactics, Burton was an alcoholic and a womanizer with many followers but few friends. Burton often angered liberals by bargaining with southern conservatives. However, Burton improved DSG fund-raising activities and distributed money to obtain the loyal support of young liberals. Many freshman Democrats respected Burton's skill as a legislator and his devotion to progressive legislation, and they owed him personally for campaign assistance. Combined with talented staff director Richard Conlon, DSG emerged as a more forceful presence. Conlon, a former newspaper reporter who came to Washington through an American Political Science Association fellowship to work with Frank Thompson and Walter Mondale, became pivotal to the reform efforts by helping craft and build support for many changes.[17]

None of these reforms was sufficient to ensure the success of direct attacks on powerful legislators. In January 1971, for instance, a founder of the Congressional Black Caucus, John Conyers, proposed that Democrats strip the Mississippi delegation of its seniority since their local party organization had been rejected by the Democratic National Convention and Democratic National Committee for racism.[18] ADA's Joseph Rauh called it absurd that the caucus was allowing individuals who were "not Democrats" to obtain seniority.[19] Jamie Whitten (D-MS) responded that the caucus did not have the authority to punish a delegation of Democrats who had been legitimately elected. The Conyers resolution secured only 55 votes. Furthermore, two reformers who ran to be Majority Leader in 1971 – Morris Udall and James O'Hara – failed to obtain a majority even when their votes were combined. In the Senate the story was similar. Liberal Democrats and Republicans still could not pass their biennial request to lower the number needed to end a filibuster. Frank Church (D-ID) and James Pearson had co-sponsored the proposal, backed by Walter Mondale, Philip Hart, and Jacob Javits.

Nonetheless, the coalition obtained procedures that did not immediately threaten influential legislators. Based on the recommendations of the Democratic Organization, Study, and Review Committee – the committee that had been established in response to DSG demands – the Democratic Caucus decided in 1971 that chairs could be selected by criteria other than seniority. The special committee chaired by the moderate Julia Butler Hansen (D-WA) included pragmatic northern and western liberals as well as southern conservatives who prided themselves on compromise.[20] The new rules adopted by the caucus in 1971 also stipulated that if ten Democrats challenged a nomination from the Committee on Committees then the caucus had to conduct an open vote. The new process did not threaten most committee chairs, who felt confident that the procedures would never be successful. Since members were required to risk challenging chairmen in the open, the rules created a disincentive for action. Hansen's committee rejected age limits for chairs on the grounds that some legislators were more effective at age 80 than others were at 40. Even liberals conceded that "disenfranchisement" at age 65 contradicted recent laws against age discrimination.[21]

Many Republicans continued to express an interest in congressional reform. Given their perpetual minority status, there were usually several members of the GOP willing to change procedure since they had less to lose. Like legislative Democrats in the reform coalition, younger moderate Republicans were often eager to shake up the procedures that benefitted the leadership. Based on a report from Barber Conable's task force, for example, in 1971 the House GOP abandoned seniority as the sole criterion for selecting ranking members. Nominations for chairs or ranking memberships would be made by a secret vote in the Republican Conference.

Yet Republicans were simultaneously skeptical about joining Democrats in an alliance for reform. There was good reason for this. The explicit purpose behind many institutional reforms was to strengthen the Democratic party and weaken the conservative coalition.[22] Although a minority, there were many senior Republicans who were deeply invested in the status quo because they obtained desired policies and positions through their alliance. Furthermore, liberal Democrats often included provisions in legislation benefitting the GOP to increase votes for reform, only to abandon them a few months later. This is exactly what happened in 1971 when the House Democratic majority revoked a guarantee of minority staffing granted the year before. The measure had been inserted by liberal Democrats in the 1970 reorganization bill to gain Republican support.

The Senate also made procedural alterations. Majority Leader Mike Mansfield accepted a proposal in 1970 to allow the Democratic Policy Committee to make policy recommendations to the Democratic Conference as long as there was a two-thirds vote to do so. Although Mansfield never took full advantage of the Democratic Policy Committee, he established a strong precedent for using this body as a party voice. Mansfield's laid-back style and preference for broad-based participation had led him to make a series of subtle reforms since taking over as Majority Leader in 1961. The reforms opened the doors to greater access within the Senate. For instance, he had broadened representation on the Democratic Policy Committee to include more than just southern conservatives.[23] The Senate also adopted a two-track approach to filibusters, which allowed the chamber to handle other business during a filibuster while conducting occasional votes to see if cloture could be obtained. This change reduced the threat of a filibuster to senators who were concerned about legislation other than the item being talked to death (it soon became clear, though, that it would increase the incentives to filibuster by causing less damage to other issues). Another example of successful incremental reform involved Senator Fred Harris (D-OK). In 1970 and 1971, Harris pushed for strengthening the Democratic Conference in the committee assignment process and weakening the power of seniority.[24] Although Mansfield blocked Harris's proposal, the Majority Leader staved off the pressure by turning what was originally meant as a memo to Harris into a formal statement to the Democrats outlining the powers of the party caucus over committees and seniority.[25] Mansfield promised to hold meetings whenever a senator requested it and appointed a committee headed by Harris and Charles Mathias to conduct hearings into seniority and committees. Mansfield's concessions were enough to call off Harris's plans for bolder action.

Although conditions were not yet right for the successful deposition of a chair, Democrats tried to use the new procedures to mount pressure on defenders of the committee process. In 1971, DSG attempted to unseat John McMillan, the conservative chair of the District of Columbia Committee. The 72-year-old McMillan infuriated liberals as a racist chairing a committee that dealt with many African-Americans. Initially seventy Democrats signed a letter supporting the challenge, many under pressure from Common Cause, the AFL-CIO, UAW, and the Leadership Conference on Civil Rights. For McMillan, reformers sought an open vote. If forced to decide in public, reformers believed, the moderates would oppose McMillan in order to save their reputation. But Albert and Ways and Means Chairman Wilbur Mills backed McMillan.[26] Albert arranged for a secret vote, and McMillan survived by a tally of 196-96. Nonetheless, the number of members willing to take such action were growing and sizable. Although McMillan survived, these figures did not go unnoticed. Some argued the challenge contributed to his loss in the 1972 Democratic primary.[27]

In addition to their interest in procedural reform, the Democratic Caucus started to take a more forceful stand in policy making. Frustrated with the war in Indochina, in 1972 the caucus accepted a DSG proposal to instruct Democrats on the Foreign Affairs Committee to report a bill to end U.S. involvement in Indochina. Although Democrats were not forced to vote for the legislation on the floor and the measure was defeated, Burton rejoiced that "for the first time, we in DSG have broken through the parliamentary barricades erected by the Republican/Dixiecrat conservative coalition and forcefully condemned the Nixon Administration's unnecessary prolongation of this bloody war."[28] There were other moves against committees. In 1972, Wright Patman (D-TX) and Les Aspin (D-WI) blocked millions of dollars in minor tax measures through which Ways and Means normally granted members benefits without debate. The following year, the Democratic Caucus adopted a rule that required committee chairmen to give advance notice of their intention to seek anything less than an open rule. This notice could trigger a party caucus based on a petition to decide what the rule should be. The action targeted the notorious closed rule, which had prevented legislators from amending a committee bill on the floor. The caucus reforms and Senate changes strengthened the parties.

### The Election of 1972

In 1972, the coalition decided to make congressional reform a major campaign issue. While there were many in Congress who were supporting reform by 1972 for various reasons, there was no force equivalent to the liberal coalition that was capable of influencing discussions about the issue and building political pressure to take action. In 1971, V. O. French (legislative assistant to the Oklahoma reformer Senator Fred Harris) had urged Common Cause to mount a "very tough" public campaign that made it "exactly clear to the liberal community, to workers, to poor people, to minorities, and to its own members, just what is really at stake in the fight for Congressional Reform."[29]

This is what happened the following year. During the summer of 1972, DSG, ADA, Common Cause, the ACLU, the League of Women Voters, the National Committee for an Effective Congress, and over forty national organizations coordinated a national campaign. As one Common Cause leader explained, "the case for Congressional Reform must be made in the context of electoral politics, in much the same fashion as the so-called bread and butter issues."[30] These groups formed the Committee for Congressional Reform. Funded by liberal philanthropist Stewart Mott, this committee planned to coordinate the activities of reform-oriented organizations. Members also sought to pressure candidates into taking public stands on reform and making certain that the media followed these activities. They wanted to make these election issues and "light a fire" under Congress.[31] While the committee itself was composed of a handful of individuals, the affiliated organizations represented a massive membership base. To maximize their impact, the reform committee focused on ending secrecy, opening committee meetings, and electing committee chairs.[32] They avoided campaign finance and filibuster reform on the grounds that the former issue created too many divisions and the latter had not been as central to liberals since the passage of civil rights.[33]

To package a compelling message for the mass media, the committee hired a reputable public relations firm.[34] The mobilization demonstrated that the reform coalition had developed a sizable infrastructure. Throughout the campaign, the affiliated organizations disseminated information through their membership networks. Pamphlets contained strategies for confronting candidates at rallies and encouraging reporters to question politicians. The publications explained that "all the questions are designed for a simple 'yes' or 'no' response.... Don't accept noncommittal answers; insist on definite positions."[35] Fearing that those working in the media did not understand most of these issues, the committee sent editors and reporters nontechnical analyses and they personally visited television stations; local papers often paraphrased draft editorials written by the committee. The press identified the committee as the driving force behind reform.[36] The committee's most publicized activity involved sending checklists to candidates that asked how they would vote on specific institutional reforms: 250 candidates responded, 91 of whom were elected.[37]

Common Cause's "Operation Open Up the System" replicated the committee by disseminating information and helping citizens to pressure candidates. Under the supervision of local Common Cause leaders, four teams were established in each congressional district. Media teams obtained local coverage about candidate positions on institutional reform. Meeting teams notified community organizations before candidates appeared and briefed citizens on how to confront politicians. Interview teams visited the candidates to obtain signed statements of their positions. Community ally teams made certain that consumer, labor, civil rights, women's, and environmental groups were aware of how their concerns were affected by "the Common Cause structure and ... government reform issues."[38]

Another source of campaign pressure emanated from Ralph Nader, whose group Congress Watch published booklets about 90 senators and 390 representatives. Using data collected by more than a thousand volunteers, the staff wrote 40-page biographies of the members. While most of the material was descriptive, it included information about abuses by politicians and analyses of interest groups that dominated their districts. One month before the election, Congress Watch distributed the profiles to public libraries, political organizations, and the media. The staff conducted 27 press conferences around the country. The press avidly reported on the findings, which offered readers an unprecedented glimpse into legislative politics. Nader and Mark Green released a book on October 3 entitled *Who Runs Congress?* that made the *New York Times* best-seller list. Most legislators were not pleased. Many conservatives and liberals dismissed the pamphlets as biased, inaccurate, and arrogant. *Time* called Nader's book "tendentious, hostile and superficial.... Hastily edited, the book is flawed by a number of factual errors and incorrect data."[39] Tempers flared at a DSG meeting when members attacked Nader for releasing this information without considering the electoral impact it might have on liberals.[40]

The election offered mixed results to the coalition. At the presidential level, Nixon defeated George McGovern by capturing 60.8 percent of the popular vote and 521 electoral votes – the third-highest electoral total in American history. Given Nixon's reputation and the fact that McGovern's campaign had targeted government corruption, reformers were dismayed. Congressional elections offered them better news: Democrats increased their majority in the Senate by two seats (to 57) and maintained a majority in the House (244 to 191), although Republicans had picked up seats. Over half of the new Senate Democrats were more liberal than their predecessors. The National Committee for an Effective Congress told its members that "the mandate to Congress is at least equal to the President's."[41]

The composition of the chamber was different. As a result of redistricting and retirement, numerous conservative Democrats had been replaced by moderate Democrats or suburban Republicans. The election of 1972 brought the most significant turnover since 1964.[42] More than forty members had not sought reelection, part of a sharp increase in voluntary retirements during the 1970s.[43] As the number of metropolitan districts increased, southern redistricting tended to favor moderate Democrats who supported civil rights and a growing number of suburban Republicans. According to *Congressional Quarterly*, 17 out of 24 Republicans and 8 out of 14 Democrats won new seats because of redistricting. Seven Democratic incumbents and two Republicans lost as a result of this factor.[44] In Texas, Barbara Jordan became the first African-American woman from the Deep South to serve in the House. Andrew Young became the first African-American elected from Georgia since Reconstruction.

Four committee chairs lost in primaries, including John McMillan and Emanuel Celler. William Colmer retired. Following the election, five standing House committees – including Rules, Judiciary, and Interior – would obtain new chairs and members. The ranking Republicans on nine committees were not returning. With 42 Democrats departing, reformers estimated that they would have a 25–40-vote advantage in the caucus.[45] Furthermore, a large number of new southerners were moderates.[46] Some of the new senators came directly out of an activist tradition. In Colorado, a 32-year-old liberal professor and grassroots activist, Democrat Patricia Schroeder, upset Republican incumbent James McKevitt.

The elections exacerbated the discrepancy between younger members and the older leadership. This was a crucial development because the majority of reforms were supported in Congress by junior and liberal members; senior members and conservatives were most likely to oppose the reforms.[47] When Congress reconvened in January, half of the new members of the House and 45 percent of senators had begun their service within the previous six years. Moreover, 316 representatives and 60 senators had been elected since 1960. In contrast, those who controlled the committees and leadership were elected in the 1930s and 1940s. The members scheduled to become chairs had been in Congress an average of 26 years. In the House, the chairs of Banking and Currency, Appropriations, Agriculture, Ways and Means, and Armed Services had entered Congress before Pearl Harbor. The average age of members in line to be committee chairs was 65, 14 years more than the average age in the House. There were 32 House Democrats with 24 or more years of service, with 15 from the South.[48]

Generational tensions within Congress played out right away as the newcomers clashed with senior chairs, who could not believe what they were witnessing. Joseph Biden, who in 1972 (at age 29) defeated incumbent Republican Delaware Senator J. Caleb Boggs in a shocking upset, recalled that "the reason I got into politics was to fight the Strom Thurmonds."[49] According to her autobiography, Patricia Schroeder obtained a position on the prestigious House Armed Services Committee over the opposition of its chair Edward Hebert (D-LA). She had done so because Wilbur Mills's wife was an admirer of Schroeder and had convinced her husband to intervene. Mills controlled committee assignments for the Democrats, since that power was vested in his Ways and Means Committee. But Schroeder did not receive a warm welcome from Hebert, who forced her and the African-American legislator Ron Dellums (D-CA) to literally share a seat in the committee room.[50]

The campaign had demonstrated that the coalition could link institutional reform to electoral politics. Notwithstanding Nixon's election, the coalition was pleased that they had forced House and Senate candidates to provide specific answers about where they stood on these pertinent issues. The reform coalition also looked favorably to the changing composition of the Democratic party.

## Party Reform (1973)

Published in January 1973, the cover for the fiftieth anniversary issue of *Time* included a picture of Speaker Joe Cannon from the front of the magazine's first issue surrounded by faces from the new Congress. The article, "Crisis in Congress," explained that the internal problems of Congress were exploding under Nixon's relentless attacks.[51] The nation was sending mixed signals to Washington, as they continued to elect large numbers of liberal legislators to Congress while simultaneously returning a Republican (albeit a moderate one) to the White House. The reasons for this discrepancy have not yet been solved by historians. Some of the factors included Nixon's ability to draw on the power of incumbency and the fact that he faced a weak Democratic opponent. Nixon was also successful at tapping into southern white votes (especially on national security and cultural issues) even when Republican congressional candidates could not yet do the same. Regardless of the reasons, the stark juxtaposition of Nixon's landslide election with a strengthened liberal Democratic majority intensified interbranch conflict.

These tensions flared in a year of crisis: 1973. Besides the war between Nixon and Congress, unemployment and inflation were hurting the economy. With the president under siege, Americans turned to Congress. When they did, its internal problems were magnified – just as they had been when liberals called on Congress to pass civil rights in the 1950s. This time, however, the problems concerned a much broader portion of the population. The perception of mounting pressure and electoral turnover induced Democratic and Republican leaders to take the reform coalition seriously.

When Congress convened in 1973, the coalition reminded the press of the pledges made in the campaign. The Committee for Congressional Reform sent the candidate checklists to local newspapers, asking each paper to verify the answers with members.[52] The committee also placed a large advertisement in the *Washington Post* calling on Democrats to enact institutional reforms.[53] The committee distributed thousands of manuals about seniority and secrecy. It also published an action sheet about how to publicize issues and another providing answers to objections raised by opponents of institutional reform.

The reform coalition focused once again on strengthening congressional parties. When the House Democratic Caucus met in January, they considered a proposal by Julia Hansen's committee to automatically conduct open votes on every committee chair at the start of each session. Burton had drafted the package. Reflecting the impact of the congressional elections, a majority of the caucus accepted an automatic vote. Controversy centered on whether that vote should be open or secret. Frank Evans (D-CO) was an active member of DSG who proposed that votes should be secret, so that those challenging senior members would not be intimidated. Evans argued that automatic voting would make committee chairs "creatures of the Caucus."[54] Evans had the support of DSG, Common Cause, the Committee for Congressional Reform, the League of Women Voters, ADA, and the National Committee for an Effective Congress.[55] But committee chairs opposed a secret vote since it would make challenges too easy. Wayne Hays warned that "the press would have a field day, what chairman received the most votes, what chairman received the least votes, they would sectionalize and factionalize the country and cause discord and dissension among the Democratic Party." Hays warned that "the press is out to destroy not only the Democratic Party but the Republican Party as well. Do any of you think that John Gardner of Common Cause has any respect for Congress? He has the utmost contempt for all of the Congress. Let us restore the respect for Congress but not by this amendment which seeks to ambush the chairmen in secret. Let us democratize this Caucus, but not on the chopping block." Moderates such as Tip O'Neill agreed.[56] Liberal committee chair Chet Holifield pleaded: "do not deal secretly and sink in a knife in the back of twenty men who have a good reputation in their districts."[57] In the end, O'Neill offered a compromise (conceived by Jonathan Bingham, D-NY) whereby 20 percent of the Caucus could obtain a secret vote on a committee chair.

The election results and the movement for institutional reform caused senior and conservative Democrats to consider bolting the party. In January, February, and March of 1973, according to Godfrey Hodgson, several frustrated congressional Democrats – primarily southern conservatives, but also several westerners and urban machine types who were angry about the direction of their party and about their treatment by Presidents Kennedy and Johnson in the 1960s – secretly negotiated with House Republicans to have forty representatives switch parties in exchange for GOP promises to forgo chairmanships and privileged assignments. Many younger Republicans were more enthusiastic than most senior GOP members, who had amassed significant power despite Democratic control. Half of the ranking committee members said privately that they would be willing to forgo their chairmanships under these conditions. This deal would have lowered the number of Democrats to 202 and increased Republican numbers to 232. Although Joe Waggonner was allegedly close to completing a deal, the revelations from the Senate Watergate hearings killed it, as many of the involved Democrats became leery about entering into a bargain with the GOP.[58] The story, which is difficult to verify, reflects the tension that existed inside Congress at this time.

The reform coalition still did not have sufficient power to use the procedures against the committee chairs. For instance, when Phil Burton obtained a secret vote on the chair of Agriculture, W. R. Poage (D-TX) still retained his seat. Senior liberals were also safe. Benjamin Rosenthal (D-NY) challenged DSG cofounder Chet Holifield for control of the Government Operations Committee, but Holifield retained his seat. Nonetheless, members of the coalition continued to remind the leadership of what threat might loom ahead if they did not accept some reforms to try and calm the storm. This is how the coalition framed its defeats. An announcer on the Common Cause radio show proclaimed that the "Old Bulls ... who ruled like dictators received a shock – they found out that there was a lot of opposition to them from their own party members."[59]

More changes followed. The caucus agreed that the Speaker, Majority Leader, and Whip would serve on the Committee on Committees (Ways and Means), which determined committee assignments. On March 7, the House required open committee meetings unless a majority of a committee voted otherwise or the hearings dealt with national security or personal issues. House committees closed only 10 percent of committee and subcommittee hearings and meetings in 1973, compared to 44 percent in 1972. Although the three major committees usually remained closed, the overall openness was notable.[60] Democrats reconstituted the Steering and Policy Committee to serve as a centralized policy-making organ. The committee would be chaired by the Speaker and included the Majority Leader, the caucus chairman, the Whip, four deputies, twelve members elected from geographic districts, and three other members appointed by the Speaker.

Membership, moreover, would be rotating. The Steering and Policy Committee gave party leaders a bigger role in the committee assignment process, although the committee's large size made the panel unwieldy and the new system made the assignment process much more transparent.[61] Finally, the caucus passed a DSG-backed amendment that cut off funds for the bombing of Cambodia. On the Republican side, Senator Robert Taft, Jr. (OH) and Senator Packwood (OR) worked with Common Cause to pass a measure deeming that seniority would not be the sole criterion for selecting ranking minority members. As a result, the Republican Conference would hold a recorded vote thereafter on every ranking member.[62]

The "Subcommittee Bill of Rights" of 1973 granted subcommittees autonomy from committee chairs. This change was a major democratization of the committee system. The Subcommittee Bill of Rights diffused power to subcommittee chairs, many of whom were not southern conservatives.[63] The reforms opened subcommittee hearings to the media and public. They also empowered subcommittee chairs in relation to their committee chairs by allowing them to hire their own staff and by mandating that legislation be reported to subcommittees. More committee votes were now required on subcommittee legislation, and the reforms clearly demarcated subcommittee jurisdiction. In 1974, the House would require committees with more than fifteen members to create at least four subcommittees. Previously some chairs had protected their own power by limiting or prohibiting subcommittees in their panel. Yet reformers were careful not to re-create the conditions that committee chairs had previously enjoyed; thus, reformers obtained support for mechanisms by which the party caucuses could deal with unruly subcommittee chairs.[64]

The reform coalition did its best to encourage these developments. Common Cause conducted a "congressional monitoring program." Volunteer teams amassed information about the key House and Senate committees,[65] which Common Cause then distributed to hundreds of staff and volunteers in congressional districts.[66] They lobbied legislators to support such provisions as the antisecrecy measure that was floated in the Senate by Delaware's William Roth. David Cohen and Ann McBride arranged meetings with professional lobbyists and field volunteers in order to share strategies for dealing with the next election.

Once the reform coalition expanded in numbers in the election of 1972, they continued their struggle to strengthen the power of parties over committees. Each time they fought for procedural change, the coalition succeeded. Each time the coalition directly challenged a chair, however, they failed. These mixed results revealed the status of congressional reform in 1973. Elections and turnover had produced enough votes for reformers to construct a legislative process that was capable of being used against congressional leaders. Yet the coalition was not strong enough to defeat a sitting chairman. This offered chairs a degree of comfort, since conventional wisdom stated that support for institutional reform would diminish as freshmen started to benefit from the existing system.

## Richard Bolling's Attack on Committee Jurisdictions

Committee jurisdictions had not been a central item on the reform agenda. Besides the memory of recent defeats, reformers had shied away from touching committee jurisdictions because it threatened almost every legislator, staffer, interest group, agency, and constituency. To committee chairs, jurisdiction meant power because it determined the areas of policy that they controlled. Average members, moreover, worked hard to serve on committees that handled policies relevant to their districts.[67] Middle-aged and senior members had waited for years to be placed on certain committees because of their jurisdiction. Interest groups and federal agencies developed intimate relationships with committees that handled the policies that were relevant to them.[68] To explain this self-enforcing system, political scientists once embraced the concept of iron triangles to describe the seemingly impenetrable bond that connected committees, interest groups, and agencies over policy. Tampering with jurisdictions challenged the heart of this relationship.[69]

The direct attack on the committee chairs in 1973 and 1974 thus marked a dramatic departure from the coalition's strategy. Until this point, the coalition had strategically focused on obtaining procedures that had long-term potential but which posed little short-term threat to committee chairs. They also concentrated on reforms that skirted the internal divisions within the coalition, especially between labor and public interest types. This time, some members of the coalition went for broke – even without the type of dramatic scandal or election mandate that was usually essential for institutional reforms that boldly attacked congressional leaders directly.

The volatile political climate of 1973 had motivated Democratic leaders to reconsider the jurisdiction issue. The election had brought a significant number of House freshmen, who were the least invested in existing jurisdictions. Shortly after the 1972 election, John Culver called for reorganizing jurisdictions since "tinkering, grafting, casual or periodic improvisation" would not suffice.[70] Proponents argued that the existing structure reflected political rather than functional criteria. In some critical areas of policy, such as energy, fragmentation was the problem. In other areas, reformers argued that jurisdiction monopolies served as the foundation of committee power. They insisted that centralized decision making would occur only by breaking the committees' hold on prized policies.

On January 31, the House formed the Select Committee on Committees to review committee structure, jurisdictions, and procedures. With Bolling as chair, the committee included John Culver, Robert Stephens (D-GA), Lloyd Meeds (D-WA), Paul Sarbanes (D-MD), Peter Frelinghuysen (R-NJ), Charles Wiggins (R-CA), William Steiger (R-WI), and Bill Young (R-FL). David Martin (R-NE) was named vice-chairman. Martin was a seventh-term conservative Republican from Nebraska who served on the Rules Committee with Bolling. Bolling was a predictable choice to chair, given his reputation as a brilliant student of congressional history. Yet Bolling's aloof personality alienated him even from those who greatly respected him.

Bolling felt confident that if his bipartisan panel could agree to a proposal then the House would pass their bill. The select committee was an eclectic group that ranged from DSG chair John Culver to Robert Stephens, Jr., a 60-year-old spokesman for southern Democrats. The most striking characteristic about the committee was its sheer intellectual caliber.[71] The staff was equally impressive. Chief-of-staff Charles Sheldon II had worked for the Congressional Research Service and as an economist with the Joint Economic Committee. Deputy chief-of-staff Melvin Miller was an attorney at HEW who had worked on the House Administration Committee. Linda Kamm, who had worked for ADA and DSG, possessed an encyclopedic knowledge of parliamentary procedure. The committee recruited two skilled political scientists, Roger Davidson of the University of California and Congressional Research Service expert Walter Oleszek.

At the first select committee meeting, Bolling warned that the committee faced a herculean task. Jurisdictional reform, he said, had never succeeded. In 1946, the Democratic leadership did not have any interest in seeing that real reforms were passed, according to Bolling. They had blocked reforms that aimed to seriously weaken committee chairs and had stood idle when reforms that did pass – such as the legislative budget – were never really implemented. Bolling warned that 1946 illustrated the "foolishness" of pushing for reform that the leadership opposed. Bolling also felt that reformers failed when their proposals avoided the internal power structure. This time he believed the leadership supported them, as was evident by Albert's willingness to create the select committee. Moreover, passage of the campaign finance bill and the changes in caucus rules suggested that institutional reform could pass.[72] Trying to avoid the mistakes of 1946, Bolling outlined a strategy whereby they would propose controversial changes up front rather than postponing unpopular decisions.[73]

Bolling fostered an academic setting that centered on ideas rather than politics.[74] Culver, too, pushed the academic approach because he did not want to "nickel and dime" reform by rejecting ideas based on how they might be received.[75] Meeting in the Cannon House Office Building, the select committee's meetings and hearings were remarkably analytic. Staffer Terrence Finn provided each member with an analysis of the political science scholarship on committees and procedures that had emerged in the 1960s.[76] In 1973 the committee benefitted from the fact that media coverage was almost nonexistent, since reporters were mesmerized by Watergate and campaign finance. Given that jurisdictions had never been seriously reorganized, most legislators expected that nothing would happen.

With the freedom of political anonymity, the select committee hearings began in May 1973. One committee that came under close scrutiny was Education and Labor. Minority Leader Gerald Ford (R-MI), a Republican who wanted to

claim institutional reform as a GOP issue, proposed that Education and Labor –
a haven for liberal policy – be divided. Ford's supporters claimed that there was
no rational reason for education and labor policies to be handled by one committee. They argued that its agenda was controlled by labor-backed Democrats,
whose primary concern was not education. The committee grilled Chairman
of Education and Labor Carl Perkins (D-KY) about his tactics. Martin accused
Perkins of maintaining inoperative subcommittees to enhance his power.[77] Wiggins charged that Democrats conducted secret meetings.[78] But liberal legislators
and the unions feared that a new labor committee would be stacked with business supporters. Frank Thompson, the highest-ranking Democrat on Education
and Labor under Perkins, added that the education issue attracted moderates
and thus balanced out the committee; a pure "labor committee" would attract
only union and business extremists.[79]

Whereas liberals were uncomfortable changing Education and Labor, conservatives were defensive about Ways and Means. Several hearing participants
had endorsed moving Medicare, unemployment compensation, and trade out of
Ways and Means. This fiscally conservative tax-writing committee was considered one of the most powerful panels in Congress. The grasp of the committee
had expanded as it gained control of large spending programs that included Social Security and Medicare. Because of his sustained budgetary attacks on the
Great Society, Wilbur Mills replaced Howard Smith as the legislator that liberals
loved to hate.

The most controversial proposal was to limit every member to one committee
assignment, a proposal backed by Bolling, Martin, and Steiger. The rationale
was that this would make it easier for representatives to fulfill their responsibilities while allowing the House to reduce the number of committees. Meeds
opposed the proposal since it would antagonize too many legislators.[80] Sarbanes
argued that serving on multiple committees offered members the opportunity to
devote some time to constituent needs and other time to panels on which they
had an intellectual interest.

Another discussion centered on empowering the Speaker to send legislation
to more than one committee. The traditional practice was for the Speaker to
consult with the Parliamentarian and send the bill directly to a single committee
with jurisdiction based on precedent.[81] Most of the select committee supported
the proposal as a permanent mechanism for the House to continually reconsider
jurisdictions.[82] The select committee wanted the Rules Committee to settle jurisdictional disputes.[83]

Following the hearings, the staff analyzed six different models for reorganizing jurisdiction.[84] They conducted mock meetings to anticipate how the select
committee would react to each model. Once the committee settled on a model,
Bolling proposed publishing a draft to dispel rumors about what the committee
was contemplating and learn what issues would cause the greatest controversy.[85]
Martin and Sarbanes cautioned that opponents would begin attacking before

Rep. Richard Bolling (on the left) talks with Common Cause's John Gardner following committee hearings in 1973 (University of Missouri at Kansas City Library, Special Collections Department).

the committee was prepared to fight. Meeds reported that there were already "horror stories" circulating.[86] In the end, Bolling obtained a consensus.[87] His most compelling argument was that a publicized draft could stimulate support among people currently unaware of jurisdictional problems.[88]

During committee meetings, Bolling claimed that he was primarily interested in procedural reform as opposed to immediate jurisdictional changes. He explained that procedural reforms could provide permanent mechanisms to handle jurisdictional problems. Alterations to current jurisdiction became dated, he said.[89] Bolling called the bill referral mechanism, which would enhance the Speaker's flexibility in deciding where to send legislation, the "most critical element" of the report.[90] Concurring, the staff noted that the history of institutional reform showed that the most "meaningful changes" were "subtle" ones that created mechanisms for future reform.[91] Paul Sarbanes felt that the most important changes "are probably not going to be perceived by many members as being very important and hopefully not perceived as being very controversial."[92]

Lloyd Meeds said "the important thing is to save the *mechanism* of reform, not the changes we suggest in jurisdiction."[93]

Yet the committee conceded that immediate jurisdictional changes were *politically* essential. Bolling explained that

we have to do what the conventional wisdom says we should do and [to] enough of a degree to satisfy not only the people on the inside, but the people on the outside, experts and non-experts. I think the more sophisticated a person is about the way Congress works today, including in the political science community, the less they are impressed by juggling committees. But I think the conventional wisdom says we have to juggle committees so clearly we have to do it.[94]

Bolling envisioned the referral mechanism and immediate jurisdictional shifts as complementary: the mechanism established a permanent process to handle these issues while the immediate shifts mandated politically popular changes among reformers.[95] The three jurisdictional changes that Bolling was most interested in were removing elections from Administration, creating an energy committee, and taking trade away from Ways and Means. He thought there was "broader willingness" to separate Labor and Education than pessimists believed. Bolling predicted in October 1973 that, if the House conducted a secret vote, they would obtain nearly unanimous support.[96]

Several members of the select committee warned Bolling that they should be paying closer attention to political feasibility of the proposals. Bolling told Sheldon that the members were realizing by October 1973 "this somewhat honorific, pleasant task that they had, turned on them. Not like a snake, but like a herd of elephants with flankers who were tigers."[97] But Bolling defended writing the boldest possible report;[98] the chairman was not even willing to craft an alternative to fall back on in negotiations. Chief-of-staff Charles Sheldon felt that Bolling was "carried away with the logic of reform" rather than the "hard-bitten" tactics needed for victory.[99] In reality, Bolling was also under pressure from select committee members.[100] Based on an erroneous vote count in 1973, Bolling expected that a sweeping measure could pass. He was depending on Andrew Biemiller's promise that labor would accept a split of Education and Labor.[101] The staff compounded Bolling's miscalculations with erroneous predictions – for example, of support from Frank Thompson because he would become the chair of an independent labor committee.[102]

The first stage of the deliberations ended in an atmosphere of political crisis. Members and staff of the committee convened in Bolling's house for a weekend retreat at the end of October. Nixon had just ordered the firing of Special Prosecutor Archibald Cox, who was fighting to force the President to release the oval-office recordings. Vice-President Spiro Agnew had resigned on October 10 because of tax evasion. Calling this the most "tumultuous week in the history of the Republic," Culver pointed to the party's failure to respond as proof that institutional reform was at a crisis point.[103] The committee spent two lengthy days debating a draft written by Martin. When the retreat concluded, Sarbanes and

Steiger promised to prepare a public draft report, which the committee released on December 7, 1973.

In the draft report, Ways and Means would lose trade, unemployment insurance, and most of health insurance. The Internal Security, Post Office and Civil Service, and Merchant Marine and Fisheries Committees were to be abolished. As expected, the report called for the separation of Education and Labor, the removal of campaign finance from the Administration Committee, and creation of an energy and environment committee. The proposal for a combined energy and environment committee had been the idea of Congress Watch, which believed that energy production should not be considered separately from conservation.[104] Besides the jurisdictional changes, the report established fifteen exclusive committees with the stipulation that members could serve on only one. Finally, the draft would empower the Speaker to refer legislation to several committees and the Rules Committee to settle jurisdictional disputes. According to the staff, the proposal would affect the assignments of 178 Democrats, 57 of whom sat on one or more of the committees to be abolished and 21 of whom chaired those committees or subcommittees. The proposal to limit members to one major committee assignment, for example, would force 71 representatives to resign from a committee.[105] At a press conference Bolling stressed that, since each component of the draft was interdependent, opponents needed to devise a complete alternative.[106]

The select committee quickly discovered its opposition. Bolling and Albert were flooded with letters from interest groups and congressmen explaining why specific reforms would be disastrous.[107] Mills and Herman Schneebeli (R-PA), the ranking Republican on Ways and Means, called the proposal to separate tax and spending in social insurance an "arbitrary and capricious" move that would have "disastrous consequences."[108] Mills was telling reporters and colleagues that this was a "kooky report prepared by kooky professors on the staff."[109] Chair of Merchant Marines and Fisheries Leonor Sullivan (D-MO) promised to fight the bill to its "death."[110] Equally troubling was the mobilization of the maritime unions, which were one of the most politically powerful sectors of the workforce. The maritime unions pressured the AFL-CIO to oppose Bolling and conducted a massive letter-writing campaign, teaming up with environmentalists.[111] Environmentalists warned that oil interests would dominate a joint committee while other programs were shifted to Agriculture, which had little interest in environmental issues.[112] Ironically, conservatives such as Dave Martin feared that environmental groups would prevent new energy initiatives.[113] Environmental organizations were supported by the powerful John Dingell (D-MI), who chaired the subcommittee that handled environmental regulations.[114] The American Postal Workers Union, the National Association of Letter Carriers, and the American Federation of Government Employees – together representing over a million workers – opposed the proposal to eliminate the Post Office and Civil Service Committee.[115]

While most of Bolling's opponents were concerned about defending their turf, their arguments offered an alternative understanding of the legislative process.

Committee members and interest groups defended historical jurisdiction by saying that the policies that committees handled were logical. Jurisdictions might not make sense when evaluated by some abstract intellectual model, but they were actually the product of arduous negotiation and compromise. When testifying before the select committee, political scientist Nelson Polsby urged caution and explained that committees were the "listening posts of Congress. They accumulate knowledge about the performance of governmental agencies and about the effects of governmental programs and performance on private citizens."[116]

It quickly became apparent that liberal Democrats were going to be a serious source of opposition. The subcommittee chairs of Education and Labor were "unanimously, vigorously and unalterably" opposed to splitting their committee.[117] Burton would have to give up one seat because of the limitations and therefore opposed the plan. Several Democrats complained to the select committee that liberals were going to get "screwed."[118] DSG published a detailed list showing how 65 Democrats would be harmed.[119] After months of working under the radar, the draft attracted attention from the media, which personalized this as a struggle between Bolling and Mills.[120]

During January and February 1974, the select committee conducted open mark-up sessions. By this point, they understood that their biggest problem would be Democrats. The committee made a few changes but stuck with most of the draft report. Most important politically, Bolling insisted on separating Education and Labor.[121] There was little reason to believe that Education and Labor could mount a united campaign with Ways and Means, given that their members were on ideologically opposite ends of the political spectrum.[122] When Meeds and Wiggins announced that they would allow Ways and Means to keep trade jurisdiction if it translated into more support for the bill, Bolling refused.[123] Repeating earlier admonitions, Meeds said that the committee assignment limitation needed to be modified or the committee should include a grandfather clause to protect existing members. He sensed that mid-ranking Democrats opposed the proposal because they would be forced to choose between assignments.[124] The committee agreed to create a handful of "minor" committees on which members could serve in addition to their major assignment.[125] At other times, Bolling was forced to avoid compromise. For instance, he still did not think it wise to remove any part of Medicare from Ways and Means. But Meeds insisted on preserving this measure since he did not understand why Ways and Means should have any power over the nontax aspects of this health care policy.[126]

Another procedural debate centered on the power of the Rules Committee to settle jurisdictional disputes. Meeds thought that the Speaker should be given this power. He, Sarbanes, and others on the committee warned that opponents were already attacking the proposal as a power grab by Bolling and Martin, both on Rules.[127] Bolling acknowledged that this was embarrassing.[128] Clarence Mitchell, the NAACP lobbyist, had even proposed abolishing Rules.[129] However, Bolling argued that – despite its flaws – Rules offered institutional flexibility in dealing with jurisdiction.[130] Nor did Bolling want the House to return to the days of "tyrannical" Speaker Cannon. Bolling was also under intense pressure from Dave Martin to keep this power in Rules. It was unreasonable, Bolling added, to expect that Rules would pass a proposal that abolished itself. A majority of the committee agreed that Rules was the logical place to vest this power.[131] The final compromise granted the Speaker unprecedented discretion in referring legislation while giving Rules increased authority to resolve jurisdictional disputes.[132]

The Select Committee on Committees unanimously approved the resolution on March 18, 1974. The final version limited members to service on one of the fifteen major committees. None could have more than 35 members. The resolution eliminated the Internal Security and Post Office and Civil Service Committees, divided Education and Labor, and created an Energy and Environment Committee. Almost all environmental policy under Merchant Marine and Fisheries would be shifted to Energy and Environment, but the former committee itself was preserved. Ways and Means would lose trade to the Foreign Affairs Committee, the nontax components of unemployment compensation to the new Labor Committee, and the nontax component of health care to the Interstate and Foreign Commerce Committee. The House Administration Committee lost campaign finance. The resolution allowed the Speaker to refer bills to several committees and to divide legislation among committees. Jurisdictional controversies would be settled by Rules, subject to approval by the House. In terms of oversight, the resolution required most standing committees to establish oversight subcommittees and strengthened the Government Operations Committee. Finally, the proposal banned proxy voting and restored the guarantee that one third of committee staff would be for the minority party.[133]

Although the media and reform organizations supported the resolution, the criticism heard in December now turned into a firestorm. On March 27, Mills met privately with twelve committee and subcommittee chairs and ranking Republicans. All of them had monitored the mark-ups through Education and Labor staffer William Cable. Mills wanted to cement an alliance between conservative chairs, liberal Democrats, and organized labor. Chair of Interstate and Foreign Commerce Harley Staggers (D-WV) promised to convince the American Truckers Association to oppose Bolling. Thompson reported that Andrew Biemiller assured him that the organization felt the proposal did "great violence" to labor. Mills and Staggers agreed that success depended on attacking the entire proposal without giving ground on any specific provision.[134] In the coming months this group spread rumors that the objective of the resolution was to make Bolling "czar of the House." They alleged that Bolling had dominated the meetings and that the final report was not bipartisan. Olin Teague (D-TX), chair of the Democratic Caucus, warned the select committee of rumors that Albert supported the plan only because he was terrified of Bolling.[135]

Behind the scenes, Mills threatened members with the formidable tools at his disposal.[136] The chairman was telling legislators and interest groups that he considered anyone who was neutral to be against him.[137] After leaving a meeting with Mills, Herman Schneebeli told one colleague that "I haven't heard that kind of language since I got out of school."[138] Ironically, Mills was at his personal weakest – struggling with back problems, alcoholism, and an addiction to painkillers. As the Bolling debate heated up, Mills was often in treatment back in Arkansas.[139] However, Mills worked through Joe Waggonner to mobilize an effective counterattack.

The opposition extended far beyond conservative southerners. Bolling had underestimated how badly liberals would react. Just as with campaign finance, committee jurisdiction brought out the tension between union representatives and many members of the reform coalition. The division of Education and Labor caused the greatest problems. Biemiller turned out to be wrong, as the AFL-CIO legislative committee voted unanimously to oppose the resolution. At the annual convention, its executive council targeted the elimination of the Merchant Marine and Fisheries Committee, the split of the Education and Labor Committee, and the abolishment of the Post Office and Civil Service Committees.[140] Biemiller told Albert in April 1974 that labor was going "all out" against the reforms.[141] Biemiller reportedly teamed up with Mills to fight against health care being transferred from Ways and Means.[142] The postal unions campaigned against eliminating the Post Office Committee, while the marine unions railed against ending Maritime Marines and Fisheries. Neutral unions encountered intense pressure to oppose the resolution.[143] The lobbyist for the United Transportation Union admitted to Bolling that they had to oppose the bill because of the AFL-CIO.[144]

The unanimity of the environmental groups took Bolling by surprise.[145] Congress Watch caught the select committee off guard by reversing its position. Although the idea for an Energy and Environment Committee originally came from their group, they now said it would become a "one-stop smorgasbord for the gluttonous appetites of the energy lobbies." Congress Watch added that the reforms were insufficient and that many of them harmed progressive committees.[146]

Despite the fact that their chairman John Culver was on the select committee, DSG remained neutral. Younger members feared Burton, who strongly opposed the plan because it could harm liberal interests.[147] Moreover, the empowerment of subcommittees had left a sufficient number of young liberals with an interest in current jurisdictions. Over drinks with select committee staffer Linda Kamm, Conlon said that his staff would not provide assistance.[148] DSG was telling its members to focus on campaign finance since there was no rush with committee reform.[149]

From the start, Bolling believed that the support of Democratic leaders was essential. But by April, Speaker Albert felt that Bolling had written a plan that could never pass. Albert feared that, when combined with the new budget process he anticipated would be enacted, radical jurisdictional realignment could bring the House to a standstill.[150] As polls indicated that Democrats (in light of Watergate) would make large gains within Congress, Albert had more to lose in 1974 by allowing an internal party fight to continue.

Whereas opponents intimidated any group that remained neutral, Bolling's allies failed to exploit divisions within the opposition. And though reform politicians believed that labor was united,[151] it was not. The UAW and the Steelworkers did not take a stand on the resolution. Bolling's committee, however, did not lobby to amplify these divisions. As a result, unions willing to accept the reform either remained silent or publicly supported the AFL-CIO. The vision of a united labor movement sent a strong message to Democrats. Likewise, Bolling failed to take advantage of the division that existed within DSG or to encourage possible defectors in the environmental movement. At most, the select committee tried to scare Democrats by warning that Republicans would capitalize on the defeat of Bolling's plan.[152]

Bolling agreed to send the proposal to the Democratic and Republican caucuses to gain their support. The Republicans endorsed the plan. However, at a Democratic whip meeting on April 25 with five members of the select committee, Chairman Teague explained that Mills, Dingell, and Hays were moving to send the proposal back to the Democratic Caucus Committee on Organization, Study, and Review (chaired by Julia Butler Hansen) for further study. Culver angrily responded that if this occurred then Republicans would turn congressional reform into their own campaign issue. O'Neill disagreed and urged compromise. Bolling said that it would establish a dangerous precedent for a party to take control of a bipartisan bill. At a whip meeting on April 25, the atmosphere was very heated. John Brademas objected to how Bolling's supporters were characterizing anyone with reservations about the report as a "bad guy," while Paul Sarbanes warned that changing many components of the bill would destroy the entire reform. After this meeting, the Speaker was warned that "No one wants to give when it comes to his piece of the pie, but that is, as you know, the only way meaningful reform will be accomplished."[153] Since the caucus vote was so close, it was impossible to obtain an accurate vote count.[154] Bolling pointed to one member who had told four people he was in favor of the select committee resolution and three that he was against it.[155]

When the Democratic Caucus secretly convened on May 9, 1974, Burton made a motion to send the plan to the Committee on Organization, Study, and Review; Mills wanted a motion to kill the resolution altogether, but Burton thought this was just a way that Democrats could still claim to support reform. William Clay (D-MO), a leading member of the Congressional Black Caucus, moved that the vote should be secret. Bolling's supporters understood that the motion to keep the final vote secret, which passed 95 to 81, was intended to allow liberals to vote against the plan without the public knowing their position. The caucus sent the plan to Hansen's committee. Given the breadth of the proposal, it was remarkable how close the vote was. The measure would have passed had a few labor-backed liberals shifted positions. Culver and Meeds protested the secret vote.

But Bolling made the calculation to accept what had taken place. In his mind, even if they could obtain an open vote the margin of victory on the second vote – with some members scared to reverse their position – would only be two or three individuals. Such a close vote would cause chaos among Democrats, Bolling said, and would diminish the leadership's chances of following up on whatever passed.[156]

Upon hearing the outcome, members of the select committee were furious.[157] Martin called the resolution a "dead duck" because the Hansen committee was stacked with opponents such as Thompson, Hays, Burton, and Waggonner. Bolling held out hope that enough Democrats would support their original plan. Given the close vote, Culver predicted that with the proper effort they could carry the caucus by twenty votes. Culver did not think the next vote would be secret since, "in the age of Watergate, they don't want to be going to the polls in November, after this heat, as being the party that killed it after 40 years of party control." He assumed that they would have the support of the media and reform organizations. At this point, Bolling admitted that he failed to anticipate how damaging labor's opposition would be. Without the Education and Labor proposal, Bolling said that "labor hacks" would have endorsed the bill and hence he would have obtained the needed votes.[158] He rejected the suggestion that handling this as a bipartisan issue had doomed the resolution.[159]

Like Culver, however, Bolling still thought that this reform could pass. He agreed that the press would continue to support them, as would reform organizations. Most important, Bolling argued that the public realized the House did not have the capacity to pass much-needed reforms of itself. There would thus be a backlash, he warned, after the next election brought freshmen with "blood in their eyes" who would force the caucus to pay for its decision. Bolling did not want to rewrite the resolution since members faced time pressure with the next election and Nixon's impeachment.[160]

The Hansen committee included liberals and conservatives from all over the nation. Hays, Waggonner, and Phil Landrum (D-GA) were opponents of most congressional reform while Burton, O'Hara, and Thompson were strong advocates of institutional reform within the caucus. Hansen was a moderate who sought to avoid setting off a civil war among Democrats. She set out to design a proposal that would help centralize decision making without undermining the committee structure. Hansen told Charles Sheldon that the select committee had done nothing right with respect to jurisdiction.[161] Hansen's panel concentrated on what was politically possible rather than theoretically sound. After a few meetings, the committee abandoned jurisdictional reform.[162]

The Hansen committee offered a revised measure on July 17, 1974, that lacked most jurisdictional changes or committee assignment limits. The procedural changes were similar to the Bolling resolution. Instead of empowering Rules, however, Hansen's panel granted the Speaker the power to resolve jurisdictional disputes. In another blow to Rules, Hansen allowed committee chairs to bypass Rules (under certain conditions) and bring legislation directly to the floor. Furthermore, Hansen's group abandoned the two measures most desired by Republicans: the ban on proxy voting and the guarantee of staff for committee minorities. The DSG endorsed the measure, as did the NEA, the AFL-CIO, Ralph Nader, Congress Watch, and environmental groups. Phil Burton boasted privately that they had enacted most of the procedural reforms from the Bolling committee – including such controversial measures as the joint referral of legislation – only because their panel was seen as a reasonable alternative to the Bolling committee.[163] Republicans attacked Democrats for sacrificing reform on the altar of vested interests.[164]

Some of the groups Bolling was counting on could not give the issue their full attention owing to the unforeseen sequence of events. Toward the end of the summer the media condemned the caucus decision as a subversion of reform and called for passage of the Bolling resolution.[165] Common Cause, the League of Women Voters, and ADA all attacked Hansen.[166] Common Cause said to its radio listeners that, according to low poll ratings, "in November, no one is going to be safe – and that worries a lot of Democrats who seemed to think it was only the other fellows who had problems in 1974."[167] However, Common Cause could provide only limited assistance: most of their resources had been used in the fight over campaign finance and Nixon's impeachment, both of which culminated during these months.[168]

On September 25, the House Rules Committee sent the Bolling plan to the floor under an open rule with the Hansen proposal as its substitute. Despite pleading by Democratic allies, Bolling refused to offer any revised version of the select committee plan. He realized that many Democrats who had supported them in the caucus now feared the resolution would tear up the party. Nonetheless, Bolling would not compromise unless so directed by the select committee.[169] Frustrated with Bolling, Martin put forth his own alternative that combined the Bolling and Hansen plans. Although Martin's measure failed, his defection broke Republican solidarity and delayed the debate enough for Hansen to seek amendments. To gain Republican votes for the Hansen measure, Democrats agreed to provide staffing for minority members and to bar proxy voting in committee. They also eliminated the plan to abolish the Internal Security Committee. Hansen even allowed the House to abandon the controversial provisions weakening Rules. During floor deliberations, Bolling's opponents tried to scare undecided members. Chet Holifield sent out a letter warning that every junior member risked being bumped from their major committee under Bolling's plan.[170] Carl Perkins branded Bolling's proposal as a "Republican package."[171] Responding to Bolling's frequent boast of GOP support, a labor lobbyist said bipartisanship was "great if you are a political scientist but it stinks if you have to work the Hill."[172] Rumors circulated that the AFL-CIO was threatening to withhold campaign contributions from Bolling supporters.[173] When Albert pleaded that something had to be done to prevent this issue from devastating the party, Bolling coolly said there was nothing he could do.[174]

On October 8, by a vote of 203 to 165, the House adopted the Hansen substitute instead of the Bolling measure; 53 Republicans joined 150 Democrats in support of the proposal while 65 Democrats joined 100 Republicans to oppose them. Almost none of the Democratic leaders voted in favor of Bolling. Over 50 percent of the freshman representatives voted against Hansen. Only two chairs supported Bolling. The final changes did not make many dents on jurisdiction, instead primarily codifying realignments that had already been established as a result of earlier parliamentarian decisions.[175] While the Hansen measure left most committees intact, it required every major committee to establish four subcommittees. Ranking minority members would be given new staff. The final measure banned proxy voting and allowed the Speaker to refer bills to more than one committee at a time (or to several committees in sequence) and to resolve jurisdictional disputes.

Although the new referral powers were extremely significant in that they offered a tool for party leaders to work around committees, the media branded this as a major defeat. The *Washington Post* reported that DSG, "which started as a hotbed of insurgency, has become the establishment."[176] The defeat took jurisdictional reform off the agenda at this pivotal moment and created animosity among many reformers toward labor.[177]

Yet the Hansen committee furthered the procedural revolution that had been taking place since 1970. Although observers focused on the loss of the jurisdictional reform, Bolling had always been most excited about the reforms that passed – namely, granting the Speaker the power to refer bills to several committees, divide legislation, and settle jurisdictional disputes. While not eliciting overwhelming public interest, these "under the radar" reforms had a crucial effect in the years to come.

## Budget Reform

The final change of the period involved the budget process. Once again, Nixon's attacks on Congress stimulated action on a procedural change that reformers had wanted for decades. Responding to the president's impoundment of funds, Congress attempted to centralize the budget process. Like the War Powers Act, which drew the support of certain prominent committee chairs, budgeting reform attracted support from numerous senior southerners. This was one of those issues that attracted the interest of an extremely broad legislative group, which ranged in the Senate from Sam Ervin to Lee Metcalf to Charles Percy (R-IL) and in the House from Richard Bolling to Jamie Whitten.

While momentum for reform built, the coalition found that it was not always in control of the debate as different political interests joined in the clamor for changing institutions. In this case the reform coalition fought a rear-guard action against conservatives who sought to use reform to secure their own power. Members of the reform coalition frequently allied with strange bedfellows to pass their measures, but with budgeting they faced the possibility of a reform that the leadership could use against them directly. When the battle came to a conclusion, liberals obtained a satisfactory compromise. The new procedures were layered over the existing power structure and posed little immediate threat to the status quo, yet they created still another procedure that could potentially undermine the committee process.[178]

Presidential power over budgeting had expanded since a reform in 1921. Previous efforts to reform the budgeting process, such as in 1946, failed. There were few individuals in the 1960s who did not think that the process was a mess. On the one hand, critics complained that the president had become the prime mover in budgeting. On the other hand, critics said that the conservative tax and spending committees controlled legislative deliberations. In this process, congressional majorities had no power. The process was also extraordinarily complex. Before 1974, there was no coordination among the multiple panels that handled this issue. Every year, the president sent Congress a budget that outlined his priorities. Thereafter, no fewer than eighteen House and fifteen Senate authorization committees and subcommittees proposed funding levels for their programs. The proposals were usually based on the previous budget. Once the authorization committees made their decisions, the House and Senate Appropriations Committees decided whether to grant the requested funds. The process was divided even further, since the House Ways and Means Committee and the Senate Finance Committee retained control over taxation and over many larger spending programs, including Social Security and Medicare. There were many forms of spending that remained outside the normal appropriations process. Given this complex process, no legislator or committee dealt with the entire budget. Rather than considering all possible funding alternatives, Congress focused on marginal changes from the previous year's budget.[179] Finally, secrecy pervaded the process.

Since WWII, liberal reformers, fiscal conservatives, and economists had endorsed some changes to centralize the process through budget committees and by requiring that Congress consider overall priorities. Concern with the budget process cut across traditional political lines. For those associated with the reform coalition, the budget process reflected the power of southern conservative chairs, the decentralized decision-making process, secrecy in politics, and congressional weakness. But fiscal conservatives also felt that the budget process prevented Congress from producing an efficient budget or curbing deficits.[180]

Although complaints about the budget process were familiar by 1972, it came under intense scrutiny as a result of Nixon's actions. On July 26, Nixon challenged Congress to place a $250-billion ceiling on the federal budget – based on a recommendation from Ways and Means. The president attacked legislators for failing to control spending. Since entering office, Nixon had used his power to impound funds, primarily to defer spending. This power to withhold appropriated expenditures was one that many twentieth-century presidents used to cut excess spending and to defer domestic spending in times of war. But in 1972 Nixon took the practice to a new level by using impoundment to punish his opponents and to block policies that he opposed.[181] When Congress refused to pass a strict $250-billion spending ceiling in October 1972, Nixon declared a right to unlimited impoundments. Following his landslide victory in November, Nixon impounded large portions of the budget. Albert warned that the constitutional balance of power was threatened.[182] The issue united conservatives such as Senator Ervin with liberals like Senator John Tunney (D-CA). Tunney warned that "we may as well go out of business."[183]

The battle was part of the larger interbranch struggle: Congress was trying to restore its power in war-making, asserting its oversight function, conducting its investigations into presidential corruption, and fighting to limit executive privilege. Some saw Nixon's attacks as an opportunity to correct structural flaws. Congress established the Joint Study Committee on Budget Control, composed of senior members from the taxing and spending panels. Standing committees perceived budget reform as a threat to their jurisdiction so they hoped to contain the extent of the change.[184] Jamie Whitten from Appropriations and Albert Ullman (D-OR) from Ways and Means chaired the hearings in January 1973. Most of the members of the committee came from the Senate and House tax and spending committees. Former Johnson budget director Charles Schultze proposed a budget committee in each chamber that would issue budget targets following the president's proposal. Once the target figures were released, Schultze explained that the authorization and appropriation committees would craft their bills. Congress would then "reconcile" the committee decisions with the original targets.[185]

The final joint committee report proposed House and Senate budget committees. Each would be two-thirds composed of members from the spending and taxing committees. The committees would report concurrent resolutions at the start of the year that established rigid spending ceilings and subceilings on specific programs. Unlike in Schultze's plan, the resolutions would be binding. This meant that, once the budget committees set the ceilings, there would be little freedom for noncommittee members to offer modifications. Senior conservatives supported the committee proposal. In fact, they would gain power by being guaranteed membership on the budget committees. The binding caps appealed to fiscal conservatives as a straitjacket on the floor. As initially planned, a budget committee dominated by conservatives would be able to establish an overall budget that reflected their interests, rendering powerless the liberals on other committees and the floor.

The proposal elicited strong opposition from the reform coalition. Liberal Democrats and groups such as ADA warned that the budget plan would subvert other reforms.[186] The coalition focused on the composition of the budget committees and the strict spending ceilings. David Obey (D-WI) concluded that the proposal ran counter to the objectives of increasing participation among all legislators and providing additional tools for the party leadership in selecting committees. Obey also warned that the budget ceiling would emasculate representatives who were not on the budget committees, including many younger liberals: "we would be replacing one solitary king in the budget-making process – the President – with a collection of 21 new and enormously powerful demi-gods – members on the budget committee itself; members with little responsibility to their colleagues because their positions on that committee will not be ratified by the Caucus."[187]

The Democratic leadership supported budget reform. However, Whitten responded to opposition from liberals and proposed initial targets rather than binding resolutions. Bolling held the third-ranking position on the Rules Committee, which was handling the reform, and he proposed a joint budget committee without quotas on membership. His plan included flexible spending and subcommittee ceilings. In the end, Bolling found a compromise. The final plan called for only ten members of the House Budget Committee to come from Appropriations and Ways and Means with the remaining thirteen seats to be chosen by the party caucus; the caucus (rather than Ways and Means) would also select the chair. Bolling's compromise stipulated that committee members could serve only four years, which satisfied liberals. When the bill was considered in the Senate, Lee Metcalf became the voice for a process that would not become a tool for conservative senior chairs. Metcalf hammered away at many recommendations that had been made by the Joint Study Committee. Senators Edmund Muskie and Charles Percy crafted a compromise between liberals, who feared that binding resolutions would be a tool of fiscal conservatives, and senior chairs who sought to empower Congress to reduce deficit spending.[188] The Rules and Administration Committee then revised the bill into one that resembled what the House had passed. The House voted in favor of the conference report on June 18 by a vote of 401 to 6, and the Senate voted in favor three days later by a vote of 75 to 0. Nixon signed the bill on July 12.

The Budget Reform Act of 1974 constituted a major institutional change by creating the House and Senate Budget Committees and a centralized legislative budget process. The 23-person House Committee would include five members from Ways and Means and five from Appropriations. The party caucuses would select the remaining thirteen members from the standing committees, as well as the majority and minority leadership. Members of the House Budget Committee could not serve for more than four years in a ten-year period. In contrast, the fifteen-person Senate panel would be composed like all other committees. The reform did not appear especially threatening, since the chairs of Appropriations and Ways and Means retained their power. Although those committees could not dominate the budget committee owing to Bolling's compromise, their role remained central. Since the final bill called for overall budget targets rather than binding resolutions, the House and Senate money committees retained significant responsibility. The regular authorization and appropriations process remained in place. Congress would then reconcile the resolution and bills, thereby revising the budget targets from the initial resolution, and committees would then adjust their figures to meet the final resolution. Control over backdoor spending was limited in that many programs were exempted. The bill also restricted presidential impoundments and created the Congressional Budget Office to make nonpartisan economic forecasts and analyze budget proposals.

That the budget process was layered over the existing system curtailed its immediate effect.[189] The change guaranteed that the types of turf wars that had buried Bolling's reorganization would become a permanent component of budgeting. However, the reform coalition had been able to fend off proposals favored by senior chairs. As a result, they obtained a compromise measure that could be used for multiple purposes. Like caucus reforms, new procedures possessed the potential to undermine committee autonomy. The theoretical weakness of the bill constituted its political strength. For the first time it was conceivable that each committee would not control its turf and that each might be forced to answer to the dictates of the legislative budget.

### Procedure in Transition

As with campaign finance, the political environment of the early 1970s enabled the reform coalition to obtain procedural changes. The coalition found that it had enough strength to achieve fundamental change, since the leadership was often willing to accept reforms that did not seem threatening to them at the time but which promised to calm down proponents of institutional reform, including the media. They were also successful when reforms didn't exacerbate the internal divisions that lurked within the coalition, especially those that pitted organized labor against the expanding ambitions of public interest reformers. The ensuing procedural changes were influential in the long run. As one Bolling staffer explained: "significant innovations are oftentimes subtle and unpublicized by the media. This very lack of publicity, of course, may aid in gaining acceptance for the change. Once in place, however, the new procedures are open to any Member who is inclined to use them."[190]

The passage of the incremental reforms that weakened the procedural autonomy of committee chairs ended the initial phase in the ground war against these critical components of the congressional era. They helped create a procedural framework that facilitated stronger parties but also kept those parties accountable to citizens and the rank and file – and susceptible to attack. The next phase was all that much more dramatic, as the coalition capitalized on a series of major focusing events to attack influential committee chairs directly and disarm them procedurally.

# 9

## Watergate Babies

The 1974 elections brought into office a group of young men and women who were determined to complete the government reforms that had started a few years earlier in order to restore America's faith in politics. While there have been debates about how much Watergate motivated voters relative to the economy, few have disputed that politicians and the media credited the scandal with having a significant impact in 1974.[1] Candidates across the nation had run on platforms that promised to clean up politics. Furthermore, a scandal brought down Wilbur Mills, who was one of the barons of Congress. In 1975, the so-called Watergate Babies held elected positions and the conditions were right for the reform coalition to use recently created procedures to attack committee leaders directly.

Within Congress, this attack was driven by a third generation of reform-oriented legislators who entered the House and Senate at a moment when the entire political system was on the defensive. These men and women were part of a generation of Americans whose distrust of the government had reached epic proportions. Many represented northern and western suburban, middle-class constituencies who were unhappy with the stories coming out of Washington. The formative events in the maturation of these legislators were Vietnam and Watergate. Many had never held elected office and came from states that had undergone sweeping institutional reforms. A large number of them defeated Republican incumbents by appealing to suburban residents – who were becoming increasingly important as redistricting and reapportionment brought them a greater voice in elections – through anticorruption messages. The Watergate Babies discovered that procedures were in place that could be used against committee chairs. Members of the reform coalition were not mavericks anymore. Part of the reason for their success was the specific historical timing within which they entered government. Unlike when Richard Bolling and Hubert Humphrey started, this generation would be assisted by veteran politicians. They also constituted a near majority and found a network of established organizations and media outlets that favored reform. There were also existing procedures that could be used against the leadership.

The institutional impact of the election became clear in 1975, as Democrats removed three sitting chairs, pressured another into resigning, and weakened the House Ways and Means Committee. Senators eased the rules for ending filibusters and increased the staff of junior members. The Senate opened most hearings to the public. Senate Democrats also agreed that they would select committee chairs by secret ballot if one fifth of the Democratic Conference requested this, and they placed several freshmen and liberal members on the powerful Finance and Armed Services Committees. Although there was never a single moment when the committee era ended, the first few months of 1975 symbolized its demise to most observers.

This did not mean that committee chairs were made irrelevant; rather, there were now more institutionalized constraints on their autonomy as they lost power to parties and noncommittee leaders. This period revealed the complex mixture of randomness and preexisting structure that produced institutional reform in the 1970s. Although the presence of a coalition and antagonistic external institutions were essential to making sure that change happened when opportunities emerged, the boldest reforms still depended on unpredictable scandal and electoral outcomes.

The Watergate Babies contributed to the deepening rift, within the Democratic party and the reform coalition, among nonsouthern rural conservative legislators. Although their policy aspirations remained unclear, a large number of Watergate Babies suggested that Democrats had to move beyond their traditional policy agenda to attract suburban middle-class constituencies. These legislators were interested in anti-inflation measures, deficit reduction, loophole-closing tax reform, environmental protection, civil liberties, and preventing government corruption. Most of them were part of what historian Lizabeth Cohen has called the "third wave of the consumer movement" in the 1970s as they attempted to reorient federal policy around the needs of suburbanites.[2] In the minds of many Watergate Babies, suburban voters were not always enthusiastic about the interests of organized labor, were skeptical about welfare, and were eager to limit taxes. "Clearly we don't think of ourselves as New Dealers at all – or proponents of the Great Society either," said James Blanchard (D-MI).[3] "We are not a bunch of little Hubert Humphreys," added Senate Democratic candidate Gary Hart.[4] AFL-CIO counsel Kenneth Young argued that "the freshman Democrat today is likely to be an upper-income type, and that causes some problems with economic issues."[5] Blue-collar workers who were once the core Democratic constituency found their political standing weakening just as the number of unionized Americans was declining.[6] Organized labor itself fissured, as several powerful union leaders grew frustrated with the direction of the AFL-CIO. In a few years these divisions would play a role in the disintegration of the reform coalition, as they had already started to do in battles over committee jurisdiction and campaign finance. Groups such as Common Cause, whose contributions in the late 1960s gave the coalition unprecedented strength, had simultaneously opened up conflicts with those who had arrived to this issue from the perspective of the liberal coalition.

But in 1975 these internal tensions generally lurked beneath the surface. Between 1974 and 1976, members of the coalition were so focused on institutional reforms that they tended to subsume their policy interests. Most in the coalition believed that, before anything else could happen, political institutions needed to be repaired or else stasis would continue. The presence of new organizations and legislators in the reform coalition created an impressive display of strength for reform on Capitol Hill.

### Watergate and an Argentinian Stripper

Although the impact of the 1972 elections on reform had been dulled by President Nixon's landslide victory, the period that directly preceded and followed the 1974 elections constituted a climactic moment in the history of American government. Congress and the entire political process completed its move from one era into another. Although there were multiple developments that produced this sea change, the famous scandals and elections of 1974 were a crucial factor in giving reformers the leverage they needed to obtain the boldest of the reforms. Distrust in government had been increasing since 1966, but public concern about corruption skyrocketed with Watergate.[7] On September 8, President Gerald Ford ensured that voters would not forget Watergate when he pardoned Nixon for crimes that he might have committed. Democrats turned the highly controversial pardon into a campaign issue, and Watergate was a central media story once again.[8] This controversial action would become the worst polling factor in Ford's presidency.[9] The renowned pollster Louis Harris told the House Democratic Steering and Policy Committee on October 1, 1974, that "anyone who tries to get out politically this fall and defend that pardon in any part of this country, North or South, is almost literally going to have his head handed to him."[10]

Republicans sensed that they were vulnerable. Besides focusing on the ailing economy, Democrats ran against Nixon by linking Republican incumbents to the former president. The Democratic National Committee was so confident that they targeted over a hundred Republican districts.[11] *Congressional Quarterly* reported that, "Whatever the size of the Democratic gain, Watergate is clearly the root of it."[12] In September, DNC reported that 62 percent of those polled disapproved of Ford's pardon and 28 percent admitted it would make them less likely to vote for Republicans. They concluded that "Democratic candidates should bend over backwards to demonstrate to citizens the honesty and openness of their campaigns and financial arrangements."[13] To make matters worse for the GOP, the party faced an unusually high number of retirements, poor success at recruiting candidates, diminished campaign funds, and indications of low voter turnout. Louis Harris reported that all "establishment institutions in America are in deep trouble."[14]

Polls were not the only sign that voters desired reform. In June, California residents passed the Political Reform Initiative, a measure promoted by Common Cause and Ralph Nader. It contained some of the strictest campaign finance and lobbying disclosure regulations in the nation. During the election, moreover, the reform-oriented and eccentric Edmund Brown, Jr., defeated two well-known incumbents in the primaries. In a special election for a vacated House seat, John Burton (brother of Phil Burton) won in a Republican district. The *New York Times* argued that "Business-as-usual politicians in both parties who think they can ride out the post-Watergate tide of public protest against political corruption and sleazy campaign practices may find they are in for a jolting surprise when the ballots are counted in November."[15] The paper's front-page story read: "California Returns Viewed as Reaction to Watergate."[16] Michigan Democrat Richard Vander Veen won Gerald Ford's seat over the president's handpicked Republican successor in a special election. The seat had not been held by a Democrat since 1910. Vander Veen focused on his opponent's relationship with Nixon. The defeat, noted one reporter, "confirmed the Nixon scandals as an issue – perhaps *the* issue – of this election year."[17]

Yet Democrats were not immune from scandal in this election season. In the early hours of October 7, the Washington, DC, park police stopped a speeding Lincoln Continental near the Jefferson Memorial at two in the morning. One of the five passengers in the car was Wilbur Mills. After the police pulled over the vehicle, passenger Annabel Battistella bolted out of the car, her face bruised, and jumped into the Tidal Basin, a large pool of water next to the memorial.[18] The police arrested the passengers. A television cameraman, who arrived at the scene after hearing police reports, captured Mills's arrest. The press discovered that the woman was a 38-year-old stripper who performed locally at the Silver Slipper as "Fanne Fox, the Argentine Firecracker" and lived next door to Mills's Virginia apartment. The intoxicated chairman had a bloody nose and scratched face. The story broke on the same day that the House was debating Bolling's proposals for jurisdictional reform. Although Mills's administrative assistant first denied that the chairman had even been present (although it was his car), Mills soon admitted otherwise. After going into seclusion for a few days, Mills released a three-page apology. During his first appearance on October 17, the 65-year-old Mills apologized to his constituents and family.

In addition to Mills's power and marriage, the story was shocking given his reputation for a technocratic knowledge of the tax code and avoidance of social events. His reputation had suffered when he made uncharacteristic policy reversals in 1972 that were geared toward his presidential bid. Subsequent revelations of illicit campaign contributions further damaged him, and a chronic back problem forced Mills to miss many committee events. Friends were concerned about how strangely he was acting, including the times he was seen drunk or making off-color jokes. Mills had uncharacteristically grown his hair long and moved with his wife from a modest Washington apartment into a fancy Virginia complex. But these troubling signs were known only to the small circle who interacted with him on a regular basis.

The scandal unfolded at a time that Mills was facing a challenger, Judy Petty, for his normally safe seat. Petty had already accused Mills of accepting illicit campaign contributions during his short run for the presidency. The *New Republic* labeled these events "Wilbur's Watergate."[19] However, Petty refused to speak about the Tidal Basin incident and told reporters it was a personal issue.[20]

Notwithstanding the impact of Watergate and the Mills scandal, the reform coalition mobilized again to ensure that their issues remained central campaign themes. Although the Committee for Congressional Reform had disbanded, Common Cause recruited 600 district steering committee coordinators and 350 publicity coordinators to handle the election. Two hundred volunteers devoted up to five days a week to orchestrating the campaign from Washington; they provided special training in campaign techniques to liaison staff and field volunteers in the districts.[21] "Open Up the System" replicated the 1972 efforts but on a grander scale. Common Cause sent questionnaires to candidates asking them their positions on specific reform proposals; they received answers from 345 victorious individuals. The answers were encouraging. A majority of respondents endorsed publicly financed congressional campaigns and stricter disclosure laws. Common Cause published more than a hundred press releases in the weeks before the election about the campaign finance practices of candidates.[22]

Campaigning in this volatile atmosphere, young Democrats embraced institutional reforms alongside other policy issues that were of concern to their particular constituencies. Colorado's second-term Republican Senator Peter Dominick faced strong opposition from the 36-year-old Gary Hart, a charismatic attorney who had never held elected office (although he had been campaign manager for George McGovern in 1972). The media-savvy Hart focused much of his campaign on milk-industry contributions that Dominick had allegedly laundered for Nixon as chairman of the Republican Senatorial Campaign Committee. To distinguish himself, Hart conducted a "people's campaign" that relied on small contributions. Hart promised voters to fight against inflation, fix the tax code, protect the environment, and reform Congress and campaign finance.[23] Although Dominick launched an intense television blitz that presented Hart as a radical, he never recovered from the charges over campaign finance.

Another Colorado candidate who made institutional reform a major issue was Timothy Wirth. This Harvard and Stanford alumnus ran in a Republican district against the popular incumbent Donald Brotzman. Like Hart, he understood the power of image. When Brotzman refused to participate in a debate, Wirth went on television anyway to sit next to an empty chair before the cameras. Most important, he tied his opponent to Nixon. Andrew Jacobs ran against Republican William Hudnut III in the Eleventh District of Indiana by insisting on the need to end secrecy in government and reform campaign finance laws (unlike many in his cohort, Jacobs had already served in Congress). New York's Thomas Downey, who entered politics because of his opposition to Vietnam, ran against the popular Republican James Grover in a Republican district. Only 25 years old, Downey lambasted Grover for having failed to take Watergate seriously. In Indiana's Ninth District, 32-year-old political scientist Philip Sharp attacked incumbent David Dennis for defending Nixon while serving on the House Judiciary Committee and for accepting undisclosed contributions from the milk industry.

Running to be senator, Democrat Richard Stone boasted that, as Florida's Secretary of State, he removed his office door to symbolize his commitment to open government. Democratic strength was evident with the surge in campaign contributions. The AFL-CIO moved ahead in contributions by spending over $1.4 million on elections, followed by the AMA and the United Auto Workers.[24] DSG's Phil Burton and Democratic Congressional Campaign Committee chairman Wayne Hays each unloaded campaign funds on challengers.[25] Although economic stagnation was equally important to Democrats, few disputed that these were the competing issues. Reform was no longer a second-class issue.

## "Improbable Members of Congress"

Democrats were elated with the election results. When the polls closed, Democrats had increased their majority by 43 seats in the House to a total of 291 and by three seats in the Senate to a total of 61. Many candidates who ran on a platform emphasizing institutional reform – such as Hart and Wirth in Colorado, Stone in Florida, Downey in New York, and Sharp in Indiana – were victorious. Although Mills survived his challenge, the margin of victory was narrow. The election culminated six years of increasing turnover in both chambers that followed the incumbent stability of the 1960s.[26] The result of this change was 92 new representatives and 11 new senators. There had not been this large a freshman class since 1949.

Given the character of the campaign, few observers doubted that corruption and institutional reform were central concerns – since many of the victorious candidates had focused on both of these issues and the critical relationship between them. The impact of Watergate seemed clear with the loss of four Republicans who served on the House Judiciary Committee during Nixon's impeachment proceedings.[27] The nature of the campaign and its impact produced an unusual political alignment that was conducive to institutional reform.

The election dealt a severe setback to Republicans. Following Nixon's first term as president, GOP loyalists believed that their party was regaining its power. But in 1974, Democrats solidified their majority in both chambers. Republican House incumbents suffered 36 defeats while only four Democratic incumbents lost.[28] The GOP was frustrated with their losses in the South, where experts had predicted that the party would make gains. What most caught the attention of commentators and GOP leaders was that Democrats were victorious among constituents who had been solidly Republican before this election, especially in the suburbs. In the House races there were several surprising results: David Evans, a high-school teacher, knocked off the twelve-term Republican incumbent William Bray in Indianapolis; Tom Downey upset James Grover in New York's suburbs; Joel Broyhill and Ben Blackburn lost in their respective suburban constituencies in Virginia and Georgia; Mark Warren Hannaford (a former political science professor) won in the 34th District of California, which had previously been overwhelmingly Republican; and Paul Tsongas defeated Republican Paul Cronin to become the first Democrat to represent the Fifth District of Massachusetts in the twentieth century.[29] In the Senate races there were surprises as well: Patrick Leahy became the first Democratic Senator in Vermont's history; Republican Marlow Cook (KY), a popular incumbent, was clobbered by Democratic Governor Wendell Ford; Gary Hart upset Peter Dominick in Colorado; and Richard Stone captured the Florida seat of retired Republican Edward Gurney.

Yet the election did more than alter the party balance. The composition of both parties continued to change. The increased youth of Congress was noticeable, which continued a trend underway since the late 1960s as the rate of voluntary retirements steadily increased.[30] The average age of House members after 1974 dropped to under 50 for the first time since WWII.[31] Similar patterns held true in the Senate. Not only was Congress younger, but many of the new members had never held elected office.[32] Tip O'Neill described them as outsiders who "hadn't come up through the state legislatures. Some of them had never run for city council or county office. Close to half of them had never campaigned for any elective office before running for Congress. Many of the new members had never rung doorbells, or driven people to the polls, or stayed late stuffing envelopes at campaign headquarters."[33] Tim Wirth explained that "JFK was our first vote, and we went through Vietnam.... We are accustomed to television.... We're part of the supermarket age, the quick fix [of social problems], and the fast shot.... We are improbable members of Congress."[34]

Unfamiliar with the incremental approach that experience in state legislatures often produced, the new generation was aggressive from the moment they were elected. Whereas the existing legislative system depended on negotiation, this generation demanded, according to one top DSG staffer, "instant gratification; the Pepsi Generation has come to Congress."[35] Many of them had been inspired watching young legislators such as Barbara Jordan and William Cohen (R-ME) emerge as the most compelling figures of the Watergate investigation. Besides generational change, the social composition of Congress continued to transform, albeit at a slow pace. In the House, the twelve female incumbents were victorious and added six new colleagues to their ranks. The delegation of African-Americans rose by one. California elected its first Japanese-American legislator, Democrat Norman Yoshio Mineta, who was victorious in a Republican district. The 1974 election furthered the ongoing change that was taking place within the Democratic party as conservative southern Democrats diminished.

The election exacerbated the ideological discrepancy between the committee chairs and the Democratic majority. Almost 60 percent of House committee chairs, 13 of 22, were more conservative than their colleagues, and the most conservative individuals headed the most powerful committees: Mills of Ways and Means, Edward Hebert of Armed Services, and George Mahon (D-TX) of Appropriations.[36] In contrast, the election continued the trend of increasing the number of moderate and nonrural southerners. This was an important trend, since it diminished support within the caucus for the existing committee process.[37] Departing incumbents were replaced by younger, educated, and metropolitan candidates (usually Democrats) representing suburban districts.[38]

The television and print media interpreted the 1974 election as indicating electoral support for institutional reform. Writing for the *New York Times*, R. W. Apple, Jr., said that Watergate had "clobbered the Republicans."[39] The *New York Times* said that "The brutal realities of inflation and recession, the fear of depression, and the memory of Watergate worked together to wreak heavy damage on the G.O.P. from New York to California."[40] The *Washington Post* stated that "the Democratic sweep owed much to two issues: Watergate and the economy."[41] Similar proclamations were offered by organizations such as ADA.[42] Speaker Albert recalled in his memoirs: "Watergate had tarnished every Republican's candidacy, and Jerry Ford's premature pardon of Nixon did nothing to help them.... Nearly all had Nixon and Ford to thank and no one else."[43] Some observers insisted that economic issues divided the candidates more than Watergate, since everyone supported reform.[44]

Yet nothing could negate the fact that government reform was a central campaign theme. One of the primary mechanisms by which the media conveyed this interpretation of the election was through countless feature stories about the freshmen. The articles included photographs, biographies, and analyses of their common characteristics (younger, assertive, independent, suburban, media-savvy, and composed of more African-Americans and women). The stories solidified the perception of a cohesive generation as opposed to a disparate group who were brought in because of local concerns.[45] The popular term "Watergate Babies" reified the conception of these legislators as a group who were born out of Nixon's scandal. Pollsters whose research was reported through the media and sent directly to legislators confirmed that reform was a central message of the election. The declining trust in institutions remained a staple feature of polling data, which revealed that citizens had entered the voting booth in November in search of new institutions. Louis Harris concluded that "the mandate from the people these days for the new Congress is far less one of simply 'throw the rascals out' than one of beginning to rebuild the structure of integrity in government at the highest levels."[46]

The 1974 election brought into Congress a new generation who were prepared to finish transforming the institution. Unlike their predecessors, this generation discovered that procedures were already in place – as a result of the work of the reform coalition and changes in legislative relationships with other institutions – that would allow them to mount this monumental challenge.

### Aiming at the Kings of the House

The reform coalition called on Congress to enact broad institutional reforms.[47] While these demands were a familiar refrain, this time the atmosphere seemed different. "There is a mood of reform in the air on Capitol Hill," proclaimed Common Cause.[48] The election translated into substantive institutional change in large part because the reform coalition had created an infrastructure to greet the freshmen. The reform coalition made sure that the cohort of 75 House freshmen carried out their mandate. As soon as the newcomers arrived, the network of established reform organizations helped them secure their footing. The legislators already had close ties to them because the National Committee for an Effective Congress and DSG had provided them with campaign funds. DSG sent them a guide explaining how Ways and Means controlled committee assignments as well as arguments for changing the legislative process.[49] NCEC granted the freshmen funds to rent an office and hire staff. Whereas politicians traditionally spent the first months arranging their offices, these freshmen designed a strategic plan to challenge committee chairs. They did so through the New Members Caucus, which was headed by Tim Wirth, Gladys Noon Spellman (D-MD), Andrew Maguire (D-NJ), and Edward Pattison (D-NY).

It is important to note that the AFL-CIO avoided the campaign against committee chairs. The relationship between the reform coalition and labor was now rather chilly. Richard Bolling was still reeling from the defeat (due in part to labor's opposition) of his reorganization plan and had severed his personal contacts with long-time friend Andrew Biemiller. The AFL-CIO would enrage many reformers at the start of session by refusing to support an amendment to end the oil industry's depletion allowance. This was an amendment seen by groups such as Common Cause as part of a broader attack on Ways and Means, which had protected this provision for decades. Labor made this choice so that they could obtain a tax cut for lower- and middle-income taxpayers.[50]

Immediately after the 1974 election, speculation had centered on the future of the House Ways and Means Committee. Many observers and politicians expected that, when the Democratic Caucus met on December 2 for their organizing session, the 75 Democratic freshmen would move to weaken this committee. They expected that Ways and Means would lose control over making committee assignments, that it would be expanded so that more liberals could be placed on the panel, and that there would be a reform of the notorious closed rule. The reform coalition was optimistic, and Common Cause released a report stating that 146 Democrats publicly favored removing committee assignments from Ways and Means. Still, John Gardner told reporters that this was their "toughest test."[51] Common Cause also wanted to limit the tenure of all chairs to four terms.[52] Shortly before the organizational caucus met, the League of Women Voters and Ralph Nader contacted Democrats to urge them to shift the appointment powers of Ways and Means into the Steering and Policy Committee.[53] The AFL-CIO endorsed changing the committee's party ratio to reflect the larger Democratic majority, as did Albert.[54] Reformers were encouraged when Mills said that committee Democrats agreed to increase Ways and Means to 31 members, a DSG proposal.

During their initial meetings of the New Members Caucus, Ways and Means was the prime target of the Watergate Babies. One Democrat, who said it was "open season," predicted that – when the caucus held its organizational meeting on December 2 – Ways and Means would be stripped of its power to make committee assignments. Tip O'Neill told a reporter that "Wilbur had an aura

Wilbur Mills with Fanne Fox after he appeared at her debut appearance after the scandal. This is one of the famous pictures (which appeared in papers around the country on December 2, 1974) that helped cause Mills's downfall. Notice the swarm of reporters that can be seen in the reflection of the mirror (Associated Press World Wide Photos).

of omnipotence that will not shine as brightly in the new Congress."[55] Despite Mills's vulnerability, there were doubts about whether freshmen would take action. Freshmen were well aware that a few months earlier Mills had eviscerated Bolling's reforms and that the Arkansan had survived his reelection despite the scandal. Patricia Schroeder explained that "It's like the dictum in English law: 'If you aim at the King, you had better not miss'." Schroeder feared that young members would "be scrambling for good committee assignments and they will be cowed by the chairmen."[56]

Two nights before the caucus met, Mills sealed his own fate. On the last day of November, Mills staggered onto the stage at Annabel Battistella's first public appearance in a Boston strip club. The shocked room of reporters covering the event could not believe their eyes. The story appeared on the front pages of newspapers around the country on the Monday morning of December 2, usually along with one of the Associated Press photographs of a drunken Mills walking onto the stage as Battistella danced or standing beside her afterward.[57] Asked if his appearance at the burlesque theater would hurt, Mills said: "This won't ruin me … nothing can ruin me."[58] But others disagreed. Charles Vanik (D-OH) said that citizens "have the right to be indignant on anything that appears to be a distraction or frivolous conduct on the part of a public official charged with such grave responsibility."[59] The *Arkansas Gazette* called on Mills to resign.

When the Democratic Caucus convened the morning after Mills's Boston appearance, one reporter sensed that a "spirit of reform, even a scent of crusaders zeal, hung in the air."[60] The first decision was to elect a new chair of the caucus. The contest pitted Phil Burton, who had assisted most of the freshmen with DSG campaign funds, against B. F. Sisk, a moderate member of the Rules Committee who helped write the legislative reorganization of 1970. The option was clear. Burton was perceived as the champion of liberalism and strong party caucuses. Supporters described Sisk as a pragmatist who could unify the fractured party.[61] Backed by almost every freshman, Burton won. In a symbolic move, Burton pushed through a proposal to fire the 28-year doorkeeper of the House, William "Fishbait" Miller, who controlled 340 patronage positions and a $3-million budget. Miller had been tied to the powerful southern conservative William Colmer.

Taking place two days after Mills's Boston appearance, the most controversial debate centered on where the caucus should locate the responsibility for making committee assignments. Proponents of institutional reform sought not to dismantle the committee process but rather to severely weaken committee chairs. Reformers perceived this decision as crucial, since Ways and Means exercised so much power by controlling the professional fate of legislators. Al Ullman was slated to succeed Mills as chair and wanted to preserve this function in Ways and Means. He promised that Ways and Means was "very willing to accept the will of the Caucus."[62] Sam Gibbons, a member of Ways and Means and DSG, half-joked that his committee was "sensitive over" being "stripped of anything right now."[63] The Floridian warned freshmen that, if the Steering and Policy Committee obtained the awesome responsibility for making committee assignments, many members would have to relinquish their seats.[64] Dismissing these arguments, Tom Foley (D-WA) and Donald Fraser recommended that the caucus shift the Committee on Committees to the revitalized Steering and Policy Committee, which they believed was more reflective of majority interests – it consisted of the Speaker, the Majority Leader, the caucus chair, twelve regional representatives, and nine members selected by the Speaker. Membership, moreover, rotated.[65] The caucus accepted this proposal 146-122, and the party secured control over committee assignments. The caucus enlarged Ways and Means from 25 to 37 members.

During the next two days, the caucus enacted additional reforms. Appropriations subcommittee chairs were made subject to a caucus vote. Another change originated with Richard Bolling, who proposed that the Speaker nominate all the Democrats on the Rules Committee (subject to caucus approval). The combination of centralized party leadership and strong noncommittee members was what Bolling hoped to achieve. This proposal, he said, would turn Rules into an instrument of the party caucus through the Speaker.[66] The caucus passed the measure and so the Speaker obtained control over Rules.

Several Democrats said that reforms were going too far. Opponents warned against returning to the days of Speaker Cannon or the "King Caucus."[67] James

Wright (D-TX) admonished his colleagues: "We have stopped some of the practices that mitigate against fair and equal consideration for junior members, but
in doing that do we now want to do the reverse?"[68] Nonetheless, warnings were
drowned out by the freshmen. The ADA boasted that "this caucus meeting will
go down as the greatest reform of House rules since George Norris knocked over
'Uncle Joe' Cannon in 1911."[69]

The relationship between the Mills scandal and reform was important. Newspapers and magazines often ran the unfolding stories right next to each other
or combined into one column.[70] Although the reforms had been contemplated
for decades, Mills's drama provided an exceptional opportunity. As Mary Russell wrote, "the Tidal Basin incident made the reforms more feasible, and Mills'
actions in Boston on the eve of the caucus made the vote a certainty."[71] Any in-
hibitions the freshmen might have exhibited in the final moments vanished after
Boston. A few days after the caucus stripped Ways and Means of its committee assignment powers, Albert told Mills to resign, calling him a "sick man."[72]
Mills announced his resignation on December 10. At the end of the month,
Mills admitted that he had been an alcoholic since 1969, and he later said
that since 1973 he had been addicted to prescription drugs given for his back
problems.[73] Battistella published a book detailing the lurid stories of the alleged
relationship.[74]

Before the congressional session started in January, the 75 freshmen met to
decide on who they wanted to elect as the committee chairs. "The freshmen,"
said Edward Hebert, the chair of the House Armed Services Committee and a
target of the reformers, "had been transformed from individuals into a mob of
crusading knights out to slay evil dragons."[75] This was a very large class of freshmen, and a majority of them were more than willing to directly challenge the
leadership. They would be the first class to participate in the selection process
that had been finalized only one year earlier.

Ignoring norms of deference, they invited the chairs to answer questions behind closed doors. Given the number of votes they constituted, the chairs had
little choice but to attend. During the meetings the freshmen grilled some of
the most powerful members of the House. Some chairs, such as Wayne Hays,
impressed them. Others, such as Hebert, insulted them. Hebert left the confrontational meeting by dismissing the freshmen to reporters as "boys and girls."
Gladys Noon Spellman commented that the 73-year-old Hebert had "underestimated the intelligence of the people he was talking to. We may be new kids
on the block, but we're not stupid."[76] Wright Patman, the 81-year-old liberal
chair of Banking, Currency and Housing, and W. R. Poage, the 75-year-old chair
of the Agriculture Committee, each experienced unpleasant meetings.

The confrontations offered the type of drama usually reserved for presidential politics. The *Washington Post* concluded that "a revolution has occurred.
The seniority system as the rigid, inviolable operating framework of the House
has been destroyed."[77] *U.S. News & World Report* said that "an all-out attack

on the 'seniority system' in the House of Representatives has created the biggest power shake-up in more than half a century – a shake-up that promises far-reaching changes in the way Congress operates.... As Henry Reuss ... put it: 'From now on, the sword of Damocles will be hanging over every chairman'."[78]

Television devoted an unusual amount of airtime to these events. Images such as Mills slurring to reporters or Hebert furiously storming out of his interrogation offered the networks compelling visual material. Like the newspapers, television reporters frequently invoked dramatic language to interpret these events.[79] CBS anchor Walter Cronkite described the meetings as "unprecedented," while Roger Mudd explained that this was the "ultimate indignity" for senior chairs.[80] He spoke of "bloodletting," and one colleague predicted that seniority "will never be again what it was."[81]

On the day that the freshmen completed their interviews, Common Cause released a detailed report analyzing the record of each chair in terms of their compliance with rules, personal and procedural fairness, and uses of power.[82] Common Cause accused Mahon, Poage, and Hays of "serious abuses"; Ray Madden, Wright Patman, and Harley Staggers of "serious shortcomings"; and Hebert of flagrantly violating every standard. The publication offered a scathing description of how Poage denied subcommittee chairs control over their staff and was "arbitrary and abusive" with members. Common Cause showed that Poage was one of six chairs who voted against the majority of his party more often than with them. According to the report, Hebert harassed members who disagreed with him. The report explained how Wayne Hays abused colleagues and threatened staff while using committee funds to settle personal scores.

Showing that reform could no longer be automatically equated with liberalism (as it had been in the 1950s and 1960s), Common Cause branded Ray Madden, the liberal chair of the Rules Committee and architect of earlier reforms, as incompetent. Moreover, the report criticized the populist Wright Patman for running his panel in a "chaotic atmosphere, lacking dignity and decorum." Because of this unflattering treatment of Patman, Congress Watch refused to endorse the report. Ralph Nader warned that "if the winds of reform are not to mock their own echoes, they should be directed toward Chairmen Hebert, Poage, and Mahon, and not against that bastion of progressivism and courage that is Wright Patman."[83] Common Cause's insistence, and the subsequent action by the caucus, revealed how far the reform movement had evolved since it was promoted by the liberal coalition.

The voting process on chairs started when the Steering and Policy Committee met on January 15. Taking over the historic function of Ways and Means, the committee rejected Poage, Hebert, and Patman as chairs. The most surprising vote took place when the committee decided to replace Hays with Frank Thompson as chair of the House Administration Committee. This plan was supported by the leadership and had been kept a tight secret. Hays's supporters believed that it was orchestrated by O'Neill to undermine Burton (his main competition for the Speakership) by dethroning Burton's ally and linking him to a corrupt chair.[84] Shortly after the vote, Hebert wrote a letter to Democrats that refuted each allegation made about his chairmanship. Hebert called Common Cause's charges so "distorted and unfair as to make the conclusion inescapable that the distortions are deliberate."[85] Like the other chairs who were being challenged, Hebert presented these decisions as a zealous campaign by unelected reformers and ambitious freshmen seeking to claim power.

On January 16, the caucus met to ratify the decisions of the Steering and Policy Committee. The caucus unseated Poage by a vote of 152-133 and Hebert by 144-141; Poage was to be replaced by Thomas Foley (chair of DSG), and Melvin Price (D-IL) would replace Hebert. The caucus decided that Patman should not resign and rejected the recommendation to remove Hays. The reason for their decision to protect Hays remains unclear. Some speculated that Hays impressed them during the meeting while cynics claimed that the freshmen were being loyal to Hays since he had provided them with campaign funds.

The caucus deliberations took on the tone of an election campaign. Seniority appeared on the ropes as senior chairs pleaded for support and were forced to justify their record. In the case of the Administration Committee, the Steering and Policy Committee needed to present their second choice for chair the following week. Before the caucus met again, intense campaigning took place. Thompson explained that the failure to remove Hays would be perceived as "approval of – or at least turning a blind eye to – the way he has abused his power as committee chairman." He told the freshmen that "if these reforms and elections mean anything at all they mean that a chairmanship is no longer an office which is inherited as a matter of right and used in whatever fashion suits one's personal whims."[86] Thompson said he wanted to make certain that Administration was not a tool of special interests and an ambitious chairman, a situation that had brought "disrepute to the House."[87] Regarding Hays, Ralph Nader wrote Democrats that the chair was "a continuing disgrace to the entire House" and not suited for a leadership position. "This type of political wheeling and dealing," Nader added, "built on conflicts of interest was widely rejected by voters in November. Surely the reform-minded members of the 94th Congress can do better than to perpetuate a man in office simply because he is directly responsive to the same old tradeoffs that have bred such cynicism about Congress in the public mind. Hays' unabashed activities warrant his removal from the chairmanship."[88]

Unlike the other deposed chairs, Hays had Burton's strong support. As was the case with Bolling's jurisdictional resolution, the reform coalition faced divisions in their ranks. This was not the first time that Burton formed a pragmatic alliance with reform opponents. Admirers said the alliances enabled him to gain influence; critics argued that it showed he lacked principle. Whatever his motivation, Burton called freshmen personally to persuade them to vote for Hays. Given the role that Burton and Hays played in providing campaign funds, the calls were heard. Through his position on the Steering and Policy Committee, Burton was helping the freshmen be placed on choice committees. Moreover, Burton remained a heroic figure for many young liberals because of his role in obtaining progressive legislation in the 1960s. Privately, some legislators appreciated the fact that Hays attacked good government groups. One representative admitted that "you've got to remember he talks back to Common Cause and Ralph Nader, who screech every time we get a new allowance and call our recesses 'vacations.' He takes a lot of heat for us, and we appreciate it. He stands up to the press too. It's like having your own hit man."[89] Equally important, word spread that Hays was promising a sizable per-diem allowance raise to legislators.

The Democratic Caucus met again on January 22. This time they voted to replace Patman with Henry Reuss from Wisconsin. Reuss was a graduate of Cornell and Harvard who had been one of the northern liberals elected to the House in 1954. He was an outspoken supporter of environmental protection and stringent financial regulations on banks. However, the caucus decided to retain Hays as chair of Administration by 161-111. The decision evoked virulent criticism. Reporter Howard Smith said on the nightly news that, while there was much to be happy about in recent caucus votes, "the new idealists betrayed a small streak of venality" by not removing Hays. Smith said that Hays had persuaded the "revolutionists to stop the revolution at his door and leave him there."[90] The *Washington Post* lamented that "self-styled congressional reformers have tackled the establishment in order to establish themselves instead."[91]

Notwithstanding the compromise on Hays, observers agreed that the removal of three senior chairs was historic. Common Cause bragged about the "toppling of the seniority system in the House."[92] John Gardner boasted: "For too long, entrenched chairmen have tyrannized within their committee empires, flouted House and caucus rules and ridden roughshod over their own committee members. That day is over."[93] Nader wrote that the reforms "put all committee chairmen, a number of whom consistently violate caucus rules and vote more often with the Republican majority than with the Democratic, on notice that they will be accountable to the Democratic majority."[94] The *New York Times* remarked that "The House Democrats have now ended the tyranny of the committee chairmen and introduced majority rule as the principle ordering their affairs."[95]

The caucus dismantled the House Un-Americans Activities Committee. Burton had despised HUAC since his youth.[96] He offered a motion to eliminate the committee, which the caucus passed. Few representatives were aware of what they had done because Burton pushed it through swiftly. Ironically, the dismemberment of a committee that had once been so controversial did not generate many sparks. This was not just as a result of Burton's cagey tactics: all Cold War institutions, including the CIA and the Pentagon, were under intense attack and had lost much credibility with the public and the press. Moreover, HUAC was a skeleton from an earlier era and had not played an influential role in the House for over a decade.

By opening up the authority structure of Congress, the reforms fostered turf wars. After the caucus granted Hays his position, much of the commentary focused on Burton's power. As a result of the caucus votes to discipline chairs and to protect Hays, Burton now stood as the central figure in the House. The conflict between Bolling and Burton – which had reached epic proportions in the subversion of jurisdictional reform – continued. Burton displaced Bolling as the most prominent voice of reform. Burton was also running into conflict with Tip O'Neill, who assumed he would replace Albert as Speaker.

The defeated chairs were outraged. On the "Today Show," Hebert accused Common Cause of having "conducted one of the most vicious and reprehensible campaigns that I've ever seen in my life," blaming them for his defeat and charging them with "misrepresentation, downright lies, downright distortions." Hebert complained: "Common Cause is running Congress. Who elected them?"[97] Warning that chairs would not be able to function, he equated these decisions to the French Revolution: "remember Danton and Robespierre all ended up in the guillotine, didn't they?"[98] The respected conservative Omar Burleson (D-TX) predicted that the new caucus would never achieve consensus and that the younger members were determined to reform even when it was not in the best interest of the institution.[99]

Yet this type of criticism did not resonate in the post-Watergate environment. By January 1975, institutional reform seemed not only logical but inevitable as well. Within a few months, the Democratic Caucus had tamed committee chairs while a new generation was ascending within the institution. For those who followed Congress, there were no doubts that this was a historic moment. The sight of Ways and Means losing its powers and senior chairs being grilled by freshmen was a far cry from the Rayburn era. The caucus made compromises, but once they had removed three senior chairs and forced another to resign, the atmosphere inside the House could never be the same. The committee process remained in place. But committee chairs could not feel that they had authority that was independent from the party caucus.

These events had also forever altered the relationship between legislators and the media. The barrier against covering sex scandals was broken with Chappaquiddick, and the media reported all the lurid details of the Mills story. The typical story included pictures of the scantily clad Battistella and descriptions about Mills's visits to the clubs.[100] Journalists understood that scandal was often the only way to bring down a powerful politician.[101] Yet some in the media felt their colleagues were going too far. One reporter concluded that "the front pages of the *New York Times* and the *Washington Post* took on the tincture of the *National Enquirer*."[102]

What was most notable was the strong defense that emerged within the press for their decision to cover these stories. As they had with Adam Clayton Powell and Thomas Dodd, most members of the media analyzed the personal scandal in the context of institutional reform. This was still the prevailing media mind-set in this era: scandal in the context of reform. NBC's David Brinkley quipped that "the private lives of public figures are assumed to be private unless they interfere with their public duties or wind up on the police blotter, as Mills did."[103]

### Limiting Filibusters

The 1974 election caused the same type of reverberations in the Senate. The reform coalition saw an opportunity to move forward with measures that had stalled for years.[104] Since Majority Leader Mike Mansfield had already diversified representation on the Democratic policy committees and turned them into more active bodies, there was strong procedural precedent for the coalition to build on. After the elections there was a strong push to broaden representation on the chamber's most powerful panels. Senators Dick Clark (IA) and Edward Kennedy targeted the Senate Finance and Armed Services Committees, two influential panels where younger liberals had made little progress in obtaining seats. Clark and Kennedy persuaded the Democratic Steering Committee to place three freshman liberals – John Culver, Gary Hart, and Patrick Leahy – on Armed Services and two liberals, William Hathaway (ME) and Floyd Haskell (CO), on Finance. Kennedy, moreover, obtained enough votes on the Democratic Steering Committee to block the assignment of James Allen to the Judiciary Committee. Instead, Democrats selected James Abourezk, the favorite of younger liberals.[105]

Only a day after the House unseated its chairs, Senate Democrats decided that their caucus would also vote on chairs by secret ballot; Senator Clark pushed through the change. Under the new rule, the Democratic Steering Committee would nominate senators to be chairs while Democrats would vote in secret on proposed candidates. If a minimum of 20 percent of the Democrats opposed a particular nominee, another secret ballot would be taken.[106] Hubert Humphrey teamed up with freshmen Mike Gravel (D-AK) and Bill Brock (R-TN) to pass a Senate resolution that increased the amount of staff available to younger members. Whereas committee chairs in the past had controlled the professional staff, senators were now granted the right to hire three staffers to report to them on committee work. The Senate Democratic and Republican caucuses also passed a proposal from Lawton Chiles (D-FL) and William Roth (R-DE) to open most committee and conference meetings. This was a reform that had passed the House two years earlier but had languished in the Senate.

The most controversial reform involved the filibuster. Cloture reform had become less pertinent to reformers ever since the Senate passed civil rights legislation and liberals started using extended debate themselves. Many liberal Senators had turned to this tactic after being faced with the fact that presidents Nixon and Ford each had enough congressional allies, in certain cases, to enact their conservative legislation.[107] For instance, a group of liberal and moderate Senators filibustered legislation to fund the supersonic transport plane, an extension of the military draft, and an antibusing bill.

Nonetheless, the reform coalition – including some legislators who had used filibusters in recent years – continued to claim that allowing a majority to end a filibuster was essential to strengthening parties. Senator James Allen's filibuster of campaign finance reform had reminded them of what a logjam this procedure could create.[108] Because historical conditions had evolved, the reform coalition strategically adjusted its rhetoric. As Mike Mansfield told his colleagues, "civil rights has passed as the dominant theme of the filibuster. But ... I think a change would be good for the Party."[109] Rather than speaking only of the link between conservatism and filibusters, proponents emphasized that institutional reform was essential for efficient policy making on issues such as energy and the economy. Sensing that reform would pass, Mansfield urged senior colleagues to accept a compromise so that the Senate did not end up with majoritarian rule. This appealed to senators such as Robert Byrd, who defended minority rights but understood that liberalizing cloture was inevitable.

When the new session started, Senators James Pearson and Walter Mondale proposed that cloture should require three fifths (rather than two thirds) of the Senate who were present and voting. This was a compromise aimed to please Mansfield, since Mondale had previously called for a majoritarian system. Mondale told the Senate that filibusters "impaired" the ability of the Senate to function. He acknowledged that the filibuster was no longer the tool of conservatives only, but in a time of economic crisis it was essential that the chamber be able to make quick decisions. Politically, the operating assumption of most legislators was still that Democratic majorities would survive and that their party would regain the White House. Few predicted the conservative tidal wave that was about to reach Washington. Mondale said that, contrary to popular myth of preventing tyrannical majorities, "the device has been used repeatedly by a small group of Senators as a method for stopping action and avoiding compromise on measures which have been carefully considered and which were favored by a vast majority of members of this body – from all sections of the country and of all political philosophies – and by an overwhelming majority of the people of this Nation."[110] Since 1917, most cloture proposals had not succeeded. Kennedy believed that the rising number of cloture votes revealed the urgency of switching to a three-fifths rule. While there had never been more than five cloture votes in one year before 1966, there had been ten each year from 1971 to 1973 and eighteen in 1974. Half of all cloture votes had taken place in the last five years.[111] Robert Packwood argued that the filibuster was the favorite media example of how Congress did not work.[112]

The president did not take a public stand on this issue. Ford was in a difficult position. His short administration would be wracked by horrible relations with Congress as he tried to save the GOP in the aftermath of Watergate. Building on the skills he learned as House Minority Leader, Ford attempted to appeal to Republican conservatives and liberals. He took a tough stand on curbing inflation and limiting federal spending while simultaneously offering some carrots to liberal Republicans. Most important, he appointed Nelson Rockefeller as vice-president. Rockefeller was a former New York governor who came directly out of New York's famous liberal Republican tradition. Congress had only confirmed Rockefeller in mid-December after a grueling hearing where Democrats grilled him about his personal finances. Many conservative Republicans were furious with Ford's decision to nominate Rockefeller.

When confronted with the filibuster issue, Ford told Rockefeller (who would have to preside over the Senate debate) that this matter should be left for the legislative body to decide.[113] Normally, presidents were reluctant to deal with the issue. There were advisors who wanted the president to oppose the proposal. Kenneth Lazarus, associate counsel to the president, said that the filibuster was "firmly" rooted in Anglo-American traditions and consistent "with the need for stability in government." But the practical implications with the large Democratic majorities were equally important. Lazarus said that the filibuster provided an "alternative to the veto in Presidential decision-making" that Ford was using with unprecedented frequency. It was one of the only ways for the Republican minority to stifle legislation. Lazarus wanted Rockefeller to rule that the filibuster should be subject to the existing filibuster rules, since the Senate was a continuing body.[114] Presidential Senate liaison Patrick O'Donnell said that Mondale's proposal would leave the administration in "deep trouble" although he did not think it would pass.[115] Bill Hildenbrand, secretary to the Senate minority, called Rockefeller to say that a ruling in favor of the reformers would "bring down the wrath of the conservatives in and out of the Senate on your first day in the new session."[116]

In the end, Ford did not give Rockefeller formal instructions despite the urging of some conservatives such as John Tower (R-TX). Ford did later praise Rockefeller before the cabinet.[117] The unproven speculation was that Ford accepted this reform as part of his effort to broaden the Republican base, which had included his appointment of Rockefeller in the first place.[118] There were also some Senate conservatives such as Strom Thurmond who were far less enthusiastic about filibusters – having been burned by liberals using the tactic against them.[119]

Rockefeller favored what he called the "northern route" of easing the cloture rules over the "southern route" of status quo. Jacob Javits, a long-time supporter of cloture reform, mediated between the reformers and Rockefeller. Javits helped guide the vice-president, who had little knowledge about these procedures.[120] Coming out of a liberal Republican tradition, Rockefeller was sympathetic to the arguments of Javits and Republican Minority Leader Hugh Scott.

As expected, opponents filibustered Mondale and Pearson's proposal. To stop this filibuster, Mondale and Pearson needed to overcome the tradition stating that the Senate was a "continuing body." Shocking Republicans and conservative Democrats, Rockefeller ruled on February 20 that a simple majority could end the debate over Pearson and Mondale's proposal. This was the decision that Mondale was hoping for.[121] Mansfield opposed Rockefeller's ruling on the grounds that it would establish a precedent for majority rule. Senator Byrd went so far as to say that he feared "for the future of this unique institution and this Republic if such a factor becomes indeed a fact."[122] But the Senate tabled a motion from Mansfield opposing the ruling that a mere majority could end debate over the Senate rules, thereby endorsing Rockefeller's decision, 51-42.

This decision marked the first time that the Senate agreed that rules could not prevent a majority from writing new rules at the start of a new Congress.[123]

When Mansfield raised a point of order against Mondale's resolution, the Senate confirmed its earlier decision by tabling it, 46-43. Rockefeller's refusal to recognize Allen at one point in this debate proved to be explosive among conservative Republicans.[124] Senator Long called it "one of the most improper decisions made by the Chair during the 26 years I have served here."[125]

The fighting intensified. Despite Rockefeller's ruling, Allen used technical rules to postpone action and warned that the change in Senate practices would result in a "disorganized mob."[126] Most reformers understood that they would need to give in on the continuing rules issue to overcome this logjam, while most southern opponents of Mondale and Pearson's motion had concluded that some kind of change was coming. Senator Long offered a compromise whereby three fifths of the Senate would be able to end debate for two years and then, in 1977, the law would revert to its current form. Mansfield, Robert Byrd, and Minority Whip Robert Griffin (R-MI) used Long's proposal as the basis for negotiation. Their goal was to overturn Rockefeller's precedent in exchange for a three-fifths cloture rule. Ford said Rockefeller had handled himself "brilliantly."[127] On March 5, the Senate reconsidered and reversed the motion to table Mansfield's second point of order, 73 to 21 (thus overturning Rockefeller's change to the "continuing body" argument) and accepted that three fifths of the Senate could end a filibuster, 56-27. The ADA called it "shabby."[128] The *New York Times* commented that it "amounts to virtually no change."[129]

Notwithstanding the critics, others were pleased. Although the compromise fell short of a majoritarian process, the revisions made it substantially easier to obtain cloture. The reduction of seven votes in an institution composed of 100 members was significant. The reform shifted the pivotal number that politicians grappled with while negotiating bills: the number required to end a filibuster.[130] The new number meshed with the new Democratic majority in the Senate, which was not quite large enough to obtain cloture under the old rules. It should be noted that many previous filibusters could have been stopped under the new rules. Apparently, both chambers had broken the stranglehold of tradition.[131] Rockefeller told Ford's cabinet that "the conservatives, the liberals, the Republicans, and the Democrats have all generally turned out to be fairly happy about it."[132] Yet feelings were so tense within the GOP that Rockefeller held a series of dinners with Senate Republicans after the battle to ease relations; some Republicans refused to attend.[133] Rockefeller informed the media the following month that conservative Republicans were trying to blackmail President Ford into forcing another change in the filibuster ruling to overturn the reform.[134]

## The New Era Begins

The committee era was fading fast. Whereas the reform coalition had treaded cautiously in the first half of the 1970s by focusing on incremental changes that did not have monumental immediate effects, events surrounding the 1974 election period had opened the floodgates for an all-out assault. Though committees were still important, committee chairs no longer reigned supreme. Their authority had been diminished. Since the caucus deposed three committee chairmen and forced the resignation of a fourth, future committee leaders would always consider this looming threat. Most chairs were deposed or defeated or simply retired or passed away.

The chamber majorities came from a new generation that had no strong identification with the committee era and who were emboldened to take action. These younger legislators provided the needed voting muscle – together with the reform coalition, a favorable institutional environment outside of Congress, and procedures enacted since 1970 – to obtain institutional and leadership changes that would have been impossible only a few months earlier. As a result of the way that many of these politicians had conducted their campaigns in the fall of 1974 and the way that the media covered them as "Watergate Babies," their very presence intensified the perception that a person's position on institutional reform could have significant electoral consequences. This was the type of perception that could move legislators on Capitol Hill, including those who were not enthusiastic about reform.

The attack on committee autonomy and the filibuster was the culmination of a sequence of institutional changes that had started in the 1950s. Some of these changes had been a direct result of the reform coalition, such as the caucuses taking a stronger stand on naming committee chairs and both chambers opening more of their business to the public. Other institutional changes had been the product of realignments in the institutions outside of Congress, such as the national media embracing a more adversarial ethic as well as the courts and Department of Justice breaking up southern rural districts that had favored conservative Democrats. These changes were gradual and were produced by multiple forces, but their cumulative effect was to push Congress into a new era.

# IO

# Scandal without Reform

In 1976, Richard Ottinger (D-NY) told his colleagues that Speaker John McCormack used to tell young members that – when they saw a committee chair – they should bow low from the waist because that was what he did. Now, Ottinger explained, it was the chair that bowed low from the waist.[1] Ottinger captured the mood on Capitol Hill. After freshman legislators forced Mills, Patman, Hebert, and Poage to relinquish their chairs and when old warhorses such as John McClellan and James Eastland passed away or retired, observers sensed that the committee era had finally ended. Though still influential, committee autonomy had significantly diminished. Congress in 1976 was a much different place than ten years earlier.

The windows of opportunity for government reform had opened rapidly, yet rapidly too did the viability of reform vanish from the political landscape. Between 1976 and 1979, Congress underwent the latter change as a new congressional era settled into place. These transitional years were marked by two competing impulses. On the one hand, a thinning reform coalition took advantage of the window that had been opened by congressional scandals and the Watergate election to pass as much as possible: stricter ethics rules, new administrative apparatuses for the House, jurisdictional realignment in Senate committees, and authorization to televise the House. The coalition also helped bring down more senior legislators such as Wayne Hays.

On the other hand, the political strength of reform was diminishing. One of the first signs of this shift was that scandals were slowly losing their close link to institutional reform. This came at a time when congressional scandals were becoming more pervasive in terms of sheer quantity and the high level of legislator regularly implicated. Between the mid-1950s and mid-1970s, the revelation of scandal and calls for institutional reform had gone hand-in-hand. Watergate and the legislation that surrounded it symbolized the marriage that had taken place in the 1970s. Like dramatic elections, scandals had provided focusing events that created political pressure for bold reform. Scandals were often a direct outgrowth of the reform coalition's efforts to root out abusive power, and they were vehicles that were employed to mobilize support for proposals that had gestated for years.[2] Likewise, the media had come to consider scandal as a legitimate way to report on the abuse of power.

The difference between this reform period and the era taking shape by the late 1970s was that scandals would no longer produce as many major changes in the way that government was structured. The marriage between scandal and institutional reform was breaking apart. Rather, scandals were becoming primarily a tool of political combat and a product of investigative organizations that focused on the revelation of corruption and individual wrongdoing rather than structural problems. Although there were many people in the media who perceived scandal as a way to stimulate reform, their stories were disseminated in a political context where few did much with the information other than bring down the individual implicated or improve a very narrow set of preexisting regulations.

Scandals were no longer part of a vibrant movement to reconstruct institutions. At the same time, the new legislative structure contained few of the countervailing forces that had generally held scandal in check since the Progressive Era. The evolution of scandal politics could be seen through three important congressional stories in this transitional period: Wayne Hays, where a personal scandal played a significant part in weakening the House Administration Committee and the subsequent creation of ethics laws; Koreagate, where a scandal involving major legislative figures produced no institutional reform; and Abscam, where a scandal triggered demands for reforming investigative institutions rather than Congress itself.

The most apparent factors behind the deteriorating strength of congressional reform was that legislators who were the issue's strongest advocates started to command significant power within the emerging process. First, Democrats retained sizable majorities throughout the second half of the 1970s. There were many reasons for this interregnum, including the temporary hold of Democrats in the South and the detrimental electoral effects of Watergate on the GOP. Whereas the new generation of Democrats was willing to use scandal as a normal form of combat, they were not as enthused about altering the institutional status quo after the mid-1970s. Second, the burst of institutional reforms in the 1970s left many former advocates of reform with a sense that they should move back to the type of bread-and-butter questions that most concerned voters amidst economic decline. Some of the pivotal organizations in the reform coalition since the 1950s, such as organized labor, could not afford to devote the same kind of resources to this fight (especially after some of the brutal battles with reformers in the early 1970s). Organizations from the civil rights movement had far fewer concerns about the legislative process since their big legislation had passed and as they now focused on promoting an affirmative action policy that centered on the federal bureaucracy and courts. Younger political scientists generally turned inward, their research focused more on esoteric methodological questions. Most foundations interested in domestic issues opened their pocketbooks to the pressing problems of poverty and unemployment. Several of the old elite liberal organizations (such as ADA) diminished in stature or disbanded. Some organizations such as Common Cause tried to tackle issues other than government reform.[3] Nonreform concerns became all the more pertinent following the 1980 election, which brought in Republican president Ronald Reagan, placed the Senate in Republican hands, and gave Republicans 33 new seats in the House. Democrats now needed to concentrate on policies that would enable them to regain power, while Republicans searched for issues to solidify their newfound stature.

Third, the new legislative process was making it difficult to pass *any* legislation, let alone measures that impinged on incumbents. There were no longer any kings in Congress. Legislators found an atmosphere where no individuals could dictate the pace of events in the same fashion as committee chairs of the past. Although parties were supposed to have become the center of the new process, in the early years their influence was limited and so those components of the legislative process favoring intense decentralization reigned supreme. Deep fissures between Democratic President Carter and Congress made the situation even worse. Finally, the diminishing salience of reform stemmed from the coalition's success. Following each victory, the thinning coalition found that it had to devote more of its resources to *defending* from retrenchment the institutional changes that had already passed.

### Defending Campaign Finance Reform, 1975–1976

Campaign finance was a prime example of how the previous accomplishments of the reform coalition turned more of the legislative debate toward the defense of existing institutions than to the creation of new ones. Before the ink on the campaign finance amendments of 1974 had dried, opponents tried to dismantle the regulations during the implementation process. The assault on campaign finance began when elected officials attempted to undermine the Federal Election Commission (FEC). For instance, President Ford delayed naming his appointees in 1975 for several months and took his time requesting funds for the commission. The House, moreover, placed two former legislators on the commission.[4] One month after its creation, Wayne Hays proposed making the FEC a part-time body.[5] The FEC itself undermined the effort to constrain the role of private money in elections through rulings that defended the right of PACs to exist.[6]

The other major challenge to campaign finance emanated from the Supreme Court.[7] On January 30, 1976, the Supreme Court overturned two components of the regulatory system. First, the Court ruled that the FEC violated the separation of powers because one branch of the government could not interfere in the elections of another. Thus Congress could not appoint commissioners to regulate presidential elections. Second, the Court concluded that spending limits were unconstitutional. The majority insisted that spending and free speech could not be disentangled in the television era. While spending limits were retained for those who accepted matching funds in presidential elections, other presidential and congressional candidates were freed from restrictions. The ruling overturned spending limits on wealthy individuals who personally financed their own campaigns. Despite these reversals the Court accepted most of the campaign finance laws, including public financing, disclosure regulations, and contribution limits.[8]

The battle over campaign finance continued as Congress attempted to reconstitute the FEC in response to the Supreme Court decision. During the debate over the FEC, legislators struggled to prevent the reconstitution of the commission or the creation of something so feeble that it would be ineffective. President Ford introduced his proposal on February 16 by warning that, if the commission became an "empty shell," public confidence in politics would continue to erode.[9] In the House, Hays wanted to eliminate the commission. Abner Mikva (D-IL) and William Frenzel (R-MN) pushed for a bipartisan compromise that created a weakened but still existent FEC.[10] Hays said that he would oppose the commission in its old form.[11] He did not want the commission to have any investigative powers, and he supported a process stipulating that if there were an apparent violation then a congressional committee would be responsible for recommending action to the Justice Department. He teamed up with labor-backed Democrats and the Democratic National Committee's Robert Strauss to add an amendment that would prohibit corporations from using general funds to solicit employees.[12] By adding amendments that favored labor, Hays imposed conditions that he thought the GOP would reject.

But with the reform coalition and media shifting into overdrive, many in the GOP avoided attacking the bill for fear of being labeled as opponents of reform. Democrats also refused to provide an advance copy of the bill until the very last minute, so Republicans did not have much time to develop their response.[13] The House Administration Committee passed legislation that reconstituted the FEC and hampered corporate committees. The bill allowed corporate committees to solicit funds from stockholders and officers of corporations. Even though Hays was unable to eliminate the FEC, the bill severely weakened it. While reformers found much to criticize, they believed that the FEC would still be effective.[14] The president attacked the legislation for its effect on corporate contributions. But before the legislation reached the Senate, advisors convinced Ford to emphasize how the bill weakened the commission.[15] Facing stiff primary competition from Ronald Reagan, the bill offered Ford an opportunity in the post-Watergate era to campaign against Democrats for opposing institutional reform. The Senate passed a more moderate bill that included a provision requiring PACs to disclose the cost of internal campaign communications to corporate or union members. The conference committee strengthened the civil enforcement mechanism of the FEC and required unions to report the costs of campaign communications. Although the final legislation placed minor restrictions on corporate PACs, it still allowed them to operate.

Even though Ford had deep reservations, he signed the bill based on the advice of several prominent Republicans.[16] The public and media, according to Ford's advisors, would see this as a "positive step." Since Ronald Reagan was having trouble obtaining funds in the Republican primary, advisors said that it would look bad for the president to waffle.[17] The bill weakened the FEC by subjecting its rulings to strong congressional scrutiny. To avoid constitutional problems, the president would appoint members and the Senate would confirm them.

The campaign finance battles revealed that the struggle over institutional reform did not end with the passage of legislation. Old and new opponents renegotiated measures during implementation. The passage of legislation had changed the terms of debate by shifting more attention to the protection and retrenchment of institutional reforms and away from their creation.

## Scandal Politics, 1976

While the reform coalition attempted to protect its legislation, Congress experienced a year of scandal in 1976. A string of legislators – some prominent and others marginal – found themselves ensnared in a web of investigations. These stories would bring an end to some careers (as Wayne Hays learned) but primarily caused embarrassment for other individuals, including those implicated in the Korean lobbying scandal. In the early part of this transitional period, scandal was still closely connected to institutional reform. The rise of scandal politics took place as the nation underwent dramatic economic decline. Whereas unprecedented rates of economic growth in the postwar years had buttressed public trust in government, rapid economic decline in the 1970s fueled general disillusionment because the government appeared incapable of sustaining a strong economy. The stagnant economy intensified the impact of scandals as Americans searched for villains to explain the decline.

One of the most shocking scandals involved the 64-year-old Wayne Hays. The chairman of the House Administration Committee was an extraordinarily powerful legislator who proved to be a major force during the battles over campaign finance. The scandal began through the media, which was not only eager to investigate but which had embraced a broader understanding of what constituted corruption in response to the reform coalition and new contemporary cultural values about sexual misconduct. In 1974, managing editor Marion Clark of the *Washington Post Magazine* was traveling on a train to Washington. When the train broke down, a fellow passenger named Elizabeth Ray confessed to Clark that she had slept with several congressmen. Clark mentioned the encounter to Rudolph Maxa, who was a 24-year-old gossip columnist for the *Post*. Although unable to contact Ray for over a year (since she had gone to Hollywood hoping to start an acting career), they learned that she had worked as a secretary for Wayne Hays. On April 6, 1976, Ray called Clark in tears to say that Hays was marrying another secretary.

Uncertain about whether their newspaper would allow them to pursue this type of investigation, Clark and Maxa approached executive editor Ben Bradlee, who had played a pivotal role in the Watergate story. Signaling how much journalistic ethics were changing, Bradlee authorized them to move forward. Clark and Maxa turned into private detectives. Bradlee authorized their request to secretly listen in on telephone conversations, a journalistic tactic that was not standard at the time. Ray revealed that she and Hays had a sexual relationship and that, during the Mills scandal, Hays threatened to use Mafia ties to silence any woman who harmed his career. Hays denied to reporters that Ray was on the payroll or that she was his mistress.[18]

On May 23 the *Washington Post* published its story. To guarantee maximum attention in the Sunday paper, Bradlee placed the piece on the front page along with three large pictures (most stories usually received one photo at most). One photograph depicted the 33-year-old Ray sitting in her office with a caption that read: "I can't type, I can't file, I can't even answer the phone." Another picture showed Hays with a quote saying "Hell's fire! I'm a very happily married man." The final picture presented a publicity photograph of the blond Ray wearing a skimpy top.[19] That the story appeared in the *Post* provided it with added legitimacy. By that time, the paper had a renowned reputation for investigative journalism. Seeking to destroy her reputation, Hays went on all three networks to call Ray a "sick girl" who was undergoing psychiatric treatment.[20] The story created a sensation in the press as newspapers, magazines, and television stations covered the lurid details.[21] Reflecting the outlook of many reporters, journalist Richard Cohen said that "the public have come to expect more from public officials and in the process the rules of the game have been changed. What used to be called gossip is now called information and some of it is as useful as the tally on a roll-call vote."[22]

But the press was not alone in uncovering this scandal. The Justice Department initiated a probe through its new Public Integrity Division, which had been created in response to Watergate.[23] Moreover, a federal grand jury heard testimony on fraud charges. All the investigations were justified on the grounds that Hays used public funds to pay for his mistress. Two days after the story appeared, Hays made a dramatic speech to the House in which he admitted to a "personal relationship" with Ray and said he committed a grave error by not disclosing all the facts. Yet Hays denied that he hired Ray because she was his mistress and urged the Ethics Committee to conduct an investigation to prove that he had done nothing wrong. Hays attacked Assistant Attorney General Richard Thornburgh for launching the investigation as a personal vendetta. He concluded by saying that "any Member of this House or of the other body is wide open to anyone who wants to make malicious statements about him and who wants to write a book or wants to get in *Playboy* magazine"[24] (Ray was scheduled to appear in September). When the speech ended, colleagues gave him a standing ovation.[25]

As details of the relationship emerged, more individuals went on the attack. One of Hays's opponents in the Ohio primary said that Hays "lied continuously through this. He tried to blame the woman and called her crazy and nuts. This reflects on his character and integrity."[26] Bella Abzug argued that the issue was not sexual conduct or marital status but rather the misuse of public funds and deception of the public. Abzug believed that "If any member of Congress is found guilty of violating the trust which the American people has placed in either him or her, I assure you that I will support any House efforts to rectify this disgraceful situation."[27] The revelations were especially explosive because Hays was notorious for attacking other legislators about payroll practices and for bullying low-level employees. Hays had headed the investigation into Adam Clayton Powell.[28]

Like Fanne Fox, Elizabeth Ray discovered that scandals could turn her into a celebrity. The *National Enquirer* tabloid stationed reporters in her lobby, and the pornographic magazine *Hustler* offered Ray $25,000 to pose nude. Ray declined, since she had already agreed to appear in *Playboy*.[29] Ray published a "fictional" book about her adventures that provided painstaking descriptions of sexual acts with congressmen.[30]

The reform coalition was still operational, even if its ranks were not as strong. Younger Democrats worked with Common Cause to draft a resolution that called for Hays to resign from his House Administration Committee and Democratic Congressional Campaign Committee (DCCC) chairmanships. His opponents claimed that "public confidence in the integrity of Congress has been shaken and prompt action is needed to begin restoring that confidence."[31] On June 1, Majority Leader Tip O'Neill urged Hays to give up his committees. As part of a deal, Hays resigned from DCCC but not from the Administration Committee. The House Ethics Committee opened hearings. Sensing another opportunity to put Democrats on the defensive about corruption, Republicans proposed removing the power over member benefits and salaries from Administration. On June 8, Hays won his primary by a narrow margin. As if scripted by a Hollywood screenwriter, two days later Hays overdosed from sleeping pills. On June 18, Hays resigned from Administration. The Ethics Committee stopped its investigation. The Justice Department and the FBI decided that they did not have sufficient evidence to pursue the case. The House weakened Administration by taking away some of its duties and established a commission to study further changes.

Scandal bred more scandal. At the height of the Hays controversy, the *New York Times* reported that the secretary of John Young (D-TX) was hired because of their sexual relationship.[32] Other sex scandals included Allan Howe, a freshman Democrat from Utah who was found guilty of prostitution charges, as was Joe Waggonner. With each story reported in the summer and fall of 1976, the press, the courts, and government investigators continued to erode the barriers that protected the private lives of politicians. "The national preoccupation with sex," wrote Warren Weaver, "has worked its way east from Hollywood and the flamboyant world of entertainers to Washington."[33]

The transformed outlook of the media was evident in each of these cases. The national media was comfortable highlighting congressional scandal.[34] Reporters jumped on these stories the minute they surfaced. Nixon's scandal had elevated the standing of journalists who fought against corruption. Nobody wanted to miss the next Richard Nixon or Wilbur Mills. Although they were

not the first to practice investigative journalism, *Washington Post* reporters Bob
Woodward and Carl Bernstein had glorified it through Watergate. Their account
of Watergate became a best-seller and a film in 1976 starring Robert Redford and
Dustin Hoffman. Investigative journalism received another boon with CBS's "60
Minutes," launched on September 24, 1968, which featured reporters exposing
corruption using dramatic visual and audio devices. The structure of the show
resembled a detective story with the top investigator, the reporter, featured in
each piece. When the show's ratings peaked around 1980, it ranked above sit-
coms like "Three's Company" and "M*A*S*H."[35]

Given recent events, there remained a perception in the press that scandal was
a legitimate means of pursuing corruption. "It would be too much to say that
money, booze and sex dominate the politics of this city, but you can hardly explain recent history around here without taking them into account," observed
James Reston:

But for the tragedy of Chappaquiddick, with its Friday night high-jinks, there is little
doubt that Senator Edward Kennedy of Massachusetts would now be the leading candidate for both the Democratic nomination and the presidency. For years, the House of
Representatives had been bridling under the power of the Ways and Means Committee
and its effective but authoritarian chairman, Wilbur Mills; but it took his splashy liaison
with Fanne Foxe, otherwise known as the Argentine Firecracker, to bring his amorous
ways and means to the rescue of the House. The latest example of reform by scandal is
the case of Wayne Hays of Ohio.[36]

This outlook encouraged the media to search for the institutional underpinnings
of questionable personal activities. Right after the *Post* published its first story
on Ray, Ben Bradlee instructed Clark and Maxa to broaden the scope of coverage
to deal with "fundamental questions of congressional misuse of power, whether
they concerned junketing, payroll padding, the seniority system or questionable campaign contributions." Clark and Maxa recounted that "it had always
been difficult to report interestingly on the congressional power structure....
The Hays affair, Bradlee said, might just be the handle that could fit the larger
story of congressional excesses, much the way Watergate had forced an examination of the role of the executive branch."[37]

Journalists in this era were determined to push the boundaries of what issues constituted legitimate stories, including the social lives of politicians. For
example, the "society" section and "women's pages" of newspapers – once reserved for homes and the parties of local elites – were starting to look more
closely at the private world of politicians. Starting with a column launched in
1969, the *Washington Post*'s Sally Quinn covered the social events and personalities of Washington in order to provide readers with a closer look at politicians.[38]
There were members of the media who were still uncomfortable discussing personal matters.[39] Fred Hechinger warned that "it is one thing to adhere to strict
standards of morality in one's personal life. It is quite another to insist that a

Congressman's sexual morality should be a matter of concern for anyone but him and his wife, and the local laws that govern such conduct."[40] Joseph Kraft believed that most of the spin-off stories were turning on "private questions important to the persons involved and their families, but not to millions of Americans who read newspapers and watch television. By pandering to prurient taste, by competitive indulgence in voyeurism, the responsible press does no service."[41]

With the Hays and other related scandals, the media fully embraced an expanded understanding of corruption that included the personal relationships of politicians. This evolving definition of abusive power was embedded in cultural and social changes that were redefining the principles that governed gender relations, sexuality, and professional privilege. In addition to the adversarial media, one of the biggest effects of the 1960s social movements had been to liberalize mainstream attitudes toward all aspects of culture regarding sexuality.[42]

More importantly, though, concern about the personal behavior of congressman was fueled by the feminist movement.[43] Stemming from the argument that the "personal was political," male public officials were being expected to uphold certain standards of behavioral conduct in the workplace and at home. During the 1960s and 1970s, feminists had popularized the concept that power often resided in the private sphere and not just in the realm of formal politics, as they called upon women to recognize that subordination took place through the way they were treated by men at home, in their communities, and in the workplace. Leading feminists challenged the traditional separation of the "private" and "public" spheres by arguing that women needed to transform their entire life experience if they were to be politically empowered. Despite various failures, the feminist movement was able to popularize the concept that personal issues were fundamentally political problems if they were directly related to women's equality.[44] These issues were said to include making men accountable for the way they behaved in all of their relationships with women – from the bedroom to the boardroom.

One of the central claims by feminists in the middle to late 1970s was that power was often asserted through sexual activities.[45] Grounded in Title VII of the 1964 Civil Rights Act, the United States government would embrace a definition of sexual harassment in employment law that was extremely broad compared to European nations in terms of what types of activities were subject to punishment – but one that centered almost exclusively on sexual abuse at the expense of other ways in which women were disadvantaged in the workplace.[46] In 1980, the Equal Employment Opportunity Commission laid out guidelines, which the Supreme Court upheld in 1986, that defined sexual harassment as (a) requiring sexual activity to retain or obtain a job or promotion and (b) creating an "intimidating, hostile, or offensive working environment."[47]

In this context, the personal behavior of politicians in government was thus a *political* issue. As these ideas gained currency nationally and as more professional women entered into politics and the media during the 1970s, there was heightened attention toward how male politicians behaved when they were not making speeches or writing legislation. The problem of sexual harassment in the workplace seemed especially acute in Congress, whose legislators were not covered by federal employment laws and where a tradition of womanizing prevailed.[48] Although the problem of "sexual harassment" was only emerging in the mid-1970s, reporters and legislators who discussed Wayne Hays frequently called for reforming hiring practices and ethics rules.[49]

Ironically, the feminist focus on the personal lives of public figures and their decision to home in on sexuality resonated with followers of the evangelical conservative movement. As religious figures and organizations entered into the political sphere during the 1970s, they focused on the moral salvation of every American in an age of liberalized cultural values.[50] Viewing politics as a moral undertaking, evangelical conservative leaders argued that politicians should live the same kind of life – which they defined as religiously moral – that they were calling for in every American family. Together, these two very different movements would thoroughly politicize the private behavior of politicians.[51]

The reform coalition remained instrumental in other types of scandals as well. Their role in political corruption cases was evident in the downfall of Robert Sikes (D-FL). In 1975, Common Cause discovered that Sikes, who was chair of the Military Construction Appropriations Subcommittee, used his position for purposes of self-interest.[52] The political atmosphere surrounding this case changed dramatically after "60 Minutes" broadcast a story about Sikes that was based on information provided by Common Cause.[53] The House Ethics Committee launched a formal investigation. Common Cause worked behind the scenes with New Jersey Watergate Baby Andrew Maguire on a letter-writing campaign in key districts.[54] When the House reprimanded Sikes by a vote of 381 to 3, he condemned the "guillotine-minded" reformers who were bringing down politicians by "subterfuge and innuendo, and rumor."[55] Six weeks after the reprimand, Sikes's constituents reelected him. Remembering Adam Clayton Powell, some colleagues felt that they did not have the right to take further action.

But younger Democrats disagreed. Leon Panetta, a new California Democrat, urged that Sikes not be renamed chair of the subcommittee. Panetta said that restoring Sikes to the same position that he abused would "reduce that reprimand to an empty gesture and invite the further disdain and disillusionment of the public."[56] Common Cause and the National Committee for an Effective Congress backed Panetta.[57] Olin Teague accused Panetta of making statements that were "blatant untruths" and insisted that Sikes had not violated any law.[58] On January 26, 1977, the Caucus voted 189 to 93 to unseat Sikes as chair. Sikes called this a vendetta from liberal "political enemies" who were angry about his support of military spending. Max Baucus (D-MT) replied that members were "concerned about the image of the Congress" and this was a "tremendous symbol."[59] Democrats understood from polls that all these and other scandals were undermining the advantage their party had enjoyed on ethics after Watergate.[60]

## Finishing the Agenda, 1977–1978

The election of 1976 maintained a legislative alignment that was still conducive to institutional reform. Although the Democratic Caucus picked moderate leaders who were not known as reformers, Tip O'Neill and Robert Byrd both had records of compromising with proponents of reform. The scandals that rocked Capitol Hill intensified the pressure to move forward with Senate committee reform, ethics rules, and televised proceedings in the House.

The election of 1976 brought a second wave of politicians who had promised to reform the entire political process. Jimmy Carter narrowly defeated Ford (by 2 million votes) with an electoral victory of 297 to 241. Carter's victory was significant to reformers since his campaign had promised to restore faith in government. The Democratic majority in the Senate increased to 62 while in the House it reached 292. The election had a similar impact on the Senate that the 1974 election had on the House. The most dramatic internal change occurred in the Senate, which experienced its largest turnover since 1958. Four Republicans elected in 1970 (three with significant help from Nixon) – Glenn Beall, Jr., Bill Brock, James Buckley, and Robert Taft, Jr. – were defeated. Nine incumbents lost. There were eighteen freshmen, ten of whom were Democrats. Many of the victors in the House and Senate, such as Al Gore, Jr. (D-TN) and Paul Sarbanes, had supported further reform. Only two House representatives elected in 1974 were defeated, one as a result of a sex scandal (Howe). There was a continued shift toward youth in both chambers.[61] There were only nineteen senators in the 94th Congress (1975–1977) who had been in office in the 85th Congress (1957–1959).[62] Reformers were optimistic.[63]

Since Speaker Carl Albert and Majority Leader Mike Mansfield both retired, each chamber needed new leaders. House Democrats chose Tip O'Neill as their new Speaker, and Senate Democrats promoted Robert Byrd to Majority Leader. Senate Republicans elected the charismatic Watergate star Howard Baker to head the minority, and the pugnacious John Rhodes was chosen to lead the GOP in the House. The most controversial race was among James Wright, Phillip Burton, John McFall (D-CA), and Richard Bolling for House Majority Leader. Bolling was the obvious candidate of reform, but the Missourian was hurt by poor personal relations and a lack of interest in wheeling and dealing. Burton, the front-runner, had strong support among freshmen. O'Neill despised Burton and privately opposed him. McFall was brought down by the unfolding scandal involving Korean lobbyists. The centrist Wright won the election by a controversial single vote.

One issue pursued by the reform coalition in 1977 was Senate committee reform. Legislators approached this issue with caution in light of the disastrous fate of the Bolling committee. The problems facing the Senate were similar to those in the House. Proponents of reform complained that senators were required to serve on too many committees and subcommittees, many of which were obsolete, while jurisdictions were irrationally based on vested interests.[64]

In 1976, Adlai Stevenson III (D-IL) and William Brock headed a temporary Select Committee to Study the Senate Committee System in order to consider plans that would shift the jurisdictions of almost every panel and drastically reduce the number of standing committees.[65] The temporary commission found that senators were worried that the public held inflated expectations given that institutional structure prevented them from meeting those goals.[66]

The reform coalition continued to insist that jurisdictional reform was integral to strengthening the Senate. Stevenson headed the effort. A Harvard Law School graduate, Stevenson was the eldest son of the famous Illinois governor who was an unsuccessful Democratic presidential candidate in the 1950s. An introvert who was much skinnier in appearance than his father, Stevenson exhibited a similar self-effacing attitude. He earned his first political stripes in Illinois politics, where he dared to take on the Cook County machine and pushed through reforms that aimed to make government more accountable. "It's not enough to talk about public policies," Stevenson once said, "we must also talk about the public institutions that implement public policy."[67] He also opposed the Vietnam war and backed civil rights. Some of his followers were disappointed when he decided to court the Chicago machine during his run for the Senate in 1970 to fill the seat of the deceased Everett Dirksen. As with that campaign, Stevenson remained keenly aware that he needed to compromise in the battle over Senate jurisdictions or he would suffer the same fate as Bolling.

The sequence of events in the 1970s was crucial. Since the Senate jurisdiction reforms came after Bolling's experience yet also at the tail end of the burst of institutional change that scandals and elections had produced, Stevenson and his colleagues were in a far better position than Bolling. They had learned from prior experience about what types of proposals to avoid, and they offered their plan at a more opportune moment. Stevenson's committee started by asking for as much as possible with the explicit intention of bargaining away reforms to build support.[68] The Stevenson committee was composed of members biased toward change: junior legislators who did not chair powerful committees.[69] Stevenson focused on obtaining what was politically possible rather than intellectually perfect. His committee proposed a reduction in Senate committees from 31 to 14. Stevenson's proposal eliminated every special, select, and joint committee as well as four standing committees. Stevenson shied away from touching Finance or Appropriations.[70] Besides jurisdictional changes, the committee proposed that senators be allowed to serve on only two standing committees and on a limited number of subcommittees; moreover, senators would be allowed to chair only one committee. As with the House, the plan endorsed the joint and sequential referral of legislation as well as ad hoc committees. Their prospects improved in 1976. Besides substantial turnover, three committee chairs whose panels Stevenson had proposed be abolished lost their elections.

When the Senate Rules Committee considered the report in January 1977, interest groups and senators threatened by the proposal fought the plan. This time the proponents of institutional reform were in a stronger position since they had

Senator Adlai Stevenson III (Senate Historical Office).

consciously avoided proposals that would threaten powerful members of organized labor, thereby creating a more united position among liberals in the reform coalition.[71] In response to critics, the Rules Committee reduced the number of committees to be eliminated and increased the number of committees and subcommittees on which senators could serve. The committee passed the revised measure 9-0 on January 25, 1977. The Republican and Democratic leadership endorsed the plan. Before the floor vote, amendments saved a few additional committees from termination. The Senate approved the plan 89 to 1 on February 4, 1977.

The final resolution reduced the number of committees to 25. It closed three minor committees and several select committees, altered jurisdictions, and stipulated that senators could only serve on two major committees and one minor committee. The number of subcommittees declined by 33 percent. Members were allowed on five subcommittees and to chair one full committee. Republicans obtained more committee staff. The package benefitted junior senators through improved subcommittee assignments.[72] The biggest jurisdictional accomplishment was that energy issues were centralized under the new Energy and Natural Resources Committee. Procedurally, the Majority and Minority Leaders gained the power to refer bills to multiple committees.

The second major institutional change in 1977 involved ethics. Amidst the scandals of 1976, the reform coalition stepped up its pressure to strengthen ethics regulations. "If Wayne Hays could only hear them now," quipped Roger Mudd, "from one end of Capitol Hill to the other, the talk is ethics, ethics, ethics ... a living testament to Wayne Hays, the very man that put their feet to the fire."[73] While ethics committees and rules existed, reformers and the media claimed that the mild codes were not enforced. Common Cause called the House Ethics Committee a "cruel hoax."[74] Based on a House commission report, Tip O'Neill announced in December 1976 that he supported an ethics bill to impose strict limits on the outside income of legislators and to require fuller disclosure. Senator Gaylord Nelson (D-WI), chair of the Special Committee on Official Conduct that was created in 1977, pushed for stricter ethics rules. In early 1977, President Carter proposed a sweeping ethics code for all federal officials. Many legislators despised ethics laws.[75] Jim Wright complained that "even if we abandon our families, and sell our homes, and pitch tents here on the lawn, somebody will criticize us for sleeping on the grass."[76]

Nonetheless, the House and Senate passed a code of ethics in 1977 that strengthened regulations created in 1958 and 1959. The scandals of 1976 had given momentum to this change.[77] The leadership helped ensure passage by tying the codes to a congressional pay raise. The new regulations mandated disclosure of financial information about members, prohibited the use of office accounts, and limited the amount of outside income that sitting politicians could earn. The Senate rules also prohibited some types of employment discrimination on the basis of race, religion, sex, or physical disability. The media contrasted these reforms favorably to what one network called the "scapegoat" approach whereby Congress punished one member while avoiding the larger problems.[78] The regulations were not drafted as statutory law, so enforcement still depended on legislators.[79] In 1978 Congress would pass the Ethics in Government Act, which enforced financial disclosure requirements and established the Office of the Independent Counsel to investigate executive branch corruption.

The final reform in 1977 centered on television. This medium had always been important to the coalition because they perceived television as a final step toward eliminating the secrecy that had haunted the committee era. The House had authorized televised committee proceedings with the Legislative Reorganization Act of 1970. Starting in the mid-1970s, there were proposals to televise all proceedings, including the floor. A majority of the House supported televised hearings.[80] Studies commissioned by several committees and foundations had confirmed the value of the medium to the institution. Proponents repeated familiar arguments. Foremost, they claimed that television would provide citizens with improved information and enable them to monitor their representatives. This was part of a broader effort to open up the halls of government and end the culture of secrecy. Finally, televised coverage would improve the visibility of the House relative to the president and Senate. Like other institutional reforms, it was understood that televised proceedings would weaken the strength of the party leadership over the floor by offering an informational tool for average members.[81] The new telegenic generation was enthused about communicating directly to the public.

Experience in the states had conditioned politicians to accept this medium. By the end of 1977, 45 states allowed some type of televised coverage of legislative floor proceedings. The frequency of coverage varied depending on the interest of the media and length of legislative sessions. Several states taped the proceedings for a one-hour nightly show. In almost all the states, the broadcasting system was owned by the media; the government neither controlled how the cameras covered the proceedings nor financed the cost. The Congressional Research Service found that the states did not experience the problems that legislators feared.[82] Reformers also pointed abroad. Canada, for example, had started to televise its House of Commons gavel-to-gavel in 1977.[83] Legislators in the United States already had experience with television, as it had become crucial to campaigns since the 1950s.[84]

The central concern about televising Congress stemmed from the nature of the communications industry. When politicians discussed televising the House in 1976 and 1977, they still conceived of a network-based industry.[85] Cable television had been in existence since 1948, but the industry had primarily been a mechanism for local entrepreneurs to bring improved reception to rural and inner city areas. Although there were attempts to introduce original programming through cable in the 1960s, the networks stopped them – as did unfavorable government regulation.[86] Starting in 1974, the FCC loosened the regulatory constraints on cable operators. Satellite technology offered entrepreneurs unprecedented opportunities to transmit stations through many cable systems.

But cable remained an experiment. There was no realistic expectation of a prominent channel that would cover legislative proceedings, unfiltered and unedited. There was not even a cable system in Washington. A majority of legislators expected that constituents would see clips selected by journalists and producers. The networks had been clear that they would not forfeit their constitutional rights by allowing politicians to regulate what would be shown.[87] President of CBS John Backe told Tip O'Neill that House control would cancel the benefits of the reform and "the credibility of what would remain would be suspect as a show staged-managed by the participants."[88] In the debate over televising the House, newspapers tended to support the constitutional claims of the networks.[89] Public television feared that they could be attacked as biased and, since they were dependent on public funds, the network could be intimidated by politicians.

Given the structure of the television industry at the time, control would likely rest in the hands of a commercial medium that was increasingly hostile toward politicians. An academic study of the network news confirmed that almost every story about the post-Watergate Congress of early 1976 presented the institution unfavorably.[90] Not surprisingly, a survey of 166 sitting legislators found that almost 92 percent felt that the media covered only conflict.[91]

The House debated television in the winter of 1977. O'Neill's closest advisors urged him to maintain control of the cameras. Jerry Colbert, a television producer whom O'Neill trusted for advice, said that television could help "Democrats get their message across – *if* they are controlled and properly developed by the Speaker." As long as they controlled the cameras, Colbert wrote, the Speaker and Democratic leaders would be able to select which portions of the debate that the networks could broadcast: "This would go a long way towards controlling what the Leadership wanted communicated.... Under the circumstances the Leadership can structure the set up of the medium to work for it – not against it." Even without such partisan considerations, Colbert warned that if the networks were allowed to handle the feed, the House would have "surrendered" their message to a few network individuals in New York who will "decide *who* will get the publicity, *what* issues will be aired and *when* they will be aired." It would be impossible, moreover, to impose control because of "cries of 'freedom of the press'."[92] Majority Whip John Brademas told O'Neill that

the power of the television screen to influence the public is enormous. It would be an act of incredible folly for the House in general – and the Speaker in particular – to allow that power to be under outside control. Once the power is delegated, it will be difficult to retrieve .... [P]utting some of that power in the Rules Committee and some of it in the hands of the networks, gives the Speaker more baronies to battle. There is virtually no way for him to win once the networks have their camera in the door and are allied with the committee setting up the rules and procedures.[93]

Brademas's assistant argued that, given the network monopoly, this situation would result in less freedom of information than the House alternative. He explained that the House plan would allow any organization access to material whereas, under private control, local affiliates would be at the mercy of the networks with regard to what clips they received.[94]

Besides constitutional principles, the networks had self-interest in mind. Controlling the feed would strengthen their monopoly. Cable, according to one commentator, had the potential to "be a liberating technology that will restore diversity and competition to our increasingly monolithic communications system."[95] O'Neill's advisor Burt Hoffman said that network control of the feed would lock out cable channels – thereby stifling "news competition" – whereas House control would permit equal access to networks, local stations, cable television, and others.[96]

Yet there were legislators who supported network control. Sisk, chair of the subcommittee investigating the issue, concluded that a network pool would protect the rights of journalists and provide legitimate broadcasts.[97] Unfortunately for the networks, O'Neill perceived Sisk as politically weak.[98] Another supporter was Republican John Anderson, who argued that "if the House attempts to operate its own broadcast system, the results will be amateurish at best, commercial networks and stations will use little or none of it due to technical quality and contract agreements, and the House will be discredited in the eyes of the public for running a slip-shod, censored operation at taxpayers' expense."[99] He noted the success of televising the Judiciary Committee Watergate hearings, which had been controlled by a network pool. Anderson also pointed to the support of such prestigious groups as the National Association of Broadcasters.[100] Seventeen industry groups displayed a rare show of unity on this issue, emphasizing the fact that forty states allowed broadcasters to control the feed.[101]

On March 2, 1977, O'Neill surprised colleagues when he announced that the House would begin a ninety-day test on closed-circuit television. The decision fit into a larger pattern within O'Neill's career. As with the recorded teller vote in 1970, O'Neill sensed the strong political support behind a particular reform and believed that, if he did not accept this, then there was a good chance the classes of 1974 and 1976 would pass it without him.[102] Seeking compromise, he worked to satisfy younger members while protecting the interests of the leadership. Chair of the Joint Committee on Congressional Operations Jack Brooks (D-TX) reiterated that this was only an "experiment" and that House employees would operate the cameras without any "extraneous panning." While Brooks said that the committee was hoping to expand coverage, he assured his colleagues that "the test will be conducted with protection of the integrity of the House, its Members, and its legislative purpose uppermost in our minds."[103]

The Rules Committee formed a select committee that was chaired by Gillis Long (D-LA) to monitor the test. Over the ninety-day period, the subcommittee discovered that most members did not feel that television had a negative effect. The full committee, in a proposal approved by the House in October 1977, urged the House to continue the test and eventually authorize a permanent system. The report also charged another subcommittee, to be headed by Long, to recommend the method for controlling the feed in February 1978. While Long's subcommittee deliberated, television received a boost when the Senate allowed coverage of the debate over the Panama Canal Treaty. The National Public Radio broadcast received tremendous praise from legislators.[104]

Because of Lionel Van Deerlin (D-CA) and Tip O'Neill's top assistant Gary Hymel, the Speaker had met with an unknown entrepreneur from the cable industry named Brian Lamb in January 1978. The two discussed the possibility of broadcasting the House gavel-to-gavel through a specialized cable channel. While the future of cable remained uncertain, the idea intrigued O'Neill because the channel would remain outside the control of the media establishment he distrusted.[105] Moreover, the very fact that cable television was such a marginal industry helped its case since it appeared as less of a threat to O'Neill. Democrats could place the House on television through a private channel that would be watched by a small number of viewers. Although they did not sign any formal agreement, O'Neill and Lamb left the meeting with the understanding that this channel would carry the feed. On February 15, 1978, the Rules Committee recommended that the House control its own system and consider relying on cable and satellite television. Despite anger from the media, in June 1978 the House supported the recommendation and granted the Speaker power over implementation by 235-150. Sisk explained to the network executives that this was the best compromise they could obtain.[106]

The decision was seen as historic, since permitting cameras into the chamber was by no means guaranteed. After all, the courts were actively resisting the most limited proposals for televised trials[107] and there was insufficient support in the Senate to pass a similar measure. Although the Senate had allowed televised coverage of some committee hearings, there were continued fears about the detrimental effects that television might have on floor proceedings. Senators already enjoyed a disproportionate amount of network coverage.[108]

### Koreagate

Despite all these victories, the legislative strength of institutional reform started to fade by the late 1970s. Several main items on the agenda of the reform coalition languished, including publicly financed congressional campaigns, stricter lobbying disclosure, and jurisdictional reform for House committees. The fading status of reform could be seen in Koreagate, which – unlike the major scandals in the first half of the 1970s – did not result in any major institutional reforms that were linked to the story.

The Koreagate scandal had started to unfold in 1976. It involved a South Korean businessman named Tongsun Park. Besides his generous donations to Democratic incumbents, Park was known for throwing lavish parties attended by politicians. The *Washington Post* broke the story on October 24, 1976, with a piece about a Justice Department investigation.[109] Members of the reform coalition and the media suspected that Park was part of a covert South Korean operation to influence American foreign policy. Park claimed that he lobbied on behalf of his personal rice business and insisted that he had no formal ties to the South Korean government. In October, former representative and Governor of Louisiana Edwin Edwards and John Brademas acknowledged that they had received campaign contributions from Park.[110] By October 28, reports speculated that twenty members were under investigation.[111] The South Korean government attacked the "malicious" and "sensational" stories.[112] Park's relationship with top officials caused Democrats concern. ABC's Brit Hume predicted that this could be the "most significant investigation ever made by Congress into the conduct of its members."[113]

In 1977, the Democratic Caucus voted to investigate Tongsun Park based on the evidence that had been produced by the initial Department of Justice inquiry. The House Ethics Committee began its own inquiry. Chaired by John Flynt (D-GA), the committee hired Philip Lacovara, a former assistant to the Watergate counsel, to be the lawyer for the committee. The House granted the committee the power to use depositions, interrogations, and subpoenas. By this time, a federal grand jury had indicted Tongsun Park, Richard Hanna (D-CA), and Hancho Kim, a businessman born in Korea who was implicated in the alleged scheme. The *Washington Post* reported on April 17 of incriminating correspondence between Park and former Senator Joseph Montoya (D-NM) and former representatives Cornelius Gallagher (D-NJ), Otto Passman (D-LA), William Minshall (R-OH), and Hanna; there were also letters between Park and John McFall (D-CA), a sitting member. The letters allegedly contradicted Park's claim that he did not lobby for South Korea.[114] By the spring of 1977, critics were complaining that the House Ethics Committee was not seriously investigating. Republican Bruce Caputo (R-NY), a charismatic 34-year-old freshman on the Ethics Committee who was elected in 1976, catapulted into the public limelight by becoming the committee's most vocal critic. Common Cause called this investigation a litmus test on how serious Congress was about reform.[115] Not only did reform organizations want guilty members to be punished, they also felt that the scandal should result in campaign finance and lobbying reforms to prevent future episodes.[116]

The Speaker was cautious about the Ethics Committee investigation because there were reports that his name, as well as that of Majority Leader Jim Wright, had surfaced in the correspondence. Twenty members of Congress had been cited in Park's federal indictment. By August, *U.S. News & World Report* wrote that 115 lawmakers might be involved.[117] During the committee hearings, former Korean CIA Chief Kim Hyung Wook explained that former representative Richard Hanna had been responsible for making Tongsun Park the middleman in the U.S. rice trade with Korea. He stated in no uncertain terms that Park worked for the South Korean government, using his private club as the base of his operations. When asked by Caputo if Park was reporting directly to the Korean Central Intelligence Agency directors, Kim said "Yes, I am very certain about that." Former Korean intelligence agent Kim Sang Keun implicated South Korean President Park Chung Hee for overseeing a $3-million government operation to lobby Congress in favor of the Korean interest.[118] There were also investigations by grand juries, the Justice Department, federal and state agencies, and other congressional committees.

The proximity of this scandal to Watergate fueled the controversy. Indeed, reporters used the term "Koreagate" to describe the story. This was part of a pattern of adding the "gate" suffix to any scandal, thereby inflating its potential implications.[119] Republicans were eager to make the comparison in order to distance the party from Nixon.

As the investigation proceeded, more high-ranking Democrats were implicated – including O'Neill. Evidence revealed that, in December 1973, Park had given a birthday party for O'Neill that was attended by many prominent officials.[120] Despite his denials of wrongdoing, O'Neill was barraged by charges whenever he met with reporters. At one press conference, the Speaker was forced to respond to accusations about junkets to Korea that he had made, dinners at Tongsun Park's house, and baseball tickets that were exchanged between Park and former Speaker Albert.[121] After considerable struggle, Park admitted to making over $100,000 in payments to former representative Otto Passman.[122] A federal grand jury indicted Otto Passman for having obtained illegal funds from Park and not reporting them on his tax returns.

Just as Elizabeth Ray discovered that scandal brought fame and economic opportunity, legislators learned the benefits of scandal politics. Bruce Caputo gained instant notoriety by badgering his Democratic colleagues on the Ethics Committee to be more diligent.[123] On national television, O'Neill charged Caputo with making unsubstantiated attacks, maintaining files about the sex lives of members, and leaking information to the press. He told Rowland Evans and Robert Novak on their syndicated television program that "It's a rare occasion a man the type of Caputo comes to the Congress of the United States, I don't think it's good for Congress."[124] The televised remarks were so harsh that colleagues pushed O'Neill to apologize on the House floor. Caputo was not alone in capitalizing on scandal. Witnesses were subject to star treatment as well. Suzi Park Thomson, who had worked in the office of Speaker Albert while she was on the payroll of the South Korean government, told Congress that Tongsun Park had operated out of O'Neill's office when he was Majority Leader. As a result, she was featured in newspapers around the country.[125]

In the end, neither of the two major pieces of legislation most closely associated with Koreagate (stricter lobbying disclosure and campaign finance reform) passed Congress. While connections were established between Park and many congressmen, there was not sufficient evidence to link them to the South Korean government. Rather, a few individuals were punished. Richard Hanna was convicted of conspiring with Park to influence Congress. Hanna was sentenced to serve up to thirty months in prison for a conspiracy to defraud the government; he ended up serving one year. On October 13, the House reprimanded Edward Roybal (D-CA) for failing to report contributions from Park. The House also reprimanded Charlie Wilson (D-CA). Overall, the story simply fizzled after years in the press. This dynamic was not isolated to Koreagate and reflected the changing climate. The same pattern was evident with other scandals in 1978 and 1979, including those that involved Senators Herman Talmadge (D-GA) and Edward Brooke as well as Representatives Charles Diggs (D-MI), Daniel Flood (D-PA), and Joshua Eilberg (D-PA). Diggs was the first member censured by the House since 1921; he was also pressured to resign from his chairmanship of the House Foreign Affairs Subcommittee on Africa after being convicted of taking kickbacks.

In each case, the *pursuit* of corruption was becoming more aggressive while ensuing institutional changes diminished. This was indeed a hallmark of the new congressional era. Of course, a politics that was filled with scandal but did not produce much in the way of institutional reform (as opposed to individual destruction) was not a new phenomenon. Throughout most of American history, this situation was far more common than periods when corruption, scandal, and institutional reform went together. The latter periods, as occurred in the Progressive Era and the 1970s, were the exceptional ones.

But the reform period in the 1970s had produced a volatile environment where the frequency of scandal increased, because the countervailing forces that held scandal politics in check during the committee era were gone. Cultural and social changes had broadened the types of behavior that were considered to be corrupt. However, since institutional reform inhabited a much lower position on the national agenda, there were fewer individuals and organizations seeking or able to translate scandals into institutional reform. As a result, what was left by the early 1980s was a legislative system in which scandals were rather easy to produce and occurred frequently, though there was little political pressure to make sure that institutional reforms were implemented as a consequence.

### The Defeat of Campaign Finance Reform, 1978

The fading political status of reform was apparent with the fate of campaign finance proposals in 1978. When Congress enacted its new regulations in 1974, many reformers were confident that publicly financed congressional elections would soon follow. As the role of political action committees increased, moreover, there was considerable speculation that PAC limitations would be the next frontier for reformers. Yet the battles of 1978, when political conditions still seemed to be ripe for reform, revealed that fewer and fewer institutional reforms were passing as Congress settled into a new era.

In 1978, there were many reasons to believe that publicly financed congressional campaigns stood a chance of passing Congress.[126] Besides Koreagate, the 1974 and 1976 elections had brought a new reform-oriented group of legislators to the helm of the Democratic party. Wayne Hays had been replaced by Frank Thompson as chairman of the House Administration Committee. Thompson sympathized with publicly financed elections. After what many perceived to be a successful experiment with the new campaign system in 1976, President Carter offered an election reform package that included public funds for congressional elections. For the first time, Democratic leaders in both chambers strongly endorsed reform. Another factor pushing some Democrats toward public funding was the rapid proliferation of corporate and right-wing PACs.[127] There were only about 100 corporate PACs in 1976 but more than 600 a mere two years later.[128] The influx of corporate and right-wing PACs caused labor and their Democratic allies to favor public funds for congressional campaigns.[129] In their minds, public finance would diminish the incentive for incumbents to rely on the funds of labor's competitors – without banning the PACs, which remained important to their political strategy.

All of these factors appeared to create an ideal opportunity for extending public finance into congressional elections. Therefore, what remained of the reform coalition mobilized in 1978.[130] Yet they immediately discovered the reality of an inhospitable political landscape. As was the case with measures associated with Koreagate, political support for any more institutional reforms, let alone campaign finance, was weak. With campaign finance, all the political incentives now seemed to be working against further reforms. Despite the position of the leadership, most Democratic incumbents were flush with PAC money and so had less interest in pushing for any changes to the system.[131] Between 1974 and 1982, corporate PACs allocated more than a third of their money to Democrats.[132] According to the FEC in 1977, most funds went to incumbents.[133] With extremely low individual contribution limits at a time when party organizations were no longer strong, PACs were an essential source of funds.[134] As President Carter distanced himself and the DNC from Congress, many congressional Democrats believed they needed to strengthen their independent financial base.[135] At the same time, Republicans had an abundance of party money as a result of their innovative fund-raising techniques. The party had less interest in stopping PACs, since labor no longer monopolized those contributions.

Partisanship now worked against campaign finance reform, and tensions within what remained of the thinning reform coalition flared. In March 1978, the House Administration Committee was marking up some minor campaign finance amendments. Just before the bill received consideration, Thompson and Brademas, two important DSG members, added a provision that lowered the amount of support a political party could give to House candidates and reduced what political action committees could spend. Right before the 1978 election, this provision targeted the Republican party committees that had been successful in recent fund-raising events by mastering the use of direct mail to build a large small-donor base (Republicans had raised $18.5 million in party funds compared to the $5.6 million of Democrats).[136] Democrats had written the provision without consulting Republicans. Common Cause, news editors, and Republicans warned that Democrats were jeopardizing the cause of reform. They had planned to offer a provision on the floor for publicly financed congressional campaigns.[137] Common Cause believed that Democrats did not want public financing and that this was their way of killing the bill. Fred Wertheimer said that "opponents of public financing could not have had better allies than House Administration Chairman Frank Thompson and Majority Whip John Brademas. Their legislative proposal to drastically cut political party limits completely sabotaged this effort to enact congressional public financing."[138] Although Thompson backed off the most stringent provisions, he did not restore the ability of parties to transfer funds between state and national committees in the bill. Republicans were so distrustful of more tricks that they rejected the offer by Democratic leaders to delete the provision on the House floor if the GOP allowed the bill to be brought up. O'Neill blamed young turks in the GOP for breaking a deal.[139] The House rejected considering the bill by a vote of 209-196; 69 Democrats joined the vote, which observers blamed on their uninterest in public financing. One source in the Democratic leadership anonymously told the *New York Times*: "Common Cause tends to cloak its tactical judgement with a mantle of righteousness. If you disagree with them in the slightest degree you're in favor of letting Uncle Julius die."[140] The proposed provision for public financing drew criticism because the plan would not apply to primaries or offer funds to match small private contributions.

The following year, the House Administration Committee considered a bill with public subsidies and a limitation on PAC spending. Republicans attacked the proposals. Newt Gingrich lambasted Common Cause for its "moral McCarthyism" because the group accused congressmen of "public prostitution," implying that they basically took bribes.[141] By the end of the year, Thompson admitted that reform was dead. Many former supporters of institutional reform voted against the measure.[142] After these failures, public financing and PAC limitations were considered to be almost impossible.

### Fractured Politics

It was not surprising that institutional reform was difficult given the emerging legislative process. Although many of the institutional changes in the early 1970s had focused on strengthening congressional parties, they had also sought to check that power by bolstering fragmentation and individual empowerment. The overall hope of the reform coalition had been to strengthen caucuses – but within a system that forced party leaders to respond to the rank and file and to splinter coalitions in the House and Senate. This was because the goal of the coalition was to avoid shifting the autocratic power of committee chairs to party leaders. One of the primary effects of the new legislative fragmentation that thrived in the late 1970s was to increase the uncertainty of policy outcomes. It was difficult, if not impossible, for any member to predict what would happen when an issue reached the floor.[143]

The lack of centralization and party discipline took many forms. One of the main outcomes was the increased use of floor amendments by representatives and senators. Procedural changes facilitated this trend: in 1973 the House started using electronic voting, which reduced the time required for voting and made it less cumbersome for a member to call for a recorded vote.[144] The increase in the staff available to all members also gave every legislator more expertise to take independent action since they were no longer so reliant on information from committee chairs or party leaders.[145]

Filibusters were another source of individual empowerment. The period witnessed the "trivialization" of filibusters, as one leading account has argued.[146] Additionally, senators no longer respected cloture and found new strategies for delay after sixty of their colleagues had voted to stop debate. Senators went so far as to stall legislation for personal vendettas. For instance, after Senator John Tower prevented a foreign policy bill from going to conference committee, William Proxmire retaliated by stifling a monetary bill that Tower wanted.[147]

The number of caucuses and subcommittees expanded dramatically in the 1970s. Caucuses were devoted to specific problems that might not be of interest to the entire party. There had been three caucuses in 1969. Between 1970 and 1974, ten were created (seven in the House and three in the Senate); by 1980, there were 57 additional caucuses.[148] The caucuses were often homes for individuals who were not sympathetic to or satisfied with the party leadership. John Conyers told fellow members of the Congressional Black Caucus, Ron Dellums (D-CA) and Gus Savage (D-IL), that he thought the Democratic leadership needed to be replaced for its incompetence.[149]

Another source of fragmentation emanated from the proliferation of subcommittees, which had been strengthened by the Subcommittee Bill of Rights in 1973. Younger members in the House used subcommittee seats to strengthen their standing, although the Senate did not experience a comparable rise of subcommittee power.[150] The Watergate Babies took advantage of the high turnover to acquire subcommittee seats. In 1981, 41 of 44 Watergate Babies who were still in the House either chaired a subcommittee or chaired one of the major full committees. Proposals to halt the subcommittee trend failed. Party leadership positions did not centralize power as expected, since both parties spread the number of slots available to members in order to be more inclusive and quell further rebellions.[151] The leadership was forced to include a broader portion of the rank and file on almost every decision.[152]

The dispersion of policy information was another tangible sign of the fragmenting forces at work in the post–committee-era Congress. The policy research industry experienced dramatic growth in the 1970s. Realizing the centrality of expertise to success, the conservative movement helped spawn this expansion by founding new think tanks. Interest groups and trade associations also decided to establish research-producing entities to distribute information about their areas of interest. A growing number of journalists trained in professional graduate schools sought homes in specialized magazines, such as the *National Journal*. By the 1980s, legislators had access to an abundance of expert information to draw on in negotiation.[153]

Even though there were moments after 1975 when critics decried the return of "King Caucus," partisan discipline usually failed. Democrats could not have found a worse time to experiment with this new uncertain process, given the terrible relations that existed between President Carter and the leaders of the Democratic Congress as well as the divisions among northern Democrats. At the same time, Republicans were becoming more forceful in tying up legislation. The story about the frustrated Congress became a staple in the national press.[154]

### Abscam

The prevalence of scandal caused great concern among legislators. By the late 1970s, there was a vast institutional infrastructure in place devoted to the exposure of corruption. In addition to the organizations and individuals that remained from the reform coalition and the adversarial media, national intelligence agencies devoted more attention to domestic corruption and white-collar crime after J. Edgar Hoover died in 1972. Federal grand juries likewise investigated government corruption. The Racketeering Influenced and Corrupt Organization Act of 1970 expanded the power of prosecutors to attack not only organized crime but all sorts of white-collar activities, including public corruption. In addition, Congress revamped its oversight activity.[155] The congressional ethics committees and ethics codes could become a professional death trap for legislators involved in or accused of wrongdoing. Specialized public interest groups focused full time on documenting political corruption, as did the media. When improprieties took place, there was thus a thick network prepared to expose these activities. From 1970 to 1979, there were 36 representatives and senators found guilty of breaking the law or the rules of Congress, compared with 13 in the preceding 25 years.[156] William Hughes (D-NJ), who supported institutional reform, admitted that "public officials are already convicted before they are tried."[157] A few journalists warned they were carrying scandal journalism too far,[158] but most moved full steam ahead.

Koreagate had shown that scandal and institutional reform were drifting apart. The "Abscam" scandal symbolized to many observers that the pursuit of corruption had reached dangerous extremes, so much that it stimulated support for reforming the organizations conducting the investigation.[159] The scandal was driven by all the institutional forces that had been created to institutionalize the pursuit of corruption in the postcommittee era. Abscam stemmed from the Department of Justice's new determination to tackle white-collar crime and government corruption under FBI Director William Webster. The investigation in June 1978 started as a sting operation involving stolen art objects and organized crime. The "sting" technique, which the FBI had previously used for high-profile espionage investigations, became routine.[160] The Supreme Court had granted lawmaking authorities broad discretion in these operations in 1973. FBI agents worked with their informant Mel Weinberg, a shady con artist who faced a possible prison sentence for various swindles. In the fall of 1978, the investigation expanded into political corruption in New Jersey. The expansion resulted from claims by informants. The third phase lasted from July 1979 to January 1980 as the FBI focused on congressional corruption. FBI agents dressed as Arab sheiks and attempted to bribe legislators on tape. The last phase of the operation was different from a traditional sting because the FBI did not wait passively for suspects but encouraged them to come forward through middlemen. Moreover, the targets were picked by the middlemen rather than by investigators on the basis of hard evidence of criminal behavior.

In February 1980, the media reported that the FBI had surveillance tape of one Republican and six Democratic legislators accepting bribes from agents who were dressed as sheiks. Federal grand juries indicted Representatives Michael Myers (D-PA), Richard Kelly (R-FL), Raymond Lederer (D-PA), John Murphy (D-NY), Frank Thompson (D-NJ), and John Jenrette (D-SC) as well as Senator Harrison Williams (D-NJ). Williams, Thompson, and Murphy were chairing committees. Common Cause said that "Representatives and Senators have an obligation to adhere to and enforce higher standards of ethical behavior than those defined by criminal statutes."[161]

The story hit the airwaves through television. Brian Ross of the NBC news bureau and field producer Ira Silverman had been tipped off about the investigation by FBI sources. NBC news officials stationed vans with tinted windows and night-vision lenses near the Washington home where some of the stings were conducted. The crews obtained footage of suspicious individuals entering and leaving the home. NBC also secretly taped the FBI coming to the homes of the legislators to inform them of the operation and tapes.[162] NBC's Jane Pauley went on the air on a Saturday-night news magazine show to break the story to viewers before the other networks knew about it. As undercover images showed politicians walking into the homes of FBI agents, NBC reporter Brian Ross said that investigators were calling this the "most important investigation of political corruption since Watergate."[163]

Abscam fit in the age of television because it was a visual scandal. As the jurors heard evidence about the case in a Brooklyn courthouse, the media obtained copies of the video tapes. Reporters published excerpts of the tapes while the case was going on.[164] Federal District Judge George Pratt allowed the networks to broadcast the tapes, although he granted a temporary stay in order to allow for an appeal of the decision. Pratt rejected claims by the defendants that they were not being treated properly or that the FBI had conducted an unethical investigation. Myers and his co-defendants complained that playing the tapes would prevent a fair trial. The U.S. Court of Appeals for the Second Circuit agreed with Pratt's decision and also granted a temporary stay. Upon reviewing the case, the Supreme Court unanimously refused to grant a stay and the existing order expired. On October 14, all three networks broadcast clips of the Mike Myers tapes before jurors had viewed the material.[165] The networks showed edited portions of the tapes with reporters providing the context. One incriminating clip revealed Myers taking an envelope with $50,000 from the agent while another had the representative saying that "money talks" in Washington. The tapes, wrote television critic Tom Shales, "had the photographic quality of a porno reel from the '50s, and one felt a similarly naughty voyeuristic fascination watching it."[166]

On August 30, 1980, Mike Myers was convicted of bribery, conspiracy, and racketeering. Although the congressmen admitted taking the money, they insisted that they had promised nothing in return. The most controversial case involved Williams: he was convicted on May 1, 1981, on nine counts of bribery and conspiracy, fined $50,000, and sentenced to three years at a federal prison in Pennsylvania; he resigned on March 11, 1982, when it became clear that the Senate was prepared to expel him. The tapes of Williams showed the senator first rejecting the bribe. The agent then encouraged him to accept shares of stock in a titanium mine for helping obtain government contracts. Williams unsuccessfully filed a civil suit against the Justice Department. The popular liberal senator claimed that the investigation had been motivated by political concerns. Williams was the fourth sitting senator in American history to be convicted on criminal charges.

Abscam triggered a fierce backlash from politicians, civil liberties organizations, and the media. The forces behind the investigation had become as much of a concern as the subjects who were being investigated. Critics accused the FBI of entrapping random legislators through a manufactured crime. As the trials

Senator Harrison Williams (D-NJ), an ardent northern liberal who was brought down in the Abscam scandal (Senate Historical Office).

were in progress, Congress held hearings into the conduct of the FBI. Editors of the *Washington Post* said that there were two kinds of corruption in this case and one was the "FBI's campaign of character assassination itself, an abuse of the police power that, in the scale of things, we would regard as probably more dangerous to people's well being than the money-corruption being charged."[167] The ACLU warned that this operation constituted a gross violation of civil liberties and called for legislation to restrict the FBI's undercover operations.[168] Many individuals were angry that the media played the video tapes during the trials, thereby undermining a fair proceeding. Attorney General Benjamin Civiletti would discipline a U.S. attorney and five FBI agents for releasing information prematurely.

Following an Ethics Committee investigation, the House expelled Myers on October 2, 1980, by a vote of 376 to 30. This was the first time the House had taken such action since 1861. Several colleagues felt that the Ethics Committee should have considered whether the FBI acted improperly. Moreover, they felt that the expulsion should not be handled in such a rushed fashion. Since it came on the day that session ended, it could appear that legislators were too eager to have an issue to take home to constituents rather than thoroughly considering the case. Myers apologized for putting the House in this position but insisted that he was "set up from the word 'go'."[169] Notwithstanding these procedural complaints, only thirty members voted against expelling Myers. The other accused legislators, except for Lederer and Williams, lost reelection in November in large part because of Abscam. In South Carolina, John Napier did not mention Abscam in his campaign against John Jenrette only because polls showed that voters were already well aware of the details.[170] Lederer resigned in May 1981, while Williams fought the charges. Myers, Murphy, Lederer, and Thompson were all required to serve prison terms.

The Senate weighed whether to expel or censure Senator Williams in March 1982. When liberal stalwarts such as Senators Thomas Eagleton (D-MO) and Leahy came out in favor of the more stringent punishment of expulsion, the senator's fate was sealed. During one of the most climactic moments of this entire saga, Eagleton said on the floor that Williams was a "knowing participant in this sleazy enterprise." Eagleton asked his colleagues: "would any of you have engaged in this tawdry, greedy enterprise? If your silent answer of inner conscience is in the affirmative, then do your soul a favor by serving out your term and passively fade into deserved oblivion."[171] Williams resigned in March 1982. Upon his departure, Williams continued to insist that the investigation was unfair and there was no evidence of his wrongdoing. Yet realizing that the Senate was prepared to take this dramatic action, Williams left. Before doing so, he said he was "completely innocent of all crime or impropriety" and warned that the constitutional barriers between the executive and legislative branches had been "shattered" by the FBI.[172]

### Working in a New Congress

The modern congressional era had thus started to take form by the early 1980s. The new process could be dynamic, porous, and volatile. While the reforms had created mechanisms for centralized parties to become more assertive than in the 1950s, they had simultaneously ensured that there would be no return to the days of Speaker Cannon in the early 1900s, when party leaders could be tyrannical.

Fragmented and decentralized governance – where strong subcommittees, caucuses, and mavericks could wield significant influence – had been institutionalized at the same time that congressional parties were strengthened. This made things difficult for Democrats. Although they controlled Congress until 1980, they found that internal divisions were making it challenging to legislate. New divisions among northerners, rather than ideological unity, had replaced the party's old regional split. A cadre of young Republicans, moreover, started to make use of the new procedural tools to stifle business. The reconstructed process offered numerous avenues for these types of battles.

The difficulties that the fragmenting components of the modern process posed became evident immediately. All proposals seemed to suffer under these conditions, including further attempts at institutional reform. The fading status of reform could be observed from the fact that scandals, which were becoming more common and ensnaring powerful members, were rarely linked to institutional reform. Nor were there any signs that, despite all the changes that had occurred, citizens felt better about Congress as a representative body. The combination of continued popular frustration, fading reform, and the difficulties of the new process hinted that Congress would have a precarious role in civic life.

# Congress in the Age of Cable Television

On March 19, 1979, representatives entered the House in the same fashion as they did on every other day. But something was different. Television cameras were present to broadcast the deliberations. Albert Gore, Jr., a baby boomer who had worked as a reporter before being elected to the House in 1976, took to the floor to praise the "marriage of the medium and our open debate." Almost two decades after his father had waged war against southern conservatives, Gore was the first member to speak before the cameras. The Tennessean promised that television would "change this institution ... the good will far outweigh the bad." Assuring viewers that there would be "no censorship," Gore predicted that television would "revitalize representative democracy."[1] During the evening news the networks showed video clips of Gore. Public television broadcast live all afternoon. Barely noticed at the time, the most significant presence was the Cable Satellite Public Affairs Network (C-SPAN), which broadcast the entire day.

Congress had opened its doors to the media right as the news industry was undergoing a second round of wrenching changes. The first big shift in the media had taken place in the 1960s with the journalistic embrace of an adversarial outlook; the second change occurred between the late 1970s and late 1980s with the success of cable television. When the House agreed to televise floor proceedings in 1978, the news industry was still dominated by the three commercial networks. By the time that the Senate televised its proceedings in 1986, cable had become a formidable industry. Suddenly, there were stations with unlimited time to cover politics and more outlets where legislators could appear. Through C-SPAN, legislators communicated instantly to political actors and constituents with minimal journalistic interference. The Cable News Network introduced a continuous, 24-hour news cycle that made it more difficult to react to or control the flow of information. The network news and national papers changed to meet the competition.

Legislators could not ignore the nature of television, even though some studies found that national stories about Congress as an institution declined after 1979.[2] Foremost, legislators had to be prepared for when they were unexpectedly pushed into the spotlight. Second, legislators frequently went on television to discuss questions that involved other branches of government. The breakdown of the committee system meant that there were a greater number of legislators eager to speak with reporters. More legislators wanted to gain attention to promote their individual area of policy specialization or their subcommittees, and fewer were hesitant to challenge committee or party leaders. In the absence of norms that discouraged average members from speaking, reporters understood that they would often find politicians eager for attention should they seek them out. Party officials, whom reporters were most interested in, no longer felt intimidated by the senior committee chairs who guarded information and discouraged public debate. Third, party leaders now considered television to be central, as the rank and file of each party expected telegenic leaders in the age of greater access to the medium.[3] There were members of Congress who believed that television was one of the most effective tools for communicating to policy networks that focused on specific issues.[4] All legislators were familiar with television since it had become increasingly crucial to campaigns, as locally based parties atrophied with the triumph of Washington-based partisanship.[5] Fourth, local television, which granted significant airtime to legislators, exhibited similar stylistic trends. Finally, many legislators who entered Congress after the 1970s believed in – even if they overestimated – the importance of television.[6]

Although it had already entered a new era by the late 1970s, Congress did not stagnate. As with the Supreme Court redistricting decisions and the rise of adversarial journalism, changes to the institutions surrounding Congress (in this case, the media) defined the character of the new legislative era. In the late 1970s and early 1980s, the television industry experienced a profound transformation revolving around technology that complemented the tendency of the new legislative environment to foster competing centers of power. One example of this was that cable-era television journalism assisted party leaders in promoting their agenda but, at the same time, offered individual legislators who disagreed with their party an equally potent forum. By empowering parties *and* mavericks, cable-era journalism created a check on both of them simultaneously.

Along with the reconstructed legislative process, the institutionalization of public interest groups, and adversarial journalism, the modern news industry constituted another formidable political force that could be hostile and destructive to legislators. The shift toward adversarial journalism started with the transformed ethics of the 1960s, but the advancing technology of the television industry in the 1980s accelerated and supported these trends. The proliferation of news shows, the expansion of the amount of time that needed to be filled, and the heightened competition for viewers all meant that broadcasters were scrambling for salacious stories about politicians that could garner high ratings. The adversarial media was all that much more difficult for politicians to handle with an ongoing 24-hour news cycle, where legislators had only seconds to react to news frenzies. As the lines between politics and news blurred in the 1980s and 1990s, interviews were conducted and analyses offered by individuals who had explicit political objectives. In short, the control of information was difficult for politicians after the 1970s owing to the speed of news dissemination, the expansion of outlets producing shows, and the type of individuals on the air.

Republican legislators from the conservative movement were among the first to take advantage of cable-era television. As with many of the institutional reforms that they had been so instrumental in passing, liberals in the reform coalition discovered that they could not contain the political uses of the new legislative process. Young conservative Republicans turned to cable news to gain instant attention and circumvent the hierarchies that remained in the chambers, including the authority of party leaders. Like liberal Democrats in the 1950s, this cohort was called "bomb-throwers." Unlike Humphrey and Bolling, however, they relied on the existing congressional process rather than fighting for a new one.

### Cable Television Arrives

Cable television finally succeeded in the 1980s because of technological and regulatory innovations. The path to success had been arduous. The networks had monopolized television news for several decades, assisted by costly technologies and anticompetitive government regulations. But deregulation in the 1970s favored cable television, and technological innovation made it nearly impossible to prevent its growth.

When television surpassed newspapers in the 1960s as the primary source of news for most Americans, the network system became the vehicle through which most citizens learned about national politics.[7] Between 1963 and 1980, CBS, ABC, and NBC dominated television news. CBS and NBC expanded the nightly news in 1963 from fifteen minutes to a half hour; ABC did the same in 1967. As commercial entities, however, there were limits to how much networks would show because executives did not want to interrupt lucrative entertainment programs.[8] This bias had been clear back in 1966 when Senator Fulbright conducted hearings about the Vietnam conflict. During the first week, all three networks played excerpts from the hearings. After watching the initial testimony, the head of CBS News Fred Friendly concluded that the public should see this historic debate. Friendly urged his network to cover the hearings live on the morning that a prominent administration official was to appear. NBC had already preempted its regular morning schedule. In the initial plan to cover a half-hour, the only show CBS would have to cancel was the children's program "Captain Kangaroo." CBS executives were concerned because they had double the morning audience of NBC and also had a sold-out advertising schedule. Regardless, CBS President Frank Stanton authorized a half-hour in the morning to show the testimony. To cover the relevant portion of the hearing when it extended beyond half an hour, the network cancelled the profitable sitcom reruns of "I Love Lucy," "The McCoys," and "The Dick Van Dyke Daytime Show."[9] In the afternoon the station preempted its lucrative daytime soap operas and game shows. Although they consented to cover several other testimonies, CBS executives called Friendly every night to remind him how much each minute cost. Fearful about the impact of these hearings on public opinion, President Johnson called Stanton and insisted that the station take them off the air.[10] When Friendly requested coverage of diplomat George Kennan, vice-president of broadcasting John Schneider refused on the grounds that housewives were not interested. Friendly resigned. Other than the nightly broadcasts or the rare coverage of live events, there were only a few national news shows – including the Sunday-morning talk shows and the news magazine "60 Minutes."

During the network era, legislators therefore had confronted a news environment where only a limited amount of information about government ever reached the air, given the sparse amount of time devoted to news programs and because there were only a few shows available to American viewers. The television news cycle was also relatively slow in the network era, thereby granting elected officials a significant amount of time during the day to respond to emerging information. Until the 1980s, the television news cycle revolved around half-hour broadcasts in the evening at 7:00. In the morning, the news division met to discuss stories in the newspapers. Executives, anchors, and producers debated which stories should be highlighted. The executive producer (with the tacit approval of the anchor) would contact the bureaus to develop the pieces that he had decided to run. By 3:30 P.M., the producers were informed about how the segments were developing, and the executive producer released a list at 4:00 P.M. that included the stories for the evening. The anchor had to approve the final decision. The deadline for final changes was 5:30 P.M. The networks used the remaining ninety minutes for editing and preparation. Late-breaking stories could be inserted, but only for major events.[11] During the show, the anchor read the stories with related images next to his head. Several times the show cut to taped stories, and toward the end of the 1960s the networks introduced short commentary sections.

The network monopoly over news and the structure of its news cycle was relatively secure until the 1980s. Local stations across the country received the network's shows through expensive land lines that were owned by the telephone monopoly AT&T. The networks were granted a steep discount from AT&T that was not offered to small competitors. Furthermore, when cable systems first attempted to broadcast original programming during the 1960s, the FCC protected the networks by implementing anticompetitive regulations that hampered the new industry. Since 1960, AT&T had leveraged its lobbying muscle to block the widespread use of domestic satellites or microwave broadcasting.[12]

But conditions had started to change in 1974. The fate of broadcasting was part of a broader deregulation policy revolution. Although regulatory arrangements benefitted many powerful economic interests, the system lost out in the 1970s to an alliance between conservative proponents of economic deregulation and public interest liberals who felt that corporations had captured regulatory commissions to the detriment of consumers.[13] The government greatly eased its restrictive regulations on cable.[14] Toward the end of his administration, Nixon consented to the advice of the White House Office of Technological Policy to promote competition in television. The FCC weakened the regulations that favored networks. In 1974 and 1975, Western Union and RCA sent domestic satellites into space. By purchasing access to these satellites, independent stations could transmit programming to cable systems for an affordable price.

The expansion of cable television took place at a furious pace over the next two decades. In 1979, cable reached one fifth of the national television audience; this amounted to approximately 14.5 million homes.[15] By 1981, cable subscribers were signing up at a rate of 250,000 per month and nearly 30 percent of U.S. households subscribed to a system.[16] In 1987, two thirds of the population had access, as cable television reached over 39 million homes.[17] Meanwhile, satellite-based stations specialized in programming such as premium movies, sports, and rock music. Unlike the networks, these stations targeted narrow segments of viewers.

## C-SPAN

Between 1979 and 1986, C-SPAN became the window through which Americans could observe Congress.[18] For legislators this station became a valuable communication tool. Like many economic innovations, entrepreneurs were a driving force in the development of cable. The person at the center of C-SPAN's creation was Brian Lamb, a midwestern independent who believed passionately in public affairs. Born in 1941, Lamb was raised by a middle-class family in Indiana. Growing up in Lafayette, Lamb fell in love with radio while working as a local disc jockey. Although he expressed little appreciation for the medium, Lamb hosted a television dance program in college.

Upon graduating from high school, Lamb attended Purdue University. Thereafter, he joined the Navy in 1964. During his last two years in the service, the Navy stationed Lamb in the Pentagon as a public affairs officer, and he briefly worked as a social aide in President Lyndon Johnson's White House. He spent much of his free time observing political events in Washington. For instance, at the court trial of Bobby Baker, Lamb was struck by how corrupt Baker looked in person. Lamb regularly sat in the visitor galleries of the House, Senate, and Supreme Court. Meanwhile, he developed an aversion to commercial news for distorting events.

Lamb returned to Washington to work as a freelance reporter for United Press International and then as press secretary for Senator Peter Dominick. Under Dominick, Lamb discovered how difficult it was for the average legislator to gain media attention. His next job brought him to the White House Office of Telecommunications Policy, where Lamb handled press relations and developed an intellectual passion for telecommunications policy. Together with director Clay Whitehead, he promoted market competition for television.

By the time Lamb left the Nixon administration, he had decided to work for the cable industry. While writing for the trade publication *Cablevision,* Lamb conceived of a financially independent cable station that was devoted exclusively to public affairs. When Home Box Office went on the air in 1975 via satellite, as did a group of local "superstations," Lamb concluded that cable could do the same for public affairs programming.

During the next few years, Lamb promoted his ideas to cable operators and legislators – including Speaker O'Neill, who saw the station as a method for circumventing the networks while satisfying reformers. Cable operators were cool to the proposal since they would have to finance it. Lamb rejected advertising or government funds. Emphasizing that a public affairs station would strengthen the image of this nascent industry, Lamb secured the backing of 22 operators. The argument especially appealed to Bob Schmidt, president of the National Cable Television Association, and his chief lobbyist Tom Wheeler, who adopted the public service argument as a lobbying tool.

C-SPAN broadcast Congress in a style that was different from network news. Building on Lamb's critique of mainstream journalism, the station eliminated personalities. For most of the day, viewers watched legislators debate on the floor or meet in committee without intervening commentary. Politicians were able to speak for long periods of time unedited by producers. Yet C-SPAN officials could not completely avoid interjecting themselves, especially after they extended their coverage from 8 to 16 hours a day in April 1982 and then to 24 hours in September. Lamb acknowledged that editorial decisions were made when the station's producers decided which hearings and debates to cover. From the day that C-SPAN went on the air, networks attacked the venture on the grounds that the House was controlling the cameras. The vice-president of NBC News said this was "quite literally the House covering itself."[19]

Notwithstanding its low-key approach, C-SPAN had to survive a series of heated controversies. At every turn, North Carolina Democrat Charles Rose made things difficult. Fortunately for the station, Gary Hymel (O'Neill's top staffer) warded off Rose's worst attacks.[20] There was also a bitter partisan fight in 1982 over the use of video clips from C-SPAN in elections. Although the House agreed in 1979 that incumbents would not be able to use video clips in campaign advertisements, challengers had been exempted. In 1982, House Republican Minority Leader Robert Michel's (R-IL) Democratic opponent used a short video clip from C-SPAN in a television ad. Michel was livid. The incident exploded into a full-scale war, as both parties amassed video libraries for future campaigns. Reacting to news about the libraries, Republican Whip Trent Lott (R-MS) quipped: "They're hollering now, because they realize they're fixing to get caught in their own device. But when you do something like that to a guy like Bob Michel, you're going to pay."[21] Democrats proposed a formal rule to punish challengers who used C-SPAN tapes. House Republicans, on the other hand, opposed such rules as censorship.[22] Chair of the Democratic Congressional Campaign Committee Anthony Coelho (D-CA) responded that, without stronger rules, incumbents would be encouraged to make only self-serving statements on the floor.[23] Yet Coelho warned that "if attacked first, we will respond and we will be able to do so effectively."[24] The stalemate ended with a tentative agreement that neither party would use video clips from C-SPAN, and they would discourage challengers from doing so.

The most dramatic controversy centered on Newt Gingrich, a former history professor elected to the House in 1978. One of his first tangible organizational achievements was to found the Conservative Opportunity Society (COS), a group of young Republican mavericks who were tied to the grassroots conservative movement that helped elect President Reagan. COS believed that, for the conservative movement to establish a secure foothold in national politics, they needed to master the new legislative process. The House Republican leadership referred to this group as "Gingrich Guerillas."[25] They were seen by the leadership as especially useful at building grassroots support for the party – as opposed to working the floor and swaying potential Democratic allies.[26]

The reconstructed institutions that emerged from the 1970s became the battleground where the conservative movement scored some of its biggest victories. Legislators affiliated with COS were among the first to benefit from the new process. Frustrated with moderate Republicans, Gingrich was a cocky politician with a natural flair for the camera. Born in 1943, he felt that "television is the dominant medium of our society ... the guys and gals in Congress who don't master it get killed."[27] While working as a professor, Gingrich had been impressed upon reading how Speaker Rayburn had banned television cameras in order to strengthen the leadership. Gingrich concluded that reversing Rayburn's practice would empower individuals such as himself.[28] Gingrich charged that Democrats were "ruthlessly partisan in changing the rules of the House, stacking committees, apportioning staff and questioning the administration."[29] Using the components of the reconstructed legislative process that favored minorities and mavericks, younger Republicans depicted those aspects of legislative procedure that favored majority rule as a tool of corrupt Democrats. Tying together several components of the process, Richard Cheney (R-WY) argued that "the apportionment of legislative districts, PAC financing, and other incumbency advantages help to explain why the signs of a Republican electoral realignment are not being reflected in House elections."[30]

Television was a potent weapon in the COS strategy. Gingrich believed that television coverage was integral to reaching out to young voters who were not tied to the Democrats.[31] Focusing on the network evening news and Sunday-morning talk shows, Gingrich sent every Republican a detailed analysis of twelve television interview shows in 1982 revealing how polished Democrats were in their appearances. He highlighted their discipline in using common themes and effective rhetoric. For example, Gingrich pointed out that, when asked embarrassing questions on television, Democrats "stick [to] their strategy and themes and keep repeating them no matter what the question is or how many times the question is repeated. The Republicans answer the question no matter how much damage their answer does to our side." Another problem that Gingrich targeted was that Republicans were bipartisan about giving credit in television interviews, while

Democrats were partisan in terms of assigning blame. Republicans, Gingrich argued, had no media plan equivalent to that of their adversaries:

Today we [the GOP] are losing the battle for the loyalty of the American people because we have no strategy, no themes, no slogans. We hope that money will make up for these failures.... A political party which focuses on the management and allocation of campaign resources, and neglects political strategy, is a party that loses. Two minutes on the evening news is watched by more people, believed by more of them, and politically, has a greater multiplier effect than paid political advertising.

To win back a majority of the House, Gingrich argued that Republicans needed to realize the urgency of learning what he called the "art of governing," which meant combining the art of passing legislation with the art of winning elections. Many Republicans, he said, were skilled legislative negotiators or ran successful campaigns, but few linked the two.

Gingrich wanted Republicans to be more conscious of the electoral implications of the bills they supported (or opposed) and to thoroughly politicize every decision.[32] He told Robert Michel that, in his mind, Republicans had lost the public relations war over the 1981 budget because Democrats were able to characterize them as having passed a bill that benefitted only the rich.[33] Based on reports from trusted pollsters, Republican leaders were afraid that they were suffering from a widespread public perception that they did not care about the "common people," female voters did not feel that there was a home for them in the party, and Reagan was seen as out of touch with the millions of unemployed.[34] Younger Republicans called on their party to embrace an aggressive approach that centered on a refined communications and media strategy. "The electronic media is where it's at today," concluded Trent Lott.[35]

In order to improve how Republicans came across to voters during their television appearances, Gingrich suggested that the national party should provide legislators with research and the skills of top political strategists before they appeared on news or talk shows; he also wanted the party to notify candidates and leaders across the country about someone who was going to appear on a show. Gingrich added: "After the show, the guest should spend an hour debriefing with the strategists, finding out what went right and what went wrong. This critique should be capsulized ... before his next appearance on T.V." Gingrich concluded by telling colleagues: "we shouldn't be surprised that our spokesmen perform on T.V. about as well as an amateur football team would perform in the Super Bowl."[36] In addition, Gingrich implored Republican leaders to designate a public spokesman for the party and to create a "leadership idea clearinghouse" to foster and refine the ideas of the party.[37] Although House leaders agreed with most of Gingrich's assessment and did develop a media strategy,[38] there were severe tensions with COS. Robert Michel's office thought that Gingrich's cohort was impossible to work with. The leadership complained that Gingrich's team did not follow through on their ideas and that their proposals aimed to wrest power from the *Republican* leadership. In the mid-1980s, House

Republican leaders were still insisting on separating the communications strategy from the internal legislative strategy for fear of crippling their effectiveness in the chamber.[39]

Most of Gingrich's initial plans in 1982 centered on the network news, since at that time cable television was only emerging as a presence. Yet C-SPAN turned out to be a political boon for COS. Gingrich felt that, since C-SPAN lacked any journalistic analysis, it offered a more hospitable forum than the "elite" networks, which leaned toward establishment Democrats and Republicans. Conservatives were not the only ones who felt this way. Ralph Nader liked the station because it allowed nonmainstream organizations such as his consumer advocacy groups to make fuller statements to the public: "people like us are now on C-SPAN every once in a while," he said, "we're shut out from the network news.... It's not only different in degree, it's different in kind, because you can't really speak the language edited into four- or five-second sound bites on the evening news.... On C-SPAN you can actually talk in sentences, paragraphs, back and forth, so it is not just a difference in degree, it's a difference in kind."[40]

Through C-SPAN, conservative mavericks took their message directly to constituents. In 1983 and 1984, Gingrich, John Vincent Weber (R-MN), and Robert Walker (R-PA) used the one-minute speeches at the start of each day and the longer "Special Order" speeches in the evening hours to attack Democrats. The number of one-minute speeches increased from 110 in March 1977 to 344 by March 1981.[41] COS met at the start of the week, and sometimes informally at the end of the day, to select issues that could be used against Democrats. David Obey warned in 1983 that these kinds of speeches "will poison the national dialogue and cripple democratic debate."[42]

Although members of COS were perceived to be mavericks, there were signs that more established Republicans were hearing their message after the crushing defeats in the 1982 elections. The press secretary for Robert Michel, for instance, agreed that the House GOP needed to work harder to define their agenda and sell issues to the public, even when this meant separating from the White House.[43] Republican leaders in 1983 embarked on an all-out partisan assault on Democrats by making one-minute speeches, writing op-ed pieces, and blitzing the rest of the press.[44] Despite their misgivings about Gingrich, Michel's staff was regularly meeting with COS about a campaign to highlight how Democrats abused their power.[45] When Gingrich's allies launched their televised attacks, COS was pursuing a strategy that Republican leaders had begun (grudgingly) to accept.

On May 8, 1984, COS used their C-SPAN speeches to hammer away at Democrats for a weak record on fighting communism. Republicans asked the accused Democrats to respond to the charges. Since the cameras only showed the person speaking, viewers were unaware that the Republicans were talking to an empty chamber. Thus it looked on television as if the Democrats had no reply when in fact they were not even present. Democrats were furious with these practices. Obey compared Gingrich to Joe McCarthy.[46] When Gingrich made a speech about O'Neill's close friend and Washington roommate, Edward Boland (D-MA), the Speaker exploded. Furious with COS, O'Neill ordered camera operators to pan across the empty chamber as Robert Walker spoke. This constituted a fundamental break from the 1978 agreement that cameras would show only the person speaking. Walker had no idea that viewers were seeing an empty chamber as he continued to pretend that the House was full – until Minority Whip Trent Lott dashed onto the floor to inform him. The next day O'Neill took to the floor to condemn Gingrich's attack as the "lowest thing" that he had seen in Congress. Democrats and Republicans yelled at each other in front of the cameras. Republicans charged that O'Neill had violated the rules of decorum. In an embarrassing move for the Speaker, his comments were stricken from the *Congressional Record*. At a press conference O'Neill called the whole thing a "sham" and said that what they were doing was "very political and extremely unfair."[47]

The Republicans launched television commercials that attacked O'Neill as a czar who disregarded House rules. Richard Cheney charged that O'Neill's "repeated attacks on the personal rather than policy or political levels are damaging the House as an institution" and were poisoning politics.[48] New York's Jack Kemp wrote Republicans that O'Neill had "altered procedure and tried to use the televising of the House to embarrass the Republicans."[49] Although O'Neill insisted that COS was using unfair tactics, observers believed that the young Republicans came away victorious. The controversy changed the perception within Washington of COS from "wild young guys to serious partisan contenders," according to Gingrich.[50] Later that summer Gingrich turned down an invitation for an interview with CBS news anchor Dan Rather and explained: "I owe C-SPAN. I don't owe CBS."[51]

For C-SPAN the controversy was beneficial. Even though "Camscam" confirmed the fears that legislators and Lamb had about television, the story made its way into the mainstream media.[52] Suddenly network reporters and viewers took notice of the station. Ironically, the media's love of scandal worked in Lamb's favor. By withstanding each controversy, C-SPAN entrenched itself into the fabric of Congress.

The next battleground for C-SPAN was the Senate, which still did not broadcast most of its proceedings. Majority Leader Howard Baker urged the Senate to televise floor debate. Like many colleagues, he believed that television was inevitable. Baker reiterated the familiar arguments of television proponents: that it would improve the public image of the Senate and break the "cocoon-like atmosphere" that gripped Washington.[53] Baker was able to point out that the House was more visible on television than the Senate. Since this debate took place after C-SPAN was operational, senators were more confident that networks would not control the broadcast. Baker told reporters that the "quality of the legislative product" had improved in the House with television.[54] Referring to C-SPAN, Baker wrote: "Early fears that members would be intimidated or bedazzled by the television cameras in their midst have by and large been proven groundless.

Shownmanship has not run amok in the House, nor have its members run off in droves to sign up for acting or elocution lessons."[55] This was an argument repeated by many supporters of the channel.[56] Moreover, technology had also solved a problem of covering legislators in a chamber where members spoke from their seats (unlike in the House, where they spoke from one of eight places). The new technology allowed for head and shoulder shots, without cameras panning an "empty chamber."[57]

But until 1984 there were enough opponents behind Russell Long to filibuster Baker's proposal. Long warned that television would result in senators playing for the camera.[58] In 1984, his allies pointed to Camscam as evidence. John Danforth (R-MO), one of Long's staunchest supporters, said that "television creates the news.... We do things in order to get on television."[59]

In 1985, Long announced that he would not seek reelection. Minority Leader Robert Byrd, once an opponent of broadcasts, concluded that television was necessary for the chamber to retain equal standing with the House.[60] The Senate moved toward a compromise by agreeing that the chamber would control the cameras and that viewers would only be able to see the person speaking. On February 27, the Senate voted 67-21 to conduct a test period. On July 29, 1986, they voted 78-21 to retain broadcasting. C-SPAN established a second channel for the Senate. Almost a year later, Byrd told his colleagues that "C-SPAN viewers are mature enough to take us warts and all and ... we have survived that scrutiny."[61]

By the time the Senate authorized television, C-SPAN was seen in more than 16 million homes. Although the channel did not attract the highest ratings, viewers were very active politically. They tended to follow politics more closely than the average citizen, vote more regularly, and participate in politically oriented civic groups.[62] Legislators who were previously skeptical about television suddenly praised the station. In his memoirs O'Neill took credit for establishing the channel.[63] C-SPAN became standard viewing for politicians, reporters, staffers, and lobbyists. By 1997 there would only be 43 members remaining in the House who had served before C-SPAN started.[64]

For legislative staff, C-SPAN became a primary source of information – ranking third behind only the *Washington Post* and cable news stations. It was also a major source of information for monitoring Congress among political elites, including legislators, governors, newspaper editors, and lobbyists.[65] Complementing C-SPAN were the improved print journals that targeted these same elites. They included the *National Journal, Congressional Quarterly,* and *Roll Call.* National Public Radio, founded in 1970, provided additional news shows with information for politically active Americans and elites.

As with many reforms of the 1970s, expanding news outlets provided legislators with substantial information about proceedings and policies, thereby depriving committee chairs of any monopoly on knowledge. This democratization of information among legislators fit with the other reforms of the 1970s that had weakened the foundations of committee power. The diffusion of information likewise offered a check against party leaders – who were emerging as new sources of authority – since they could not keep crucial information locked away from rank-and-file legislators as committee chairs had done in the previous era. In a business where knowledge was a form of capital used in negotiations and in framing issues, this transformation in the accessibility of information altered the congressional playing field.

## Cable News Network

The Cable News Network introduced a continuous and live television news cycle. The medium could serve as a strategic tool for attacking opponents; however, given the difficulty of controlling information, it was also a network that politicians had to monitor constantly and react to. The entrepreneur at the heart of CNN could not have been more different from Brian Lamb. Robert "Ted" Turner III was brash, boisterous, and always visible. For different reasons, Turner and Lamb shattered the network news monopoly and redefined the presentation of political information. Although the history of CNN did not center on Congress, its significance to the institution would be equally important since it reconfigured the length and speed of the news cycle.

Born on November 19, 1938, Turner experienced a rough childhood. His demanding father, who owned a billboard business, moved his family from Cincinnati to Savannah when his son was 9. Turner's parents sent him to the Georgia Military Academy, where he earned a reputation as a brawler. After being expelled from Brown University, Turner entered the family billboard business. But his divorced and alcoholic father became depressed and committed suicide when Ted was only 24. Turner transformed the indebted family business into a profit maker. He then sold the company in 1970 and invested all proceeds into a small Atlanta television station that broadcast on the weak UHF frequency.

Satellite technology elicited the same reaction from Turner as it did from Brian Lamb. When HBO went on the air in 1975, Turner decided that he would use satellites to make his station national at a cheap price. By 1982 the station reached 20 million homes in 48 states, earning $18 million in profit.[66] While Turner was building WTBS into a commercial success, the second key player in this story – Reese Schonfeld – was fighting the network news monopoly. Schonfeld had been educated at Dartmouth and Columbia. He was a physically imposing figure with a strong temper. A long-time critic of the networks, Schonfeld held several positions in his 20s and 30s with companies that competed with the network news. Schonfeld and his employer Burt Reinhardt even attempted to legally force AT&T to provide lower rates to nonnetwork stations. They were unsuccessful. In 1974 Schonfeld moved to Colorado, where he worked for Television News Incorporated, a syndication service that provided local stations with nonnetwork news stories produced from a politically conservative perspective. After Colorado, Schonfeld founded the Independent Television News Association. During these years, Schonfeld arranged meetings with representatives from various organizations to discuss the possibility of bringing a news station to cable television through satellite.

At this time, Turner was entertaining similar ideas. Turner lacked interest in the news but saw this as an unclaimed niche. He was thinking about a station that resembled the successful 24-hour news radio station in New York City, one that would broadcast a continuous cycle of half-hour news segments. When Turner became serious about the project, he teamed up with Schonfeld to have someone with news expertise.

Schonfeld and Turner believed that the style and format would distinguish the station. The biggest difference from the networks would be that the station would present the news live throughout the day. Although there would be increased risk of error, the ongoing schedule would allow them to make corrections almost immediately. Turner also wanted to broaden the types of stories that were covered, complaining that the networks "dwell on catastrophe – dictators assassinated, seagulls covered with oil, volcanoes erupting, charred bodies.... The only time they tell you what's going on in Washington is when some Senator has gotten caught with his hand in the till."[67]

Seeking professional credibility, Turner and Schonfeld recruited seasoned broadcasting veterans such as Daniel Schorr.[68] The duo also signed reputable executives such as NBC's Jim Kitchell and Burt Reinhardt from Paramount Pictures. Turner used hardball tactics when confronted with challenges. Shortly before CNN aired, the RCA satellite SATCOM III – through which they were to transmit their signal – was lost in space. When RCA informed Turner that they would not be able to carry his channel, Turner threatened to destroy them financially through the courts. Turner forced RCA into transmitting CNN through an older satellite by filing a multimillion-dollar lawsuit.

Following a year of intense planning, CNN went on the air on June 1, 1980, with six domestic bureaus, several foreign correspondents, and headquarters located in an antebellum mansion in Atlanta. The station offered unprecedented technological and editorial freedom to the producers at the bureaus to dictate what went on the air. Other than the senior executives from the networks, most of the production staff was composed of individuals in their 20s and 30s who were seeking to be part of a broadcasting experiment. Approximately 2 million homes received the station in 1980, and the figure increased to 4.3 million by the end of the year. Because of a limited number of cameramen, reporters, and news bureaus, CNN reached agreements with thirty independent local stations to provide them with footage.[69] The daily schedule was divided into thirty-minute segments with each focusing on different subject areas: sports, entertainment, business, politics, and more. Seeking to interest viewers other than news junkies, Turner wanted to replicate the format of magazines.[70] Headlines were shown every half-hour. The centerpiece was the two-hour evening news show. The station was always prepared to interrupt scheduled shows to report on live stories. The scheduling flexibility, combined with a rhythmic delivery of headlines, defined the station over the next two decades.

CNN established itself as a legitimate institution in the news industry. This was evident in June 1981, when ABC and Westinghouse Broadcasting launched their own cable news station: the Satellite News Channel. Rather than backing down, Turner responded with CNN-2, Headline News. Turner promised cable operators that he would not charge for CNN-2 if they subscribed to CNN. Moreover, he relied on his personal relationships with local cable operators to convince them to retain CNN. Beginning in January 1982, CNN-2 started playing half-hour news shows all day. ABC's station shut down after Turner bought it out for $25 million.[71] NBC unsuccessfully attempted to start a similar station in 1985.

By the mid-1980s, CNN had emerged from its status as a marginal station to one that was redefining news. According to one study conducted in the mid-1990s, congressional staffers ranked CNN in the first tier of media sources, along with the *Washington Post* and *Congressional Quarterly Weekly Report*, and ahead of the networks or the *New York Times*.[72] "The explosion of news is beginning to affect our story selection," said NBC anchor Tom Brokaw in 1983, "When people tune us in they may already have seen someone reporting from in front of the White House. So we have to think about doing something unique while still fulfilling our obligation to give them the news."[73]

Like Lamb, Turner played an important role in shaping legislative politics through his influence on the news, even though he had no part in the battles over congressional reform. As the networks started to abandon public affairs or mimic cable, CNN established the tone for the industry. For legislators the change meant having to deal with a 24-hour news cycle where information appeared instantly on the air. As a result of the cable news cycle, politicians had less time to respond to stories before the public saw them. Given that journalists had become so adversarial, this environment could be perilous.

### Journalism in the Cable Age

Except for C-SPAN, news about legislators was filtered through a journalistic lens. Like any professional community, journalists working in the era of television favored particular narrative strategies for interpreting events and also favored certain types of stories.[74] They also influenced the strategies that political actors chose in anticipation of how they would play on camera. Although the print media remained integral,[75] the news was then filtered through the lens of television (the print media, moreover, adjusted its own reporting and presentation to compete with television by mirroring the medium). It is important to remember that television was not solely responsible for the character of journalism in the 1980s. The shaping of the media was a multidimensional process with numerous factors at work, ranging from the legitimation of adversarial journalism to the evolving cultural environment within which stories were disseminated. But the adversarial tendencies of journalism – including the taste for scandal and conflict – were greatly amplified by television technology. Because of cable technology, moreover, the news business became much more dangerous to politicians owing to how quickly information hit the airwaves and also to the vast expansion in the number of shows that were reporting stories.[76]

Since its advent, three structural constraints have influenced the content of television news. The first was economic. As part of a medium devoted to entertainment, television news needed to present stories that could attract viewers. Producers competed for a fixed pool of viewers as well as for "inadvertent viewers" who were waiting for their entertainment shows.[77] Therefore, stories had to be visually appealing, they needed to revolve around colorful personalities and conflict, and they had to be easy to follow.[78] Second, television news faced legal regulations on what they could broadcast, such as the requirement to provide equal access for all candidates whose support reached a certain threshold. Journalists still recalled how the Nixon administration in the early 1970s had intimidated the networks through regulation.[79] The final constraint was time.[80] In the network era, the international and national news received only about 21 minutes of coverage per day. Producers needed issues that could be compressed into a one- or two-minute time frame; two-minute segments included a maximum of 250 words.[81] Even though cable expanded the amount of time that was available, most stories still received only a few minutes.

Given these constraints, dramatic conflict and scandal played well on television and garnered decent ratings. Like election campaigns and up-and-coming legislators, scandal was one of those items that the networks considered as "newsworthy" enough to capture public attention.[82] During the 1987 Iran-Contra hearings into whether President Reagan's administration had illegally sold arms to Iran, CNN's coverage received a 70-percent increase in audience against the shows they competed with. The networks preempted popular daytime soap operas to cover a portion of the hearings.[83] When a key witness testified, approximately 55 million viewers tuned in to see the debate on the networks. This was five times more than the audience for "General Hospital."[84] "The event is high drama," said Jeff Gralnick, vice-president and executive producer of special programming for the ABC news division, "this is a piece of historic theater that's being played out here. The key word is historic, but it is also theater."[85]

Politics and entertainment sometimes converged: NBC interrupted its regular programs to show the testimony of Fawn Hall, the attractive blond secretary of Lieutenant Oliver North. Although NBC insisted that they were covering Hall because she was an important player, most agreed that the station had ignored much bigger players.[86] The hearing's strongest competition was images of the married Democratic presidential candidate Gary Hart vacationing on a yacht with liquor bottles in the background and a young woman dressed only in a bikini.[87] After Hart stepped down from the presidential race because of the revelations, *Newsweek* captured the tenor of these years with a cover story entitled "Sex, Politics and the Press."[88]

Indeed, during the cable era, television journalists became more interested in and comfortable with discussing salacious sex scandals like Hart's. The troubles of Kennedy, Mills, and Hays had already weakened conventional taboos among journalists, although always on the grounds that the private behavior of these men influenced their public responsibilities. That tenuous link evaporated in the 1980s as the news media proved willing to examine sex scandals for their own sake. Throughout television, film, radio, and print, sex was presented more frequently and explicitly. Listeners could turn on the radio to hear Howard Stern discuss a celebrity guest's breast size. The boundaries of legitimate issues expanded as voyeuristic talk shows eroded the barrier that had separated entertainment from the "hard" news.[89] In 1991, NBC's "Expose" – one of the news magazines that the networks had created in response to heightened competition – broadcast an interview with a woman acknowledging that she had sexual relations with Virginia's Senator Charles Robb while he was governor. This broadcast (together with subsequent statements by Robb in response to the story) produced an explosion of investigative pieces about the Senator's past drug use and his sexual relationships. Those caught up in these scandals continued to find themselves at the center of media attention for a short time. According to *Time,* "It is hard to exaggerate the way people caught up in scandal, sensation or fragrant doings can parlay a puddle of notoriety into oceans of money plus exotic lifestyles. Culprits do it, victims do it, innocent bystanders do it."[90]

One of the most lurid congressional sex scandals began on June 30, 1982. The CBS "Evening News" broadcast a story featuring two young House pages whose faces were hidden by silhouette settings.[91] The male pages claimed to have had sexual relationships with congressmen in exchange for promises of promotion. They told the reporter that they had organized a homosexual prostitution ring for members. CBS had learned about this by hearing of an investigation that the FBI was conducting into the charges. As respected news outlets flocked to the story, the charges escalated to include cocaine use. When visiting their districts during the Fourth of July recess, legislators heard from angry constituents who were concerned about the stories: "The people were outraged," reported Bill Alexander (D-AR), "incensed and repulsed."[92] The interview triggered an unusually swift investigation by the House Ethics Committee after Speaker O'Neill said that he was "deeply disturbed by the allegations in the media."[93] Senate Majority Leader Howard Baker told reporters: "I never thought I'd see the day when I'd rather talk about abortion and gun control."[94] The committee was granted the same sweeping subpoena powers that had been used in previous investigations into Abscam and Koreagate.[95] Two pages made formal reports of sexual misconduct.

In addition to the committee, a House commission, the Justice Department's Public Integrity Section, and the FBI each conducted their own investigations; the Drug Enforcement Agency and the DC police looked into the charges of an alleged cocaine distribution ring on Capitol Hill (based on accusations by California Republican Robert Dornan). There were rumors from inside Congress that the accusations about the pages were based on highly questionable witnesses, but there were serious fears that substantial evidence existed regarding drug traffic among the staff in members' offices.[96] The inquiries took place only three months before the elections. But in December, the House Ethics Committee reported that most of the charges had been fabricated by pages who were searching for media attention. One of the pages admitted that he had lied about everything and failed a lie detector test. Joseph Califano, the former aide to President Johnson who headed the $400,000 congressional investigation, told reporters that "every one of the original highly publicized allegations of homosexuality made by these pages" had resulted from "out-and-out fabrication, overactive teenage imagination stimulated by a journalist, or teenage gossip."[97] The report was critical of CBS for how it handled the initial story; one page admitted to the investigators that CBS reporter John Ferrugia had given him leading questions about the scandal, asking him to confirm the information.[98]

Nonetheless, during the course of the investigation two legislators were discovered to have had sexual relationships with underage pages in previous years.[99] The House censured Gerry Studds (D-MA) in 1983 for having sex with a 17-year-old page ten years earlier as well as Daniel Crane (R-IL) for sleeping with a 17-year-old page in 1980. When the Ethics Committee originally recommended a milder reprimand, Gingrich called for the strictest punishment of expulsion. Robert Michel worked out a compromise of censure. Crane's constituents voted him out of office the next year although Studds was reelected. The House Ethics Committee would finish a sixteen-month investigation in 1983 that concluded they did not have enough evidence to prove allegations of drug use.

The television networks' appetite for scandal was fed by a generation of journalists who by the mid-1980s tended to convey negative opinions about Congress.[100] This was not surprising in that most reporters came from cosmopolitan, middle-class communities that had become alienated from mainstream institutions during the 1960s.[101] Political cynicism in the media also stemmed from the professional advances that journalists had made in the postwar period. By the 1980s, journalists were providing the public much more information about government, they were offering an interpretive context along with facts, and they were developing more coherence between the stories that were presented by different news organizations and within individual organizations.[102] In this context, television news increasingly focused on congressional scandal and ethics violations, rather than policy making. Starting in the mid-1980s, the nightly news aired only three stories on policy issues for every one on congressional scandal, whereas in the previous period the networks broadcast thirteen stories on policy issues for every one on ethics violations.[103] Even congressional investigations into corruption, which had traditionally earned extensive praise from reporters, were treated critically.[104] Reporters often ignored strong expert evidence that directly challenged supporters of reform and instead turned to groups like Common Cause.[105] The tone of the news mirrored fictional television shows, which also portrayed politicians unfavorably.[106]

In addition to scandal, television journalism favored conflict.[107] The 1980s election coverage focused on the competition between candidates rather than on the policies or issues in dispute. Reporters did not usually examine the policies that candidates discussed in their campaigns but searched instead for an electoral motive behind every statement or appearance. In covering campaigns as horse races, reporters were drawn to personal flaws that ranged from sexual affairs to political corruption.[108] The same held true with fights over legislation, such as the health care proposals in 1993 and 1994; the media was more enthused about power struggles between politicians and interest groups, outrageous statements, colorful personalities, and backroom maneuvering than about careful analyses and evaluations of the proposals.[109]

This atmosphere could be dangerous. Legislators who entered presidential campaigns were often tripped up under the klieg lights. One of the most famous incidents was broadcast on November 4, 1979, when NBC's Roger Mudd asked Ted Kennedy, only days before he announced his candidacy, why he wanted to be president. Because Kennedy rambled without offering a definitive answer, his campaign was hamstrung from the start. Kennedy also had to deal with Chappaquiddick, an issue that television did not forget.[110] In August 1987, Senator Joseph Biden made a speech (taped by C-SPAN) in Iowa in which he used words from a speech by Neil Kinnock, leader of the British Labour Party. The discovery raised accusations of plagiarism in this and other work. "Biden was strangled with C-SPAN," according to *Newsweek*.[111]

Yet television did not treat all blunders, conflicts, or scandals equally. The media shied away from stories that lacked simplicity or drama. News stories required a dramatic lead, a clear narrative, and then a closer.[112] The most notable scandal that took a very long time to gain national attention was the savings and loan crisis. After Congress deregulated their industry in the early 1980s, savings and loan officials took advantage of the deregulation to make risky investments that generated quick profits. Several prominent congressmen had received campaign contributions from industry officials who had been deregulated but who continued to be protected – by federal insurance – from investment losses. The financial crisis cost taxpayers billions of dollars and involved top law firms, politicians, and two government agencies. But the story did not make it into the national news until the end of the decade, despite the fact that local reporters had been covering the controversy.[113] One of the reasons for this failure was that the story was complex and technical.[114] Besides technical complexity, economic conflict of interest mitigated against televised coverage of certain economic scandals. This problem became worse with the dominance of television, since stations and networks were owned by conglomerates that handled multiple ventures. Although television stations claimed that they protected the news division from commercial pressure, the boundaries were never impermeable. The same factors were sweeping the print industry, as large chains swiftly bought city newspapers.[115] During wartime, commercial pressures often encouraged the media to refrain from controversial stories that could be seen as "unpatriotic" by viewers and thus cause a decline in ratings.

Nonetheless, commercialization did not prevent journalism from tackling sensitive issues. After all, the mainstream media did eventually report on the savings and loan scandal. Moreover, they covered many explosive issues as the centrality of scandal coverage increased. What was more significant to the relationship between journalism and scandal in the 1980s and 1990s was the context within which these stories were reported – namely, the declining vitality of the reform coalition and hence the diminished interest in doing anything about these issues when they emerged.

While cable-era television nurtured an interest in scandal and conflict, the new technology and the competition among shows to broadcast a story first meant that information could go out to the public in seconds, thereby diminishing the amount of time a legislator had to respond. Improved recording and surveillance technologies, for instance, allowed reporters around the world to bring to the public sights and sounds directly from the halls of power.[116] It also allowed them to go undercover. In 1990, ABC's "PrimeTime Live" played a video (secretly taped in Barbados) of eight members of the House Ways and Means Committee vacationing as guests of lobbyists for insurance and computer companies with interests in legislation that the committee was working on.[117] The tremendous expansion of broadcasting space that resulted from cable encouraged the growth of the number of news shows on the air. Cable television offered around-the-clock news broadcasts, and networks responded by producing more news magazine shows and slicker evening newscasts. Radio, which also broadcast news instantly, experienced a renaissance with the formation of dozens of all-news radio channels, extended noncommercial radio news shows, and political talk shows.[118]

Those involved with politics understood by the 1990s that responding to television was a time-consuming and full-time process. George Stephanopoulos, a top advisor to President Clinton, recalled the dynamic as follows: "Stopping CNN was key. If they ran the story all day, however briefly, other news organizations could cite them to justify running their own stories. Our denials would be folded into the accounts, but the damage would be done."[119] Furthermore, there were more reporters searching for stories. Between 1983 and 1991, the number of accredited print reporters increased from 2,300 to approximately 4,100, while the number of television and radio journalists rose from 1,000 in 1983 to over 2,400 in 1990.[120] At the same time that the number of news shows expanded, moreover, the overall pool of nightly news viewers declined.[121] News shows were under more pressure to produce ratings and earn advertising profits. There were many reasons for this change in the 1980s. For instance, both local television and the national CBS show "60 Minutes" were profitable, demonstrating that news shows which succeeded at attracting audiences could make substantial amounts of money. Indeed, by the 1980s the revamped news divisions of the networks were generating impressive advertising dollars, as were the specialized news magazines that competed in prime time.[122] Moreover, the corporate takeovers of the 1980s placed networks in the hands of companies that were in debt.[123]

Legislators tried to take advantage of this heightened competition even as they were getting caught up in the frenzy of a scandal. For example, in 1991 the Senate Ethics Committee was investigating Alfonse D'Amato (R-NY). The senator was forced to respond to a negative story on "60 Minutes" that centered on unfavorable ethics accusations against him. D'Amato responded with a news blitz against the show. Before the program aired, D'Amato took the unusual step of holding a news conference to lambaste the show. He invited the three accusers in the piece to show up at a public event to debate the charges. Knowing they would not, the picture of the senator next to three empty chairs was intended to be an effective public relations stunt. After "60 Minutes" refused to interview the senator live so that he could respond without editing, D'Amato went to a competitor, ABC's "PrimeTime," which offered him airtime.[124] He also purchased a $100,000 commercial in New York.[125] Some said the media campaign backfired by calling more attention to the charges.[126] During the 1990s, D'Amato would again find himself under continual media attack, this time from CNN's "Crossfire," a cable show where co-host Michael Kinsley criticized the senator weekly for his investigations of President Clinton's administration.

Competition for advertising dollars and scarce viewers encouraged producers to release information as soon as possible. As soon an interesting story emerged, stations and shows entered into frenzies to get at the information as quickly as possible and to obtain the most salacious details.[127] One Republican leader's press secretary in the mid-1990s explained that, whereas the network news was useful for framing issues, through CNN "you can get in to influence the news spin much more quickly. You can also get in to influence the way people are interpreting the events as they happen. By contrast, the networks are much later in the debate. They frame events, but they don't influence the course of events."[128] Breaking news could literally happen before a viewer's eyes. In 1996, presidential candidate Robert Dole announced on CNN's "Larry King Live" that he was selecting New York Representative Susan Molinari to deliver the keynote speech at the Republican convention. Molinari was eating dinner with her husband at an Italian restaurant when she unexpectedly received a call from her staff and Dole's handlers informing her about the broadcast. She instantly called in to the show from a pay phone to accept the invitation.[129] By the following morning she was at the center of a massive media frenzy.

Another important characteristic of journalism in the cable television era was that the reporters who interviewed legislators were taking a more prominent role in the news, accelerating a trend that started in the Progressive Era. Constant appearances on television made celebrity status easier to obtain for journalists than did the relative anonymity of newspaper writing.[130] In the mid-1980s, all three network anchors earned over $1 million a year, while many television reporters and correspondents received six-figure salaries. Reporters found gainful employment on the lecture circuit.[131] The networks revamped their Sunday-morning talk shows to include more telegenic hosts such as Tim Russert.[132] Russert was well known for getting controversial statements out of politicians. When Newt Gingrich appeared shortly before taking over as Speaker in 1994, Russert provoked Gingrich into making his controversial claim that a quarter of the White House staff had used drugs in recent years.[133] When politicians offered hostile responses,

Russert was not shy about expressing his opinion. Statements on his show often kicked off the news narrative for the upcoming work week.

Politicians were interviewed and reported on by pundits who were not only more prominent and tougher than their predecessors but were often closely involved in politics as well. The line that separated politics and the media blurred. The conservative movement had conducted a campaign to get allies onto the airwaves in the 1980s and 1990s as part of their effort to win in the marketplace of ideas. Patrick Buchanan, a member of the Nixon and Reagan administrations, wrote a syndicated column and was a regular on television talk shows despite his own political ambitions.[134] After observing the tremendous success of conservative Republicans, Democrats in the 1990s would embrace the exact same strategy.

The style of this journalism was not confined to television. Reeling from the competition, newspapers replicated the format of television.[135] News chains purchased many of the newspapers and standardized this television-based style. First published in the 1980s, Gannett's *USA Today* was a national newspaper that used color photographs and short articles to attract readers. Market research about consumers, once reserved for advertising, was now being used by the news divisions. Just as with television, the words of politicians were further squeezed from the story. Local newspapers gained national attention by breaking the news of a scandal (for example: the *Miami Herald* with Gary Hart; the *Richmond Times-Dispatch* and the *Virginian-Pilot* with Virginia's Senator Charles Robb). The most prestigious publications, including the *New York Times,* appropriated these styles as well. The *Times* after 1986 started to use more captions, pictures, and graphs to increase its appeal. The op-ed page, which the *New York Times* inaugurated on September 21, 1970, became a centerpiece of the paper. The page offered room for a larger number of experts to enter into legislative debates and created another arena that politicians needed to engage.

### On the Air

Legislators were forced to consider the nature of cable-era television journalism as they crafted legislative strategy. Given the constraints on power in the new legislative process, the media – now defined by television – was perceived as an integral tool with which to shape legislative debate. Party leaders, for example, could not afford to maintain the reclusive posture that individuals such as Richard Russell or Sam Rayburn had embraced decades earlier. Mavericks understood that the media was their best opportunity to make a national mark. Nor could legislators avoid cable-era journalism and the dangers that the medium posed, since many politicians were ensnared in its web regardless of their wishes.

There were numerous examples of how legislators dealt with television. Senate Democrats picked George Mitchell (D-ME) as their Majority Leader in a three-way race in 1988, although he had barely gotten his feet wet since entering the chamber eight years earlier. One of the biggest reasons behind his victory was that colleagues felt Mitchell would fare well on television.[136] As chair of the House Armed Services Committee in 1991, Wisconsin Democrat Les Aspin built support for the congressional vote on the Persian Gulf War by appearing on CNN's "Larry King Live," the syndicated "John McLaughlin's One on One," and NBC's "Meet the Press," and by publishing two op-ed pieces in the *Washington Post*.[137] New York's Senator Patrick Moynihan, according to his biographer, often "used a television talk show, a television interview or an op-ed piece in the *New York Times*" to promote his ideas instead of committee hearings or speeches.[138] Jesse Helms (R-NC) had spent two decades honing his media skills as a newspaper writer and television broadcaster before entering the Senate. Helms gained a tremendous amount of national exposure by goading and attacking the "elite liberal media."[139] Legislators who responded fast to unfolding events could obtain national exposure. California's Maxine Waters appeared on television news shows constantly for several weeks following the 1991 beating of an African-American male by police in her Los Angeles district. The attention allowed her to promote her policy goals for the inner cities despite only recently having arrived to Congress.[140] Furthermore, legislators used splashy visual and audio material to get the attention of cameras. On C-SPAN, Silvio Conte (R-MA) attacked pork-barrel spending in 1983 by making a speech while wearing a pig nose.[141] Politicians who refused to accommodate television ran the risk of not appearing on the news at all unless they were drawn in by attacks from an opponent or a scandal.

Most legislators thus adjusted to the medium regardless of how enthusiastic they were. One of the most striking cases involved Speaker Tip O'Neill, who had dismissed television for most of his career. Yet the Speaker could not ignore television indefinitely. In his first year as Speaker (1977), O'Neill had more television coverage than his predecessors.[142] O'Neill was forced to change tactics after the 1980 election, when Republicans ran vicious ads depicting him as the quintessential machine politician. President Reagan, a former actor, dominated the airwaves through a sophisticated media strategy.[143] Facing media-savvy Republicans, the Speaker realized that he needed to improve his television presence. In 1981, O'Neill hired Chris Matthews as his new administrative assistant. A former speechwriter for President Carter, the fast-talking and exuberant Matthews was an expert in media relations. From the moment he arrived at the Speaker's office, his mission was to teach O'Neill how to operate on television. His lessons emphasized the importance of repeating short messages and positioning his body in certain angles. Matthews encouraged his boss to appear on the Sunday-morning talk shows (which he had avoided until that time) and to grant interviews with television reporters whenever they wanted them. In Matthews's mind, political battles were fought not only in the halls of Congress but also in the arena of television. One of Matthews's first accomplishments came in 1981 when the White House proposed cutting Social Security benefits in its budget proposal. Guided by Matthews, O'Neill bombarded television shows

Brian Lamb conducts an interview for C-SPAN with Speaker Tip O'Neill on September 18, 1986 (C-SPAN Archives).

to warn that the GOP was threatening the future of this program. Republicans acknowledged that the House Democrats were convincing voters that the GOP was attempting to balance the budget on the backs of the elderly – as opposed to the GOP interpretation of Democrats selling out future retirees for immediate electoral needs.[144] The battle was a bruising experience for Reagan and congressional Republicans. O'Neill also revamped his daily press conference to make it more interesting to reporters.[145] On the lighter side, he appeared as a guest on the NBC's hit sitcom "Cheers" in 1983. The transformation of O'Neill's television image was remarkable, from Tammany Hall leader to Santa Claus. By the end of his speakership in 1986, O'Neill had been remade into a compassionate and friendly bearlike figure.[146]

O'Neill was not alone. House Ways and Means Committee Chair Dan Rostenkowski (D-IL), the quintessential legislative insider, hired a media consultant and high-profile speech writer to help him with a battle over tax reform in 1985 and 1986. Rostenkowski used a prime-time televised appearance in 1985 to take back the issue of tax reform from Republicans and ensure that Ways and Means played a central role in the legislation. In the widely praised speech, Rostenkowski said that the Democratic version of reform would benefit average citizens and stand for principles of fairness. Emphasizing his ethnic Chicago dialect, the chair told viewers in endearing terms to write "R-O-S-T-Y" if they wanted to take a stand in favor of fair taxes, which thousands of voters did. Rostenkowski became a national celebrity at the same time that he, the Democrats, and the Ways and Means Committee secured a central spot in this tax reform debate.[147] Legislators also made sure they obtained good television press in the district by sending stations a steady flow of press releases and satellite feeds, participating in local cable and radio call-in shows, and alerting members of the press to upcoming speeches that they would make on C-SPAN.[148]

The television bug spread fast. In 1984, Chief Deputy Whip Bill Alexander admitted to his colleagues that "with the advent of TV ... we have a facility for communicating with the public, but we don't schedule and manage things properly. We don't make it easy for the American people."[149] During the 1980s, congressional Democrats reduced the length of their responses to presidential addresses to fit network programming formats;[150] they also started to coordinate the party's media campaign on television and radio.[151] The media could be an excellent political tool in partisan interbranch battles. When the White House charged that Democrats were withholding a preliminary draft report on the Iran-Contra scandal because it proved that the president was innocent, Senator Patrick Leahy of the Senate Select Committee on Intelligence leaked the report to NBC news, which showed a copy of the document to viewers. Republican party chairman Haley Barbour was famous for relentless telephone calls to C-SPAN in the 1990s requesting that they televise party events in Washington.[152]

These tactical adjustments by parties and legislators were essential for success, given that misreading the pulse of journalism could be costly. For example, Rostenkowski made an enormous mistake following a Medicare decision in 1988 that had raised taxes on wealthier seniors to pay for new benefits. Rostenkowski went to speak in 1989 at a local senior citizens center in his Chicago neighborhood. His Washington staff failed to consult with colleagues in the district and they overlooked unusual calls from the national networks about this apparently minor event. After the speech there was a planned protest outside the center by a local activist group opposed to the tax increase. When Rostenkowski left the building he found himself caught in an onslaught of senior protesters who surrounded him and his car. After making the initial mistake of stopping to talk with a local reporter, Rostenkowski dashed to his car when the protesters kept taunting him in front of the cameras. The protesters yelled out

"Liar!" "Impeach!" and "Recall!"[153] As Rostenkowski grumbled into the micro-phone that "these people are nuts," the protesters surrounded his automobile. A 69-year-old woman climbed onto the hood while other protesters screamed and pounded the vehicle. Unfortunately for Rostenkowski, the event was a pub-lic relations disaster. The network evening news shows played images of the incident.[154] The visual images became symbolic of an entrenched senior incum-bent who was out of touch with his constituents.[155]

There were other, similar examples of bad television moments. Emboldened by the landslide Republican victories of 1994, the GOP decided to take on Presi-dent Clinton in a budget battle. The strategy backfired when the media broadcast stories about Gingrich's erratic personality and zeroed in each night on the per-sonal impact of a government shutdown, including stories about government workers without paychecks, tourists being turned away at national parks, and citizens denied their passports.[156] The media also kept playing a video tape of Robert Livingston (R-LA) screaming on the House floor that the Republicans would stay their ground until "doomsday." The clip turned into a symbol for op-ponents of how the GOP was incapable of compromise. During another famous incident in this battle, Gingrich complained that the president had ignored him on an overseas flight to attend the funeral of the assassinated Israeli Prime Minis-ter, Yitzhak Rabin. After the *New York Daily News* posted a headline that read "CRY BABY" next to a cartoon of Gingrich, Democrats brought a cardboard blowup to the House floor for C-SPAN audiences and the rest of the media. Re-publicans were dealt another major blow after the 2002 elections. Trent Lott, who was to become the Senate Majority Leader, made an off-the-cuff remark about Strom Thurmond's 1948 campaign at an event broadcast on C-SPAN; it cost him his leadership position and turned into a major public relations fiasco for the GOP.

Not catching the attention of the media could be just as problematic. Fred Thompson (R-TN) grew frustrated by the fact that television coverage of his committee hearings into the campaign finance abuses of 1996 was sporadic at best. Although Thompson leaked a few salacious stories that captured the media's attention, the overall lack of coverage was widely believed to be a major reason that the investigation fizzled. The hearings were carefully managed in a judicious fashion that appealed to lawyers on the committee but not to con-temporary reporters. Other than a handful of stories, almost nothing reached the air. In addition, the White House conducted a highly effective response by stationing a presidential counsel outside the hearings to instantly dismiss to re-porters harmful information as "old news" or partisan politics.[157]

Additionally, party leaders were sensitive to the fact that the proliferation of media outlets had offered avenues around them. As Dan Rostenkowski explained when discussing why chairmen such as himself no longer had the same grip as those in the previous era, "now members of Congress are independent contrac-tors ... they can get bits on the television news if they raise enough cain."[158] With House Democrats such as Rostenkowski unsupportive of his plan to renew a program that benefitted the unemployed in 1985, Ohio's Donald Pease provided economic data to reporters, wrote op-ed pieces, appeared on C-SPAN and in *Congressional Quarterly,* and helped organize a televised rally where he used a fast-food spatula to symbolize Reagan's plan for the unemployed. Although Pease's legislation was ultimately defeated, he put the plight of the unemployed in the national spotlight.[159] In the mid-1990s, Senator John McCain frustrated Republican leaders by using his television and radio interviews to build momentum for controversial campaign finance legislation. McCain blitzed the airwaves, where he was a popular guest owing to his inclination to make controversial statements.[160]

### Exposed

The triumph of cable-era television thus meant more to politicians than switching from print to the tube. Cable television amplified certain journalistic trends that had emerged since the 1960s, such as adversarial journalism. The medium was important not only in itself but also because it caused the network news shows and national newspapers to alter their styles in response to the competition. The stylistic traits of the cable era became more pronounced as younger reporters entered the business by directly taking jobs in television.[161] Most important, cable television reconstructed the length and speed of the news cycle for everyone in the media. People could observe politics in real time. Events, scandals, and conflicts unfolded live on their living room television sets. Moreover, the sheer number of news shows that were produced – a consequence of the space that cable offered – was breathtaking. The cautious pace and rigid editorial standards that were still evident at the time of Watergate deteriorated as the media felt intense pressure to release gripping details fast.[162] Together, these developments made the news a more explosive and uncontrollable environment than it had been in the days of the Vietnam war.

Television was an important part of the transformed media that legislators confronted when they campaigned and governed. This was no less significant than the diminished procedural autonomy of committees or the reduction of secrecy. In many respects, the influence of cable on the news was as significant as the introduction of television itself. Despite the consolidation of media ownership during these decades, the fragmentation of media outlets available in the era of cable and the lengthened news cycle offered numerous opportunities for the competing centers of power in Congress to get their message out. At the same time, the constant news cycle and fragmentation of news outlets made it all the more difficult for any politician to truly control the flow of information.

The media was one more obstacle to imposing tight internal control over congressional proceedings. There were also more celebrity reporters seeking heated interviews and commentators with an explicit political affiliation. Many politicians attempted to use the cable-era media for their own gain. Sometimes they were successful, but sometimes they ended up on the cutting-room floor.

Younger conservatives were among the first to take advantage as they hammered away at Democrats through cable television. At the same time, every politician was forced – from the moment of entering office until the time of leaving – to navigate through difficult terrain. Many of the Republicans who relied on television to quickly make their presence known in Congress soon fell victim to the medium after they had established themselves.

# 12

# The Contemporary Era

Newt Gingrich's topsy-turvy career epitomized the contemporary Congress. Gingrich was a Republican who won the former seat of senior conservative committee chair John Flynt, a Democrat who had retired after becoming alienated from his party and weakened by the suburbanization of his southern district. Elected in 1978, Gingrich rose to power by taking advantage of the reconstructed legislative process. Republicans elected him as Minority Whip in 1989 and, following the election of 1994, as Speaker. Using the recently acquired tools of the House majority, Gingrich helped the GOP pass welfare reform and deficit reduction. Despite his initial success, however, the Speaker confronted the pitfalls and constraints of the contemporary Congress. Many of his policy proposals failed, and Gingrich fell victim to scandal warfare when Democrats, some Republicans, and the media turned against him.

The contemporary era that produced and destroyed Newt Gingrich evolved out of the 1970s institutional changes. Throughout these years, congressional parties exhibited the type of aggressive stance that would have seemed impossible only a few decades earlier. At times both parties showed the ability to keep their members in line and to dictate the terms of debate inside the institution. Yet the resurgence of strong partisanship did not mean that life inside the legislative branch had become any smoother than before. While legislators such as Gingrich, Tom DeLay (R-TX), and Trent Lott amassed significant power, partisanship and scandal warfare meant that bipartisan compromise and cooperation were rare. The majority caucuses depended on overwhelming unity within their party as well as a super-majority of senators to overcome a filibuster. Divided government throughout most of this period also meant that much legislation that survived this process still needed to overcome the threat of a presidential veto.

Party leaders also remained on a short leash because the 1970s institutional changes had created numerous fragmenting mechanisms to prevent excessive centralized authority. In the new era, Congress fluctuated between extreme moments of decentralization and partisan centralization. There were thus multiple avenues of influence for the rank and file: the existence of codified rules of behavior, and the remaining power of committee and subcommittee chairs. When party leaders overstepped their bounds there were congressional committees, independent commissions, prosecutors, and ethics codes that might be used to bring them down. Nor had the external constraints on Congress diminished. Every legislator faced an adversarial media that disseminated stories instantly and which offered several outlets for politicians. The fractured world of interest groups, activists, and think tanks made political alliances unreliable. Divided government posed an enormous obstacle to those pursuing bold policy initiatives. Despite measures to reinvigorate congressional power, the executive branch and Supreme Court remained strong. Policy also influenced politics, as large deficits and pre-committed spending allowed for only slight alterations to existing policy. Finally, the rightward shift in politics had placed all politicians on alert, including the conservatives who found themselves in power. The conservative movement popularized political arguments that focused almost entirely on the ineptitude and corruption of the federal government.

These conditions created a paradoxical situation. Although most legislators felt confident that voters would return them to office given the tremendous incumbent advantage after the 1970s, once they returned to Capitol Hill for each new session the challenges of governing seemed no less – if not greater – than before the period of reform had begun. Liberals also found a Congress that was not as hospitable as they had hoped for.

### Revitalizing Congressional Parties

During the administration of Jimmy Carter, it had appeared as if congressional parties would not be rejuvenated. But congressional parties soon reasserted themselves in the 1980s with an intensity not experienced since the 1910s. With Ronald Reagan in the White House, Democratic and Republican leaders started to use the new procedural weapons available to them to wage partisan battles.

The return of partisanship took time. Despite controlling the presidency and Congress until 1980, Democrats had failed to achieve internal party discipline. This situation was evident in 1981 when Reagan allied with conservative House Democrats to pass income-tax reduction. In fact, the renewed prominence of the "Southern Coalition" caused some animosity among Republicans who felt that political observers were overlooking the strong unity that was achieved by the GOP.[1] Nonsouthern Democrats still harbored ideological divisions that made voting coalitions unpredictable.[2] Nor were Republicans as united as some claimed. House Minority Leader Robert Michel, who tended to compromise with Democrats, struggled with the Conservative Opportunity Society (COS). Even after the GOP gained control of the Senate in 1981, a group of liberal Republicans frequently forced staunch conservatives to compromise.[3] Furthermore, fiscal conservatives clashed with supply-side Republicans over taxes. For example, several Republicans defied presidential demands in 1983 by supporting a tax increase. The rebellious moderate Lowell Weicker (R-CT) proclaimed on the Senate floor: "The President is not going to get his way, not as far as this Republican is concerned."[4] In short, ten years after committee chairs lost their dominance, parties had not yet replaced them.

After 1984, however, congressional partisanship thrived. More roll-call votes took place along party lines and a greater number of battles were defined by partisan interests. The change was due in large part to the decline of moderates in both parties. Constituents were voting for legislators whose preferences closely resembled the fellow members of their party. Underlying the change in voting was a basic shift in the regional orientation of the two major parties, as Republicans secured control over the West and South while Democrats locked in northern states.[5] Redistricting and recession resulted in 81 freshmen entering the House in 1982. By 1984, many Boll Weevils had either switched to the GOP or abandoned their alliance with Republicans. Many moderate northeastern Republicans were replaced by right-wing Republican conservatives or liberal Democrats. The decline of the center eliminated those legislators who were traditionally important to crafting compromises on major issues.[6] Both parties learned how to manipulate the post–Warren Court districting system so as to secure seats for incumbents and diminish the number of competitive positions that were available in the House. As they did so, politicians gained a stronger incentive to play to the most partisan part of their districts, who tended to be the most active in primaries.

While southern Democrats remained more conservative than their northern colleagues on cultural and foreign policy issues, their differences on civil rights and economics diminished.[7] Twenty out of 23 freshman Democrats from the South and Southwest in 1982, for example, were loyal supporters of the Democratic agenda. The party unity score of southern Democrats increased from an average of 53 percent in the 94th Congress (1975–1976) to 78 percent in the 100th to 103rd Congress (1987–1994).[8] The unity of nonsouthern Democrats increased as the GOP moved further to the right, thereby reminding northerners how much they had in common. In 1987, 64 percent of House votes were along party lines, compared with 27 percent in 1972.[9] Party voting in the Senate shifted from an average of 43 percent of each vote between the 1950s and 1980s to approximately two thirds of all votes in 1995–1996.[10] With fewer internal ideological divisions, the rank and file had a stronger incentive to follow their parties.[11] A new generation of centrist Democrats would not be able to make much headway within Congress and would focus instead on the promotion of moderate Democratic presidential and gubernatorial candidates.

Besides this strong electoral incentive to avoid bipartisanship, party control of Congress became less predictable and so intensified the need for Democrats and Republicans to remain at each other's throats. Congressional Republicans emerged as a competitive alternative to the Democrats. This was true even in the former Democratic stronghold of the South.[12] Although Democrats controlled Congress between 1986 and 1992, the fact that the GOP held the Senate between

1980 and 1986 and all of Congress for most of the period after 1994 (with the exception of a brief interlude in 2001 and 2002) was historically significant. They had broken the hold that Democrats had maintained on Congress since 1932 (with the exception of 1946–1948 and 1952–1954). While the House remained relatively stable, three factors produced anxiety in that chamber: the fact that the party controlling the House did not always enjoy a Senate under sympathetic hands, razor-thin margins through much of the 1990s, and the seismic shift in party control that occurred in 1994. All of this added to the tensions that arose from divided government.

When electoral conditions were ripe for partisanship, procedures were now in place to facilitate this style of politics. Party leaders turned to the budget process, special rules, caucuses, and other centralizing mechanisms to try to overcome opposition from freshmen, mavericks, committee and subcommittee chairs, and the occasional bipartisan coalition. One procedure that party leaders employed was the budget process. From the time of its creation in 1974, the budget process offered party leaders a vehicle to maneuver around committees and curtail floor opposition. According to the original reform, the budget committees would offer a spending plan in the nonbinding "first budget resolution." The authorizing and appropriations committees were supposed to follow the resolution. The budget committees later passed a second resolution that included reconciliation instructions to each committee that explained how they needed to cut their figures to meet the final budget. To enhance the prospect of centralized decisionmaking, Senate filibusters were barred and the Congressional Budget Office offered budgetary information to all legislators (information once monopolized by the chairs).

However, there had been two obstacles preventing either party from taking advantage of the process before 1980. First, there were no viable enforcement mechanisms. Second, the Senate Budget Committee operated on a bipartisan basis in the 1970s under Edmund Muskie (D-ME) and Henry Bellmon (R-OK).

Starting in 1980, Congress strengthened the budget process. Hoping to reduce deficits, Democrats authorized the budget committees to include reconciliation instructions with the first budget resolution rather than the second. In 1981, Reagan, the Republican Senate, and a bipartisan House coalition passed reconciliation instructions *before* the first budget resolution in order to force $130 billion in specific spending cuts. Leon Panetta called this reconciliation bill "the most extensive legislation that a Congress has acted on in the history of this institution."[13] The decision to use the process this way followed even more dramatic attempts to eliminate the role of the authorizing committees altogether.[14] Although some Democrats fought these developments tooth and nail, they "didn't win," as one member explained, "the Republicans won and the Administration dictated the exact terms of the budget, reconciliation, and the tax cut to Congress."[15] "Reconciliation," said Richard Bolling (who chaired the House Rules Committee from 1979 to 1982), "is the most brutal and blunt instrument used by a president in an attempt to control the congressional process since Nixon used impoundment."[16]

One of the least-known technical procedures from the 1974 budget reforms had been brought out of the shadows.[17] Democrats were furious that Reagan had successfully turned this legislative-strengthening reform into a tool of the executive branch. Chair of the House Budget Committee James Jones (D-OK) warned his colleagues that "although reconciliation was designed as a procedure to improve budgetary responsibility and control by the Congress," it had since become "an executive tool for domination of the Congress."[18] At the same time that the budget process gained sharper teeth, partisanship expanded its reach over the Senate Budget Committee following the Republican Senate takeover in 1980. Party cohesion on Senate budget votes rose from 40 percent in 1975–1979 to 61 percent between 1980 and 1984.[19] Chairman Pete Domenici (R-NM), who began his term in 1981 by working with the senior Democrat Ernest "Fritz" Hollings (D-SC), gave in to a more partisan approach by 1983.[20] Given the procedural advantages granted to the budget process, after unified control of Congress returned in 1986 the parties started to place all types of programs into omnibus budget legislation and relied on high-level summits between the leadership and the president to circumvent legislators.[21] As deficits became the big issue in the 1980s, party leaders applied pressure on members to remain loyal.[22] The budget process did not really restrain spending, but it did offer caucuses a tool to centralize decisions.

To achieve their objectives, party leaders also used special rules to limit floor amendments and referred bills to multiple committees. The main reason the caucuses accepted such rules was that most chairs now supported the party.[23] The percentage of special rules (granted by the Rules Committee) restricting floor amendments in the House increased from 15.7 percent in 1975–1976 to 28.8 percent in 1981–1982 and to 44.6 percent in 1985–1986.[24] Using another recently enacted procedure, the Speaker referred legislation to multiple committees, the most relevant surviving product of the Bolling committee reforms. By referring bills to many committees, the Speaker weakened the jurisdictional lock that any single panel maintained over policy.[25] Jurisdictional fragmentation became more prevalent.[26]

Senate leaders maintained less control because filibusters guaranteed that any individual could block legislation, barring a super-majority. Yet Senate parties expanded their influence. For example, during the 1980s and 1990s, party leaders used complex Unanimous Consent Agreements (UCAs) to limit floor debate. Although obtaining a UCA required making concessions to each senator, the agreements prevented filibusters and limited postcloture debate. Party leaders maintained the upper hand by including more legislation in budget bills, since the process barred filibusters. Party leaders also used task forces to work around committees, scheduled debate in advantageous ways, provided more in-kind services to members, and took advantage of their access to the media.[27] Sometimes the Senate's individualistic rules merged with partisanship: filibusters became a standard party tactic.[28]

Campaign finance likewise facilitated partisanship. After the campaign finance reforms of 1974, previously underutilized party committees adopted a prominent role. The committees worked closely with political action committees as well as organizational and individual contributors. Party committees were essential to legislators, who faced escalating campaign costs, strict contribution limits, and no public funding. Four committees dealt with financing congressional elections: the Democratic Congressional Campaign Committee and the National Republican Campaign Committee in the House as well as the Democratic Senatorial Campaign Committee and the National Republican Senatorial Committee. While subject to most of the same regulations as interest groups, parties were granted more opportunities by Congress and the FEC to distribute and raise funds. In short, the parties adapted to candidate-centered politics by providing campaign resources.[29] Tony Coelho and Guy Vander Jagt (R-MI) modernized their respective House committees.[30] Republican leaders proved to be equally effective at raising campaign funds.[31] By the late 1980s, campaign committee chairs were perceived among colleagues and the news media as influential congressional leaders.[32] Richard Lugar (R-IN), who headed one of the Senate committees, bluntly explained that "centralized fund-raising and the campaign support we are able to provide produces heightened camaraderie among Senate Republicans which translates into increased unity on roll call votes."[33]

Finally, the party leaders made use of the revitalized caucuses. Under Gillis Long (D-LA) and Richard Gephardt (D-MO), for example, the House Democratic Caucus met every other week and frequently released material to the media. Additionally, the parties expanded leadership positions so that more members gained a direct stake in party success.[34] On those rare occasions when committee chairs ignored the parties, there were threats of retribution. In 1987 the caucus warned Les Aspin – who two years earlier had successfully challenged Charles Melvin Price (on the grounds that he was too supportive of Reagan) for the chair of the Armed Services Committee – that he was becoming too conservative. Aspin changed his behavior.

Speaker James Wright personified the new stature of party leaders. After the House elected Wright as Speaker in 1987, he made full use of his procedural authority to push party bills.[35] Wright was a tough politician: "he has managed one feat no one thought possible," noted two reporters, "Jim Wright has made the departing Tip O'Neill look like a statesman."[36] When Dan Rostenkowski published an op-ed supporting policies that the Speaker opposed, Wright threatened to replace him as chair of Ways and Means.[37] One of the Speaker's most controversial actions took place on October 29, 1987, when conservative Democrats and Republicans defeated a bill containing a tax increase. After the vote, Wright brought the bill up for a second vote using a little-known procedure. When time expired, Wright left the electronic vote open long after the usual fifteen-minute vote time had expired in order to allow Democrats sufficient time to find one member who would change his vote: James Chapman (D-TX). While the roll call was held open, Republicans booed and screamed on the floor. Connie Mack (R-FL) later said of the Speaker's action: "It has totally broken down cooperation between Democrats and Republicans.... I have absolutely no respect for Jim Wright."[38] Wright, complained Minority Whip Richard Cheney, was a "heavy-handed son of a bitch [who] will do anything he can to win at any price."[39] Constantly appearing in the press was another tactic that Wright used as leader. Whereas Speaker Rayburn shunned talk shows, Wright – and his successor Tom Foley – craved airtime.[40]

Yet revitalized partisanship could not replicate the type of power that committee chairs once enjoyed. Instead of replacing the fractured process created in the 1970s, renewed partisanship was layered over it. Rank-and-file members were willing and able to threaten party leaders through congressional procedures or the media. When they were a congressional minority, for example, young conservative Republicans such as Newt Gingrich used the mechanisms available to the rank and file to push their senior party leaders to the right of the political spectrum and to attack top Democrats. The influence of subcommittee chairs was significant after the 1970s. Nor had reformers rendered committees powerless – just less autonomous.[41] In those moments when party leaders unified their colleagues, they still had to grapple with the tremendous external constraints that Congress faced, such as the adversarial television media and a powerful president. Finally, several of the most influential senior Democrats by the early 1990s were the Watergate Babies, whose professional affinity was still to resist hierarchical control.[42] Thus parties were central and influential mechanisms, but their leaders faced considerable internal and external constraints, including a process that facilitated decentralization.

The new partisanship also differed significantly from that of the nineteenth century because the two major parties did not reestablish strong connections to most citizens. A majority of Americans did not vote in presidential or congressional elections, let alone involve themselves in party activities. Although partisanship in Congress did reflect strong ideological tensions polarizing the electorate, it did not result from Americans having become more engaged in mass political parties that involved them in politics on a regular basis. The result was highly partisan institutions in a country where parties were not altogether very strong and where most citizens remained rather disconnected from the institutions of the federal government. Americans seemed to be more interested in the latest *Rambo* movie than in attending parades and picnics that were organized by Democrats or Republicans. Those who wanted to support their party tended to do so through financial contributions.

## The Impact of Partisanship

Besides producing a preponderance of party-based roll-call votes, heightened partisanship in Congress had corrosive effects on legislative relations in the 1980s and 1990s. Whereas the main source of authority in the previous era – committee chairs – were adept at producing compromise (to the frustration of many on the left and right), the new barons of Congress in the 1980s and 1990s – party leaders – created conditions that stifled legislative negotiation.

The effects of partisanship could be seen through incessant partisan warfare in these years. Democrats and Republicans turned to the Office of the Independent Counsel to attack one another.[43] Although Republicans had attempted to eliminate the office in the 1980s, Democrats blocked the effort. Then, in 1988, the Supreme Court deemed the office constitutional. The largest investigation took place during President Reagan's second term. Independent counsel Lawrence Walsh conducted a multimillion-dollar investigation into National Security Council officials who had surreptitiously traded weapons for hostages and cash while providing support to Central American anticommunist military operations despite an explicit congressional ban. But investigators failed to turn up any "smoking gun" that proved Reagan had knowledge of the violations. The congressional hearings, which were carried on cable television, generated mixed reactions. Although a bipartisan majority on the joint investigative committees criticized the administration, all the House Republicans joined two Senate Republicans in a dissenting report. Republican opponents charged that the case was driven by liberal Democrats who were frustrated with Reagan's popularity. The dissenters stated that the committee report "reads as if it were a weapon in the ongoing guerilla warfare, instead of an objective analysis."[44] While the Iran-Contra affair dealt with serious charges, the investigation became ensnared in partisanship: many Democrats sought to humiliate Reagan while several Republicans defended the president to protect their party.

Senate confirmations were another arena for partisan battles. There were many policies at stake in judicial confirmations, since the legislature had increasingly abdicated such key issues as abortion and affirmative action to the courts. Partisan fighting reached epic proportions in 1987 when President Reagan nominated the conservative judge Robert Bork to replace Lewis Powell on the Supreme Court. Liberal Democrats had terrible opinions about Bork, who as Solicitor General had fired Archibald Cox in the "Saturday night massacre." Bork was also an outspoken critic of Supreme Court decisions to protect African-American and women's civil rights. Senator Ted Kennedy told his colleagues that "Bork's America is a land in which women would be forced into back alley abortions, blacks would sit at segregated lunch counters, rogue police could break down citizens' doors in midnight raids, and schoolchildren could not be taught about evolution."[45] When Bork tried to appear flexible during the hearings, Kennedy attacked his sincerity.[46] The attacks did not center on Bork's professional competence, the traditional focus of these hearings, but rather on his ideology and integrity and on predictions of how he would rule in specific cases.[47] Kennedy felt that "most Americans would agree that the man who fired Archibald Cox does not deserve to be promoted to Justice on the Supreme Court."[48] Women's and civil rights organizations mounted intense public relations and lobbying campaigns against Bork. Judiciary voted 9-5 to send Bork's case to the floor with a negative recommendation. Only one Republican, Arlen Specter (PA), supported the committee's decision. The Senate rejected Bork by a vote of 42-58 with only two southern Democrats supporting him and six Republicans in opposition.

Two years later, the same organizations and individuals mobilized to defeat President George H. W. Bush's nomination for Secretary of Defense, former senator John Tower. Although the confirmation of cabinet choices was usually pro forma, liberal groups alleged that Tower had a serious drinking problem, a reputation for womanizing, a record of sexual harassment, and highly questionable connections to defense contractors. Ironically, the charges about his "moral character" were first made by conservative activist Paul Weyrich.[49] Senator Sam Nunn (D-GA), chair of the Armed Services Committee, warned that the Secretary of Defense "must be a person suited by personal conduct, discretion, and judgment to serve second only to the President in the chain of command for military operations; to set the highest leadership example for the men and women in uniform and civilian employees of the Department of Defense and to restore public confidence in the integrity of defense management.... Tower cannot meet these standards."[50] Often relying on information that was leaked by Democrats but based on unreliable FBI files, the media reported on rumors that undermined Tower's standing.[51] Tower's staff referred to NBC's Andrea Mitchell as the "High Priestess of the Lynch Mob."[52] The Armed Services Committee voted to reject Tower's nomination with a party-line vote of 11 to 9. On March 9, 1989, Democrats finished off the Tower nomination with a Senate vote of 47 to 53. Nancy Kassebaum of Kansas was the only Republican to oppose Tower, while just three Democrats supported him. Watergate star William Cohen said that this process had involved the "trial, the conviction and, indeed, the political execution" of Tower.[53]

While Democrats demonstrated their skill in investigation and confirmation, Republicans used ethics codes and the new cable media to destroy several senior Democrats between 1988 and 1994. Congressional Republicans were determined to present the Democratic majority as corrupt. In response to the continued Democratic control of Congress after 1986 and the strong-arm tactics of leaders such as Wright, congressional Republicans were paying more attention to the types of ideas that Gingrich and his allies had been promoting for years. Acknowledging the need for a stronger party voice, House leaders turned their attention to improving coordination within the party in order to home in on refined messages.[54] Robert Michel told the Republican Conference in 1990 of the need to balance the requirements of governing with the need to fight back when necessary using selective "guerilla warfare" tactics. New York's Gerald Solomon mapped out a plan in December 1990 that would wage an "all-out, aggressive counteroffensive" against Democratic leaders through a campaign that focused on how Democrats were abusing the procedural power of the majority. They would use one-minute speeches, letters to the Speaker and Rules Committee chairs, public hearings, and regular press releases and briefings.[55] Sounding like COS in the early 1980s, House Republicans officially called attention in 1988 to the "Broken Branch of the Federal Government" by offering graphs and charts showing how Democrats were abusing procedure. Trent Lott quipped that "rules seem to change more frequently than Washington's weather."[56] Some of the procedures highlighted included the reliance on restrictive rules, budget reconciliation legislation that barred the filibuster, the avoidance of committees so that Democrats could bring bills directly to the floor, and the use of proxy voting. Republicans wrote letters to specific committee chairs such as John Dingell of the Committee on Energy and Commerce to complain about instances where they said Democrats had abused their power.[57]

In 1987 and 1988, Gingrich spearheaded an attack based on media stories against Speaker Wright by accusing him of questionable relationships with business (he was joined by Common Cause). Gingrich said that the House was facing an "ethics crisis" because of Wright.[58] Democrats responded by firing off attacks about Gingrich's own practices.[59] Downplaying his opponents, Wright said that Gingrich and his allies "remind you of gnats…. A gnat can't do you any real harm, but the worst he can do is irritate you by flying around in your ear."[60] Gingrich was not scared off. He had already faced the sting of scandal warfare when Democrats circulated a controversial article in a left-wing magazine that reported on his divorce, alleged extramarital affairs, and rumors of his making sexual advances.[61] The House Ethics Committee started to investigate Wright on June 9, 1988, in response to the accusations of Gingrich and Common Cause.

When Republicans elected Gingrich as the House Republican Whip in 1989, the attacks on Wright became even fiercer. According to journalist Chris Matthews, former aide to Speaker O'Neill, "Gingrich has the political sensitivity of a Beirut car-bomber…. The Democrats got Robert Bork. The Republicans got Michael Dukakis. The Democrats got John Tower. The Republicans will get … Jim Wright."[62] Gingrich charged that the Speaker unethically required trade associations to purchase his book, *Reflections of a Public Man,* when he spoke to their members; Gingrich said the "book" was merely a collection of speeches thrown together to circumvent ethics rules. Although Wright had followed the ethics rules regarding outside income limits, the Speaker had violated the intent of the restrictions. "The House," Gingrich said, "has never before had to deal with allegations of unethical conduct at the Speaker's level."[63] Concluding its ten-month investigation in April 1989, the Ethics Committee charged Wright with sixty counts of ethics rules violations.[64] The "ethics monster," as one journalist called it, was "devouring" congressional leaders.[65] Toward the end of the investigation, Democrats suffered another blow with the downfall of Majority Whip Tony Coelho owing to media revelations of ethics problems; the charges were first mentioned in a *Newsweek* article about Wright.[66] Coelho's resignation fueled speculation about Wright. "We are in danger of establishing standards that the Pope couldn't keep," quipped Charlie Wilson (D-TX).[67] The carnage kept getting worse. Toward the climactic moments of the Wright scandal, the

Speaker's trusted lieutenant Bill Alexander accused Gingrich of violating House rules and filed a complaint with the ethics committee.[68] Besides the alleged ethics violation, Alexander attacked Gingrich for practicing "confrontational, demagogical" politics that relied on "vicious remarks which are unparalleled in the history of the House."[69] Approximately one month later, the news took another bad turn for Wright. The *New York Times* reported on its front page of a secret meeting where influential Democrats told Wright he could not survive.[70] Realizing his tenuous support among Democrats, on May 31 the Speaker said he would step down. He warned that "all of us in both political parties must resolve to bring this period of mindless cannibalism to an end."[71] Wright became the first Speaker to be forced out of office in the middle of a term. One Republican staffer called this resignation, along with Coelho's demise and some other scandals, a Democratic "meltdown."[72]

The influence of partisanship during these investigations was usually easy to glean. In 1991, the Senate Ethics Committee investigated four Senate Democrats and one Republican for having assisted Charles Keating, the owner of a defunct savings and loan association, with federal regulators. The "Keating Five," as they were called, had received campaign contributions from Keating. The Senate Ethics Committee declared that John McCain, John Glenn (D-OH), Dennis DeConcini (D-AZ), and Don Riegle (D-MI) were guilty of poor judgment. There were two legislators whom most observers agreed should not have been part of this investigation: McCain and Glenn. Both were placed on the list for partisan reasons: McCain was included by Democrats who wanted to implicate at least one Republican while the GOP targeted John Glenn as retribution for McCain. Alan Cranston (D-CA), whom the committee accused of the most serious infractions, was reprimanded by the Senate. Critics complained that the punishments were mild because senators did not want to tackle the relevant institutional or policy problems (most legislators had supported the deregulation of the industry and routinely accepted contributions from interests influenced by the jurisdiction of their committees).[73]

Shortly after the savings-and-loan scandal, Republicans triggered an investigation into the House Bank. The GOP publicized a report by the General Accounting Office in 1991 that revealed 269 sitting representatives (and 56 who were out of office) had bounced checks at the House Bank but were not required to pay any penalties. The House Bank was actually a checking service offered through the Sergeant-at-Arms. Representatives deposited their paychecks into this service, and any bad checks they wrote were covered by the pool without additional cost. When Democratic leaders initially downplayed the allegations, Republicans pressured the Ethics Committee to investigate. The committee was chaired by Matthew McHugh, a Watergate Baby who started with a limited inquiry that kept secret most of the names of the accused.[74]

Republicans pushed for a broader inquiry. The attack came from the media-savvy and confrontational "Gang of Seven," which included John Boehner (R-OH), Richard Santorum (R-PA), and James Nussle (R-IA).[75] Nussle stood before

C-SPAN cameras on the floor with a paper bag over his head, urging his colleagues to name those who were guilty. Robert Michel was unable to stop these attacks. Tom Foley continually underestimated how far the GOP would push this investigation, and he himself came under fire for how he had lost control of the debate. Texas Democrat John Bryant said, "political leadership is not a responsibility which he relishes. I call on [Foley] to retire."[76] In the spring of 1992, the Ethics Committee released the names of the worst offenders, which included 252 sitting lawmakers. Most were Democrats although there were Republicans as well. More than 60 percent of House members had written at least one overdraft, although there was a wide range in terms of how many had been written. The Justice Department hired a special counsel to investigate the most egregious cases. Republicans pressured Democrats into releasing the information of the House investigation to the counsel.

The drama of the bank scandal was heightened when the 1992 elections resulted in the largest House turnover in over forty years: 110 new members. Of the 269 sitting members implicated in the scandal, 77 retired or were defeated. Although the scandal caused a significant number of retirements and primary defeats and also lowered the normal rate of reelection, the electoral consequences were mixed because many notorious overdraft writers survived.[77] Nonetheless, the retirements of those implicated and the losses of others were substantial. The scandal and the one that later rocked the House Post Office resulted in the 1992 creation of a House Administrator, who was given responsibility over nonlegislative and financial issues such as staff payrolls and internal mail. The fears had driven Democratic freshmen in 1993 to insist that Speaker Foley push for reforms to cleanse their party image.[78]

Furthermore, there were enough cases of powerful legislators who were destroyed to keep politicians on their toes. Chairman of the House Ways and Means Committee Dan Rostenkowski was another senior member severely damaged by scandal. Whereas *U.S. v. Daniel D. Rostenkowski* revolved around ethics rules created by Democrats in the 1970s, the chairman's actual downfall took place in a charged partisan atmosphere. Rostenkowski's problems began with an investigation by Jay Stephens (the Reagan-appointed U.S. Attorney for the District of Columbia) into the House Post Office, a haven for Democratic patronage. A federal grand jury found evidence that post office employees had embezzled funds and sold cocaine. The House learned that the grand jury had subpoenaed expense account records from three Democrats, including Rostenkowski. Republicans attacked Speaker of the House Tom Foley and his wife (who was his chief of staff) for failing to oversee House Postmaster Richard Rota when they were aware that problems existed. "The issue," according to the conservative *Washington Times,* "is what the speaker and his wife may have done to keep the lid on another political scandal in an environment already poisoned by revelations about check writing at the House bank and unpaid bills at the House restaurant."[79] Gingrich claimed that "this entire cocaine and theft scandal has been handled by the Democratic leadership as a partisan coverup of their patronage problems."[80] As the Department of Justice moved forward with legal proceedings, the House instructed the Administration Committee to hold hearings. The U.S. Capitol Police conducted a thorough investigation into Rota's employees.[81] The General Accounting Office discovered a host of problems, such as one employee mixing personal and Post Office funds and a complete absence of internal controls on employees.[82] Rota resigned in April 1992. With Democrats delaying further hearings, Republicans filed a formal complaint that led to an Ethics Committee investigation. In July 1993, Rota pled guilty to having allowed representatives – including Rostenkowski – to sell stamps in exchange for cash. Stephens referred charges about Rostenkowski to a grand jury. The jury would find that Rostenkowski had received $55,000 for cashing in his stamps between 1986 and 1992, more than any other member. Rostenkowski refused to testify before the grand jury on the grounds that this was a "political witch hunt."[83]

Yet it was a witch hunt that produced results, leading one commentator to write that "Beltway barons like former House speaker Jim Wright or former senator John Tower do not seem to understand their vulnerability to scandal until it is too late."[84] Based on ethics rules adopted in 1977, Rostenkowski was indicted on May 30, 1994, for seventeen counts of misusing public funds, including purchasing goods at the House stationery store for constituents, padding the payroll by hiring family friends, and selling stamps for cash. Still, Rostenkowski refused to plead guilty. The Democratic Caucus forced him to resign as chair of Ways and Means as provided by the House ethics rules. Thereafter he endured a bruising two-year trial. In the middle of the trial, Rostenkowski was defeated for reelection in November 1994. Facing skyrocketing legal costs, he pled guilty in 1996 to lesser charges such as placing friends on the payroll. On April 9, 1996, Judge Norma Holloway Johnson sent Rostenkowski to a federal penitentiary.

From Iran-Contra through Rostenkowski, scandal warfare between the parties thrived during the contemporary era. According to one study, there was a 1,515-percent increase in how many federal officials were indicted for corruption between 1975 and 1991.[85] Numerous institutions fueled this trend, including the media, the Department of Justice, the FBI, independent counsels, and grand juries. Also important was the vast number of public interest organizations whose numbers and diversity continued to expand after the reform coalition was gone.[86] Politicians did not believe there was any statue of limitations for actions taken earlier. They were willing to reach back farther and farther into a person's past for material. Responding to Democratic claims that Republican attacks on 1992 presidential candidate Bill Clinton (for draft dodging during the Vietnam conflict) were "ancient history," Robert Dornan argued as follows:

Bork's rejection for a seat on the U.S. Supreme Court was based, in larger part, on articles and opinions from 25 years earlier. Douglas Ginsburg was denied a Supreme Court seat because he had many years earlier smoked marijuana. During Clarence Thomas' confirmation hearing, Senators asked what his views were on Roe v. Wade when he was in law school, almost 20 years earlier. Chappaquiddick may be ancient history, but it has *forever* put an end to Ted Kennedy's quest for the presidency.[87]

The defense of such attacks was that the character of a politician mattered. "It is important to know how each candidate dealt with the major events that shaped their outlook on the world, their country and their own personal life.... These are character-forming incidents that say a lot about each man."[88]

When charges emerged, party leaders and mavericks alike were prepared to take advantage of them. The party leadership was now interested in using rather than inhibiting scandal warfare. At the same time, the parties only had limited ability to contain such fighting when it did not serve their interests. Institutional reforms could still emerge from scandals – such as the Ethics Reform Act of 1989, which (in response to Wright) closed loopholes in the 1978 Ethics in Government Act – but the types of extensive institutional reform that seemed common in the 1970s were now rare. Whereas the 1970s had featured the creation of ethics rules, progress during the 1980s and 1990s was limited to fixing omissions and errors within them. When they passed, institutional reforms in the contemporary era focused on resolving the specific problems that were highlighted by a particular scandal rather than turning attention more broadly to the entire legislative process. Once the connection between sweeping institutional reforms and congressional scandal had come undone, there was almost no end to how far legislators were willing to go. This is not to say that scandal was all that mattered, as many battles were still fought over policy. But scandal did become an extremely common phenomenon that reached all levels of government.

### Outside Pressure

After the 1970s, Congress encountered a bewildering array of external constraints on its power. Although the reform coalition had promised that the end of the committee era would strengthen Congress in relationship to other government institutions, legislators soon discovered that this was not the case. With a large number of constraints bearing down on them, Congress found it no less difficult than before to claim a preeminent role in the polity.

One of the biggest constraints was the federal budget. As government grew in the twentieth century, the "institutional thickening" of government made it increasingly difficult for the most prominent political actors to preside over monumental innovations.[89] Budgetary policy in the 1980s and 1990s challenged any politician seeking to effect significant change.[90] There was simply less money for politicians to fight over. Persistent inflation and recession, the tax reductions of 1981, and the inflation-indexed tax code had cut the revenue that federal income taxes normally generated. Since federal tax hikes were politically unpopular, there was little money for new programs. Discretionary funds declined from 70.4 percent of the federal budget in 1963 to 37.2 percent in 1993.[91] Republicans did not overhaul the federal government, settling instead on a path of preventing any growth of the status quo and curbing what was put in place between the New Deal and the 1960s.[92] While Ronald Reagan's administration experienced mostly frustration when attempting to retrench government programs directly, they were more successful at draining financial resources from government through tax reduction.[93] At the same time, over 60 percent of the federal budget was now devoted to spending programs (e.g., Social Security, Medicare, and farm subsidies) for which the federal government had made strong commitments that would be extremely risky to overturn. A precommitted federal budget, large deficits and debt, and diminished tax revenue left the government in what one economist called a "fiscal straitjacket."[94] There were even steep declines in military funding, an area once considered sacrosanct.[95] Further, the Budget Enforcement Act of 1990 imposed stringent fiscal rules. Discretionary spending was subjected to annual budget caps: any legislated entitlement increase had to be offset by reductions in another program or by raising taxes. Until economic growth generated revenue, Congress had to raise taxes or cut spending to compensate for shortfalls. When surpluses temporarily returned in the late 1990s, legislators faced the option of reforming programs rather than launching new initiatives.[96]

To be sure, legislation was not impossible to obtain.[97] For instance, Congress reformed Social Security in 1983, closed major tax-code loopholes in 1986, enacted landmark deficit reduction in 1990, eliminated Aid to Families with Dependent Children (AFDC) in 1996, and made large reductions in farm assistance via the Federal Agricultural Improvement and Reform Act of 1996. Yet most of the big legislation in this era involved incremental expansion, retrenchment, and alterations of existing programs rather than breakthrough initiatives.[98] Moreover, many of these policy reforms did not last very long, as became evident with the rapid proliferation of tax loopholes in the mid-1990s and the growth in spending on farm programs in the late 1990s and early 2000s.[99] Also, many of the most important policy developments since the 1970s (such as affirmative action) were now being handled through the courts, commissions, and bureaucracies.[100]

Legislating became more challenging as the number of actors interacting with Congress continued to proliferate.[101] Thus the collective power of interest groups increased and the influence of any single organization diminished.[102] Elected officials found it difficult to develop stable relationships with interest groups, think tanks, or policy experts because there were so many of them. Unlike the committee era, legislators were negotiating in a hypercompetitive environment. The number of lobbyists and interest groups grew exponentially between the 1970s and 1990s,[103] a phenomenon that was not limited to corporations and trade associations. Liberal interest groups that focused on such "quality of life" issues as the environment emerged as an important presence.[104] In a world once dominated by the AMA, the AFL-CIO, and the Chamber of Commerce, thousands of individual corporations, unions, and specialized trade associations set up permanent offices in Washington.[105] Besides interest groups, there were more think tanks, policy experts, specialized publications, and pollsters.[106] Most of the tight alliances (or "iron triangles") that existed in the committee period loosened as the number of relevant actors mushroomed.[107] With so many organizations offering campaign contributions, information, and lobbying, tight coalitions rarely coalesced. Legislators had more freedom to maneuver around almost any particular interest group by allying with others. Although this freed politicians from dependence on any one group, the result was fewer stable long-term relationships.

The transformation was most evident in the domains of farm and health policy. In the committee era, the principal need of a legislator interested in farm policy was to develop a relationship with the American Farm Bureau Federation; those seeking to make a mark in health care needed a strategy, be it adversarial or cooperative, for handling the AMA. But in the 1980s and 1990s, the situation was more complicated. Legislators had to deal with multiple specialized interest groups. In the health care industry, there were distinct trade associations representing nonprofit and for-profit hospitals, insurers, nurses, doctors, staff workers, medical schools, medical specialists, medical technology and research manufacturers, and managed care providers, as well as lobbyists speaking for specific regions, states, and localities. In farm policy, the Bureau gave way to an arena filled with the National Farmers Union and commodity-based groups, such as the National Wheat Growers Association. Upon any legislative proposal, most of these groups sprung into action. Given how specialized their interests were, it was difficult to predict what position various groups would take and there were usually significant conflicts among them.

Divided government through much of this period was another factor that made things difficult for legislators who sought dramatic policy change. Certainly, as political scientist David Mayhew has shown, divided government has not prevented Congress from passing legislation. Indeed, since the 1940s, Congress has proven that it could be productive when different parties control the White House and Congress.[108] Yet divided government has not offered the most hospitable climate for passing "big ticket" legislation or for fostering bursts of major policies that transform the infrastructure of government, as occurred with the New Deal and Great Society.

In an era of divided government, Congress also encountered a powerful executive branch. Reagan reinvigorated the presidency to try and push through his conservative agenda. Once the conservative coalition had disintegrated, many Republicans looked to a strengthened presidency as the institution through which they could advance their agenda. Reagan and his allies brazenly made use of executive power to overcome liberal Democratic strength in Congress. For instance, Reagan relied on the Office of Management and Budget to make controversial decisions through the administrative process without congressional or judicial scrutiny.[109] In foreign policy, the War Powers Resolution had done little to negate the acceleration of executive power.[110] Reagan authorized military operations in Lebanon, Grenada, and Libya without asking for congressional consent. Some reforms that had been intended to strengthen Congress, such as the legislative veto, were overturned or fell into disuse.[111] Although the president was subject to multiple constraints before and after the era of the "Imperial Presidency," Congress continued to negotiate with a powerful office.

The media was another force that constrained Congress, as the trends discussed in the previous chapter persisted. C-SPAN matured as an organization, with the House and Senate channels each achieving a significant presence on cable systems. CNN's coverage of the Gulf War in 1991 established it as a viable all-news station that could seriously compete with the major network broadcasters. After the war, those networks would never reclaim their dominant role in the medium. The news cycle of cable was firmly established. The number of 24-hour news channels increased when NBC launched CNBC (1989) and MSNBC (1996). Specialized channels like the Christian Broadcast Network devoted extensive time to news. Even in the rather stuffy journalism from inside the Beltway, there were changes in this direction. In 1985, the new majority owner of *Roll Call* expanded the journal's coverage to include much more about the social scene of Washington. *The Hill* was an upstart competitor that covered more of the same. There were more Americans who normally did not pay much attention to political news who were now obtaining a greater amount of information about politics through the "soft news," meaning entertainment shows such as "Late Night with David Letterman," "The Tonight Show," "Entertainment Tonight," "The Daily Show," and "The Oprah Winfrey Show." The producers of these shows discovered that sometimes presenting news information could attract viewers – as long as the selected information was packaged in a style that emphasized individual drama, scandal, and intrigue.[112] Despite all the reforms, polls consistently showed that legislators still worked in a national culture that harbored negative sentiment toward Congress.[113]

Therefore, legislators in the new era confronted numerous external constraints on their collective and individual power. Some of those constraints had existed in the previous era, such as a strong president, while others were new, including the 24-hour adversarial media. But together they meant that Congress was not the dominant branch of government that many in the 1970s had promised.

## The Republican Revolution, 1992–1999

Bill Clinton was the first president to serve two terms when the new legislative process was firmly in place. Although members of the liberal coalition in the 1950s might have predicted that his presidency would be an ideal situation – given that it started with a moderate Democratic president and a Democratic Congress with strong party caucuses – they would have been sorely disappointed with the outcome. As president he would confront both the fragmenting and centralizing components of the new legislative process, neither of which tended to work in his favor. The Clinton years revealed how difficult it had become to obtain major legislation and – after the electoral terrain of America shifted rightward – how powerful conservative Republicans had become in the post–committee-era Congress.

Clinton's saga began in 1992, when he defeated President Bush and independent Ross Perot. Clinton secured 370 electoral votes but received only 43 percent

President Bill Clinton (second from right), Newt Gingrich (far right), and Robert Dole (far left), 1993 (Library of Congress).

of the popular vote. During the primaries, Clinton barely survived allegations of an extramarital affair and constant attacks on his character. Despite predictions of large Republican gains due to redistricting, the GOP obtained only ten additional seats in the House, leaving Democrats in the majority with 258. Democrats retained control of the Senate with 57 seats.

With Democrats controlling the presidency and Congress in 1993, there were predictions of a bold period in public policy. But optimism quickly faded. Clinton found himself under continuous investigation throughout his first term. Heeding calls from Republicans, the Justice Department appointed an independent counsel to investigate an Arkansas real-estate transaction from Clinton's days as governor. Congress conducted limited hearings that did not produce incriminating evidence. Prosecutors also examined the firing of the White House travel office staff. The suicide of Deputy White House Counsel Vincent Foster, a friend of the Clintons, fueled speculation about corruption at the highest levels.

Clinton was not the only politician grappling with scandal. One of the most explosive stories involved Senator Robert Packwood, a moderate Republican who had been praised for his role in the 1986 tax reform and his support of women's rights. Days after the 1992 election, the *Washington Post* reported that ten female staffers as well as several campaign workers and lobbyists had accused Packwood of sexual harassment.[114] Although the women did not say he was coercive, they accused him of such actions as grabbing a staff member and kissing her on the lips; fondling a campaign worker and forcing his tongue into her mouth; and making sexual advances toward the elevator operator at the Capitol.[115] Packwood's case arose at a potent moment. The election of 1992 had galvanized women's organizations in response to how the Senate Judiciary Committee had treated Anita Hill, a female lawyer who accused Supreme Court nominee Clarence Thomas of sexual harassment in 1991. The hearings on the Thomas confirmation, many argue, did more than almost anything else to popularize the problem of sexual harassment to the American public. Another media story revealed that Navy and Marine aviators physically and verbally assaulted women, including Navy officers, at the Tailhook Association's convention in Las Vegas. The relatively large number of female legislators subsequently elected in 1992 greatly increased the pressure on male politicians to deal more forcefully with women's civil rights, especially the rising demand to clamp down on inappropriate sexual behavior in the workplace.[116] The news media encouraged this through its extensive coverage (compared to a country such as France, for example) of sexual harassment scandals implicating powerful politicians. Media stories on sexual harassment in this country reached an all-time high between 1991 and 1998.[117]

The Senate Ethics Committee began an inquiry into Packwood on December 1, 1992. When the Senator revealed that he kept a comprehensive diary with pertinent information that could absolve him of the charges, the Ethics Committee subpoenaed the entire document because they were interested in other potential abuses, such as claims that Packwood pressured a lobbyist to find employment for his wife. With Packwood resisting, in 1993 the Supreme Court forced him to turn over the diary. Relying on standards of evidence that would most likely not have been permissible in a court of law, the Ethics Committee staff concluded there was sufficient evidence to show that Packwood had acted improperly.[118] "We're not talking about verbal harassment or lewd remarks, which were things that might have been acceptable at one time," said Patricia Ireland, president of the National Organization for Women, "it's an insult to the Senate and the men in the Senate that he or anybody else would not have known it was wrong to tear at a woman's clothing, to stand on her toes, to stick his tongue in her mouth."[119] Packwood's case became even more dramatic when he took over as chairman of the Senate Finance Committee in 1995. Barbara Mikulski

(D-MD), the sole woman in the Ethics Committee, insisted on public hearings and gained the support of five female legislators and prominent women's groups. Packwood denounced the idea of public hearings and convinced the chairman of the Ethics Committee, Mitchell McConnell (R-KY), to support him. After committee Republicans blocked the proposal, Barbara Boxer (D-CA) introduced a resolution for public hearings on the floor. Mikulski said, "I lived through the Anita Hill debacle ... the U.S. Senate raised questions whether this institution could ever deal with allegations related to sexual misconduct."[120] But Republicans lined up to oppose Boxer and her allies, with only three in the GOP dissenting. Republicans feared the effect of such hearings on their party, since they were planning to run on "family values" in the upcoming election against a president who was notorious for womanizing and who was himself facing a sexual harassment lawsuit.[121] Boxer's female allies attacked the GOP for not taking a serious stand on sexual harassment. Shortly before the Ethics Committee released its final report, it started to look into a charge that Packwood had made unwanted sexual advances toward a 17-year-old intern. A furious Packwood named the intern on a cable television show while challenging her credibility and calling for public hearings to defend himself. Republicans who had gone out on a limb to *oppose* such hearings were livid that Packwood had reversed his position. The Senate Ethics Committee charged Packwood with sexual misconduct, misusing public office for personal gain, and obstructing justice by altering diary entries. The committee unanimously called for his expulsion. With the Senate prepared to expel Packwood, he resigned on October 1, 1995.

In this atmosphere of scandal and investigation, President Clinton failed to develop a strong working relationship with Congress. The few victories that he enjoyed early on resulted either from bipartisan deals that infuriated congressional Democrats or from heavy-handed partisan action. The success of the North American Free Trade Act, for instance, received strong bipartisan support but angered liberal congressional Democrats. On the other hand, the deficit reduction bill of 1993 obtained no Republican support. Democratic leaders used the budget process to stifle floor opposition and to intimidate ambivalent colleagues into supporting the bill. The Democratic use of restrictive rules to prevent floor debate in 1993 and 1994 frustrated Republicans.[122]

The tension between Clinton and Congress exploded over his health care proposal in 1993. The health care problem had become critical, with over 40 million people lacking insurance. Skyrocketing health care costs posed a serious fiscal challenge to government and business. This issue, as a special Pennsylvania Senate election revealed in 1991, appealed to suburban middle-class voters. The constrained budgetary environment of the 1990s limited the options that were available to Clinton. The President's Task Force on Health Care Reform, headed by First Lady Hillary Clinton, drafted a plan that combined government intervention with cost-saving managed competition.[123] The plan called on the federal government to regulate health purchasing alliances consisting of individual and organizational purchasers of health care in a specific state or region. Under this system, insurance companies would compete for the business of these alliances by offering low-cost plans. The proposal would raise revenue through tobacco taxes and would use savings from proposed cuts in Medicare and Medicaid to take care of the uninsured. Operating in the stringent budgetary environment of the 1990s, Clinton abandoned plans that necessitated significant tax and spending increases and instead chose a proposal that centered on regulations and managed care. Every component of the proposal was crafted with administration officials anticipating how the Congressional Budget Office would "score" the proposal in terms of cost.[124]

There were many reasons that Clinton's health care bill failed, including a spirited counterattack by a segment of the insurance industry, a fragmented and divided health care industry, corporate resistance to taxation or employer mandates, insufficient government revenue, and tepid public support. This already difficult situation was made that much more challenging by the fragmented legislative process.[125] Although 20 percent of House bills were referred to multiple committees in the 1990s, 40 percent of health care legislation was sent to more than one committee.[126] For Clinton this meant that five House committees and two Senate committees shared control over health care. Since his proposal had to move through each committee, opponents found numerous opportunities to attack the legislation and it was difficult to mobilize supporters behind any single bill. There were also many places from which committee chairs could launch their attacks. Chairman of the Senate Finance Committee Patrick Moynihan lobbed a political grenade at Clinton during NBC's "Meet the Press" on September 19, 1993, when he called the budgetary figures behind their emerging plan a "fantasy."[127] Besides jurisdictional fragmentation, scandal brought down the pivotal figures of Rostenkowski and Packwood right in the middle of the debate. Although diminished in number, moderates could wreak havoc. This was evident when Tennessee Democrat James Cooper doggedly pursued a moderate compromise that drained support from his party. Facing severe internal divisions, Democratic leaders did not feel confident using procedures such as special omnibus committees.[128]

Unlike the debate over Medicare in 1965, when the AMA was the primary interest group, Clinton now faced a dizzying number of organizations. It was no longer possible to focus on outflanking one or two major interest groups. Attacks could come from anywhere, since each group was capable of inflicting serious damage through the fragmented legislative process and the televised media environment. For instance, the Health Insurance Association of America (HIAA), a group of small and middle-sized insurance companies, launched a devastating television campaign against Clinton's proposal. Hillary Clinton inadvertently publicized the ads nationally (though they were carried in only a few key northeastern markets) by denouncing them on television. When the staff of the House Energy and Commerce Committee chairman John Dingell leaked to the media a compromise that he had drafted, lobbyists representing several trade associations and individual businesses such as Pizza Hut and JCPenney conducted a massive letter-writing campaign that sabotaged the plan.[129]

Republicans were more united than Democrats on this issue and so were able to mount greater partisan pressure as their members voted in unison. Because there was strong unity among most in the GOP, moderates such as John Chafee (R-RI) who supported compromise were squeezed out of the debate. Most Republicans opposed a federal health care plan. When Senate Minority Leader Robert Dole met with pollsters in May 1994, he concluded that it would be better politically to prevent a bill from passing than to accept a compromise. Republicans used all the tools available to them to stifle any further progress. In the Senate, the GOP filibustered a tenuous compromise crafted by George Mitchell. The GOP also used the media. House Minority Leader Richard Armey (R-TX) published an op-ed in the *Wall Street Journal* on October 13, 1993, along with a chart that visually mocked how dangerously complicated Clinton's plan would be.[130] Television news shows picked up on Armey's column – particularly his flow chart, which he showed there as well as on C-SPAN.[131] In the end, no version of a health care bill was brought to a vote.

Republicans used the health care fiasco as part of a massive campaign mobilization in 1994. The GOP conducted a retreat in Maryland with media consultants and pollsters. Following the health care battle and other victories, Republicans felt confident and wanted to "create our own policies and present them forcefully, persistently, and intelligently."[132] After this retreat the GOP produced their "Contract with America," a slick, ten-point platform that called for reforming Congress and passing vital conservative legislation in the first hundred days of Republican rule. Advised by pollster Frank Luntz, Republicans drew on extensive survey and market research data when planning the document.[133]

More than 300 Republican legislators appeared outside the Capitol on September 27, 1994, to promote the "Contract." They signed the document as a symbolic promise to voters that they would fulfill their campaign pledges – unlike the Democrats, who (it was claimed) were nothing more than career politicians playing to vested interest groups. All the networks covered the event.[134] Using the document to nationalize the congressional elections, the GOP published a tear-out version of the "Contract" in *TV Guide* as a scorecard for readers to retain. Furthermore, Republicans appeared on conservative radio talk shows and purchased television ads to promote their message. GOP campaign committees channeled funds to candidates running for open seats.[135] Within Congress, Republicans blocked legislation so that Democrats could not claim major victories.[136] The GOP also continued to use the nontraditional media. Republican leaders, for instance, formed a close relationship with the controversial conservative radio host Rush Limbaugh.[137]

Republicans scored a stunning victory in the 1994 elections by taking control of the House and Senate. Senate Republicans raised their total numbers to 52 by

Minority Whip Newt Gingrich addresses Republican congressional candidates on Capitol Hill on September 27, 1994, during a rally where they pledged a "Contract with America" (Associated Press World Wide Photos).

gaining eight seats; that majority soon increased to 54 when two Democrats announced that they were switching parties. Alabama Democrat Richard Shelby announced his switch the day after the election. He proclaimed that "I thought there was room in the Democratic Party for a conservative Southern Democrat such as myself. But I can tell you, there is not."[138] Support for Clinton's most activist proposals – including health care, gays in the military, and tax increases – harmed allied Democratic incumbents who faced strong challengers in marginal southern and midwestern districts.[139] House Republicans took over the majority with 230 seats. Not only did the election bring the GOP control of Congress for the first time since 1952, it also further solidified the position of the conservative Republican wing.[140] The biggest GOP gains were in the South, Midwest, and West (regions that had been steadily gaining representation with reapportionment), while House Democrats managed to minimize their defeats in the East.[141]

The regional effects of reapportionment finally took hold, as Democrats in the Northeast and Midwest lost nineteen seats to the South and West. The new GOP leadership reflected the shift in the growth of the population from the Frost Belt to the suburban Sunbelt: Speaker Gingrich represented the Atlanta suburbs; Majority Leader Richard Armey represented the Dallas suburbs; and

Majority Whip Tom DeLay represented the Houston suburbs. This shift, one of the biggest demographic changes in the U.S. population since World War II, was finally being allowed to affect the character of congressional representation as a result of reapportionment and redistricting.[142] Indeed, suburbs were likewise doing well in the Democratic party: Minority Leader Richard Gephardt was a representative of the St. Louis suburbs and Minority Whip David Bonior represented suburban Macomb County, just outside of Detroit.[143] As a result of the 1994 elections, the GOP claimed a majority of southern House seats for the first time since Reconstruction. "The old Southern bull Democrat," Trent Lott announced, "is now a Republican."[144] Southern and southwestern Senate Republicans were big victors. Although a few campaigns involved the dramatic defeat of senior incumbents (e.g., Rostenkowski and Speaker Foley), most of the victories in 1994 involved Republicans winning open seats and defeating young Democratic incumbents.[145]

With redistricting, Republicans had once again used the procedures born out of the 1960s and 1970s to achieve their pivotal political objective. They turned court-ordered redistricting, the Voting Rights Act, and the problem of vote dilution to their advantage. The Republican National Committee had promoted redistricting in the early 1990s. Entering into unusual alliances with African-American legislators, they championed redistricting with the intention of creating more solidly conservative Republican districts by concentrating African-Americans outside their core areas of support. This removed African-American voters who were a moderating force in districts that otherwise leaned toward the conservative end of the spectrum. As a result, Republicans who represented these areas could move more forcefully toward the right of the political spectrum.[146]

After taking control of Congress, Republicans passed a series of institutional reforms in 1995 that further weakened committee chairs and solidified the process put into place during the 1970s. The reforms grew out of the work of the Joint Committee on the Organization of Congress, established in 1992, whose recommendations had been stalled in the Rules Committee. Remembering that autonomous chairs could be problematic if they pursued their own agendas or formed alliances with the other party, the Republican leadership wanted to retain authority in their own hands.

The direction of their reforms revealed that the new generation of Republicans was quite comfortable with – indeed, dependent on – the legislative process that congressional liberals had done so much to construct. Whereas the GOP in the 1980s relied on those aspects of the legislative process that favored minorities and individual legislators, they now reversed course to focus on the majority-strengthening components. The schizophrenic character of the modern legislative process enabled this reversal. After more than a decade of attacking Democrats for using special rules to manhandle the minority, Republicans turned to the same provisions as a way to bury legislation or stifle looming threats to the party agenda from Democrats or uncontrollable Republicans. House Republicans weakened proxy voting; they also imposed a six-year term limit on committee and subcommittee chairs as well as an eight-year term limit on the Speaker. With a plan to keep committee chairs under the control of the party, Republicans reversed the subcommittee bill of rights by eliminating their control over staff and by allowing committee chairs to help appoint subcommittee chairs. Speaker Gingrich took on the responsibility of appointing subcommittee chairs. The House Republicans also limited the number of committee assignments that any member could have to two full committees and four subcommittees while cutting committee staff by a third. Gingrich relied on task forces and advisory counsels, rather than committee chairs, and he flagrantly violated seniority by appointing chairs (to Appropriations, Commerce, and Judiciary) who were not in line for the position. The House required members to follow the labor laws that private-sector employees faced, fulfilling one of the unheeded demands from the mid-1970s. In 1995 Congress passed the Congressional Accountability Act, which protected those who worked as employees in Congress and created internal protections for congressional staff, also granting them the right to take job claims to court. Members retained considerable flexibility in hiring, promotions, and firing. Nonetheless, Congress now fell under the Civil Rights Act of 1964, the Occupational Safety and Health Act of 1970, the Americans with Disability Act of 1990, the Family and Medical Leave Act of 1993, and more. The Congressional Accountability Act established formal procedures for compliance and established the Compliance Office to handle complaints by employees.[147]

Yet Gingrich knew he must heed the freshmen lest they cause him significant problems. This was not the omnipotent Speaker that some in the press at first depicted. From the beginning, Gingrich's strategy was to depend on the freshmen voting as a solid bloc. The 73 freshmen were an extremely cohesive group of individuals who were convinced they had a mandate and cared little about their political future.[148] Ed Gillespie, a spokesman for Dick Armey, said that "there's a strong synthesis between the freshmen and the sophomores and the House Republican leadership."[149] When the newly appointed Robert Livingston tried to remove first-year member Mark Neumann (R-WI) from the defense appropriations subcommittee, the freshmen intimidated Gingrich into overriding Livingston. Nor was the GOP able to ride roughshod over committees. When David Dreier's (R-CA) committee recommended sweeping jurisdictional changes, Republicans were forced to water down the plan, eliminating only committees (including the Post Office and Civil Service, the Merchant Marine and Fisheries, and the District of Columbia committees) that had primarily served Democratic interests. While committees were facing stronger party leaders and reduced staff resources (by 1996, committee staff had been cut by a third), the reduction of subcommittees had given them some increased power, which was praised as a positive development by 67 percent of thirteen chairs and five ranking minority members interviewed in 1996. Revealing the continued sense of importance among committee chairs, the one reform that did not sit well was the term limits imposed on them; when surveyed in 1996, 69 percent of the chairs and ranking minority members said that Republicans should rethink those limits.[150]

Given the protections afforded to individual rights, institutional reforms in the Senate did not go as far in centralizing authority. But there were notable changes that completed the move against committees. Republicans imposed a six-year limit on chairs and started voting on a legislative agenda. Senate Republicans also decided to vote on committee chairs. One senior Republican complained: "Each of us operates on the graces of our colleagues now."[151] Notwithstanding the failure to remove the chair of Appropriations, senior members realized that younger senators were prepared to challenge them.[152]

Republican leaders learned that they had taken over in an era where the constraints upon governance and the long-term power of every legislator, including party leaders, were enormous. Although Gingrich initially held frequent televised press conferences and opened many inside meetings to reporters, he quickly backed off when media coverage of him turned negative (he still appeared on television more than any of his predecessors, an indication of how important television had become).[153]

Scandal consumed Gingrich's speakership. Under relentless attack from Minority Whip David Bonior (D-MI), Gingrich was forced to return a $4.5-million book advance that he had received from a publishing company owned by Rupert Murdoch, who had spent the past year lobbying for deregulation of the broadcast industry. The House Ethics Committee, which was investigating whether Gingrich misused campaign contributions, started to look into the deal as well.[154] In terms of legislating, Republicans stumbled when they squared off with Democrats over the budget. The GOP decided to use omnibus budget legislation in 1995 to pass a bold package of spending and tax cuts as well as a historic reform of Medicare and Medicaid. They promised that cuts would balance the budget by 2002. The reconciliation measure passed 237 to 189 in the House (with one Republican opposing the package and five Democrats supporting it) and 52 to 47 in the Senate (where there were no Democratic supporters and only one Republican opponent). Despite his inclination to compromise, Clinton's advisors persuaded the president to oppose the package. Facing intense pressure from the freshmen to hold the line, Gingrich was again reminded of the limits of authority as he was unable to develop a compromise.[155] One top advisor to Clinton explained: "the freshmen had become Newt's Frankenstein monster – and my new best friend. The more they dug in, the better off we were."[156]

Clinton relied on television news and advertisements to attack the GOP for undermining Medicare to finance upper-income tax cuts; Medicare was one of those costly precommitted and enormously popular social programs that had taken up major space in the federal budget. Events also played against conservatives. On April 19, 1995, a tragedy in Oklahoma City – where two men with links to right-wing paramilitary groups bombed a federal building and killed 168 people – resulted in charges that conservatism was fueling dangerous extremism. Dismissing such claims, Gingrich and the Republicans stood firm. Gingrich called such charges "grotesque and offensive."[157] The Speaker contributed to the attacks by making a series of statements that played into negative media portraits of him.

When Clinton vetoed a few reconciliation bills, the partisan struggle resulted in several shutdowns of the federal government between October 1995 and January 1996. During the conflict, the media portrayed Gingrich as immature and unreasonable. The Speaker lost the support of conservative Democrats when he refused to budge. He also faced a determined freshman class that was unwilling to compromise. As the Speaker explained, the freshmen "really think this is life and death for their country, and think their careers are trivial in the balance; and mean it with total sincerity. They don't regard being defeated as the end of their life, just as a change in jobs."[158] This stance troubled many Senate Republicans – including future presidential candidate Robert Dole, who had a stake in being productive and had spent much of his career seeking bipartisan compromises. Many voters, especially the elderly, were outraged by the proposed cuts to Medicare. Clinton coopted their position by accepting legislation to balance the budget in seven years, but based on data from the Office of Management and Budget rather than the Congressional Budget Office. After one final prolonged shutdown, the GOP closed on a deal under pressure from Senate Republican Leader Dole.

The polarized partisan approach that shaped the budget process was not an aberration. The number of votes that divided the parties rose from half of recorded votes in 1991–1992 to nearly two thirds in 1995–1996.[159] Senators filibustered in unprecedented fashion for partisan purposes. In 1995, almost 44 percent of the major legislation considered was delayed as a result of extended debate.[160] Sounding like liberal Democrats in the 1950s attacking Democratic committee chairs, House Democrats in the 1990s focused on the new source of authority – Republican party leaders – for stifling the rights of minorities by blocking votes on legislation and limiting minority rights on investigative committees.[161] They blamed their own legislative failures on the ability of the Republican majority to use procedures against them.[162] Republicans responded that Democratic leaders were using procedures to block action through delay and to tie up the legislative agenda.[163] The GOP also believed that Democrats were simply grandstanding for partisan purposes by attacking procedures that they themselves had used as a majority.[164] Republicans claimed that Democrats were highlighting exceptional decisions by the Republicans and presenting them as part of a broader trend: "just as 'one swallow does not a summer make'," said the chief of staff for the House Rules Committee, "one rule on an unreported bill does not an ominous trend make."[165]

The tense environment did not change after the 1996 elections. Republicans retained control of Congress and Clinton defeated Robert Dole by winning 370 electoral votes, including some key southern and western states that tended to lean Republican. The GOP majority in the House fell to 227 Republicans (versus 206 Democrats) while Senate Republicans increased their lead by two seats to 55. Democrats were able to regain some standing in the West and in a few midwestern states. The new congressional leadership solidified conservative control of the GOP. Gingrich retained the Speakership. Trent Lott had replaced Robert Dole when he stepped down as Majority Leader. The other positions were filled by staunch conservatives as well, including Majority Whip Tom DeLay, Majority Leader Dick Armey, and Senate Whip Donald Nickles (R-OK). Democratic Minority Leader Richard Gephardt and Senate Minority Leader Tom Daschle (D-SD) were equally partisan, having learned to legislate in the polarized 1980s. The election of 1996 witnessed the continued exodus of moderates.[166] The unusually large number of retirees blamed incivility, fund-raising, and distrust in government.[167] *Congressional Quarterly* ended its feature on the conservative coalition, inaugurated in 1957, by proclaiming: "the conservative coalition – a tool of political analysis for much of the century – became moribund in 1998."[168]

Partisanship remained strong after the health care and budget battles, but Democrats and Republicans backed down from bold policy proposals. Whereas Clinton feared another health care fiasco, Republicans had been wounded by the budget confrontation. Gingrich was also cautious, since he knew that his own support within the party was weak.[169] But more than party strategy was at work here.

Politicians were coming to terms with how hard it was to legislate in the contemporary congressional era. Clinton focused on protecting existing programs through his veto power, obtaining legislation that offered incremental change, and achieving policy outside the legislative process by using executive orders. In 1997, Clinton and the Republican Congress agreed on legislation to balance the budget by 2002. This removed the central policy issue of the decade from the table. Economic growth and lower health care costs ensured that the budget was balanced as a result of rising tax revenue. Both parties focused on modest legislation that accomplished less but elicited milder opposition.

Instead of legislation, Democrats and Republicans fought through the politics of investigation. Congressional Democrats had been attacking Gingrich's ethics since he became Speaker. By December 1995, a special counsel for the House Ethics Committee was investigating whether his televised town hall meetings and a college course that he had taught between 1993 and 1995 – which many saw as a promotional tool for the GOP – were financed by tax-deductible contributions diverted from his political action committee, GOPAC. Gingrich claimed the course was nonpartisan and thus eligible for the funds. The course, according to Democrats, was a tool to mobilize political support and thus not eligible for tax-deductible funds. The Ethics Committee named James Cole to investigate whether Gingrich had violated the tax laws, while David Bonior leveled a series of charges against the Speaker. Few missed the irony of this situation. "It was Newt Gingrich who pioneered the inquisitorial style that David Bonior now practices against him," noted the *New Republic*.[170]

Following the 1996 elections, dissenting Republicans forced Gingrich to fight for his position. Cole would explain the findings from his investigation during a televised hearing on January 17, 1997. That day, after the release of Cole's report and the televised hearings, the Ethics Committee reported that Gingrich had been reckless with the House ethics rules. With only one dissenting member, the committee recommended that he be reprimanded and fined. Based on a deal that the Speaker had negotiated with them, the House fined Gingrich $300,000 and reprimanded him by a vote of 395 to 28 on January 21. He earned the dubious distinction of becoming the first sitting Speaker reprimanded by his colleagues for failing to adhere to House ethics rules. Despite the partisan fighting, the final vote took place on bipartisan lines. Gingrich admitted that he had not provided full information to the Ethics Committee and acknowledged that he should have checked more closely with his lawyers about handling the funds. He claimed, however, that he accepted the verdict to preserve the stability of the House rather than because he was guilty. The reprimand came at a time when Gingrich's support within his own party was shaky: younger Republicans were frustrated with his willingness to compromise on the budget, his unpopularity and ethics problems, and rumors of his own personal indiscretions. Between March and July of 1997, a coup against Gingrich was attempted that included a coalition of younger and senior GOP officials. Soon after the unexpected Republican losses in the 1998 elections – when one GOP operative said that "the problem for the party is that Newt is the face of the party" – Gingrich was forced by his colleagues to retire from office.[171] Before he stepped down, Gingrich decried the "cannibals" in his party.[172]

Meanwhile, Republicans pursued their investigations into the administration. Congress conducted no fewer than 37 investigations into the White House between 1995 and 1998,[173] which culminated in Clinton's impeachment proceedings. The charges stemmed from his sexual relationship with an intern and his failure to acknowledge this relationship during a sexual harassment lawsuit that had been allowed by the Supreme Court.[174] The legislative process through which the Clinton scandal was handled was rooted in the broader institutional changes that had transformed the entire political system during the 1960s and 1970s. The investigation was driven by an independent counsel, framed by the new sexual workplace norms, and judged within a partisan and televised legislative process. Cable and Internet organizations dominated the news coverage. Conservative organizations and philanthropists funded many of the legal cases and investigations into the President. Clinton's impeachment revealed just how much government institutions had changed since the days of Rayburn and Johnson.

### The Turbulent World of Congress

Although once envisioned as a path toward progressive legislation in the 1950s, the new legislative process was just as important to Republicans as it was to Democrats. In the 1980s and 1990s, Republicans relied on C-SPAN and cable news to communicate with supporters; expanded their vast network of individual campaign supporters, who were extremely important given the contribution limitations imposed in 1974; created alliances with new specialized interest groups and think tanks; supported court-ordered redistricting to create solidly conservative constituencies; used their party caucuses to ensure discipline, as well as the tools of minorities and mavericks when they were not in control of the chambers; and attacked powerful Democrats through scandal warfare. As the minority party, the GOP thus used the decentralizing aspects of the process to hamstring Democrats and launch attacks on the leadership, while as the majority they used it to maintain party discipline and to shape the congressional agenda.

For critics, the modern congressional era was dysfunctional because partisanship and scandal eroded the willingness to compromise and trust among legislators. Congress was not as powerful, efficient, or trusted as many had hoped for after Nixon's downfall. Liberals lamented that the decline of the committee era had not meant a resurgence of progressive policies. For other observers, the process worked well. Indeed, Congress was now more open and porous. Parties finally asserted the type of centralizing influence that liberal Democrats had yearned for in the 1950s, even though this came at the cost of bipartisan agreement. Yet the party leaders were kept honest by mavericks and chamber minorities who could shake up the system as well as by committee and subcommittee chairs, who retained significant roles. Any politician could be punished for violating ethics rules. No leader, from the Speaker to the Senate Majority Leader, enjoyed autocratic power. Furthermore, Congress as an institution was kept in line by powerful external forces that were far from subservient in dealing with the legislative branch. These forces included television reporters who disseminated stories about corruption, interest groups fighting for virtually every issue imaginable, and extremely powerful presidents.

# 13

# Epilogue

Some observers dismiss congressional procedural changes of the 1970s by saying that they did not have a dramatic effect on the types of policies that resulted. While this latter claim is debatable, the argument of this book is that democracy is as much defined by the political process as by the specific policies produced. In addition to questions about who should have the right to vote, American political history has been animated by heated struggles over the actual mechanisms of representative democracy. For it is at this nitty-gritty level of debate that the character of government comes alive.[1]

Changes that swept through institutions in the 1970s fundamentally altered the national political experience. Congress became more open to public and media scrutiny, legislators were more susceptible to nonelectoral attacks, congressional parties were empowered while their leaders were constrained, ethics codes made it easier to punish certain forms of behavior, and a greater number of interest groups, think tanks, and activists obtained access to the system. Understanding how political institutions have changed as well as the successes – and failures – of earlier reforms is crucial to evaluating current strategies for improving government on a sound historical basis.

This book began by asking how and why America's Congress exited the committee era and entered the contemporary era in the 1970s. This shift was part of a broader reconstruction of American politics that moved the nation away from an insulated, hierarchical, and stable governing structure into one that was uncertain, partisan, fragmented, and highly conflictual. The political parties, for instance, underwent significant changes as reformers wrested remaining power away from machine operatives and lodged decision making about candidates within the primary system. Moreover, bureaucracies were reconfigured as new laws and regulations ensured that public interest groups, the media, and the courts would retain access to the administrative process. Election campaigns came to involve disclosure, public monies, contribution limits, and a diverse and diffuse donor base. Finally, the Office of the Independent Counsel, grand juries, and the FBI institutionalized the apparatus necessary for conducting constant investigations into political corruption.

This book shows that government reform is a slow, messy, and complex process. The case examined here fits well with new research on institutions that shows how change takes a long time and does not tend to occur in the dramatic bursts of innovation often depicted in high-school and college textbooks.[2] Institutional change started with the formation of a reform coalition in the 1950s. This coalition of dissatisfied political elites was pivotal to the downfall of the committee process, since the issue never elicited strong electoral pressure. With numerous politicians demanding to fix the legislative branch, it was this coalition that placed "congressional reform" on the national agenda and defined the issues in ways that were politically potent.

With representatives from civil rights organizations, unions, academia, foundations, and the Democratic party, this coalition emerged directly out of the political arena. They invested their resources into convincing the public that process had a monumental impact on what government could or could not do, linking it to some of the most turbulent social questions of the period. The coalition began as an outgrowth of twentieth-century liberalism and involved individuals and organizations who believed that institutional reforms were essential if Congress was ever going to pass legislation for neglected African-American, urban, and labor constituencies. The need for federal civil rights legislation was initially the driving force in this coalition, since that issue bridged the concerns of internal factions and also highlighted conservative southern Democrats and the committee process as a common target.

The coalition swelled by the 1960s to include public interest groups such as Common Cause and individuals like Ralph Nader, who claimed to represent the interests of the suburban middle class and picked up on the anticorruption tradition in American politics. These public interest groups demanded government reform as an end in itself rather than merely as an avenue to obtain policies. Like those who created the coalition in the 1950s, these groups were not shy about jumping into the political fray and believed that they, too, should become an institution of American politics. The public interest groups perceived the problems they were targeting as chronic in that government institutions were so developed and entrenched. They frequently found themselves in conflict with labor liberals who remained determined to protect the programs and government organizations that benefitted their main constituencies.

Despite internal differences and competing objectives, most in the coalition agreed that the existing political leaders were tightly bound to the legislative process. Based on this argument, they stated that institutional reform was essential to obtaining almost any new type of policy and leadership. It was also necessary if the nation wanted to restore public faith in the federal government and to curtail excessive political power in those cases where constitutional checks and balances had fallen short.

The coalition communicated across institutions through informal networks. Its members sold a message to the public and policy makers by pressuring the media, lobbying, and electioneering. Sensitive to the importance of short-term electoral calculations to legislators, the coalition focused on obtaining incremental reforms that weakened the institutional foundation of the committee process. This was an important strategic tactic that brought considerable rewards to the coalition. Instead of trying to overcome the political and electoral fears of congressional leaders through brute force (which they most often did not have), the coalition usually tried to work around those fears. This tactic worked, since even the most powerful committee leaders often accepted such incremental reform proposals because they did not perceive them as an immediate threat to themselves. They were confident that, in the short term, the mechanisms would never be used against them.

During debates over each specific reform, legislators in the coalition joined voting alliances with other factions interested in the particular measure at hand, such as Republicans seeking to enhance their party's position. The coalition also accepted important compromises to keep its members together on the broader reform agenda. While the coalition's growth and its ad hoc alliances caused internal friction, the benefits at first outweighed the costs since they helped pressure incumbents into responding to reform.

As the coalition evolved, the external institutional environment surrounding Congress altered in ways that did not favor continuation of the committee process. The Supreme Court embraced an activist stance toward redistricting. This created short-term uncertainty for southern conservative Democrats – right as the battle over institutions was heating up – by eliminating population inequality in districts and weakening the electoral power of rural areas. Over the long term, the decisions helped create a more ideologically cohesive Democratic Caucus that had far less interest in tolerating autonomous committee chairs. The news media were transformed in the 1960s by the triumph of the professional ethos of adversarial reporting. Cable television technology then produced an ongoing news cycle in the 1980s that imposed more burdens on legislators and made it harder for them to control information. Legislators also confronted a highly fragmented environment of nonprofit advocacy and other special interest groups, where predictable alliances were not common. Finally, presidents remained antagonistic to Congress: Kennedy and Johnson were each frustrated by southern conservative chairs, and Richard Nixon launched an institutional war against the entire Congress.

The reform coalition and the reorientation of institutions surrounding Congress (the media, the Supreme Court, the presidency, interest groups, and more) established a strong foundation for institutional reform to succeed. But this was not enough. Dramatic events during the first half of the 1970s – such as the Wilbur Mills scandal and the post-Watergate elections – were the final step because they created the political support necessary for the coalition to directly attack committee chairs and to dismantle their most important procedural prerogatives.

By themselves, these events could easily have fizzled or had little institutional impact. But the maturation of the reform coalition and changes within the nation's major political institutions had established the preconditions necessary for these events to produce concrete outcomes. The events enabled the coalition to turn procedures that (to committee chairs) had previously appeared harmless into potent political weapons. The divisions that emerged within the reform coalition as it expanded its membership were impossible to overcome in some cases (such as with committee jurisdiction and restricting political action committees), as were certain differences that emerged with the legislative factions whom the coalition allied with. Nonetheless, in an unusually large number of instances, Congress accepted reform in the 1970s. Although many of these reforms seem inconsequential today because of unintended or unanticipated consequences or because of a familiarity with the style of politics that emerged, at the time they were dramatic and were perceived as a transformation in the way that Congress worked.

Together, this sequence of developments ushered Congress into the contemporary era. Congress was very different in the 1990s than it had been in the committee era. Parties were much stronger in the contemporary Congress, although legislative leaders (now also party heads) were more susceptible to challenge than committee chairs of the past. The new Congress still offered many opportunities for independent entrepreneurs and mavericks to exert influence, and the legislative branch was now more open to public and media scrutiny. Legislators faced more rules and regulations on their behavior, and the new process created multiple entry points for interest groups and activists to enter the debate.

Yet the institutional changes of the 1970s did not produce many of the outcomes that proponents of reform had hoped for. Congress has not emerged as the dominant branch of government, it is not an icon of efficiency, it has not regained public favor, and it has certainly not become a factory of progressive policy. There were many reasons why the dramatic changes did not produce these desired effects.

Foremost, committee chairs – the pivot of the older era – were not replaced with a source of authority that was any more forceful or efficient. Congress had become an institution that facilitated both centralized and decentralized authority in order to nurture competing centers of power. In the contemporary era, there have been stronger party caucuses where the leaders remained susceptible to challenge, since the legislative process now offers room to such decentralized forces as specialized caucuses, subcommittees, and mavericks. Although no longer the center of the action, committee chairs had not been totally disempowered and so they, too, continued to exercise influence. For example, House Ways and Means Committee chairman Bill Thomas (R-CA) often gave the Republican White House and congressional leaders considerable headaches in 2003 by driving debates rather than following orders.

The new sources of authority in Congress, moreover, did not favor legislative compromise. When subcommittees, caucuses, and mavericks exerted influence, Congress could be chaotic as the fragmenting tendencies of the institution made it hard to pull together broad coalitions. During periods of intense partisanship, legislative success depended on an unusual set of circumstances: near total agreement among members of one party, enough senators to overcome a filibuster, and a president who would not veto the final product. Members of the opposition party rarely entered into bipartisan agreements because their caucuses possessed similar tools to punish defectors. Partisan and scandal warfare had eroded trust among members.

Additionally, the internal transformation of Congress did little to reverse the external challenges that legislatures faced. Congress was operating in a period when strong presidents and the courts continued to engage the legislature in battle. The fractured world of interest groups, activists, and think tanks made durable alliances difficult to achieve. And the adversarial news media that operated around the clock made life more challenging for politicians. All this occurred at a time when the federal budget offered legislators in both parties little room for innovation.

Although liberals had been crucial to the coalition that helped the reform movement develop its political muscle, the conservative movement that swept through America after the 1970s proved remarkably adept at working in the new legislative process. Liberals learned that a new political process did not inherently mean a more progressive policy agenda. Political context was everything. Instead of developing a new reform agenda, legislators who were allied with the conservative movement took advantage of the reconstructed process. When they were a minority, Republicans used the process to stifle Democratic legislation and to bring down several of the most powerful leaders.

When the electoral winds of America blew in conservative majorities, the new legislative process turned into a liberal nightmare. Republicans paralyzed the Clinton administration during its second term. When the era of divided government ended with the election of President George W. Bush, the GOP used the process to severely weaken the fiscal infrastructure of the American state. Democrats were stifled and frustrated as the Republican leadership prevented them from offering amendments, prohibited substitute bills on the floor, delayed spending legislation to limit debate, loaded conference committees, and much more. Republicans also overturned some of their own reforms from 1994 that hampered party leaders.[3] There were many factors behind the success of the conservative movement, but their skillful use of the legislative process was instrumental.

Moreover, the institutional changes of the 1970s did not reverse the broader trends that were fueling popular discontent with the political system. Reformers were unable to prevent the flow of private money into campaigns or prevent the type of corruption that citizens detested. The negative outlook of the national media and other producers of political culture continued to disseminate

images of politicians as hopelessly corrupt. The institutional barriers that separated citizens from politics remained high. The resurgence of partisanship did
not produce the type of parties America witnessed in the nineteenth century,
which had created points of close contact for voters and politicians. Further, the
conservative movement shaped a national culture that exacerbated the antistatist
sentiments of American political life. In some cases the reforms strengthened aspects of the congressional process, such as rabid partisanship, that were turning
off voters instead of reengaging them with the ebbs and flows of politics.

The traumatic events following September 11, 2001, created the potential for
the start of a new era. The terrorist attacks on the World Trade Center and
the Pentagon produced unprecedented fear among American citizens about the
threats that loomed from international forces, revealing the desperate need for
extensive changes in government surveillance and military strategy. Like previous wars, this one stirred intense feelings of patriotism and made it risky for
politicians to continue their old practices of partisan vitriol and scandal warfare.
After the 2002 elections, the federal government was under unified control. In
terms of policy innovation, the wartime emergency and unified partisan control
of government have allowed Congress to overcome some of the obstacles they
faced in the 1990s, as evidenced by passage of sweeping "homeland security"
changes and continued tax cuts.

Thus far, however, there are few signs of a new reform period emerging that
could move Congress into a new historical era. Currently, America's Congress
is firmly rooted in the postcommittee era. At this point, none of the three major
components that produced institutional reform in the 1970s is evident. Foremost, there is not a strong reform coalition promoting a coherent alternative to
the process that defines the contemporary era. Most individuals and organizations who campaign for institutional reform today are committed to correcting
the flaws of the existing system rather than searching for a fundamentally new
type of process. This was evident during the Republican revolution of 1994, when
most GOP reforms continued to focus on weakening committees and strengthening parties. It was also clear with the most pertinent recent institutional change:
the Bipartisan Campaign Reform Act of 2002 did not create a new regulatory
structure; instead, it closed loopholes in the structure that was created in 1974.
The bill was driven not by a coalition fighting for wholesale government reform
but by a handful of legislators and advocacy groups who were concerned about
shoring up the 1974 campaign finance laws. This is a far cry from the broad demands of the early 1970s.

In most cases, proponents of reform rail in abstract terms against corruption
without presenting any coherent alternative or explanation of how the current
institution works. They have established few concrete links to today's major
social problems and movements. The powerful discourse of the previous era,
which bound together the reform coalition despite its internal differences, no
longer exists. There is not a reform coalition that is tightly connected by informal networks or a coherent discourse. Whereas institutional reform in the 1960s

and 1970s was tied to mass political movements such as civil rights, pacifism, feminism, the New Left, and conservatism, current proponents of institutional reform lack any similar kind of broader connection.

Furthermore, the institutions that surround Congress do not threaten the contemporary process. In fact, the situation is the opposite. The individuals who have been president since Jimmy Carter, for example, have been fully prepared to engage the legislative branch in scandal, partisan, and media warfare. This has been the case even when a single party controlled both branches of government. Despite its conservative turn, the Supreme Court did not turn back the clock to the period before 1962; it has continued to impose certain restrictions on redistricting, and the composition of existing districts has favored strong partisanship. Minority-based districts have created Democratic constituencies who encourage legislators to move to the left (given the high number of African-American residents) as well as strong Republican districts that push legislators to the right (because they have been drained of almost any liberal constituents). Gerrymandering to protect incumbents, moreover, has increased the incentive of elected officials to play to the most active (i.e., the least moderate) elements of their constituencies during the primaries.

Within the media, trends continue to buttress a constant adversarial outlook in many areas of politics. Computer technology created a medium that removed almost any barrier to the dissemination of information and which also lowered the cost of entry into the news business. Control of information kept slipping away. Even in those issue areas (e.g., military conflict) where the media has been more restrained during recent years, television and print news continues to demonstrate a willingness to challenge politicians when the time is right and when opinions among Washington's political elites are divided.[4]

Although "focusing" events have taken place since the 1970s, they have not resulted in institutional change. Many of the biggest events, such as 9/11 and corporate scandals, were not directly related to Congress. Other events that were linked to Congress, such as the impeachment of President Clinton, did not have a serious institutional effect because a vibrant reform coalition and external institutions unfavorable to the status quo did not exist. Without such preconditions, the focusing events either lent support to the existing process or faded into obscurity.

The future of the current legislative era remains unclear. Some citizens are content with a system that they believe holds politicians accountable, ensures constant surveillance for corruption, is relatively open to the public and media, and allows parties to influence policy. Others fear that the prominence of partisanship and scandal warfare has poisoned relations among legislators to the point that policymaking is almost impossible. Some of the nation's finest citizens, critics add, refuse to enter into the turbulent fray. All of this has become particularly troubling as the nation is thrust into a new and dangerous era of warfare. Recent actions by presidential candidates have also threatened to render many 1970s reforms irrelevent. What this book demonstrates, however, is that moving into a new legislative era would require the nation to reconstruct the entire process and culture that have defined congressional politics – indeed, national politics – since the 1960s. This would be a gradual process, requiring a strong coalition that could work over time to reform the interconnected processes that define today's Congress and depending on institutions other than the legislative branch to change in ways that favor a new politics.

The history of congressional reform in the post–World War II period demonstrates that government institutions *can* be changed in American politics – even if it is extraordinarily difficult to achieve the changes and even though the effects of such reforms often turn out to be different than anticipated. Notwithstanding the age-old admonitions about government reformers, dating back to New York City machine politician George Washington Plunkitt's criticism of reformers as "morning glories" who look "lovely in the mornin' and withered up in a short time," this history shows that fundamental government reform can happen despite the enormous staying power of the status quo.[5] In the year 2004, there seems to be the political space for another round of reform because it is clear that many Americans are profoundly dissatisfied with the quality of their government and the nature of the political process. Most damaging of all is the fact that many of these citizens express their feelings by opting out of the political system. Whether we are approaching another era of reform akin to the 1900s or 1970s will only become clear as the new millennium unfolds. Yet what reformers can take from this history is that they should not be seduced by the promises of optimists, who insist that reform can be easily accomplished through some quick fix, nor deterred by the progeny of George Washington Plunkitt, who claim that government institutions can never be changed.

# Notes

## Chapter 1

1. The decade has only recently begun to receive serious historical attention: Bruce J. Schulman, *The Seventies: The Great Shift in American Culture, Society, and Politics* (New York: Free Press, 2001); David Frum, *How We Got Here: The 70's – The Decade That Brought You Modern Life – For Better or Worse* (New York: Basic Books, 2000).
2. Richard Hofstadter, *The Age of Reform* (New York: Vintage, 1955).
3. The political science literature in the subfield of congressional studies is enormous. Its books and articles can be found scattered throughout my footnotes. Congressional studies, however, has focused primarily on one issue: what factors motivate legislators to oppose or reject particular congressional reform proposals at any given moment in time (modernization, partisanship, electoral self-interest, institutional pride, and more). My book draws on many of the analytic insights and data from this impressive literature while also stressing several issues that they have downplayed. First, whereas political scientists tend to examine the role of legislators and other political actors in isolation from one another, I emphasize the importance of a reform coalition whose members were located in different institutions and connected through policy networks. Second, I stress how noncongressional institutions – such as interest groups, public interest lobbies, the mass media, and the Supreme Court – reconfigured the legislative experience. Third, I emphasize the importance of unpredictable political events, such as scandals or dramatic elections. Scandal politics has been overlooked by most political scientists – except for David Mayhew, who has shown how a key aspect of congressional history is how members try to shape public opinion through actions such as public investigations. See David R. Mayhew, *America's Congress: Actions in the Public Sphere, James Madison through Newt Gingrich* (New Haven, CT: Yale University Press, 2000). This, I argue, is a big part of what scandal is about. Fourth, although each period of congressional reform has been driven by an amalgamation of different interests, I argue that many political scientists have underestimated the coherence that can still emerge behind any push for reform. Despite the multiplicity of interests supporting most reforms, the coherence derives from the strength of those whom reform proponents are targeting as well as the fact that the various interests in a coalition consistently draw on the same package of reforms to achieve their objectives. The final and most critical distinguishing feature of my

analysis is that, rather than organizing my book around specific reform topics (e.g., committee or budgetary reform), as is the tendency in political science, this work is structured chronologically and looks at the complex relationship between different areas of reform over time. The book is especially concerned with the alignment of policy and political goals across organizations and their ability to influence the legislative process.

4. I use the term institutional *change* to describe the outcome of a shift from one institutional structure to another. I use the term institutional *reform* as a description of the attempt to obtain, or the ideas for, institutional change. The two are not always the same: sometimes institutions change without any concerted reform effort. My analysis builds on interdisciplinary scholarship about how institutions change that has emerged in the fields of American Political Development and political sociology. Key works include Richard Bensel, "Of Rules and Speakers: Toward a Theory of Institutional Change for the U.S. House of Representatives," *Social Science History* 24 (Summer 2000): 349–66; Elizabeth S. Clemens and James M. Cook, "Politics and Institutionalism: Explaining Durability and Change," *Annual Review of Sociology* 25 (1999): 441–66; Karen Orren and Stephen Skowronek, "Regimes and Regime Building in American Government: A Review of Literature on the 1940s," *Political Science Quarterly* 113 (1998/1999): 689–702; William H. Sewell, Jr., "A Theory of Structure: Duality, Agency, and Transformation," *American Journal of Sociology* 98 (July 1992): 1–29; Walter W. Powell and Paul J. DiMaggio, Eds., *The New Institutionalism in Organizational Analysis* (University of Chicago Press, 1991). For excellent reviews of the new historical institutionalism, see Paul Pierson and Theda Skocpol, "Historical Institutionalism in Contemporary Political Science," and Karen Orren and Stephen Skowronek, "The Study of American Political Development," both in Ira Katznelson and Helen V. Milner, Eds., *Political Science: The State of the Discipline* (New York: Norton, 2002), pp. 693–754.

5. I argue that there have been four eras in congressional history: the experimental era (1780s–1820s); the partisan era (1820s–1900s); the committee era (1910s–1960s); and the contemporary era (1970s–today). See "Introduction," in Julian E. Zelizer, Ed., *The Reader's Companion to the American Congress* (Boston: Houghton-Mifflin, forthcoming).

6. On the nineteenth century, see Joel H. Silbey, *The American Political Nation, 1838–1893* (Stanford, CA: Stanford University Press, 1991); Paula Baker, "The Domestication of Politics: Women and American Political Society 1780–1920," *American Historical Review* 89 (June 1984): 620–47; Jean Baker, *Affairs of Party: The Political Culture of Northern Democrats in the Mid-Nineteenth Century* (Ithaca, NY: Cornell University Press, 1983). For a review of the historical literature on the Progressive Era, see Daniel T. Rodgers, "In Search of Progressivism," *Reviews in American History* 10 (December 1982): 113–32.

7. Some scholars have challenged the concept of a committee period. See, for instance, Gary W. Cox and Mathew D. McCubbins, *Legislative Leviathan: Party Government in the House* (Berkeley: University of California Press, 1993). In this interpretation, Democratic leaders relied on the committee system to overcome deep sectional divisions and to obtain legislation that was close to the party median. Moreover, party leaders controlled what issues entered onto the agenda. While reminding us that parties were not inconsequential, this interpretation downplays several factors. First, it understates how party leaders and average members often felt compelled to anticipate

the position of committee chairs. Second, this interpretation tends to stress high-profile issues rather than the large number of decisions where most members do not have a strong preference. In these cases, committee chairs were more influential in this era than party leaders. Third, this interpretation does not account for the tremendous frustration with, and deference to, committee chairs that party leaders and average members expressed in the 1940s and 1950s. Finally, the interpretation does not account for the fact that, barring extraordinary actions, there were few institutional constraints on the independence of committee chairs.

8. For an excellent review of the literature critiquing Hofstadter, see Rodgers, "In Search of Progressivism." One of the best recent works to show other groups involved in the progressive period that were firmly rooted in social movement and legislative politics is by Elizabeth Sanders, *The Roots of Reform: Farmers, Workers, and the American State, 1877–1917* (University of Chicago Press, 1999).

9. R. Douglas Arnold, *The Logic of Congressional Action* (New Haven, CT: Yale University Press, 1990), pp. 30, 269.

10. For an introduction into the role of networks in institutional development, see Daniel P. Carpenter, *The Forging of Bureaucratic Autonomy: Reputations, Networks, and Policy Innovation in Executive Agencies, 1862–1928* (Princeton, NJ: Princeton University Press, 2001).

11. David Mayhew argues that generating public interest in issues has been a central concern of legislators. See Mayhew, *America's Congress*, pp. 81–102.

12. On the critical role of ideas in institutional change, see Mark Blyth, *Great Transformations: Economic Ideas and Institutional Change in the Twentieth Century* (Cambridge University Press, 2002).

13. Eric Schickler has examined how multiple interests push for most reforms. See Schickler, *Disjointed Pluralism: Institutional Innovation and the Development of the U.S. Congress* (Princeton, NJ: Princeton University Press, 2001).

14. The concept of focusing events comes from John W. Kingdon, *Agendas, Alternatives, and Public Policies* (Glenview, IL: Scott-Foresman, 1984), pp. 99–100. American Political Development scholars have argued that focusing events are constrained by preexisting institutions. They have developed the useful concept of "critical junctures," which are dramatic periods featuring bursts of change within institutional constraints. See Jacob S. Hacker, "The Historical Logic of National Health Insurance: Structure and Sequence in the Development of British, Canadian, and U.S. Medical Policy," *Studies in American Political Development* 12 (Spring 1998): 77–80. Kingdon himself points to the limits of focusing events in isolation (pp. 103–6). I argue that political scandals and electoral mandates are given particular meanings by preexisting institutions and actors in the political arena, be they a reform coalition, the press, or others.

15. Lisa McGirr, *Suburban Warriors: The Origins of the New American Right* (Princeton, NJ: Princeton University Press, 2001); Rick Perlstein, *Before the Storm: Barry Goldwater and the Unmaking of the American Consensus* (New York: Hill & Wang, 2001); Jonathan M. Schoenwald, *A Time For Choosing: The Rise of Modern Conservatism* (New York: Oxford University Press, 2001); Godfrey Hodgson, *The World Turned Right Side Up: A History of the Conservative Ascendancy in America* (Boston: Houghton-Mifflin, 1996); E. J. Dionne, Jr., *Why Americans Hate Politics* (New York: Simon & Schuster, 1991); George H. Nash, *The Conservative Intellectual Movement in America Since 1945* (New York: Basic Books, 1976).

## Chapter 2

1. Ira Katznelson, Kim Geiger, and Daniel Kryder, "Limiting Liberalism: The Southern Veto in Congress, 1933–1950," *Political Science Quarterly* 108 (1993): 283–302; David M. Kennedy, *Freedom from Fear: The American People in Depression and War, 1929–1945* (New York: Oxford University Press, 1999), p. 783; David Plotke, *Building A Democratic Political Order: Reshaping American Liberalism in the 1930s and 1940s* (Cambridge University Press, 1996), pp. 226–61, 350–1; V. O. Key, Jr., *Southern Politics in State and Nation* (New York: Knopf, 1950), pp. 314–82. Like Katznelson and his co-authors, I use the standard definition of the South that was used by political observers in the 1930s and 1940s, which includes the ex-Confederate states of Alabama, Arkansas, Florida, Georgia, Louisiana, Mississippi, North Carolina, South Carolina, Tennessee, Texas, and Virginia, plus Kentucky and Oklahoma.

2. A more extended version of this section appears in Julian E. Zelizer, Ed., *The Reader's Companion to the American Congress* (Boston: Houghton-Mifflin, forthcoming).

3. Michael F. Holt, "Change and Continuity in the Party Period: The Substance and Structure of American Politics, 1835–1885," in Byron E. Shafer and Anthony J. Badger, Eds., *Contesting Democracy: Substance and Structure in American Political History, 1775–2000* (Lawrence: University Press of Kansas, 2001), pp. 93–115; Joel H. Silbey, *The American Political Nation, 1838–1893* (Stanford, CA: Stanford University Press, 1991); Michael E. McGerr, *The Decline of Popular Politics: The American North, 1865–1928* (New York: Oxford University Press, 1986); Richard L. McCormick, *The Party Period and Public Policy: American Politics from the Age of Jackson to the Progressive Era* (New York: Oxford University Press, 1986).

4. Sarah A. Binder, *Minority Rights, Majority Rule: Partisanship and the Development of Congress* (Cambridge University Press, 1997).

5. Morton Keller, *Affairs of State: Public Life in Late Nineteenth Century America* (Cambridge, MA: Belknap Press, 1977).

6. Paul Kleppner, *The Cross of Culture: A Social Analysis of Midwestern Politics, 1850–1900* (New York: Free Press, 1970).

7. Richard F. Bensel, *The Political Economy of American Industrialization, 1877–1900* (Cambridge University Press, 2000); Theda Skocpol, *Protecting Soldiers and Mothers: The Political Origins of Social Policy in the United States* (Cambridge, MA: Harvard University Press, 1992).

8. David Rothman, *Politics and Power: The United States Senate: 1869–1901* (Cambridge, MA: Harvard University Press, 1966).

9. Gerald Gamm and Steven S. Smith, "Policy Leadership and the Development of the Modern Senate," in David W. Brady and Mathew D. McCubbins, Eds., *Party, Process, and Political Change in Congress: New Perspectives on the History of Congress* (Stanford, CA: Stanford University Press, 2002), pp. 290–1.

10. John Mark Hansen, *Gaining Access: Congress and the Farm Lobby, 1919–1981* (University of Chicago Press, 1991).

11. Eric Schickler, *Disjointed Pluralism: Institutional Innovation and the Development of the U.S. Congress* (Princeton, NJ: Princeton University Press, 2001), pp. 53–9, 93–8.

12. David W. Brady, Richard Brody, and David Epstein, "Heterogenous Parties and Political Organization: The U.S. Senate, 1880–1920," *Legislative Studies Quarterly* 14 (1989): 214.

13. Richard F. Fenno, Jr., *Congressmen in Committees* (Boston: Little, Brown, 1973).

14. Steven S. Smith and Gerald Gamm, "Emergence of the Modern Senate: Party Organization, 1937–2002," paper presented at the 2002 American Political Science Association Convention, Boston.

15. Steven S. Smith, *Call to Order: Politics in the House and Senate* (Washington, DC: Brookings Institution, 1989), pp. 20–4, 88–92.

16. Despite a debate over why freshmen refrained, there is agreement that senior southerners were not frequently challenged. See Richard L. Hall, *Participation in Congress* (New Haven, CT: Yale University Press, 1996); Donald R. Matthews, *U.S. Senators and Their World* (Chapel Hill: University of North Carolina Press, 1960); Barbara Sinclair, *The Transformation of the U.S. Senate* (Baltimore: Johns Hopkins University Press, 1989).

17. Sarah A. Binder and Steven S. Smith, *Politics or Principle? Filibustering in the United States Senate* (Washington, DC: Brookings Institution, 1997), pp. 87–9.

18. Joseph Cooper, *Congress and Its Committees: A Historical Approach to the Role of Committees in the Legislative Process* (New York: Garland, 1988).

19. Jeffery A. Jenkins, "Property Rights and the Emergence of Standing Committee Dominance in the Nineteenth-Century House," *Legislative Studies Quarterly* 23 (November 1998): 493–519.

20. Robert C. Byrd, *The Senate 1789–1989: Addresses on the History of the United States Senate*, v. 2 (Washington, DC: U.S. Government Printing Office, 1991), p. 223.

21. George Goodwin, Jr., "The Seniority System in Congress," *American Political Science Review* 53 (June 1959): 418–20.

22. Barbara Hinckley, *The Seniority System in Congress* (Bloomington: Indiana University Press, 1971); Nelson Polsby, Miriam Gallaher, and Barry Spencer Rundquist, "The Growth of the Seniority System in the U.S. House of Representatives," *American Political Science Review* 63 (September 1969): 787–807.

23. Nelson Polsby, "Institutionalization of the U.S. House of Representatives," *American Political Science Review* 62 (March 1968): 144–68. See also N. Polsby, Ed., *Explorations in the Evolution of Congress: H. Douglas Price* (Berkeley, CA: Institute of Governmental Studies, 1998).

24. DSG, "Age & Tenure of House Committee Chairmen," 1 February 1971, CAP, Legislative Files, Box 148, File: 5.

25. H. Douglas Price, "The Electoral Arena," in Polsby, *Explorations in the Evolution of Congress*, pp. 3–32; Jonathan N. Katz and Brian R. Sala, "Careerism, Committee Assignments, and the Electoral Connection," *American Political Science Review* 90 (March 1996): 21–33.

26. Robert E. Mutch, *Campaigns, Congress, and Courts: The Making of Federal Campaign Finance Law* (New York: Praeger, 1988), pp. 24–52.

27. Key, *Southern Politics in State and Nation*, pp. 470–85.

28. Robert A. Caro, *The Path to Power: The Years of Lyndon Johnson* (New York: Knopf, 1983), pp. 606–71.

29. Alexander Heard, *The Costs of Democracy: Financing American Political Campaigns*, rev. ed. (Garden City, NY: Doubleday, 1962), pp. 111–17; Edwin M. Epstein, *Corporations, Contributions, and Political Campaigns: Federal Regulation in*

*Perspective* (Berkeley, CA: Institute of Governmental Studies, 1968), p. 74; William H. Jones, "Political Muscle Desire Began Payoffs," *Washington Post,* 4 January 1976, Section B; Walter Pincus, "Silent Spenders in Politics – They Really Give at the Office," 1971, GMA, Department of Legislation, Box 7, Folder 20.

30.  The term "redistricting" is used to describe governmental reshaping of existing districts, whereas "reapportionment" means changing the number of districts as a result of increases or decreases in the population. In most cases the two went hand in hand, and activists often used the phrases interchangeably. Reapportionment was not a problem at the federal level because the U.S. government did change the number of representatives a state received if there were shifts in the population. There were differences in the dynamics of districting for the U.S. Congress and state legislatures. The Constitution stated that the number of representatives a state received would be based on its population. In a cornerstone of federalism, the states retained the power to elect representatives in the fashion they saw best. Methods for electing state legislatures varied dramatically between states, since the Constitution had not specified a formula for determining state districts. At first, most states relied on at-large elections where large geographic areas voted on their delegation to the House. It was only in 1842 that Congress decreed that districts should be the method of election for representatives. Although districts became the primary method for congressional election at the federal level, at-large elections were still used when states gained representatives so that existing districts did not have to be redrawn. In 1872 Congress had required districts to be as equal in population as possible, but it dropped that requirement in 1929. As a result of the 1929 legislation, the composition of federal districts remained essentially under the control of the states.

31.  Andrew Hacker, *Congressional Districting: The Issue of Equal Representation* (Washington, DC: Brookings Institution, 1964), pp. 79–99.

32.  Michael Perman, *Struggle for Mastery: Disfranchisement in the South, 1888–1908* (Chapel Hill: University of North Carolina Press, 2001); Stephen D. Kantrowitz, *Ben Tillman and the Reconstruction of White Supremacy* (Chapel Hill: University of North Carolina Press, 2000); J. Morgan Kousser, *The Shaping of Southern Politics: Suffrage Restriction and the Establishment of the One-Party South, 1880–1910* (New Haven, CT: Yale University Press, 1974).

33.  J. Morgan Kousser, *Colorblind Injustice: Minority Rights and the Undoing of the Second Reconstruction* (Chapel Hill: University of North Carolina Press, 1999), pp. 203–4.

34.  Hacker, *Congressional Districting,* p. 99.

35.  Mark J. Rozell, *In Contempt of Congress: Postwar Press Coverage on Capitol Hill* (Westport, CT: Praeger, 1996), pp. 11–25.

36.  Leo C. Rosten, *The Washington Correspondents,* reprint (New York: Arno Press, 1974), p. 106.

37.  Donald A. Ritchie, *Press Gallery: Congress and the Washington Correspondents* (Cambridge, MA: Harvard University Press, 1991), p. 222.

38.  Joe S. Foote, "Rayburn, the Workhorse," in Everette E. Dennis and Robert W. Snyder, Eds., *Covering Congress* (New Brunswick, NJ: Transaction, 1998), pp. 143–5.

39.  Douglass Cater, *The Fourth Branch of Government* (Boston: Houghton-Mifflin, 1959), pp. 53–4.

40.  John F. Stacks, *Scotty: James B. Reston and the Rise and Fall of American Journalism* (Boston: Little, Brown, 2003), pp. 94–101.

41. George E. Reedy, *The U.S. Senate: Paralysis or a Search for Consensus?* (New York: Crown, 1986), p. 86.
42. Markus Pryor, "The Incumbent in the Living Room – The Rise of Television and the Incumbency Advantage in the House," unpublished manuscript.
43. Michael Schudson, *Discovering the News: A Social History of American Newspapers* (New York: Basic Books, 1978), pp. 121–94.
44. John H. Summers, "What Happened to Sex Scandals? Politics and Peccadilloes, Jefferson to Kennedy," *Journal of American History* 87 (December 2000): 842.
45. Cater, *The Fourth Branch of Government*, pp. 55–6.
46. Robert D. Dean, *Imperial Brotherhood: Gender and the Making of Cold War Foreign Policy* (Amherst: University of Massachusetts Press, 2001).
47. William S. White, *Citadel: The Story of the U.S. Senate* (New York: Harper & Row, 1957).
48. John R. Hibbing and Elizabeth Theiss-Morse, *Congress as Public Enemy: Public Attitudes toward American Political Institutions* (Cambridge University Press, 1995), pp. 34–5.
49. Hinckley, *The Seniority System in Congress,* pp. 38–9.
50. Katznelson, Geiger, and Kryder, "Limiting Liberalism," p. 285.
51. Gilbert C. Fite, *Richard B. Russell, Jr., Senator from Georgia* (Chapel Hill: University of North Carolina Press, 1991), p. 200.
52. Key, *Southern Politics in State and Nation*, pp. 345–82.
53. James Patterson, *Congressional Conservatism and the New Deal: The Growth of the Conservative Coalition in Congress, 1933–1939* (Lexington: University of Kentucky Press, 1967), p. 17.
54. Mary Elizabeth Poole, "Securing Race and Ensuring Dependence: The Social Security Act of 1935," Ph.D. dissertation, Rutgers University, New Brunswick, NJ, 2000.
55. Howard L. Reiter, "The Building of a Bifactional Structure: The Democrats in the 1940s," *Political Science Quarterly* 116 (Spring 2001): 112; Barbara Sinclair, *Congressional Realignment, 1925–1978* (Austin: University of Texas Press, 1982), pp. 65–6.
56. Nicol C. Rae, *Southern Democrats* (New York: Oxford University Press, 1994), p. 39.
57. Josephus Daniels to Franklin Roosevelt, 5 July 1935, PPF 86.
58. Robert C. Lieberman, *Shifting the Color Line: Race and the American Welfare State* (Cambridge, MA: Harvard University Press, 1998); Jill S. Quadagno, *The Color of Welfare: How Racism Undermined the War on Poverty* (New York: Oxford University Press, 1994).
59. David Plotke, *Building a Democratic Political Order: Reshaping American Liberalism in the 1930s and 1940s* (Cambridge University Press, 1996), p. 179.
60. Everett Carll Ladd with Charles D. Hadley, *Transformations of the American Party System: Political Coalitions from the New Deal to the 1970s* (New York: Norton, 1978), pp. 42–6.
61. Edwin Amenta, *Bold Relief: Institutional Politics and the Origins of Modern American Social Policy* (Princeton, NJ: Princeton University Press, 1998), pp. 4–5.
62. Julian E. Zelizer, "The Forgotten Legacy of the New Deal: Fiscal Conservatism and the Roosevelt Administration, 1933–1938," *Presidential Studies Quarterly* 30 (June 2000): 331–58; Mark H. Leff, *The Limits of Symbolic Reform* (Cambridge University Press, 1984).
63. On antistatism, fiscal concerns, and the Supreme Court, see Michael K. Brown, *Race, Money, and the American Welfare State* (Ithaca, NY: Cornell University Press,

1999); James Patterson, "Congress and the Welfare State: Some Historical Reflections," *Social Science History* 24 (Summer 2000): 372–3; Gareth Davies and Martha Derthick, "Race and Social Welfare Policy: The Social Security Act of 1935," *Political Science Quarterly* 112 (Summer 1997): 217–35.

64. Reiter, "The Building of a Bifactional Structure," pp. 114–17.

65. Bruce J. Schulman, *From Cotton Belt to Sunbelt: Federal Policy, Economic Development, and the Transformation of the South, 1938–1980* (New York: Oxford University Press, 1991), pp. 43–51.

66. Alan Brinkley, *The End of Reform: New Deal Liberalism in Recession and War* (New York: Vintage, 1995), pp. 20–30.

67. Patterson, *Congressional Conservatism and the New Deal*, pp. 146–8.

68. Cited in William E. Leuchtenburg, *Supreme Court Reborn: The Constitutional Revolution in the Age of Roosevelt* (New York: Oxford University Press, 1995), pp. 158–9.

69. Josephus Daniels to Franklin Roosevelt, 8 March 1937, and Daniels to Roosevelt, 9 February 1939, PPF 86.

70. Diaries of Henry Morgenthau, 17 May 1937, HMD, Roll 19.

71. "Roosevelt Meets with Eight Liberals," *New York Times,* 22 December 1937.

72. James T. Patterson, "A Conservative Coalition Forms in Congress, 1933–1939," *Journal of American History* 52 (March 1966): 762.

73. John O'Connor to Franklin Roosevelt, 22 April 1938, PSF, Box 129, Subject File: Congress 1932–1940.

74. Diaries of Harold Ickes, 2 March 1938, HID, pp. 2634–5. See also the entry on 17 March 1938, pp. 2660–1.

75. Harold Ickes to Maury Maverick, 1938, PSF, Box 129, Subject File: Congress 1932–1940.

76. Henry Wallace to Franklin Roosevelt, 25 July 1937, PSF, Box 165, Subject File: January–July 1937.

77. Vernon Allen Fagin, "Franklin D. Roosevelt, Liberalism in the Democratic Party and the 1938 Congressional Elections: The Urge to Purge," Ph.D. dissertation, University of California, Los Angeles, 1979.

78. Diaries of Harold Ickes, 15 September 1938, HID, p. 2959.

79. "Text of Two Addresses Made by President Roosevelt in Georgia; Barnesville," *New York Times,* 12 August 1938.

80. Franklin Roosevelt to Harold Ickes, 17 August 1938, PPF 3650.

81. "Vandenberg Sees Dictator's Aim in Roosevelt's Fight on O'Connor," *New York Times,* 8 September 1938.

82. Pollster George Gallup reported that 77 percent of those asked if they would have supported every bill recommended by Roosevelt in the past two years said No. See George Gallup, "Roosevelt 'Purge' Seen Called Off," *New York Times,* 7 August 1938.

83. See, for example, "Major Readjustments Face Both Old Parties," *New York Times,* 13 November 1938.

84. Jamie L. Carson, "Electoral and Partisan Forces in the Roosevelt Era: The U.S. Congressional Elections of 1938," *Congress & the Presidency* 28 (Autumn 2001): 162, 168–80.

85. William E. Leuchtenburg, *Franklin D. Roosevelt and the New Deal, 1932–1940* (New York: Harper & Row, 1963), p. 272.

86. Patterson, "A Conservative Coalition Forms in Congress," pp. 769–72.
87. Reedy, *The U.S. Senate*, p. 49.
88. Joe Martin, *My First Fifty Years in Politics* (New York: McGraw Hill, 1960), pp. 84–5; A. James Reichley, *The Life of the Parties: A History of American Political Parties* (New York: Free Press, 1992), p. 279.
89. Allen Drury, *A Senate Journal 1943–1945* (New York: McGraw-Hill, 1963), p. 4.
90. Daniel Kryder, *Divided Arsenal: Race and the American State During World War II* (Cambridge University Press, 2000).
91. Drury, *A Senate Journal*, pp. 140–1.
92. Katznelson, Geiger, and Kryder, "Limiting Liberalism," pp. 283–306. See also John W. Malsberger, *From Obstruction to Moderation: The Transformation of Senate Conservatism, 1938–1952* (Selinsgrove, PA: Susquehanna University Press, 2000).
93. Brown, *Race, Money, and the American Welfare State*, pp. 102–34; David L. Porter, *Congress and the Waning of the New Deal* (Port Washington, NY: Kennikat, 1980).
94. Franklin Roosevelt to Sam Rayburn, 23 December 1940, PSF, Box 129, Subject File: Congress 1932–1940.
95. Gary Gerstle, *American Crucible: Race and Nation in the Twentieth Century* (Princeton, NJ: Princeton University Press, 2001), pp. 187–237; Meg Jacobs, " 'How About Some Meat?': The Office of Price Administration, Consumption Politics, and State Building from the Bottom Up, 1941–1946," *Journal of American History* 84 (December 1997): 910–41; Nelson Lichtenstein, "From Corporatism to Collective Bargaining: Organized Labor and the Eclipse of Social Democracy in the Postwar Era," in Steve Fraser and Gary Gerstle, Eds., *The Rise and Fall of the New Deal Order, 1930–1980* (Princeton, NJ: Princeton University Press, 1989), pp. 122–52.
96. Roger H. Davidson, "The Advent of the Modern Congress: The Legislative Reorganization Act of 1946," *Legislative Studies Quarterly* 15 (August 1990): 361–2.
97. American Political Science Association, *The Reorganization of Congress: A Report of the Committee on Congress of the American Political Science Association* (Washington, DC: Public Affairs Press, 1945).
98. George Galloway, "On Reforming Congress," JCLR, RG 128, Box 321, File: 27.
99. George Galloway to Senator La Follette and Representative Monroney, 14 November 1945, JCLR, RG 128, Box 321, File: 37.
100. George Galloway to Wayland Brooks, 23 October 1945, NA, RG 128, Box 321, File: 37.
101. David C. King, *Turf Wars: How Congressional Committees Claim Jurisdiction* (University of Chicago Press, 1997), pp. 59–62.
102. John C. Coleman, *Party Decline in America: Policy, Politics, and the Fiscal State* (Princeton, NJ: Princeton University Press, 1996), p. 64.
103. D. B. Hardeman and Donald C. Bacon, *Rayburn: A Biography* (Lanham, MD: Madison Books, 1987), p. 319.
104. Davidson, "The Legislative Reorganization Act of 1946," p. 364.
105. Cooper, *Congress and Its Committees*, pp. 240–95.
106. Mark J. Rozell, "Press Coverage of Congress, 1946–92," in Thomas E. Mann and Norman J. Ornstein, Eds., *Congress, the Press, and the Public* (Washington, DC: American Enterprise Institute / Brookings Institution, 1994), pp. 60–2.
107. Richard F. Fenno, Jr., *The Power of the Purse: Appropriations Politics in Congress* (Boston: Little, Brown, 1966), pp. 122, 629.
108. White, *The Citadel*, p. 68.

## Chapter 3

1. Hubert Humphrey, "Hubert Humphrey Speaks Out on Human Rights," 14 July 1948, HHP, Box 150.A.8.1, File: July 14, 1948.

2. The only books that have paid attention to them have been works about Lyndon Johnson, rather than the liberal coalition itself. See, for example: Robert A. Caro, *Master of the Senate: The Years of Lyndon Johnson* (New York: Knopf, 2002); Robert Dallek, *Lone Star Rising: Lyndon Johnson and His Times, 1908–1960* (New York: Oxford University Press, 1991). The three most comprehensive accounts of the 1950s Congress that examine liberal legislators on their own terms are Robert Mann, *The Walls of Jericho: Lyndon Johnson, Hubert Humphrey, Richard Russell, and the Struggle for Civil Rights* (New York: Harcourt Brace, 1996); James L. Sundquist, *Politics and Policy: The Eisenhower, Kennedy, and Johnson Years* (Washington, DC: Brookings Institution, 1968); and Roger Biles, *Crusading Liberal: Paul H. Douglas of Illinois* (Dekalb: Northern Illinois University Press, 2002).

3. Thomas J. Sugrue, "Jim Crow's Last Stand: Civil Rights in the Suburban North," paper presented at the State University of New York at Albany, 28 April 2003.

4. See Democratic Study Group (DSG), "The Republican–Southern Democratic Coalition – 1937–1959," MMP, Series XIV, Box 50, File: 6; Sundquist, *Politics and Policy*.

5. See, for example, Thomas J. Sugrue, *The Origins of the Urban Crisis* (Princeton, NJ: Princeton University Press, 1996).

6. Interview with Richard Bolling, 23 February 1959, HTOHC.

7. Jennifer A. Delton, *Making Minnesota Liberal: Civil Rights and the Transformation of the Democratic Party* (Minneapolis: University of Minnesota Press, 2002).

8. Richard Bolling to President Harry Truman, 18 December 1950, HTP, President's Personal File, Box 585, File: PPF 4379.

9. Joseph Rauh to Editor, 19 January 1957, JRP, Box 13, File: ADA January–June 1957.

10. Delton, *Making Minnesota Liberal*, pp. 40–60, 111–59.

11. In addition to the biographies cited in the footnotes, these portraits rely on John Arthur Garraty and Marc C. Carnes, Eds., *American National Biography* (New York: Oxford University Press, 1999).

12. Barbara Sinclair, *The Transformation of the U.S. Senate* (Baltimore: Johns Hopkins University Press, 1989), p. 33.

13. Eugene McCarthy, "The 87th Congress: Brookings Institution Lecture," 23 February 1961, EMP, Box 147.A.2.8(F), File: 2/23/61.

14. Charles Lloyd Garrettson III, *Hubert H. Humphrey: The Politics of Joy* (New Brunswick: Transaction, 1993), pp. 9–10.

15. James Loeb, Jr., to James Roosevelt, 27 April 1948, ADA, Series II, Box 29, File: 9.

16. Hubert Humphrey, "The Senate on Trial," *American Political Science Review* 44 (September 1950): 651.

17. Mann, *The Walls of Jericho*, p. 98.

18. Transcript, WTIC Radio, 10 October 1951, HHP, Box 150.D.10.9(B), File: S.Res. 41 – Cloture; Hubert Humphrey to Editors in the South, November 1951, HHP, Box 150.A.10.1(B), File: Letters to Southern Editors 1948–1951.

19. Hubert Humphrey, "The Facts About Our Budget," 20 October 1951, ADA, Series V, Box 34, File: 1.

20. Ronald L. Heinemann, *Harry Byrd of Virginia* (Charlottesville: University Press of Virginia, 1996).

21. Hubert Humphrey to Walter White, 8 February 1955, HHP, Box 150.A.17.7, File: Civil Rights – General; Dallek, *Lone Star Rising*, p. 336.
22. Cited in Caro, *Master of the Senate*, p. 460.
23. George Reedy to Lyndon Johnson, January 1957, LJS, Files of George Reedy, Box 420, File: Reedy Memos – January 1957.
24. Biles, *Crusading Liberal*, pp. 30–53.
25. Paul H. Douglas, *In The Fullness of Time: The Memoirs of Paul H. Douglas* (New York: Harcourt Brace Jovanovich, 1972), pp. 196–221; P. H. Douglas, "The Surrender to the Filibuster," 17 March 1949, PDP, Box 108, File: Paul Douglas; P. H. Douglas, "On The Seniority System," 1949, PDP, Box 159, File: Seniority System.
26. Law Department, National Association of Manufacturers, 19 September 1955, NAM, Series III, Box 851.1, File: 2.
27. Steven M. Gillon, *Politics and Vision: The ADA and American Liberalism, 1947–1985* (New York: Oxford University Press, 1987), p. 41.
28. Kevin Mattson, *Intellectuals in Action: The Origins of the New Left and Radical Liberalism, 1945–1970* (University Park: Pennsylvania State Press, 2002), pp. 17–18.
29. Stephen Hess, *The Ultimate Insiders: U.S. Senators in the National Media* (Washington, DC: Brookings Institution, 1986), pp. 26–7.
30. Edwin R. Bayley, *Joe McCarthy and the Press* (Madison: University of Wisconsin Press, 1981); Rodger Streitmatter, *Mightier Than the Sword: How the News Media Have Shaped American History* (Boulder, CO: Westview, 1997), pp. 157–8.
31. Joseph Bruce Gorman, *Kefauver: A Political Biography* (New York: Oxford University Press, 1971), p. 98; Charles L. Fontenay, *Estes Kefauver: A Biography* (Knoxville: University of Tennessee Press, 1980), p. 182.
32. Jack Lait and Lee Mortimer, *Washington Confidential* (New York: Dell, 1951).
33. Ronald Garay, *Congressional Television: A Legislative History* (Westport, CT: Greenwood, 1984), p. 52.
34. Douglas B. Harris, "The Rise of the Public Speakership," *Political Science Quarterly* 113 (Summer 1998): 198.
35. Transcript, "The American Forum of the Air," 30 March 1952, ECP, Box 240, File: Televising Congress.
36. Walter Cronkite, *A Reporter's Life* (New York: Knopf, 1996), pp. 184–5.
37. Nancy E. Bernhard, *U.S. Television News and Cold War Propaganda, 1947–1960* (Cambridge University Press, 1999).
38. E. E. Schattschneider, *Party Government* (New York: Farrar & Rinehart, 1942).
39. For an excellent discussion of this literature see Delton, *Making Minnesota Liberal*, pp. 19–39.
40. James MacGregor Burns, *Congress on Trial: The Legislative Process and the Administrative State* (New York: Harper, 1949), p. xi.
41. Caro, *Master of the Senate*, pp. 488–515, 557–80.
42. Dallek, *Lone Star Rising*, pp. 477–8; Steven S. Smith and Marcus Flathman, "Managing the Senate Floor: Complex Unanimous Consent Agreements since the 1950s," *Legislative Studies Quarterly* 14 (August 1989): 354–74. Johnson took advantage of – but did not create – these party-strengthening devices, which had been evolving since the 1890s. See Gerald Gamm and Steven S. Smith, "Party Leadership and the Development of the Modern Senate," in David W. Brady and Mathew D. McCubbins, Eds., *Party, Process, and Political Change in Congress: New Perspectives on the History of Congress* (Stanford, CA: Stanford University Press, 2002), pp. 287–311;

G. Gamm and S. Smith, "Emergence of the Modern Senate: Party Organization, 1937–2002," paper presented at the 2002 American Political Science Association Convention, Boston.

43. Research Division, Democratic National Committee, "Analysis of 1956 Election," ADA, Series V, Box 23, File: 11.

44. Hubert Humphrey to Mike Mansfield, 3 December 1956, MMP, Series XVIII, Box 25, File: 3.

45. Transcript, "Face the Nation," CBS Television, 15 April 1956, ADA, Series II, Box 76, File: 1.

46. ADA, Press Release, 24 March 1956, JRP, Box 14, File: ADA February–March 1956.

47. Minutes of the ADA Executive Committee Meeting, 9 April 1956, ADA, Series II, Box 35, File: 8.

48. Paul Douglas to Friend, 28 December 1956, ACP, Box 44, File: 19; Senators Irving Ives and Douglas, Press Release, 26 December 1956, PDP, Box 107, File: Filibuster Articles and Materials.

49. Paul H. Douglas, "The Fight Against the Filibuster," *New Republic*, 12 January 1953, p. 6.

50. "Statement of American Jewish Congress," 3 October 1951, NAACP, Washington Bureau, Box 5, File: American Jewish Congress, 1949–1959. See also, Walter White to Hubert Humphrey, 12 January 1955, HHP, Box 150.A.17.7, File: Civil Rights – General.

51. Nelson W. Polsby, "The Making of the Modern Congress," in William H. Robinson and Clay H. Wellborn, Eds., *Knowledge, Power, and the Congress* (Washington, DC: Congressional Quarterly, 1991), p. 86.

52. D. B. Hardeman and Donald C. Bacon, *Rayburn: A Biography* (Lanham, MD: Madison Books, 1987), p. 346.

53. Neil MacNeil, *Forge of Democracy: The House of Representatives* (New York: David McKay, 1963), p. 107; Ronald M. Peters, Jr., *The American Speakership: The Office in Historical Perspective,* 2nd ed. (Baltimore: Johns Hopkins University Press, 1997), pp. 92–145.

54. Caro, *Master of the Senate,* pp. 474–5.

55. Jacob K. Javits with Rafael Steinberg, *Javits: The Autobiography of a Public Man* (Boston: Houghton-Mifflin, 1981), p. 260.

56. Smith and Gamm, "Emergence of the Modern Senate."

57. Roy Wilkins, James Carey, and Joseph Rauh, Jr., to Vice President Nixon, 29 October 1956, JRP, Box 13, File: ADA October–December 1956.

58. Arnold Aronson to All Supporting Organizations, 25 June 1952, ADA, Series II, Box 30, File: 2.

59. "Resolution Adopted by 1952 Leadership Conference on Civil Rights," 18 February 1952, ADA, Series V, Box 7, File: 2.

60. Walter White to Participants in Civil Rights Conference, 31 May 1951, ADA, Series V, Box 7, File: 2; White to Violet Gunther, 14 November 1951, ADA, Series V, Box 18, File: 1; ADA, "Draft: Program for Federal Civil Rights Legislation," December 1950, ADA, Series V, Box 7, File: 1.

61. Richard Bolling, *House Out of Order* (New York: Dutton, 1965), p. 179.

62. LCCR, "Background Memo on Civil Rights," October 1956, ADA, Series V, Box 12, File: 3.

63. AJC, "Draft: A Model Code of Fair Procedure for Congressional Investigating Committees," 29 December 1953, ADA, Series V, Box 17, File: 1; Estes Kefauver, Press Release, 27 May 1954, HLP, Senate Papers, File: Senate Rules on Senate Conference Reports; ACLU, "Statement of the American Civil Liberties Union on S. Con. Res. 2," July 1949, ACLU, Box 1031, File: 13; ACLU, "Congressional Ethics Committee Supports ACLU Proposals," 5 November 1951, ACLU, Box 1036, File: 10.

64. Samuel Lubell, *The Future of American Politics* (New York: Harper, 1951), p. 196.

65. Richard Franklin Bensel, *Sectionalism and American Political Development, 1880–1980* (Madison: University of Wisconsin Press, 1984), p. 175.

66. Lyndon Johnson, Press Release, 21 November 1955, HLP, Special Files: 32, Robert Baker. See also George Reedy to Johnson, 13 July 1956, LJS, Files of George Reedy, Box 419, File: Memos 1956.

67. George Reedy to Lyndon Johnson, 25 November 1956, LJS, Files of George Reedy, Box 419, File: Memos 1956.

68. Dallek, *Lone Star Rising,* pp. 510–11.

69. Caro, *Master of the Senate,* pp. 492–515.

70. Robert Griffith, *The Politics of Fear: Joseph R. McCarthy and the Senate* (Lexington: University of Kentucky Press, 1970).

71. David Daniel Potenziani, "Looking to the Past: Richard B. Russell and the Defense of Southern White Supremacy," Ph.D. dissertation, University of Georgia, Athens, 1981.

72. Anthony Badger, "Southerners Who Refused to Sign the Southern Manifesto," *Historical Journal* 42 (1999): 526.

73. LCCR, "Background Memo on Civil Rights."

74. Timothy Thurber, "Civil Rights," in Julian E. Zelizer, Ed., *The Reader's Companion to the American Congress* (Boston: Houghton-Mifflin, forthcoming).

75. Mann, *The Walls of Jericho,* pp. 172–3; Caro, *Master of the Senate,* pp. 795–6.

76. ADA, Press Release, 21 September 1956, EMP, Box 145.E.13.1B, File: ADA.

77. George E. Reedy, *The U.S. Senate: Paralysis or a Search for Consensus* (New York: Crown, 1986), p. 106.

78. Hubert Humphrey to Paul Butler, 7 February 1956, HHP, Box 150.D.5.6(F), File: Civil Rights.

79. Denton L. Watson, *Lion in the Lobby: Clarence Mitchell, Jr.'s Struggle for the Passage of Civil Rights Laws* (New York: Morrow, 1990), p. 352.

80. "JFK – Report No. 1," 28 February 1961, ADA, Series II, Box 76, File: 2, pp. 22–3.

81. Caro, *Master of the Senate,* pp. 829–30.

82. Ibid., pp. 858–9.

83. Lewis L. Gould and Nancy Beck Young, "The Speaker and the Presidents: Sam Rayburn, the White House, and the Legislative Process, 1941–1961," in Roger Davidson, Susan Webb Hammond, and Raymond W. Smock, Eds., *Masters of the House: Congressional Leadership over Two Centuries* (Boulder, CO: Westview, 1998), pp. 196–214.

84. Hardeman and Bacon, *Rayburn,* pp. 420–1.

85. Gayle B. Montgomery and James W. Johnson, *One Step from the White House: The Rise and Fall of Senator William F. Knowland* (Berkeley: University of California Press, 1998), p. 213.

86. Paul H. Douglas, "The Struggle for Civil Rights During the Last Century," 1958, PDP, Box 489, File: "The Struggle for Civil Rights During the Last Century," p. 19.

87. Caro, *Master of the Senate,* pp. 685–1040.
88. Paul Douglas, "Sentry Duty on Civil Rights," 18 June 1957, HHP, Box 150.D.13.8.F., File: Civil Rights 1957 (3).
89. Nadine Cohodas, *Strom Thurmond and the Politics of Southern Change* (New York: Simon & Schuster, 1993), pp. 295–6.
90. Mark J. Rozell, *In Contempt of Congress: Postwar Press Coverage on Capitol Hill* (Westport, CT: Praeger, 1996), pp. 18–20.
91. Hugh Davis Graham, *The Civil Rights Era: Origins and Development of National Policy, 1960–1972* (New York: Oxford University Press, 1990), p. 23.
92. Wayne Morse to Herbert Lehman, 2 November 1957, HLP, Senate Papers, Special File 641A: Wayne Morse.
93. Nelson Lichtenstein, *State of the Union: A Century of American Labor* (Princeton, NJ: Princeton University Press, 2002), pp. 162–71.
94. Joseph Rauh to President Eisenhower, 27 July 1955, ADA, Series V, Box 45, File: 10.
95. Biles, *Crusading Liberal,* p. 75.
96. George Reedy to Lyndon Johnson, 15 February 1957, LJS, Files of George Reedy, Box 420, File: Memos – February 1957.
97. "Minutes of Meeting – Democratic Policy Committee," 20 February 1956, LJS, Files of Democratic Leader, Box 364, File: Senate Democratic Policy Committee, Minutes of March 8, 1955 – June 24, 1960.
98. Douglas, *In the Fullness of Time,* p. 192.
99. Wayne Morse to Herbert Lehman, 7 January 1957, HLP, Senate Papers, Special File 641A: Wayne Morse.
100. NAM, 1956, "Citadel of Government," NAM, Series III, Box 851.1, File: 4.
101. Charles R. Sligh, Jr., "Congress, Labor Unions, and the Public," 31 July 1958, NAM, 1411 Series I, Box 530, File: 58-2734.
102. Walter Reuther to George Meany, 5 August 1959, ACP, Department of Legislation, Box 10, File: 27.
103. Charles Plontek to Herbert Lehman, 20 February 1956, HLP, Senatorial Papers, File: Election Bill C78-1.
104. David W. Rohde, Norman J. Ornstein, and Robert L. Peabody, "Political Change and Legislative Norms in the U.S. Senate, 1957–1974," in Glenn R. Parker, Ed., *Studies of Congress* (Washington, DC: Congressional Quarterly, 1985), pp. 158–61.
105. Sinclair, *Transformation of the U.S. Senate,* pp. 30–50.
106. David B. Walker, "The Age Factor in the 1958 Congressional Elections," *Midwest Journal of Political Science* 4 (February 1960): 1–26.
107. George Reedy to Lyndon Johnson, 16 June 1959, LJS, Files of George Reedy, Box 429, File: Reedy Memos May–June 1959.
108. Lee Metcalf, George Rhodes, and Frank Thompson to Emanuel Celler, 14 November 1958, ECP, Box 249, File: 1. See also ADA, "A *New* New Deal for the 1960s," December 1958, ADA, Series VI, Box 14, File: 6.
109. Democratic Advisory Council, Press Release, 14 June 1959, LJS, Box 409, File: Legislative Program for 1959.
110. Transcript, "Celebrity Parade," 5 July 1959, AKP, Box 40, File: Joseph McCarthy.
111. Gould and Young, "The Speaker and the Presidents," pp. 203–5.
112. Sinclair, *Transformation of the U.S. Senate,* pp. 30–50.

113. George Reedy to Lyndon Johnson, 12 December 1958, LJS, Files of George Reedy, Box 428, File: Reedy Memos – January 1959; George Reedy to Lyndon Johnson, 10 July 1959, LJS, Files of George Reedy, Box 429, File: Reedy Memos – July 1959.

114. Julius Edelstein to Senator Lehman, 25 July 1959, HLP, Senate Papers, Special File 431: Lyndon Johnson.

115. National Committee for an Effective Congress, "Congressional Report," 30 April 1962, EMP, Box 145.E.7.10(F), File: NCEC.

116. DSG, "The Republican–Southern Democratic Coalition – 1937–1959."

117. Andree E. Reeves, *Congressional Committee Chairmen: Three Who Made an Evolution* (Lexington: University of Kentucky Press, 1993), pp. 31, 43–4, 83–4.

118. Joseph Clark to Harry Byrd, 9 December 1960, MMP, Leadership Collection, Box 19, File: 8.

119. Roy Wilkins to Styles Bridges, 23 January 1959, NAACP, Washington Bureau, Box 128, File: 1958.

120. Taylor Branch, *Parting the Waters: America in the King Years, 1954–1963* (New York: Simon & Schuster, 1988), p. 248.

121. George Reedy to Lyndon Johnson, LJS, Files of George Reedy, Box 430, File: Memo File 1960.

122. Hyman Bookbinder to Andrew Biemiller, Walter Mason, George Riley, and Jack Curran, 10 December 1958, ACP, Department of Legislation, Box 44, File: 20.

123. Allen Ellender, interview with Hugh Cates, 30 April 1971, RROHP.

124. Samuel Ervin, Jr., interview with Hugh Cates, 28 April 1971, RROHP.

125. Minutes of the Senate Democratic Conference, 7 January 1960 and 12 January 1960, in Donald A. Ritchie, Ed., *Minutes of the U.S. Senate Democratic Conference, 1903–1964* (Washington, DC: U.S. Government Printing Office, 1998), pp. 515–43.

126. Joseph Clark to Lyndon Johnson, 26 March 1959, LJS, Papers of Democratic Leader, Box 365, File: Clark. See also Democratic Policy Committee, "Minutes of Meeting," 14 April 1959, LJS, Papers of the Democratic Leader, Box 364, File: Senate Democratic Policy Committee Minutes of March 8, 1955 – June 24, 1960; "Comment on Senator Clark's Letter to Senator Johnson," 1958, MMP, Leadership Collection, Series XXII, Box 89, File: 1.

127. NCEC, "The 86th Congress – The Quiet Crisis," 30 June 1959, EMP, Box 145.E.7.7B, File: NCEC.

128. Minutes of the Democratic Conference, 7 January 1960, in Ritchie, *Minutes of the U.S. Senate Democratic Conference,* p. 519.

129. Smith and Gamm, "Emergence of the Modern Senate."

130. James A. Robinson, *The House Rules Committee* (Indianapolis, IN: Bobbs-Merrill, 1963), p. 82.

131. Peters, *The American Speakership,* p. 136.

132. DSG, "Opposition in the House of Representatives to a Change in the Rules," 20 October 1960, ADA, Series V, Box 55, File: 6.

133. Joseph Cooper, *Congress and Its Committees: A Historical Approach to the Role of Committees in the Legislative Process* (New York: Garland, 1988), pp. 261–2.

134. "What's Wrong With Congress – 118 Members Answer," *U.S. News & World Report,* 12 September 1960, pp. 56–77.

135. ADA National Board Meeting, 19–20 November 1960, ADA, Box 68, File: 1.

136. New York Americans for Democratic Action, "Issues That Count!" 28 December 1960, ACLU, Box 1022, File: 11.

137. Conference on Majority Rule in Congress, "Majority Rule in Congress," 28 December 1960, PDP, Box 108, File: Rule 22-1961.

138. John D. Morris, "Halleck Expects House Coaction to Curb Kennedy," *New York Times,* 21 November 1960.

139. Irving Bernstein, *Promises Kept: John F. Kennedy's New Frontier* (New York: Oxford University Press, 1991), p. 283.

140. Library of Congress, Congressional Research Service, "Refusal of a Committee Post for Party Disloyalty," 18 November 1960, ACP, Department of Legislation, Box 11, File: 18.

141. "Battle Is Hinted on House Change," *New York Times,* 16 November 1960.

142. ADA, "Minutes of ADA National Board Meeting," 19–20 November 1960, JRP, Box 12, File: ADA 1960; DSG, "Analysis of Proposals to Overcome Legislative Obstruction by the Rules Committee," 26 October 1960, JBP, Box 143.G.12.6(F), File: Legislation 1960.

143. George Reedy to Lyndon Johnson, 28 June 1956, LJS, Files of George Reedy, Box 419, File: Reedy Papers 1956.

144. Editorial, "Mr. Kennedy and the 87th," *New York Times,* 3 January 1961; Editorial, "Breaking the Rules," *New Republic,* 21 November 1960, pp. 3–4.

145. Tom Wicker, "Again That Roadblock in Congress," *New York Times,* 7 August 1960, Section 6.

146. For correspondence about the show see HSP, Box 81.

147. Herblock, "Gateway to the New Frontier," *Washington Post,* 17 November 1960.

148. Howard Smith, Memos, 23 November and 17 November 1960, HSP, Box 79, File: Change in Rules Committee.

149. Hardeman and Bacon, *Rayburn,* p. 452.

150. William R. MacKaye, *A New Coalition Takes Control: The House Rules Committee Fight of 1961* (New York: McGraw-Hill, 1963), pp. 11–12.

151. Patrick J. Maney, "Hale Boggs: The Southerner as National Democrat," in Davidson et al., *Masters of the House,* pp. 231–2.

152. Howard Smith, Memos, 11 November 1960, 5 December 1960, 6 December 1960, and Howard Smith to Phil Landrum, 21 November 1960, all in HSP, Box 79, File: Change in Rules Committee.

153. Hardeman and Bacon, *Rayburn,* p. 455.

154. NCEC, Congressional Report, 4 March 1961, EMP, Box 145.E.7.10(F), File: NCEC.

155. Peters, *The American Speakership,* p. 138.

156. Bernstein, *Promises Kept,* p. 283.

157. Mary L. Dudziak, *Cold War Civil Rights: Race and the Image of American Democracy* (Princeton, NJ: Princeton University Press, 2000).

158. Howard Smith to Carl Vinson, 28 January 1961, HSP, Box 79, File: Change in Committee on Rules January 1961.

159. Oral History Interview with John McCormack, 5 January 1971, JMP, Box 196, Audio Reel.

160. U.S. Congress, House of Representatives, 31 January 1961, *Congressional Record,* 87th Congress, 1st Session, pp. 1576–9.

161. Ibid.

162. National Committee for an Effective Congress, "Congressional Report," 10 July 1961, EMP, Box 145.E.7.10(F), File: NCEC.

163. The vote breakdown comes from Milton C. Cummings, Jr., and Robert L. Peabody, "The Decision to Enlarge the Committee on Rules: An Analysis of the 1961 Vote," in Robert L. Peabody and Nelson W. Polsby, Eds., *New Perspectives on the House of Representatives* (Chicago: Rand-McNally, 1963), pp. 167–94; NCEC, "Congressional Report," 4 March 1961.

164. Watson, *Lion in the Lobby*, pp. 606–7.

165. Ibid., p. 608; Mann, *The Walls of Jericho*, p. 408.

166. Arnold Aronson to Cooperating Organizations, "Cloture At Last!" 10 June 1964, LCCR, Box 1, File: 2.

167. "Election Changes in House of Representatives As They Affect Standing Committees," 9 November 1964, RBP, Box 129, File: 10.

### Chapter 4

1. Earl Warren, *The Memoirs of Earl Warren* (Garden City, NY: Doubleday, 1977), pp. 306–11.

2. Alexander Keyssar, *The Right to Vote: The Contested History of Democracy in the United States* (New York: Basic Books, 2000), pp. 284–98.

3. Lucas Powe, Jr., "The Warren Court and Congress," in Julian E. Zelizer, Ed., *The Reader's Companion to the American Congress* (Boston: Houghton-Mifflin, forthcoming).

4. Earl Black and Merle Black, *The Rise of Southern Republicans* (Cambridge, MA: Belknap Press, 2002).

5. For examples see David W. Rohde, *Parties and Leaders in the Postreform House* (University of Chicago Press, 1991); John H. Aldrich, Mark M. Berger, and David W. Rohde, "The Historical Variability in Conditional Party Government, 1877–1994," in David W. Brady and Mathew D. McCubbins, Eds., *Party, Process, and Political Change in Congress: New Perspectives on the History of Congress* (Stanford, CA: Stanford University Press, 2002), pp. 17–35.

6. See the essays in Chandler Davidson and Bernard Goffman, Eds., *Quiet Revolution in the South: The Impact of the Voting Rights Act, 1965–1990* (Princeton, NJ: Princeton University Press, 1994).

7. "Statement by William Taylor to Subcommittee No. 2 of the House Judiciary Committee," 27 July 1959, ADA, Box 48, File: 7.

8. Eugene J. McCarthy, "Who Says the Majority Rules?" *The Reporter,* 18 March 1952, p. 23. See also Alfred De Grazia, *Apportionment and Representative Government* (New York: Praeger, 1962), pp. 132–44.

9. American Veterans Committee, "Working Conference on Reapportionment: Report of Proceedings," 28 November 1960, ACP, Department of Legislation, Box 41, File: 44.

10. "Statement of Andrew Biemiller Before the House Judiciary Committee," 29 July 1959, ACP, Department of Legislation, Box 41, File: 44.

11. Richard S. Childs to Members, 30 June 1959, ACLU, Box 1141, File: 5.

12. Ralph Goldman to Members of the American Political Science Association Executive Committee, 18 November 1955; Committee on Reapportionment of Congress, American Political Science Association, Press Release, 22 December 1955; Committee on Reapportionment of Congress, American Political Science Association, "The Reapportionment of Congress," March 1951, ADA, V, Box 48, File: 7.

13. Lucas A. Powe, Jr., *The Warren Court and American Politics* (Cambridge, MA: Belknap Press, 2000), p. 249.

14. J. Morgan Kousser, *Colorblind Injustice: Minority Rights and the Undoing of the Second Reconstruction* (Chapel Hill: University of North Carolina Press, 1999), p. 203.

15. *Colegrove v. Green*, 328 U.S. 549 (1946).

16. *Gomillion v. Lightfoot*, 364 U.S. 339 (1960).

17. Del Dickson, Ed., *The Supreme Court in Conference (1940–1985): The Private Discussions Behind Nearly 300 Supreme Court Decisions* (New York: Oxford University Press, 2001).

18. American Veterans Committee, "Working Conference on Reapportionment."

19. Justice Harlan to Charlie and Potter, 11 October 1961, JMHP, Box 135, File: No. 6 Memoranda.

20. Richard C. Cortner, *The Apportionment Cases* (Knoxville: University of Tennessee Press, 1970), pp. 28–94.

21. John F. Kennedy, "The Shame of the States," *New York Times*, 18 May 1958.

22. Dickson, *The Supreme Court in Conference*, pp. 845–6.

23. Ibid., p. 846.

24. *Baker v. Carr*, 369 U.S. 186 (1962), p. 270.

25. "Bigger Voice for Big Cities," *Newsweek*, 9 April 1962, p. 30.

26. Gordon E. Baker, *The Reapportionment Revolution: Representation, Political Power, and the Supreme Court* (New York: Random House, 1966), p. 40.

27. Kousser, *Colorblind Injustice*, p. 205.

28. *Gray v. Sanders*, 372 U.S. 368 (1963).

29. Jimmy Carter, *Turning Point: A Candidate, a State, and a Nation Come of Age* (New York: Times Books, 1992), pp. 41–2.

30. Powe, *The Warren Court and American Politics*, p. 203.

31. Dickson, *The Supreme Court in Conference*, p. 853.

32. *Wesberry v. Sanders*, 376 U.S. 1 (1964), pp. 14, 20.

33. Bench Memorandum, "Wesberry v. Sanders," 17 October 1963, JMHP, Box 191, File: No. 22 Memoranda.

34. Editorial, " 'Out of Whole Cloth'," *Richmond Times-Dispatch*, 26 February 1964.

35. Warren Weaver, Jr., "Democrats Report Record Total of 280 Negroes in Elective Jobs," *New York Times*, 23 December 1964.

36. Baker, *The Reapportionment Revolution*, p. 81.

37. ACLU, Press Release, 11 March 1965, ACLU, Box 1140, File: 2; Powe, *The Warren Court and American Politics*, p. 245.

38. *Reynolds v. Sims*, 377 U.S. 533 (1964).

39. Powe, "The Warren Court and Congress."

40. James Blacksher and Larry Menefee, "At-Large Elections and One Person, One Vote: The Search for the Meaning of Racial Vote Dilution," in Chandler Davidson, Ed., *Minority Vote Dilution* (Washington, DC: Howard University Press, 1984), p. 207.

41. *Lucas v. Colorado 44th General Assembly*, 377 U.S. 713 (1964).

42. James E. Alt, "The Impact of the Voting Rights Act on Black and White Voter Registration in the South," in Davidson and Goffman, *Quiet Revolution in the South*, pp. 366–9; Steven F. Lawson, *Black Ballots: Voting Rights in the South, 1944–1969* (New York: Columbia University Press, 1976), pp. 342–8.

43. David T. Cannon, *Race, Redistricting, and Representation: The Unintended Consequences of Black Majority Districts* (University of Chicago Press, 1999), p. 63.

44. Bernard Grofman, Lisa Handley, and Richard G. Niemi, *Minority Representation and the Quest for Voting Equality* (Cambridge University Press, 1992), p. 22.

45. Baker, *The Reapportionment Revolution,* p. 7.

46. U.S. Congress, House of Representatives, Committee on the Judiciary, *Hearings: State Legislative Apportionment,* 89th Congress, 1st Session, 23 June 1965, HJC, Box 199, File: 2, pp. 106–7.

47. U.S. Congress, House of Representatives, Committee on the Judiciary, *Hearings: Apportionment of State Legislatures,* 88th Congress, 2nd Session, 23 July 1964, HJC, Box 354, File: 2, pp. 96–8, 109.

48. Emanuel Celler, Handwritten Notes, 1964, ECP, Box 293, File: Reapportionment 2.

49. Leo Bodine to Emanuel Celler, 6 August 1964, HJC, Box 356, File: 2.

50. U.S. Congress, House of Representatives, Committee on the Judiciary, *Hearings: Reapportionment of State Legislatures,* 88th Congress, 2nd Session, 5 August 1964, HJC, Box 454, File: Hearings – Transcripts, p. 344.

51. National Committee for Fair Representation, "News Bulletin," 4 June 1965, ACLU, Box 1140, File: 2.

52. U.S. Congress, House of Representatives, Committee on Judiciary, *Hearings: State Legislative Apportionment,* 89th Congress, 1st Session, 4 August 1965, HJC, Box 199, File: Report of Proceedings, p. 6.

53. ADA, *Legislative Newsletter,* 13 April 1966, ECP, Box 292, File: Reapportionment 1.

54. ADA, *Legislative Newsletter,* 11 August 1965, ECP, Box 292, File: Reapportionment 1.

55. Andrew Biemiller to Sir and Brother, 23 February 1965, ACP, Department of Legislation, Box 41, File: 46.

56. "Statement of Howard Squadron to the Subcommittee on Constitutional Amendments of the Senate Committee on the Judiciary," 14 May 1965, NAACP, Washington Bureau, Box 197, File: Reapportionment Miscellaneous 1965.

57. U.S. Congress, House of Representatives, Committee on the Judiciary, *Hearings: State Legislative Apportionment,* 89th Congress, 1st Session, 25 June 1965, HJC, Box 199, File: 1, p. 325. See also Arnold Aronson to Cooperating Organizations, 10 August 1965, LCCR, Box 1, File: 3.

58. National Committee for Fair Representation, "News Bulletin," 4 June 1965.

59. Editorial, "Hit Inflation and Waste with Robertson, Byrd, Smith," *Richmond Times-Dispatch,* 3 July 1966.

60. Howard Smith to Andrew Farley, 28 July 1966, HSP, Box 208, File: Campaign 1966.

61. Senator A. Willis Robertson's Third District Campaign Committee to Fellow Richmonder, 23 June 1966, WSP, Box 142, File: 1966 Civil Rights and Race.

62. Ralph Eisenberg to Senator William Spong, Jr., 14 October 1966, WSP, Box 140, File: 1966 Campaign and Analysis of General Election; "Potential Sources of Strength for Spong and Boothe in 1966," WSP, Box 140, File: 1966 Campaign Analysis of General Election; Alexander P. Lamis, *The Two-Party South,* 2nd ed. (New York: Oxford University Press, 1998), pp. 147–9.

63. James J. Kilpatrick, "Nothing Is Sacred in Virginia," *Sunday Star,* 17 July 1966.

64. Editorial, "The Political Earthquake," *Richmond Times-Dispatch,* 13 July 1966.

65. Editorial, "Broken Traditions," *Washington Post,* 14 July 1966.

66. Lamis, *The Two-Party South,* pp. 145–62; Jack Bass and Walter DeVries, *The Transformation of Southern Politics: Social Change and Political Consequence Since 1945* (New York: Basic Books, 1976), p. 350.

67. Nelson W. Polsby, "Political Change and the Character of the Contemporary Congress," in Anthony King, Ed., *The New American Political System,* 2nd ed. (Washington, DC: American Enterprise Institute, 1990), pp. 38–45.

68. Charles S. Bullock III, "Redistricting and Congressional Stability, 1962–1972," *Journal of Politics* 37 (May 1975): 569–75.

69. Robert G. Dixon, Jr., *Democratic Representation: Reapportionment in Law and Politics* (New York: Oxford University Press, 1968), pp. 436–543; Peyton McCrary and Steven F. Lawson, "Race and Reapportionment, 1962: The Case of Georgia Senate Redistricting," *Journal of Policy History* 12 (2000): 293–320.

70. Mathew McCubbins and Thomas Schwartz, "Congress, the Courts, and Public Policy: Consequences of the One Man, One Vote Rule," *American Journal of Political Science* 32 (May 1988): 391.

71. Peyton McCrary, "Bringing Equality to Power: How the Federal Courts Transformed the Electoral Structure of Southern Politics, 1960–1990," paper presented at the 2002 Organization of American Historians Convention, Washington, DC.

72. Gary W. Cox and Jonathan N. Katz, *Elbridge Gerry's Salamander: The Electoral Consequences of the Reapportionment Revolution* (Cambridge University Press, 2002), p. 8.

73. Timothy G. O'Rourke, *The Impact of Reapportionment* (New Brunswick, NJ: Transaction, 1980); T. G. O'Rourke, "The Impact of Reapportionment on Congress and State Legislatures," in Mark E. Rush, Ed., *Voting Rights and Redistricting in the United States* (Westport, CT: Greenwood, 1998), pp. 195–224; Milton C. Cummings, Jr., "Reapportionment in the 1970s: Its Effects on Congress," and Charles O. Jones, "Commentary," in Nelson W. Polsby, Ed., *Reapportionment in the 1970s* (Berkeley: University of California Press, 1971), pp. 209–47; Larry M. Schwab, *The Impact of Congressional Reapportionment and Redistricting* (Lanham, MD: University Press of America, 1988).

74. Black and Black, *The Rise of Southern Republicans,* pp. 174–204.

75. Richard F. Fenno, Jr., *Congress at the Grassroots: Representational Change in the South, 1970–1998* (Chapel Hill: University of North Carolina Press, 2000).

76. Congressional Research Service, "Congressional Districting: The Constitutional Standard in the Decade of the '70s," 20 January 1971, BAP, Box 173, File: Reapportionment and Redistricting General, pp. 47–8.

### Chapter 5

1. Through his excellent biography of Allard Lowenstein, William Chafe provided an insightful examination of this tension that existed within American liberalism during the 1960s: *Never Stop Running: Allard Lowenstein and the Struggle to Save American Liberalism* (New York: Basic Books, 1993), p. xvii.

2. Julian E. Zelizer, "The Constructive Generation: Thinking About Congress in the 1960s," *Mid-America: An Historical Review* 81 (Fall 1999): 263–96.

3. R. Douglas Arnold, *The Logic of Congressional Action* (New Haven, CT: Yale University Press, 1990), pp. 30–1, 68, 267–74.

4. For example, when Senator Albert Gore, Sr., was pushing a proposal to strengthen the Democratic Policy Committee in 1960, his opponent Harry Byrd warned colleagues that it would harm the party since the media would interpret the move as an attempt to overthrow the leadership. He cited a *Washington Post* article to prove his point. See Minutes of the Senate Democratic Conference, 12 January 1960, in Donald A. Ritchie, Ed., *Minutes of the U.S. Senate Democratic Conference, 1903–1964* (Washington, DC: U.S. Government Printing Office, 1998), p. 534.

5. Thomas E. Patterson, *Out of Order* (New York: Vintage, 1994), p. 80.

6. Larry J. Sabato, *Feeding Frenzy: How Attack Journalism Has Transformed American Politics*, rev. ed. (New York: Free Press, 1993), p. 26. See also Mark J. Rozell, "Press Coverage of Congress, 1946–1992," in Thomas E. Mann and Norman J. Ornstein, Eds., *Congress, the Press, and the Public* (Washington, DC: American Enterprise Institute / Brookings Institution, 1994), pp. 63–73.

7. "Congressional Reform: Special Report," *Congressional Quarterly*, 1 April 1964.

8. "Nationwide Backing for Congressional Reforms," December 1964, RBP, Box 129, File: 11; Walter Lippmann, "A Critique of Congress," *Newsweek*, 20 January 1964, pp. 18–19 (cover story); "Wanted: A Modern House," *New Republic*, 21 November 1964, pp. 11–12; Stewart Alsop, "The Failure of Congress," *Saturday Evening Post*, 7 December 1963, pp. 23–5.

9. The quote on Mudd can be found in Robert Blanchard, Ed., *Congress and the News Media* (New York: Hastings House, 1974), pp. 68–9. On Vietnam, see William M. Hammond, *Reporting Vietnam: Media and Military at War* (Lawrence: University Press of Kansas, 1998); Daniel C. Hallin, *The "Uncensored War": The Media and Vietnam* (New York: Oxford University Press, 1986); Chester J. Pach, Jr., "And That's the Way It Was: The Vietnam War on the Network Nightly News," in David Farber, Ed., *The Sixties: From Memory to History* (Chapel Hill: University of North Carolina Press, 1994), pp. 90–118.

10. Robert J. Donovan and Ray Scherer, *Unsilent Revolution: Television News and American Public Life, 1948–1991* (Cambridge University Press / Washington, DC: Woodrow Wilson International Center for Scholars, 1992), pp. 257–82; Leo Bogart, "Changing News Interests and the News Media," *Public Opinion Quarterly* 32 (Winter 1968/1969): 560–74.

11. Ben H. Bagdikian and Don Oberdorfer, "Bobby Was the Boy to See," *Saturday Evening Post*, 7 December 1963, p. 26.

12. Minutes of the Senate Democratic Conference, 27 July 1964, in Ritchie, *Minutes of the U.S. Senate Democratic Conference*, p. 645.

13. Charles V. Hamilton, *Adam Clayton Powell, Jr.: The Political Biography of an American Dilemma* (New York: Atheneum, 1991), p. 273.

14. "Must Adam Leave Eden?" *Newsweek*, 16 January 1967, p. 28.

15. Migel Acoca, "An Armed Powell Defends His Hideout," *Life*, 9 December 1966, pp. 101–6.

16. David S. Broder, *Behind the Front Page: A Candid Look at How the News Is Made* (New York: Simon & Schuster, 1987), pp. 214–16.

17. Editorial, "Not Just Powell," *New York Times*, 23 September 1966. For other examples of the press linking Powell's behavior to congressional operations and norms, see the following articles: Editorial, "Mr. Powell ... Absent," *New York Times*, 8 February 1963; Editorial, "Indolence and Arrogance," *New York Times*, 17 September

1966; Editorial, "Rebuke for Powell," *New York Times,* 10 January 1967; Vermont Royster, "One Man's Vote," *Wall Street Journal,* 10 January 1967; Editorial, "What People Think of Congress," *Wall Street Journal,* 13 February 1967; Editorial, "The Larger Ethics Issue," *Wall Street Journal,* 27 February 1967; Editorial, "A Necessary Journey," *Wall Street Journal,* 30 August 1967; Arlen J. Large, "Is Powell Right? Do They All Do It?" *Wall Street Journal,* 22 March 1967; Editorial, "House Discipline," *Washington Post,* 11 January 1967; Richard L. Lyons, "59 in House GOP Open Ethics Committee Drive," *Washington Post,* 26 February 1967; Editorial, "Riot Button on Powell," *Washington Post,* 2 March 1967; "Out of Powell Case: Reforms in Congress?" *U.S. News & World Report,* 16 January 1967, pp. 29–30; Editorial, "What to Do About Adam Powell?" *Life,* 13 January 1967, p. 6.

18. Editorial, "Escalator on Capitol Hill," *New York Times,* 5 January 1967. See also Richard Bolling, "What the New Congress Needs Most," *Harper's,* January 1967, p. 79.

19. CBS "Evening News," 3 January 1969, TNA.

20. ADA, "Clean Up Congress or Leave Powell Alone, Rauh Says," 1967, ADA, Unprocessed, Box 3, File: 13. See also Andrew Jacobs, *The Powell Affair: Freedom Minus One* (Indianapolis, IN: Bobbs-Merrill, 1973).

21. Press Release, "Joint Statement on the Seating of Adam Clayton Powell," 19 April 1967, RBP, Box 353, File: 10.

22. Editorial, "Powell Aftermath," *Washington Post,* 3 March 1967; "And Now ... What about Jim Eastland?" *New York Post,* 24 September 1966; Editorial, "Power 'Refined'," *Boston Herald,* 24 September 1966.

23. Clarence Mitchell to John McCormack, 29 December 1966, RBP, Box 353, File: 11.

24. *Powell v. McCormack,* 395 U.S. 486 (1969).

25. Lucas A. Powe, Jr., *The Warren Court and American Politics* (Cambridge, MA: Belknap Press, 2000), p. 271.

26. For some notable examples, see the following: Jack Anderson, "Dodd, Agent Skirt Act's Intent," *Washington Post,* 26 January 1966; Drew Pearson and Jack Anderson, "Dodd Aid to Foreign Agent Cited," *Washington Post,* 29 January 1966; Drew Pearson and Jack Anderson, "Klein Wrote Letters for Dodd," *Washington Post,* 18 February 1966; Drew Pearson and Jack Anderson, "Spanel Pushed by Dodd as Envoy," *Washington Post,* 1 March 1966; Drew Pearson and Jack Anderson, "Committee Pondered Dodd Ouster," *Washington Post,* 7 March 1966; Drew Pearson and Jack Anderson, "Dodd Started Campaign in '61," *Washington Post,* 25 March 1966; Drew Pearson and Jack Anderson, "How Dodd Rewarded Contribution," *Washington Post,* 22 April 1966; Drew Pearson and Jack Anderson, "Dodd's Double Standard Angers Public," *Washington Post,* 25 April 1967.

27. Oliver Pilat, *Drew Pearson: An Unauthorized Biography* (New York: Harper's Magazine Press, 1973), p. 265.

28. Drew Pearson to Katharine Graham, 11 April 1966, DP, Box G 271 (1 of 3), File: Thomas J. Dodd I.

29. Radio Script, 1 May 1966, DP, Box G 153, File: Radio Scripts April-May-June 1966.

30. "Keeping Faith with Adam" and "Dogging Dodd," *Newsweek,* 24 April 1967, pp. 26–7; "Dodd and Powell," *Nation,* 27 March 1967, pp. 387–8; "The Powell and Dodd Cases – How They Differ," *U.S. News & World Report,* 1 May 1967, pp. 35–7.

31. William F. Buckley, Jr., "Senator Dodd's Censure," *National Review,* 16 May 1967, p. 509.

32. For a sampling of other local newspapers that tied Dodd's case to calls for broader institutional changes, see DP, Box G270, File: Thomas J. Dodd II and File: Thomas J. Dodd V.

33. Editorial, "Campaign $$ Without Strings," *Boston Globe,* 7 April 1967; Editorial, "Making Money by the Book," *Chicago Daily News,* 10 December 1965; Editorial, "Favor Reform of Campaign Finance Laws," *Chicago Tribune,* 7 March 1966; Editorial, "New Campaign Fund Law Needed," *Des Moines Register,* 4 April 1967; Editorial, "No Will to Reform?" *Detroit News,* 17 June 1967; Editorial, "Misused White House Power," *Evening Bulletin,* 8 April 1967; Editorial, "The Super Duper Club for the Elite," *Hartford Courant,* 30 August 1966; Editorial, "It Seemed to Be a Good Idea," *Louisville Times,* 7 April 1967; Editorial, "President's Club Should Go Out of Business," *Milwaukee Journal,* 30 August 1966; "Campaign Funds," *Newsday,* 7 April 1967; Editorial, "Advertising the Great Society," *New York Times,* 13 December 1965; "Congress Ducks Again on Campaign Fund Reforms," *Providence Journal,* 22 March 1966; James Deakin, "Dinners Put Democrats in the Black," *St. Louis Post-Dispatch,* 23 July 1967; Editorial, "Raising Money the Democratic Way," *Wall Street Journal,* 13 December 1965; Jerry Landauer, "Political Fund-Raising: A Murky World," *Wall Street Journal,* 28 June 1967; Editorial, "The Economics of Elections," *Wall Street Journal,* 7 April 1967; David Broder, "Money Is the Root," *Washington Post,* 11 April 1967; Rowland Evans and Robert Novak, "The Mysterious $6000," *Washington Post,* 9 October 1966.

34. Editorial, "Censure for Dodd," *New York Times,* 28 April 1967. See also Editorial, "What About the Money?" *Detroit Free Press,* 3 May 1966.

35. "Dodd – Unfinished Business," *New Republic,* 28 May 1966, p. 7. See also Editorial, "Sen. Dodd Should Resign," *Los Angeles Times,* 28 April 1967; Editorial, "Make the Inquiry Complete," *Billings Gazette,* 3 May 1966; Editorial, "No Senator an Island," *Wall Street Journal,* 28 June 1966; Jerry Landauer, "The Dodd Case," *Wall Street Journal,* 11 May 1966 and Editorial, "The High Cost of Politics," *Wall Street Journal,* 23 May 1966; Jerry Landauer, "Senator's Political Career Likely to End, but Congress Still Faces Ethics Problem," *Wall Street Journal,* 28 April 1967; Editorial, "Senatorial Gifts," *Washington Post,* 21 April 1966; Editorial, "Censure for Dodd," *Washington Post,* 28 April 1967; Editorial, "A Code for the Senate," *Washington Post,* 20 June 1967; "Senators Are Different," *Nation,* 11 July 1966, pp. 36–7; Editorial, "A Shadow Falls Across the Senate," *Los Angeles Times,* 28 March 1966; "A Close Look Inside Today's Congress," *U.S. News & World Report,* 10 April 1967, pp. 44–8; Editorial, "Senator Dodd's Dinners," *Tulsa World,* 25 April 1966.

36. Editorial, "A Toothless Code of Ethics," *Life,* 5 April 1968, p. 4.

37. Transcript, "Firing Line," 16 July 1966, DP, Box G270, File: Thomas Dodd IV.

38. Senator Dodd, Memorandum, 17 May 1967, ACLU, Box 1023, File: 10.

39. "Senator Dodd's Report to the People of Connecticut," 14 May 1967, ACLU, Box 1023, File: 10.

40. William White, "Dodd Case Lesson ... Climate of Snoopery Exposed," *Washington Post,* 17 April 1967.

41. National Committee for Justice for Dodd to Editors and Correspondents, 26 May 1967, DP, Box G270, File: Thomas Dodd V; Russell Long to Mike Mansfield, 12 June 1967, MMP, Series XXII, Box 66, File: 23.

42. "Senator Dodd's Report to the People of Connecticut"; "Dodd Says Pearson Tries Case in Press," *New York Times,* 1 June 1966.
43. Drew Pearson, "Anybody for Cops and Robbers?" *Washington Post,* 30 March 1966.
44. Julius Klein to Drew Pearson, 3 May 1966, DP, Box G270, File: Thomas Dodd I.
45. Transcript, "CBS Evening News with Walter Cronkite," 24 July 1966, DP, G270, File: Thomas Dodd Various Columns.
46. Drew Pearson and Jack Anderson, "Columnists Under Investigation," *Washington Post,* 1 April 1966.
47. Jack Anderson and Drew Pearson to Thomas Dodd, 7 May 1966, DP, Box G270, File: Thomas J. Dodd II.
48. Frederick C. Klein, "The Muckraker," *Wall Street Journal,* 25 May 1966; Richard Harwood, "Dodd's Image in Connecticut Unstained by Charges," *Washington Post,* 3 April 1966; Ben Franklin, "Senator Dodd's Ride on the 'Merry-Go-Round'," *New York Times,* 15 May 1966, Section IV.
49. Editorial, "Pearson's Hot Potato," *Nation,* 11 April 1966, p. 410.
50. Neil MacNeil, *Forge of Democracy: House of Representatives* (New York: David McKay, 1963).
51. Drew Pearson and Jack Anderson, *The Case Against Congress: A Compelling Indictment of Corruption on Capitol Hill* (New York: Simon & Schuster, 1968).
52. Robert Bendiner, *Obstacle Course on Capitol Hill* (New York: McGraw-Hill, 1964).
53. James Boyd, *Above the Law* (New York: New American Library, 1968).
54. Michael Schudson, *Watergate in American Memory: How We Remember, Forget, and Reconstruct the Past* (New York: Basic Books, 1992), p. 118.
55. Robert L. Peabody and Nelson W. Polsby, *New Perspectives on the House of Representatives,* 2nd ed. (Chicago: Rand-McNally, 1969), p. vii.
56. Charles L. Clapp, *The Congressman: His Work As He Sees It* (Washington, DC: Brookings Institution, 1963).
57. Roger H. Davidson, David M. Kovenock, and Michael K. O'Leary, *Congress in Crisis: Politics and Congressional Reform,* 2nd ed. (New York: Wadsworth, 1968), p. 39.
58. James Burnham, *Congress and the American Tradition* (Chicago: Henry Regnery, 1959).
59. Davidson, Kovenock, and O'Leary, *Congress in Crisis,* pp. 17–34. The categorization of the literature that I state here comes from this work.
60. Joseph S. Clark and Other Senators, *The Senate Establishment* (New York: Hill & Wang, 1963), p. 22. See also J. Clark, Ed., *Congressional Reform: Problems and Prospects* (New York: Thomas Crowell, 1965).
61. Joseph S. Clark, *Congress: The Sapless Branch* (New York: Harper & Row, 1964), p. 113.
62. Richard Bolling, *House Out of Order* (New York: Dutton, 1965). See also R. Bolling, *Power in the House: A History of the Leadership of the House of Representatives* (New York: Dutton, 1968), and Clem Miller with John Baker, *Member of the House: Letters of a Congressman* (New York: Scribner's, 1962).
63. James MacGregor Burns, *The Deadlock of Democracy: Four-Party Politics in America* (Englewood Cliffs, NJ: Prentice-Hall, 1963), p. 248. See also James MacGregor Burns, *Presidential Government: The Crucible of Leadership* (Boston: Houghton-Mifflin, 1965).

64. For examples see James A. Robinson, *The House Rules Committee* (New York: Bobbs-Merrill, 1963); George Goodwin, "The Seniority System in Congress," *American Political Science Review* 53 (June 1959): 412–36; James L. Sundquist, *Politics and Policy: The Eisenhower, Kennedy, and Johnson Years* (Washington, DC: Brookings Institution, 1968); Milton C. Cummings, Jr., and Robert L. Peabody, "The Decision to Enlarge the Committee on Rules: An Analysis of the 1961 Vote," in Peabody and Polsby, *New Perspectives on the House of Representatives*, pp. 253–81; James T. Patterson, *Congressional Conservatism and the New Deal: The Growth of the Conservative Coalition in Congress, 1933–1939* (Lexington: University of Kentucky Press, 1967); T. Richard Wittmer, "The Aging of the House," *Political Science Quarterly* 79 (December 1964): 526–41.

65. Stephen K. Bailey, *The New Congress* (New York: St. Martin's Press, 1966), p. vii. See also Raymond E. Wolfinger and Joan Heifetz, "Safe Seats, Seniority, and Power in Congress," *American Political Science Review* 59 (June 1965): 349.

66. Charles O. Jones, "Joseph G. Cannon and Howard W. Smith: An Essay on the Limits of Leadership in the House of Representatives," *Journal of Politics* 30 (August 1968): 617–46.

67. Robert G. Dixon, Jr., *Democratic Representation: Reapportionment in Law and Politics* (New York: Oxford University Press, 1968).

68. Richard Bolling, "The House," *Playboy*, November 1969, pp. 125–6, 254.

69. Norman C. Thomas and Karl A. Lamb, *Congress: Politics and Practice* (New York: Random House, 1964), p. 131.

70. William J. Keefe and Morris S. Ogul, *The American Legislative Process: Congress and the States* (Englewood Cliffs, NJ: Prentice-Hall, 1964), p. 463.

71. Bolling, *House Out of Order*, pp. 243–4. See also Bolling to Charles Bolte, 18 March 1963, RBP, Box 326, File: 35.

72. See, for example, American Assembly, "Report of the Twenty-Sixth American Assembly: The Congress and America's Future," 29 October – November 1964, RBP, Box 129, File: 9.

73. David B. Truman, "Introduction: The Problem in Its Setting," in David B. Truman, Ed., *The Congress and America's Future* (Englewood Cliffs, NJ: Prentice-Hall, 1965), pp. 1–2.

74. Committee on Campaign Contributions and Expenditures to Senators and Representatives in Congress, 4 November 1958, GMA, Department of Legislation, Box 7, File: 21.

75. Michael Schudson, *The Good Citizen: A History of American Civic Life* (Cambridge, MA: Harvard University Press, 1999), pp. 182–5.

76. Ralph Huitt to Mike Monroney, 2 December 1964, MMOP, Box 1, File: 2; APSA, "Report of the Executive Director, 1965–1966," FHP, Box 30, File: 12.

77. Nelson W. Polsby and Eric Schickler, "Landmarks in the Study of Congress Since 1945: Sketches for an Informal History," paper presented at the 2001 American Political Science Association Convention, 30 August – 2 September 2001, San Francisco. The best example of this is Stephen Kemp Bailey, *Congress Makes a Law: The Story Behind the Employment Act of 1946* (New York: Columbia University Press, 1950).

78. "Introduction," in Nelson W. Polsby, Ed., *Explorations in the Evolution of Congress: H. Douglas Price* (Berkeley, CA: Institute of Governmental Studies, 1998), p. xiii.

79. Albert Somit and Joseph Tanenhaus, *The Development of American Political Science: From Burgess to Behavioralism* (Boston: Allyn & Bacon, 1967), pp. 173–94; Demetrios Caraley, "The Political Behavior Approach: Methodological Advance or New Formalism? – A Review Article," *Political Science Quarterly* 79 (March 1964): 96–108; David Easton, "The New Revolution in Political Science," *American Political Science Review* 63 (December 1969): 1051–61.

80. George Homans, *The Human Group* (New York: Harcourt Brace, 1950); Talcott Parsons and Edward A. Shils, Eds., *Toward a General Theory of Action* (Cambridge, MA: Harvard University Press, 1951); Robert K. Merton, *Social Theory and Social Structure* (Glencoe, IL: Free Press, 1957); Talcott Parsons, *The Social System* (Glencoe, IL: Free Press, 1961); Robert A. Dahl, "The Behavioral Approach in Political Science: Epitaph for a Monument to a Successful Protest," *American Political Science Review* 55 (December 1961): 770.

81. Louis Galambos, "Parsonian Sociology and Post-Progressive History," *Social Science Quarterly* 50 (June 1969): 25–45; David Easton, "An Approach to the Analysis of Political Systems," *World Politics* 9 (April 1957): 383–400; John C. Wahlke, Heinz Eulau, William Buchanan, and LeRoy C. Ferguson, *The Legislative System: Explorations in Legislative Behavior* (New York: Wiley, 1962). One of the most influential earlier articles suggesting this approach was Ralph K. Huitt, "The Congressional Committee: A Case Study," *American Political Science Review* 48 (June 1954): 340–65.

82. Richard F. Fenno, Jr., "The House Appropriations Committee as a Political System: The Problem of Integration," *American Political Science Review* 56 (June 1962): 310–24. Although he downplayed the theories, they still informed the introduction and analysis of his pathbreaking book, *The Power of the Purse: Appropriations in Congress* (Boston: Little, Brown, 1966), pp. xiii–xxix. Fenno's research articulated this approach for an entire generation.

83. Roland Young, *The American Congress* (New York: Harper, 1958), p. 267.

84. Donald R. Matthews, *U.S. Senators and Their World* (Chapel Hill: University of North Carolina Press, 1960), pp. 102–3. See also Roger H. Davidson, *The Role of the Congressman* (New York: Pegasus, 1969), p. 190, and John F. Manley, *The Politics of Finance: The House Committee on Ways and Means* (Boston: Little, Brown, 1970).

85. Dale Vinyard, *Congress* (New York: Scribner's, 1968), p. 115.

86. Ralph K. Huitt and Robert L. Peabody, "Forward," in John S. Saloma III, *Congress and the New Politics* (Boston: Little, Brown, 1969), pp. ix–x.

87. Fenno, *The Power of the Purse*, p. 689.

88. John Bibby and Roger Davidson, *On Capitol Hill: Studies in the Legislative Process* (New York: Holt, Rinehart & Winston, 1967).

89. Nelson W. Polsby, "The Institutionalization of the U.S. House of Representatives," *American Political Science Review* 62 (March 1968): 144–68; Nelson W. Polsby, Miriam Gallaher, and Barry Spencer Rundquist, "The Growth of the Seniority System in the U.S. House of Representatives," *American Political Science Review* 63 (September 1969): 787–807.

90. Nelson W. Polsby, *Congress and the Presidency* (Englewood Cliffs, NJ: Prentice-Hall, 1964), pp. 32–41. See also Ralph K. Huitt, "The Outsider in the Senate: An Alternative Role," *American Political Science Review* 55 (September 1961): 566–75; Randall B. Ripley, "Power in the Post–World War II Senate," *Journal of Politics* 31

(May 1969): 465–92; Barbara Hinckley, "Seniority in the Committee Leadership Selection of Congress," *Midwest Journal of Political Science* 13 (November 1969): 613–30; B. Hinckley, *The Seniority System in Congress* (Bloomington: Indiana University Press, 1971); James W. Dyson and John W. Soule, "Congressional Committee Behavior on Roll Call Votes: The U.S. House of Representatives, 1955–1964," *Midwest Journal of Political Science* 14 (November 1970): 626–47.

### Chapter 6

1.  Keith W. Olson, *Watergate: The Presidential Scandal That Shook America* (Lawrence: University Press of Kansas, 2003), pp. 22–42.
2.  Allen Matusow, *The Unraveling of America: A History of Liberalism in the 1960s* (New York: Harper & Row, 1984); Terry H. Anderson, *The Movement and the Sixties* (New York: Oxford University Press, 1996).
3.  Jonathan Rieder, "The Rise of the 'Silent Majority'," in Steve Fraser and Gary Gerstle, Eds., *The Rise and Fall of the New Deal Order, 1930–1980* (Princeton, NJ: Princeton University Press, 1989), p. 243.
4.  Minutes, ADA National Board Meeting, 26–27 September 1970, JBP, Box 149.G.8. 7(B), File: ADA 1970–1971.
5.  Byron E. Shafer, *Quiet Revolution: The Struggle for the Democratic Party and the Shaping of Post-Reform Politics* (New York: Russell Sage Foundation, 1983).
6.  George McGovern, Press Release, 25 October 1972, GMP, Box 779, File: Corruption.
7.  Wes Barthelmes, "The Greening of Congress," *Nation*, 30 November 1970, p. 553.
8.  John Jacobs, *A Rage for Justice: The Passion and Politics of Phillip Burton* (Berkeley: University of California Press, 1995), p. xxiv.
9.  LaVerne McCain Gill, *African-American Women in Congress: Forming and Transforming History* (New Brunswick, NJ: Rutgers University Press, 1997), p. 27.
10. Steven M. Gillon, *The Democrats' Dilemma: Walter F. Mondale and the Liberal Legacy* (New York: Columbia University Press, 1992).
11. Adam Clymer, *Edward M. Kennedy: A Biography* (New York: Morrow, 1999), pp. 130–3.
12. Editorial, "… And Scott's Success," *Washington Post*, 4 January 1969.
13. John W. Finney, "Challenge to the Senate 'Old Guard'," *New York Times*, 26 January 1969.
14. Linda Witt, Karen M. Paget, and Glenna Matthews, *Running As a Woman: Gender and Power in American Politics* (New York: Free Press, 1994), p. 48.
15. Robert Singh, *The Congressional Black Caucus: Racial Politics in the U.S. Congress* (Thousand Oaks, CA: Sage, 1998), p. 53.
16. Susan Webb Hammond, "Congressional Caucuses and Party Leaders in the House of Representatives," *Political Science Quarterly* 106 (Summer 1991): 277–94.
17. Alexander Heard, *The Costs of Democracy: Financing American Political Campaigns*, rev. ed. (Garden City, NY: Doubleday, 1962), pp. 196–203.
18. Herbert E. Alexander, *Money in Politics* (Washington, DC: Public Affairs Press, 1972), p. 33.
19. Democratic National Committee, "Financial Report," 25 March 1965, LJP, Files of Marvin Watson, Box 19, File: DNC/Financial Reports.
20. Democratic National Committee, Financial Records, 1965 and 1966, LJP, Files of Marvin Watson, Box 19, File: DNC/Financial Reports.

21. Minutes, Senate Democratic Conference, 16 November 1970, MMP, Series XXII, Box 90, File: 11.
22. Morris Udall to Democratic Colleagues, 25 July 1969, RBP, Box 129, File: 1.
23. Lawrence O'Brien to Members and Friends of the Democratic Party, 27 December 1970, RBP, Box 131, File: 4.
24. Garry Orren, "Fall from Grace: The Public's Loss of Faith in Government," in Joseph S. Nye, Jr., Philip D. Zelikow, and David C. King, Eds., *Why People Don't Trust Government* (Cambridge, MA: Harvard University Press, 1997), pp. 80–1.
25. Seymour Martin Lipset and William Schneider, *The Confidence Gap: Business, Labor and Government in the Public Mind* (New York: Free Press, 1983), p. 43.
26. John Gardner, "Pre-History of Common Cause & On the Road to Common Cause 1968 through 1970," 24 August 1976, CCP, Box 10, File: John Gardner's Pre-History of Common Cause.
27. William Frenzel to John Gardner, 7 July 1971, CCP, Box 23, File: 1971.
28. Michael W. McCann, *Taking Reform Seriously: Perspectives on Public Interest Liberalism* (Ithaca, NY: Cornell University Press, 1986), pp. 46–7.
29. Robert D. Putnam, *Bowling Alone: The Collapse and Revival of American Community* (New York: Simon & Schuster, 2000); Matthew A. Crenson and Benjamin Ginsberg, *Downsizing Democracy: How America Sidelined Its Citizens and Privatized Its Public* (Baltimore: Johns Hopkins University Press, 2002), pp. 122–51; Theda Skocpol, "Advocates without Members: The Recent Transformation of American Civic Life," in Theda Skocpol and Morris P. Fiorina, Eds., *Civic Engagement in American Democracy* (Washington, DC: Brookings Institution / New York: Russell Sage Foundation, 1999), pp. 461–509.
30. Minutes, Executive Meeting of the Policy Council, 4 November 1970, CCP, Box 30, File: September 1970 – January 1972.
31. John Gardner to Friend, 16 December 1970, CCP, Box 10, File: Early C.C. Memos September–December 1970.
32. John Gardner, "Sources of Common Cause Strength," 12 August 1974, CCP, Box 22, File: Memos July–December 1974.
33. John Gardner, "The Crisis in Confidence," 13 May 1970, CCP, Box 24, File: Speeches – June 1970.
34. Elizabeth Drew, "Conversation With a Citizen," *New Yorker,* 23 July 1973, pp. 43–4.
35. Andrew S. McFarland, *Common Cause: Lobbying in the Public Interest* (Chatham, NJ: Chatham House, 1984); Lawrence S. Rothenberg, *Linking Citizens to Government: Interest Group Politics at Common Cause* (Cambridge University Press, 1992).
36. David Vogel, *Kindred Strangers: The Uneasy Relationship Between Politics and Business in America* (Princeton, NJ: Princeton University Press, 1996), pp. 141–65.
37. Frederick Dutton to John Gardner, 18 October 1971, CCP, Box 27, File: Tom Mathews – 1971.
38. Ralph Nader, *Unsafe at Any Speed: The Designed-in Dangers of the American Automobile* (Washington, DC: Grossman, 1965).
39. Steven M. Gillon, *Politics and Vision: The ADA and American Liberalism, 1947–1985* (New York: Oxford University Press, 1987), pp. 226–31.
40. Leon Shull to Officers, 5 October 1970, ADA, Unprocessed Material, Box 1, File: 25.
41. Mrs. S. Peter Karlow to State and Local League Presidents, 24 July 1970, LWV, Box IV 214, File: 4.

42. "House Democratic Study Group Increases Activities Budget," *National Journal,* 8 November 1969, pp. 103–6.

43. DSG, "Campaign Activity Report," 1969, RBP, Box 129, File: 4.

44. Michael Schudson, *Discovering the News: A Social History of American Newspapers* (New York: Basic Books, 1978), p. 183.

45. Thomas E. Patterson, *Out of Order* (New York: Vintage, 1993), pp. 81–2.

46. Frederick Logevall, *Choosing War: The Lost Escalation for Peace and the Escalation of War in Vietnam* (Berkeley: University of California Press, 1999), pp. 134–53, 284–7; F. Logevall, "Congress and the Vietnam War," in Julian E. Zelizer, Ed., *The Reader's Guide to the American Congress* (Boston: Houghton-Mifflin, forthcoming); Robert Mann, *A Grand Delusion: America's Descent into Vietnam* (New York: Basic Books, 2001).

47. Both citations are in Bruce J. Schulman, *From Cotton Belt to Sunbelt: Federal Policy, Economic Development, and the Transformation of the South, 1938–1980* (New York: Oxford University Press, 1991), p. 146.

48. Randall Bennett Woods, *Fulbright: A Biography* (Cambridge University Press, 1995), pp. 515–16.

49. "Diary of White House Leadership Meetings – 91st Congress," 7 October 1969, RTH, Box 106, File: White House – Congressional Leadership Meeting 10/7/69.

50. Bryce Harlow to President Nixon, 6 October 1969, RNP, White House Central Files, Subject Files FG 31-1, Box 5, File: 4.

51. "Diary of White House Leadership Meetings – 91st Congress."

52. Denis S. Rutkus, "Opposition Party Access to the Broadcast Networks to Respond to the President," 2 March 1977, TOP, Jack Lew Files, Box 36, File: Network Fairness Doctrine.

53. Joe S. Foote, *Television Access and Political Power: The Networks, the Presidency, and the "Loyal Opposition"* (Westport, CT: Praeger, 1990).

54. Maurice Rosenblatt to Walter Mondale, 10 March 1970, WMP, Box 154.1.9.11.B, File: Meetings March 1970.

55. Rutkus, "Opposition Party Access to the Broadcast Networks to Respond to the President."

56. Ibid.

57. Foote, *Television Access and Political Power,* p. 48.

58. DSG, "The Most Corrupt Administration in History," DSG, Box 22, File: Issue Report #13.

59. Arthur M. Schlesinger, Jr., *The Imperial Presidency* (Boston: Houghton-Mifflin, 1973).

60. John Conyers to Colleague, 21 December 1972, CAP, Legislative Series, Box 181, File: 70.

61. Fraser and Gerstle, *The Rise and Fall of the New Deal Order.*

### Chapter 7

1. For a comprehensive history, see Julian E. Zelizer, "Seeds of Cynicism: The Struggle over Campaign Finance, 1956–1974," *Journal of Policy History* 14 (Winter 2002): 73–111.

2. Twentieth Century Fund, *Voter's Time: Report of the Twentieth Century Fund Commission on Campaign Costs and Electronic Data* (New York: Twentieth Century Fund, 1969).

3. Terry Robards, "Election Funds May Set Record," *New York Times,* 31 March 1968; "Campaign Spending Regulation: Failure of the First Step," *Harvard Journal of Legislation* 8 (1971): 642.

4. Robert E. Mutch, *Campaigns, Congress, and Courts: The Making of Federal Campaign Finance Law* (New York: Praeger, 1988), p. 69.

5. Lucas A. Powe, Jr., *The Warren Court and American Politics* (Cambridge, MA: Harvard University Press, 2000), pp. 303–35.

6. Ken Davis to Senator Scott, 19 January 1971, SHSP, Box 101, File: Campaign Reform (1 of 3).

7. Philip Hart and James Pearson to Fred Harris, 5 August 1969, and National Committee for an Effective Congress, July 1969, FHP, Box 279, File: 12.

8. James Abourezk to Carl Albert, 22 September 1971, CAP, Legislative Files, Box 147, File: 5.

9. U.S. Congress, Senate, Committee on Commerce, Subcommittee on Communications, *Hearings: Federal Election Campaign Act of 1971,* 92nd Congress, 1st Session, 2–31 March and 1 April 1971, pp. 146–8.

10. Common Cause, "Making Congress Work," November 1970, CCP, Box 216, File: Open-Up-The-System.

11. "Statement on John W. Gardner Re Common Cause Lawsuit," 11 January 1971, CCP, Box 27, File: Tom Mathews – 1971.

12. Mutch, *Campaigns, Congress, and Courts,* p. 45.

13. Numerous examples can be found in U.S. Congress, Senate, Committee on Commerce, Subcommittee on Communications, *Hearings: Federal Election Campaign Act of 1971,* pp. 220–79.

14. U.S. Congress, Senate, Committee on Rules and Administration, Subcommittee on Privileges and Elections, *Hearings: Federal Election Campaign Act of 1971,* 92nd Congress, 1st Session, 24–25 May 1971, pp. 92–3.

15. Mutch, *Campaigns, Congress, and Courts,* p. 189.

16. Press Release, 23 June 1971, CAP, Box 147, File: 91.

17. Andrew Biemiller to Edward Kennedy, 9 June 1971, ACP, Department of Legislation, Box 7, File: 20.

18. Ken Davis to Senator Scott, 10 February 1971, SHSP, Box 101, File: Campaign Reform (2 of 3).

19. Everett Erlick to Hugh Scott, 12 February 1971, SHSP, Box 101, File: Campaign Reform (2 of 3).

20. Lowell Beck to John Gardner, 21 June 1971, CCP, Box 28, File: Tom Mathews – 1971 III.

21. John Gardner to Senator Frank Moss, 27 June 1971, CCP, Box 28, File: Tom Mathews – 1971 III.

22. Robert Gallamore to John Gardner, 23 July 1971, CCP, Box 28, File: Tom Mathews – 1971 III.

23. John Barriere to Carl Albert, 17 January 1972, CAP, Legislative Files, Box 238, File: 9.

24. Al Barkan to George Meany, 11 November 1971, ACP, Office of the President, Box 95, File: Political Education, 1970–1972.

25. Herbert E. Alexander, *Financing the 1972 Election* (Lexington, KY: Lexington Books, 1976), p. 461.

26. George Melloan, "Playing Politics," *Wall Street Journal,* 17 February 1964.

27. John Barriere to Carl Albert, 23 November 1971, CAP, Legislative Files, Box 238, File: 8.

28. Minutes, Common Cause Governing Board Meeting, 8–9 June 1973, CCP, Box 31, File: February–June 1973.

29. Minutes, Common Cause Governing Board Meeting, 13 September 1972, CCP, Box 30, File: 13 September 1972.

30. Minutes, Common Cause Executive Committee Meeting, 26 July 1972, CCP, Box 30, File: February–July 1972; Common Cause, Press Release, "The Federal Election Campaign Act of 1971 – Is It the Real Thing, or Only a Sham," 24 February 1972, CCP, Box 136, File: January–March 1972.

31. John W. Gardner, "We, The People of the United States and Common Cause: Remarks Delivered to Common Cause Membership Meeting," 1 February 1973, CCP, Box 25, File: Speeches – March 1973.

32. Minutes, Common Cause Governing Board Meeting, 13 September 1972.

33. Alexander Barkan to Victor Riesel, 23 January 1973, ACP, Office of the President, Box 95, File: Political Education, 1972–1973.

34. Larry Gold to Tom Harris, Ken Young, and Mary Zon, 1 June 1973, ACP, Department of Legislation, Box 7, File: 20.

35. Herbert E. Alexander, *Money in Politics* (Washington, DC: Public Affairs Press, 1972), p. 171.

36. AFL-CIO, "Proceedings of the Tenth Constitutional Convention," v. II, 18–23 October 1973, ACP, pp. 368–71.

37. Larry Gold to Tom Harris, Ken Young, and Mary Zon.

38. Democratic Study Group, "Alice in Wonderland of Campaign Reform," 24 June 1974, DSG, Box 27, Unfiled.

39. Nelson Lichtenstein, *State of the Union: A Century of American Labor* (Princeton, NJ: Princeton University Press, 2002), pp. 185–91.

40. Byron E. Shafer, *Quiet Revolution: The Struggle for the Democratic Party and the Shaping of Post-Reform Politics* (New York: Russell Sage Foundation, 1983), pp. 86–8, 92–8, 361–2.

41. Taylor E. Dark, *The Unions and the Democrats* (Ithaca, NY: Cornell University Press, 1999), pp. 85–6.

42. *Pipefitters v. United States,* 407 U.S. 385 (1972).

43. George Meany to Presidents of Internationals, 2 August 1972, ACP, Office of the President, Box 95, File: Political Education, 1972–1973.

44. Jack M. McLeod, Jane D. Brown, and Lee B. Becker, "Watergate and the 1974 Congressional Elections," *Public Opinion Quarterly* 41 (Summer 1977): 182.

45. Gladys Engel Lang and Kurt Lang, *The Battle for Public Opinion: The President, the Press, and the Polls During Watergate* (New York: Columbia University Press, 1983), pp. 75–6, 92, 147–80.

46. "The Senate and the Watergate," CBS Television, 13 May 1973, TNA.

47. "Campaign '72: A Matter of Money," CBS Television, 3 September 1972, TNA.

48. NBC "Nightly News," 8 May 1973, TNA.

49. Minutes, Senate Democratic Conference, 9 May 1973, MMP, Series XXII, Box 91, File: 1, p. 22.

50. Bill Brock to Carl Albert, 4 May 1973, CAP, Legislative Files, Box 160, File: 1.

51. "Frenzel Predicts Congress Will Pass Sweeping Changes in Election Laws," 25 May 1973, GVP, Box 143, File: Election Reform.

52. Minutes, Senate Democratic Conference, 9 May 1973.
53. James O'Hara, "Remarks at the St. Clair Rotary Club, St. Clair, Michigan," 13 August 1973, JOP, Box 33, File: Speeches January–August 1973.
54. U.S. Congress, Senate, Committee on Rules and Administration, Subcommittee on Privileges and Elections, *Hearings: Federal Election Reform, 1973,* 93rd Congress, 1st Session, 11–12 April and 6–7 June 1973, pp. 66–7.
55. Minutes, Common Cause Governing Board Meeting, 8–9 June 1973.
56. David Cohen to Publicity Coordinators, 18 September 1973, CCP, Box 116, File: September 1973.
57. See, for example, "Summary of John Gardner's News Conference," 13 September 1973, CCP, Box 116, File: September 1973.
58. Center for Public Financing of Elections, 1974, WP, Box M80–71, File: Campaign Financing.
59. Minutes, Senate Democratic Conference, 9 May 1973.
60. George Gallup, *The Gallup Poll: Public Opinion, 1972–1977,* v. 1 (Delaware: Scholarly Resources, 1978), pp. 146, 186; GPA; Steven M. Gillon, *"That's Not What We Meant to Do": Reform and Its Consequences in Twentieth-Century America* (New York: Norton, 2000), p. 203.
61. Gallup Poll, 4 June 1973, GPA.
62. Minutes, Senate Democratic Conference, 21 May 1973, MMP, Series XXII, Box 91, File: 1.
63. Minutes, Senate Democratic Conference, 9 May 1973.
64. Common Cause, "Editorial Memorandum: A Wave of State Legislative Reform Sweeps Country," May 1974, CCP, Box 137, File: Press Releases May–August 1974.
65. Minutes, Senate Democratic Conference, 9 May 1973.
66. "Talk to the Nation: Interview of Mike Mansfield," ABC News, 1 February 1974, MMP, Oral History Collection, Tape: OH 22-172a.
67. Minutes, Senate Democratic Conference, 19 February 1974, MMP, Series XXII, Box 90, File: 11.
68. President Richard Nixon to Speaker Carl Albert, 27 March 1974, RNP, White House Subject Files, FG 34, Box 15, File: 2 of 3.
69. Minutes, Republican Leadership Meeting with the White House, 20 February 1974, SHSP, Box 8, File: Leadership Notes on Meetings 1974.
70. Minutes, Common Cause Governing Board Meeting, 19–20 April 1974; "Public Financing Fight Moves to House," *In Common: News for Common Cause Activists,* 26 April 1974, SHSP, Box 165, File: Campaign & Elections Campaign Finance Reform (2 of 2).
71. Ibid.
72. John Jacobs, *A Rage for Justice: The Passion and Politics of Phillip Burton* (Berkeley: University of California Press, 1995), pp. 254–6.
73. Ken Cole to President Ford, 21 August 1974, GFP, White House Central Files, Box 77, File: PL2.
74. Ken Cole to President Ford, 26 August 1974, WTP, Box 2, File: Campaign Financing Reform Legislation.
75. William Timmons, "Meeting with Rep. Hays," 12 September 1974, WTP, Box 5, File: Meeting with Representatives & Senators – Briefing Papers September 1974.
76. NBC "Nightly News," 17 September 1974, GFVC, Weekly News Summary Videos, Tape 1, File: F073.

77.  David Cohen, "Robust Political Competition: Voting, Redistricting and Campaign Finance," 16 January 1981, CCP, Box 200, File: Government Board Meeting 1981.

78.  William Timmons to President Ford, 9 October 1974, WTF, Box 2, File: Campaign Financing Reform Legislation.

79.  Walter Mondale, News Release, September 1974, WMP, Box 154.K.1.2.F, File: Press Releases August–September 1974.

80.  CBS "Nightly News," 13 September 1974, GFVC, Weekly News Summary Videos, Tape IV, F069B.

81.  Minutes, Common Cause Governing Board Meeting, 15–16 November 1974, CCP, Box 32, File: 27 July – 16 November 1974.

82.  CBS "Nightly News," 13 September 1974.

83.  Richard Zimmer to Gilman Spencer, 24 September 1974, and Frank Thompson to Robert Willis, 18 September 1974, FTP, Box 306, File: Campaign Reform Conference Committee.

84.  Herbert E. Alexander, "Political Finance Regulation in International Perspective," in Michael J. Malbin, Ed., *Parties, Interest Groups, and Campaign Finance Laws* (Washington, DC: American Enterprise Institute, 1980), p. 336.

## Chapter 8

1.   Eric Schickler, *Disjointed Pluralism: Institutional Innovation and the Development of the U.S. Congress* (Princeton, NJ: Princeton University Press, 2001), pp. 189–248.

2.   In addition to my archival research, this chapter builds on two excellent books that examine these battles: Burton D. Sheppard, *Rethinking Congressional Reform: The Reform Roots of the Special Interest Congress* (Cambridge, MA: Schenkman, 1985); and Roger H. Davidson and Walter J. Oleszek, *Congress Against Itself* (Bloomington: Indiana University Press, 1977).

3.   ABC "Nightly News," 17 February 1970, TNA.

4.   Morris Udall to John McCormack, 27 November 1968, JMP, Box 118, File: No Title.

5.   John W. Finney, "Vote on McCormack Is Blocked As House Reform Drive Opens," *New York Times,* 19 February 1970.

6.   Gilbert Gude, Fred Schwengel, Alphonzo Bell, Donald Riegle, Daniel Button, and Lawrence Coughlin to John Anderson, 12 October 1970, RTH, Box 45, File: Congressional Reorganization.

7.   DSG, "Secrecy in the House of Representatives," 24 June 1970, DFP, Box 149.G.8.3(B), File: Congressional Reform.

8.   V. O. French, "Taking on Mills and Long: A New Fight for Congressional Reform," 16 December 1971, CCP, Box 216, File: Open-Up-The-System.

9.   John Aloysius Farrell, *Tip O'Neill and the Democratic Century* (Boston: Little, Brown, 2001), p. 272.

10.  Steven S. Smith and Christopher J. Deering, *Committees in Congress,* 2nd ed. (Washington, DC: Congressional Quarterly, 1990), p. 47.

11.  Common Cause, "Report from Washington," November 1970, CCP, Box 128, File: November 1970 – September 1971.

12.  DSG, "Special Report: The First Year of Record Teller Voting," 27 January 1972, RBP, Box 132, File: 19.

13. Donald M. Fraser, "The Eclipse of Partisanship in the Legislative Process," January 1974, DFP, Box 149.G.8.3(B), File: Speeches 1974.
14. Select Committee on Committees Meeting, 28 October 1973, Audio Tape, RBP.
15. Ronald M. Peters, Jr., *The American Speakership: The Office in Historical Perspective*, 2nd ed. (Baltimore: Johns Hopkins University Press, 1990), pp. 146–208.
16. Farrell, *Tip O'Neill and the Democratic Century*, pp. 295–7, 316–17.
17. John Jacobs, *A Rage for Justice: The Passion and Politics of Phillip Burton* (Berkeley: University of California Press, 1995), pp. 217–41.
18. John Conyers to Colleague, 15 January 1971, RBP, Box 131, File: 16.
19. Joseph Rauh to Chapters, Officers, and National Board Members, 7 December 1970, ADA, Unprocessed, Box 9, File: 16.
20. William Cable, interview with Julian Zelizer, 20 August 2000.
21. Minutes, Committee on Organization, Study and Review of the Democratic Caucus, 24 November 1970, JBHP.
22. Sarah A. Binder, *Minority Rights, Majority Rule: Partisanship and the Development of Congress* (Cambridge University Press, 1997), p. 162.
23. Francis R. Valeo, *Mike Mansfield: Majority Leader, A Different Kind of Senate, 1961–1976* (Armonk, NY: M.E. Sharpe, 1999), pp. 6–47, 208–9.
24. Fred Harris to Senators, 1 February 1971, FHP, Box 233, File: 21; F. Harris, "Senate Reform," 1971, MMP, Box 101, File: 11.
25. Minutes of the Senate Democratic Conference, 10 February 1971, MMP, Box 90, File: 11. See also the draft of Mansfield to Fred Harris, 26 January 1971, MMP, Box 101, File: 11.
26. Memorandum, February 1971, CCP, Box 27, File: Tom Mathews – 1971.
27. Leroy N. Rieselbach, *Congressional Reform* (Washington, DC: Congressional Quarterly, 1986), p. 48.
28. "Statement by DSG Chairman Phillip Burton," 20 April 1972, RBP, Box 132, File: 15.
29. French, "Taking on Mills and Long: A New Fight for Congressional Reform."
30. John Lagomarcino to the Common Cause Governing Board, February 1972, CCP, Box 30, File: September 1970 – January 1972.
31. Committee for Congressional Reform, "Reform Committee Proposal," 1972, ADA, Unprocessed, Box 21, File: 28.
32. Minutes, "Exploratory Meeting on Congressional Reform of Religious and Citizen Action Groups," 20 July 1972, ADA, Unprocessed, Box 21, File: 28.
33. Minutes, Committee for Congressional Reform, 31 July 1972, ADA, Unprocessed, Box 21, File: 28.
34. Virginia L. Burch to Organizations Supporting Congressional Reform, 3 November 1972, ADA, Unprocessed, Box 21, File: 28.
35. Committee for Congressional Reform, "Congressional Reform," 1972, ADA, Unprocessed, Box 21, File: 28.
36. Committee for Congressional Reform, "What Have We Done?" 1972, ADA, Unprocessed, Box 21, File: 28.
37. Committee for Congressional Reform, "1973 Legislative Action," 1973, ADA, Unprocessed, Box 21, File: 29.
38. Common Cause, "Guidelines for Activist Members: Operation Open Up The System," 1972, and "Operation Open Up The System: A Common Cause Manual for the 1972 Congressional Elections," CCP, Box 216, File: Open-Up-The-System.

39. "Nader's Bird Watchers," *Time,* 16 October 1972, p. 23.

40. Paul L. Leventhal, "Congressional Report/Political Reaction Overshadows Reform Aim of Massive Nader Congress Study," *National Journal,* 23 September 1972, pp. 1484, 1491.

41. Sidney Scheuer and Russell Hemenway to Member of Congress, 8 June 1972, WP, Box M77–190 (1 of 2), File: Congressional Reform.

42. Norman J. Ornstein, "House Reform: Another Year of Seniority," *Washington Post,* 17 December 1972.

43. John R. Hibbing, "Voluntary Retirements from the House in the Twentieth Century," *Journal of Politics* 44 (November 1982): 1020–34.

44. "House: Republican Gain of 12, New Count of 244-191," *Congressional Quarterly Almanac* (1972): 1020.

45. "Democratic Caucus Changes," 1973, DFP, Box 149.G.8.3(B), File: Congressional Reform.

46. ADA, "House Democrats More Liberal in '73, Southern Democrats More Moderate," 11 February 1974, ADA, Unprocessed, Box 31, File: 5.

47. Eric Schickler, Eric McGhee, and John Sides, "Remaking the House and Senate: Personal Power, Ideology, and the 1970s Reforms," *Legislative Studies Quarterly,* forthcoming.

48. Common Cause, "Why the Seniority System in Congress Must Be Changed," December 1972, CCP, Box 136, File: October–December 1972.

49. Kevin Merida, "The Seniority of Strom Thurmond," *Washington Post,* 26 April 2001.

50. Pat Schroeder, 24 *Years of House Work ... And the Place Is Still a Mess: My Life in Politics* (Kansas City, MO: McMeel, 1998), pp. 39–42.

51. "Crisis in Congress," *Time,* 15 January 1973, pp. 12–19.

52. Committee for Congressional Reform, "1973 Legislative Action."

53. Committee for Congressional Reform, "In the Next Two Weeks You Have a Chance to Begin Restoring People's Faith in Congress," *Washington Post,* 2 January 1973.

54. Minutes, House Democratic Caucus, 22 January 1973, DCP.

55. Phil Burton to DSG Members, 19 January 1973, DFP, Box 149.G.8.3(B), File: Congressional Reform.

56. Minutes, House Democratic Caucus, 22 January 1973.

57. Ibid.

58. Godfrey Hodgson, *The World Turned Right Side Up: A History of the Conservative Ascendancy in America* (Boston: Houghton-Mifflin, 1996), pp. 124–7.

59. Transcript, "Speaking Out for Common Cause," 24 May 1973, CCP, Box 187, File: Transcripts.

60. "Senate and House Open Up Their Sessions in 1973," *Congressional Quarterly Almanac* (1973): 1074; Common Cause, "Most Committees in House of Representatives Switch to Open Bill-Drafting Sessions in 1973 under New Anti-Secrecy Requirement," January 1974, FTP, Box 298, File: Common Cause.

61. Steven S. Smith and Bruce A. Ray, "The Impact of Congressional Reform: House Democratic Committee Assignments," *Congress & The Presidency* 10 (Autumn 1983): 219–40.

62. Common Cause, "Seniority Reform in the Republican Caucus," January 1973, CCP, Box 216, File: Open-Up-The-System.

63. Norman J. Ornstein, "Subcommittee Reforms in the House," in Norman J. Ornstein, Ed., *Congress in Change: Evolution and Reform* (New York: Praeger, 1975), pp. 102–3.

64. David W. Rohde, *Parties and Leaders in the Postreform House* (University of Chicago Press, 1991), pp. 26–8.

65. Minutes, Common Cause Governing Board Meeting, 8–9 June 1973, CCP, Box 31, File: February–June 1973.

66. Information Minutes, Common Cause Governing Board Meeting, 8–9 February 1974, CCP, Box 32, File: 11 January – 20 April 1974.

67. E. Scott Adler, *Why Congressional Reforms Fail: Reelection and the House Committee System* (University of Chicago Press, 2002).

68. Parts of this section cite internal memoranda and letters from Gladys Uhl, Eleanor Lewis, Linda Kamm and Bill Cable. Uhl, Lewis, and Kamm were staffers for Bolling and the select committee who met privately with members and interest groups. They also sat in on meetings. These events were recorded as they reported on the incidents to Bolling. Cable, moreover, was an Education and Labor staffer who was allowed to sit in on all committee meetings and hearings. As I discuss in this section, Cable wrote lengthy descriptive reports to his superiors, a group of chairmen following the debates closely.

69. Ernest S. Griffith, *Congress: Its Contemporary Role* (New York: New York University Press, 1951); Arthur Mass, *Muddy Waters: The Army Engineers and the National Rivers* (Cambridge, MA: Harvard University Press, 1951); Douglass Cater, *Power in Washington: A Critical Look at Today's Struggle to Govern in the U.S.A.* (New York: Random House, 1964).

70. John Culver to Colleague, 29 December 1972, WOP.

71. Sheppard, *Rethinking Congressional Reform*, pp. 122–4.

72. Minutes, Select Committee on Committees, 31 January 1973, RBP, Box 232, File: 15.

73. Minutes, Select Committee on Committees, 21 February 1973, RBP, Box 232, File: 17.

74. John Culver to Richard Bolling, 27 February 1973, RBP, Box 232, File: 14.

75. Select Committee on Committees Meeting, 27 October 1973, Audio Tape, RBP.

76. Terence Finn to Members of the Select Committee, 1973, WOP.

77. U.S. Congress, House of Representatives, Select Committee on Committees, *Committee Organization in the House*, v. 1, part I, 93rd Congress, 1st Session, 9 May 1973, pp. 114–18.

78. Ibid., p. 130.

79. William Cable, interview with Julian Zelizer.

80. Minutes, Select Committee on Committees, 30 January 1974, RBP, Box 347, File: 19.

81. David C. King, *Turf Wars: How Congressional Committees Claim Jurisdiction* (University of Chicago Press, 1997), pp. 33–55.

82. "Select Committee on Committees Hearing Summary," 14 September 1973, RBP, Box 232, File: 11.

83. There were a few changes that were immediately shot down as politically impossible, such as Common Cause's call for rotating membership on all committees every six to eight years. See "Select Committee on Committees Hearing Summary," 4 October 1973, RBP, Box 232, File: 11; Select Committee on Committees Meeting, 28 October 1973; Select Committee on Committees Meeting, 16 October 1973, Audio Tape, RBP.

84. Select Committee on Committees Meeting, 12 September 1973, Audio Tape, RBP.

85. Select Committee on Committees Meeting, 18 October 1973, Audio Tape, RBP.

86. Select Committee on Committees Meeting, 19 September 1973, Audio Tape, RBP.

87. Minutes, Select Committee on Committees Meeting, 28 November 1973, WOP.

88. Select Committee on Committees Meeting, 18 October 1973.

89. Select Committee on Committees Meeting, 16 October 1973.

90. Bill Cable to Don Baker, 25 February 1974, WOP.

91. Select Committee on Committees Meeting, 26 September 1973, Audio Tape, RBP. See also Committee Staff to Members of the Select Committee, 3 October 1973, RBP, Box 344, File: 21.

92. Select Committee on Committees Meeting, 28 October 1973.

93. Minutes, Select Committee on Committees, 30 January 1974, p. 4.

94. Select Committee on Committees Meeting, 28 October 1973.

95. Select Committee on Committees, "Mark-Up Sessions," 6 March 1974, Audio Tape, RBP.

96. Select Committee on Committees Meeting, 18 October 1973.

97. Ibid.

98. Select Committee on Committees Meeting, 19 September 1973; Select Committee on Committees Meeting, 16 October 1973.

99. Charles Sheldon, "Critique of the Evaluation of the Reorganization Effort 1973–1974," RBP, Box 347, File: 8.

100. For example, Bolling wanted to remove only trade from Ways and Means, fearing that touching Medicare would be politically impossible. But he was overruled by Meeds, Sarbanes, and Steiger. See Select Committee on Committees Meeting, 28 October 1973.

101. "Select Committee on Committees Hearing Summary," 3 October 1973, RBP, Box 232, File: 11; Davidson and Oleszek, *Congress Against Itself,* p. 110.

102. Staff, Select Committee on Committees, Member Analysis, December 1973, WCP.

103. Select Committee on Committees Meeting, 28 October 1973.

104. Joan Claybrook and Nancy Chasen to Members of the Select Committee on Committees, 28 November 1973, WOP.

105. Furthermore, the abolition of the Internal Security, Merchant Marine and Fisheries, and Post Office and Civil Service Committees, as well as the elimination of some select committees, would cost 57 members an assignment – although some would retain seniority or a chairmanship on another committee. See Staff, Select Committee on Committees, "Impact of Select Committee on Committees Draft Proposals on Committee and Subcommittee Assignments of Democratic Members," December 1973, WCP.

106. Press Conference, 7 December 1973, Audio Tape, RBP.

107. W. R. Poage and William Wampler to Richard Bolling, 28 February 1974, WOP; John Heinz III to Bolling, 28 February 1974; Roy Taylor to Bolling, 22 February 1974; James Hanley to Bolling, 23 January 1974; Joe Evins to Bolling, 18 December 1973; Mario Biaggi to Bolling, 20 December 1973; John Dingell to Bolling, 7 January 1974; W. R. Poage and William Wampler to Bolling, 5 February 1974, all in WOP.

108. Wilbur Mills and Herman Schneebeli to Richard Bolling, 23 January 1974, RBP, Box 348, File: 1.

109. Minutes, Select Committee on Committees, 30 January 1974.
110. Iric Nathanson, "Shaking Up the House," *New Republic,* 9 February 1974, p. 17; Leonor Sullivan to Speaker Albert, 31 January 1974, WOP.
111. Davidson and Oleszek, *Congress Against Itself,* p. 161.
112. Sierra Club, "Congressional Reform Proposals Being Drafted: Environmental Jurisdictions in Jeopardy," *National News Report,* 15 February 1974, WOP.
113. Select Committee on Committees, "Mark-Up Hearings," 7 March 1974, Audio Tape, RBP.
114. John Dingell to Richard Bolling, 21 January 1974, WOP.
115. Francis Filbey, James Rademacher, and Clyde Webber to Thaddeus Dulski, 14 February 1974, RBP, Box 352, File: 2.
116. U.S. Congress, House of Representatives, Select Committee on Committees, *Committee Organization in the House,* v. 1, part 2, 93rd Congress, 1st Session, 9 May 1973, pp. 9–10.
117. Carl Perkins, Frank Thompson, John Dent, Dominick Daniels, John Brademas, James O'Hara, Augustus Hawkins, and William Ford to Richard Bolling, 6 February 1974, WOP.
118. Gladys Uhl to Richard Bolling, 15 February 1974, RBP, Box 348, File: 27. See also Linda Kamm to Richard Bolling, 8 August 1974, RBP, Box 347, File: 16.
119. Eleanor Lewis to Richard Bolling, 14 February 1974, RBP, Box 348, File: 27.
120. Marjorie Hunter, "Rep. Bolling Faces Reform Plan Test," *New York Times,* 22 January 1974; Shirley Elder, "Jealous House Powers Cool to Bolling Reform Plan," *Washington Star-News,* 17 February 1974; Taylor Branch, "The Approaching Struggle Over Reform in the House," *New York Times,* 28 April 1974.
121. Transcript, Select Committee on Committees, "Mark-Up Hearings," 23 February 1974, RBP, Box 237, File: 1, p. 556.
122. Burton, *Rethinking Congressional Reform,* p. 156.
123. Bill Cable to Don Baker, 25 February 1974, WOP; Cable to Baker, 20 February 1974, WOP.
124. Bill Cable to Don Baker, 20 February 1974, WCP.
125. The committee rejected a grandfather provision, as they did any stringent changes that would mandate specific subcommittee structures, on the grounds that the caucus should control assignments.
126. Select Committee on Committees, "Mark-Up Hearings," 6 March 1974; Select Committee on Committees, "Mark-Up Hearings," 7 March 1974.
127. Select Committee on Committees, "Mark-Up Hearings," 21 February 1974, RBP, Box 236, File: 1, p. 459.
128. Bill Cable to Don Baker, 21 February 1974, WCP.
129. "Select Committee on Committees Hearing Summary," 10 October 1973, RBP, Box 232, File: 11.
130. Select Committee on Committees, "Mark-Up Hearings," 21 February 1974, p. 469.
131. Bill Cable to Don Baker, 20 February 1974, WOP.
132. Bill Cable to Don Baker, 25 February 1974, WOP.
133. U.S. House of Representatives, Select Committee on Committees, *Report: Committee Reform Amendments of 1974,* 93rd Congress, 2nd Session, 21 March 1973.
134. Memorandum, 27 March 1974, RBP, Box 347, File: 15.
135. Linda Kamm, "Report from Charles on Meeting with Tiger Teague," 8 April 1974, RBP, Box 347, File: 4.

136. Gladys Uhl to Richard Bolling, 12 April 1974, RBP, Box 347, File: 16.

137. Gladys Uhl to Richard Bolling, 29 April 1974, RBP, Box 347, File: 16. He allegedly pressured multinational corporations to lobby on his behalf. See Eleanor Lewis to Richard Bolling, 26 September 1974, RBP, Box 347, File: 15.

138. Gladys Uhl to Richard Bolling, 25 April 1974, RBP, Box 347, File: 16.

139. Eleanor Lewis to Richard Bolling, 19 February 1974, RBP, Box 348, File: 1; Editorial, "The 'Decline' of Mills," *Arkansas Gazette,* 20 March 1974.

140. AFL-CIO Executive Council, "Proposed Restructuring of Committees of the House of Representatives," 25 February 1974, RBP, Box 347, File: 17.

141. Eleanor Lewis to Richard Bolling, 4 April 1974, RBP, Box 347, File: 16.

142. Eleanor Lewis to Richard Bolling, 26 April 1974, RBP, Box 347, File: 16.

143. Gladys Uhl to Richard Bolling, 7 May 1974, RBP, Box 347, File: 4.

144. Gladys Uhl to Richard Bolling, 5 March 1974, RBP, Box 347, File: 8.

145. "Mistakes Made by the Bolling Committee," 1974, WOP.

146. Joan Claybrook and Nancy Chasen to Phillip Burton, 15 July 1974, WOP; Claybrook and Chasen to Richard Bolling, 7 May 1974, RBP, Box 349, File: 9.

147. Gladys Uhl to Richard Bolling, 12 April 1974, RBP, Box 347, File: 4.

148. Eleanor Lewis to Richard Bolling, 4 April 1974, RBP, Box 347, File: 16.

149. Linda Kamm to Richard Bolling, July 25, 1974, RBP, Box 347, File: 15.

150. Peters, *The American Speakership,* p. 184.

151. Eleanor Lewis to Richard Bolling, 22 August 1974, RBP, Box 347, File: 15.

152. Memorandum, 3 April 1974, WOP.

153. Staff, Memorandum for the Speaker, 25 April 1974, CAP, Legislative Files, Box 190, File: 3.

154. Gladys Uhl to Richard Bolling, 26 April 1974, RBP, Box 347, File: 16.

155. Select Committee on Committees Staff Meeting, 10 May 1974, Audio Tape, RBP.

156. Select Committee on Committees Staff Meeting, 10 May 1974.

157. John Culver to Julia Butler Hansen, 17 May 1974, CAP, Legislative Files, Box 181, File: 71.

158. Select Committee on Committees Meeting, 16 May 1974, Audio Tape, RBP.

159. Select Committee on Committees Staff Meeting, 10 May 1974.

160. Ibid.

161. Charles Sheldon to Richard Bolling, 13 May 1974, RBP, Box 347, File: 13.

162. William Cable, interview with Julian Zelizer.

163. "DSG Meeting on Hansen Committee Recommendations," August 1974, RBP, Box 347, File: 12.

164. "That Congress Is 'Loafing'," *U.S. News & World Report,* 27 May 1974, p. 30.

165. Charles Sheldon II to John Barriere, 14 June 1974, RBP, Box 347, File: 8.

166. "Democrats Junk Committee Plan in Secret," *In Common,* 24 May 1974; "Telephone Alert on Bolling Committee Reorganization Plan for the House of Representatives," 28 August 1974; Leon Shull to House Members, 19 July 1974, WOP.

167. Transcript, "Speaking Out for Common Cause," 11 June 1974, CCP, Box 191, File: Transcripts.

168. Eleanor Lewis to Richard Bolling, 19 August 1974, RBP, Box 347, File: 15.

169. He said there were three groups on the reform issue: "all-out enemies," "the compromisers," and those "who want a reasonable debate on our plan." See Minutes, Select Committee Meeting, 6 August 1974, WOP.

170. "Statement of Congressman Holifield on Bolling Committee Reform," 2 October 1974, WOP.

171. Carl Perkins to Carl Albert, 19 September 1974, WOP.

172. Linda Kamm to Richard Bolling, 4 April 1974, RBP, Box 347, File: 16.

173. Gladys Uhl to Richard Bolling, 27 September 1974, RBP, Box 347, File: 15.

174. Davidson and Oleszek, *Congress Against Itself,* pp. 241–2.

175. King, *Turf Wars,* pp. 62–7.

176. Editorial, "The Reorganization of the House," *Washington Post,* 12 October 1974.

177. "The AFL-CIO: How Much Clout in Congress," *Congressional Quarterly Weekly,* 19 July 1975, p. 1533.

178. The best analysis of this can be found in Allen Schick, *Congress and Money: Budgeting, Spending and Taxing* (Washington, DC: Urban Institute, 1980).

179. Aaron Wildavsky, *The Politics of the Budgetary Process* (Boston: Little, Brown, 1964).

180. Schick, *Congress and Money,* p. 42.

181. James L. Sundquist, *The Decline and Resurgence of Congress* (Washington, DC: Brookings Institution, 1981), p. 203; Louis Fisher, *Presidential Spending Power* (Princeton, NJ: Princeton University Press, 1975), pp. 147–201; DSG, "Special Report: Presidential Impoundment of Funds," 15 February 1973, DSG, Box 18, File: Unmarked.

182. Carl Albert, "The Domestic Balance," *New York Times,* 13 February 1973.

183. Minutes, Senate Democratic Conference, 18 January 1973, MMP, Leadership Series, Box 91, File: 1.

184. Schick, *Congress and Money,* p. 56.

185. Sundquist, *The Decline and Resurgence of Congress,* pp. 210–11.

186. John Barriere to Carl Albert, 3 August 1973, CAP, Legislative Files, Box 238, File: 12; Leon Shull to Congressmen, 14 May 1973, FTP, Box 256, File: Joint Study Committee on Budget Control; Leon Shull to Congressman, 1 May 1973, ADA, Unprocessed, Box 21, File: 15.

187. David Obey to DSG Members, 15 May 1973, DFP, Box 151.H.2.6(F), File: Democratic Caucus 1973. The United Auto Workers offered an alternative plan, endorsed by ADA and Common Cause, for budget committees with term-limited memberships. See Jack Beidler to Congressmen, 18 May 1973, FTP, Box 256, File: Joint Study Committee on Budget Control.

188. Allen Schick, *Congress and Money,* p. 66.

189. Schickler, *Disjointed Pluralism,* p. 193; Schick, *Congress and Money,* pp. 59–60, 78.

190. Committee Staff to Members of the Select Committee, 3 October 1973, RBP, Box 349, File: 21.

## Chapter 9

1. For the scholarly debate about what motivated voters, see Eric M. Uslaner and Margaret Conway, "The Responsible Congressional Electorate: Watergate, the Economy, and Vote Choice in 1974," *American Political Science Review* 79 (September 1985): 788–803; Gary C. Jacobson and Samuel Kernell, *Strategy and Choice in Congressional Elections,* 2nd ed. (New Haven, CT: Yale University Press, 1983); "Interpreting the 1974 Congressional Election," *American Political Science Review* 80 (June 1986): 591–6.

2. Lizabeth Cohen, *A Consumer's Republic: The Politics of Mass Consumption in Postwar America* (New York: Knopf, 2003), pp. 345–97.

3. David W. Rohde, *Parties and Leaders in the Postreform House* (University of Chicago Press, 1991), p. 48.

4. "The AFL-CIO: How Much Clout in Congress," *Congressional Quarterly Weekly,* 19 July 1975, p. 1533.

5. Taylor E. Dark, *The Unions and the Democrats* (Ithaca, NY: Cornell University Press, 1999), p. 95.

6. Thomas Byrne Edsall, "The Changing Shape of Power: A Realignment in Public Policy," in Steve Fraser and Gary Gerstle, Eds., *The Rise and Fall of the New Deal Order, 1930–1980* (Princeton, NJ: Princeton University Press, 1989), pp. 269–93.

7. Hazel Erskine, "The Polls: Corruption in Government," *Public Opinion Quarterly* 37 (Winter 1973/1974): 628–44; Seymour Martin Lipset and William Schneider, "The Decline of Confidence in American Institutions," *Political Science Quarterly* 98 (Autumn 1983): 382.

8. Gladys Engel Lang and Kurt Lang, *The Battle for Public Opinion: The President, the Press, and the Polls During Watergate* (New York: Columbia University Press, 1983), p. 210.

9. Stanley I. Kutler, "Clearing the Rubble: The Nixon Pardon," and Mark J. Rozell, "In Defense of President Ford's Pardon of Richard M. Nixon," in Bernard J. Firestone and Alexej Ugrinsky, Eds., *Gerald R. Ford and the Politics of Post-Watergate America* (Westport, CT: Greenwood, 1993), pp. 36, 40; Mark J. Rozell, *The Press and the Ford Presidency* (Ann Arbor: University of Michigan Press, 1992), pp. 51–85.

10. U.S. Congress, House of Representatives, *Hearings Before the Committee on Democratic Steering and Policy,* 1 October 1974, CAP, Legislative Series, Box 182, File: 6, p. 5.

11. Minutes, Democratic National Committee, Executive Committee Meeting, 16 September 1974, Box 27, File: Bound, p. 95.

12. Congressional Quarterly, *The 1974 Election Report,* 12 October 1974, p. 2711.

13. Democratic National Committee, "Up-to-Date Information for Candidates," 27 September 1974, TSP, General Series, Box 62, File: Democrats 1 of 2.

14. The Harris Survey, "Public Confidence in Institutions Mostly Lower," 30 September 1974, TOP, Eleanor Kelley Files, Box 6, File: Polls 1975.

15. Editorial, "The California Vote," *New York Times,* 6 June 1974.

16. Wallace Turner, "California Returns Viewed as Reaction to Watergate," *New York Times,* 6 June 1974.

17. "A Vote of No Confidence," *Newsweek,* 4 March 1974, p. 16.

18. The story was widely reported by the media. For the coverage by the *New York Times,* see the following articles: "Mills Called Occupant of Car Police Stopped," 9 October 1974; John M. Crewdson, "Mills in Seclusion after Report He Was Intoxicated in Car Stopped by Police," 10 October 1974; Crewdson, " 'Embarrassed' Mills Acknowledges That He Was in Limousine Stopped by Police," 11 October 1974; William Safire, "The Need to Know," 17 October 1974; Roy Reed, "Mills Apologizes to His Constituents," 18 October 1974; "Mills Forced to Campaign Hard Following Tidal Basin Incident," 19 October 1974. For the coverage by the *Washington Post,* see the following articles: Alfred E. Lewis and Martin Wed, "Riders in Mills' Car Involved in a Scuffle," 9 October 1974; Stephen Green, "Mills Hurt, Intoxicated in Incident, Police Say," 10 October 1974; Green, "Mills Admits Being

Present During Tidal Basin Scuffle," 11 October 1974; Margot Hornblower and Megan Rosenfeld, "Police Identify Driver in Rep. Mills Incident," 15 October 1974; "The Incident at the Tidal Basin," 20 October 1974. See also "A Bit of the Bubbly," *Time,* 28 October 1974, p. 21. Some people spelled the name as "Fox"; others, as "Foxe."

19. Brooks Jackson, "Wilbur's Watergate," *New Republic,* 14 September 1974, p. 9.
20. CBS "Nightly News," 10 October 1974, GFL, Weekly News Summary Videos, Tape III, F101A.
21. Minutes, Common Cause Governing Board Meeting, 8–9 February 1974, CCP, Box 32, File: 11 January – 20 April 1974.
22. Minutes, Common Cause Governing Board Meeting, 15–16 November 1974, CCP, Box 32, File: 27 July – 16 November 1974.
23. James P. Sterba, "Democrats Take Colorado Races," *New York Times,* 6 November 1974.
24. "Labor and A.M.A. Top List in '74 Spending on Politics," *New York Times,* 29 October 1974.
25. John Jacobs, *A Rage for Justice: The Passion and Politics of Phillip Burton* (Berkeley: University of California Press, 1995), pp. 252–3.
26. Leroy N. Rieselbach, *Congressional Reform* (Washington, DC: Congressional Quarterly, 1986), p. 45.
27. Gerald C. Wright, Jr., "Constituency Response to Congressional Behavior: The Impact of the House Judiciary Committee Impeachment Votes," *Western Political Quarterly* 30 (September 1977): 401–10.
28. Richard Conlon to DSG Members, 6 November 1974, FTP, Box 296, File: DSG.
29. "1974 Elections: A Major Sweep," *Congressional Quarterly Almanac* (1974): 839–40.
30. Joseph Cooper and William West, "Voluntary Retirement, Incumbency, and the Modern House," *Political Science Quarterly* 96 (Summer 1981): 279–300.
31. Lawrence C. Dodd and Bruce I. Oppenheimer, "The House in Transition," in L. Dodd and B. Oppenheimer, Eds., *Congress Reconsidered* (New York: Praeger, 1977), p. 25.
32. Burdett Loomis, *The New American Politician: Ambition, Entrepreneurship, and the Changing Face of Political Life* (New York: Basic Books, 1988), p. 33.
33. Tip O'Neill with William Novak, *Man of the House: The Life and Political Memoirs of Speaker Tip O'Neill* (New York: Random House, 1987), p. 283.
34. Sanford J. Ungar, "Bleak House: Frustration on Capitol Hill," *Atlantic Monthly,* July 1977, p. 32.
35. DSG Staffer, interview with Sidney Waldman, 19 May 1976, SWOHI.
36. John Isaacs, "Dems Sweep Congress; Women, Blacks, Browns Make Big Gains," and Iric Nathanson, "Caucus Talk," in *ADA World,* November/December 1974, pp. 3, 8.
37. Richard Franklin Bensel, *Sectionalism and American Political Development, 1880–1980* (Madison: University of Wisconsin Press, 1984), p. 354; Mathew D. McCubbins and Thomas Schwartz, "Congress, the Courts, and Public Policy: Consequences of the One Man, One Vote Rule," *American Journal of Political Science* 32 (May 1988): 388–415.
38. Larry M. Schwab, *The Impact of Congressional Reapportionment and Redistricting* (Lanham, MD: University Press of America, 1988), pp. 91–200.

39. R. W. Apple Jr., "National Vote Pattern: A Sweep If Not a G.O.P. Debacle," *New York Times,* 7 November 1974.

40. Editorial, "Up to the Democrats," *New York Times,* 7 November 1974.

41. Editorial, "For the Democrats," *Washington Post,* 7 November 1974. For other accounts that stress the economy and Watergate, see the following: "The Price of Trusting Nixon," *Time,* 18 November 1974, p. 25; "Election Woes at White House," *U.S. News & World Report,* 18 November 1974, p. 16; "Impact '74 Election," *U.S. News & World Report,* 18 November 1974, pp. 19–24; "The Big Sweep: What Now?" *Newsweek,* 18 November 1974, pp. 24–7; Robert Shogan, "GOP Founders in Riptides of Watergate, Pardon, Economy," *Los Angeles Times,* 6 November 1974; Editorial, "What the American Voter Said," *Los Angeles Times,* 7 November 1974; Editorial, "The Verdict was National," *Boston Globe,* 7 November 1974; Editorial, "But What Did the Voters Say?" *Chicago Tribune,* 7 November 1974; Harry Kelly and Jon Margolis, "Voters Shift U.S. Power Balance," *Chicago Tribune,* 7 November 1974; "Democrats Tighten Grip on Congress," *Atlanta Constitution,* 6 November 1974; Editorial, "The Voters' Message in 1974 is Easy to Read," *Kansas City Times,* 7 November 1974; Albert R. Hunt, "Republicans Are Routed as Voters React to Watergate and Economy," *Wall Street Journal,* 7 November 1974; Alan T. Otten, "A Campaign with Few Hurrahs," *Wall Street Journal,* 7 November 1974.

42. Leon Shull, "Happy Days Are Here Again, Maybe," *ADA World,* November/December 1974, p. 4.

43. Carl Albert with Danney Goble, *Little Giant: The Life and Times of Speaker Carl Albert* (Norman: University of Oklahoma Press, 1990), pp. 367–8.

44. NBC "Nightly News," 23 October 1974, GFL, Weekly News Reports Videos, Tape II, File: F120; CBS "Nightly News," 4 November 1974, GFL, Weekly News Reports Videos, Tape I, File: F133.

45. "Democrats: Now the Morning After," "Impressive Freshman Class," and "New Faces and New Strains," *Time,* 18 November 1974, pp. 8–25; "A Crowd of New Faces – Any Prospects For '76?" *U.S. News & World Report,* 18 November 1974, pp. 30–1; "The 94th Congress: Younger, Restless, More 'Liberal'," *U.S. News & World Report,* 20 January 1975, pp. 27–8; "Rookies of the Year" and "The Aggressive 94th," and Bill Moyers, "The Morning After," *Newsweek,* 18 November 1974, pp. 27–35, 116; "Good Day at the Polls," *Nation,* 16 November 1974, pp. 482–3.

46. The Harris Survey, "Restoring Integrity in Government Should Be Congress' First Priority," 2 December 1974. See also Democratic National Committee, "Analysis of Recent Polls – XI," 20 October 1975. Both documents are in TOP, Eleanor Kelley Files, Box 6, File: Polls 1975.

47. John Gardner to Committee Member, 20 January 1975, and Gardner to Senator, 9 January 1975, CCP, Box 23, File: 1975.

48. Common Cause, "Editorial Memorandum: Congress Returns to Face Major Reform Proposals," January 1975, CCP, Box 137, File: Press Release January–April 1975.

49. Democratic Study Group, "Committee Assignments for New Members," 14 November 1974, and "Model Committee Caucus & Committee Rules," 20 January 1975, DSG, Box 18, File: Unmarked.

50. "The AFL-CIO," pp. 1531–3.

51. Common Cause, Press Release, 20 November 1974, CCP, Box 216, File: Open-Up-The-System.

52. John Gardner to Representative, 13 November 1974, CCP, Box 216, File: Open-Up-The-System.

53. Ruth Clusen to Democratic Members of the House of Representatives, 27 November 1974, DFP, Box 151.H.2.6(6), File: Democratic Caucus 1974; Ralph Nader to Representative, 25 November 1974, DFP, Box 151.H.2.6(F), File: Democratic Caucus 1974.

54. George Meany to Carl Albert, 21 November 1974, and Albert to Meany, 23 November 1974, CAP, Legislative Files, Box 181, File: 71.

55. Albert R. Hunt, "Ebbing Influence," *Wall Street Journal,* 29 November 1974.

56. Nathanson, "Caucus Talk," p. 8.

57. "Mills Does a Walk-on with Stripper," *New York Times,* 2 December 1974; Martha Hamilton, "Mills Derided in Congress over Link to Stripper," 2 December 1974; "Mills Takes a Curtain Call with His 'Argentine Hillbilly'," *Los Angeles Times,* 2 December 1974; Richard Martin and Nick King, "A Most Unusual Visit," *Boston Globe,* 2 December 1974; "Rep. Mills, Starmaker?" *Chicago Tribune,* 2 December 1974; "Fanne's Co-Star," *Atlanta Constitution,* 2 December 1974; "Mills Visits Fanne Foxe," *Kansas City Times,* 2 December 1974. See also Julian E. Zelizer, *Taxing America: Wilbur D. Mills, Congress and the State, 1945–1975* (Cambridge University Press, 1998), pp. 349–72.

58. "CBS News Special: 1974 A Television Album," 29 December 1974, The Museum of Television and Radio (New York City), T81: 0089, 002908.

59. ABC "Nightly News," 3 December 1974, GFL, Weekly News Reports Videos, Box: Tape I, File: F178.

60. ABC "Nightly News," 2 December 1974, GFL, Weekly News Reports Videos, Tape I, File: F178.

61. U.S. Congress, House of Representatives, Democratic Caucus, *Hearings Before the Committee for the Organization of the 94th Congress,* 2 December 1974, DCP, p. 11.

62. Ibid., pp. 90–1.

63. Ibid., p. 105.

64. Ibid., pp. 106–7.

65. Ibid., pp. 96–7.

66. U.S. Congress, House of Representatives, Democratic Caucus, *Hearings Before the Committee for the Organization of the 94th Congress,* 3 December 1974, CAP, Legislative Files, Box 219, File: 46, pp. 202–3.

67. Ibid., pp. 203–5.

68. U.S. Congress, House of Representatives, Democratic Caucus, *Hearings Before the Committee for the Organization of the 94th Congress,* 4 December 1974, DCP, pp. 302–3.

69. "House Democrats: Freshmen and Reformers Lead Rebellion," *ADA Legislative Newsletter,* v. 3, no. 21, 15 December 1974, HHP, Box 150.G.3.3(B), File: Congressional Reform.

70. For examples see David E. Rosenbaum, "House Democrats End Mills's Rule Over Committees" and "Mills Derided in Congress Over Link to Stripper," *New York Times,* 3 December 1974; "Return of King Caucus" and "The Fall of Chairman Wilbur Mills," *Time,* 16 December 1974, pp. 17–19; "Mills's Problems – Among Many for Democrats in the House," *U.S. News & World Report,* 16 December 1974,

p. 17; "Wilbur in Nighttown" and "A Hurricane Blows Through the Old House," *Newsweek,* 16 December 1974, pp. 21–4; "Wilbur Mills' Ways and Means," *Nation,* 11 December 1974, pp. 5–6; "Democrats Vote to Expand Panel in New Mills Rebuff," *Los Angeles Times,* 3 December 1974; Editorial, "The Look of Reform in the House," *Los Angeles Times,* 4 December 1974; Robert Healy, "Bow Won't Do Much for Mills," and David Nyhan, "Caucus Attacks Powers of Mills," *Boston Globe,* 2 December 1974; Editorial, "The Class of 94," *Boston Globe,* 4 December 1974; Arthur Siddon, "Mills Stripped of Leading Role," *Chicago Tribune,* 3 December 1974; "Mills' Retreat" and "And Defeat," *Atlanta Constitution,* 3 December 1974; Paul Houston, "Democrats Strip Mills of Power to Name Panels," *Los Angeles Times,* 3 December 1974.

71. Mary Russell, "Democrats End Hill Era," *Washington Post,* 8 December 1974. See also Cartoon, "Wait! Let Go – Not That Kind of Strip Routine," *Washington Post,* 3 December 1974.

72. CBS "Nightly News," 4 December 1974, GFL, Weekly News Summary Tapes, Tape II, File: F179.

73. "Text of the Statement by Mills," *New York Times,* 31 December 1974; CBS "Evening News," 30 December 1974, TNA.

74. Annabel Battistella and Yvonne Duleavy, *Fanne Fox* (New York: Pinnacle, 1975).

75. F. Edward Hebert with John McMillan, *"Last of the Titans": The Life and Times of Congressman F. Edward Hebert of Louisiana* (Lafayette: Center for Louisiana Studies, 1976), p. 442.

76. Richard L. Lyons, "Freshmen Assess House Chairmen," *Washington Post,* 14 January 1975.

77. Editorial, "The Democratic Caucus in Command," *Washington Post,* 20 January 1975.

78. "As the Old Order Begins to Crumble on Capitol Hill," *U.S. News & World Report,* 3 February 1975, p. 23. See also "A Whiff of Rebellion in the 94th," *Time,* 27 January 1975, pp. 26–7; Iric Nathanson, "The Caucus vs. the Barons," *Nation,* 11 January 1975, pp. 6–9; Paul R. Wieck, "Freshmen on the Move," *New Republic,* 1 February 1975, pp. 8–9; "Reuss Beats Patman for Chairmanship of House Panel, Maps Bold Course," *Wall Street Journal,* 23 January 1975; Editorial, "The House Revolution," *New York Times,* 11 January 1975.

79. See, for examples, NBC "Nightly News," 8 January 1975, GFL, Weekly News Summary Video, Tape II, File: F194A, and NBC "Nightly News," 16 January 1975, GFL, Weekly News Summary, Tape III, File: F201B.

80. CBS "Nightly News," 8 January 1975, GFL, Weekly News Summary Video, Tape II, File: F194A.

81. CBS "Nightly News," 18 January 1975, GFL, Weekly News Summary, Tape III, File: F201B.

82. Common Cause, "Report on House Committee Chairmen," 13 January 1975, Revised Version, CCP, Box 216, File: Open-Up-The-System.

83. Ralph Nader to Representatives, 15 January 1975, RBP, Box 177, File: 2.

84. Burton D. Sheppard, *Rethinking Congressional Reform: The Reform Roots of the Special Interest Congress* (Cambridge, MA: Schenkman, 1985), p. 203.

85. Edward Hebert to Colleague, 14 January 1975, DFP, Box 151.H.2.6(F), File: Democratic Caucus 1975.

86. Frank Thompson, "An Approach to the Frosh," January 1975, FTP, Box 547, File: Hays-Thompson.

87. Frank Thompson to Fellow Democrat, 22 January 1975, FTP, Box 547, File: Hays-Thompson.

88. Ralph Nader to Representative, 20 January 1975, RBP, Box 177, File: 2.

89. Jacobs, *A Rage for Justice*, p. 271.

90. ABC "Nightly News," 24 January 1975, TNA.

91. Editorial, "The Trouble with Mr. Hays," *Washington Post*, 22 January 1975.

92. Common Cause, "Report on House Committee Chairmen."

93. "Seniority System Toppled by Reform Wave," January 1975, CCP, Box 128, File: November 1974 – October 1975.

94. The Ralph Nader Congress Project, *Ruling Congress* (New York: Grossman, 1975), p. xv.

95. Editorial, "House in Order," *New York Times*, 23 January 1975.

96. Jacobs, *A Rage for Justice*, pp. 264–5.

97. "Rep. Hebert Castigates Citizen Unit," *Washington Post*, 6 February 1975.

98. NBC "Nightly News," 18 September 1975, GFL, Weekly News Summary Video, Tape III, File: F201B.

99. Omar Burleson, interview with Sidney Waldman, 17 July 1975, SWOHI.

100. "A Firecracker Exploded," *Newsweek*, 21 October 1974, p. 42.

101. Walter Shapiro, "Wilbur Mills: The Ways and Means of Conning the Press," *Washington Monthly* 6 (December 1974): 4–13. This piece was reprinted in newspapers; see e.g. Walter Shapiro, "How Wilbur Conned the Press – And Public – All Those Years," *Kansas City Star*, 5 January 1975.

102. Nicholas von Hoffman, "Wilbur Mills and Journalistic Malaise," *Washington Post*, 9 December 1974. See also William Safire, "The Need to Know," *New York Times*, 17 October 1974; Editorial, "Wilbur Mills' Statement," *Washington Post*, 2 January 1975.

103. NBC "Nightly News," 10 December 1974, GFL, Weekly News Summary Videos, Box: Tape I, File: F181.

104. Common Cause, "Editorial Memorandum: Congress Returns to Face Major Reform Proposals."

105. "Other Caucus Actions," *Congressional Quarterly Almanac* (1975): 40.

106. Dick Clark to William Proxmire, 6 January 1975, WPP, Box M77–307, File: Letters To and From Other Senators 1975.

107. "Senate," *Congressional Quarterly Almanac* (1975): 36.

108. Common Cause, "Editorial Memorandum: Senate Considers Adjustment of Filibuster Rule," February 1975, CCP, Box 137, File: January–April 1975.

109. Minutes, Senate Democratic Conference, 26 January 1971, MMP, Leadership Series, Box 90, File: 12.

110. "Statement of Senator Walter F. Mondale," 17 January 1975, WMP, Box 154.K.12F, File: Press Releases January–April 1975.

111. U.S. Congress, Senate, *Congressional Record*, 94th Congress, 1st Session, 20 February 1975, p. 3848.

112. Ibid., p. 3852.

113. Gerald Ford to Nelson Rockefeller, 13 January 1975, GFP, White House Central Files, Subject File LE1: Filibusters, Box 3.

114. Kenneth Lazarus to Philip Buchen, 13 January 1975, JCP, Box 2, File: Rule XXII (Senate Cloture Rule) Changes.

115. Patrick O'Donnell to Max Friedersdorf, 9 January 1975, WKF, Box 4, File: Rule XXII.

116. Jim Cannon to Nelson Rockefeller, 10 January 1975, JCP, Box 2, File: Rule XXII (Senate Cloture Rule) Changes.

117. Dick Cheney to Jack Marsh and Phil Buchen, 10 January 1975, KLF, Box 21, File: LE1 Filibustering.

118. Michael J. Malbin, "Congress Report/Compromise by Senate Eases Anti-Filibuster Rule," in *National Journal Reprints* (Washington, DC: Government Research Corporation, 1976), p. 24.

119. David E. Rosenbaum, "The Filibuster Change Falls Far Short of Revolution," *New York Times,* 9 March 1975, Section IV.

120. Jacob K. Javits with Rafael Steinberg, *Javits: The Autobiography of a Public Man* (Boston: Houghton-Mifflin, 1981), pp. 374–7.

121. William Kendall to Max Friedersdorf, 10 January 1975, GFL, White House Central Files, Subject File LE1: Filibusters, Box 3; Staff to Walter Mondale, January 1975 and Memo from Walter Mondale's Staff to Walter Mondale (n.d.). Both documents in WKF, Box 4, File: Rule XXII.

122. U.S. Congress, Senate, *Congressional Record,* 94th Congress, 1st Session, 20 February 1975, p. 3836.

123. Sarah A. Binder and Steven S. Smith, *Politics or Principle? Filibustering in the United States Senate* (Washington, DC: Brookings Institution, 1997), p. 181.

124. Jack Marsh to Gerald Ford, 27 February 1975, GFP, Presidential Handwriting File – Labor Management Relations, Box 28, File: Legislation – Filibustering.

125. U.S. Congress, Senate, *Congressional Record,* 94th Congress, 1st Session, 26 February 1975, p. 4370.

126. NBC "Nightly News," 26 February 1975, TNA.

127. Notes, Cabinet Meeting, 12 March 1975, RNP, Box 294, File: March 12, 1975 – Cabinet Meeting Notes.

128. ADA, Press Release, 3 March 1975, ADA, Unprocessed, Box 30, File: 31.

129. Editorial, "Hollow Victory," *New York Times,* 7 March 1975.

130. Keith Krehbiel, *Pivotal Politics: A Theory of U.S. Lawmaking* (University of Chicago Press, 1998).

131. "Trimming the Filibuster," *Time,* 17 March 1975, p. 9.

132. Minutes, Cabinet Meeting, 12 March 1975.

133. Marjorie Hunter, "Rockefeller Joins Effort to Ease Relations with G.O.P. Senators," *New York Times,* 21 March 1975.

134. Philip Shabecoff, "Rockefeller Says Filibuster Role Evoked Attempts at 'Blackmail'," *New York Times,* 10 April 1975.

### Chapter 10

1. U.S. Congress, House of Representatives, Democratic Caucus, *Hearings on the Organization of the Democratic Caucus for the 95th Congress,* 8 December 1976, DCP, p. 336. See also Sanford J. Ungar, "Bleak House: Frustration on Capitol Hill," *Atlantic Monthly,* July 1977, p. 33.

2. Most scholars have tended to dismiss the importance of scandals. For an alternative view, see John B. Thompson's *Political Scandal: Power and Visibility in the Media Age* (Cambridge, U.K.: Polity, 2000).

3. Minutes, Governing Board of Common Cause, 15 January 1975, CCP, Box 32, File: 24 January – 26 April 1975.

4. CBS "Evening News," 20 February 1975, TNA.

5. Bill Frenzel to Max Friedersdorf, 19 December 1974, RTH, Box 24, File: Federal Elections Commission.

6. In 1975, the commission decided that corporate PACs were legal. The issue arose in a case that involved the Sun Oil corporation, which had raised voluntary campaign funds from employees and distributed them to candidates. The Justice Department referred to the St. Louis Pipefitters case and informed the FEC that it would not prosecute corporate PACs. The FEC allowed Sun Oil to continue its activities as long as donations were received from specified types of managerial employees. Frank Thompson warned that "every one of us in our Congressional districts could be totally inundated by corporate money." See also Richard Thornburgh to John Murphy, 3 November 1975, LLF, Box 9, File: Federal Election Campaign Act Amendments (6); and U.S. Congress, House of Representatives, Democratic Caucus, *Hearings: Special Meeting*, 24 March 1976, CAP, Legislative Files, Box 220, File: 2, p. 6.

7. The case began on January 2, 1975. Senator James Buckley (Conservative-NY), Eugene McCarthy, the New York Civil Liberties Union, the Mississippi Republican Party, the American Conservative Union, and the conservative magazine *Human Events* filed a suit against the new law. The plaintiffs argued that contribution and spending limits curbed freedom of speech, that public financing provisions punished minority parties (since it was difficult for them to receive public funds), and that the provisions amounted to an unconstitutional extension of federal funds into elections. The FEC hired its own counsel when it realized that the Justice Department would not provide a strong defense. See Thomas Curtis to Edward Levi, 5 June 1975. See also Curtis to Gerald Ford, 9 June 1975, Levi to Curtis, 30 May 1975, Curtis to Levi, 27 May 1975, all in GFL, White House Central Files, Box 203, File: FG 387 5/1/75–4/18/76.

8. *Buckley v. Valeo,* 424 U.S. 1 (1976); Brice M. Clagett to the Plaintiffs in Buckley v. Valeo, 1975, NYSCP, Series 10, Box 1, File: Buckley v. Valeo – Motions & Correspondence.

9. The White House, Press Release, 16 February 1976, LLF, Box 9, File: Federal Election Campaign Act Amendments (4).

10. Common Cause, "Legislative Report," 23 April 1976, CCP, Box 131, Folder: Legislative Reports 1976.

11. "News Conference – Wayne Hays," 5 February 1976, FTP, Box 551, File: FEC Newspaper Clippings.

12. Philip Buchen to President Ford, 20 February 1976, GFL, LLF, Box 9, File: Federal Election Campaign Act Amendments (4).

13. Louis Wilson Ingram, Jr., to Minority Members of the Committee on House Administration, 23 February 1976, LLF, Box 9, File: Federal Election Campaign Act Amendments (4).

14. Frank Thompson, Handwritten Notes, Meeting with Common Cause, John Brademas, Frank Thompson, Mooney, Bill Cable, and Howell, 19 March 1976, FTP, Box 551, File: FEC Newspaper Clipping.

15. Philip Buchen to Jim Connor, 1 March 1976, PBP, Box 14, File: Federal Election Campaign Act Amendments-1976 (2); Bo Callaway to President Ford, 29 January 1976, GFL, JJF, Box 21, File: Federal Election Commission (2).

16. Charles Leppert, Jr., to Max Friedersdorf, 29 April 1976, LLF, Box 9, File: Federal Elections Campaign Act Amendments (7); Max Friedersdorf to Dick Cheney and Jack Marsh, 20 April 1976, GFP, White House Central File, Box 203, File: FG 387 5/1/75–4/18/76; Charles Leppert, Jr., to Max Friedersdorf, 20 April 1976, LLF, Box 9, File: Federal Election Campaign Act Amendments (6); "GOP Leadership Meeting," 27 April 1976, GFP, Robert Wolthuis Files, Box 2, File: Congressional Leadership Meetings: GOP 4/27/76; Philip Buchen to the President, 10 May 1976, PBP, Box 15, File: Federal Election Commission Act Amendments 1976 (6).

17. Mike Duval, Foster Chanock, and Dave Gergen to Dick Cheney, 26 April 1976, JJF, Box 21, File: Federal Election Commission (2).

18. Insider accounts of the reporter's story can be found in Aaron Latham's "How the *Washington Post* Got the Goods on Wayne Hays," *New York,* 21 June 1976, pp. 33–9.

19. Marion Clark and Rudy Maxa, "Closed-Session Romance on the Hill," *Washington Post,* 23 May 1976.

20. "Hays Denies Aide Was His Mistress," *Boston Globe,* 24 May 1976; Arthur Siddon and James Coates, "Mistress? – 'She's Sick,' Hays Says," *Chicago Tribune,* 24 May 1976; "Why 'Mistress' Revealed Role," *Dallas Times Herald,* 25 May 1976.

21. See, for example: "Indecent Exposure on Capitol Hill," *Time,* 7 June 1976, pp. 12–15; "Sex Scandal Shakes Up Washington," *Time,* 14 June 1976, pp. 9–11; David M. Alpern with Anthony Marro and John Lowell, "An Overdose of Scandal," *Newsweek,* 21 June 1976, pp. 31–2; Tom Mathews with Henry W. Hubbard and Anthony Marro, "Capitol Capers," *Newsweek,* 14 June 1976, pp. 18–20; Tom Mathews with Henry W. Hubbard, Elaine Shannon, and Anthony Marro, "Congressman's Lady," *Newsweek,* 7 June 1976, pp. 26–8; "The Bonfire the Hays Case Lit under Congress," *U.S. News & World Report,* 14 June 1976, p. 20.

22. Richard Cohen, "Concorde Arrival Quieter Than Song of Hays' Aide," *Washington Post,* 25 May 1967.

23. "Swift Moves by Prosecutors – What More to Expect," *U.S. News & World Report,* 14 June 1976, p. 23.

24. U.S. Congress, House of Representatives, *Congressional Record,* 94th Congress, 2nd Session, 25 May 1976, p. 15346.

25. Don Shannon, "Hays Admits Affair with Secretary," *Los Angeles Times,* 26 May 1976.

26. George Esper, "Hays' Admission Likened to 'Checkers' Talk," *Washington Post,* 28 May 1976.

27. Bella Abzug to Frank LeBoutillier, 11 June 1976, BAP, Box 166, File: Wayne Hayes.

28. Mary McGrory, "No Sympathy for Despotic Rep. Hays," *Boston Globe,* 26 May 1976.

29. Marion Clark and Rudy Maxa, "The Odyssey of Elizabeth Ray," *Washington Post,* 2 June 1976.

30. Elizabeth L. Ray, *The Washington Fringe Benefit: A Novel* (New York: Dell, 1976). See also Marion Clark and Rudy Maxa, *Public Trust, Private Lust: Sex, Power and Corruption on Capitol Hill* (New York: Morrow, 1977).

31. Bob Bergland, Richardson Preyer, Lee Hamilton, Frank Evans, Abner Mikva, James O'Hara, and Marty Russo to Democratic Colleague, 2 June 1976, RBP, Box 354, File: 2.

32. John Crewdson, "Congressman's Ex-Aide Links Her Salary to Sex," *New York Times,* 11 June 1976, and J. Crewdson, "U.S. Studies Charge of Sex-for-Vote Bid," *New York Times,* 12 June 1976; ABC "Nightly News," 16 June 1976, TNA.

33. Warren Weaver, Jr., "Washington Sex: Always Available," *New York Times,* 20 June 1976.

34. Michael J. Robinson, "Three Faces of Congressional Media," in Thomas E. Mann and Norman J. Ornstein, Eds., *The New Congress* (Washington, DC: American Enterprise Institute, 1981), pp. 55–96.

35. Richard Campbell, *60 Minutes and the News: A Mythology for Middle America* (Urbana: University of Illinois Press, 1991).

36. James Reston, "Reform by Scandal," *New York Times,* 4 June 1976. See also "The Hays Scandal," *Nation,* 5 June 1976, pp. 674–6; "Scandal in Congress: Will It Lead to a Cleanup?" *U.S. News & World Report,* 7 June 1976, pp. 24–6; David M. Alpern with Henry Hubbard, James Bishop, Jr., Stephan Lesher, Anthony Marro, and John J. Lindsay, "Questions of Ethics," *Newsweek,* 14 June 1976, pp. 21–7.

37. Clark and Maxa, *Public Trust, Private Lust,* p. 157.

38. Timothy Noah, "What David Broder Could Learn from Sally Quinn," *Washington Monthly,* December 1984, pp. 12–27. Tom Wolfe wrote of the "new journalism" expanding the news to include fictional techniques that highlighted personality and character. See T. Wolfe, *The New Journalism* (New York: Harper & Row, 1973).

39. David Broder, "Hays' Abuse of Power," *Washington Post,* 16 June 1976.

40. Fred M. Hechinger, "The New Moralism," *New York Times,* 7 July 1976.

41. Joseph Kraft, "The Fruits of Scandal," *Washington Post,* 20 June 1976. See also Tom Wicker, "Congress, Sex and the Press," *New York Times,* 22 June 1976; "Everybody's Affair," *New Republic,* 12 June 1976, pp. 7–8.

42. Kenneth Cmiel, "The Politics of Civility," in David Farber, Ed., *The Sixties: From Memory to History* (Chapel Hill: University of North Carolina Press, 1994), pp. 263–90.

43. E. J. Dionne, Jr., *Why Americans Hate Politics* (New York: Touchstone, 1991), p. 41.

44. Maurice Isserman and Michael Kazin, *America Divided: The Civil War of the 1960s* (New York: Oxford University Press, 2000), pp. 295–6.

45. Catherine A. MacKinnon, *Sexual Harassment of Working Women: A Case of Sex Discrimination* (New Haven, CT: Yale University Press, 1979).

46. Vicki Schultz, "Reconceptualizing Sexual Harassment," *Yale Law Journal* 107 (April 1998): 1683–1805; Abigail C. Saguy, "Employment Discrimination or Sexual Violence? Defining Sexual Harassment in American and French Law," *Law and Society Review* 34 (2000): 1091–1128.

47. Equal Employment Opportunity Commission, 29 C.F.R. §§ 1604.11(a)(1980); 45 Fed. Reg. 74676 (1980); *Meritor Savings Bank, FSB v. Vinson Et Al.,* 477 U.S. 57 (1986). Sexual harassment, according to the National Women's Law Center in 1991, included unwelcome sexual advances, requests for sexual favors, verbal or physical conduct of a sexual nature, or a situation when submitting to such conduct was the basis for employment decision or when such conduct created a hostile or offensive work environment. See National Women's Law Center, "Fact Sheet on Sexual Harassment," 1991, ADA, Unprocessed, Box 29, File: 23.

48. Capitol Hill Women's Political Caucus, "Sexists in the Senate? A Study of Differences in Salary by Sex Among Employees of the U.S. Senate," May 1975, BAP, Box 634, File: Politics – General. Those who legitimated congressional freedom from regulation did so on the grounds that the work of legislators was thoroughly political and thus should not be subject to private-sector rules. Politicians, they said, also needed the freedom to hire staffers who would be loyal to them. Moreover, defenders of the system said that if the executive branch could start regulating legislative employment, this would constitute a violation of the separation of powers.

49. For examples, see Editorial, "Cleaning Up the House," *Washington Post,* 16 June 1976; Editorial, "House Out of Order," *New York Times,* 29 May 1976; "Fanny Hill," *Nation,* 26 June 1976, p. 772.

50. Michael Kazin, *The Populist Persuasion: An American History* (New York: Basic Books, 1995), p. 256.

51. Peter Beinhart, "How the Personal Became Political," *New Republic,* 15 February 1999, pp. 21–5.

52. Minutes, Common Cause Governing Board Meeting, 24 October 1975, CCP, Box 32, File: 26 July – 25 October 1975.

53. Minutes, Common Cause Governing Board Meeting, 23 April 1976, CCP, Box 33, File: Corporate Papers I.

54. "Common Cause Briefing: Victory over Sikes," 26 January 1977, Audio Tape, CCP, Box 117, File: Tapes.

55. U.S. Congress, House of Representatives, *Congressional Record,* 94th Congress, 2nd Session, 29 July 1976, pp. 24384–5.

56. Leon Panetta to New Members of the 95th Congress, 24 January 1977, FTP, Box 545, File: Democratic Caucus. See also Philip Heynmann to John Flynt, 11 May 1976, RBP, Box 203, File: 19.

57. National Committee for an Effective Congress to Member of Congress, 25 January 1977, DFP, Box 151.H.2.6(F), File: Democratic Caucus 1977.

58. Olin Teague to Colleague, 25 January 1977, DFP, Box 151.H.2.6(F), File: Democratic Caucus 1977.

59. NBC "Nightly News," 26 January 1977, CBS "Evening News," 26 January 1977, and ABC "Nightly News," 26 January 1977, TNA.

60. John A. Farrell, *Tip O'Neill and the Democratic Century* (Boston: Little, Brown, 2001), p. 407.

61. "Characteristics of Members of 95th Congress," *Congressional Quarterly Almanac* (1977): 34.

62. Norman J. Ornstein, Robert L. Peabody, and David W. Rohde, "The Changing Senate: From the 1950s to the 1970s," in Lawrence C. Dodd and Bruce I. Oppenheimer, Eds., *Congress Reconsidered* (New York: Praeger, 1977), p. 4.

63. Common Cause, "Majority of U.S. House of Representatives Pledges Support for Broadcast of Congressional Proceedings, Other Key Reforms," 3 December 1976, CCP, Box 138, File: Press Releases – December 1976.

64. Frank Moss to Mike Mansfield, 24 January 1975, MMP, Leadership Series, Box 67, File: 12; Walter J. Oleszek, "Overview of the Senate Committee System," 23 April 1976, MMP, Series XVIII, Box 38, File: 8, p. 16.

65. U.S. Congress, Senate, *Temporary Select Committee to Study the Senate Committee System,* 94th Congress, 2nd Session, 20–22 July 1976.

66. Commission on the Operation of the Senate, "Interim Report of the Commission on the Operation of the Senate," 31 March 1976, MMP, Leadership Series, Box 26, File: 1.

67. William Barry Furlong, "The Adlai III Brand of Politics," *New York Times,* 22 February 1970.

68. Judith H. Parris, "The Senate Reorganizes Its Committees, 1977," *Political Science Quarterly* 94 (Summer 1979): 331.

69. Ibid., p. 321.

70. Common Cause, "Editorial Memorandum: Winds of Change May Rejuvenate Senate Committees," December 1976, CCP, Box 138, File: Press Releases – December 1976.

71. Parris, "The Senate Reorganizes Its Committees, 1977," p. 325.

72. Eric Shickler, *Disjointed Pluralism: Institutional Innovation and the Development of the U.S. Congress* (Princeton, NJ: Princeton University Press, 2001), p. 208.

73. CBS "Evening News," 3 February 1977, TNA.

74. John Gardner, "The House Ethics Committee – A Cruel Hoax," September 1976, CCP, Box 138, File: Press Releases – September 1976.

75. When Common Cause called on the Senate Ethics Committee to clean up interest group corruption, Senator John Melcher (D-MT) reminded president David Cohen that he was just like every interest group. See Warren Brown, "Common Cause, Senators Trade Barbs on Ethics," *Washington Post,* 3 February 1977.

76. ABC "Nightly News," 2 March 1977, TNA.

77. "Ethics – Congressional," in *Congress A to Z* (Washington, DC: Congressional Quarterly, 1999); retrieved 17 June 2003 from CQ Electronic Library, CQ Congress Collection: ce120800.

78. ABC "Nightly News," 2 March 1977, TNA.

79. Eliot Marshall, "Behavior Modification," *New Republic,* 12 November 1977, pp. 9–11.

80. Common Cause, "Majority of U.S. House of Representatives Pledges Support for Broadcast of Congressional Proceedings, Other Key Reforms."

81. Comment by Tony Coelho, "The Drive to Televise House Floor Debates," 19 March 1999, C-SPAN, Videotape #121911, Purdue Research Foundation, Lafayette, IN.

82. Stanley Bach, Congressional Research Service, "Television Coverage of State Legislative Floor Proceedings," 25 January 1978, and Daniel Melnick, "The Likely Impact on the Public of Televising Proceedings of the U.S. House of Representatives: A Review of Recent Relevant Studies," 20 January 1978, RBP, Box 226, File: 2.

83. Terry Dean to Patti Tyson, 24 January 1978, RBP, Box 226, File: 1; "When Parliament Goes on Camera, 'It's Better Than Soap Opera'," *U.S. News & World Report,* 19 June 1978, p. 58.

84. Sig Mickelson, *The Electric Mirror: Politics in an Age of Television* (New York: Dodd, Mead, 1972).

85. Brian Lamb, interview with Julian Zelizer, 21 July 2000.

86. "The Cable-TV Industry Gets Moving Again," *Business Week,* 21 November 1977, p. 154.

87. Roon Arledge to Speaker O'Neill, 3 February 1978, TOP, Eleanor Kelley Files, Box 6, File: Organization and Committee Appointments, 1977–1979; Bill Ferguson to Gillis Long, 21 December 1977, RBP, Box 226, File: 3; Howard Monderer to Walter Kravitz, 7 November 1969, WKP, File: Television Broadcasting.

88. John Backe to Tip O'Neill, 17 January 1978, NNCR, Working Files – Freedom of the Press, Box 76, File: 1.

89. See, for example, Editorial, "Broadcasting in the House," *Washington Post,* 10 March 1976; Neal R. Peirce, "Can Television Get into Congress?" *Washington Post,* 12 April 1977; Editorial, "Not-So-Candid Camera in the House," *New York Times,* 10 January 1978; Editorial, "The House, Live," *New York Times,* 12 March 1978.

90. Michael J. Robinson and Kevin R. Appel, "Network News Coverage of Congress," *Political Science Quarterly* 94 (Fall 1979): 407–18.

91. American University, Press Release, 19 December 1978, RBP, Box 226, File: 1.

92. Jerry Colbert to Thomas P. O'Neill, 17 February 1976, TOP, Eleanor Kelley Files, Box 8, File: TV Coverage of the House, 1976.

93. John Brademas to Thomas P. O'Neill, 4 March 1976, TOP, Eleanor Kelley Files, Box 8, File: TV Coverage of the House, 1976.

94. Burt Hoffman to Scott Aiken, 1 February 1978, NNCR, Working Files – Freedom of the Press, Box 76, File: 1.

95. Douglas Davis, "Let's Hear It for the Cable," *Newsweek,* 21 November 1977, p. 29. See also Kevin Phillips, "Busting the Media Trusts," *Harper's,* July 1977, pp. 23–34.

96. Burt Hoffman to Thomas P. O'Neill, 12 January 1978, TOP, Eleanor Kelley Files, Box 6, File: Organization and Committee Appointments.

97. B. F. Sisk, "Controlling TV Cameras on Capitol Hill," *New York Times,* 11 February 1978.

98. "Background Memo: Control of Broadcasting," 1977, TOP, Eleanor Kelley Files, Box 6, File: Organization and Committee Appointments, 1977–1979.

99. John Anderson to Gillis Long, 19 January 1978, RBP, Box 226, File: 2.

100. John Anderson to Tip O'Neill, 29 December 1977, NNCR, Working Files – Freedom of the Press, Box 76, File: 1.

101. "Media Coalition Pushing for Operation of House-TV System," *Communicator,* January 1978, NNCR, Working Files – Freedom of the Press, Box 76, File: 1.

102. Comment by Tony Coelho, "The Drive to Televise House Floor Debates."

103. Jack Brooks to Colleague, 15 March 1977, TOP, Party Leadership Files, Box 6, File: TV Coverage of the House, 1977–1984.

104. Ronald Garay, *Congressional Television: A Legislative History* (Westport, CT: Greenwood, 1984), pp. 95–6.

105. Stephen Frantzich and John Sullivan, *The C-SPAN Revolution* (Norman: University of Oklahoma Press, 1996), pp. 34–5.

106. Comment by Tony Coelho, "The Drive to Televise House Floor Debates."

107. The National News Council, "Statement on Cameras in the Courtroom," 9 March 1979, NNCR, Working Files – Freedom of the Press, Box 75, Series: 8.

108. Michael J. Robinson, "A Twentieth-Century Medium in a Nineteenth-Century Legislature: The Effects of Television on The American Congress," in Norman J. Ornstein, Ed., *Congress in Change: Evolution and Reform* (New York: Praeger, 1975), p. 254.

109. Maxine Cheshire and Scott Armstrong, "Seoul Gave Millions to U.S. Officials," *Washington Post,* 24 October 1976.

110. CBS "Evening News," 25 October 1976, and CBS "Evening News," 26 October 1976, TNA.

111. CBS "Evening News," 28 October 1976, TNA.

112. John Saar, "S. Korea Accuses *Post* of 'Malicious, Sensational' Reporting," *Washington Post,* 29 October 1976.

113. ABC "Nightly News," 15 December 1976, TNA.

114. Maxine Cheshire and Charles R. Babcock, "Letters Reveal Legislators' Ties to Korean," *Washington Post,* 17 April 1977; Scott Armstrong, "13 Congressmen Aided Tongsun Park," *Washington Post,* 27 April 1977.

115. "Backsliding on Ethics," *In Common* 8 (Fall 1977), CCP, Box 128, File: Winter–Fall 1977; David Cohen to John Flynt, 22 June 1977, CCP, Box 212, File: Ethics-in-Government 1976, 1977.

116. "Congress Faces Four-Way Ethics Test," *Frontline,* January/February 1977, CCP, Box 129, File: Frontline III, pp. 1–6.

117. "New Scandal in Congress," *U.S. News & World Report,* 1 August 1977, p. 9.

118. U.S. Congress, House of Representatives, Committee on Standards of Official Conduct, *Hearings: Korean Influence Investigation: Part 1,* 95th Congress, 1st Session, 19–21 October 1977, pp. 62, 120.

119. Michael Schudson, *Watergate in American Memory: How We Remember, Forget, and Reconstruct the Past* (New York: Basic Books, 1992), pp. 148–64. For example, see David M. Alpern with Lea Donosky, "All About 'Koreagate'," *Newsweek,* 1 August 1977, pp. 17–21; Jack Anderson, "Carter to Publicize Achievements," *Washington Post,* 26 January 1977; Haynes Johnson, "The Most Unhappy Talk of This Town," *Washington Post,* 17 July 1977.

120. Transcripts, "Face the Nation," 20 February 1977 and "Face the Nation," 22 January 1978, CBS Television, TOP, Press Relations, Box 22, File: Face the Nation.

121. "Daily Press Briefing," 4 April 1978, TOP, Press Relations, Box 13, File: Staff Press Briefings January–May 1978. Making matters worse, the FBI was investigating separate allegations that O'Neill had used his position to influence private business deals in his district.

122. U.S. Congress, House of Representatives, Committee on Standards of Official Conduct, *Hearings: Korean Influence Investigation: Part 2,* 95th Congress, 2nd Session, 3–11 April 1978, p. 29.

123. Myra MacPherson, "Why Do They Say Such Nasty Things About Bruce Caputo?" *Washington Post,* 13 February 1978.

124. Richard L. Lyons, "House Speaker Denounces Freshman N.Y. Republican," *Washington Post,* 17 February 1978.

125. Robert L. Jackson, "Park Often Used O'Neill's Office, Investigators Told," and "O'Neill Denies Report That Park Used His Office," *Los Angeles Times,* 30 August 1977.

126. Minutes of the Governing Board of Common Cause, 13 November 1976, CCP, Box 33, File: Corporate Papers II.

127. Frank J. Sorauf, *Inside Campaign Finance: Myths and Realities* (New Haven, CT: Yale University Press, 1992), pp. 68–9; Steven M. Gillon, *"That's Not What We Meant to Do": Reform and Its Unintended Consequences in Twentieth Century America* (New York: Norton, 2000), pp. 216–17; Thomas Byrne Edsall, "The Changing Shape of Power: A Realignment in Public Policy," in Steve Fraser and Gary Gerstle, Eds., *The Rise and Fall of the New Deal Order, 1930–1980* (Princeton, NJ: Princeton University Press, 1989), pp. 269–93; David Vogel, *Fluctuating Fortunes: The Political Power of Business in America* (New York: Basic Books, 1989).

128. Al Barkan to George Meany, 7 August 1978, GMA, Office of the President: George Meany Files, Box 96, File: Political Education, 1978–1980.

129. Al Barkan to George Meany, December 1978, ACP, Office of the President: George Meany Files, Box 96, File: Political Education, 1978–1980.

130. Minutes, Governing Board of Common Cause, 4 February 1978, CCP, Box 34, File: Corporate Papers 1978.

131. U.S. Congress, House of Representatives, House Committee on Administration, *An Analysis of the Federal Election Campaign Act, 1972–1978,* 96th Congress, 1st Session, October 1979, Government Document 51-403.

132. Gary C. Jacobson, "Money in the 1980 and 1982 Congressional Elections," in Michael J. Malbin, Ed., *Money and Politics in the United States: Financing Elections in the 1980s* (Washington, DC: American Enterprise Institute / Chatham, NJ: Chatham House, 1984), p. 43.

133. "House Races: More Money to Incumbents," *Congressional Quarterly Almanac* (1977): 31-A.

134. House Committee on Administration, *An Analysis of the Federal Election Campaign Act, 1972–1978,* pp. 1–5.

135. John Brademas to Tip O'Neill, 16 February 1977, TOP, Eleanor Kelley Files, Box 2, File: Correspondence with Colleagues 1977.

136. Edsall, "The Changing Shape of Power: A Realignment in Public Policy," pp. 280–1.

137. Minutes of the Governing Board of Common Cause, 4 February 1978.

138. Mary Russell, "House, in Blow to Leadership, Spurns Election Fund Bill," *Washington Post,* 22 March 1978.

139. "Daily Press Briefing," 20 March 1978, TOP, Press Relations, Box 13, File: Staff Press Briefings January–May 1978.

140. Russell, "House, in Blow to Leadership, Spurns Election Fund Bill."

141. U.S. Congress, House of Representatives, Committee on House Administration, *Hearings: Public Financing of Congressional Election,* 96th Congress, 1st Session, 21 March 1979, p. 314.

142. Common Cause, "Briefing: Campaign Defeat in House Administration," 24 May 1979, Audio Tape, CCP, Box 117, File: Tapes.

143. Stanley Bach and Steven S. Smith, *Managing Uncertainty in the House of Representatives: Adaptation and Innovation in Special Rules* (Washington, DC: Brookings Institution, 1988), pp. 1–37.

144. Steve Smith, *Call to Order: Floor Politics in the House and Senate* (Washington, DC: Brookings Institution, 1989), pp. 16, 28–9, 88.

145. Harrison W. Fox, Jr., and Susan Webb Hammond, "The Growth of Congressional Staffs," in Harvey C. Mansfield, Sr., Ed., *Congress Against the Presidency* (New York: Academy of Political Science, 1975), pp. 112–24; "Evolution of the Congressional Staff: Changes of 1974–1979," in *Guide to U.S. Congress,* v. 1 (Washington, DC: Congressional Quarterly, 2000); retrieved 17 June 2003 from CQ Electronic Library, CQ Congress Collection: g2con1-98-612:307592.

146. Sarah A. Binder and Steven S. Smith, *Politics or Principle? Filibustering in the United States Senate* (Washington, DC: Brookings Institution, 1997), pp. 83–4.

147. "A Few Frustrate Many," *Congressional Quarterly Almanac* (1976): 4. On February 22, 1979, Robert Byrd was able to curtail some of these postcloture filibusters by obtaining a time limit on how long senators could speak after cloture.

148.  Susan Webb Hammond, "Congressional Caucuses and Party Leaders in the House of Representatives," *Political Science Quarterly* 106 (Summer 1991): 278–80.

149.  Jackie to Michael Johnson, 31 July 1981, RMP, Press Series, Box 1, File: Memoranda 1981–1988 (1).

150.  Christopher J. Deering and Steven S. Smith, "Subcommittees in Congress," in Lawrence C. Dodd and Bruce I. Oppenheimer, Eds., *Congress Reconsidered,* 3rd ed. (Washington, DC: Congressional Quarterly, 1985), pp. 272–87.

151.  Burdett Loomis, *The New American Politician: Ambition, Entrepreneurship, and the Changing Face of Political Life* (New York: Basic Books, 1988), pp. 46, 161–9, 174–8.

152.  Barbara Sinclair, *Majority Leadership in the U.S. House* (Baltimore: Johns Hopkins University Press, 1983), pp. 55–85; Sidney Waldman, "Majority Leadership in the House of Representatives," *Political Science Quarterly* 95 (Fall 1980): 373–93.

153.  Allen Schick, "Informed Legislation: Policy Research versus Ordinary Knowledge," in William H. Robinson and Clay H. Wellborn, Eds., *Knowledge, Power, and the Congress* (Washington, DC: Congressional Quarterly, 1991), pp. 99–119.

154.  See, for example, James M. Naughton, "The Lost Innocence of Congressman Aucoin," *New York Times,* 31 August 1975; "Freshman Democrats: Tamed by Realities," *U.S. News & World Report,* 11 August 1975, pp. 29–30; Editorial, "The 94th Congress," *Washington Star,* 5 October 1976.

155.  Joel D. Aberbach, *Keeping a Watchful Eye: The Politics of Congressional Oversight* (Washington, DC: Brookings Institution, 1990); Leroy N. Rieselbach, *Congressional Reform* (Washington, DC: Congressional Quarterly, 1986), pp. 61–3.

156.  Nicholas Lemann, "Putting the House (and Senate) in Order," *Washington Post,* 10 February 1980.

157.  U.S. Congress, House of Representatives, Democratic Caucus, *Hearings on Organization of the 96th Congress,* 6 December 1978, DCP, pp. 33, 53, 152, 166.

158.  Robert M. Kaus, "The Smokeless Gun: Billygate and the Press," *Washington Monthly,* October 1980, pp. 38–52.

159.  The term "Abscam" came from Judge George C. Pratt, presiding at the trials, who said that it stood for "Abdul Scam." The name that the FBI gave to the fake Arab business involved was Abdul Enterprises, an import–export firm.

160.  Jerry J. Berman, "The Lessons of Abscam: A Public Policy Report by the American Civil Liberties Union," 10 October 1982, NNRC, Reference Files, Box 156, File: 4, p. 4.

161.  David Cohen to Chuck Sauvage, 29 February 1980, CCP, Box 171, File: Congressional Code of Conduct/Ethics 1978–1981.

162.  John Carmody, "NBC's 'Sting' Stakeout on W. Street," *Washington Post,* 5 February 1980.

163.  NBC "Nightly News," 2 February 1980, TNA.

164.  See, for example, Jack Anderson, "Thompson on Tape: A Shabby Side," *Washington Post,* 4 August 1980; J. Anderson, "'Ya Deal with Mafia through … Me'," *Washington Post,* 7 August 1980.

165.  ABC and NBC "Nightly News" and CBS "Evening News," 14 October 1980, and "Nightline," 14 October 1980, TNA.

166.  Tom Shales, "The Abscam Tapes on TV," *Washington Post,* 15 October 1980.

167.  Editorial, "ABSCAM: Two Kinds of Corruption," *Washington Post,* 11 February 1980. See also James Kelly, "The FBI's Show of Shows," *Time,* 1 September 1980, p. 19.

168. Berman, *The Lessons of Abscam,* pp. i–ii.
169. U.S. Congress, House of Representatives, *Congressional Record,* 96th Congress, 2nd Session, 2 October 1950, pp. 28954–5, 28967.
170. Charles R. Babcock, "Abscam Playing Dominant Role in Five House Reelection Drives," *Washington Post,* 29 October 1980.
171. U.S. Congress, Senate, *Congressional Record,* 97th Congress, 2nd Session, 9 March 1982, pp. 3645–6.
172. U.S. Congress, Senate, *Congressional Record,* 97th Congress, 2nd Session, 4 March 1982, p. 3298.

### Chapter 11

1. U.S. Congress, House of Representatives, *Congressional Record,* 96th Congress, 1st Session, 19 March 1979, p. 5411.
2. Stephen Hess, *Live from Capitol Hill: Studies of Congress and the Media* (Washington, DC: Brookings Institution, 1991), pp. 36–7, 105; Timothy E. Cook, "House Members as Newsmakers: The Effects of Televising Congress," *Legislative Studies Quarterly* 11 (May 1986): 203–26.
3. Stephen Hess, *The Ultimate Insiders: U.S. Senators in the National Media* (Washington, DC.: Brookings Institution, 1986), pp. 85–112.
4. Karen M. Kedrowski, *Media Entrepreneurs and the Media Enterprise in the U.S. Congress* (Cresskill, NJ: Hampton, 1996), pp. 192–4; Samuel Kernell, *Going Public: New Strategies of Presidential Leadership,* 2nd ed. (Washington, DC: Congressional Quarterly, 1993), pp. 230–1.
5. Edie N. Goldenberg and Michael W. Traugott, "Mass Media in U.S. Congressional Elections," *Legislative Studies Quarterly* 22 (August 1987): 334.
6. Hess, *Live from Capitol Hill,* p. 106; Burdett Loomis, *The New American Politician: Ambition, Entrepreneurship, and the Changing Face of Political Life* (New York: Basic Books, 1988), pp. 76–107; Patrick J. Sellers, "Congress and the News Media: Manipulating the Message in the U.S. Congress," *Harvard International Journal of Press and Politics* 5 (Winter 2000): 22–31; Timothy Cook, *Making Laws and Making News: Media Strategies in the U.S. House of Representatives* (Washington, DC: Brookings Institution, 1989), pp. 9, 72.
7. Michael J. Robinson, "Public Affairs Television and the Growth of Political Malaise: The Case of 'The Selling of the Pentagon'," *American Political Science Review* 70 (June 1976): 409, 427.
8. Thomas E. Patterson, "The United States: News in a Free Market Society," in Richard Gunther and Anthony Mughan, Eds., *Democracy and the Media: A Comparative Perspective* (Cambridge University Press, 2000), pp. 241–65.
9. Fred W. Friendly, *Due to Circumstances Beyond Our Control...* (New York: Random House, 1967), p. 221.
10. Randall Bennett Woods, *Fulbright: A Biography* (Cambridge University Press, 1995), p. 405.
11. Reese Schonfeld, *Me and Ted Against the World: The Unauthorized Story of the Founding of CNN* (New York: HarperCollins, 2001), pp. 3–4. See also Herbert J. Gans, *Deciding What's News: A Study of CBS Evening News, NBC Nightly News, Newsweek, and Time* (New York: Pantheon, 1979).
12. Robert Britt Horwitz, *The Irony of Regulatory Reform: The Deregulation of American Telecommunications* (New York: Oxford University Press, 1989), pp. 146–53.

13. Martha Derthick and Paul J. Quirk, *The Politics of Deregulation* (Washington, DC: Brookings Institution, 1985).

14. Robert W. Crandall and Harold Furchtgott-Roth, *Cable TV: Regulation or Competition* (Washington, DC: Brookings Institution, 1996), pp. 1–23; Vernone Sparkes, "Cable Television in the United States: A Story of Continuing Growth and Change," in Ralph M. Negrine, Ed., *Cable Television and the Future of Broadcasting* (London: Croom Helm, 1985), pp. 15–46; Stanley M. Besen, Thomas G. Krattenmaker, A. Richard Metzger, Jr., and John R. Woodbury, *Misregulating Television: Network Dominance and the FCC* (University of Chicago Press, 1984).

15. "Cable TV: The Lure of Diversity," *Time,* 7 May 1979, p. 82.

16. Harry F. Waters, "Cable TV: Coming of Age," *Newsweek,* 24 August 1981, pp. 44–9; Cable Information Services, "Data on Cable TV," 1984, ACLU, Box 39, File: 4.

17. Austin Ranney, "Broadcasting, Narrowcasting, and Politics," in Anthony King, Ed., *The New American Political System,* 2nd ed. (Washington, DC: American Enterprise Institute, 1990), p. 191.

18. Stephen Frantzich and John Sullivan, *The C-SPAN Revolution* (Norman: University of Oklahoma Press, 1996). In covering the internal history of C-SPAN's formation and early evolution, this section relies heavily on this excellent work as well as an oral history that I conducted with Brian Lamb on 21 July 2000. Moreover, Stephen Frantzich, a professor at the U.S. Naval Academy, generously lent me his research notes for the book. For more detailed information, readers might also wish to consult Casey Peters, "The Cable Satellite Public Affairs Network: C-SPAN in the First Decade of Congressional Television," Master's thesis, University of California, Los Angeles, 1992.

19. NBC "Nightly News," 22 February 1979, TNA. See also Ron Nessen, "It's Live. It's Different. It's Drama. It's Real Life," *TV Guide,* 7 July 1978.

20. Comment by Brian Lamb, "The Drive to Televise House Floor Debates: Panel at the Woodrow Wilson Center," Washington, DC, 19 March 1999, C-SPAN, Videotape #121911, Purdue Research Foundation, Lafayette, IN.

21. Steven R. Roberts, "A House Divided: Ads and Those TV Cameras," *New York Times,* 18 April 1984.

22. Guy Vander Jagt to Tony Coelho, 4 May 1984, TOP, Party Leadership Files, Box 30, File: Democratic Congressional Campaign Committee 1984.

23. Tony Coelho, "Wearing Bags Over Our Heads Won't Work," *Washington Post,* 5 May 1984.

24. Tony Coelho to Guy Vander Jagt, 11 May 1984, TOP, Party Leadership Files, Box 30, File: Democratic Congressional Campaign Committee 1984.

25. Mike Johnson to Robert Michel, 20 September 1981, RMP, Press Releases, Box 1, File: Memoranda 1981–1988 (1).

26. Mike Johnson to Robert Michel and Trent Lott, 18 May 1981, RMP, Press Releases, Box 1, File: Memoranda 1981–1988 (1).

27. Brian Lamb and the Staff of C-SPAN, *C-SPAN: America's Town Hall* (Washington, DC: Acropolis, 1988), p. 117.

28. Comment by Newt Gingrich, "Newt Gingrich: Backbencher," 30 July 1999, C-SPAN, Videotape #151796, Purdue Research Foundation, Lafayette, IN.

29. Newt Gingrich to Republican Colleague, 8 February 1983, TOP, Kirk O'Donnell Files, Box 1, File: Newt Gingrich, 1982–1985. See also Gingrich to Paul Weyrich, 18 December 1980.

30. Dick Cheney to Republican Colleague, 20 June 1985, TOP, Kirk O'Donnell Files, Box 5, File: DCCC Campaign 1984, 1984–1985.

31. Eleanor Clift and Tom Brazaitis, *War Without Bloodshed: The Art of Politics* (New York: Touchstone, 1996), p. 224.

32. Newt Gingrich to Fellow Republican, 18 March 1982, TOP, Kirk O'Donnell Files, Box 1, File: Newt Gingrich, 1982–1985.

33. Newt Gingrich to Robert Michel, 29 April 1982, RMP, Box 1, Press Series, File: Memoranda 1981–1988 (2).

34. Tim Wyngaard and Mike Johnson to Robert Michel and Richard Cheney, 14 April 1982, RMP, Press Series, Box 1, File: Memoranda 1981–1988 (2); Mike Johnson (press secretary to Robert Michel), Handwritten Notes, House Republican Leadership Meeting, 22 February 1982, RMP, Press Series, Box 1, File: Memoranda 1981–1988 (2).

35. Roberts, "A House Divided."

36. Gingrich to Fellow Republican, 18 March 1982.

37. Michael Johnson to Robert Michel (n.d.), RMP, Press Series, Box 1, File: Memoranda 1981–1988 (1).

38. Bill Pitts to Michael Johnson, 12 January 1981, RMP, Press Series, Box 1, File: Memoranda 1981–1988 (1).

39. Michael Johnson to Robert Michel, 5 May 1982, RMP, Press Series, Box 1, File: Memoranda 1981–1988 (2).

40. Ralph Nader, interview with Steven Frantzich (n.d.), SFR.

41. Roger H. Davidson and Walter J. Oleszek, *Congress and Its Members* (Washington, DC: Congressional Quarterly, 1981), p. 138.

42. David Obey to House Members, 2 August 1983, TOP, Kirk O'Donnell Files, Box 1, File: Newt Gingrich, 1980–1984.

43. Mike Johnson to Robert Michel, 5 January 1983, RMP, Press Series, Box 1, File: Memoranda 1981–1988 (2).

44. "Republican Agenda for the Remainder of 1983," 17 October 1983, RMP, Press Series, Box 1, File: Memoranda 1981–1988 (2).

45. Mike Johnson to Robert Michel, 30 November 1983, RMP, Press Series, Box 1, File: Memoranda 1981–1988 (2).

46. David Obey to Tony Coelho, 3 May 1984, TOP, Kirk O'Donnell Files, Box 1, File: Newt Gingrich, 1980–1984.

47. Speaker's Press Conference, 14 May 1984, TOP, Press Relations, Box 12, File: Press Conferences, Transcripts January–May 1984.

48. Richard Cheney, Press Release, 29 July 1984, TOP, Kirk O'Donnell Papers, Box 1, File: Dick Cheney 1984.

49. Jack Kemp to Friend, 1984, TOP, Kirk O'Donnell Files, Box 1, File: Newt Gingrich, 1982–1985.

50. John A. Farrell, *Tip O'Neill and the Democratic Century* (Boston: Little, Brown, 2001), p. 636.

51. Dick Williams, *Newt! Leader of the Second American Revolution* (Marietta, GA: Longstreet, 1995), p. 106.

52. See, for example, Alessandra Stanley, "Tip Topped!" *Time,* 28 May 1984, p. 36; "Tip and Newt," *National Review,* 29 June 1984, pp. 15–16; "TV Stirs a Capitol Tempest," *U.S. News & World Report,* 28 May 1984, p. 13; CBS "Evening News," 15 May 1984, TNA. See also ABC "Nightly News," 15 May 1984, TNA.

53. U.S. Congress, Senate, Committee on Rules and Administration, *Hearings: Television and Radio Coverage of Proceedings in the Senate Chamber,* 97th Congress, 1st Session, 8–9 April and 5 May 1981, p. 5.

54. Howard H. Baker, "On Need for the Senate to Enter the TV Age," *New York Times,* 31 October 1981.

55. Howard H. Baker, "It's Time to Put the Senate on TV," *Washington Post,* 29 January 1982.

56. See, for example, the local news editorials in SHBSP, Legislative Subject File, Box 9, File: 4.

57. Ralph Griffith to Howard Liebengood, 15 September 1981, SHBSP, Legislative Subject File, Box 9, File: 4.

58. Robert Mann, *Legacy to Power: Senator Russell Long of Louisiana* (New York: Paragon, 1992), p. 384.

59. Richard F. Fenno, Jr., "The Senate Through the Looking Glass: The Debate Over Television," *Legislative Studies Quarterly* 14 (August 1989): 325.

60. Robert C. Byrd, *The Senate 1789–1989: Addresses on the History of the United States Senate,* v. 2 (Wendy Wolff, Ed.) (Washington, DC: U.S. Government Printing Office, 1991), p. 614.

61. U.S. Congress, Senate, *Congressional Record,* 100th Congress, 1st Session, 2 June 1987, pp. 14274–5.

62. Maura E. Clancey, "The Political Knowledge, Participation, and Opinions of C-SPAN Viewers: An Exploratory Assessment of Mass Media Impact," Ph.D. dissertation, University of Maryland, College Park, 1990.

63. Tip O'Neill with William Novak, *Man of the House: The Life and Political Memoirs of Speaker Tip O'Neill* (New York: Random House, 1987), p. 289. See also "Today Show," NBC, 19 August 1985, TOP, Tip O'Neill Audio Visual Material, Tape 11: Interviews 1985–1986.

64. Brian Lamb, "Debunking the C-SPAN Myths: Speech to the National Press Club," 6 January 1997, C-SPAN, Videotape #77658, Purdue Research Foundation, Lafayette, IN.

65. Frantzich and Sullivan, *The C-SPAN Revolution,* pp. 242–4.

66. William A. Henry III, "Shaking Up the Networks," *Time,* 9 August 1982, p. 51.

67. "Terrible Ted vs. the Networks," *Time,* 9 June 1980, p. 68.

68. Daniel Schorr, *Staying Tuned: A Life in Journalism* (New York: Toronto Books, 2001), pp. 304–5.

69. Hank Whittemore, *CNN: The Inside Story* (Boston: Little, Brown, 1990), pp. 112–13.

70. Ingrid Volkmer, *News in the Global Sphere: A Study of CNN and Its Impact on Global Communication* (Bedfordshire, U.K.: University of Luton Press, 1999), p. 132.

71. Sally Bendell Smith, "Turner Buys Sole Rival in Cable News Market," *New York Times,* 13 October 1983.

72. Kedrowski, *Media Entrepreneurs and the Media Enterprise in the U.S. Congress,* p. 147.

73. Sally Bedell Smith, "The Great Chase in Network News," *New York Times,* 28 November 1983.

74. Barbie Zelizer, *Covering the Body: The Kennedy Assassination, the Media, and the Shaping of Collective Memory* (University of Chicago Press, 1992), pp. 8–10; Leon V. Sigal, *Reporters and Officials: The Organization and Politics of Newsmaking*

(Lexington, MA: D.C. Heath, 1973), pp. 39–42; Todd Gitlin, *The Whole World Is Watching: Mass Media in the Making and Unmaking of the New Left* (Berkeley: University of California Press, 1980), pp. 1–123.

75. Michael Schudson, *The Good Citizen: A History of American Civic Life* (Cambridge, MA: Harvard University Press, 1999), p. 287.

76. To be sure, some of the traits of journalism in the cable television era, such as a bias toward sensational scandal and the privileging of celebrity reporters, could be found in other historical periods. For an interesting history of these issues see Mitchell Stephens, *A History of News: From the Drum to the Satellite* (New York: Viking, 1988).

77. Stephen Ansolabehere, Roy Behr, and Shanto Iyengar, *The Media Game: American Politics in the Television Age* (New York: Macmillan, 1993), pp. 45–7.

78. Timothy E. Cook, *Governing With the News: The News Media As a Political Institution* (University of Chicago Press, 1998), pp. 100–1; Robinson, "Public Affairs Television and the Growth of Political Malaise," pp. 428–30; James H. Kuklinski and Lee Sigelman, "When Objectivity Is Not Objective: Network Television News Coverage of U.S. Senators and the 'Paradox of Objectivity'," *Journal of Politics* 54 (August 1992): 815; Chester J. Pach, Jr., "And That's the Way It Was: The Vietnam War on the Network Nightly News," in David Farber, Ed., *The Sixties: From Memory to History* (Chapel Hill: University of North Carolina Press, 1994), p. 101.

79. Julius Duscha, Paul S. Green, and Charles B. Seib, "The Media in the Washington Area: Effects of Changing Competitive Patterns on Availability of Information, A Preliminary Report to the National News Council," 1 December 1981, NNCR, Working Files – Freedom of the Press, Box 81, File: 9, p. 7.

80. David L. Altheide and Robert P. Snow, *Media Logic* (Beverly Hills, CA: Sage, 1979), pp. 78–80.

81. Austin Ranney, *Channels of Power: The Impact of Television on American Politics* (New York: Basic Books, 1983), pp. 42–55. Ranney outlines these constraints.

82. Kuklinski and Sigelman, "When Objectivity is Not Objective," p. 815.

83. Lisa Belkin, "Shows Being Pre-Empted for Iran-Contra Hearings," *New York Times,* 5 May 1987.

84. David Thelen, *Becoming Citizens in the Age of Television* (University of Chicago Press, 1996), p. 18.

85. Peter J. Boyer, "North Outdraws the Top Show on Daytime TV," *New York Times,* 11 July 1987.

86. Peter J. Boyer, "NBC Only Major Network to Carry Hall Testimony," *New York Times,* 9 June 1987.

87. John Corry, "Hearings in Congress," *New York Times,* 12 May 1987. See, for example, ABC "Evening News," 3 May 1987 and 6 May 1987; CBS "Evening News," 5 May 1987 and 8 May 1987; NBC "Evening News," 6 May 1987. All in TNA.

88. "Sex, Politics, and the Press: Gary Hart Self-Destructs," *Newsweek,* 18 May 1987, Cover.

89. Howard Kurtz, *Media Circus: The Trouble With America's Newspapers* (New York: Time Books, 1994), p. 153.

90. Ezra Bowen, "On the Springboard of Notoriety," *Time,* 12 October 1987, p. 64.

91. CBS "Evening News," 30 June 1982, TNA.

92. "Fighting Its Image Problem," *Time,* 26 July 1982, p. 12.

93. Francis X. Clines, "House to Check Sex Reports on Members and Pages," *New York Times,* 2 July 1982.
94. "Capitol Scandal," *Time,* 12 July 1982.
95. Walter Pincus and Joe Pichirallo, "House to Probe Sex–Drug Allegations," *Washington Post,* 14 July 1982.
96. Memorandum for the File, 9 July 1982, RMP, Press Series, Box 1, File: Memoranda 1981–1988 (2).
97. CBS "Evening News," 14 December 1982, TNA.
98. Leslie Maitland, "House Unit Finds No Truth in Sex Allegations," *New York Times,* 15 December 1982.
99. Suzanne Garment, *Scandal: The Culture of Mistrust in American Politics* (New York: Time Books, 1991), pp. 66–9.
100. Michael J. Robinson, "Three Faces of Congressional Media," in Thomas E. Mann and Norman J. Ornstein, Eds., *The New Congress* (Washington, DC: American Enterprise Institute, 1981), pp. 55–96.
101. S. Robert Lichter, Stanley Rothman, and Linda S. Lichter, *The Media Elite* (Bethesda, MD: Adler & Adler, 1986), p. 294.
102. Michael Schudson, "Social Origins of Press Cynicism in Portraying Politics," *American Behavioral Scientist* 42 (March 1999): 998–1008.
103. S. Robert Lichter and Daniel R. Amundson, "Less News Is Worse News: Television News Coverage of Congress, 1972–1992," in Thomas E. Mann and Norman J. Ornstein, Eds., *Congress, the Press, and the Public* (Washington, DC: American Enterprise Institute / Brookings Institution, 1994), p. 136.
104. Mark J. Rozell, *In Contempt of Congress: Postwar Press Coverage on Capitol Hill* (Westport, CT: Praeger, 1996), pp. 65–72.
105. Frank J. Sorauf, "Campaign Money and the Press: Three Soundings," *Political Science Quarterly* 102 (Spring 1987): 25–42.
106. S. Robert Lichter, Linda S. Lichter, and Daniel Amundson, "Government Goes Down the Tube: Images of Government in TV Entertainment, 1955–1998," *Harvard International Journal of Press and Politics* 5 (Spring 2000): 98–9, 102.
107. Doris A. Graber, *Mass Media and American Politics,* 2nd ed. (Washington, DC: Congressional Quarterly, 1984), p. 78.
108. Thomas E. Patterson, *Out of Order* (New York: Vintage, 1993).
109. Theda Skocpol, *Boomerang: Clinton's Health Security Effort and the Turn Against Government in U.S. Politics* (New York: Norton, 1996), pp. 128–30; Joseph N. Cappella and Kathleen Hall Jamieson, "Public Cynicism and News Coverage in Campaigns and Policy Debates," paper presented at the 1994 American Political Science Association Convention, New York; Tom Hamburger, Ted Marmor, and Jon Meacham, "What the Death of Health Reform Teaches Us About the Press," *Washington Monthly* 26 (November 1994): 35–42.
110. "20/20," ABC, 19 July 1979, TNA.
111. Jonathan Alter and Howard Fineman, "The Fall of Joe Biden," *Newsweek,* 5 October 1987, p. 28.
112. David L. Altheide, *Creating Reality: How TV News Distorts Events* (Beverly Hills, CA: Sage, 1976), p. 73.
113. Kurtz, *Media Circus,* pp. 53–74; Bartholomew H. Sparrow, *Uncertain Guardians: The News Media As a Political Institution* (Baltimore: Johns Hopkins University Press, 1999), pp. 153–61.

114. Martin Mayer, *The Greatest Ever Bank Robbery: The Collapse of the Savings and Loan Industry* (New York: Scribner's, 1990), pp. 18–19.

115. Sparrow, *Uncertain Guardians*, pp. 73–104; Norman E. Isaacs, *Untended Gates: The Mismanaged Press* (New York: Columbia University Press, 1986), pp. 183–203.

116. John B. Thompson, *Political Scandal: Power and Visibility in the Media Age* (Cambridge, U.K.: Polity, 2000), p. 59; Martin Mayer, *Making News* (Garden City, NY: Doubleday, 1987), pp. 143–4.

117. "Congressional Junket Is Filmed by TV Crew," *New York Times*, 27 October 1990.

118. Michael Schudson, *The Power of News* (Cambridge, MA: Harvard University Press, 1995), pp. 173–4.

119. George Stephanopoulos, *All Too Human: A Political Education* (Boston: Little, Brown, 1999), p. 55.

120. Larry J. Sabato, *Feeding Frenzy: How Attack Journalism Has Transformed American Politics,* rev. ed. (New York: Free Press, 1993), p. 49.

121. Lamb, "Debunking the C-SPAN Myths."

122. Mayer, *Making News*, p. 145.

123. Daniel C. Hallin, *We Keep America on Top of the World: Television Journalism and the Public Sphere* (London: Routledge, 1994), pp. 99, 177.

124. Alfonse D'Amato, *Power, Pasta and Politics: The World According to Senator Al D'Amato* (New York: Hyperion, 1995), pp. 165–81, 316.

125. "Counterattacks on the Ethics Front," *Newsweek*, 3 June 1991, p. 19.

126. Suzanne Daley, "D'Amato Holds Forum for No-Show Accusers," *New York Times*, 3 May 1991.

127. Sabato, *Feeding Frenzy*.

128. Ibid., p. 150.

129. Susan Molinari with Elinor Burkett, *Representative Mom: Balancing Budgets, Bill, and Baby in the U.S. Congress* (New York: Doubleday, 1998), pp. 205–6.

130. There were exceptions, of course, such as Walter Lippman. But these print celebrities were few and far between relative to those on television. See Robert J. Donovan and Ray Scherer, *Unsilent Revolution: Television News and American Public Life, 1948–1991* (Cambridge University Press / Washington, DC: Woodrow Wilson International Center for Scholars, 1992), pp. 294–6; James Fallows, "The New Celebrities of Washington," *New York Review of Books,* 12 June 1986, pp. 41–9; Jacob Weisberg, "The Buckrakers," *New Republic,* 27 January 1986, pp. 16–18; Charlotte Hays and Jonathan Rowe, "Reporters: The New Washington Elite," *Washington Monthly* 17 (July/August 1985): 21–7.

131. Lichter, Rothman, and Lichter, *The Media Elite*, pp. 24–5.

132. David Brinkley, *David Brinkley: A Memoir* (New York: Ballantine, 1995), pp. 234–41.

133. Howard Kurtz, *Hot Air: All Talk All the Time* (New York: Basic Books, 1997), p. 189.

134. Eric Alterman, *Sound and Fury: The Making of the Punditocracy,* rev. ed. (Ithaca, NY: Cornell University Press, 1999), pp. 115–19.

135. Doug Underwood, *When MBA's Rule the Newsroom: How the Marketeers and Managers Are Reshaping Today's Media* (New York: Columbia University Press, 1993), pp. 7, 55–70.

136. Norman J. Ornstein, Robert L. Peabody, and David W. Rohde, "The U.S. Senate in an Era of Change," in Lawrence C. Dodd and Bruce I. Oppenheimer, Eds.,

*Congress Reconsidered,* 5th ed. (Washington, DC: Congressional Quarterly, 1993), pp. 29–30.

137. Kedrowski, *Media Entrepreneurs and the Media Enterprise in the U.S. Congress,* p. 61. See also Les Aspin in Cook, *Making Laws and Making News,* pp. 156–7.

138. Godfrey Hodgson, *The Gentleman from New York: Daniel Patrick Moynihan* (Boston: Houghton-Mifflin, 2000), pp. 371–2.

139. Ernest B. Furgurson, *Hard Right: The Rise of Jesse Helms* (New York: Norton, 1986).

140. Kedrowski, *Media Entrepreneurs and the Media Enterprise in the U.S. Congress,* p. 3.

141. Frantzich and Sullivan, *The C-SPAN Revolution,* p. 265.

142. Douglas B. Harris, "The Rise of the Public Speakership," *Political Science Quarterly* 113 (Summer 1998): 196.

143. Donovan and Scherer, *Unsilent Revolution,* pp. 177–95; Schudson, *The Power of News,* pp. 124–41.

144. Mike Johnson to Robert Michel, 20 September 1981.

145. Harris, "The Rise of the Public Speakership," pp. 196–201.

146. Farrell, *Tip O'Neill,* pp. 563–606.

147. Jeffrey H. Birnbaum and Alan S. Murray, *Showdown at Gucci Gulch: Lawmakers, Lobbyists, and the Unlikely Triumph of Tax Reform* (New York: Vintage, 1987), pp. 96–100.

148. David E. Price, *The Congressional Experience: A View from the Hill* (Boulder, CO: Westview, 1992), pp. 115–16.

149. Steven V. Roberts, "House Democrats Seeking Better TV Image," *New York Times,* 10 May 1984.

150. Joe S. Foote, *Television Access and Political Power: The Networks, the Presidency, and the "Loyal Opposition"* (Westport, CT: Praeger, 1990), pp. 116–17.

151. Bill Drayton to Al From, Jack Lew, and Ari Weiss, TOP, Jack Lew Files, Box 36, File: Drayton Media Plan. See also Memorandum, 1982, TOP, Jack Lew Files, Box 36, File: Drayton Plan; Price, *The Congressional Experience,* pp. 83–4.

152. Kurtz, *Hot Air,* p. 160.

153. "House Panel Leader Jeered by Elderly in Chicago," *New York Times,* 19 August 1989.

154. See, for example, NBC "Evening News," 18 November 1989, TNA.

155. Richard E. Cohen, *Rostenkowski: The Pursuit of Power and the End of the Old Politics* (Chicago: Ivan R. Dee, 1999), pp. 187–90.

156. See, for example, CBS "Evening News," 1 January 1996, 4 January 1996, and 6 January 1996; CNN "Evening News," 3 January 1996; NBC "Evening News," 27 December 1995, 28 December 1995, 2 January 1996, and 4 January 1996; ABC "Evening News," 22 December 1995, 4 January 1996, and 6 January 1996. All broadcasts in TNA.

157. Elizabeth Drew, *The Corruption of American Politics: What Went Wrong and Why* (Secaucus, NJ: Birch Lane, 1999), pp. 110, 126; Howard Kurtz, *Spin Cycle: How the White House and the Media Manipulate the News,* rev. ed. (New York: Touchstone, 1998), pp. 224–41.

158. Susan F. Rasky, "For the Chairman of a Powerful Committee, the House Is No Longer Home," *New York Times,* 20 November 1989.

159. Cook, *Making Laws and Making News,* pp. 132–48. For an example of national coverage on the issue, see CBS "Evening News," 2 April 1985, TNA.

160. Elizabeth Drew, *Citizen McCain* (New York: Simon & Schuster, 2002), pp. 9, 44–5, 64–5, 134–42.

161. Stephen Hess, *The Washington Reporters* (Washington, DC: Brookings Institution, 1981), pp. 30–1.

162. David S. Broder, *Behind the Front Page: A Candid Look at How the News Is Made* (New York: Simon & Schuster, 1987), pp. 112–13.

## Chapter 12

1. Anna Holmquist to Robert Michel (n.d.), RMP, Press Series, Box 1, File: Memoranda 1981–1988 (1).

2. Barbara Sinclair, "Majority Party Leadership Strategies for Coping with the New U.S. House," in Frank H. Mackaman, Ed., *Understanding Congressional Leadership* (Washington, DC: Congressional Quarterly, 1981), p. 184; B. Sinclair, "Coping with Uncertainty: Building Coalitions in the House and Senate," in Thomas E. Mann and Norman J. Ornstein, Eds., *The New Congress* (Washington, DC: American Enterprise Institute, 1981), pp. 178–220.

3. Nicol C. Rae, *The Decline and Fall of the Liberal Republicans: From 1952 to the Present* (New York: Oxford University Press, 1989), pp. 174–82.

4. U.S. Congress, Senate, *Congressional Record,* 98th Congress, 1st Session, 12 May 1983, p. 12082.

5. Nichole Elizabeth Mellow, "A House Divided: Regional Conflicts, Coalitions, and Partisanship in Postwar America," Ph.D. dissertation, University of Texas, Austin, 2003.

6. Ibid.; Nicol C. Rae, *Southern Democrats* (New York: Oxford University Press, 1994), pp. 19–20; Sarah A. Binder, "The Disappearing Political Center," *Brookings Review* 14 (Fall 1996): 36–9; S. A. Binder, *Stalemate: Causes and Consequences of Legislative Gridlock* (Washington, DC: Brookings Institution, 2003), pp. 79–81, 127–9.

7. Kenneth A. Shepsle, "The Changing Textbook Congress," in John E. Chubb and Paul E. Peterson, Eds., *Can the Government Govern?* (Washington, DC: Brookings Institution, 1989), pp. 256–9; Stanley P. Berard, *Southern Democrats in the U.S. House of Representatives* (Norman: University of Oklahoma Press, 2001), pp. 111–42; Rae, *Southern Democrats,* pp. 65–110; Earl Black and Merle Black, *Politics and Society in the South* (Cambridge, MA: Harvard University Press, 1987), p. 253.

8. Burdett Loomis, *The Contemporary Congress* (New York: St. Martin's, 1996), p. 121.

9. David W. Rohde, *Parties and Leaders in the Postreform House* (University of Chicago Press, 1991), pp. 14–15.

10. Barbara Sinclair, "Evolution or Revolution? Policy-Oriented Congressional Parties in the 1990s," in L. Sandy Maisel, Ed., *The Parties Respond: Changes in American Parties and Campaigns,* 3rd ed. (Boulder, CO: Westview, 1998), pp. 281–2. See also Eric M. Uslaner, "Is the Senate More Civil Than the House?" in Burdett A. Loomis, Ed., *Esteemed Colleagues: Civility and Deliberation in the U.S. Senate* (Washington, DC: Brookings Institution, 2000), p. 42.

11.  Rohde, *Parties and Leaders in the Postreform House,* pp. 1–39. See also Gary W. Cox and Mathew D. McCubbins, *Legislative Leviathan: Party Government in the House* (Berkeley: University of California Press, 1993), pp. 277–8. For the best analysis of centrist Democrats, see Kenneth S. Baer, *Reinventing Democrats: The Politics of Liberalism from Reagan to Clinton* (Lawrence: University Press of Kansas, 2000).

12.  Earl Black and Merle Black, *The Rise of Southern Republicans* (Cambridge, MA: Belknap Press, 2002), pp. 36–9; Jonathan S. Krasno, *Challengers, Competition, and Reelection* (New Haven, CT: Yale University Press, 1994); Alan I. Abramowitz and Jeffrey A. Segal, *Senate Elections* (Ann Arbor: University of Michigan Press, 1992).

13.  Presentation attached to Gillis W. Long to Colleague, 19 June 1981, RBP, Box 280, File: 18.

14.  James Jones to Colleagues, 19 February 1981, RBP, Box 280, File: 19.

15.  James Jones to Richard Bolling, 21 September 1981, RBP, Box 280, File: 17.

16.  Joseph White and Aaron Wildavsky, *The Deficit and the Public Interest: The Search for Responsible Budgeting in the 1980s* (Berkeley: University of California Press / New York: Russell Sage Foundation, 1989), p. 138.

17.  Lance T. Leloup, "After the Blitz: Reagan and the U.S. Congressional Budget Process," *Legislative Studies Quarterly* 7 (August 1982): 325.

18.  James Jones to Colleagues, 4 May 1981, RBP, Box 280, File: 18.

19.  John W. Ellwood, "The Great Exception: The Congressional Budget Process in an Age of Decentralization," in Lawrence C. Dodd and Bruce I. Oppenheimer, Eds., *Congress Reconsidered,* 3rd ed. (Washington, DC: Congressional Quarterly, 1985), p. 336.

20.  Richard F. Fenno, Jr., *The Emergence of a Senate Leader: Pete Domenici and the Reagan Budget* (Washington, DC: Congressional Quarterly, 1991), pp. 54–72.

21.  Barbara Sinclair, *Unorthodox Lawmaking: New Legislative Processes in the U.S. Congress* (Washington, DC: Congressional Quarterly, 1997), pp. 92–5.

22.  James A. Thurber, "The Senate Budget Committee: Bastion of Comity?" in Loomis, *Esteemed Colleagues,* pp. 246–54.

23.  Steven S. Smith and Christopher J. Deering, *Committees in Congress,* 2nd ed. (Washington, DC: Congressional Quarterly, 1990), pp. 132–4; Loomis, *The Contemporary Congress,* pp. 89–90.

24.  Smith and Deering, *Committees in Congress,* p. 186. See also Stanley Bach and Steven S. Smith, *Managing Uncertainty in the House of Representatives: Adaptation and Innovation in Special Rules* (Washington, DC: Brookings Institution, 1988).

25.  Roger H. Davidson, "Congressional Committees in the New Reform Era: From Combat to the Contract," in James A. Thurber and Roger H. Davidson, Eds., *Remaking Congress: Change and Stability in the 1990s* (Washington, DC: Congressional Quarterly, 1995), pp. 28–9.

26.  David C. King, *Turf Wars: How Congressional Committees Claim Jurisdiction* (University of Chicago Press, 1997), p. 140.

27.  Norman J. Ornstein, Robert L. Peabody, and David W. Rohde, "The U.S. Senate: Toward the Twenty-First Century," in Lawrence C. Dodd and Bruce I. Oppenheimer, Eds., *Congress Reconsidered,* 6th ed. (Washington, DC: Congressional Quarterly, 1997), pp. 15–19; Steven S. Smith, "Forces of Change in Senate Party Leadership and Organization," in Lawrence C. Dodd and Bruce I. Oppenheimer, Eds., *Congress Reconsidered,* 5th ed. (Washington, DC: Congressional Quarterly,

1993), pp. 259–90; Barbara Sinclair, "The Dream Fulfilled? Party Development in Congress, 1950–2000," in John C. Green and Paul S. Herrnson, Eds., *Responsible Partisanship? The Evolution of American Political Parties Since 1950* (Lawrence: University Press of Kansas, 2002), pp. 121–40.

28. Sarah A. Binder and Steven S. Smith, *Politics or Principle? Filibustering in the United States Senate* (Washington, DC: Brookings Institution, 1997), pp. 11, 83–115.

29. Frank J. Sorauf and Scott A. Wilson, "Political Parties and Campaign Finance: Adaptation and Accommodation Toward a Changing Role," in L. Sandy Maisel, Ed., *The Parties Respond: Changes in American Parties and Campaigns,* 2nd ed. (Boulder, CO: Westview, 1994), pp. 235–53; James W. Ceaser, "Political Parties – Declining, Stabilizing, or Resurging?" in Anthony King, Ed., *The New American Political System,* 2nd ed. (Washington, DC: American Enterprise Institute, 1990), pp. 87–137.

30. A. James Reichley, *The Life of the Parties: A History of American Political Parties* (New York: Free Press, 1992), pp. 353–81.

31. Gary Jacobson, "The Republican Advantage in Campaign Finance," in John E. Chubb and Paul E. Peterson, Eds., *The New Direction in American Politics* (Washington, DC: Brookings Institution, 1985), p. 155; Frank J. Sorauf, *Inside Campaign Finance: Myths and Realities* (New Haven, CT: Yale University Press, 1992), p. 125.

32. Robin Kolodny, *Pursuing Majorities: Congressional Campaign Committees in American Politics* (Norman: University of Oklahoma Press, 1998), p. 182.

33. Reichley, *The Life of the Parties,* p. 372.

34. Steven M. Smith, "New Patterns of Decisionmaking in Congress," in Chubb and Peterson, *The New Direction in American Politics,* pp. 227–8; Barbara Sinclair, *Majority Leadership in the U.S. House* (Baltimore: Johns Hopkins University Press, 1983), pp. 55–85.

35. Rohde, *Parties and Leaders in the Postreform House,* pp. 105–13.

36. Douglas A. Harbrecht and Howard Gleckman, "The New Speaker Is Stepping on Everyone's Toes," *Business Week,* 12 January 1987, p. 55.

37. James L. Merriner, *Mr. Chairman: Power in Dan Rostenkowski's America* (Carbondale: Southern Illinois University Press, 1999), p. 234.

38. Jonathan Fuerbringer, "Tax Rise is Passed in the House," *New York Times,* 30 October 1987.

39. Eric M. Uslaner, *The Decline of Comity in Congress* (Ann Arbor: University of Michigan Press, 1993), p. 32.

40. Douglas B. Harris, "The Rise of the Public Speakership," *Political Science Quarterly* 113 (Summer 1998): 198–202.

41. Tim Groseclose and David C. King, "Little Theatre: Committees in Congress," in Herbert F. Weisberg and Samuel C. Patterson, Eds., *Great Theatre: The American Congress in the 1990s* (Cambridge University Press, 1998), pp. 135–51; Richard L. Hall and Gary J. McKissick, "Institutional Change and Behavioral Choice in House Committees," in Dodd and Oppenheimer, *Congress Reconsidered,* 6th ed., pp. 212–28.

42. Christopher Madison, "Congress – A Class Apart," *National Journal,* 9 March 1991.

43. Benjamin Ginsberg and Martin Shefter, *Politics by Other Means: The Declining Importance of Elections in America* (New York: Basic Books, 1990).

44. U.S. Congress, Joint Congressional Committee Investigating the Iran-Contra Affair, *Report of the Congressional Committees Investigating the Iran-Contra Affair,* 100th Congress, 1st Session, 17 November 1987, p. 438.

45. U.S. Congress, Senate, *Congressional Record,* 100th Congress, 1st Session, 1 July 1987, p. 18519.

46. Howard Fineman, "The Grilling of Judge Bork," *Newsweek,* 28 September 1987, p. 29.

47. Ginsberg and Shefter, *Politics by Other Means,* pp. 154–5.

48. U.S. Congress, Senate, Committee on the Judiciary, *Hearings: Nomination of Robert H. Bork to Be Associate Justice of the Supreme Court of the United States,* 101st Congress, 1st Session, 19 September 1987, p. 845.

49. U.S. Congress, Senate, Committee on Armed Services, *Hearings: Nomination of John G. Tower to Be Secretary of Defense,* 101st Congress, 1st Session, 25 January 1989, pp. 241–2.

50. U.S. Congress, Senate, *Congressional Record,* 101st Congress, 1st Session, 2 March 1989, p. 3253.

51. Cited in Larry J. Sabato, *Feeding Frenzy: How Attack Journalism Has Transformed American Politics,* rev. ed. (New York: Free Press, 1993), pp. 179–80.

52. John G. Tower, *Consequences: A Personal and Political Memoir* (Boston: Little, Brown, 1991), p. 329.

53. U.S. Congress, Senate, *Congressional Record,* 101st Congress, 1st Session, 2 March 1989, p. 3261.

54. Mike Johnson to Robert Michel and Bill Pitts, 29 April 1987, and "Long-Term Strategy for Achieving Majority Status," 14 July 1987, RMP, Press Series, Box 1, File: Memoranda 1981–1988 (3).

55. Gerald Solomon to Robert Michel, 6 December 1990, RMP, Staff Series, Karen Buttaro, Box 13, File: Legislative Agenda for 102nd Congress.

56. Press Release, "House Republican Leaders Assail the Broken Branch of Government," 24 May 1988, RMP, Leadership Series, Box 18, File: Special Order, "Broken Branch of Government" (1).

57. Norman Lent, Edward Madigan, et al. to John Dingell, 7 August 1987, RMP, Leadership Series, Box 18, File: Special Order, "Broken Branch of Government" (1).

58. Newt Gingrich to Colleagues, 17 February 1988, JWP, RC Box 18-4, The Capital, Suite H324, Steering and Policy Committee, File: Newt Gingrich.

59. Beryl Anthony, Jr., to Democratic Colleague, 25 February 1988, and Newt Gingrich to Colleagues, 17 February 1988, JWP, RC Box 18-4, The Capital, Suite H324, Steering and Policy Committee, File: Newt Gingrich. See also Debra J. Saunders, "Gingrich Wasted More Than $200,000 in Prime Example of Republican Welfare," *Atlanta Constitution,* 25 February 1988.

60. Dave Montgomery, "Gingrich Tactics Rile Politicians in Both Parties," *Fort Worth Star-Telegram,* 20 December 1987.

61. David Osborne, "Newt Gingrich: Shining Knight of the Post-Reagan Right," *Mother Jones,* November 1984.

62. Christopher Matthews, "Gingrich and the Cycle of Revenge," *Dallas Morning News,* 30 March 1989.

63. Newt Gingrich to Colleague, 15 December 1987, TFP, Box 135, File: Newt Gingrich, 1988.

64. U.S. Congress, House of Representatives, Committee on Standards of Official Conduct, *Statement of Alleged Violation in the Matter of Representative James C. Wright, Jr.,* 101st Congress, 1st Session, 13 April 1989.

65. Hugh Sidney, "The Ethics Monster," *Time,* 29 May 1989, p. 32.

66. Rich Thomas and David Pauly, "The Wright Man to See," *Newsweek*, 29 June 1987, pp. 44–5.
67. Gloria Borger, "The Last Stand of Speaker Jim Wright," *U.S. News & World Report*, 24 April 1989, p. 27.
68. Complaint Before the Committee on Standards of Official Conduct of the House of Representatives, "In the Matter of a Complaint by Representative Bill Alexander Against Representative Newt Gingrich," 6 April 1989, and Newt Gingrich to Colleagues, 17 February 1988, JWP, RC Box 18-4, The Capital, Suite H324, Steering and Policy Committee, File: Newt Gingrich.
69. Bill Alexander to Colleagues, 7 April 1989, and Newt Gingrich to Colleagues, 17 February 1988, JWP, RC Box 18-4, The Capital, Suite H324, Steering and Policy Committee, File: Newt Gingrich.
70. Michael Oreskes, "Gloom on Wright Shakes Gathering of Key Democrats," *New York Times*, 18 May 1989.
71. U.S. Congress, House of Representatives, *Congressional Record*, 101st Congress, 1st Session, 31 May 1989, p. 10440.
72. Douglas Harbrecht, "The Democrats' Meltdown on the Hill," *Business Week*, 12 June 1989, p. 25.
73. Martin Tolchin and Susan J. Tolchin, *Glass Houses: Congressional Ethics and the Politics of Venom* (Boulder, CO: Westview, 2001), p. 58.
74. U.S. Congress, House of Representatives, Committee on Standards of Official Conduct, *Inquiry into the Operation of the Bank of the Sergeant-at-Arms*, 102nd Congress, 2nd Session, 10 March 1992.
75. Donald R. Wolfensberger, *Congress and the People: Deliberative Democracy on Trial* (Washington, DC: Woodrow Wilson Center Press / Baltimore: Johns Hopkins University Press, 2000), p. 152.
76. Nancy Traver, "Why Foley Stood Idle," *Time*, 13 April 1992, p. 29.
77. For an interesting debate on the electoral consequences of the banking and other congressional scandals, see the following articles: Gary C. Jacobson and Michael A. Dimock, "Checking Out: The Effects of Bank Overdrafts on the 1992 House Elections," *American Journal of Political Science* 38 (August 1994): 601–24; John Alford, Holly Teeters, Daniel S. Ward, and Rick K. Wilson, "Overdraft: The Political Cost of Congressional Malfeasance," *Journal of Politics* (August 1994): 788–801; Timothy Groseclose and Keith Krehbiel, "Golden Parachutes, Rubber Checks, and Strategic Retirements from the 102nd House," *American Journal of Political Science* 38 (1994): 75–99; M. Dimock and G. Jacobson, "Checks and Choices: The House Bank Scandal's Impact on Voters in 1992," *Journal of Politics* 57 (November 1995): 1143–59; John G. Peters and Susan Welch, "The Effects of Charges of Corruption on Voting Behavior in Congressional Elections," *American Political Science Review* 74 (September 1980): 697–708.
78. Thomas Foley to Karen, 10 September 1993, TFP, Box 179, File: House Reform – Campaign Finance, 1993.
79. Editorial, "The Postmaster and the Speaker's Wife," *Washington Post*, 11 February 1992.
80. "Parties Trade Bitter Charges Over Post Office Inquiry," *Congressional Quarterly Weekly Report*, 8 February 1992, p. 289.
81. Steven R. Ross to Robert Rota, 12 February 1992, TFP, Box 179, File: House Post Office, 1991–1992.

82. Milton Socolar to Donald K. Anderson, 2 April 1992, TFP, Box 179, File: House Post Office, 1991–1992.

83. Merriner, *Mr. Chairman,* p. 263.

84. Bob Cohn with John McCormick, "Rostenkowski's Choice," *Newsweek,* 30 May 1994, p. 49.

85. Norman J. Ornstein and Amy Schenkenberg, "Congress Bashing: External Pressures for Reform and the Future of the Institution," in Thurber and Davidson, *Remaking Congress,* pp. 121–3.

86. Kay Lehman Schlozman and John T. Tierney, *Organized Interests and American Democracy* (New York: Harper & Row, 1986), pp. 74–5, 82; Jeffrey M. Berry, *The New Liberalism: The Rising Power of Citizen Interest Groups* (Washington, DC: Brookings Institution, 1999).

87. Robert Dornan to Republican Colleagues, 5 October 1992, GSP, Box 50, Unprocessed.

88. Ibid.

89. Stephen Skowronek, *The Politics Presidents Make: Leadership from John Adams to George Bush* (Cambridge, MA: Harvard University Press, 1993).

90. Eric M. Patashnik, "Budgeting More, Deciding Less," in Martin A. Levin, Marc K. Landy, and Martin Shapiro, Eds., *Seeking the Center: Politics and Policymaking at the New Century* (Washington, DC: Georgetown University Press, 2001), pp. 35–53.

91. Paul Pierson, "The Deficit and the Politics of Domestic Reform," in Margaret Weir, Ed., *The Social Divide: Political Parties and the Future of Activist Government* (Washington, DC: Brookings Institution, 1998), p. 134.

92. Mark Tushnet, *The New Constitutional Order* (Princeton, NJ: Princeton University Press, 2003).

93. Paul Pierson, *Dismantling the Welfare State? Reagan, Thatcher, and the Politics of Retrenchment* (Cambridge University Press, 1996).

94. C. Eugene Steuerle, "Financing the American State at the Turn of the Century," in W. Elliot Brownlee, Ed., *Funding the Modern American State, 1941–1995: The Rise and Fall of the Era of Easy Finance* (Cambridge University Press / Washington, DC: Woodrow Wilson Center Press, 1996), pp. 409–44. See also Pierson, "The Deficit and the Politics of Domestic Reform," pp. 126–78.

95. Lance T. LeLoup, "The Fiscal Straitjacket: Budgetary Constraints on Congressional Foreign and Defense Policy-Making," in Randall Ripley and James M. Lindsay, Eds., *Congress Resurgent: Foreign and Defense Policy on Capitol Hill* (Ann Arbor: University of Michigan Press, 1993), pp. 37–66.

96. Paul Pierson, "From Expansion to Austerity: The New Politics of Taxing and Spending," in Levin et al., *Seeking the Center,* pp. 74–5.

97. For examples of dramatic policy breakthroughs, see Marc K. Landy and Martin A. Levin, Eds., *The New Politics of Public Policy* (Baltimore: Johns Hopkins University Press, 1995); Gary Mucciaroni, *Reversals of Fortune: Public Policy and Private Interests* (Washington, DC: Brookings Institution, 1995); and R. Kent Weaver, *Ending Welfare As We Know It* (Washington, DC: Brookings Institution, 2000).

98. For explorations of this theme, see the essays in Levin et al., *Seeking the Center.*

99. Eric P. Patashnik, "After the Public Interest Prevails: The Political Sustainability of Reform," *Governance* 16 (April 2003): 203–34.

100. Sidney M. Milkis, *Political Parties and Constitutional Government: Remaking American Democracy* (Baltimore: Johns Hopkins University Press, 1999), pp. 103–73; Gareth Davies, "The Great Society after Johnson: The Case of Bilingual Education," *Journal of American History* 88 (March 2002): 1405–29; Hugh Davis Graham, "Since 1964: The Paradox of American Civil Rights Regulation," in Morton Keller and R. Shep Melnick, Eds., *Taking Stock: American Government in the Twentieth Century* (Cambridge University Press / Washington, DC: Woodrow Wilson Center Press, 1999), pp. 187–218; Landy and Levin, *The New Politics of Public Policy.*

101. This was a process that had started in the 1960s. See Barbara Sinclair, *The Transformation of the U.S. Senate* (Baltimore: Johns Hopkins University Press, 1989), pp. 51–70.

102. Robert H. Salisbury, "The Paradox of Interest Groups in Washington – More Groups, Less Clout," in King, *The New American Political System,* pp. 203–29.

103. Jonathan Rauch, *Government's End: Why Washington Stopped Working* (New York: Public Affairs Press, 1995), pp. 86–7; Larry J. Sabato, *PAC Power: Inside the World of Political Action Committees* (New York: Norton, 1980), pp. 10–16; Thomas Byrne Edsall, "The Changing Shape of Power: A Realignment in Public Policy," in Steve Fraser and Gary Gerstle, Eds., *The Rise and Fall of the New Deal Order, 1930–1980* (Princeton, NJ: Princeton University Press, 1989), pp. 271–2; Loomis, *The Contemporary Congress,* p. 35; Salisbury, "The Paradox of Interest Groups in Washington," pp. 203–29.

104. Berry, *The New Liberalism.*

105. King, *Turf Wars,* pp. 143–4.

106. James Allen Smith, *The Idea Brokers: Think Tanks and the Rise of the New Policy Elite,* rev. ed. (New York: Free Press, 1993); David M. Ricci, *The Transformation of American Politics: The New Washington and the Rise of Think Tanks* (New Haven, CT: Yale University Press, 1993).

107. William P. Browne, *Cultivating Congress: Constituents, Issues, and Interests in Agricultural Policymaking* (Lawrence: University Press of Kansas, 1995); Hugh Heclo, "Issue Networks and the Executive Establishment," in Anthony King, Ed., *The New American Political System* (Washington, DC: American Enterprise Institute, 1978), pp. 90–121.

108. David R. Mayhew, *Divided We Govern: Party Control, Lawmaking, and Investigations, 1946–1990* (New Haven, CT: Yale University Press, 1991).

109. Samuel P. Hays, *Beauty, Health, and Permanence: Environmental Politics in the United States, 1955–1985* (Cambridge University Press, 1987), pp. 497–8.

110. Louis Fisher and David Gray Adler, "The War Powers Resolution: Time to Say Goodbye," *Political Science Quarterly* 113 (Spring 1998): 1–20; L. Fisher, "War and Spending Prerogatives: Stages of Congressional Abdication," *St. Louis University Public Law Review* 19 (2000): 7–63.

111. On the legislative veto, see Jessica Korn, *The Power of Separation: American Constitutionalism and the Myth of the Legislative Veto* (Princeton, NJ: Princeton University Press, 1996).

112. Lauren Bayne Anderson, "Capitol Hill Tabloids Compete for Attention of Political Elite," *Wall Street Journal,* 21 July 2003. For an excellent account of the "soft news," see Matthew A. Baum, *Soft News Goes to War: Public Opinion and*

*American Foreign Policy in the New Media Age* (Princeton, NJ: Princeton University Press, 2003).

113.  John R. Hibbing and Elizabeth Theiss-Morse, *Congress as Public Enemy: Public Attitudes Toward American Political Institutions* (Cambridge University Press, 1995).

114.  Florence Graves and Charles E. Shepard, "Packwood Accused of Sexual Advances," *Washington Post,* 22 November 1992.

115.  U.S. Congress, Senate, Select Committee on Ethics, *Documents Related to the Investigation of Senator Robert Packwood,* 104th Congress, 1st Session, 1995, pp. 2–5.

116.  Linda Witt, Karen M. Paget, and Glenna Matthews, *Running as a Woman: Gender and Power in American Politics* (New York: Free Press, 1994), pp. 14, 229.

117.  Abigail C. Saguy, "Sexual Harassment in the News: The United States and France," *Communication Review* 5 (2002): 119.

118.  Tolchin and Tolchin, *Glass Houses,* pp. 89–100.

119.  Trip Gabriel, "The Trials of Bob Packwood," *New York Times,* 29 August 1993, p. 38.

120.  U.S. Congress, Senate, *Congressional Record,* 104th Congress, 1st Session, 2 August 1995, p. 21496.

121.  Warren B. Rudman, *Combat: Twelve Years in the U.S. Senate* (New York: Random House, 1996), pp. 200–1.

122.  Wolfensberger, *Congress and the People,* p. 157.

123.  On the origins of this plan, see Jacob S. Hacker, *The Road to Nowhere: The Genesis of President Clinton's Plan for Health Security* (Princeton, NJ: Princeton University Press, 1997).

124.  Theda Skocpol, *Boomerang: Clinton's Health Security Effort and the Turn Against Government in U.S. Politics* (New York: Norton, 1996), pp. 67–9.

125.  Ibid., p. 101; Mark A. Peterson, "The Politics of Health Care Policy: Overreaching in an Age of Polarization," in Weir, *The Social Divide,* p. 185. On the other opponents who have fought against health care in the twentieth century, see Jennifer Klein, *For All These Rights: Business, Labor and the Shaping of America's Public–Private Welfare State* (Princeton, NJ: Princeton University Press, 2003); Colin Gordon, *Dead on Arrival: The Politics of Health Care in the Twentieth Century* (Princeton, NJ: Princeton University Press, 2003); Marie Gottschalk, *The Shadow Welfare State: Labor, Business, and the Politics of Health Care in the United States* (Ithaca, NY: Cornell University Press, 2000).

126.  C. Lawrence Evans, "Committees and Health Jurisdictions in Congress," in Thomas E. Mann and Norman J. Ornstein, Eds., *Intensive Care: How Congress Shapes Health Policy* (Washington, DC: American Enterprise Institute / Brookings Institution, 1995), pp. 33–4.

127.  Eleanor Clift and Tom Brazaitis, *War Without Bloodshed: The Art of Politics* (New York: Touchstone, 1996), p. 143.

128.  Skocpol, *Boomerang,* pp. 61–3, 102.

129.  Cathie Jo Martin, "Dead on Arrival? New Politics, Old Politics, and the Case of National Health Reform," in Levin et al., *Seeking the Center,* pp. 284–6.

130.  Dick Armey, "Your Future Health Plan," *Wall Street Journal,* 13 October 1993.

131.  Meanwhile, the Project for the Republican Future disseminated messages through popular magazines such as *Reader's Digest.* See Skocpol, *Boomerang,* pp. 144–50.

132. Robert Michel to Republican Colleague, 27 January 1994, RMP, Leadership Series, Box 17, File: 103rd, "Setting Legislative Goals."

133. John B. Bader, "The Contract with America: Origins and Assessments," in Dodd and Oppenheimer, *Congress Reconsidered,* 6th ed., p. 355.

134. CBS "Evening News," ABC "Evening News," NBC "Evening News," 27 April 1994. All in TNA.

135. Paul S. Herrnson, "Money and Motives: Spending in House Elections," in Dodd and Oppenheimer, *Congress Reconsidered,* 6th ed., p. 107.

136. Clift and Brazaitis, *War Without Bloodshed,* p. 255.

137. Rodger Streitmatter, *Mightier Than the Sword: How the News Media Have Shaped American History* (Boulder, CO: Westview, 1997), pp. 227–31.

138. Jim Impoco, "Sea Change," *U.S. News & World Report,* 21 November 1994, p. 40.

139. John Ferejohn, "A Tale of Two Congresses: Social Policy in the Clinton Years," in Weir, *The Social Divide,* pp. 56–60.

140. Barry C. Burden and Aage R. Clausen, "The Unfolding Drama: Party and Ideology in the 104th House," in Weisberg and Patterson, *Great Theatre,* p. 155.

141. Timothy J. Barnett, *Legislative Learning: The 104th Republican Freshmen in the House* (New York: Garland, 1999), p. 61.

142. Timothy G. O'Rourke, "The Impact of Reapportionment on Congress and State Legislatures," in Mark E. Rush, Ed., *Voting Rights and Redistricting in the United States* (Westport, CT: Greenwood, 1998), p. 217. For an excellent analysis of how these demographic changes altered the character of legislators sent to Washington in the 1980s and 1990s, see Nelson Polsby, *How Congress Evolves: Social Bases of Institutional Change* (New York: Oxford University Press, 2003).

143. "Suburbia: Land of Varied Faces and a Growing Political Force," *Congressional Quarterly Weekly Report,* 24 May 1997, pp. 1209–18.

144. Jerelyn Eddings, "Welcome to Gingrich Nation," *U.S. News & World Report,* 21 November 1994, p. 44.

145. Lawrence C. Dodd and Bruce I. Oppenheimer, "Revolution in the House: Testing the Limits of Party Government," in Dodd and Oppenheimer, *Congress Reconsidered,* 6th ed., p. 34.

146. Carol M. Swain, *Black Faces, Black Interests: The Representation of African Americans in Congress* (Cambridge, MA: Harvard University Press, 1993), pp. 205–6. See also Kenny J. Whitby and Franklin D. Gilliam, Jr., "Representation in Congress: Line Drawing and Minorities," and Elliot E. Slotnick and Sheldon Goldman, "Congress and the Courts: A Case of Casting," both in Weisberg and Patterson, *Great Theatre*; David T. Cannon, *Race, Redistricting, and Representation: The Unintended Consequences of Black Majority Districts* (University of Chicago, 1999); Bernard Grofman, Lisa Handley, and Richard G. Niemi, *Minority Representation and the Quest for Voting Equality* (Cambridge University Press, 1992).

147. "The Congressional Workplace: Workplace Compliance," in *Guide to U.S. Congress,* v. 1 (Washington, DC: Congressional Quarterly, 2000); retrieved 17 June 2003 from CQ Electronic Library, CQ Congress Collection: g2con-1-98-6123-307639.

148. Barnett, *Legislative Learning,* pp. 55–181.

149. Robin Toner, "73 Mr. Smiths, of the G.O.P., Go to Washington," *New York Times,* 8 January 1995.

150. House Committee on Rules, "Report on Survey of House Committee Chairmen and Ranking Minority Members on Committee Operations, Staffing, and Procedures," 5 September 1996, GSP, Box 15.

151. Cited in Elizabeth Drew, *The Corruption of American Politics: What Went Wrong and Why* (Secaucus, NJ: Birch Lane, 1999), p. 37.

152. Steven S. Smith and Eric D. Lawrence, "Party Control of Committees in the Republican Congress," in Dodd and Oppenheimer, *Congress Reconsidered,* 6th ed., pp. 176–7.

153. Harris, "The Rise of the Public Speakership," p. 211.

154. U.S. Congress, House of Representatives, Committee on Standards of Official Conduct, *Inquiry into Various Complaints Filed Against Representative Newt Gingrich,* 104th Congress, 1st Session, 12 December 1995.

155. Barnett, *Legislative Learning,* pp. 11–25.

156. George Stephanopoulos, *All Too Human: A Political Education* (Boston: Little, Brown, 1999), p. 406.

157. Robert Wright, "Did Newt Do It?" *New Republic,* 15 May 1995, p. 4.

158. Cited in Adam Clymer, "G.O.P. Revolution Hits Speed Bumps on Capitol Hill," *New York Times,* 21 January 1996.

159. Sinclair, "Evolution or Revolution?" p. 281.

160. Sinclair, *Unorthodox Lawmaking,* p. 49.

161. See, for example, Joseph Moakley, Anthony Beilenson, Martin Frost, and Tony Hall to Gerald Solomon, 23 January 1996, and "Statement by House Democratic Leader Richard A. Gephardt on Republican Ruling to Deny Vote on Minimum Wage Increase," 16 April 1996, GSP, Box 15, Unprocessed.

162. "Statement of David E. Bonior," 16 April 1996. See also Richard Gephardt, David Bonior, and John Joseph Moakley to Newt Gingrich, 16 April 1996. Both documents in GSP, Box 15, Unprocessed.

163. Gerald Solomon to Rules Committee Republicans, 30 April 1996, and Solomon to House Republicans, 1 May 1996, GSP, Box 15, Unprocessed.

164. Committee on Rules, "Democrats Engage in 'Nit-Picking, Partisan Hypocrisy' Over July 4th Adjournment Resolution; Missed Same Budget Deadlines Every Year in 101st–103rd Congress," 27 June 1996. See also Chairman Solomon to Rules Committee Republicans, 4 March 1996, GSP, Box 15, Unprocessed.

165. Don Wolfensberger to Juliet Eilperin, 18 March 1996, GSP, Box 15, Unprocessed.

166. Binder, "The Disappearing Political Center," pp. 36–9.

167. Eliza Newlin Carney, "Exodus," *National Journal,* 20 January 1996.

168. "Influential Since the 1940s, the Conservative Coalition Limps into History in 1998," *Congressional Quarterly Almanac* (1998): B-9.

169. Jerry Gray, "G.O.P. Support for Gingrich Begins to Waver," *New York Times,* 29 December 1996.

170. "Wright and Wrong," *New Republic,* 20 January 1997, p. 7.

171. James Carney, "A Wing and a Prayer," *Time,* 5 December 1994, p. 47.

172. Romesh Ratnesar, "A Deal Cutter with a Bit of a Temper," *Time,* 16 November 1998, p. 43.

173. Ronald Brownstein, "Life in the Time of Scandal," *U.S. News & World Report,* 27 April 1998, p. 15.

174. Richard Posner, *An Affair of State: The Investigation, Impeachment, and Trial of President Clinton* (Cambridge, MA: Harvard University Press, 1999); Peter Baker,

*The Breach: Inside the Impeachment and Trial of William Jefferson Clinton* (New York: Scribner, 2000).

## Chapter 13

1. This is a theme explored in the essays in Meg Jacobs, William J. Novak, and Julian E. Zelizer, Eds., *The Democratic Experiment: New Directions in American Political History* (Princeton, NJ: Princeton University Press, 2003).
2. Paul Pierson, *Politics in Time: History, Institutions, and Social Analysis* (Princeton, NJ: Princeton University Press, forthcoming).
3. Jim VandeHei and Juliet Eilperin, "GOP's Power Play," *Washington Post*, 26 July 2003.
4. Jonathan Mermin, *Debating War and Peace: Media Coverage of U.S. Intervention in the Post-Vietnam Era* (Princeton, NJ: Princeton University Press, 1999).
5. William L. Riordan, *Plunkitt of Tammany Hall* (Terrence J. McDonald, Ed.) (New York: Bedford, 1994), p. 57.

# Index